A Dictionary of
Environment and Conservation

Chris Park is a Professorial Fellow and Director of the Graduate
School at Lancaster University. His previous publications include
more than 50 journal articles and 10 books, including *The Envi-
ronment: Principles and Applications* (2001, Routledge).
Michael Allaby has written many books on environmental
science and especially on climatology and meteorology. He is the
General Editor of several Oxford Dictionaries, including the
Dictionaries of *Earth Sciences*, *Ecology*, *Plant Sciences*, and
Zoology.

(((⊕))) SEE WEB LINKS

Many entries in this dictionary have recommended web links.
When you see the above symbol at the end of an entry go to the
dictionary's web page at www.oup.com/uk/reference/resources/
environment, click on **Web links** in the Resources section and
locate the entry in the alphabetical list, then click straight
through to the relevant websites.

Oxford Paperback Reference

The most authoritative and up-to-date reference books for both students and the general reader.

Many of these titles are also available online at
www.Oxfordreference.com

A Dictionary of

Environment and Conservation

SECOND EDITION

CHRIS PARK
MICHAEL ALLABY

OXFORD
UNIVERSITY PRESS

OXFORD
UNIVERSITY PRESS

Great Clarendon Street, Oxford, OX2 6DP,
United Kingdom

Oxford University Press is a department of the University of Oxford.
It furthers the University's objective of excellence in research, scholarship,
and education by publishing worldwide. Oxford is a registered trade mark of
Oxford University Press in the UK and in certain other countries

First Edition published in 2007
First published as an Oxford University Press paperback 2008
Second Edition 2013

Impression: 1

British Library Cataloguing in Publication Data

Data available

Library of Congress Cataloging in Publication Data

Data available

ISBN 978-0-19-964166-6

Printed in Great Britain by
Clays Ltd, St Ives plc

Contents

Preface

Nature never errs. Things always follow their principles. Though complex, they are never chaotic. Though many, they are not confused.

Wang Pi (Chinese philosopher, AD 226–49)
Quoted by Adelaine Yen Mah (2001) Watching the tree to catch a hare.
Harper Collins.

According to Simon Winchester (The Meaning of Everything, 2003, OUP) the first Oxford English Dictionary was published in 1928. It came in twelve volumes, totalled 15 490 pages, contained 414 825 definitions and had taken a team of writers 70 years to complete. This dictionary was written in less than 3 years, very much on a part-time basis in the gaps between day-job and the-rest-of-life, by one person with a small PC. It contains just under 9000 definitions and around 240 000 words.

Wang Pi's advice has informed much of my thinking and decision-making in writing this dictionary, because my aim has been to make clear the principles on which nature operates. Taking on this challenge has involved many choices as I have sought to produce a collection of definitions that is comprehensive but accessible, which embraces words and terms that are in common use throughout much of the English-speaking world (particularly in the UK, North America, and Australasia), and which will not date too quickly. I have also resisted the temptation to include long lists of names (of plants and animals, for example), and tried to balance science and non-science entries. To reinforce Wang Pi's observation that the principles of nature are many but not confused, I have tried to cross-reference entries as much as seems useful, using two conventions—the standard convention *See also*, *Compare* and *Contrast*, and using an asterisk before a term that is defined in its own right (e.g. *niche).

Inevitably, the source material that I have drawn on is very diverse, widely scattered, and rooted in many different disciplines. I have tried hard to weave many different threads together into a coherent tapestry, and (to change the metaphor) to impose one voice on this disparate material, in the rather optimistic hope of turning a cacophony into a symphony! I dread to think quite how lexicographers of old managed to do their work without access to the Internet, notebook-sized computers, and software that allows us to word-process, save back-up copies, and (most importantly!) instantly sort vast amounts of text.

I have adopted a style that I hope works well for the informed lay reader. To this end, whilst a great many technical and specialized terms are included, I have sought to distil what is sometimes complex material down to manageable sound bites and to explain things as clearly as possible without being patronizing.

I owe a great debt of thanks to a number of people who have played a part in the creation of this dictionary. I would never have been brave or stupid enough to think of writing a dictionary (on anything) had not Ruth Langley, Commissioning Editor at OUP, first approached me and suggested this one. Her faith was stronger than mine to start with, but I soon warmed to the idea, and I thank her for the bold approach and for her sustained support and interest during the writing. Jo Walker and Angela Carpenter offered invaluable suggestions for improving the text, for which I am enormously grateful. Bridget Johnson's attention to detail while copy-editing the text was meticulous, and is greatly appreciated. My closest family have sacrificed time with me while I soldiered on with the research and writing, and even when I was able to spend time with them, my mind was often elsewhere. My parents Alex and Margaret have been wonderful; always there in the background, quietly proud and supportive, even when they have little idea what I am doing. Sadly, my mother died while I was writing this dictionary, but her memory lives on through all that I do. My two eldest, Emma and Andrew, have flown the nest but are still very dear to me. My youngest offspring Sam and Elizabeth, both still in the nest, are resigned to having a Dad who seems to do little else but sit silently at the keyboard evening after evening; they tolerate my behaviour with charitable indifference. The true hero of the piece is my wife and travelling companion Penny, who keeps me grounded and brought the sunshine back into my life. I dedicate this dictionary to her, with love.

Chris Park

Lancaster, UK
February 2006

Preface to the Second Edition

Six years have passed since Chris Park completed the first edition of this dictionary. That seems a short time, but it is long in the lifetime of disciplines expanding as rapidly as the environmental sciences and the theory and application of conservation principles and techniques. Expansion implies a broadening, as practitioners borrow ideas from adjacent disciplines, as well as advances resulting from environmental and conservation research. New ideas and new discoveries bring with them or generate their own vocabularies. Consequently, if scientific and technical dictionaries are to remain relevant, from time to time the words and expressions from those new vocabularies must be added. Older terms retain their meanings, of course, but even those may require revision as newly acquired information provides a deeper understanding of their true significance. Six years is not long between editions.

I am privileged to have been invited to prepare a second edition. I began the task by compiling a list of several hundred new entries that I hoped would accommodate the broadening of the topic. These included a number of chemical substances, including pesticides, ecological and biogeographical terms, terms from atmospheric science, and reference soil groups in the FAO–UNESCO World Soil Classification. Then I worked my way through the existing definitions, revising and updating as I went, and inserting the new entries at the same time. As Chris Park noted in his preface, modern computing power has made this much easier than it was in the days when dictionary entries were stored on index cards and a new edition involved typing the entire work.

Dictionaries tend to grow longer with each edition. That is because in any living language new terms are coined faster than old terms become so completely obsolete they can be deleted. This edition is, therefore, longer than the first edition. I hope that the new entries and my substantial revisions will have given the dictionary a new lease of life, so it will continue to help and inform students and everyone interested in the environment and conservation for years to come.

I am grateful to Chris Park for having provided me with such a strong first edition as a solid base on which to build. I must also thank Judith Wilson and Jamie Crowther for entrusting the revision to me and for their encouragement. And I thank you, the reader, for buying and using the book.

Michael Allaby

Tighnabruaich, Argyll
www.michaelallaby.com
May 2012

aa Volcanic *lava rock that is thick and porous and has a rough, jagged surface when it cools. It is a Hawaiian word, pronounced *ah-ah*.

abandoned well Any *well that has not been used for a long time and/or is not properly sealed, and is so poorly maintained that it cannot be used for the purpose for which it was intended.

abatement The elimination or reduction of emissions that create *pollution. Examples include smoke abatement and noise abatement.

abatement debris Waste materials produced by *remediation activities.

Abbey, Edward US author (1927–89) who wrote the book *Desert Solitaire* and is remembered for his strong criticism of public land policies and his passionate advocacy of environmental issues.

abiotic Devoid of life, not *biotic, non-biological. Examples of the abiotic environment include climate, geology, and atmosphere.

ablation 1. The process by which *snow or *ice is lost from a *glacier or *ice cap by *melting, *sublimation, and *evaporation, which produces *meltwater. 2. The removal of rock particles by wind action.

ablation zone (ablation area, zone of ablation) The lower part of a glacier, where more ice melts than accumulates over a year. *Contrast* ACCUMULATION ZONE.

Aborigines *See* INDIGENOUS PEOPLES.

abrasion (corrasion) The *physical weathering or mechanical weathering of rock or sediment by running water, glaciers, or wind loaded with fine particles, through such processes as scratching, rubbing, grinding, or wearing away by friction.

absolute age Age that is expressed in number of years, rather than age relative to a particular event. In geology absolute age is considered misleading because ages are subject to error. *Contrast* RELATIVE AGE.

absolute chronology A *chronology that determines the age of a feature or event in years. *Contrast* RELATIVE CHRONOLOGY.

absolute dating A range of methods for determining the *absolute age of an object or material, for example using *radiometric dating which measures the *decay product produced by *radioactive decay in minerals, or via *dendrochronology. *Contrast* RELATIVE DATING. *See also* GEOCHRONOLOGY.

absolute humidity A measure of *humidity, or the actual mass of *water vapour in a given volume of air, usually expressed in grams of water per cubic metre of air (g m^{-3}). This measure takes no account of changes in humidity due to variations in the volume of air caused by changes in temperature and pressure. *Contrast* RELATIVE HUMIDITY. *See also* SPECIFIC HUMIDITY; DEW POINT; MIXING RATIO; VAPOUR PRESSURE.

absolute instability The meteorological condition in which a rising *parcel of air continues to rise because the *dry adiabatic lapse rate (DALR) is lower than the *environmental lapse rate, so the rising air is always warmer, and less dense, than the surrounding air. If the rising air reaches its *lifting condensation level its water vapour will start to condense, releasing *latent heat. The air will then cool at the *saturated adiabatic lapse rate, which is lower than the DALR, increasing the instability.

absolute poverty An extreme state of *poverty, in which the standard of living is below the minimum that is needed for the maintenance of life and *health. *Contrast* RELATIVE POVERTY.

absolute relief The maximum elevation of a particular area above *sea level. *Contrast* RELATIVE RELIEF.

absolute scarcity A condition that exists when there is not enough of a *resource in existence to satisfy existing demand for it. *Contrast* RELATIVE SCARCITY.

absolute zero A temperature of $-273.15°C$, $-459.67°F$, the zero point on the *Kelvin temperature scale, at which atomic and molecular motion stops, at least theoretically.

absorb To take something in (such as the penetration of a solid substance by a liquid, by capillary, osmotic, solvent, or chemical action). In energy terms, to take in energy and then not re-emit it.

absorbed dose (internal dose) The amount (*dose) of a chemical substance that is absorbed by, and thus enters the body of, an organism exposed to it. Most commonly expressed as milligrams per kilogram body weight per day $(mg\,kg^{-1}day^{-1})$.

absorbency The ability of a substance to *absorb, which reflects its *porosity.

absorption 1. The penetration of one substance into or through another, such as the absorption of water into soil, or the uptake of water and nutrients by a cell or organism which *absorbs them. *Contrast* ADSORPTION; DESORPTION; INGESTION. **2.** A way of containing an *oil spill, in which oil is absorbed onto special materials from which it can be squeezed out for reuse or disposal.

absorption tower A vertical cylinder in which components of a rising gas are absorbed by a falling liquid. Such devices are commonly used as *scrubbers.

absorptive capacity The maximum amount of waste material that can be naturally absorbed by the environment on a sustainable basis, without causing environmental damage.

abstraction The action of removing something, such as the abstraction of water from a river, lake or *groundwater, for use in industry. Also known as **extraction**, particularly when applied to a *rock or *mineral.

abstractive use *See* OFFSTREAM USE.

abundance The number or amount of something. *See also* SPECIES ABUNDANCE; RELATIVE ABUNDANCE.

abyss *See* OCEAN FLOOR.

abyssal hill A hill on the ocean floor, commonly 50–250 m in height and several kilometres in diameter.

abyssal plain The flat, deep part of the ocean floor that lies offshore from the *continental rise, below about 2000 m below the ocean surface. It usually has a very low slope (less than 1:1000) and is covered by a thick layer of sediment.

abyssal zone An ecological zone within the ocean that accounts for three-quarters of the deep ocean floors. Conditions are cold (temperatures remain steady at about 4°C) and dark in this zone, more than 2000 m below the ocean surface.

acaricide A chemical substance used to kill ticks (order Acarina).

accelerated erosion An increased rate of *erosion above natural levels. This can be natural (for example, caused by hurricane damage) but is often caused directly or indirectly by human activities. It removes soil much faster than soil naturally develops and can lead to serious environmental damage, both where it occurs (because it reduces plant productivity and can lead to *mass movement of soils and sediments) and downslope or downstream where it is deposited (where it can, for example, infill reservoirs and lakes, change river channels and increase the growth of a *delta).

acceptable daily intake The largest daily amount of a substance that a typical person can consume or be exposed to over a lifetime, without producing unwanted health risk, usually expressed in milligrams per kilogram (of body mass) per day $(mg\,kg^{-1}\,day^{-1})$.

acceptable risk The level of *risk that is regarded as acceptable by the community or authorities, below which no specific action by local government is deemed necessary other than making the risk known. *Contrast* AVOIDABLE RISK; UNACCEPTABLE RISK.

accident profile A description of an accident that includes relevant preceding and succeeding events as well as details of the accident itself. Preceding events may reveal steps that might prevent a recurrence of the accident. Succeeding events may expose inadequacies in measures taken to rescue and treat injured persons and repair environmental damage.

accident scenario A simulation of a major disaster that is held to test the response of emergency services and assess the extent of damage and injury.

accident site The location of an accident. Examples include the failure of a pipe in a factory that leads to the release of hazardous chemicals, or the site of an accidental release of pollutants into a lake or river.

accident type The accident event that causes, or the circumstances that give rise to, injury to people or damage to property. Examples include road traffic accidents, an explosion in a building, or a flood that drowns people.

acclimation An adjustment that occurs in an individual organism that allows it to tolerate a change (often in a single factor, such a temperature) in its environment, or to tolerate a new environment. The adjustment is usually gradual and reversible, and it can be physiological or behavioural, or both. The term is usually applied to organisms used in laboratory experiments and exposed to a change in a single factor. A response to a change in several factors is known as acclimatization. *See also* ADAPTATION.

acclimatization *See* ACCLIMATION.

accounting The systematic recording, reporting, and analysis of transactions, particularly financial ones, in order to support effective management and decision-making, by providing the required information. *See also* ENVIRONMENTAL ACCOUNTING; INTERNALIZATION.

accretion A process of growth by accumulation and adhesion. Examples include the build-up or accumulation of *sediment, and the process by which *precipitation particles grow, by the collision of an ice crystal or snowflake with a supercooled liquid droplet that freezes upon impact. On a large scale, the term is also used to describe primitive planetary growth, and to describe the addition of material at the edges of pre-existing continents.

accumulated temperature The sum of the amount by which the air temperature deviates from a datum level over a protracted period. If the temperature on a particular day is m degrees above (positive) or below (negative) the datum and it remains there for n hours (i.e. $n/24$ days), the accumulated temperature is $mn/24$ degree days. Adding daily accumulated temperatures yields the accumulated weekly, monthly, seasonal, or annual temperature.

accumulation rate The speed at which something (such as a layer of sediment on the floor of a lake or ocean, or layers of ice on the surface of a glacier) accumulates or builds up. Usually expressed as depth per unit time (for example millimetres per year, mm year^{-1}).

accumulation zone (zone of accumulation) An area where accumulation of material occurs. **1.** The upper part of a glacier, where snow and ice accumulate because annual snowfall exceeds loss by *ablation. *Contrast* WASTAGE ZONE. **2.** The lower part of a hillslope, where sediment transported downhill by *mass movement processes accumulates.

ACE *See* US ARMY CORPS OF ENGINEERS.

acetaldehyde (ethanal) A direct oxidation product (CH_3CHO) of *ethanol. It is made industrially from ethene (C_2H_4) and it can be further oxidized to *acetic acid. Acetaldehyde is an important raw material for certain organic compounds, has medicinal uses, and its volatility allows it to be used as solid pellets to fuel cooking stoves. It is also used as a food additive with the flavour of apple.

acetic acid (ethanoic acid) The acid in vinegar and an important industrial raw material ($CH_3.COOH$) that is obtained from *alcohols by *fermentation.

acetone (propanone) An industrial and laboratory solvent (CH_3COCH_3) that is *miscible with water and is a raw material for making plastics.

acetylcholine (ACh) A substance that is released at many nerve endings, thereby transmitting impulses to other nerve cells or to effectors. Following secretion it is rapidly destroyed by the *enzyme cholinesterase.

acetylene (ethyne) A colourless hydrocarbon used industrially as a fuel for welding, in the synthesis of *acetic acid, and as a starting material for many chemicals including *polyvinyl chloride.

ACh *See* ACETYLCHOLINE.

acid An organic or inorganic compound that contains hydrogen and releases hydrogen ions (H^+) when dissolved in water. Acids also react with metals to release hydrogen, and with bases to form salts. All acids turn litmus paper red and have a *pH of less than 7.0. Many have a sour taste and can cause severe skin burns in humans. *Contrast* ALKALI.

acid aerosol Acidic liquid or solid particles small enough to become airborne. High concentrations can irritate the lungs and have been associated with respiratory diseases, e.g. asthma.

acid deposition *See* ACID RAIN.

acid dipping The process of immersing a metal object in a bath of acid or a mixture of acids in order to remove scale and clean the surface. The process may release hazardous gases and acid mists.

acid grassland (grass heath) Grassland that develops over nutrient-poor, acidic soils, often as a result of a long period of grazing or burning of woodland.

acid loading The total amount of acid material that is added to a particular habitat or area over a given period of time, usually expressed as grams per square metre per year ($g\,m^{-2}\,year^{-1}$).

acid mine drainage The drainage of water from areas that have been mined for coal or other mineral ores (including gold, silver, *copper, iron, *zinc, and *lead). The water has high acidity (low *pH, sometimes less than 2.0) because it has been in contact with material that contains sulphur, producing *sulphuric acid (H_2SO_4) which is strongly corrosive and dissolves metals such as lead, zinc, copper, *arsenic, *selenium, *mercury, and *cadmium into ground water and surface water. Acid mine drainage can poison *groundwater and drinking water, and it is harmful to aquatic organisms and habitats.

acid neutralizing capacity *See* BUFFERING CAPACITY.

acid precipitation *See* ACID RAIN.

Acid Rain Program A major air pollution control initiative in the USA, established under the *Clean Air Act Amendments of 1990, which established a *cap and trade system for reducing

emissions of *sulphur dioxide from power plants.

acid rock An *igneous rock that contains more than 60% *silica by weight, most of which is as silicate materials, with the excess of about 10% as free quartz. Acid rock is low in magnesium. Acid rocks tend to be much lighter in colour than *basic rocks, they tend to disintegrate around the mineral *crystals, and they often weather into coarse-textured and rather infertile *soils.

acid shock (acid surge) A sudden increase in the level of *acidity of surface waters (lakes, streams, and rivers) in mid-latitude areas, caused by the melting in spring of snow that has accumulated through the winter, and stored dry fallout of acidic precipitation. An acid shock can cause significant damage to freshwater species and habitats.

acid smut *See* ACID SOOT.

acid soil Soil with a *pH of less than about 6.6, caused by *acidification. Acidification occurs either naturally beneath *coniferous forest which sheds acidic needles and creates acidic litter, or as a result of air pollution by *acid deposition.

acid soot (acid smut) Particles of carbon (i.e. soot) about 1–3 mm in diameter that are emitted during combustion and that are held together by water. Combination with sulphur trioxide (SO_3) renders the particles acidic so that they contribute to acid deposition (*see* ACID RAIN). Emissions can be reduced by using low-sulphur fuels and reducing the airflow to minimize SO_3 formation, by making *flues airtight, and by raising the temperature, e.g. by insulating chimneys.

Fig. 1 Acid rain cycle

ACID RAIN (ACID DEPOSITION, ACID PRECIPITATION)

A form of *air pollution that is created by the transformation within the atmosphere of gaseous pollutants, principally *sulphur dioxide (SO_2) and *nitrogen oxides (NO_x), which are emitted mainly from coal-fired power stations and vehicle exhausts, respectively (see Fig. 1). These oxides interact with sunlight and other atmospheric contaminants such as *ozone, *photo-oxidants, *hydrocarbons, and *moisture. The chemical chain-reactions turn the *primary pollutants into a variable cocktail of *secondary pollutants. It can occur as *dry deposition and as *wet deposition. Acid rain has a *pH of less than 5.6, and the deposition of acidic material on the ground causes acidification of soils, water bodies, and vegetation. Acidified lakes are noted for large-scale fish deaths and declining fish populations, and acidified forests suffer from *tree dieback and tree death. Acidification affects plant growth by damaging leaves, impairing *photosynthesis, and damaging root hairs. The oxides can remain active for at least seven days, during which time they can be blown thousands of kilometres by wind systems to create *trans-frontier pollution. Swedish scientists estimate that up to nine-tenths of the sulphur deposited on Sweden is blown in from other countries (particularly the UK, France, and Germany). The USA is also accused of exporting acid rain from industrial centres in the north-east, across the Canadian border into the province of Ontario. From the early 1920s onwards many lakes and rivers in southern Scandinavia have displayed signs of acidification, including large-scale fish deaths, declining fish populations, and falling rates of reproduction. But only since the late 1960s have scientists beyond Scandinavia taken the acid rain problem seriously. In 1972 the *Organisation for Economic Co-operation and Development (OECD) launched a major research programme designed to measure air quality at 70 sites, in order to examine the long-range transport of air pollutants. By 1977, OECD studies had shown that the areas receiving acid rain were growing (in size and number), and that acid rain crosses national boundaries, so that some countries (such as Britain) are net exporters whilst others (such as Sweden) are net importers. The first international initiatives designed to deal with acid rain came in 1979 when a *convention was drafted by the United Nations Economic Commission for Europe (ECE). This convention grew out of the *Long-Range Transport of Air Pollutants (LRTAP) project and it aimed to reduce acid rain by reducing and controlling emissions of SO_2 and NO_x using the 'best available control technology economically feasible'. Thirty-one countries signed initially, but the convention was not legally binding and the commitment of some countries quickly evaporated. The Scandinavians were not satisfied with the 1979 convention, which they saw as inadequate to deal with the problem. They proposed that signatories should be responsible for reducing their emissions of SO_2 by 30% between 1980 and 1993. As a result a group of LRTAP countries met in Ottawa in 1984 to form what has since been called the *Thirty Percent Club. By July 1985, 21 of the LRTAP countries had joined the club by promising to cut their emissions by at least 30%. The USA and UK initially refused to join the club and reduce emission levels, insisting that there was not yet enough firm evidence linking SO_2 emissions with observed damage to forests and lakes. The UK had a change of heart and joined in 1986. Tackling acid deposition will require action on a broad front, because there are a number of options for reducing the two main gases (SO_2 and NO_x) that create the problem.

acid surge *See* ACID SHOCK.

acidic A material, liquid, or solid that has a high *acid content. The acidity of solutions (including water in soil) is measured using the *pH scale; acidic means with a pH of less than 7.0.

acidification The process by which *acids are added to a water body or soil, causing a decrease in *buffering capacity and leading to a significant decrease in *pH that may lead to the water body or soil becoming acidic (having a

pH less than 7.0). This is a common form of *water pollution, and when pH drops below about 6.5 it damages aquatic ecosystems. For sensitive organisms the chemical *threshold of acid water is about pH 5.5 (zero *alkalinity); below this many aquatic species disappear from the waterbody.

acidity A measure of how acid a material, liquid, or solid is as expressed using the *pH scale. A *pH of less than 7.0 is described as *acidic (the lower the pH value the greater the acidity); a pH of more than 7.0 is described as *alkaline (the higher the pH value the greater the alkalinity).

acquired land General term for land in the USA which is owned by the government and was obtained through purchase or as a gift or donation, by exchange, or to exploit the timber growing there.

acquired trait A *phenotype characteristic of an *organism, that is acquired during the growth and development of an individual, such as the large muscles that an athlete develops as a result of exercise and training. An acquired trait is not genetically based and so it cannot be passed on to the next generation.

acquired value A value (monetary or otherwise) that people attach to something because of its perceived usefulness. *Contrast* INTRINSIC VALUE. *See also* INSTRUMENTAL VALUE.

acre-foot The volume of a substance (usually water) that will cover one acre of a level surface to a depth of one foot, i.e. 43 560 ft^3; 1232.75 m^3.

acrid Bitter or sharp-tasting, usually with an unpleasantly strong or bitter smell.

acrisols *Acid soils that have an *illuvial horizon rich in *silicate *clays with a *cation-exchange capacity lower than 24 cmol$_c$/kg (centimoles cation per kilogram). Acrisols are a reference soil group in the *World Soil Classification.

acrotelm The upper layer of a peat *bog, in which organic matter decomposes aerobically and much more rapidly than in the underlying, anaerobic catotelm. As litter accumulates at the surface the size of the catotelm increases, because the thickness of the acrotelm is limited to the depth at which aerobic respiration can occur. Although the rate of decomposition per unit volume of material is much greater in the acrotelm than in the catotelm, a point is reached at which the difference in volume between the two layers is such that the total rate of decomposition in the catotelm is equal to that in the acrotelm. This limits the thickness to which the bog can grow. Should there be a climate change (e.g. an increase in precipitation) growth can resume. Bogs therefore preserve a record of climatic conditions. Most water movement occurs within this layer, because the *hydraulic conductivity of the acrotelm is about one hundred times that of the catotelm.

acrylic resins A group of synthetic *resins, including acrilan and Perspex, that are derived by polymerization from acrylic (propenoic) acid. The resins are transparent and resistant to light, weak *acids, *alkalis, and *alcohols, but are attacked by oxidizing acids, *organo-chlorines, *ketones, and *esters.

act A legal document that codifies the result of deliberations by a committee, society, or legislative body. *See also* STATUTE.

actinide (actinoid) Any of a series of *radio-active elements that have an *atomic number of between 89 and 103.

actinoid *See* ACTINIDE.

action level The *threshold level of *contamination, defined in a regulatory programme, that defines when action or a response is formally required. For example, in the US *Superfund programme, the action level makes clear when a particular form of contamination is high enough to warrant action or trigger a response under *SARA and the *NCP. Also in the USA, the *Environmental Protection Agency has defined action levels for levels of indoor *radon, levels of pesticide residues in foodstuffs, and for other environmental factors.

action research Learning by doing. A particular type of applied research that often involves researchers and practitioners working closely together, in which a group of people identifies a problem, does something to resolve it, reflects on how successful their efforts were, and, if not satisfied, tries again. *See also* ADAPTIVE MANAGEMENT.

activated alumina A granular form of aluminium oxide that is porous and capable of absorbing water, oil vapour, and certain other fluids. It is used in pollution control, *chromatography, and as a catalyst.

activated carbon (activated charcoal) A highly absorbent carbon-rich material, made from burnt wood, that is used to remove odours and toxic substances from liquid or gas emissions by absorbing the solutes onto the activated *carbon. It is used, for example, to remove dissolved organic matter (including *pesticides) and some inorganic solutes (including chlorine) from waste water. *See also* GRANULAR ACTIVATED CARBON TREATMENT.

activated charcoal *See* ACTIVATED CARBON.

activated sludge A process for treating *sewage and primary effluent water using an active population of *micro-organisms that feed on organic wastes. Raw sewage is mixed with bacteria-laden sludge, and the mixture is then shaken and aerated (oxygen is added) to speed the breakdown of organic matter in *secondary wastewater treatment. The process converts soluble organic matter into solid *biomass. Half of the sewage in Britain is treated like this.

activator The activity of a *catalyst, such as a chemical that is added to a *pesticide to increase its activity.

active fault A geological *fault that is still active rather than *dormant, meaning that significant displacement or movement has occurred on it within about the last 10 000 years.

active ingredient The component in any *pesticide that kills or controls the target pests, and that determines how that pesticide is regulated.

active layer A seasonally thawed surface layer, between a few centimetres and about 3 m thick, that lies above the permanently frozen ground in a *periglacial environment. It may be subject to considerable expansion on freezing because of the water it contains, and especially if silt-sized particles dominate, with important engineering implications.

active restoration The use of active measures, such as hand-planting trees and shrubs and removing *exotic plants and animals, in *habitat restoration. *See also* NATURAL PROCESS RESTORATION.

active solar heating A form of *solar heating that uses *solar energy to heat buildings indirectly. *Solar collectors are used to heat water which can then be stored and circulated around a building by pumps and pipes to heat water and space. *Contrast* PASSIVE SOLAR HEATING.

active transport The passage of a substance from a region of low concentration to one of high concentration (i.e. against the concentration gradient) through the expenditure of energy. It most commonly occurs across cell membranes.

activism *See* ENVIRONMENTAL ACTIVISM; GRASSROOTS ACTIVISM.

Activities Implemented Jointly (AIJ) A pilot programme established by the *United Nations Framework Convention on Climate Change, designed to encourage a cooperative international approach to tackling global warming caused by air pollution. It allowed private bodies and organizations in one country to reduce, *sequester, or avoid reducing *greenhouse gas emissions through funding or running a project in a different country that reduces emissions there. The AIJ programme ended in 2000 and has evolved into *joint implementation under the *Kyoto Protocol.

activity plan A detailed plan for managing a single resource programme, designed to achieve specific objectives, and usually developed only when needed to support more general *land use plan decisions. An example is a habitat management plan for the *conservation of a particular wildlife *habitat.

actual evaporation The amount of *evaporation that takes place from open water. *Contrast* POTENTIAL EVAPORATION.

actual evapotranspiration The rate at which water is lost from vegetation and soil by a combination of *evaporation (from any water surface) and *transpiration (from plants), which is usually lower than *potential evapotranspiration.

acute In general, extremely serious or severe. Relating to disease, severe and of short duration. *Contrast* CHRONIC.

acute dose A fatal level of exposure to some factor (such as radiation) that is experienced over a short period of time.

acute effect A sudden, rapid onset in any organism of severe symptoms or adverse effects as a result of exposure to some factor (such as high concentrations of particular pollutants), which often disappear after the exposure stops. *Contrast* CHRONIC EFFECT.

acute exposure A single, brief, intense exposure to a hazardous material (such as a toxic substance) or situation that may cause serious injury or death in an organism (including people). Such exposure often lasts less than a day, but can have long-lasting consequences. *Contrast* CHRONIC EXPOSURE.

acute poverty A serious shortage of income or of access to the range of resources that usually provide the basic necessities for life for humans, such as food, shelter, sanitation, clean water, medical care, and education.

acute reference dose (ARfD) An estimate of the amount of a substance that a person might consume over a short (acute) duration of 24 hours or less without appreciable risk to the consumer's health. It is most commonly used in setting limits for pesticide residues in food.

(●) **SEE WEB LINKS**
• WHO guidance on setting of acute reference dose for pesticides.

acute toxicity The short-term effects of a single large exposure to a *toxic substance, which are apparent usually within 24 to 96 hours. See also CHRONIC TOXICITY; TOXICITY.

adaptability (adaptive capacity) A measure of the extent to which a *species or *ecosystem is able to adjust to environmental change (such as *global warming). Such *adaptation can be planned or unplanned, and it can be carried out in response to or in anticipation of changes in conditions.

adaptation A change in the structure or habit of an *organism that makes it better adjusted to its surroundings. Short-term change is physiological (for example, *acclimation) or behavioural (*phenotypic adaptation), and long-term change is genetic (*genotypic adaptation). Particular genetic adaptations in a population become frequent and dominant if they enhance an individual's ability to survive in the environment, for example as climate changes through time. See also EVOLUTION; NATURAL SELECTION.

adaptive capacity See ADAPTABILITY.

adaptive management (monitor-and-modify approach) An approach to the management of *natural resources that is based on learning by doing, and on making decisions as part of an on-going process of monitoring, review, and adaptation. A planned course of action is kept under constant review, and is adapted where appropriate as new information becomes available from the monitoring of results, publication of new scientific findings and expert judgements, and changing needs of society. See also ACTION RESEARCH.

adaptive radiation A burst of evolution, with new forms diverging from a single ancestral form, that results from the exploitation of an array of *habitats that have newly become accessible. The term is applied at many taxonomic levels. For example, Charles *Darwin observed that over many generations 13–15 (depending on the classification) *species of finches descended from a single ancestral species had adapted to the availability of different food sources on islands in the Galápagos by developing different shapes of beak. See also CLADOGENESIS; SPECIATION.

(●) **SEE WEB LINKS**
• Darwin's finches

adaptive strategy The means by which *species cope with competition and environmental change over the long term, on an evolutionary time scale. See also GENOTYPIC ADAPTATION.

additionality A reduction in or avoidance of *greenhouse gas emissions that exceeds what would have occurred under a *business-as-usual scenario. Under the *Kyoto Protocol, such reductions must be real and measurable.

additive A substance that is added to improve or preserve something. Examples include the chemicals that are added to food and the lead that was previously added to gasoline to reduce engine wear in vehicles.

additive effect The combined effect of two or more changes that is equal to the sum of their individual effects. Contrast SYNERGISM.

ADEOS II A *satellite *remote sensing system, launched in 1999, that monitors surface wind speeds and directions over the *oceans.

adhesion 1. The ability to stick to something. 2. Intermolecular attraction between unlike substances where adjacent surfaces cling together.

adiabatic Any change in temperature, pressure, and volume in a parcel of air that is caused by the expansion (cooling) or compression (warming) of the air as it rises or descends in the atmosphere. The parcel of air does not exchange heat with the surrounding atmosphere. Contrast DIABATIC.

adiabatic lapse rate The rate at which the temperature of a parcel of air decreases when the air is lifted (or the rate of increase of temperature when air sinks), without any exchange of heat or energy with the surrounding air, by *adiabatic change. When lifted, a parcel of unsaturated air cools at the *dry adiabatic lapse rate; a parcel of saturated air cools at the *saturated adiabatic lapse rate. When it descends, the parcel of air warms at the corresponding rate.

adiabatic process A process that occurs with no exchange of heat or energy between a system (such as a parcel of air) and its environment (the surrounding atmosphere).

adit A more or less horizontal tunnel from a *hillside into an underground *mine, open to the surface at one end, that is used for access or drainage.

adjustment Change or adaptation within a *system that serves to accommodate the factor(s) that are promoting the change and produce a new *equilibrium. A system changes when it is forced to, otherwise it tends to remain stable and unchanging. *See also* HOMEOSTASIS.

adjuvant A substance that modifies the effect of another substance. Adjuvants are often added to *vaccines to enhance the recipient's response to an *antigen.

administered dose (intake, potential dose) In exposure assessment, the amount (*dose) of a substance that is given to a test subject (a human or animal) to determine *dose–response relationships.

adsorption The process by which molecules of a gas, liquid, or dissolved substance (in a condensed form) adhere to the surface of a solid material, or less frequently of a liquid. This process is used, for example, in advanced wastewater treatment, using *activated carbon to remove organic matter from the water. *Contrast* ABSORPTION.

advanced air emission control device Equipment for controlling air pollution after it has been initially treated (for example by low-energy *scrubbers). Examples include *electrostatic precipitators and high-energy scrubbers.

advanced character *See* DERIVED CHARACTER.

Advanced Very High Resolution Radiometer (AVHRR) The main sensor on US polar orbiting *satellites, which is used for monitoring changing levels of radiation as well as visible and infrared light. It can produce cloud images even at night.

advanced wastewater treatment (tertiary treatment) Any treatment of sewage and wastewater that goes beyond the secondary (biological) stage and includes the removal of nutrients such as *phosphorus and *nitrogen, and a high percentage of *suspended solids. *See also* PRIMARY TREATMENT; SECONDARY TREATMENT.

advection The horizontal transfer of properties (such as heat or moisture) or substances (such as air or water pollutants) by the flow of a current of water or air. *See also* FOG; ADVECTION FOG.

advection fog A *fog that forms by *advection when warm air flows over a cold surface (such as a cold ocean current). The air cools from below until air temperature falls to the *dew point, *saturation occurs, and *water vapour condenses to form fog. This type of fog is quite common and can be persistent, lasting longer and dispersing more slowly than *radiation fog.

advection frost *See* FREEZE.

advection inversion A temperature *inversion caused by *advection as warm air passes over a cool surface.

adventitious root A plant root that grows in an unusual location (for example, from a stem). *See also* ROOT CLIMBER.

adverse effect/impact An effect that damages the environment or reduces environmental quality, which can include human health and quality of life to an unacceptable degree.

advisory A term used in the USA to refer to guidance issued by the authorities, usually in a particular area. It usually relates to the incidence of a specific *environmental hazard (such as adverse weather) that is likely to cause significant inconvenience to people but is not serious enough to issue a *warning. *Compare* CAUTION.

AEC *See* ATOMIC ENERGY COMMISSION.

Aedes aegypti *See* YELLOW-FEVER MOSQUITO.

aeolian (eolian) Wind-blown or involving wind. For example, *loess is an *aeolian deposit, and a *dune is a *landform produced by aeolian action.

aeolian deposit Fine sediments that are transported and deposited by wind. Examples include *loess, *dunes, desert sand, and some *volcanic ash.

aeolian erosion *See* WIND EROSION.

aeolian soil Soil that has been deposited by wind, usually made up of silt or sand.

aeration To oxygenate or allow air to penetrate something. This process is used to promote biological degradation of *organic matter in water, by exposing it to air. The process may be passive (when waste is simply exposed to air), or active (when a mixing or bubbling device introduces the air into the liquid, generating bubbles and aerosols that lead to the

a

release of the dissolved gases). *See also* DIF-FUSED AIR.

aeration tank A chamber used to inject air into water to speed the *aeration process.

aeration zone (unsaturated zone, vadose zone, zone of aeration) The subsurface zone between the ground surface and the *water table, where the pores in soil and rock contain both air and water.

aerial logging The removal of logs from a timber harvest area by helicopter, which allows access to previously inaccessible sites but causes less environmental damage because fewer access roads need to be built.

aerial photograph (air photograph) A photograph of the Earth's surface that is taken from the air, usually at regular intervals along a *transect. Interpretation of such photographs provides valuable information about *land use, *vegetation, and *landforms, etc.

aerial plankton Bacteria, spores, and other minute organisms and particles of biological origin that are blown from the ground and carried aloft by air currents. Air movements may then transport them considerable distances.

aeroallergen Any of a variety of *allergens (such as pollens, grasses, or dust) that are carried in the air and dispersed by winds.

aerobe (aerobic organism) An organism that can live and grow only in the presence of oxygen. *Contrast* ANAEROBE.

aerobic A process that occurs, or life that exists, only in the presence of oxygen. *Contrast* ANAEROBIC.

aerobic biological oxidation Any waste treatment process that uses *aerobes to reduce the pollution load or oxygen demand of organic substance in water.

aerobic composting A method of composting organic waste using *aerobic bacteria. The waste is exposed to air either by turning or by forcing air into it through pipes. This process is reasonably odour-free, and it generates more heat and is faster than *anaerobic composting. Temperatures may become high enough to destroy *pathogens and weed seeds.

aerobic digestion (aerobic treatment, sludge processing) The decomposition of *organic matter by *aerobic organisms in the presence of oxygen, which results in the formation of mineral and simpler organic compounds.

aerobic organism *See* AEROBE.

aerobic treatment *See* AEROBIC DIGESTION.

aerodynamic A body shape which is *streamlined to reduce air resistance and thus allow easy movement through air. *Compare* HYDRODYNAMIC.

aerodynamics The study of objects in air flow, or of objects moving through air.

aerosol A suspension of tiny liquid droplets or solid particles in a gas which are so small that they do not settle out under the influence of gravity and so remain suspended in the air. Natural aerosols include *fog and minute particles that originate from wind-blown sea salt or dust, volcanic eruptions, and the burning of *vegetation. Manufactured aerosols include fine sprays used in perfumes, insecticides, and antiperspirants. Aerosol particles provide nuclei for the *condensation of water droplets and for the growth of ice crystals, and they also absorb and scatter *solar radiation, through which they influence the *radiation budget of the atmosphere, which in turn influences *climate on the surface of the Earth.

aerosol spray A device that releases a substance under pressure, in the form of an *aerosol.

aerovane *See* ANEMOMETER.

aesthetic Pleasing to the eye or judged to have beauty, particularly as relating to visual appearance, such as a view or *landscape.

aesthetic degradation Any reduction in environmental quality that people interpret as making it less attractive, for example the adverse impact on a natural *landscape of building a large power station.

aesthetic injury level *See* ECONOMIC INJURY LEVEL.

aesthetic resource The intangible natural qualities of a place that make it appeal to people, such as a sense of solitude, of being in close contact with nature, and of being inspired and emotionally recharged by the experience of being there. *Contrast* CULTURAL RESOURCE. *See also* RESOURCE.

aesthetic zoning Land use *zoning which regulates property in order to protect *aesthetic values.

aesthetics The study of beauty, and the basis of judgments about beauty.

aestivation (estivation) Dormancy or sluggishness that occurs in some animals (e.g. snails and hagfish) during a period when conditions are hot and dry. Aestivation is analogous to *hibernation in cold environments and normally lasts the length of the dry period or season.

aetiology The study of the causes of *diseases.

affected public A North American term for the people who are adversely affected by exposure to a *toxic pollutant in food, water, air, or soil, perhaps by living near or working in a hazardous waste site.

affinity A chemical attraction that causes the atoms of certain elements or compounds to combine with atoms of another element or compound, and then remain in the combined state. The term is also used to describe how likely such a reaction is to occur.

afforestation (forestation) The process of establishing and growing *forests on bare or cultivated land which has not been forested in recent history. As well as creating new *habitats for wildlife, and new supplies of timber, afforestation provides valuable *carbon sinks which absorb *carbon dioxide and thus help to reduce *global warming. *Contrast* DEFORESTATION; REFORESTATION.

aflatoxin A *toxin that is produced by *moulds in stored crops (particularly in peanuts) and is *carcinogenic.

African-Indian desert floral region Part of the African subkingdom of R. Good's palaeotropical kingdom (*The Geography of the Flowering Plants*, 1974). The flora is relatively poor and specialized, the number of *endemic genera probably just exceeding 50. *Phoenix dactylifera* (the date palm) belongs to this region, but, not surprisingly perhaps, there are no garden plants.

African wave *See* EASTERLY WAVE.

Afrotropical realm A *biogeographical realm which covers most of Africa and is dominated by *tropical forest, *savanna, and *desert.

afterburner Equipment used in an *incinerator, in which the exhaust gases are passed through a burner to remove smoke and odours. This helps to completely combust unburned or partially burned carbon compounds.

aftershock A lesser *earthquake that follows a stronger one.

Aftonian The earliest (1.3–0.9 million years ago) of four *interglacial stages in North America, marked by mild summers and winters warmer than those in present-day North America.

age class 1. An age grouping of any organism, including people. 2. A grouping of trees, forests, stands, or forest types into 20-year age classes (1–20, 21–40, and so on) employed by foresters.

age distribution (age structure) The proportions of a population that fall in different *age classes, or into different groups such as pre-reproductive (subadult), reproductive, and post-reproductive.

Age of Reason *See* ENLIGHTENMENT.

age pyramid A diagram that shows the proportions within each *age class of a population.

age ratio The proportion of young individuals to adults in a population. This has an impact on productivity and population growth.

age structure *See* AGE DISTRIBUTION.

agency 1. A form of action or intervention. 2. An organization or government department that provides a particular service.

agency capture A term used in the USA for the situation in which a regulatory process is 'captured' by those it is supposed to regulate, and then turned to their advantage.

agent (environmental agent, stressor) In environmental science, any physical, chemical, or biological entity that can affect (benefit or injure) an *organism, people, or the *environment.

Agent Blue *See* ARSENICAL HERBICIDES.

agent of disease Any factor (such as a *micro-organism, a chemical substance, or a form of *radiation) that is essential for the occurrence of a *disease.

agent orange A toxic *defoliant that was used by the USA in the Vietnam War. Based on a mixture of several *herbicides, it is believed to be a *carcinogen because it includes *dioxin. The name comes from the orange-banded barrels in which the defoliant was marketed.

AGENDA 21

A comprehensive, long-term plan of action on environmental and development issues that was drawn up at the 1992 *United Nations Conference on Environment and Development (UNCED) and is being implemented globally, nationally, and locally in order to relieve *poverty in developing countries and promote *sustainable development. The main focus of Agenda 21 is the sustainable management of economic, social, and natural capital (including *biodiversity) in order to meet the needs of present and future human generations, with particular emphasis on the needs of the most disadvantaged. Agenda 21 proposals include various ways of saving biodiversity, including: creating a world information resource for biodiversity; protecting biodiversity; offering *indigenous peoples the chance to contribute to biodiversity conservation; making sure that poor countries share equally in the commercial exploitation of their products and experience; protecting and repairing damaged habitats; conserving endangered species; assessing every big project (dams, roads, etc.) for its *environmental impact. The estimated total cost of implementing all of the recommendations in Agenda 21 is nearly $600000 million (at 1992 prices), and a number of sources of funding were identified. UNCED proposed that $460000 million (77%) would come from local sources, and the remaining $140000 million (23%) from international sources including foreign aid and the *World Bank. It was agreed that each country should meet the costs of implementing Agenda 21 from its own resources, but that additional funding would be needed for the *developing countries and this would come mainly from official development assistance, the *Global Environment Facility (GEF) set up by the World Bank, the *United Nations Development Programme (UNDP) and the *United Nations Environment Programme (UNEP), and the International Development Association, the branch of the World Bank that provides interest-free loans to the lowest-income countries. *See also* GLOBAL ENVIRONMENT FACILITY; LOCAL AGENDA 21.

agglomerate 1. To collect or gather together fine particulates into a larger mass. **2.** A type of volcanic rock.

agglomeration 1. In general, the process of gathering together. **2.** The process by which precipitation particles grow larger, by collision or contact with *cloud particles or other precipitation particles, until they are large enough to fall as *precipitation.

aggradation The accumulation of unconsolidated sediments, which builds up the land surface. *Contrast* DEGRADATION.

aggregate 1. A mass or cluster of material, such as the particles in a *soil. **2.** A mixture of rock and mineral fragments that resemble a rock.

aggregation 1. The process of cementing or binding together of soil particles into an *aggregate. **2.** A method by which ice crystals grow around nuclei in the atmosphere, by colliding with other crystals and sticking together. **3.** A collection of organisms that live closely together but are not physically connected. *See also* COLONY.

agrarian Relating to *agriculture or *farming.

agrarian civilization A society that depends on an *agricultural economy, and which is therefore settled, as opposed to *hunter-gathering.

Agreement on the Conservation of Polar Bears An international agreement reached in Oslo on 15 November 1973 between the governments of Canada, Denmark, Norway, the USSR (now the Russian Federation), and the USA. It forbids the hunting, killing, or capturing of polar bears except under special circumstances and requires governments to protect polar bear *habitats.

(🌐) **SEE WEB LINKS**

• Text of the Agreement on the Conservation of Polar Bears.

agribusiness Large-scale, industrialized agriculture controlled by corporations, which includes all of the operations involved in the production, storage, processing, distribution, and wholesale marketing of farm products.

agricultural diversification The process of seeking supplementary or replacement income streams for farms, beyond agricultural activities themselves. Farm-based tourism is an example.

agricultural economy An economic system that is based primarily on crop production.

agricultural intensification The management of increased production in *agriculture by making greater use of *agrochemicals and mechanization. *See also* INTENSIVE AGRICULTURE.

agricultural pollution The liquid and solid wastes produced by any type of agricultural activity. These include runoff and leaching of chemicals (*pesticides and *fertilizers) from fields, *soil erosion and dust from ploughing, animal manure and carcasses, and crop residues. Some such pollution (for example, from large feedlots) is *point source, but much (for example blowing dust, or nutrients from fields) is *non-point source.

Agricultural Revolution A major shift in human society and culture that began about 10000 years ago, in which people started to raise domesticated livestock and cultivate crops. Agriculture replaced a nomadic mode of living, based on hunting and gathering, and it allowed people to adopt a more settled mode of living. *See also* GREEN REVOLUTION; INDUSTRIAL REVOLUTION.

agricultural runoff The surface water that leaves an area of agricultural land use, which may be enriched with nutrients, sediment, and agricultural chemicals. *See also* EUTROPHICATION.

agricultural sewage Liquid waste material that is produced through the agricultural processes of cultivating soil, producing crops, or raising livestock.

agricultural system *Agriculture viewed as an *open system, including the input and output of materials and energy from farms.

agricultural waste The waste products created by agriculture, including animal *byproducts, *manure, *agricultural sewage, residual materials in liquid or solid form, and the residues from harvesting of grain, vegetables, and fruit.

agricultural zoning A type of *natural resource zoning that allows only *agriculture and other low-density uses.

agriculture (farming) The practice of cultivating the soil, growing crops, or raising livestock for human use, including the production of food, feed, fibre, fuel, or other useful products. *See also* TRADITIONAL AGRICULTURE.

Agriculture and Consumer Protection Act (1973) US legislation, some sections of which authorized a forestry incentives programme for non-industrial private landowners for tree planting and timber stand improvement in order to produce marketable timber crops and other values. These sections were repealed and supplanted by the *Cooperative Forestry Assistance Act (1978).

Agriculture Department *See* US DEPARTMENT OF AGRICULTURE.

agrochemicals Synthetic chemicals that are used in agriculture to fertilize soil (*fertilizers), and to control animal pests (*pesticides) and weeds (*herbicides).

agroecological zone A large area of land that has relatively uniform soils and climate, across which agricultural productivity is also relatively uniform.

agroecosystem An agricultural system viewed as an *ecosystem or *open system, where the objective is sustainable management of the interrelationships between system components (including crops, pastures, livestock, other flora and fauna, atmosphere, soils, *groundwater, and *drainage networks) and environmentally sensitive management of uncultivated land and *wildlife.

agroforestry A form of *agriculture that is based on the cultivation of *trees with other crops, animals, or both. This is usually done for multiple objectives, including improving the quality of wildlife *habitat, increasing access by humans and wildlife, and growing more woody plant products (including trees, shrubs, palms, or bamboos). *See also* AGROSYLVICULTURAL SYSTEM; SYLVOPASTORAL SYSTEM.

agrometeorology The study of how atmospheric conditions and processes affect agriculture.

agronomy The science of soil management and crop production.

agropastoral system A system of land use based only on crops and livestock, without trees.

agrosilvicultural system An *agroforestry system of land use in which trees and shrubs are grown with herbaceous food crops, pastures, and animals.

A-horizon The upper layer of soil within a *soil profile. This is the fertile topsoil of a mineral soil, that contains much organic material (from the decomposition of litter) and minerals, and is the location of much biological activity (by earthworms and other soil organisms). The organic-rich layer in the A-horizon is termed the *O-horizon. Fine materials (such as iron, aluminium oxides, and silicate clays) are washed out (*leached) from the A-horizon and deposited in the lower horizons, by *eluviation, so this horizon is also sometimes known as the **zone of leaching**. *See also* B-HORIZON; C-HORIZON; SOIL HORIZON.

AIDS Acquired immune deficiency syndrome, an often fatal disease that destroys the human immune system and is spread through direct contact with the bodily fluids of an infected person, especially by sexual contact or via contaminated needles.

AIJ *See* ACTIVITIES IMPLEMENTED JOINTLY.

air 1. A mixture of gases that makes up the Earth's *atmosphere. It comprises 78.08% *nitrogen, 20.95% *oxygen, 0.93% argon, 0.039% *carbon dioxide, and smaller amounts of other gases, as well as varying amounts of *water vapour. **2.** The region above the ground, also known as the *sky or *atmosphere.

air cleaning An approach to the management of indoor air quality based on removing particulates and/or gases from the air, using procedures such as *particulate filtration, *electrostatic precipitation, and gas *sorption.

air conditioning Regulation by mechanical means of the temperature, humidity, cleanliness, and circulation of air within a particular enclosed area, such as a building. *See also* VENTILATION.

air current The movement of air. *See also* WIND.

air curtain A device that forces air bubbles from a perforated pipe in order to create an upward flow of water in a waterbody. This is used for example to contain an oil spill or to stop fish from entering polluted water.

air drainage wind *See* KATABATIC WIND.

air emission Any gas that is released into the air as a result of human activities, including *ozone, *carbon monoxide, *nitrogen oxides, *nitrogen dioxide, and *sulphur dioxide.

air exchange rate The rate at which outside air replaces indoor air in a space, expressed either as the number of air changes per hour or

the rate at which a volume of outside air enters (in cubic metres per minute, $m^3 \ min^{-1}$).

air mass A large body of air in which the characteristics (temperature, humidity, and *lapse rate) are approximately constant at every height. Weather changes are most marked at the boundary zone (the *frontal system) between adjacent air masses. Air masses typically cover a substantial part of a continent or ocean. They are classified in terms of temperature and moisture content—tropical (T) and equatorial (E) air masses are warm, whereas arctic (A) and polar (P) air masses are cold; continental air masses (c) are normally dry, and maritime air masses (m) are usually wet. These categories are combined as cA, cP, cT, mT, mP, mA, and mE; there is no cE because oceans cover almost all the equatorial area.

air mass thunderstorm A *thunderstorm produced by local *convection within an unstable *air mass. *Contrast* FRONTAL THUNDERSTORM.

air monitoring A programme of sampling and measuring the pollutants present in the atmosphere at a particular place, on a continuous, regular, or intermittent basis. *See also* MONITORING.

air parcel A theoretical concept of a body of air with properties and transformations that may be determined through the application of laws of physics and mechanics. The concept is widely used in atmospheric physics.

air photograph *See* AERIAL PHOTOGRAPH.

air pollutant A gas or aerosol that is present in the air in a concentration capable of causing injury to living organisms, including humans. Some pollutants are from natural sources, but there are also more than a hundred man-made substances including solids, *sulphur compounds, *volatile organic compounds, *nitrogen compounds, *oxygen compounds, *halogen compounds, *radioactive compounds, and odours that cause *air pollution.

Air Pollution Control Act (1955) The first piece of US federal legislation to address the problem of air pollution (the first state law was passed in California in 1947). The Act mandated federal research into the effects of air pollution on health and welfare in order to empower the Secretary of Health, Education, and Welfare to define air quality criteria and to award grants to local and state air pollution agencies.

air pollution control device Equipment that cleans emissions generated by a source (such as an *incinerator, industrial *smokestack, or vehicle exhaust system) by removing pollutants that would otherwise be released to the atmosphere.

air pollution episode A period when the concentration of *air pollutants is unusually high, often as a result of low winds and *temperature inversion. Prolonged or severe episodes can cause illness and death amongst people, as happened during the *Great London Smog episodes of the 1950s.

air pressure *See* ATMOSPHERIC PRESSURE.

air quality A general term that describes the condition of the air in a particular place and time, reflecting the degree to which it is pollution-free (particularly in terms of *sulphur dioxide, *nitrogen oxides, *carbon monoxide, ground level *ozone, and airborne particles).

air quality class A designation given to geographical areas of the USA in which *air quality is better than the national standards. Allowable increases in pollutants are specified for each class, with Class II allowed the greatest increase and Class I allowed the least.

air quality control region An area in the USA, designated by the federal government, in which communities share a common *air pollution problem. Such a region can sometimes involve more than one state.

air quality criteria Threshold levels of *air pollution and lengths of exposure, above which there may be adverse effects on human health and welfare.

Air Quality Framework Directive A *directive of the *European Commission which has a framework for limits for a range of *air pollutants.

Air Quality Index (AQI) A numerical scale to indicate how polluted the air is in a particular place. It was developed by the US *Environmental Protection Agency for measuring pollution levels for the major air pollutants that are regulated under the *Clean Air Act. It replaced the *Pollution Standards Index (PSI) in 1999.

air quality standard The maximum level of air pollutants (particularly *sulphur dioxide, *nitrogen oxides, ground level *ozone, and *airborne particles), defined to protect human health and prescribed by law or regulation, which must not be exceeded during a given time in a defined area.

air sampling The collection and analysis of samples of air to measure *air quality, particularly the concentration of radioactive substances, particulate matter, or chemical pollutants. *See also* AIR MONITORING.

air stripping A system of treating water pollution that involves removing *volatile organic compounds from contaminated *groundwater or *surface water, by forcing a stream of air through the water and causing the compounds to evaporate and be separated from the water.

airborne infection An infectious agent that is transmitted through the air, carried, e.g, on particles, dust, bacteria, viruses, or spores.

airborne particle A *particle that exists in the *atmosphere as a solid or liquid. It can come from natural and/or human sources, and can vary in size from coarse (bigger than 3 μm (*micrometres) in diameter) to fine (less than 3 μm).

airborne particulate The suspended matter that exists in the *atmosphere as tiny solid particles or liquid droplets. It comes from many sources, including windblown dust, emissions from industrial processes, smoke from the burning of wood and coal, and the exhaust of motor vehicles. The chemical composition of

AIR POLLUTION

The presence in the air of any *air pollutant that reduces *air quality enough to threaten the health and welfare of people, plants, and animals, to adversely affect materials and structures, and/or to interfere with the enjoyment of life and property. Although there are a number of important *natural sources of air pollution (including forest fires and volcanic eruptions), the term is usually applied to substances released into the atmosphere as a result of human activities, which can be either deliberate (such as the continual release of gases from factory chimneys) or accidental (such as the release of material from the damaged *Chernobyl nuclear power station, and the *Bhopal explosion).

the particulates varies widely, depending on location and the time of year.

airborne pollutant *See* AIR POLLUTION.

airborne release The deliberate or accidental release into the air of any gas or object, including *pollutants.

airshed 1. A geographical area that frequently shares the same air because of topography, meteorology, and/or climate. 2. The catchment area (after *watershed) for air pollutants around known emission sources.

Alamogordo cattle A herd of 32 Hereford cattle that was probably situated 16–23 km north-east of ground zero of the first atomic bomb test at Alamagordo, New Mexico, in July 1945. The cattle were exposed to *fallout and were subsequently removed to Oak Ridge, Tennessee, where the effects of radiation exposure were studied. The animals developed patches of grey hair, horn-like growths on the skin that took longer than ordinary tissue to heal when wounded, and three cows developed skin cancer. Otherwise their general health and reproductive efficiency were no different from those of 74 control cattle.

Alar The trade name of a *pesticide (daminozide) that can be sprayed on apples to regulate their growth, make it easier to harvest them, and improve their colour. It was registered with the US Food and Drug Administration from 1963 to 1989, but was banned as a result of public concern over a controversial study which found that Alar residue could produce *tumours in mice and that residues in apple juice might harm children if ingested in extremely large amounts.

ALARA *See* AS LOW AS REASONABLY ACHIEVABLE.

Alaska National Interest Land Conservation Act (ANILCA) (1979) US legislation that offered protection to over 100 million acres of federal lands in Alaska, doubling the size of the country's *national park and *refuge system, and tripling the amount of land designated as *wilderness.

albedo A measure of ability to reflect light (reflectivity), which is the ratio of the amount of light reflected by a surface to the amount of incident light. Dark surfaces reflect relatively little light so they have a low albedo; for example rock surfaces 12–18%, green grass and forest 8–27%, sand up to 40%. Light surfaces have a high albedo; for example fresh *snow up to 90%; cloud surfaces have an albedo of around 55% on

average, but it can be as high as 80% for thick *stratocumulus clouds. The Earth's albedo averages around 30% at the edge of the atmosphere.

albeluvisols Soils that have an *illuvial horizon rich in *silicate *clays and with an irregular upper boundary. Albeluvisols are a reference soil group in the *World Soil Classification.

alcohol A group of organic chemical compounds composed of *carbon, *hydrogen, and *oxygen that occurs naturally and is commonly obtained by fermentation. It is used in solvents, antifreezes, chemical manufacture, beverages, and as a fuel.

aldehyde An organic compound that contains *carbon, *hydrogen, and *oxygen, produced by the oxidation of an *alcohol. Some (such as *formaldehyde) are manufactured and some are emitted in vehicle exhausts. Aldehydes appear to be *carcinogenic, and formaldehyde was listed as a hazardous air pollutant in the 1990 US *Clean Air Act.

aldrine An *organochlorine *insecticide that was used as a dressing for seeds but led to population decline in some birds of prey (which ate seed-eating birds). Its use has been restricted and controlled since the 1960s.

ALERT *See* AUTOMATED LOCAL EVENT REPORTING IN REAL TIME.

Aleutian low A semi-permanent area of low atmospheric pressure in the North Pacific that is centred at about 50°N, over the Aleutian Islands. It covers a large area and generates many storms that travel eastward and tend to merge. Pressure is lowest in January, but the low is present most of the winter. *See also* ICELAND LOW.

alfalfa A *perennial plant in the pea family that is rich in vitamins, minerals, and protein and is widely cultivated to be made into *hay or used for *forage. *See also* MEADOW.

alfisol A type (*order) of soil that typically develops beneath broadleaved *forest. It has a much thicker *A-horizon than most other soils, because leaves and other litter decompose quickly during the mild, wet winters. The A-horizon often has a white layer, indicating *eluviation of nutrients into the soil. An alfisol also has a relatively thick *B-horizon where clay and plant nutrients accumulate by *illuviation.

algae Simple, aquatic, non-vascular plants (without roots, stems, and leaves), a member of the *Protoctista kingdom. They contain *chlorophyll and live in *colonies, either floating or suspended in sunlit freshwater (*phytoplankton), or attached to structures, rocks, or other submerged surfaces (*periphyton). Algae vary in size from minute single-celled forms to large multicellular seaweeds such as giant kelp (which can often grow to longer than 30 m). Like all aquatic plants, algae *photosynthesize, add oxygen to the water, affect *pH, and are important in the food chain—they provide food for fish and small aquatic animals. Algae grow in proportion to the amount of available nutrients, and excess algal growth (*algal blooms) can reduce water quality and alter water chemistry. *See also* EUTROPHICATION.

algal bloom A sudden rapid growth of *algae (or often *cyanobacteria), which develops in surface waters (lakes, streams, ponds, reservoirs, and marine waters) due to an increase in nutrients such as nitrogen and phosphorus. It can occur naturally or as a result of pollution. The bloom reduces the availability of oxygen in the water, and can kill fish and other aquatic organisms through oxygen deprivation. *See also* EUTROPHICATION; NUTRIENT ENRICHMENT; RED TIDE.

algal mat An accumulation of *cyanobacteria that develops in shallow marine environments as well as in lakes and swamps. The bacteria cover the sediment surface and trap sediment, producing alternating *laminations of bacterial layers and sediment layers.

algicide A substance or chemical that is used specifically to kill or control algae.

algology *See* PHYCOLOGY.

alien (exotic species, introduced species) A non-native species, especially one introduced to an area outside of its historically known natural range through human action (by accident or design) or by other agents. *Contrast* NATIVE SPECIES; INDIGENOUS.

aliphatic Applied to organic compounds that contain open chains of carbon atoms; the group comprises *paraffins, olefins, and *acetylenes together with their derivates and substitution products. *Compare* AROMATIC.

alisols Soils that have an *illuvial horizon rich in *silicate *clays, with a *cation-exchange capacity of more than 24 $cmol_c$/kg (centimoles cation per kilogram) clay and a *base saturation of less than 50% within 100 cm of the surface. These are soils with high concentrations of alu-

minium. Alisols are a reference soil group in the *World Soil Classification.

alkali A compound that dissolves in water, giving *hydroxide ions. Alkalis neutralize *acids to form a salt and water. Alkalis have a *pH of more than 7.0, turn litmus paper blue, and can cause severe burns to the skin. Common commercial alkalis include sodium carbonate (soda ash), lime, potash, caustic soda, and regular mortar. Alkali is the opposite to acid, and is also known as a *base.

alkalination The process of increasing the pH of a soil to more than 7.0, usually by increasing its content of carbonates of calcium, magnesium, potassium, and, more specifically, sodium.

alkaline Having the qualities of an *alkali, or a solution with an excess of *hydroxide ions (with a *pH greater than 7.0).

alkaline soil A soil that contains a relatively large amount of alkaline salts (usually sodium carbonate), has a *pH greater than 7.0, and restricts the growth of most crop plants.

alkalinity The *buffering capacity of water. This means its capacity to neutralize an acid solution by its content of bicarbonates, carbonates, or hydroxides, adding *carbon to the water and preventing the *pH of the water from becoming too *basic or too *acidic, stabilizing it at a pH of around 7.0. The lower the alkalinity, the less capacity the water has to absorb acids without becoming more acidic. The alkalinity can be raised by adding a *buffer.

alkaloid One of a group of more than 1000 basic, nitrogenous, normally heterocyclic compounds of a complex nature that exist in combination with organic acids in plants belonging to approximately 1200 species. Alkaloids are secondary plant compounds that in some species may confer a degree of protection against attacks by herbivores. Many alkaloids are very poisonous to humans and in small amounts are the active ingredients in many therapeutic drugs. Pharmacologically powerful alkaloids derived from plants include atropine, caffeine, cocaine, morphine, nicotine, quinine, and strychnine.

alkyl mercury Ethyl mercury and methyl mercury, which are highly toxic organic compounds that were formerly used in fungicides and seed dressings.

all-aged stand A stand of forest in which trees of different ages are found growing together. *See also* EVEN-AGED STAND, UNEVEN-AGED STAND.

Allee effect The social dysfunction and failure to mate successfully that occurs in some species when their population density falls below a certain threshold. This is believed to have caused the extinction of the American passenger pigeon (*Ectopistes migratorius*), probably because *habitat destruction and hunting reduced the population density to a level at which individuals lacked the social stimulation necessary to prompt mating. The effect was first described in 1949 by W. C. Allee, O. Park, A. E. Emerson, T. Park, and K. P. Schmidt.

allele One of several alternative forms of a *gene which occupy the same relative position on paired *chromosomes, and which control the inheritance of one characteristic.

allelochemical Any substance that affects allelopathic reactions. *See also* ALLELOPATHY.

allelopathy The release into the soil by one plant species of substances that inhibit the growth or *germination of other plants.

Allen's rule A 19th century *ecogeographical rule that the warmer the climate the longer the appendages (ears, legs, wings) of warm-blooded animals in comparison with closely related taxa from colder climes. *See also* BERGMANN'S RULE; GOLGER'S RULE.

allergen Any substance that is capable of causing an allergic reaction. These include dust, pollen, certain foods and drugs, fur. *See also* AEROALLERGEN.

allergy Hypersensitivity to a substance (*allergen) that is normally harmless.

Allerød A period during the last *glacial that marks a prolonged *interstadial during the general phase of ice retreat in north-western Europe. *Carbon dating suggests it lasted from about 12000 BP to 10800 BP. Pollen records for the north-west European area indicate a cool temperate flora with birch (*Betula* species) widespread, in marked contrast to the preceding and following, colder, *Dryas phases.

alley cropping The planting of crops in strips, with rows of trees or shrubs grown on either side of the produce.

Alliance of Small Island States (AOSIS) A coalition of small, low-lying island countries formed during the Second World Climate Conference in 1990 that includes 35 states from the Atlantic, Caribbean, Indian Ocean, Mediterranean, and Pacific, most of which are members of the *Group of 77, and all of which are particularly vulnerable to *sea level rise. These countries share the threat that *global warming and *climate change pose to their survival, and have called on developed countries to rapidly reduce their emissions of *greenhouse gases.

allocation The process of assigning activities, costs, or facilities to particular people, or of designating certain resources for particular purposes.

allochthonous 1. Not *indigenous, introduced. Can be used to describe flora, fauna, or people. **2.** In geology, a deposit that originated elsewhere than its current position. *Contrast* AUTOCHTHONOUS.

allometry A differential rate of growth of an organism such that the size of one or more parts of its body change as a proportion of another part, or the whole body, at a constant exponential rate.

allomone An *allelochemical that can be produced by a species and influences the behaviour or growth of another species. *See also* SEMIOCHEMICAL.

allopatric Applied to *species that occupy *habitats that are geographically separated, so the species do not occur together naturally. *Contrast* SYMPATRIC.

allotment 1. In the UK, a small plot of land rented by local people (usually from the local authority) on which they can cultivate food and flowers. **2. (range allotment)** In the USA, the area of land designated for use by a prescribed number of livestock for a prescribed period of time.

allotrope Two or more different physical forms in which a particular element exists. For example, *carbon has three allotropes, diamond, graphite, and buckminsterfullerene.

allotropy The existence of two or more forms (*allotropes) of the same element.

allowable annual harvest The volume or acreage of timber that can be harvested each year from a particular area of forest, defined by the objectives of management.

allowable cut The amount of wood that may be harvested annually or periodically from a particular area of forest over a stated period of time, defined by the objectives of management.

allowable use The level of use of *rangeland that is sustainable, defined by the objectives of management. To maintain a range in good to excellent condition, use of 40% to 50% of the annual growth is often allowed; less use will be allowed if the aim is to restore overgrazed land.

alloy A material made of two or more *metals.

alluvial (riverine) Composed of or relating to *alluvium, or caused by or related to river action. *Compare* COLLUVIAL.

alluvial cone *See* ALLUVIAL FAN.

alluvial deposit *See* ALLUVIUM.

alluvial fan A mass of sediment that builds up at a point on a stream course where there is a sudden decrease in gradient (for example, in a mountain canyon). Adjacent alluvial fans are commonly found in arid and semi-arid environments, and they can coalesce to form a *bajada.

alluvial plain *See* FLOODPLAIN.

alluvial river A river that flows through *alluvium, that it can move and refashion, as opposed to a *bedrock river that flows through or over solid rock.

alluvial soil Soil that has developed on alluvium that has recently been deposited, with as yet little or no modification of the original material by soil-forming processes.

alluvium (alluvial deposit) Loosely compacted sediment that is deposited by a river, which can include particles ranging in size from clay, silt and sand, to gravel. Stones and boulders are often worn by the water into rounded shapes. *Contrast* COLLUVIUM. *See also* ALLUVIAL FAN; ALLUVIAL PLAIN; FLOODPLAIN.

alp 1. A high mountain. **2.** Relatively flat area of grazing land in a mountain environment, which is covered by snow during winter but free from snow in the summer.

alpha decay Process of radioactive decay in which the nucleus of an atom emits an *alpha particle.

alpha diversity (local diversity) The diversity of *species within a particular area or *ecosystem, expressed by the number of species (*species richness) present there. A measure of *biodiversity. *See also* BETA DIVERSITY; GAMMA DIVERSITY.

alpha particle A *helium nucleus given out by some *radioactive substances during *alpha decay. Alpha particles cannot penetrate very far into materials, even soft tissue, but if they enter the body (by inhalation or through a wound) they can cause great biological damage.

alpha radiation Emission of *alpha particles from a material that is undergoing nuclear transformation. *See also* RADIATION.

alpine Relating to or growing above the *tree line in high mountain areas, higher than about 1500 metres above sea level in middle latitudes, where the mean summer temperature is below 10°C, making it too cold for trees to grow. The term is also used to describe things that are typical of high mountain areas, or related to or found in them.

alpine glacier A type of valley *glacier that is fed by *cirque glaciers that show a positive *mass balance. Such glaciers are common in the European Alps and in the coastal mountains of Alaska.

alternation of generations *See* HAPLOID.

alternative agriculture (alternative farming) An approach to farming that reflects traditional practices such as using organic rather than chemical *fertilizers and *pesticides, increased use of *crop rotations, reduced tillage of the soil, greater use of *renewable energy sources and of *intermediate technology, compared with modern high-energy, chemical-dependent *agribusiness. *Contrast* CONVENTIONAL AGRICULTURE. *See also* ECOFARMING; ORGANIC AGRICULTURE.

alternative compliance An approach to *pollution control or the reduction of *environmental risk that is based on setting targets but allowing those responsible to choose amongst a variety of different methods for achieving them, rather than *command and control regulations that define standards and specify how to meet them.

alternative crop Any non-traditional crop that can be grown in an area to diversify *crop rotations (and thus increase soil fertility and productivity) and increase income.

alternative energy Energy that is produced from sources other than *fossil fuels, which includes sources such as compressed *natural gas, *solar, *hydroelectric, or *wind energy.

alternative farming See ALTERNATIVE AGRICULTURE.

alternative fuel A non-petroleum (not gasoline or diesel) fuel, in liquid or gas form, that is used to power vehicles and produces less pollution. Examples include *biofuels or ALCOHOL fuels (such as *ethanol and *methanol), mineral fuels, *natural gas, *hydrogen, and fuel cells.

alternative technology *Technology that has been developed or is used to reduce the generation of *hazardous waste, promote *recycling, or develop alternative disposal methods.

altimeter An instrument that indicates the *altitude of an object above a fixed level, usually sea level. Pressure altimeters use an *aneroid barometer with a scale graduated in altitude instead of pressure.

altiplano A high plateau in south-eastern Peru and western Bolivia, at an elevation of about 3500 m.

altithermal 1. In general, any period of high temperature. **2. (hypsithermal, Climatic Optimum)** A period in the mid-*Holocene, between about 4000 and 8000 years ago, when the climate was generally warmer (particularly during summer) than before or since.

altitude (elevation) Height above *sea level or ground level.

altitudinal migration A vertical pattern of *migration in which populations that breed in the *alpine or subalpine zones during the summer move to lower levels in winter, to avoid harsh climate and snow cover, and then return to the higher level the following spring. See also ALP.

altitudinal zonation The pattern of variation of plant and animal species relative to elevation, in response to vertical differences in climate (particularly temperature and precipitation).

altocumulus (Ac) A genus of *clouds which have a *cumulus shape and are found at medium altitude, about 2400–6100 m (8000–20000 feet). They are composed of water droplets, and consist of grey-white sheets or soft, rounded patches 1–5° across, which are usually larger and darker than those in *cirrocumulus and smaller than those in *stratocumulus. Altocumulus are associated with weather changes, and often appear in middle latitude *cyclones.

altostratus (As) A genus of *cloud that is found at medium altitude, about 2400–6100 m (8000–20000 feet), and generally consists of uniform grey sheets or layers that are lighter than *nimbostratus but darker than *cirrostratus. The cloud may be striated, fibrous, or uniform, and is composed of water droplets. Altostratus often covers the whole sky, and often arrives ahead of a *frontal system, signalling that weather changes are about to occur. See also STRATUS.

altricial Applied to young mammals (e.g. rats, mice, cats, dogs) that are helpless at birth. Their eyes and ears are sealed, and they cannot walk, maintain their body temperature, or excrete without assistance. Compare PRECOCIAL.

altruism Sacrifice made by an individual that others may benefit. Many animals display what appears to be altruistic behaviour.

alum (potash alum) Aluminium potassium sulphate. A white or colourless crystalline compound that is used to dress leather, as a pigment in dyes, and that has a wide range of other uses.

aluminium (Al) A naturally occurring, light, metallic element that is silver-grey in colour, conducts heat and electricity, is easy to weld, and is resistant to corrosion. It is the third most abundant element in the Earth's crust, and is used in alloys with *copper, *zinc, *manganese, and *magnesium. It is a very versatile metal with a wide variety of uses, including utensils, vehicle and airplane bodies, building materials, electrical conductors, explosives and fireworks, abrasives, cosmetics, paints, and even food additives. It is an important ingredient in the Earth's *continental crust (it accounts for 8.13% by mass) and occurs naturally in soil, water, and air. Inhalation of the fine powder can produce serious damage to lungs (pulmonary fibrosis).

aluminium sulphate A compound that is used in sewage treatment and for the purification of drinking water. It causes dirt and other particles to clump together and fall to the bottom of *settling basins. It is also used in the paper industry and as a fire-proofing agent.

alveoli The many small sacs in the lungs through the walls of which oxygen enters and carbon dioxide leaves the bloodstream.

amalgam A solution of a metal in mercury.

Amazon floral region Part of R. Good's *Neotropical floral kingdom (Geography of the Flowering Plants, 1974), corresponding to one of the blocks of the rain forest. Because of extensive flooding by the Amazon river, the vegetation can be divided into that which is above the flood level, called 'terra firme', and that which is below it, called 'igapo' or 'varzea'. The flora of this vast region is one of the richest in the world.

Amazonia The Amazon Basin of South America. It covers an area of 5.8 million km^2 of Peru, Colombia, and Brazil, and is dominated by *grassland, *wetland, *shrubland, lakes, and *tropical forests.

amber The fossilized *resin of conifer trees. It is hard, translucent, yellowish to brownish in colour, and used for the manufacture of ornamental objects including jewellery.

ambient Surrounding environmental conditions, such as pressure, temperature, or humidity.

ambient air The open air or surrounding air.

ambient air quality standard In the US, the permissible upper limit for a pollutant in *ambient air, established by the state or federal government, that serves as a target in local air quality improvement or protection programmes. It is based on the maximum acceptable average concentrations of *air pollutants during a specified period of time. The primary standard protects public health, and the secondary standard protects public welfare. *See also* CRITERIA POLLUTANT; HAZARDOUS AIR POLLUTANT; NATIONAL AMBIENT AIR QUALITY STANDARDS; PRIMARY AMBIENT AIR QUALITY STANDARDS; SECONDARY AMBIENT AIR QUALITY STANDARDS.

ambient level The general level of any particular substance or *pollutant in the environment, expressed as an average over a suitably long time and large area.

ambient measurement A measure of the concentration of a particular substance or *pollutant within the immediate vicinity of an organism, which can be related to the maximum amount of possible exposure.

amelioration *See* REMEDIATION.

amenity The useful or desirable features of a place, that provide non-monetary benefits to those who use it but which are not necessary for its use. An amenity can be natural (such as an attractive location or accessible woods or water) or made by people (such as a swimming pool or garden).

amenity horticulture (hobby farming) Gardening or cultivation for leisure or *aesthetics rather than for commercial reasons.

amenity planting Planting trees and shrubs for non-commercial purposes, for example to make a landscape more attractive rather than to produce a crop for sale.

amenity resource Any resource that is valued for non-monetary characteristics, such as its beauty or uniqueness. For example, attractive natural scenery can inspire creativity and promote well-being.

amenity value The non-monetary, intangible value of goods or services.

amensalism An interaction of *species *populations, in which one population is inhibited while the other (the amensal) is unaffected. It is the opposite of *commensalism.

amictic Applied to a lake in which no thermal stratification of the water occurs and there is no overturn. Such lakes occur in the Arctic.

amide herbicide A group of about 30 products used to kill a wide range of broad-leaved and annual grass weeds before these emerge. They prevent leaves from emerging and have no effect on plants that have emerged above the soil. Amides break down rapidly and disappear quickly.

amines Compounds that are formed by replacing hydrogen atoms in ammonia (NH_3) with organic radicals (R). Amines are classified according to the number of hydrogens replaced as primary (NH_2R), secondary (NHR_2), and tertiary (NR_3).

amino acid An organic compound that contains both an amino group (NH_2) and a carboxyl group (COOH). Amino acids are the building blocks of *protein molecules in living things. There are 20 common amino acids that can be combined to form proteins.

amino-acid dating A method of *absolute dating of organic materials that is based on the chemical change that amino acids undergo. This is dependent on both time and temperature.

ammonia (NH_3) A colourless gas with a strong smell. It is a compound of *nitrogen and *hydrogen that is formed naturally when bacteria decompose nitrogen-containing compounds such as manure, and is used to manufacture *fertilizers and nitrogen-based compounds. Ammonia is extremely soluble in water and it reacts with *nitrogen oxides to form ammonium nitrate in soils and streams. *See also* NITROGEN CYCLE.

ammonia fixation The *adsorption of ammonium ions by *clay minerals, which makes them insoluble and non-exchangeable.

ammonification The biochemical process in which *ammonia is produced by *micro-organisms through the *decomposition of organic matter.

ammonifying bacteria *Nitrifying bacteria (e.g. *Pseudomonas* species) that break down *protein in plant and animal tissues with the release of ammonia.

ammonium (NH$_4$) An *ion derived from *ammonia; the primary form in which *nitrogen is applied in *fertilizers.

ammonium nitrate A colourless, crystalline salt that is used in explosives, *fertilizers, and veterinary medicine.

ammonium sulphate A chemical compound that is used as a *fertilizer. It is quite acidic, and will lower the *pH of a soil.

Amoco Cadiz A Liberian-registered oil tanker owned by Amoco International Oil, which ran aground and broke in two off Portsall, Brittany, France, on 17 March 1978, releasing its entire cargo of 1.6 million barrels of oil, mostly light crude. Almost all the oil drifted on to the Brittany coast.

amphibian A *cold-blooded, smooth-skinned *vertebrate animal of the class Amphibia that can live on land or in water but which returns to the water to breed. Amphibians usually hatch as aquatic larvae, breathe by means of gills, and metamorphose to an adult form with air-breathing lungs. Examples include *frogs, *toads, and salamanders. *See also* HERPETOFAUNA.

amphidromous Applied to the behaviour of fish that migrate between fresh water and the sea at some stage of the life cycle for feeding, overwintering, etc., but not for breeding. *Compare* ANADROMOUS; CATADROMOUS; DIADROMOUS; POTAMODROMOUS.

anabatic wind (upslope wind) A gentle local wind that blows up a *hillslope when the sloping ground has been warmed by the sun. *Compare* KATABATIC WIND.

anabiosis Resuscitation after apparent death (e.g. following dessication of a plant).

anabolism (biosynthesis, constructive metabolism) The process by which a living cell or organism constructs the *proteins, *carbohydrates, and fats which form tissue and store energy. *See also* METABOLISM.

anadromous Applied to the behaviour of fish that spend most of their lives in the sea but migrate to fresh water to spawn, e.g. Atlantic salmon (*Salmo salar*). *Compare* AMPHIDROMOUS; CATADROMOUS; POTAMODROMOUS.

anaemia A condition in which there are low levels of red blood cells or red blood cells that are deficient in haemoglobin. Can be due to iron deficiency or loss of blood and causes tiredness.

anaerobe An organism (such as bacteria) that does not need oxygen to respire. The opposite is an *aerobe.

anaerobic (anoxic) Applied to organisms or processes that do not require oxygen, or which oxygen would damage. *Contrast* AEROBIC.

anaerobic biological treatment (anaerobic digestion) A process commonly used in the treatment of municipal waste that uses *anaerobic organisms (without air) to reduce the organic matter in wastes.

anaerobic composting Composting based on *anaerobic decomposition. *Contrast* AEROBIC COMPOSTING.

anaerobic decomposition The breakdown of organic matter caused by *anaerobic *micro-organisms in an oxygen-free environment.

anaerobic digestion *See* ANAEROBIC BIOLOGICAL TREATMENT.

ana-front A weather *front in the atmosphere, along which warmer air rises rapidly over a layer of cold air. Ana-fronts are very active, and are associated with uplift, condensation, and pronounced weather changes. *See also* KATA-FRONT.

analogue Similar in structure, appearance, or function but not in origin or development. *See also* CLIMATIC ANALOGUE.

anatomy 1. The structure of an *organism or one of its parts. **2.** The study of those structures.

ancestor Any *organism, *population, or *species from which another organism, population, or species is descended.

ancient countryside In Britain, an area in which most of the features were present prior to 1700.

ancient forest A *forest that is typically older than about 250 years with large trees, dense canopies, and great diversity of wildlife. In North America this is described as *old growth forest.

ancient woodland Woodland in Britain that originated before AD 1600 and has had a continuous cover of trees since then. Ancient woodland can also be *secondary woodland, which might have previously been cleared for *underwood or timber production.

Andean floral region Part of R. Good's *Neotropical floral kingdom (*The Geography of the Flowering Plants*, 1974). The region is elongated and extends from Colombia to southern Chile, spanning both tropical and temperate climates; it also includes the Galápagos Islands, because they have only two important endemic genera, *Leiocarpus* and *Scalesia*, although they have numerous endemic (*see* ENDEMISM) species. The mainland flora is rich in endemic genera, however, and has supplied many economic and garden plants.

andesite A fine-grained, *intermediate, volcanic rock characterized by *feldspars which formed by the ejection of *lava in continental areas. Named after the Andes mountains in South America.

andosols Soils that have developed from volcanic material and either have a horizon containing more than 10% volcanic glass more than 30 cm below the surface, or have weathered (*see* WEATHERING) volcanic material within 25 cm of the surface. Andosols are a reference soil group in the *World Soil Classification.

androgyny Possessing both masculine and feminine characteristics. *See also* HERMAPHRODITE.

anechoic Applied to a surface that is almost completely sound-absorbent.

anemometer An instrument that is used to measure surface *wind speed. There are several types. The *rotating-cups anemometer is the type most widely used. The aerovane comprises a propellor mounted on a bullet-shaped body with a vane that keeps it heading into the wind, so it also measures wind direction. The swinging-plate anemometer is preferred for

measuring wind gusts and the *pressure-tube anemometer is also used.

aneroid barometer An instrument that is used to measure atmospheric *pressure based on variations in the height or thickness of a sealed metal box from which most of the air has been evacuated. The box has a flexible top that rises or falls in response to changes in atmospheric pressure; variations in the height or thickness of the box are recorded on a pressure scale.

angiosperm A flowering plant in which the seeds are fully enclosed in an ovary which matures into a fruit. *Contrast* GYMNOSPERM.

Angiosperm Phylogeny Group (APG) A group of botanists engaged in plant *taxonomy who aim to establish a classification of flowering plants (angiosperms) based on *phylogeny, previous systems not having been based on *monophyletic groups. They published their first classification in 1998 and updated it in 2003 and 2009. *Gymnosperms were added in 2005. The APG classification is now widely used and is being adopted by major institutions.

(⊕) SEE WEB LINKS

• Home page of the Angiosperm Phylogeny Group.

angle of incidence The angle at which any ray or wave meets a surface, such as the angle at which the Sun's rays strike the Earth's surface.

angle of repose The steepest angle in which *unconsolidated sediment will lie without sliding down. It is an important measure in determining the stability of a slope and its susceptibility to *mass movement.

angle of slide The slope at which unconsolidated sediment will start to slide, which is slightly greater than the *angle of repose (because of friction).

Anglian 1. A glacial stage of the middle *Pleistocene in Britain. **2.** A middle Pleistocene, cold-climate series of deposits. The highest terraces of the Thames may belong to this period.

angstrom (Å) A unit of length equal to 10^{-10} m that is used to measure wavelengths and intermolecular distances. It has been replaced by the nanometre (nm): $1 Å = 0.1$ nm.

angular momentum The tendency of a spinning body or mass of air or water to continue to spin.

angular unconformity An *unconformity in which the *bedding planes of the rocks above and below are not parallel to each other. This occurs, for example, where older underlying beds have undergone alteration and been eroded prior to deposition by younger overlying beds.

anhydrous Containing no water. The term is applied specifically to oxides, salts, and other compounds to indicate that they contain neither water of crystallization nor chemically combined water.

ANILCA *See* ALASKA NATIONAL INTEREST LAND CONSERVATION ACT.

animal Any member of the *animal kingdom (Animalia), which comprises all multicellular *organisms that obtain energy, actively acquire their food and digest it internally, have well-developed nervous systems, have cells organized into tissues, and reproduce sexually. This includes multicellular marine organisms, worms, insects, spiders, crustaceans, fish, amphibians, reptiles, birds, and mammals.

animal community The characteristic assemblage of *animals that is associated with a particular ecosystem.

animal kingdom The taxonomic *kingdom (Animalia) that comprises all living or extinct *animals.

animal rights The belief that *animals possess rights similar to those afforded to humans, and that those rights deserve to be respected and protected.

animal unit *See* LIVESTOCK UNIT.

animal waste methane recovery The capture and reuse of *methane produced from the *decomposition of animal waste, before the *manure or *fertilizer is spread on fields. Recovery technologies include the *anaerobic digester, and machines that use the methane to produce energy.

Animalia In *taxonomy, the *animal kingdom.

anion A negatively charged *ion. *See also* CATION.

anion exchange capacity A measure of the surface charge of an *anion, expressed in equivalents of exchangeable ions per unit weight of the solid.

anisotropy Having different properties in different directions. For example, variations in hydraulic properties of *groundwater in an *aquifer. *Contrast* ISOTROPY.

annelid A member of the phylum Annelida, comprising worms with a distinct head and clear segmentation, including earthworms, sandworms, and leeches. They occur in marine, freshwater, and terrestrial environments, and some are parasitic.

Annex A Gases The *greenhouse gases whose emissions are regulated by the *Kyoto Protocol (as defined in Annex A) in order to reduce *global warming and slow down *climate change. The gases are *carbon dioxide, *methane, *nitrous oxide, *hydrofluorocarbons, *perfluorocarbons, and *sulphur hexafluoride.

Annex B Countries The list of industrialized countries and *economies in transition that have their *greenhouse gas emissions capped under the *Kyoto Protocol (as listed in Annex B). The Protocol also defines legally binding obligations on each country to reduce their emissions by set amounts within a defined period of time. For example, most European countries are required to decrease their emissions by 8% (relative to 1990 levels) during the first commitment period from 2008 to 2012, whilst Iceland is allowed to increase its emissions by up to 10% over the same period (because it is at a lower stage of industrial development).

Annex I Countries/Parties Countries that committed themselves specifically to the aim of reducing their emissions of *greenhouse gases to 1990 levels by the year 2000. The list, which appears in Annex I to the *United Nations Framework Convention on Climate Change, includes all the countries in the *Organisation for Economic Cooperation and Development, plus countries designated as *economies in transition. By default other countries were referred to as Non-Annex I countries. When these countries ratified the *Kyoto Protocol they accepted further emission targets for the period 2008–12, and the Annex I list and the *Annex B list are almost interchangeable. Strictly speaking, it is the Annex I countries which can invest in *Joint Implementation (JI) and *Clean Development Mechanism (CDM) projects, as well as host JI projects, and non-Annex I countries which can host CDM projects.

Annex II Countries/Parties The countries listed in Annex II to the *United Nations

Framework Convention on Climate Change that have a special obligation to help developing countries with financial and technological resources required to reduce *greenhouse gas emissions and curb *global warming. This includes all 24 original member countries of the *Organisation for Economic Cooperation and Development plus the *European Union.

annual A plant that completes its *life cycle (germination, growth, flowering and fruiting, then death) in a single growing season and so has a *lifespan of 1 year. *See also* BIENNIAL; PERENNIAL PLANT; SEASONAL PLANT.

annual cycle The yearly cycle of changes in the climate system and related environmental systems, caused by variations in the amount of solar radiation that reaches the Earth as it orbits the Sun.

annual growth The amount of new *biomass produced by a plant per year, usually measured as above-ground production.

annual maximum series Flow records that are used in *flood frequency analysis, which include only the highest *discharge each year (the annual maximum). *Contrast* PARTIAL DURATION SERIES.

annual pasture A *pasture consisting of *introduced *forage species that have been planted to grow for only one year or season. *Contrast* PERMANENT PASTURE.

annual ring *See* GROWTH RING.

annular drainage pattern A type of *drainage pattern in a river system. It develops on a dome where concentric outcrops of rocks with different resistance to erosion are exploited by river erosion.

anomaly The difference between a particular measurement (for example of weather elements such as temperature or precipitation) and the mean or expected value.

Anopheles The *genus of mosquito that transmits *malaria.

anoxic Lacking oxygen or oxygen-free. *See also* ANAEROBIC.

ant mosaic The three-dimensional mosaic within a habitat that is created by the non-overlapping territories of dominant ants. This in turn has a significant influence on the diversity and species composition of other organisms, including plants, *vertebrates, and *invertebrates.

antagonism The interaction of two or more substances with opposing effects which partially or wholly cancel each other out, or (for organisms such as *bacteria) where the growth of one inhibits that of the other. *Contrast* SYNERGISM.

Antarctic Circle Latitude 66°30′S, to the south of which there is at least one day each year when the sun fails to rise above the horizon and one day when the sun fails to sink below the horizon.

Antarctic circumpolar current (West Wind Drift) A large ocean current that is driven by the wind and flows completely around *Antarctica from west to east.

Antarctic Convergence A sharp change in the physical characteristics of the Atlantic, Indian, and Pacific oceans between latitudes 48° and 60°S. Here, warmer waters moving south from the mid-latitude oceans meet and mix with colder waters moving north from *Antarctica, and there is a steep temperature gradient within the ocean water which effectively isolates life in the *Southern Ocean (i.e. the area within the Antarctic Convergence).

Antarctic ozone hole The seasonal depletion of *ozone over much of *Antarctica. *See also* OZONE HOLE.

Antarctic realm A *biogeographical realm in the southern hemisphere, which contains a variety of *ecosystems from *temperate forest and *grassland in New Zealand to *tundra and *ice sheets in *Antarctica.

Antarctic Treaty An international treaty that is designed to preserve the unique environment of *Antarctica by limiting development there. It was signed in 1959 by the seven countries (Norway, France, Australia, New Zealand, Chile, Great Britain, and Argentina) which claim sovereign rights over the continent, plus twelve other countries, and it dedicated the whole continent to peaceful scientific investigations. All existing territorial claims were suspended when the treaty came into effect in 1961. Since it was signed, international concern has grown over the prospect of renewed mineral prospecting in and around Antarctica, and there have been repeated calls for the continent to be designated a *world park and protected for ever against development. In 1991, 24 countries approved a protocol to the treaty (the Madrid Protocol) that would ban oil and other mineral exploration for at least 50 years.

a

ANTARCTICA

The fifth largest and by far the coldest of the seven continents. It is centred on the *South Pole, located mostly within the *Antarctic Circle, covered with ice (which in places is more than 2000 metres thick), and surrounded by sea ice, particularly during the winter. The outer limits of Antarctica are defined by the *Antarctic Convergence. It is, in effect, a *cold desert, with an average annual precipitation in the interior of about 50 mm. Climate in the interior is dominated by extreme cold and light snowfall, and temperatures are milder and precipitation is much higher (up to about 380 mm a year) around the coastal fringe. Over 95% of the land surface is currently covered by ice, and the ice cover is variable in thickness but sometimes thicker than about 2000 m. This thick ice cover makes Antarctica the highest continent overall, with an average elevation of about 2300 m above sea level. Wildlife on the ice-covered areas is extremely limited; the most prominent examples are the penguins (particularly Adelie and emperor penguins) which breed on ice and live on ice and in the surrounding oceans. The sea has more abundant life, including six species of seal and large numbers of whales which feed on krill (small, shrimp-like crustaceans that swarm in dense shoals and feed on tiny diatoms). The human population of Antarctica is extremely small, because there is no native population and most residents are short-term scientific visitors. Antarctica is widely regarded as the last great wilderness. Until relatively recently its natural environments have been preserved more by lack of exploitation (because the continent is so remote, inaccessible, and uninviting) than by purposeful action. But this is changing, as geological exploration reveals more details of the large deposits of valuable mineral resources (particularly *coal, *oil, and *natural gas) beneath the cold continent and its surrounding *continental shelf. Pressures on Antarctic marine resources are also mounting, with extensive commercial exploitation of whales and krill. West Antarctica contains enough ice to raise *sea level by between five and six metres, and there is mounting concern about the rapid melting of this ice, which is occurring faster than previously thought, and appears to be associated with, if not directly caused by, *global warming. *See also* ANTARCTIC TREATY.

antecedent moisture (antecedent soil water) The degree of wetness of the soil at the beginning of a period of *runoff, usually expressed as the total inch-depth-equivalent of water stored in the soil.

antecedent river A *river network in which an initial pattern, established in the geological past, has been preserved while the area has been uplifted. Rates of river downcutting must have been higher than rates of *uplift for this to occur.

antecedent soil water *See* ANTECEDENT MOISTURE.

antediluvian The period before the Biblical flood (described in Genesis, Chapter 7).

anthophilous Living or growing on flowers, as certain insects do.

anthracene An *aromatic *hydrocarbon obtained during *coal *pyrolysis that is used as an intermediate in the production of dyes, and also in insecticides and wood preservatives. It is considered to be persistent, bioaccumulative (*see* BIOACCUMULATION), and toxic for aquatic organisms.

anthracite A hard, black *coal that burns slowly with little flame or smoke but gives off intense heat, formed at the later stages of the coal cycle by the folding and hardening of sedimentary strata containing *bituminous coal. This is the most highly metamorphosed form of coal, containing 92 to 98% of fixed *carbon.

anthropic Relating to the period during which humans have existed on Earth.

anthropocentric (homocentric) Human-centred. Based on the belief that only humans have value and thus they have a privileged position in nature, that the environment exists only for the benefit of humans, and that nature has no rights. *Contrast* ECOCENTRIC.

anthropocentrism A *worldview that sees humans as the source of all value, since the concept of value itself is a human creation, and that sees nature as of value merely as a means to the ends of human beings. *See also* ECOCENTRISM; HUMAN EXCEPTIONALISM PARADIGM.

anthropogenic Originally, pertaining to the study of human origins. More recently applied to substances or processes made by humans or phenomena resulting from human activities.

anthropoid A member of the primate infra-order Simiiformes (formerly the suborder Anthropoidea) that comprises monkeys, apes, and humans.

Anthropological Reserve See NATURAL BIOTIC AREA/ANTHROPOLOGICAL RESERVE.

anthropology The study of human cultural variations, including language, biology, and society. *See also* ETHNOGRAPHY.

anthropomorphism The attribution of human motivation, characteristics, or behaviour to non-human things, which leads to the treatment of animals, gods, inanimate objects, or natural phenomena as if they have human feelings and emotions.

anthrosols Soils that have been strongly affected by human activities such as ploughing, *irrigation, or the addition of *manure. Anthrosols are a reference soil group in the *World Soil Classification.

antibiotic A chemical produced or synthesized by living micro-organisms (such as yeast) that destroys or inhibits the growth of other organisms, especially *bacteria. Used to treat or prevent infections by inhibiting the growth of bacteria and *fungi that produce disease.

antibody A special *protein that is produced by the immune system within an organism in response to an invading foreign *antigen (such as *bacteria, *dust, or *pollen).

anticarcinogen A substance or agent that opposes the action of *carcinogens.

anticline A common type of *fold in rock. It takes the form of a symmetrical fold, arched upward in the middle, in which the rocks at the centre are usually the oldest. *Contrast* SYNCLINE.

anticlinorium A series of small-scale *anticlines and *synclines which may be small enough to be viewed in outcrop.

anticyclone (high) A large area of high *atmospheric pressure around which the winds blow clockwise in the northern hemisphere (and anticlockwise in the southern hemisphere) and which usually results in calm, fine *weather.

antidote A remedy designed to relieve, prevent, or counteract the effects of a poison, usually by eliminating it, neutralizing it, or absorbing it.

anti-environmental group A group comprising those who disagree with and challenge extreme environmentalist views, while supporting practical policies aimed at protecting the natural environment and conserving wildlife. Examples from the USA include *think-tanks such as the *Cato Institute, *Heartland Institute, *Heritage Foundation, legal groups such as the *Mountain States Legal Foundation, and *front groups such as the Climate Council, *Coalition for Vehicle Choice, *Global Climate Coalition, *National Wetlands Coalition, and *Wise Use Movement.

anti-equitable effect An effect that leads to less *equity and more *inequality.

antigen A substances that the body regards as foreign, which results in the production of *antibodies.

antigibberellin An organic compound that causes stunted growth in plants or has effects opposite to those of *gibberellins. *Maleic hydrazide is an antigibberellin.

antinode See STANDING WAVE.

antiquities The collective name for prehistoric and historic artefacts, objects, structures, ruins, sites, and monuments that have some cultural or scientific significance and are considered to be older than 100 years.

Antiquities Act (1906) US legislation that protects ruins or objects of antiquity on *federal lands.

anvil cloud The top part of a *cumulonimbus cloud which spreads horizontally outward in the vicinity of the *tropopause and looks like a blacksmith's anvil.

ANWR See ARCTIC NATIONAL WILDLIFE REFUGE.

AONB See AREA OF OUTSTANDING NATURAL BEAUTY.

AOSIS See ALLIANCE OF SMALL ISLAND STATES.

aphelion The point in the Earth's orbit when it is farthest from the sun (152.5 million km), which occurs on the 3rd or 4th of July each year. The opposite is *perihelion.

aphicide A *pesticide that kills aphids.

aphotic (disphotic) Totally dark. *Contrast* PHOTIC.

apiculture Beekeeping in order to produce honey. *Contrast* BOMBICULTURE.

apodous Without feet; legless.

apomorphic character See DERIVED CHAR-ACTER.

application factor The ratio between the dose of a substance that produces a chronic toxic response and the dose that causes the death of 50% of the organisms exposed to it (the *LD_{50} dose). The figure is used to estimate an *acceptable daily intake for humans.

applied dose In exposure assessment, the amount (*dose) of a substance that is in contact with the parts of an organism (such as the skin, lung tissue, or gastrointestinal track) through which it can be absorbed.

appropriate technology See INTERMEDI-ATE TECHNOLOGY.

apterygote A wingless insect of a group that is believed never to have had wings in its evolutionary past. *Contrast* PTERYGOTE.

AQI See AIR QUALITY INDEX.

aquaculture (fish farming, mariculture, pisciculture) The cultivation of marine or freshwater food fish or shellfish, such as oysters, clams, salmon, and trout, and the farming of aquatic plants, under controlled conditions to be sold for human consumption.

aquanaut A person who is trained to live in underwater installations and to conduct, assist in, or be a subject of scientific research.

aquarium A tank, pool, or building in which living aquatic animals and plants are kept under controlled conditions for pleasure, study, exhibition, or as a form of *ex situ* conservation.

aquasilvicultural system An *agroforestry system that combines trees with fish farming. *See also* AQUACULTURE.

aquatic Related to, living, or growing in or on water.

aquatic resources The living resources of aquatic habitats, which include fish, invertebrates, and *amphibians.

aqueduct A long channel or raised bridge-like structure built to transport water from a remote source, usually by gravity. *See also* INTERBASIN TRANSFER.

aqueous Containing water, dissolved in water, or composed mainly of water.

aqueous solubility The extent to which a substance will dissolve in water.

aquiclude (aquifuge) An effectively *impermeable layer of rock that confines an *aquifer by preventing the flow of *groundwater. *See also* PERCHED AQUIFER.

aquifer A body of *permeable and/or *porous *rock that is underlain by *impermeable rock and through which *groundwater is able to flow. *See also* AQUICLUDE; AQUITARD; ARTESIAN WELL; CONFINED AQUIFER; PERCHED AQUIFER.

aquifer depletion (groundwater mining, overdraft) Withdrawing *groundwater from an *aquifer faster than it is naturally replenished.

aquifer mining The withdrawal of *groundwater from an *aquifer, over a period of time, at a rate that exceeds the rate of natural *recharge.

aquifuge See AQUICLUDE.

aquitard The less *permeable beds in a rock sequence, that may be permeable enough to transmit water but not permeable enough to allow water to be abstracted from *wells within them.

arable 1. Land that is suitable for cultivation. 2. A farming system in which crops (such as cereals) are raised, rather than livestock.

arachnid Air-breathing *arthropod belonging to the class Arachnida such as a spider scorpion, or mite, that has book lungs or tracheae derived from gills, a body made of two segments (except mites), and four pairs of legs.

Aral Sea A very large *freshwater *lake (formerly the world's fourth largest lake) on the border between Kazakhstan and Uzbekistan in Central Asia. Since the 1960s the lake has been drying up and shrinking as a result of a loss of water due to the diversion of *river flow to a major *irrigation project designed to make the area *self-sufficient in cotton, and to increase rice production. The surface area of the Aral Sea has shrunk by nearly half since 1960, and its volume has decreased by two-thirds. Steps are now being taken to bring water back to the sea.

(((●))) SEE WEB LINKS

• Shrinking Aral Sea.

arbitration A formal process for resolving disputes, in which there are strict rules of evidence, cross-examination of witnesses, and a legally-binding decision made by the arbitrator that all parties must obey.

arboreal Relating to or living in or amongst *trees.

arboretum A collection of specimen *trees from which seeds and cuttings can easily be gathered as part of a *living collection.

arboriculture The cultivation and management of *trees. *See also* SILVICULTURE.

arbovirus A *virus that is transmitted by an *arthropod (such as a mosquito or tick), which includes encephalitis, *yellow fever, and dengue fever.

Archaea Single-celled organisms including the *methanogens, sulphur-reducing organisms, and *extremophiles. **1.** In the widely used five-kingdom system of classification, the Archaea (also called Archaebacteria) is ranked as one of the two subkingdoms within the *kingdom *Bacteria. **2.** In the three-domain system of classification, Archaea is one of the *domains, comprising organisms formerly known as the archaebacteria and placed in a kingdom of that name. The former kingdom Archaebacteria has been split into two kingdoms: Crenarchaeota and Euryarchaeota.

Archaean The eon of geological time extending from about 3.8 to 2.5 billion years ago (the start of the *Proterozoic), during which the Earth's crust formed. The earliest part of *Precambrian time. Rocks of this age contain fossils of single-celled organisms, which are the earliest forms of life on Earth.

(((●))) SEE WEB LINKS

• The Archaean eon of Precambrian time.

Archaebacteria *See* ARCHAEA.

Archaeological and Historic Preservation Act (1974) US legislation that provides for recovery, protection, and preservation of significant cultural resources that will be irreparably lost or destroyed by alteration of terrain from any federal construction project or federally licensed activity or programme.

archaeological resource All remaining physical evidence of past human occupation, other than historical documents, which can be used to reconstruct life styles of ancient cultural groups. This includes skeletons, sites, monuments, *artefacts, environmental data, and all other relevant information.

archaeological site Any place that contains physical evidence of past human activity, and which provides scientific, cultural, or historical evidence relating to the history of that place.

archaeology The study of past human cultures through the analysis of material remains (as fossil relics, *artefacts, and monuments), which are usually recovered through excavation.

archetype The original form or body plan from which a group of *organisms develops.

Arctic air A very cold and dry *air mass that generally forms north of the Arctic Circle but moves southwards, cooling the areas it passes over.

Arctic Circle Latitude 66°30′ N, to the north of which there is at least one day each year when the sun fails to rise above the horizon and one day when the sun fails to sink below the horizon.

Arctic front 1. A weather *front at the boundary between the very cold dense arctic *air mass that is associated with the cold arctic *anticyclone, and warmer air to its south. **2.** A front that advances southwards across North America with arctic air behind it. **3.** A shallow front that forms over snow and ice in winter when the wind is weak or blows parallel to the edge of sea ice.

Arctic haze A persistent thin mist, sometimes extending to a height of more than 9 km, that lies over the Arctic during the winter months, possibly associated with by the long-range transport of *air pollutants that originate in mid-latitude countries.

Arctic high A very cold zone of high *atmospheric pressure that originates over the Arctic Ocean.

Arctic National Wildlife Refuge (ANWR) A *National Wildlife Refuge that covers about 80000 km^2 in north-eastern Alaska, in the North Slope region. The area has been protected since 1960, but the refuge was expanded in 1980 under the *Alaska National Interest Lands Conservation Act.

Arctic Ocean The ice-covered waters that surround the *North Pole, which are largely a

ARCTIC

The area lying above 66.5° North that is dominated by the Arctic Ocean but also includes large land areas in Canada, Russia, Greenland, Scandinavia, Iceland, and Alaska. Some of the land areas, including most of Greenland, are permanently covered in ice and *pack ice is common throughout the Arctic Ocean. Climate in this high latitude zone is extreme, with short cool summers and long cold winters. Temperatures are particularly low in the interior—average mid-winter temperatures on the Greenland *ice cap are around −33°C, for example. Precipitation is generally low (less than 250 mm a year on average), and well distributed throughout the zone. Large river and lake systems are rare, because of the low precipitation, but shallow lakes, ponds, and marshes are common in areas underlain by *permafrost. Although the Arctic has the appearance of a vast, frozen desert, it does support wildlife. Signs of life are difficult to find during the cold, dark winter months but some species of mammals and birds carry extra insulation (such as fat) to survive the winter. The Arctic appears to wake up in spring. More than 400 species of flowering plant grow in the Arctic, and most of the land which is not covered in ice is *tundra, with a natural vegetation of low creeping *shrubs, grasses, thick growths of *lichens and *mosses, and *herbs and *sedges. The Arctic region is home to a wide variety of birds and fish, and the mammals include polar bear, arctic fox, arctic wolf, walrus, seal, caribou, reindeer, the infamous lemming, and many species of whale.

covered with solid ice or with *ice floes and *icebergs.

Arctogea A zoographic region that comprises the northern continents, as well as Africa and Indo-China. It is usually subdivided into the *Palaearctic and *Nearctic (together *Holarctica), Ethiopian, and *oriental faunal regions. *Compare* NEOGEA; NOTOGEA.

arcuate In the shape of an arc, bow, or fan.

area mining 1. (area strip mining) A type of *strip mining that is practised on relatively flat land, which involves cutting a trench through the *overburden in order to expose the deposit of *mineral or *ore to be removed. The overburden is placed on unmined land adjacent to the cut, and the mineral or ore is then removed. A second cut is then made parallel to the first, the overburden from which is deposited in the first cut. This process is continued until the mineral or ore is all extracted. 2. Surface mining, on a large scale, in an area of level or gently rolling ground.

area of critical environmental concern An area of public land in the USA where management is directed towards the protection of fish and wildlife, important historic, cultural, or scenic values, or other natural systems or processes. *See also* FRAGILE OR HISTORIC LANDS.

Area of Outstanding Natural Beauty (AONB) An area of protected *countryside in the UK, designated under the National Parks and Access to the Countryside Act 1949 on the

basis of attractive *landscape, in which development is tightly controlled.

area source Any source of *air pollution that is released over a relatively small area but is not a *point source. Sources include vehicle exhausts, houses, and small businesses. Similar to a *non-point source. *See also* EMISSION SOURCE.

area strip mining *See* AREA MINING.

area-sensitive species Species that respond badly if the *patch size of their *habitat decreases.

arenaceous rock Medium-grained sandy *clastic *sedimentary rocks, such as *sandstone, with particles ranging in size from 0.06 to 2.0 mm.

arene *See* AROMATIC.

arenosols Weakly developed, coarse-textured soils that are a soil reference group in the *World Soil Classification.

arête A long, sharp, knife-edged ridge with a serrated top, formed when *glaciers erode adjacent *cirques on the opposite sides of a mountain ridge. *See also* COL; HORN.

argillaceous rock Fine-grained *clastic *sedimentary rocks, such as *siltstones and *marls, made of *clay and *silt particles smaller than 0.06 mm.

argon (Ar) A natural, colourless, odourless, *inert *gas that is the third most abundant constituent of dry air (it comprises 0.93% of the Earth's *atmosphere).

arid Dry, lacking moisture.

arid region An area with a dry climate which cannot support the growth of trees, woody plants, or most crops (without *irrigation), and with a *biome in which only drought-resistant vegetation naturally survives.

aridisol A desert type (*order) of soil that develops in an *arid region, with little or no organic content but significant amounts of calcium carbonate (*gypsum) and other deposited salts. With little if any vegetation growing on the soil surface, there is no surface *litter, no *humus, and no dark organic layer in the *A-horizon. There is a relatively deep *B-horizon where soluble compounds accumulate which are leached down from above. Aridisols are often affected by *salinization.

aridity index A measure of the lack of moisture in a place, based on the level of water deficit. In equation form the index is $100 \times$ water deficit/potential evaporation. The term was first used in the *Thornthwaite climate classification.

arithmetic growth A pattern of growth that increases at a constant rate over a specified time period, such as 1, 2, 3, 4 or 1, 3, 5, 7. *Contrast* EXPONENTIAL GROWTH; GEOMETRIC GROWTH.

Army Corps of Engineers *See* US ARMY CORPS OF ENGINEERS.

aromatic (arene) A major group of unsaturated *hydrocarbons, such as *benzene or *toluene, which have a specific type of benzene ring structure and are added to *gasoline to increase octane. Some are toxic; all have a strong but not unpleasant odour.

aromatic acid herbicides A group of *herbicides, based on synthetic *auxins, that are taken up by plant roots and leaves and inhibit plant growth.

arrested development An incomplete ecological *succession that has not reached the natural climax stage, usually as a result of human disturbance or alteration which is reflected in *subclimax and *plagioclimax vegetation.

Arrhenius, Svante A Swedish physicist and chemist (1859–1927) who predicted that the release of *carbon dioxide into the atmosphere

would lead to *global warming, and estimated the magnitude of the *greenhouse gas effect.

arroyo A small, deep gully or channel with steep or vertical walls and a flat floor, which is eroded into the surface of a dry *desert by an intermittent stream. The bed is usually dry, and the arroyo contains *streamflow only after rain.

arsenic (As) A metalloid element that occurs naturally in the Earth's crust, which *bioaccumulates and is highly *toxic and *carcinogenic to humans. It is used in the production of glass, enamels, ceramics, oil, cloth, linoleum, electrical semiconductors, pigments, fireworks, pesticides, fungicides, veterinary pharmaceuticals, and wood preservatives.

arsenical herbicides A group of *herbicides that are compounds of *arsenic. They include monosodium methyl arsenate, also used as a *fungicide, that is less toxic than the others and is widely used to destroy weed grasses on golf courses and to burn marking lines into sports fields. The group also includes Agent Blue, a mixture of sodium cacodylate and cacodylic acid that was used to destroy rice crops during the Vietnam War.

arsenical insecticides *Arsenic compounds that are used to kill insects. They are probably the most ancient of insecticides, arsenic oxide having been used in China in 900 CE and against ants in Europe in 1699. Their use is declining as less toxic products replace them.

artefact An object made by humans, usually for a practical purpose, which has been preserved and can be studied to learn about the period it was made and used.

artesian aquifer A confined *aquifer in which *groundwater is held between two *impermeable layers (*aquitards), under *hydrostatic pressure, which is significantly greater than *atmospheric pressure and forces the water to flow out of an *artesian well, boreholes or springs, so long as the aquifer is constantly recharged.

artesian well A *well sunk in an *artesian aquifer, from which *groundwater is naturally forced to the surface by *hydrostatic pressure so the well is free flowing. *See* FLOWING WELL.

arthropod A member of the *phylum Arthropoda, which is by far the largest in the *animal kingdom, comprising about 75% of all animal species, and includes many different *invertebrates having an *exoskeleton with jointed limbs, such as *arachnids (spiders, mites), *insects (bees, ants, moths), and *crustaceans (shrimps, crabs).

artificial fertilizer A chemical that is added to soil to increase fertility and enhance crop production.

artificial rain *See* CLOUD SEEDING.

artificial recharge Adding water to an *aquifer to restore *groundwater.

artificial reef A large, permanent structure made on the seabed in shallow water, often from solid waste materials, either to restrict the entrance to a harbour for defence purposes or, more commonly, to provide cover for marine organisms. The practice is ancient and improves local inshore fisheries management.

(()) SEE WEB LINKS

• Assessment by the FAO Fisheries and Aquaculture Department

artificial regeneration Establishing a new *forest by planting seedlings or by direct seeding, often after *deforestation. *Contrast* NATURAL REGENERATION.

artificial selection The process by which humans breed animals and crops to ensure that future generations have specific desirable characteristics, by exploiting the process of *natural selection. Breeders select the most desirable variants in a plant or animal population, and then selectively breed them with other desirable individuals. Examples include particular plants that are resistant to disease, high yielding, or attractive in appearance, and particular breeds of cattle which produce more meat or milk. Domesticated animals such as dogs, cats, and farm animals are the product of selective breeding.

artificial wetland An engineered *wetland, often constructed to treat *sewage or other organic wastes.

artiodactyls Mammals belonging to the order Artiodactyla of even-toed *ungulates including camels, pigs, hippopotamuses, cattle, sheep, and goats, in which the first digit is absent and the second and fifth often reduced or lost. The digits end in hoofs, the third and fourth of equal size.

Arusha Declaration The declaration that was issued in 1961 at the end of an *IUCN conference at Arusha, Tanzania, recognizing the importance of the survival of wildlife in Africa 'as a source of wonder and inspiration [and as] an integral part of our national resources and of our future livelihood and well-being'.

As Low As Reasonably Achievable (ALARA) An approach to the control of radiation in order to protect public health and the environment, based on keeping radiation emissions and exposures to levels set as far below regulatory limits as is reasonably possible.

asbestos A group of naturally occurring fibrous minerals that can be spun and woven. They are strong, do not corrode or burn, are good at insulating heat and electricity, and were formerly used for insulation, construction, and brake linings. Asbestos minerals separate into fibres that can cause air and water pollution, and cause cancer or *asbestosis when inhaled by humans. Their use is now banned or severely restricted.

asbestos abatement Measures used to control the release of dangerous fibres from materials that contain asbestos. These include removal, enclosure, and encasement.

asbestosis A lung disease in humans, associated with chronic exposure to asbestos and inhalation of asbestos fibres, which results from scarring of the lung tissues by the fibres. The disease makes breathing progressively more difficult and can be fatal.

Ascencion and St Helena floral region Part of R. Good's *Palaeotropical floral kingdom (*The Geography of the Flowering Plants*, 1974), within the African subkingdom, comprising just two islands. This is probably the smallest floral region. There are five *endemic genera, three of them being woody members of the aster family (Asteraceae).

asexual reproduction A mode of reproduction, common among lower animals, micro-organisms, and plants, in which offspring are created by a single parent so they inherit only the *genes of that parent.

ash 1. The mineral content of a product that remains after complete combustion, which consists mainly of minerals in oxidized form. *See also* FLY ASH. **2.** Volcanic dust that erupts from a *volcano, and either flows out (as a *pyroclastic flow) or forms a cloud.

ash cone A steep-sided *volcano composed of fine *volcanic ash erupted from the volcano.

Ashby, Eric (1904–92) A British botanist who held many public offices and professorships at the universities of Sydney and Manchester. He was president, vice-chancellor, and chancellor (1970–83) of Queen's University, Belfast, master of Clare College, Cambridge, and vice-chancellor of Cambridge University (1967–9). Lord Ashby chaired the working party on environmental pollution in preparation for the *United Nations Conference on the Human Environment and was a member of the Royal Commission on Environmental Pollution. He wrote two books on environmental topics: *Reconciling Man with the Environment* (1978) and (with Mary Anderson) *The Politics of Clean Air* (1981).

ask *See* OFFER.

ASOS *See* AUTOMATED SURFACE OBSERVING SYSTEM.

aspect The direction in which a slope or feature faces, usually expressed in terms of points on a compass. For example, an aspect of 90° is due east, 180° is due south and 315° is northwest. *See also* AZIMUTH.

asphyxia Suffocation dues to inhalation of toxic gases.

asphyxiant A vapour that can cause unconsciousness or death due to a lack of oxygen (suffocation). Chemical asphyxiants like *carbon monoxide (CO) reduce the ability of the blood to carry oxygen; those like *cyanide interfere with the way the body uses oxygen.

assay Analysis of a specific chemical, microbe, or biological response. *See also* BIOASSAY; LIMIT OF DETECTION.

assemblage A group of plants and/or animals that is indicative of a particular environment. *See also* COMMUNITY.

asset Anything owned by an individual or group that has a value, whether financial or otherwise.

assigned amount (emissions budget) The total amount of *greenhouse gas that each country is allowed to emit during the first *Commitment Period of the *Kyoto Protocol, taking into account certified *emissions reductions acquired via the *Clean Development Mechanism.

assimilation The process by which organisms take in and convert nutrient substances for growth, reproduction, or repair.

assimilative capacity The ability of a body of water to naturally purify itself of *pollutants.

association Two or more species living in the same place at the same time. *See also* COMMUNITY.

association, index of A measure of the likely occurrence of two particular species together, in *association.

Association for Biodiversity Information *See* NATURERESERVE.

asteroid A small, rocky, or metallic celestial body that orbits the Sun in the asteroid belt between Mars and Jupiter. There are probably more than two million asteroids in the asteroid belt. They are part of the original matter of the solar system that never became a planet owing to perturbations caused by Jupiter's gravity. The risk of an asteroid impact on Earth is measured using the *Torino scale. *See also* COMET.

asthenosphere The weak upper part of the *mantle within the *Earth's interior, just below the *lithosphere.

astronomy The study of the universe and celestial bodies.

asulam A *systemic herbicide of the *carbamate group that is used to control docks in grassland and orchards, and bracken in grassland, forest plantations, and upland pastures.

asynchronous Not coinciding in time. *Contrast* SYNCHRONOUS.

at risk species Species whose survival is not guaranteed. These are often classified as *endangered, *threatened, or *species of concern. *See also* IMPERILLED SPECIES.

Atlantic Basin The *Atlantic Ocean north of the equator, the Caribbean Sea, and the Gulf of Mexico.

Atlantic conveyor *See* OCEANIC CONVEYOR BELT.

Atlantic North American floral region Part of R. Good's boreal kingdom (*The Geography of the Flowering Plants*, 1974). It has a large and extensive flora with 100–200 *endemic genera. *Robinia* (false acacia) is a well-known example, and there is also *Franklinia*, a garden tree (not hardy in Britain) that was obtained from a single plant of a single species, and which is now extinct in the wild. As a whole the flora strongly resembles those of temperate Eurasia, China, and Japan.

Atlantic Ocean The Earth's second largest *ocean, which covers about a fifth of its surface, and is bounded by North and South America to the west and by Europe and Africa to the east. It is relatively shallow, and is the warmest and most *saline of the major oceans.

Atlantic Period *See* CLIMATIC OPTIMUM.

atmophile Applied to the elements most typical of, and concentrated in, the Earth's atmosphere (e.g. H, C, N, O, I, and inert gases). These may occur uncombined or combined (e.g. water (H_2O), carbon dioxide (CO_2), and methane (CH_4)).

atmosphere 1. The air surrounding the Earth. The atmosphere has no precise upper limit, but for all practical purposes the absolute top can be regarded as being at about 200 km. The density of the atmosphere decreases rapidly with height, and about three-quarters of the mass of the atmosphere is contained within the lowest major layer, the *troposphere, whose depth varies between about 10 km and 17 km, being generally smaller further from the equator. **2.** A unit of pressure (abbreviation: atm.). Its value is approximately the average pressure of the atmosphere at sea level, the figure adopted being the pressure at sea level in the International Standard Atmosphere (760 mm of mercury, or 1013.25 millibars). In SI units, 1 atm = 101 325 pascals. *See also* ATMOSPHERIC STRUCTURE.

atmospheric boundary layer *See* BOUNDARY LAYER.

atmospheric brown cloud A widespread layer of brownish haze that is a *plume of pollutants, mainly *aerosol particles, on a regional scale. The particles are mainly of black carbon (soot) and organic carbon and the most extensive clouds occur over southern Asia.

atmospheric deposition The deposition of solids, liquids, or gaseous materials from the air onto land or oceans. *See also* ACID RAIN.

atmospheric pressure (air pressure, barometric pressure) The force exerted by the weight of the overlying *atmosphere. *Pressure is measured with a *barometer and expressed scientifically in *pascals but also in *bars or millibars (mb), and pressure readings are normally adjusted to sea level equivalents in order to eliminate the effects of altitude. Mean atmospheric pressure on Earth is 101.325 kilopascals (kPa) (1013.25 mb). High pressure cells within the atmosphere, which generally produce stable weather conditions, have pressures up to about 101.6 kPa (1060 mb); low pressure cells, which can result in storms, have pressures down to about 0.94 kPa (940 mb).

atmospheric structure The broadly horizontal layering of the *atmosphere, the layers

ATMOSPHERE

1. The mixture of *gases that surrounds the *Earth, which includes *nitrogen (78.08%), *oxygen (20.94%), and *carbon dioxide (0.035%). It is a major *environmental system, which interacts with the *lithosphere, the *hydrosphere, and the *biosphere. It contains a variable amount of fine solid material, held up in suspension by air currents, wind systems, and convection currents, which comes from a variety of sources and in a variety of forms, including *dust (for example from volcanoes and desert sandstorms), *pollen and mould spores (from natural vegetation), *smoke (from natural forest fires, and from air pollution), and salt spray (from the oceans). There is no definite outer limit to the atmosphere, it simply becomes less dense with increasing height above the ground until it eventually becomes part of the solar atmosphere (at an altitude of about 1000 km) and merges into space where near-vacuum conditions exist. *Weather is mostly confined to the lowest 16 km of the atmosphere, although air movements in the lowest 30 km affect weather patterns and changes. The atmosphere is composed of a number of vertical layers or zones, each of which is quite clearly defined and has distinctive physical properties (particularly temperature and pressure). Abrupt changes in temperature and pressure mark the boundaries between successive zones. It is convenient to think in terms of three main layers within the atmosphere—the lower atmosphere (*troposphere, which contains three-quarters of the mass of the atmosphere), the middle atmosphere (*stratosphere), and the upper atmosphere (*mesosphere, *thermosphere and beyond into the *exosphere). **2.** A unit of pressure equal to *atmospheric pressure at *sea level.

being distinguished by differences in the rate of change of temperature with height, which either favour or discourage the development of vertical exchanges (convection). From the surface of the Earth upwards the layers are: (*a*) the *troposphere, in which convection is often prominent, especially over warm regions, extending to the *tropopause at a somewhat variable height, generally about 11 km over middle and higher latitudes and 17 km near the equator; (*b*) the *stratosphere, in which there is much less vertical motion, and which extends from the tropopause to about 50 km at the *stratopause; (*c*) the *mesosphere, in which there is once again more convection, extending from the stratopause to a height of about 80 km at the *mesopause; and (*d*) the *thermosphere, extending from the mesopause to the effective limit of the atmosphere, at about 200 km.

atmospheric transport The movement of *air pollutants from one region to another via the *atmosphere, which may be for hundreds or even thousands of kilometres and can cross national boundaries to create international or *trans-frontier pollution.

atmospheric window Part of the infrared band in the *electromagnetic spectrum at a wavelength of about 10 micrometres (μm) at which the atmosphere is transparent to radiation. Radiation from the Earth's surface at this wavelength passes through the atmosphere unimpeded; at shorter wavelengths (about 7 μm) radiation is absorbed by water vapour and at longer wavelengths (about 15 μm) it is absorbed by carbon dioxide.

atoll A low-lying island composed of *coral reef, which is usually circular or horseshoe-shaped, with a *lagoon in the middle.

atom The smallest part of an *element that can exist. An atom is composed of a nucleus containing protons and neutrons surrounded by *motile electrons. *See also* ELECTRON; PROTON; NEUTRON; SUBATOMIC.

atomic energy Energy that is released in a nuclear reaction, either by *fission or *fusion.

Atomic Energy Commission (AEC) The US federal agency responsible for all aspects of nuclear energy.

atomic number (Z) The number of protons in the *nucleus of an *atom, which defines and identifies the element, indicating its place in the *periodic table of the elements. The atomic number is also equal to the number of electrons in the atom.

atomic pile North American term for a *nuclear reactor.

atomic weight *See* RELATIVE ATOMIC MASS.

atomization The dividing of a liquid into very small particles, thus increasing the total surface area.

attainment area A geographical area in which levels of a *criteria air pollutant meet the *national ambient air quality standard for that pollutant. An area may have an acceptable level for one criteria air pollutant but not for others, so it could be both an attainment and a non-attainment area at the same time. *See* NON-ATTAINMENT AREA.

attenuation Weakening, such as the dilution of concentration of a compound or agent, or a reduction in the size and energy of a signal (such as a *seismic wave).

Atterberg limits A series of thresholds that are observed when the water content of a soil is steadily changed. The 'contraction limit' occurs when sufficient water is added to a dry soil for contraction cracks to close. The addition of further water leads to plastic deformation at the 'plastic limit'. The 'liquid limit' occurs when just enough water is then added for the soil to behave like a liquid. Knowledge of these limits is important for understanding and predicting hill-slope failure. The limits were devised in 1911 by the Swedish soil physicist Albert Mauritz Atterberg (1846–1916).

attractant A chemical agent that attracts insects or other pests by stimulating their sense of smell.

attributable risk The difference between the *incidence rate (of a disease or effect) in groups who have been exposed to an environmental risk and that in non-exposed groups.

attrition The wearing or grinding down of a substance by friction.

auction *See* EMISSIONS AUCTIONING.

audit An inspection or systematic examination of a process or activity, often carried out by an independent or external specialist, designed to ensure compliance with requirements. *See also* ENVIRONMENTAL AUDIT.

Audubon, John James A US wildlife artist (1785–1851) who published the book *Birds of*

America (a collection of 435 life-size prints). His name is synonymous with birds and bird conservation worldwide, although he played no role in the organization that bears his name (the *National Audubon Society).

auger An instrument that is used for drilling holes, mainly for extracting samples of soil or peat.

auger mining A type of surface *mining that involves drilling large, closely spaced holes into a deposit, where the slope is too steep for *contour strip mining or where there is a lot of *overburden relative to the workable deposit.

aurora Spectacular lights and colours (usually green, red, or yellow) in the sky that can sometimes be seen within the *ionosphere, most often above latitude 67° at midnight and 76° by day, but occasionally in latitudes as low as 40°. These are the aurora borealis (northern lights) in the *northern hemisphere and the aurora australis (southern lights) in the *southern hemisphere. They are caused by the interaction of *solar wind particles with oxygen and nitrogen atoms in the upper atmosphere.

austral Relating to high southern latitudes. *See also* BOREAL.

Australian faunal subregion A region that is distinguished by a unique marsupial (Marsupialia) fauna, including herbivores, carnivores, and insectivores. These evolved in isolation from the placental mammals (Eutheria), which now dominate the other continental faunas. In addition to marsupials there are also very primitive mammals (Monotremata), the spiny anteater and the platypus; and small rodents which are relatively recent (probably *Miocene) immigrants.

Australian realm A *biogeographical realm which is largely *desert, surrounded by *tropical forest and *savanna.

autecology The study of individual *organisms or *species, with particular reference to their interaction with their environment. *See also* GENECOLOGY. *Contrast* SYNECOLOGY.

autochthonous Formed *in situ*, in its present location. **1.** A rock whose main constituents were formed in that position rather than being transported from elsewhere. Organic deposits that turn into *coal are of this type. **2.** Organic matter produced within the given *habitat, *community, or *ecosystem. *See also* ENDOGENOUS. *Contrast* ALLOCHTHONOUS.

Automated Local Evaluation in Real Time (ALERT) A network of automated meteorological and hydrological sensors in the USA that transmit data via VHF and UHF radio link to a base station. Some sites are also equipped with other sensors to report temperature, wind, pressure, river stage, or tide level.

Automated Surface Observing System (ASOS) A network of meteorological stations across the US, operated by the National Weather Service, that provide weather information for airports by automatically measuring surface *atmospheric pressure, *temperature, *wind speed and direction, runway visibility, cloud ceiling height, cloud types, and precipitation intensity. These are augmented by a separate system to warn of *thunderstorms, operated by the Federal Aviation Administration.

automated weather station An unmanned station that has a range of sensors to measure weather elements such as *temperature, *wind, and *pressure and that transmits these readings for use by meteorologists in *weather forecasting.

autotroph (primary producer) An *organism that makes its own food by synthesizing organic matter from inorganic substances, unlike a *heterotrophic organism which derives food from *organic matter. Higher plants and algae use *carbon dioxide as a source of *carbon and obtain their energy from the Sun, via *photosynthesis, and are called *photoautotrophs. Bacteria and other autotrophs oxidize inorganic substances such as *sulphur, *hydrogen, ammonium, and nitrate salts, and are called *chemoautotrophs.

autumn The *season of the year, between *summer and *winter, when temperatures at mid-latitudes decrease as the Sun approaches the winter solstice. Astronomically this is the period between the *autumnal equinox and the *winter solstice, which covers the months of September, October, and November in the northern hemisphere, and March, April, and May in the southern hemisphere. Until the 17th century the season was known as the fall, a Germanic word, which is the name it retains in North America.

autumnal equinox The *equinox at which the Sun approaches the southern hemisphere and passes directly over the equator, which occurs at present on 22–23 September each year. *See also* VERNAL EQUINOX.

auxin A *hormone that promotes longitudinal growth in the cells of higher plants. Typically, low concentrations of auxin promote growth whereas high concentrations inhibit it. Auxins are produced at the growing points of stems and roots, and promote growth by increasing the rate of cell elongation rather than that of cell division. They are involved in the curvature of parts of the plant towards light (phototropism) or gravity (geotropism), and may control fruit growth or leaf fall. Auxins have been synthesized, and are widely used to regulate growth in a variety of plants of agricultural and horticultural importance. Some of these may have differential effects on different plants. For example, 2, 4-dichlorophenoxyacetic acid (2, 4-D) is toxic to *dicotyledons but not to *monocotyledons, and is used to control weeds in cereal crops and lawns.

auxotroph An organism (usually a bacterium) that, as a result of a *mutation, has lost the ability to synthesize a particular substance essential for its growth, e.g. an *amino acid or a sugar. The organism must be able to obtain this component from its environment if it is to survive and grow. *Compare* PROTOTROPH.

available element *See* AVAILABLE NUTRIENT.

available nutrient (available element) An element in the soil solution that can readily be taken up by plant roots, usually only a fraction of the total amount of a nutrient that is present in the soil.

available relief Part of a landscape that is higher than the floors of the main valleys. It is therefore available for destruction by the agents of *erosion, controlled by the local base level. Available relief is measured as the vertical distance between hilltops and valley floors.

available water The water in soil that can be taken up by plant roots. *Contrast* UNAVAILABLE WATER.

avalanche A sudden, rapid *mass movement process like a *landslide, but involving a large mass of snow, ice, and rock crashing down a mountainside under its own weight. Most avalanches occur in spring when the snow starts to melt, although some are triggered by *earthquakes.

avalanche wind A blast of air that is pushed ahead of an *avalanche. A major slab avalanche can generate a wind of up to 300 km/h.

average life expectancy The average number of years that a person can expect to live, in a particular country or area, counted either from birth or from a particular age.

avermectin A naturally occurring *toxic *antibiotic that is produced by the bacterium *Streptomyces avermitilis* and is often used to control mites.

avian Having to do with *birds.

aviary A building or large enclosure in which *birds are kept.

avicide A *pesticide which can be used to kill *birds.

aviculture The rearing of *birds in captivity.

avifauna The *birds of a particular region, *habitat, or period of time.

avoidable risk A *risk which it is not necessary to take because the individual or public goals that it entails can be achieved by other means, at the same or lower total cost, without taking the risk. *Contrast* ACCEPTABLE RISK; UNACCEPTABLE RISK.

avoidance Emissions of *greenhouse gases that have not occurred, either because of improvements in energy efficiency (thus less energy is used) or because of a switch in energy sources (from high to low or no emission).

avoidance cost The actual or estimated cost of preventing environmental damage by adopting alternative production and consumption processes, or by reducing or abstaining from particular activities.

avoided emissions Emissions of *greenhouse gases that would have been made under a *business-as-usual scenario, but have been avoided through the implementation of an *emissions reduction project.

avulsion The lateral displacement of a stream from its main channel into a new course across its *floodplain. Normally it is a result of the instability caused by channel *aggradation. The avulsion of a stream into an adjacent valley may explain some cases of apparent *river piracy.

azimuth The angle along the Earth's horizon made with *magnetic north, which is measured clockwise. *See also* ASPECT.

azoic Devoid of life, or before life began.

azonal soil A poorly developed soil with young and evolving *horizons. Examples include *alluvium and *loess. Through time these types of soils are likely to mature and develop into a *zonal soil. *See* *GREAT SOIL GROUP.

Azores high A semi-permanent *anticyclone centred over the Azores, about 1290 km west of Portugal and often extending westwards as far as Bermuda, when it is known in North America as the Bermuda high. The difference in surface pressure between the Azores high and the *Iceland low drives weather systems across the Atlantic from west to east. Period variations in this pressure difference are known as the *North Atlantic Oscillation.

Bacillariophyta (golden-brown algae) *See* DIATOM.

Bacillus thuringiensis **(Bt)** A naturally occurring *bacterium that produces a *protein which kills caterpillars and some moths and butterflies. It is a *biopesticide that is used extensively by the *microbial *pesticide industry. The genes encoding for the Bt toxin have been inserted into certain crop plants to make them resistant to insect attack. *See* GENETIC ENGINEERING.

backcountry A general term used in North America for all parts of *wildlands in which there are no permanent, improved, or maintained access roads or working facilities (such as lumber mills, ski resorts, or settlements with permanent residents). Any current uses of the area only have primitive facilities, such as cabins, base camps, or undeveloped campgrounds.

backcountry recreation A simple or primitive recreation experience in a roadless *backcountry area, where travel is mostly by horse, foot trails, or canoe.

backfill The process of filling in an excavation, and the material that is used in doing so.

backfit *See* RETROFIT.

backflow A reverse flow condition in a *potable water supply system, caused by a difference in water pressures, which makes water flow back into the distribution pipes from a unintended source.

background The part of a scene or *landscape that is furthest away from the viewer. *See also* FOREGROUND; MIDDLEGROUND.

background concentration *See* BACKGROUND LEVEL.

background extinction The normal rate of *extinction of species, which reflects changes in local environmental conditions, in the absence of human influences. *See also* MASS EXTINCTION.

background level The *ambient or typical level of a substance that occurs in an environmental medium (air, water, or soil) in a particular place or area, through natural processes or from natural sources. This is often used as a *baseline against which to measure changes that result from human activities, including *pollution control.

background radiation Low-intensity *radiation in the natural environment that originates from cosmic rays and from the naturally *radioactive elements of the Earth. *See also* RADON.

backing An anti-clockwise change in *wind direction.

backwash The return flow of water down a beach after a wave has broken.

backwater A small, generally shallow body of stagnant water that is attached to the main channel but has little or no current of its own.

backwoods A remote, undeveloped area where few people live.

backyard composting The composting of organic food waste and organic garden waste in one's yard, using bacteria and fungi to decompose it into a humus-like product. It is regarded as a *source reduction form of waste management.

BACM *See* BEST AVAILABLE CONTROL MEASURES.

BACT *See* BEST AVAILABLE CONTROL TECHNOLOGY.

bacteria Eleven main groups of *prokaryotes: purple (photosynthetic); Gram positive; *cyanobacteria; green non-sulphur; spirochaetes; flavobacteria; green sulphur; Planctomyces; Chlamydiales; Deinococci; and Thermatogales. Bacteria are almost universal in distribution and may live as *saprotrophs, *parasites, *symbionts, *pathogens, etc. They have many important roles in nature, e.g. as agents of decay and mineralization, and in the recycling of elements (such as nitrogen) in the *biosphere. Bacteria are also important to humans, e.g. as symbiotic gut flora aiding digestion, as causal agents of certain diseases, as agents of spoilage of food and other commodities, and as useful agents in the industrial production of commodities such as vinegar, *antibiotics, and many types of dairy products. In the widely used five-kingdom system of classification, Bacteria is one of the kingdoms, and the only kingdom in the superkingdom Prokarya. In the three-*domain system of classification, Bacteria is one of the domains (with *Archaea and *Eukarya).

bacterial agent A live *pathogenic *organism that can cause disease, illness, or death.

bactericidal That which destroys bacteria, such as *antibiotics and *disinfectants.

bacteriophages A group of *viruses whose hosts are *bacteria.

bacteriostatic Applied to an agent that prevents the growth of at least some types of *bacteria without actually killing them.

badland Steep, barren land, usually broken by narrow channels and sharp crest ridges that result from rapid erosion, often of *unconsolidated sediments. Most common in dry areas.

bag limit The maximum number of animals that a hunter may legally harvest during one hunting season. See also GAME BAG; GAME SPECIES.

baghouse filter A fabric filter device that is used to remove *particulate pollutants from air.

bahada See BAJADA.

bajada (bahada) A gentle slope of *unconsolidated material where several *alluvial fans overlap at the foot of a mountain.

baleen In whales of the suborder Mysticeti, sheets of keratin that hang transversely from the roof of the mouth, their lower edges fringed with hairs which form a comb-like structure used to filter *plankton.

baling The compacting of solid waste, or other material, into blocks, in order to reduce volume.

ballast water Water that is carried in the lower hold of ships to make them heavier, which causes them to float lower in the water and thus be less likely to roll. The water is discharged from the ship when it enters harbour.

banded iron ore formation A *sedimentary rock composed of alternating layers of *chert and ferric iron oxides (haematite and limonite).

bank erosion The wearing back of a river bank, usually during a *flood.

bankfull The height (*stage) of water in a river channel that equals the level of the surrounding *floodplain, so that *flooding would occur if the water level increased further. See also FLOOD STAGE.

Bankhead-Jones Farm Tenant Act (1937) US legislation that authorized federal acquisition of eroded and exhausted farm lands, which were ultimately designated *National Grassland.

bankside On the side of a river or stream.

banner cloud A stationary, undulating layer *cloud that extends downwind from an isolated mountain peak, resembling a flag. It is produced by the rising and subsidence of air downwind of the mountain peaks.

BAP See BIODIVERSITY ACTION PLAN.

bar 1. A shoal of coarse-grained *sediment (sand, gravel, and pebbles) that has been deposited either on the bed of a *river (see also POINT BAR) or along a *coast, offshore from the *beach (see also LONGSHORE DRIFT). **2.** A measure of *atmospheric pressure based on an approximate value for the average sea-level pressure (1.01325 bar) and equal to 0.1 megapascals (MPa). Weather forecasts often report pressure in *millibars (mb); 1 bar = 1000mb. See also KILOBAR.

barban A *systemic herbicide of the *carbamate group that is used to control wild oat and other weed grasses in cereal crops, beans, and sugar beet. It is harmful to fish and can cause contact dermatitis in humans.

Barcelona Convention An agreement as part of the *Regional Seas Programme signed on 16 February 1976 by nations bordering the Mediterranean, which came into force on 12 February 1978. It forbids the discharge of a wide range of substances into that sea, including organosilicon compounds, all petroleum hydrocarbons, all radioactive wastes, and acids and alkalis.

(⊕) **SEE WEB LINKS**

• Text of the Barcelona Convention.

barchan A crescent-shaped *dune form common in sandy deserts with winds that blow predominantly from one direction (see Fig. 2). The convex side faces upwind and the concave side faces downwind. The horns of the barchan point downwind, and the dunes migrate continuously downwind across the desert floor.

barium (Ba) A soft, silver-grey, alkaline-earth metal that is naturally abundant in nature and is found in plant and animal tissue. It has many uses, e.g. in various alloys, paints, soap, paper, rubber, ceramics, glass, and insecticides. Barium can *bioaccumulate in the human skeleton and it can cause muscular problems if ingested.

bark The tough protective outer covering of the branches and roots of *trees and other woody plants.

bark beetle An insect that bores through the *bark of forest trees to eat the inner bark and lay its eggs. Many forest trees are killed by diseases transmitted by bark beetles.

barograph A *barometer that provides a continuous record of variations in *atmospheric pressure through time.

barometer An instrument that measures *atmospheric pressure, which is used in making *weather forecasts. The two most common types are the *aneroid barometer and the *mercury barometer.

barometric gradient *See* PRESSURE GRADIENT.

barometric pressure *See* ATMOSPHERIC PRESSURE.

barothermograph An instrument that records *atmospheric pressure, *relative humidity, and temperature simultaneously as pen lines on a chart carried on a rotating drum, for use in making *weather forecasts.

barrage A dam across a river or estuary.

barrel, petroleum A unit of volume that is equal to 42 US gallons, 35 UK gallons.

Fig. 2 Barchan dune

barren Devoid of life, incapable of sustaining life.

barren land Land that is uninhabited wilderness, often in a hostile climate, and offers no prospect of being developed or used for agriculture or other economic activities. *See also* FORESTLAND.

barrier bar A major *longshore bar of gravel or sand the surface of which is below mean still-water level. Normally it is formed off a depositional coast of low gradient and with ample unconsolidated sediment.

barrier beach A relatively small, shingle feature that protects a steep coast.

barrier hedge A hedge that is grown to help prevent *runoff and *soil erosion from a field. *See also* CONTOUR HEDGE; HEDGE.

barrier island A long, low, narrow, sandy *island that forms offshore from a *coastline, parallel to the *coast. Such features help to protect the mainland during hurricanes, tidal waves, and other maritime hazards.

barrier reef A *coral reef that is separated from a mainland or island shore by a lagoon.

basal ice The ice at the bottom of a glacier, which is in direct contact with (and both affects and is affected by) the sediment and rock beneath the glacier.

basal lamina A layer of *proteins and glycoproteins that surrounds tissues in a body.

basal metabolic rate (BMR) The rate at which an animal must release energy metabolically in order to maintain itself at rest. Since the BMR of different body tissues varies, the BMR for a particular animal is determined by the composition of its tissues; for a group of animals BMR is inversely proportional to body weight (i.e. small animals usually have a higher BMR than large ones).

basal sediment The sediment (*till) that is transported at, or deposited from, the bottom of a *glacier.

basal sliding/slip The process by which the bottom of a *glacier slides directly over the bedrock below, often lubricated by *meltwater.

basalt A fine-grained, dark-coloured, *basic, *extrusive *igneous rock. It is the most common type of volcanic rock in the Earth's *crust, and is rich in *iron and *magnesium and has a relatively low *silica content. Under suitable climatic conditions basalt can weather into deep productive *soils.

base A metal *oxide, *hydroxide, or compound (such as *ammonia) that gives off hydrogen ions in aqueous solution. *See also* ALKALI.

base exchange capacity *See* CATION EXCHANGE CAPACITY.

base level The level below which a river cannot erode. This is usually *sea level, but local base levels are provided by resistant layers of rock or the level of a lake or *reservoir. *See also* LONG PROFILE; WATERFALL.

base map A map that shows important basic information, on which can be superimposed more specialized information relevant to a particular study or purpose.

base metal A non-precious metal, such as *copper, *lead, or *zinc, which is inferior in value to *gold and *silver but still has commercial uses and value. Base metals easily corrode, *oxidize, and tarnish in air, moisture, or heat.

base neutral acid compound *See* SEMI-VOLATILE ORGANIC COMPOUND.

base pair The pair of complementary, nitrogen-rich molecules within a strand of *DNA which are held together by weak chemical bonds. The bonds between the base pairs hold the two strands of DNA held together in the shape of a *double helix.

base saturation The extent to which the exchange sites on the surface of soil particles are occupied (i.e. saturated) by exchangeable basic *cations, or by cations other than hydrogen and aluminium, expressed as a percentage of the total *cation exchange capacity.

base year In environmental regulation, the year for which a national inventory is to be taken, or the baseline year against which changes are measured. For *Annex I countries, for example, the base year is 1990. Under the *Kyoto Protocol, the base year for *hydrofluorocarbons, *perfluorocarbons, and *sulphur hexafluoride is 1995.

baseflow The portion of *streamflow that comes from the seepage of *groundwater and *throughflow into the channel, rather than from *direct runoff or *precipitation.

Basel Convention on the Control of Transboundary Movements of Hazardous Wastes and their Disposal (1992) An international *convention that seeks to minimize the generation of *hazardous wastes, ensure that such wastes are disposed of in the countries that generate them, and control the import, export, and movement of hazardous waste.

baseline emission The emissions that would occur in a *business-as-usual scenario, without any change or intervention. Estimates of what these emissions would be are needed in order to determine the effectiveness of *emissions reduction programmes.

baseline information Information collected at the start of a study or programme which gives an initial or known value as a standard against which later measurements can be compared.

baseline study A description and analysis of the existing conditions and trends in a location or area where some form of change is proposed or likely, such as a change in *land use, or the likelihood of air or water pollution. This provides a reference point from which effects of proposed actions might be predicted, or against which observed effects can be compared.

basement The oldest rocks in a given area. Usually a complex of *metamorphic and *igneous rocks underlying *sedimentary formations.

base-rich Containing an abundance of *basic (less *acidic) materials.

basic *See* ALKALINE.

basic needs The basic items and services that a person needs to ensure a reasonable standard of living.

basic rock Rock with a relatively high concentration of *iron, *magnesium, and *calcium, and with 45–53% silica by weight. Basic rocks tend to be darker than *acidic rocks and many of them are weathered by *chemical weathering which breaks down the *crystal structure into the main *mineral constituents. Basic rocks produce more fertile and productive *soils than acidic rocks because *nutrients are more freely available for plants. *See also* ACID; INTERMEDIATE; ULTRABASIC.

basin 1. An area of land that drains into a lake or river. *See also* DRAINAGE BASIN. 2. A circular depression of rock *strata which dips towards the centre. 3. The site where a large thickness of *sediments accumulates by deposition.

basin and range *Topography dominated by numerous mountain ranges separated by broad valleys (basins), found in the west and south-west of the USA.

bastion A large rock *outcrop which projects out from the side of a valley or from an ice field.

BAT *See* BEST AVAILABLE TECHNOLOGY.

Bates, Henry Walter (1825-92) An English naturalist who, in 1848, accompanied A. R. *Wallace on an exploration of the Amazon, where he collected nearly 15 000 species of insects, 8000 of which were new to science. His studies of them led him to propose the way in which the mimicry named after him can arise among unrelated species. He received enthusiastic support from Charles *Darwin and Sir Joseph Hooker, and Darwin wrote an introduction to his only book, *The Naturalist on the River Amazons*, published by John Murray in 1863 and still in print.

Batesian mimicry A form of *mimicry first described by Henry Walter *Bates, in which one non-poisonous *species (the Batesian mimic) evolves to resemble the coloration, body shape, or behaviour of another species that is protected from *predators by some defensive adaptation (such as a venomous sting or a bad taste). This adaptation gives the mimic species a much better chance of survival. *Contrast* MÜLLERIAN MIMICRY.

bathing water quality The state of purity or pollution of water that people have access to for swimming, usually along a coastline.

batholith The largest and most common type of *discordant igneous *intrusion, most often composed of granite, similar in form to but much larger than a *laccolith. They vary in size between 100 and several thousand square kilometres. Batholiths often form the core of major mountain ranges, such as parts of the Sierra Nevada and Rocky Mountains in the USA.

bathyal zone The upper boundary of the *continental shelf, comprising the *continental slope and *continental rise.

bathymetry Measurement of the depths of large bodies of water (particularly seas and oceans) in order to determine the bottom *topography.

bathypelagic zone The deep *aphotic zone of the ocean, into which no light penetrates, so no *photosynthetic organisms are found here. It extends from 700-1000 m to 2000-4000 m below the surface. *Contrast* PHOTIC ZONE.

BATNEEC *See* BEST AVAILABLE TECHNIQUES NOT ENTAILING EXCESSIVE COSTS.

batrachotoxins Toxins secreted by *Dendrobates* and *Phillobates* species of South American frogs and that are also found in the skin and feathers of *Pitohui* and *Ifrita* species of birds found in New Guinea. The birds acquire the batrachotoxins from *Choresine* species of beetles on which they feed. These beetles also occur in South America and may also be the source of the frog poison, although this has not been confirmed. They are the most powerful poisons produced by any vertebrate animal; they are 250 times more toxic than strychnine and in tropical South America are used to poison the tips of blowdarts and arrowheads.

bauxite A rock composed mainly of *hydroxides of aluminium, formed by *weathering of aluminate silicate rocks in tropical areas with good drainage. Bauxite is the major ore of aluminium, from which the metal is extracted.

bay A large curved inlet of the sea.

bayhead barrier A barrier that partially closes the mouth of a *bay.

bbl Barrel of oil; 1 bbl = 42 US gallons; 34.9723 UK gallons; 158.9873 litres.

BCIS *See* BIODIVERSITY CONSERVATION INFORMATION SYSTEM.

BDAT *See* BEST DEMONSTRATED AVAILABLE TECHNOLOGY.

beach A strip of land that borders the sea. The upper and lower limits of a beach are usually defined by the *high water mark and the *low water mark, respectively.

beach dune A sand *dune on a *beach, formed by deposition of fine particles of sediment that are carried by the wind, in the same way that dunes develop in hot *deserts.

beach nourishment *See* BEACH REPLENISHMENT.

beach replenishment (beach nourishment) The deliberate addition of sand to beaches where erosion is a major problem, in order to stabilize losses and restore badly eroded (and sometimes unsightly) beaches. *Contrast* SAND MINING.

beach seining *See* FISH TRAPPING.

Beaufort scale A scale that is widely used to describe wind speed. It was defined in 1806 by

Admiral Sir Francis Beaufort (1774–1857), and uses the effect that wind has on certain familiar objects such as trees and the sea surface. The scale is given in Appendix 3.

becquerel (Bq) The *SI unit for measuring *radioactivity. 1 Bq represents the activity of a *radionuclide which decays on average at one spontaneous nuclear transition per second. This unit replaced the *curie and *picocurie.

bed (stratum) A layer of deposited *sediment within a *sedimentary rock.

bedding plane The junction between the layers in a *sedimentary rock (such as sandstone), which shows the original surface onto which *sediment was deposited. See also DIP.

bedform Patterns that are produced on the surface of sediment by the flow of air or water, such as *ripples in water or *dunes in a desert.

bedload The coarse portion of the *sediment load in a river that is too large or too heavy to move in the body of water as *suspended load, but instead rests on the river bed and is pushed or rolled along by the flow of water.

bedrock A general term for the solid, unweathered *rock that lies beneath *soils or *deposits and is often exposed at the ground surface. See also OUTCROP.

bedrock river A river that flows directly on *bedrock, rather than through *alluvium.

benchmark A reference point or standard for comparison. For example, a site for measuring natural processes or features, where there has been no human impact, or a set of observations that is used to establish standards by which to compare the effectiveness of alternative policies or strategies. See also REFERENCE SITE; REFERENCE YEAR.

beneficial use A use of the environment or of some part of it that benefits a human population and should therefore be protected so it may continue. Recreation, agriculture, and water storage are examples of beneficial uses.

beneficiation The separation of a mineral from its surrounding rock in order to increase the grade of the *ore.

benefit The degree to which effects are judged desirable, through giving advantage, profit, or gain.

benefit–cost analysis See COST–BENEFIT ANALYSIS.

benefit value An estimate or projection of the expected positive results or outputs of a proposed activity, project, or programme, expressed in either monetary or non-monetary terms. See also COST–BENEFIT ANALYSIS.

Benguela current The eastern boundary *current of the South Atlantic subtropical *gyre, which flows north from the *Southern Ocean that surrounds *Antarctica and moves cold water along the west coast of Africa.

benign A mild, non-lethal illness or disease, which carries no long-term threat to health. Contrast MALIGNANT.

benthic Of or relating to the *benthos.

benthic–pelagic coupling The cycling of nutrients in a body of water between the water itself and the sediments on the bottom.

benthic region/zone The bottom layer of a body of water.

benthos All the organisms that live on (*epifauna) or burrow into (*infauna) the bottom sediment of a body of water such as a river, lake, or sea. Nearly 98% of all marine animals are benthic organisms. See also MACROBENTHOS; MEIOBENTHOS; MICROBENTHOS. Contrast PELAGIC.

bentonite A type of clay, derived from weathered *volcanic ash, that is highly plastic and expands when wet, and is used to seal *landfills, *lagoons, and *wells. See also MONTMORILLONITE.

benzene A colourless, highly flammable liquid *hydrocarbon present in coal tar and petroleum, from which it is distilled for use as a solvent and in making dyes and drugs. See also AROMATIC.

bequest motive See EXISTENCE VALUE.

bequest value The value that people place on knowing that future generations will have the option to enjoy a particular environmental *asset, which is usually measured by *willingness to pay.

Bergmann's rule A 19th century *ecogeographical rule that the colder the climate (or higher the latitude), the larger the body size of a *warm-blooded animal when compared with close relatives in warmer regions. See also ALLEN'S RULE; GLOGER'S RULE.

bergschrund A deep gap (*crevasse) that forms between the ice and headwall (back wall) in a *cirque glacier as the ice is pulled away from the headwall and moves downslope.

Berlin Mandate A proposal under the *United Nations Framework Convention on Climate Change that was adopted in 1995 and was designed to make reductions of *greenhouse gas emissions mandatory. Under the Framework Convention, developed countries pledged to take measures designed to return their greenhouse gas emissions to 1990 levels by the year 2000. The Berlin Mandate established a process that would enable countries to take appropriate action for the period beyond 2000, including a strengthening of *developed country commitments, through the adoption of the *Kyoto Protocol in 1997.

berm 1. A narrow embankment (often made from earth, bales of hay, or timber framing) along a slope, which is often used as *dike or *dam. **2.** A strip of large rocks placed at the bottom of a spoil pile to help hold the material in position. **3.** A small mound of earth piled up on the outer edge of a mountain or secondary road. **4.** An embankment at the rear of a *beach, above the *high tide mark.

Bermuda high A semi-permanent *anticyclone in the vicinity of Bermuda that is a westward extension of the *Azores high.

Berne Convention An international nature conservation treaty, signed by 40 nations in 1979, which came into force in 1982. Its full title is the Convention on the Conservation of European Wildlife and Natural Habitats, and it seeks to conserve wild flora and fauna and their natural habitats.

berylliosis (chronic beryllium disease, CBD) An allergic lung disease caused by the inhalation of particles of *beryllium or its compounds. It is incurable and reduces lung function.

beryllium (Be) A greyish-white, brittle, toxic, metallic substance that occurs naturally in certain rocks, soils, and volcanic dust. It is one of the lightest of all metals, resists oxidation in air, and is non-magnetic. It is used in nuclear reactors, radio and television tubes, fluorescent tubes, and powders, is discharged by machine shops, ceramic and propellant plants, and foundries, and also enters the environment through the fly ash from combustion of coal and fuel oil. It can cause severe skin problems and is hazardous to human health if inhaled (*see* BERYLLIOSIS).

Best Available Control Measures (BACM) An approach to *pollution control in the USA that is based on adopting the most effective methods of controlling emissions of pollutants from sources such as roadway dust, soot and ash from woodstoves, and open burning of timber, grasslands, or rubbish.

Best Available Control Technology (BACT) An approach to *pollution control in the USA that is based on adopting, for any specific source, the technology that is currently available and produces the greatest reduction in emissions of air pollutants, taking into account energy, environmental, economic, and other costs. In the USA, major sources are required to use BACT unless they can show that it is not feasible for energy, environmental, or economic reasons.

Best Available Techniques Not Entailing Excessive Costs (BATNEEC) An approach to *pollution control in the UK that is based on adopting the most effective techniques for an operation at the appropriate scale which are commercially available and where the benefits gained are more than the costs of obtaining them.

Best Available Technology (BAT) An approach to *pollution control in the USA that is based on adopting the best technology, treatment techniques, or other means which are available, taking account of cost.

Best Demonstrated Available Technology (BDAT) An approach to *pollution control in the USA that is based on adopting the most effective commercially available means of treating specific types of *hazardous waste.

Best Management Practice (BMP) An approach to *pollution control in the USA that is based on adopting methods that have been determined to be the most effective, practical means of preventing or reducing *water pollution from non-point sources.

Best Practicable Environmental Option (BPEO) An approach to *pollution control in the UK that is based on seeking to establish the option which causes the least damage to the environment at an acceptable cost, taking into account the total pollution from a process and the technical possibilities for dealing with it.

best practicable means A concept applied to the control of air pollution in Britain, whereby the best possible level of control is obtained within constraints imposed by the technological and economic capabilities of the industrial plant in question.

Best Practical Control Technology (BPCT) An approach to *pollution control that is based on adopting the *best technology for pollution control available at reasonable cost and operable under normal conditions.

best-current-data approach An approach to decision-making in *resource management that uses current data collected through new or existing sampling programmes. Managers analyse the data using the latest techniques, assess their management options, and then choose the best option to implement.

beta decay The process of *radioactive decay in which a *neutron is converted to a *proton (emitting an *electron and an antineutrino) or a proton is converted to a neutron (emitting a positron and a neutrino). The result is that an unstable atomic nucleus becomes stable by altering its proton number.

beta diversity (species turnover) The difference in diversity of *species between two or more *ecosystems in an area, expressed as the total number of species that are unique to each of the ecosystems being compared. A measure of *biodiversity. *See also* ALPHA DIVERSITY; GAMMA DIVERSITY.

beta particle A high-energy *electron that is emitted from a nucleus during *beta decay. It has a single negative electric charge, is halted by a thin sheet of metal, and can cause skin burns.

bet-hedging The behavioural response of a species *population to a K-selecting environment in which occasional fluctuations in conditions affect the mortality rate of juveniles to a much greater extent than of adults. In such a situation adults release young into several different environments to maximize the chance that some will survive. *See also* K-SELECTION; R-SELECTION.

Bhopal The location in India of the world's worst industrial accident in terms of loss of life. A major explosion at the Union Carbide *pesticide factory there, in December 1984, released nearly 40 tonnes of *methyl isocyanate which blew over the residential area nearby. Nearly 200 000 people were exposed to the poison, and within ten years more than 4000 had died as a result. Many more have suffered long-term ill-health and disability because of exposure to the *toxic cloud.

B-horizon The intermediate layer in a *soil profile, beneath the *A-horizon and above the *C-horizon. The B-horizon is dominated by the deposition (*illuviation) of material *leached from the A-horizon, so it is a zone of accumulation and enrichment. It contains little organic material, and is usually more compacted than the A-horizon because *clay washed down from the A-horizon fills many of the voids between particles. *See also* SOIL HORIZON.

bicarbonate A sodium salt ($NaHCO_3$) of *carbonic acid that can act as a *buffer and resists changes in the *pH of soil and waterbodies.

bid The price that a prospective buyer is willing to pay in *greenhouse gas *emissions trading.

biennial A plant that completes its life cycle in two years, producing leaves in the first year, blooming and producing seed in the second year, and then dying. *Contrast* ANNUAL; PERENNIAL.

big game The collective term for large mammals, such as deer, elk, bear, bison, and antelope, that are hunted for sport. *See also* GAME.

bilateral trade/transaction A direct trade between two parties, on a one-to-one basis, with no intermediary exchange or third party involvement.

bilharzia *See* SCHISTOSOMIASIS.

bill A piece of legislation introduced by government that is intended to become law.

billow cloud A distinctive type of *cloud in the form of broad parallel bands oriented at right angles to the wind, with distinct clear areas between the bands.

binding target An agreed or mandatory environmental standard (such as a reduction in emissions of *greenhouse gases) that a country must meet in the future, usually within a defined period of time.

binomial nomenclature *See* LATIN NAME.

bio- Referring to living organisms.

bioaccumulant A substance that increases in concentration through time in living organisms, as they take in contaminated air, water, or food, because the substance is used or excreted only very slowly. *See also* BIOACCUMULATION.

bioaccumulation (bioamplification, biological amplification, bioconcentration, biological concentration, biomagnifications, biological magnification) The tendency for a *pollutant (particularly a *toxic substance, such as *mercury, *PCBs, and some *pesticides) to accumulate in the tissues of plants or animals because it is absorbed faster than the organism can break it down through *metabolism. The organism absorbs the pollutant either through exposure to it or through digestion (via food), and organisms towards the top of the *food chain can have high levels of a particular pollutant through consuming other organisms further down the food chain.

bioamplification See BIOACCUMULATION.

bioarchaeology The study of plant and animal remains collected from *archaeological sites, in order to reconstruct the *environment in which they grew.

bioassay A laboratory test using living organisms (tissues, cells, live animals, or humans), designed to measure the effects of various substances on them.

bioassessment See BIOLOGICAL ASSESSMENT.

bioaugmentation The deliberate addition of *microbes to soil or groundwater in order to enhance *biodegradation or the *bioremediation of organic contaminants.

bioavailability The degree to which chemicals (such as *contaminants) can be absorbed by organisms.

bioavailable Available for biological uptake.

biobarrier An obstruction (such as a filled trench or a *membrane) that inhibits living tissue. Used, for example, to control plant root growth in contaminated soils.

biocatalyst An enzyme that activates or speeds up a biochemical reaction in a *bioprocess. See also BIOTECHNOLOGY; INDUSTRIAL BIOCATALYST.

biocentric See ECOCENTRIC.

biocentrism See ECOCENTRISM.

biochemical Chemicals that are present in living organisms, and reactions associated with them.

biochemical decay The breakdown of pollutants in water through the action of *bacteria.

biochemical oxygen demand (BOD) See BIOLOGICAL OXYGEN DEMAND.

biochemical precipitate A *sedimentary rock, such as *limestone, that has formed from elements extracted from seawater by living organisms.

biochemicals Chemicals (such as hormones, pheromones, and enzymes) that are found naturally occurring in living organisms and are synthesized by them. Biochemicals can be very effective *pesticides by disrupting the mating pattern of insects, regulating growth, or acting as repellents.

biochemistry The chemistry of living organisms, especially the chemical components, their processes, and reactions.

biocide A chemical agent that kills a wide range of organisms.

bioclastic rock A *sedimentary rock made up of broken fragments of organic skeletal material.

biocoenosis See ECOSYSTEM.

bioconcentration See BIOACCUMULATION.

biocontrol See BIOLOGICAL CONTROL.

bioconversion (biotransformation) The conversion of a compound from one form to another by the actions of organisms or enzymes.

biocriteria Biological measures of the health of an environment, such as the incidence of a particular disease in a particular species.

biodegradable Capable of being decomposed rapidly by natural biological processes. Most organic waste such as food, wood, paper, wool, and cotton is biodegradable.

biodiesel A *renewable, *biodegradable, *alternative fuel or fuel additive for diesel engines, produced from organic material such as soybean or sunflower seed oil.

Biodiversity Action Network (Bionet) An international network of *non-governmental organizations working to strengthen *biodiversity policy and law.

biodiversity action plan (BAP) A national plan, programme, or strategy for the *conservation and *sustainable use of biological diversity, drawn up in response to the *United Nations Framework Convention on Biological Diversity.

Biodiversity Conservation Information System (BCIS) An international initiative that

BIODIVERSITY

Short for biological diversity. A measure of variation (the number of different varieties) amongst living things. The word is most commonly used to describe 'species diversity'—the number and relative abundance of different species, within a particular area (*local biodiversity) or within the world (*global biodiversity), which is not the same as *species richness (the count or number of *species). A number of ways of measuring biodiversity are in use, the most common of which is the *Shannon–Wiener index. The term biodiversity is also sometimes used to describe the number of genetic strains (differences) within species, and the number of different *ecosystems in an area. The most common expression of biodiversity is the number of different species within a particular area (local biodiversity), a specific habitat (*habitat biodiversity), or the world (global biodiversity). The *United Nations Framework Convention on Biological Diversity, agreed by the *United Nations Conference on Environment and Development in 1992, is a framework for international action in protecting biodiversity. *See also* ALPHA DIVERSITY; BETA DIVERSITY; GAMMA DIVERSITY.

seeks to support environmentally sound decision-making and actions affecting the status of *biodiversity and *landscapes at the local, national, regional, and global levels through cooperative provision of data, information, advice, and related services.

Biodiversity Convention *See* UNITED NATIONS CONVENTION ON BIOLOGICAL DIVERSITY.

Biodiversity Forum A web-based forum funded by the US National Science Foundation, that allows people to express and exchange views on topics related to *biodiversity loss and conservation.

biodiversity hotspot A biogeographical region define by *Conservation International (CI) that is both a significant reservoir of *biodiversity and threatened with destruction. The CI list includes 25 hotspots that cover 1.4% of the land area of the Earth but support nearly 60% of the world's plant, bird, mammal, reptile, and amphibian species. The CI hotspots are larger than the *ecoregions identified by the *Worldwide Fund for Nature in their *Global 200 initiative, and they only cover terrestrial areas whereas the latter also include *freshwater and *marine ecoregions.

biodiversity prospecting The search for new products among genes found in wild organisms, which may be of potential commercial value.

bioenergy Energy that is made available by the combustion of materials derived from biological sources.

bioengineering The application to biological science of engineering principles or equipment.

bioerosion Erosion or decay caused by living things.

bioethics The study of the ethical implications of biological research and applications, including *biomedicine and *biotechnology.

biofilm A layer of micro-organisms that is attached to a surface such as the rocks in natural streams.

biofuel An *alternative fuel that is produced from biological materials including crops (especially trees) and animal wastes. Examples include *ethanol, *methanol, and *biodiesel.

biogas A mixture of *methane and *carbon dioxide that is generated by the *anaerobic fermentation of organic matter such as plant residues and animal *manure, and can be used as a *renewable fuel or a *fertilizer.

biogenic Material that results from the activity of living things.

biogenic source Biological sources, such as plants and animals, that emit *air pollutants such as *volatile organic compounds.

biogenically reworked zone The upper zone within a *sediment that is actively burrowed by *benthic organisms.

biogeochemistry The study of the exchange of materials between living (*biotic) and non-living (*abiotic) components of the *biosphere.

biogeocoenosis *See* ECOSYSTEM.

biogeographical Relating to the geographical distribution of plants and animals.

biogeographical barrier A barrier that prevents the migration of species. It may be

b

BIOGEOCHEMICAL CYCLE (MINERAL CYCLE)

One of the large-scale long-term environmental cycles that circulates elements (such as *carbon, *nitrogen, *oxygen, *hydrogen, *calcium, and *sulphur) between the *biotic and *abiotic components of the *environment (including the *atmosphere, *soil, *water cycle, and *ecosystems) by living organisms, geological processes, or chemical reactions. Biogeochemical cycles function at the global scale, and *nutrient cycles are those biogeochemical cycles that involve the elements necessary for life. Flow through the environment is cyclic because of the finite supply and the relatively constant form of the individual elements. Individual cycles can be identified for each of the elements, but they all have in common a basic two-part structure involving an *inorganic component (comprising the abiotic or non-living parts of the environment, with sedimentary and atmospheric phases), and an *organic component (comprising plants and animals, living and dead, and their physical and chemical interactions). Natural biogeochemical cycles are being disrupted by a range of human activities, including changes in *land use and the burning of *fossil fuels. The nitrogen, carbon, and sulphur cycles are particularly important to the functioning of the biosphere, and they are also closely linked to the climate system. Despite recent advances in our understanding of how these great cycles work (partly a result of the *IGBP studies), many uncertainties and gaps remain. Many of the more pressing global and regional environmental problems we face today—such as *greenhouse gases, *eutrophication, *acid rain, and *ozone depletion—are closely related to these cycles.

climatic, involving temperature and the availability of water, or physical, involving, for example, mountain ranges or expanses of sea water.

biogeographical province/realm One of the eight geographical regions from which particular assemblages of plants and animals evolved and dispersed. *See also* AFROTROPICAL REALM; ANTARCTIC REALM; AUSTRALIAN REALM; INDOMALAYAN REALM; NEARCTIC REALM; NEOTROPICAL REALM; OCEANIAN REALM; PALAEARCTIC REALM.

biogeography The study of the geographical distribution of organisms, past and present. *See also* ISLAND BIOGEOGRAPHY.

biogeophysical feedback A *feedback mechanism that connects the biological and geophysical parts of the climate system.

biohazard The health risk to humans or animals that is posed by the possible release of a *pathogen into the environment.

bioherm A build-up of largely *in situ* organisms that produces a *reef or mound of organic origin.

biohydrology The study of the interactions between the *water cycle and plants and animals.

bioindicator (environmental indicator) An organism (plant or animal species) that has a known sensitivity to particular types of stress (such as pollution) at relatively low levels, so that its population and health can be used as an *indicator of environmental quality. *See also* INDICATOR.

bioinformatics (computational biology) The use of computers and statistical methods in the classification, storage, retrieval, and analysis of biological information, particularly relating to *genomes. *See also* INFORMATICS.

biointermediate elements Elements that are partially depleted in surface waters due to biological activity. Four biointermediate elements are known: *barium, *calcium, *carbon, and *radium.

biolimiting Any factor that determines or restricts the growth of a particular *life form.

biolimiting elements The elements *nitrogen, *phosphorus, and *silicon, which are almost totally depleted in surface waters, relative to deep water, by biological activity. As these elements are essential to living organisms, the depletion limits further biological production until the scarce elements are replaced, e.g. by *upwelling.

biological additive A microbiological *culture, *enzyme, or nutrient additive that is deliberately introduced into an oil discharge to promote *biodegradation in order to reduce the effects of the discharge.

biological amplification *See* BIOACCUMULATION.

biological assessment (bioassessment) An evaluation of the biological condition of a population or habitat.

biological bench-marking The use of plant or animal species to measure pollution levels, based on assessments (bench-marks) of *population level and fitness against which changes can be evaluated. For example, *lichens are used to estimate levels of *sulphur dioxide.

biological classification A means of arranging *species on the basis of the degree of their evolutionary relatedness. Thus members of a particular group share a more recent common ancestor than the ancestor of any other group. This classification is based on the order of evolutionary branching rather than on present similarities and differences. The most common system of *taxonomy for classifying organisms was developed by Carolus *Linnaeus, who divided the plant kingdom into several *divisions (now often called *phyla), and the animal kingdom into phyla (singular phylum). Divisions and phyla are, in turn, divided into *classes, which are further subdivided into *orders. Orders are divided into *families, which are subdivided into *genera (singular genus), and genera into *species. Modern classification groups kingdoms into three *domains. Thus the normal classification scheme is hierarchical, descending from the domain (highest level) to the species (lowest level): domain → kingdom → division/phylum → class → order → family → genus → species. *See also* CLADISTICS; EVOLUTIONARY CLASSIFICATION; PHENETIC CLASSIFICATION; TAXONOMY.

biological concentration *See* BIOACCUMULATION.

biological contamination The presence of infectious agents (such as viruses, bacteria, fungi, and mammal and bird antigens) in an environment. *See also* CONTAMINATION.

biological control The use of natural predators, pathogens, or competitors to regulate *pest populations. Examples include introduced or naturally occurring predators such as wasps, or hormones that inhibit the reproduction of pests.

biological diversity *See* BIODIVERSITY.

biological half-life *See* HALF-LIFE.

biological integrity The ability of an *ecosystem to support and maintain a balanced, adaptive *community of *organisms that has a species composition, diversity, and functional organization comparable to that of natural *habitats within the same region. *See also* INDEX OF BIOLOGICAL INTEGRITY.

biological invasion Processes by which species become established in *ecosystems to which they are not native. The invading species are often weeds, pests, or disease-causing organisms.

biological magnification *See* BIOACCUMULATION.

biological monitoring (biomonitoring) Measurement of the levels of particular chemicals that are present in biological materials (such as blood or urine) in order to determine whether chemical exposure has occurred.

biological oxidation The decomposition of complex organic materials by bacteria and micro-organisms, as occurs in the self-purification of water bodies and in *activated sludge *wastewater treatment.

biological oxygen demand (biochemical oxygen demand, BOD) An indirect measure of the concentration of biologically degradable material that is present in organic wastes, usually based on the amount of oxygen that is consumed in five days in 1 litre of effluent held at $20°C$ by biological processes breaking down the organic waste. *See also* CHEMICAL OXYGEN DEMAND.

biological pesticide (biopesticide) A substance that is biological in origin, such as a *virus, *bacteria, *pheromone, or natural plant compound, used as a *pesticide. *See* BACILLUS THURINGIENSIS.

biological productivity The amount of organic matter, *carbon, or energy content that is accumulated in a given area over a given period of time. Usually expressed in terms of weight per unit area per unit time (grams per metre squared per year, $g\ m^{-2}\ year^{-1}$).

biological shield A thick (usually 3–4 m) wall, usually made from concrete, that surrounds the core of a *nuclear reactor. It protects personnel by absorbing *neutrons and *gamma rays.

biological simplification The reduction of *biodiversity that results from altering the environment in ways that favour certain *species over others, either directly (through management) or indirectly (for example, through pollution).

biological species concept The most commonly used definition of *species, as a group of natural populations that interbreed between themselves but not with other such groups from which they are reproductively isolated. *Compare* CLADISTIC SPECIES CONCEPT; ECOLOGICAL CONCEPT; RECOGNITION SPECIES CONCEPT.

biological stressor An organism that is introduced, by accident or design, to a habitat in which it does not naturally belong, and that has an adverse effect on existing species.

biological survey (biosurvey) The collection, processing, and analysis of a representative sample of a *community of plants and animals in order to determine the structural and/or functional characteristics of that community.

biological treatment A *waste treatment technology that uses bacteria to consume waste material.

biological warfare The intentional use of micro-organisms or toxins derived from living organisms to cause death or disease in humans, animals, or plants. *See also* BIOTERRORISM.

biological weapon Any biological substance (such as a deadly *virus or *bacterium) that can be used to kill or injure people, animals, and plants. A type of *weapon of mass destruction.

biologically unique species A *species that is the only living representative of an entire *genus or *family.

biologicals (biologics) A collective term for preparations (such as vaccines and cultures) that are made from living organisms and their products, and are used in diagnosing, immunizing, or treating humans or animals, or in related research.

biologics *See* BIOLOGICALS.

biology The study of living organisms.

bioluminescence The production of light without heat by living organisms. The process occurs in many *bacteria and *protists, as well as in certain animals and fungi. It is a chemical process that should not be confused with *phosphorescence

(⊕) SEE WEB LINKS
- Chemistry of bioluminescence.

biomagnetism **1.** The *magnetic field that is created by a living organism. **2.** The effect of an external magnetic field on living organisms.

biomagnification *See* BIOACCUMULATION.

biomarker A chemical compound that is produced by an organism which can be used as an indicator of the presence or health of that organism.

biomass **1.** The total weight of all living organisms in an area. The term is sometimes used to refer specifically to organisms of one type. **2.** Living material (such as wood and vegetation) that is grown or produced for use as fuel.

biomass burning The burning of organic matter for energy production, forest clearing, and agricultural purposes, which releases *carbon dioxide and other *greenhouse gases into the air.

biomass energy Energy that is produced from burning organic waste, such as sawmill wood waste or crop waste.

biomass fuel Organic material produced by plants, animals, or micro-organisms that can be burned directly as a heat source or converted into a gaseous or liquid fuel. Examples include wood and forest residues, animal manure and waste, grains, crops, and aquatic plants.

biomass generation plant A plant that produces electricity from *biomass fuel.

biomass harvesting A forest harvest method in which whole trees are chipped and used as fuel.

biome A large naturally occurring regional *ecosystem that contains *communities of plants and animals that are adapted to the conditions in which they occur. Biomes are strongly influenced by climate, and their distributions often coincide with climate regions, although many other factors also influence the distribution of plants and animals. Biomes are characterized by a dominant vegetation, and defined by the *species within them. Examples include *desert, *tundra, *grassland, *savanna, *woodland, *coniferous forest, *temperate deciduous forest, and *tropical rain forest. Species composition can vary from place to place within a biome because of local differences in soils, drainage, *topography, *microclimate, and other factors. It can also vary within and between continents for a given type of biome, reflecting *adaptation to the environment and local *speciation in widely separated populations.

biomedicine The study of the ability of organisms to cope with environmental stress, and the application of basic sciences to problems in clinical medicine.

biometric A measurable physical characteristic or personal behavioural trait that can be used to recognize or confirm the identity of an individual.

biometrics 1. (biometry) The science of measuring and statistically analysing biological data. *See also* BIOSTATISTICS. **2.** The use of biological properties (such as fingerprints, retina scans, or voice recognition) to identify individuals.

biometry *See* BIOMETRICS.

biomonitor A *species that is sensitive to changes in the environment, such as changes in pollution levels, and shows measurable responses to them.

biomonitoring *See* BIOLOGICAL MONITORING.

BIONET *See* BIODIVERSITY ACTION NETWORK.

biopesticide *See* BIOLOGICAL PESTICIDE.

biopharmaceuticals *Proteins produced by living organisms that have medical or diagnostic uses.

biophile Applied to those elements required by, or found in, living plants and animals, including *carbon, *hydrogen, *oxygen, *nitrogen, *phosphorus, *sulphur, *chlorine, *iodine, *bromine, *calcium, *magnesium, *potassium, *sodium, *vanadium, *iron, *manganese, and *copper.

biopile A mound of soil built to allow *aerobic *bioremediation by *aeration.

biopiracy (ecopiracy) The unauthorized and uncompensated collection of biological resources (indigenous plants and animals) by individuals or companies who then use or patent them for their own benefit. Illegal *bioprospecting or biological theft.

bioprocess A process in which living cells, or components of them (such as enzymes), are used to produce a desired product. *See also* BIOCATALYST; BIOTECHNOLOGY.

bioprospecting The search for economically valuable new genetic and biochemical resources from nature that may serve as sources for natural products. *See also* BIOPIRACY.

bioreactor A large container in which *micro-organisms are grown for the production of biologically useful materials, such as *enzymes and insulin.

bioreclamation *See* BIOREMEDIATION.

bioregion A territory defined by natural boundaries (such as *drainage basins or *ecosystems), rather than by political or administrative units. An area of relatively homogeneous ecological characteristics, or a specific assemblage of ecological communities. Similar to a *biome but smaller and with more specific characteristics. *See also* BIOREGIONAL PLANNING; ECOREGION.

bioregional planning Planning based on seeking to preserve the integrity of a *bioregion rather than a political or administrative unit.

bioremediation (bioreclamation) The use of living organisms to clean up *oil spills or remove pollutants from soil, groundwater, or wastewater. Short for biological *remediation. *See also* LAND FARMING.

bioreserve An area of natural *ecosystems and high *biodiversity that has been designated and protected for *nature conservation purposes. *See also* BIOSPHERE RESERVE.

biosafety Safety from exposure to infectious *agents, particularly those created by *biotechnology.

biosecurity Biological security, particularly protection against *bioterrorism and the use of *biological weapons.

biosolids *See* SEWAGE SLUDGE.

biosphere (ecosphere) The part of the Earth in which living organisms exist and interact, which includes the *atmosphere, *hydrosphere, and *lithosphere; the sum of all *ecosystems. The biosphere extends from less than 11 km below *sea level, to the *tropopause which is less than 17 km above sea level. This gives it a maximum thickness of 38 km—roughly 0.5% of the radius of the Earth (6371 km). The concept of the biosphere as the Earth's integrated living and life-supporting system was first proposed in the 1920s, but only in recent decades has it been widely adopted and used. Originally, the concept was applied just to the Earth's surface where plants and animals obviously make their home. But it has more recently been extended by the *Gaia hypothesis to include parts of the atmosphere and subsurface geology that were previously thought of as *abiotic.

Biosphere II A man-made, closed *ecological system that was constructed in the Arizona desert between 1987 and 1989, in which experiments were conducted to study how *ecosystems operate and to evaluate whether people could live and work in a closed *biosphere (for example during colonization of other planets). It involved artificially recreating a range of habitats under a geodesic glass dome, using nearly 4000 natural species representing *tropical rainforest, *saltmarsh, *desert, *coral reef, *savanna, and intensive agriculture. Eight humans were part of the experiment, and they lived on a self-sufficient basis inside the sealed dome for two years, effectively isolated from the outside world. The dome was self-contained and self-sufficient, except for some electricity fed in from outside.

Biosphere Reserve A large, protected area of natural habitat, established by *UNESCO under the *Man and the Biosphere Programme. Designed to create a representative network of the world's *ecosystems where research and monitoring activities are conducted, with the participation of local communities, to protect and preserve healthy natural systems threatened by development. Each reserve contains a *core area (dedicated to preserving *biodiversity with no human interference) and a *buffer zone. *See also* BIORESERVE.

biostatistics The use of statistics to analyse biological data. *See also* BIOMETRICS.

biostimulation The addition of nutrients to a population of micro-organisms in order to stimulate growth and activity during *bioremediation or *biotreatment.

biostratigraphy The organization of layers of *sedimentary rock into units, based on their *fossil content, for the purposes of *dating and *correlation. *Contrast* LITHOSTRATIGRAPHY.

biostrome A layered, sheet-like accumulation of *in situ* organisms. It differs from a *bioherm in its geometry, lacking a mound-like or *reef-like form.

biosurvey *See* BIOLOGICAL SURVEY.

biosynthesis The production of a chemical substance by a living organism. *See also* ANABOLISM.

biota All of the living organisms (including animals, plants, fungi, and micro-organisms) that are found in a particular area.

biotechnology Any technology that uses living organisms (or parts of organisms) to make or modify products, improve plants and animals, or develop micro-organisms for specific use. An example is the use by industry of *recombinant DNA. *See also* BIOCATALYST; GENETIC ENGINEERING; INDUSTRIAL BIOTECHNOLOGY.

biotelemetry A remote-sensing method for monitoring animal movements which uses small transmitters attached externally to the body of the animal or implanted within the body cavity. It enables the precise locations of animals to be followed, and may also be used to monitor changes in heartbeat (e.g. in response to stress). It is especially useful for studying migratory animals in remote areas and is an important aid to the study of bird migration.

bioterrorism The unlawful use of biological agents, such as a deadly *virus or *bacteria, to kill or harm people, animals, or plants. *See also* BIOLOGICAL WARFARE; BIOSECURITY; TERRORISM.

biotic Living, containing life. *Contrast* ABIOTIC.

biotic association *See* BIOTIC COMMUNITY.

biotic community (biotic association) A natural assemblage of plants and animals that live in the same environment and are mutually sustaining and interdependent. *See also* BIOME.

biotic index A rating that is used in assessing the ecological quality of an environment. For example, the presence of certain invertebrate groups in fresh water can be awarded a score that indicates the quality of the water. A scheme employing biotic indices has a scale ranging from 10 (clean water with diverse fauna) to 0 (grossly polluted water with no fauna or with only a few anaerobic organisms).

((●)) SEE WEB LINKS

• The use of the biotic index as an indication of water quality.

biotic potential The maximum reproductive rate of an organism, given unlimited resources and ideal environmental conditions.

biotope *See* ECOTOPE.

biotrade Trade in biological resources within and between countries. *See also* BIOPIRACY; CITES.

biotransformation *See* BIOCONVERSION.

biotreatment The process of reducing pollution in waste streams, such as industrial wastewater, by biological treatment (particularly the use of micro-organisms).

biotroph An organism that derives nutrients from the living tissues of another organism (its *host).

bioturbation The mixing of a *sediment by the burrowing, feeding, or other activities of living organisms.

biotype A group of genetically identical individuals.

biounlimiting elements Elements (e.g. *boron, *magnesium, strontium, and *sulphur) that show no measurable depletion in surface waters compared to deep waters as a result of biological activity.

bioweapon See BIOLOGICAL WEAPON.

bipedalism The ability to walk upright on two legs, as in humans.

bird A *warm-blooded *vertebrate animal that lays eggs and has two legs, feathers, and wings. Most birds can fly.

birth cohort A group of individuals who are born during a specific period of time.

birth control Any method that is used to reduce births, including celibacy, delayed marriage, contraception, and sterilization. See also FAMILY PLANNING.

birth rate (natality) The number of live births per year per 1000 population.

bitter lake A general term for a saltwater lake.

bitumen A black, sticky, *hydrocarbon substance that is obtained naturally or from *petroleum, used for surfacing roads.

bituminous coal A soft, black *coal that burns with a smoky yellow flame, derived from the *lithification of *lignite. It can be turned into *anthracite by folding and hardening.

bivalve A mollusc of the phylum Bivalvia in which the body is laterally compressed, there is no distinct head, and the body is enclosed between two valves (shells) of unequal size hinged together. There are more than 20000 species including oysters, clams, scallops, and mussels.

bivoltine Having two broods and generations in a year or season. See also VOLTINISM. Contrast MULTIVOLTINE; UNIVOLTINE.

black blizzard A *dust storm in which the dust consists mainly of dark-coloured soil particles. Such a storm occurred in May 1934, covering an area of 3.5 million km^2 from Canada to Texas and extending to a height of 5 km.

black body A body that absorbs all the electromagnetic radiation falling upon it and reradiates its absorbed energy at a wavelength inversely proportional to its absolute temperature. See also EMISSIVITY.

black body temperature The temperature that the surface of a body (such as a *planet, like the *Earth) would be if it were not warmed by the retention of heat in its own *atmosphere. It can be calculated using the *Stefan–Boltzmann equation. The black body temperature of the Earth is $-23°C$, but the actual surface temperature is about $15°C$. The difference ($38°C$) is the amount by which the planet is warmed by the absorption of *radiation within its atmosphere, by the natural *greenhouse effect.

black box In systems terms, an unknown and often unknowable mechanism, process, or system which is judged solely by observing its inputs and outputs.

black earth A dark-coloured *chernozem soil with a high *humus content, which is often deep and very fertile.

black ice Thin, new ice that forms when rain close to freezing falls on to surfaces that are below freezing and freezes instantly. It appears black because it is transparent and can create hazardous driving conditions because it often cannot be seen.

black lignite See SUB-BITUMINOUS COAL.

black shale A type of *sedimentary rock that is deposited in conditions with very little oxygen. It is generally dark-coloured and has a high *organic content.

black smoke Smoke produced when *hydrocarbons are decomposed by heat (cracked), then cooled rapidly, releasing particles of carbon, which are black.

black smoker A vent in a geologically active region of the ocean floor from which superheated water laden with minerals (sulphide precipitates) flows out into the ocean, looking like black smoke.

black water Wastewater that contains animal, human, or food waste. *Contrast* GREY WATER; WHITE WATER.

blade The green leaf of a grass or cereal plant.

blanket bog A *peatland formed in areas of high rainfall and humidity that covers large areas of flat and gently sloping ground.

bleaching *See* CORAL BLEACHING.

blizzard A severe storm characterized by blowing snow, low temperatures, strong winds (56 km h^{-1} or higher), and reduced visibility (less than 0.40 km). It usually lasts for three hours or longer.

BLM *See* US BUREAU OF LAND MANAGEMENT.

block fault A type of geological faulting in which the topography is divided by *faults of different heights and orientations.

blocking In *synoptic meteorology, the establishment in the mid-latitudes of a high-pressure system that interrupts or diverts for a considerable period the typically eastward movement of *depressions and other synoptic features in the *zonal flow. Over western Europe, for example, blocking often forces depressions to move northwards towards Scandinavia or southwards over southern France and Spain.

bloom *See* ALGAL BLOOM.

blowout 1. A depression in the surface of sand or dry soil that is caused by wind erosion. 2. A sudden release of oil or gas from a well due to the failure of the seal.

blue moon 1. The second full moon in a calendar month. 2. A sky condition caused by the presence of large quantities of suspended particles in the atmosphere which selectively remove the longer visible wavelengths more than the blue or green wavelengths.

blue-green algae *See* CYANOBACTERIA.

Blueprint for Survival A book published by *The Ecologist* in 1971 as a manifesto for radical changes in *lifestyle and patterns of *economic development, which had a significant impact on attitudes towards the *environment, and on the development of modern *environmentalism.

bluff A high steep bank or cliff.

BMP *See* BEST MANAGEMENT PRACTICE.

BMR *See* BASAL METABOLIC RATE.

boardwalk A walkway made of wooden planks that is used in fragile sites which are heavily used by people, such as on sand or across boggy ground.

BOD *See* BIOCHEMICAL OXYGEN DEMAND; BIOLOGICAL OXYGEN DEMAND.

body burden The total amount of a chemical that is stored in the body of an organism at a given time, particularly a potential *toxin (such as *lead) to which the organism has been exposed.

bog (peat bog) A poorly drained area of shrubby *peat dominated by specialized acid-tolerant vegetation including shrubs, sedges, and peat moss. It is a spongy *wetland habitat with a high *water table, and has a high content of organic remains. A bog is similar to, but more acidic than, a *fen.

bog forest A forest that develops as a *bog fills and dries. In *boreal North America and Eurasia bog forests develop in post-glacial *kettle holes which filled with water and were later colonized by bog plants, especially *Sphagnum* mosses. As the sites dry out further, trees become established, eventually producing forests typically dominated by *Picea mariana* (black spruce), *Larix laricina* (tamarack), and *Pinus banksiana* (jack pine), with associated herbs and shrubs. In tropical regions bog forests develop in coastal regions; those in Asia are often dominated by *Shorea albida* (alan).

boghead coal *Coal containing finely divided plant remains, mainly algal and fungal in origin, and rich in *kerogen.

boiling water reactor (BWR) A type of *light-water nuclear reactor that uses water as a *moderator and boiling water to produce steam which drives a turbine to generate electricity. *Contrast* PRESSURIZED WATER REACTOR.

bole 1. The main trunk of a tree. 2. A reddish clay.

boll weevil A small, greyish beetle (*Anthonomus grandis*) that is common throughout the south-eastern USA. It has destructive larvae that hatch in and damage cotton bolls.

Bølling interstadial A relatively warm period that occurred towards the end of the last *glaciation in north-western Europe, and which is named after the type site in Denmark. The event took place about 13 000–12 000 *radiocarbon years BP. In Britain, the Bølling is not usually distinguished from the *Allerød. *See also* *DRYAS.

bolson In arid regions, a basin that is filled with *alluvium and intermittent *playa lakes, and has no outlet.

bomb calorimeter A sealed apparatus that is used to calculate the energy content of a substance by measuring the heat produced by its combustion.

bombiculture The use of bees as pollinators of specific crops such as hothouse tomatoes and other fruit. *Contrast* APICULTURE.

bond The force that holds together two atoms in a molecule or crystal.

bonding 1. The physical and chemical processes that join substances together (such as atoms in a molecule or individual *crystals to make *minerals). **2.** The making of close relationships between individual of the same species.

Bonn Convention An international treaty, formally called the Convention on the Conservation of Migratory Species of Wild Animals, which came into force in 1983. Its aim is the to protect those species of wild animals that migrate across or outside national boundaries, and the species covered include marine mammals, sea turtles, and sea birds.

boom 1. A floating device that is used to contain oil on a body of water. **2.** Equipment used to apply pesticides from a tractor or other vehicle.

bora A cold north or north-easterly *katabatic wind that blows along the coast of the Adriatic Sea, usually in winter and associated with heavy *precipitation. The name is from Boreas, the Greek god of the north wind.

Bordeaux mixture A *fungicide that contains copper sulphate, lime, and water and is used as a spray on grapevines to fight fungal diseases.

bore (tidal bore) A tidal wave that surges upstream in an *estuary, and occurs during high *tides (particularly during *spring tides).

boreal Relating to cool or cold temperate regions at high latitudes in the northern hemisphere. *See also* AUSTRAL.

boreal climate *See* SUBPOLAR CLIMATE.

boreal forest The belt of *coniferous forest that extends across northern North America and Eurasia as the largest terrestrial *biome on Earth.

borehole A hole drilled into the ground either for subsurface exploration (for example in the search for reserves of *oil or *gas) or for extraction (for example the pumping *groundwater from an *aquifer).

Borlaug, Norman (1914–2009) American agronomist considered by some to be the 'father of modern agriculture'. Winner of the Nobel Peace Prize in 1970 for his contribution to the *Green Revolution because of his work developing new, short-strawed wheat varieties and his contribution to introducing them in the 1960s into agricultural production in Pakistan and India, thereby saving more than a billion people from starvation.

(⊕) SEE WEB LINKS

• Nobel Peace Prize biography.

boron (B) A *trace element that occurs naturally as boric acids in soil solutions and in the ore borax. It is a *micronutrient that is important for plant growth, essential for bone development in animals, and can be *toxic at high concentrations in humans.

boss *See* STOCK.

botanical Relating to plants and plant life.

botanical garden A facility in which trees and shrubs are cultivated for exhibition, or preserved for *conservation or *reintroduction, as part of a *living collection. *See also* ZOO.

botanical insecticide *See* BOTANICAL PESTICIDE.

botanical medicine The use of plants or plant extracts for medicinal purposes.

botanical pesticide An *organic *pesticide that is derived from another plant, for example *pyrethrin or *rotenone.

botany (phytology) The study of plants and their structures and functions.

bottle bank A place where glass bottles can be deposited for *recycling.

bottom ash The heavy residue from burning coal in a boiler which falls to the bottom of the boiler and is removed mechanically. It may include *toxic compounds.

bottom berg An *iceberg that originates from near the base of a *glacier. They are usually black (from trapped rock material) or dark blue (made from old, coarse, bubble-free ice), and are heavy so they sit low in the water.

bottom fish *See* GROUNDFISH.

bottom land A North American term for low-lying land along a waterway.

bottom water The dense, cold water at the deepest depths of the ocean, near the ocean floor, which has different properties (such as temperature, *salinity, and *dissolved oxygen content) from the overlying deep water.

botulism A disease caused by the bacterium *Clostridium botulinum* that can cause many wildfowl deaths during hot summers when water levels fall. The disease also affects other animals including humans, and it can be fatal.

boulder A large particle of *sediment, which has a *particle size greater than 256 mm.

boulder clay (drift, glacial diamicton, glacial drift, till) A glacial deposit, consisting of unsorted *boulders and smaller particles in a matrix of *clay, that is laid down beneath a *glacier or *ice sheet.

boundary The edge between two adjacent things. **1.** In ecology, the edge between adjacent habitats (*ecotone). **2.** In a system, the defining limit across which matter and energy can move (in an *open system) or within which matter and energy are confined (in a *closed system). **3.** The outer edge of a political or organizational unit, including a national boundary or frontier.

boundary current The northward- or southward-directed ocean-water current that flows parallel and close to a continental margin. Such currents are caused by the deflection of eastward- and westward-flowing currents by the continental *landmasses. Boundary currents on the western margins of ocean basins, such as the Gulf Stream and Kuroshio Current, are deep, narrow, fast-moving currents; currents along the eastern boundaries, such as the Canaries and California Currents, tend to be relatively shallow, broad, diffuse, and slow-moving.

boundary layer **1.** The layer of fluid that is in contact with a surface. *Contrast* MAINSTREAM FLOW. **2. (atmospheric boundary layer, planetary boundary layer, surface boundary layer)** The layer of air closest to the ground (up to about 500 m), which is affected by exchanges of heat, moisture, or momentum with the surface.

boundary water A river or lake that is part of the *boundary between two or more countries or provinces that have rights to the water.

Boundary Water Treaty A treaty that was signed in 1909 providing the principles and mechanisms to help resolve disputes and to prevent future ones relating to water quantity and water quality along the *boundary between Canada and the USA.

bovids Members of the *artiodactyl family Bovidae, comprising cattle, antelopes, goat antelopes, gazelles, sheep, and goats.

bovine Relating to *bovids.

Bovine Spongiform Encephalopathy (BSE) Mad cow disease. A chronic, progressive and ultimately fatal disease that affects the brains and central nervous systems of adult cattle. Humans have been known to develop new variant *CJD as a result of eating the meat of affected animals.

BP The number of years before the present time, the present taken as 1950.

BPCT *See* BEST PRACTICAL CONTROL TECHNOLOGY.

BPEO *See* BEST PRACTICABLE ENVIRONMENTAL OPTION.

Bq *See* BECQUEREL.

BR *See* US BUREAU OF RECLAMATION.

brachiopods (lamp shells) A phylum (Brachiopoda) of *benthic, *marine animals that have hinged half shells and a soft body, and attach themselves to the sea floor with a stalk.

bracken A large coarse fern (*Pteridium aquilinum*), often several feet high, with a widespread distribution. Common on *moorland.

brackish (briny) Mixed fresh water and seawater, as occurs in a river *estuary. *See* VENICE SYSTEM.

Braer A Liberian-registered tanker that lost power in heavy seas off the southern coast of the mainland of Shetland on 5 January 1993. It eventually ran aground, losing its entire cargo of 86 000 tonnes of light crude oil and 5000 tonnes of heavy fuel oil. Despite heavy contamination of the coastline and damage to salmon farms, continuing heavy seas broke up the slick and there was no serious harm to wildlife.

Braess's paradox In traffic planning, the tendency for traffic flows (and thus congestion) to increase when new links are added to a transport network such as a highway or motorway.

braided river A river that carries coarse sediment as *bedload, and flows through multiple channels with islands in between them.

bramble Any prickly shrub or bush, such as a blackberry.

Brandt Commission See INDEPENDENT COMMISSION ON INTERNATIONAL DEVELOPMENT.

breaker zone In the *sea, the zone within which waves approaching the *shore start to break, normally in water depths of between 5 and 10 m. See also SURF ZONE.

breccia A *clastic *sedimentary rock composed of angular pieces of broken rock cemented together by a fine matrix. Contrast VOLCANIC BRECCIA.

breed 1. To produce more of a species; animals have babies and plants produce seeds or spores. **2.** A group of animals or plants that are related by descent from common ancestors and look similar. One species can have numerous breeds, which can look very different. Breeds are often domesticated or cultivated by humans.

breed at risk Any *breed that is in danger of becoming *extinct if the factors that are causing a decline in its numbers are not removed or controlled.

breed not at risk Any *breed in which the population size is increasing, and there are more than 1000 breeding females and more than 20 males.

breeder nuclear fission reactor See BREEDER REACTOR.

breeder reactor (breeder nuclear fission reactor, fast breeder) A *nuclear reactor that produces more *fuel than it consumes, by bombarding *isotopes of *uranium and *thorium with high-energy *neutrons. This converts inert (unreactive) atoms to ones that can be split (*fission), which sustains the nuclear *chain reaction.

breeding 1. The sexual activity of conceiving and bearing offspring. **2.** The production of animals or plants by *inbreeding, *outbreeding, or *hybridization.

breeding dispersal The movement between successive breeding sites of individuals that have reproduced. See also DISPERSAL.

breeding ground A place where animals breed.

breeding line The genetic history of an individual or species of plant or animal, which breeders need to know in order to *breed new *varieties.

breeding parasitism See BROOD PARASITISM.

breeding population A group of individuals (plants or animals) that tends to reproduce among itself, and much less frequently with individuals from other members of the same species. These separated subpopulations are important sources of migrants, and their genetic variability can prove critical to the survival of a species as a whole.

breeding rate The number of new individuals that are born in a given period of time.

breeding stock 1. Individuals (usually animals) that are kept specifically for *breeding purposes. **2.** The group of individuals within a given population which is capable of breeding.

breeze Light *wind, or a local air movement such as a *sea breeze or *land breeze. In the *Beaufort wind scale, a wind blowing at 6–50 km/h).

brine A salt solution. Water that is saturated with or contains a large amount of salts, especially of *sodium chloride.

brine mud Waste material that comes from well-drilling or mining and is composed of mineral salts or other inorganic compounds.

briny See BRACKISH.

British thermal unit (Btu) A unit of measurement for *heat. It is the amount of energy that is required to raise the temperature of 1lb of water by one degree from 62–63°F (about the amount of energy released when a match tip burns). One Btu is equal to 252 *calories or 1055 joules.

broadcast application The process of spreading a chemical (such as a *pesticide) over an area.

broadcast burn A controlled fire that is started deliberately and is allowed to burn a designated area. Such fires are used to remove organic debris after a clear-cut *deforestation project, and as part of ongoing vegetation management to reduce wildfire hazards, improve *forage for wildlife and livestock, and encourage successful *regeneration of trees.

broadcast seeding Scattering seed on the surface of the *soil. *Contrast* DRILL SEEDING.

broadcaster Equipment that is used to scatter (broadcast) seeds.

broadleaved Any tree with broad leaves rather than scale or needle-like leaves. This includes both *evergreens (such as holly) and *deciduous trees (such as oak). They belong to the *angiosperm group of plants.

broadleaved evergreen forest Forest that is dominated by *broadleaved, *evergreen tree species. In temperate regions of the northern hemisphere broadleaved evergreen forest is confined to the coastal plain of the Gulf of Mexico, southern Japan, and central China. In the southern hemisphere most broadleaved forests are evergreen, except in Chilean Patagonia.

broadleaved–sclerophyll forest A North American *chaparral type of forest vegetation with a closed canopy of trees which are adapted to drought by having small, broad, waxy-coated leaves. It is found in dry areas such as California (e.g. on the western foothills of the Sierra Nevada).

broken clouds *Clouds that cover between six-tenths and nine-tenths of the sky.

broker In *greenhouse gas *emissions trading, a broker acts as an intermediary between a buyer and a seller, for which they usually charge a commission.

bromine (Br) A *halogen chemical that works as a disinfectant, and is often used as an alternative to *chlorine to kill bacteria and algae in the water of pools and spas. It is one of the most common chemicals found in seawater. It exists as a volatile liquid at room temperature and is also used for petrol additives. Liquid bromine is harmful to human tissue, and the vapour irritates the eyes and throat.

Bronze Age The *prehistoric period of human culture in Europe from about 2000 BC to about 1000 BC, during which bronze (an alloy of *copper and tin) was the main material used for making tools and weapons. It followed the *Stone Age and ended with the start of the *Iron Age.

brood The young of certain animals, particularly young birds and fowl, that are hatched and cared for one at one time.

brood cover Low vegetation (such as grasses or herbs) that offers protection for ground nesting birds to raise their young.

brood parasitism (breeding parasitism, nest parasitism) A form of *parasitism in which a bird of one species (such as a cuckoo) lays an egg in the nest of a bird of a different species, and the latter then looks after the young.

Brower, David US environmental campaigner and activist (1912–2000) who founded many environmentalist organizations including the Sierra Club Foundation, the John Muir Institute for Environmental Studies, *Friends of the Earth, the League of Conservation Voters, Earth Island Institute, North Cascades Conservation Council, and Fate of the Earth Conferences. He was nominated for the Nobel Peace Prize three times, served as the first Executive Director of the *Sierra Club between 1952 and 1969, and served on its board three times between 1941 and 2000.

brown earth soil A type of soil that develops under *deciduous forest on calcium-rich parent material, has a high *base status, and lacks a well-developed *illuvial horizon.

brown smoke Smoke that contains particles of tar-like compounds, produced when *coal is burned at a low temperature.

brownfield An abandoned industrial or commercial site where expansion or redevelopment is compromised by the possibility that it may be contaminated with hazardous substances from operations on the site. After *remediation it may be reclassified as a *greenfield site. *See also* INFILL.

browse 1. Leaves, young shoots, herbs, shrubs, trees, and other vegetation that serve as food for livestock and wildlife. **2.** The act of eating such food. *See also* GRAZE.

browse line (grazing line) The height limit on trees and tall shrubs to which livestock and big game browse.

Brundtland Commission *See* WORLD COMMISSION ON ENVIRONMENT AND DEVELOPMENT.

brush 1. (undergrowth, underwood) A type of woody vegetation, comprising shrubs and small trees. **2.** Material such as twigs that are cut from undergrowth.

brush control The deliberate removal or reduction of *brush in order to reduce the accumulation of *wildfire fuel, or to allow the growth of plant species that are preferred for growing timber or *forage.

brush management The management of stands of *brush using mechanical, chemical, or biological methods, or by *prescribed burning.

brushing In *silviculture, the removal from beneath the trees of *brush and *weed species, which compete with seedlings for sunlight, water, and soil nutrients.

bryophyte A plant of the division Bryophyta (a moss, liverwort, or hornwort) that grows in damp places. *Contrast* VASCULAR PLANT.

bryozoans (moss animals) A phylum (Ectoprocta) of small, aquatic, colonial animals, many of which possess a well-developed *calcite skeleton comprising microscopic, box-like divisions, each housing an individual animal possessing ciliated tentacles and a coelom. Food is collected by the tentacles surrounding the mouth. Reproduction takes place by asexual budding and by the release of larvae which give rise to new colonies. Bryozoans have occurred from the *Ordovician to the present day. Fossilized branched colonies are common in some rocks. They were important reef-builders in the *Phanerozoic, and underwent several great *adaptive radiations.

BSE *See* BOVINE SPONGIFORM ENCEPHALOPATHY.

Btu *See* BRITISH THERMAL UNIT.

bubble A concept used in *air pollution control, based on the idea that reductions anywhere within a specific area should count towards a common reduction goal. *See also* EMISSIONS BUBBLE; EU BUBBLE.

bubble approach (bubble policy) In *pollution control, an approach that allows polluters to discharge more pollutants at one source, if an equivalent reduction occurs at other sources within the *bubble. *See also* EMISSIONS BUBBLE; EMISSIONS TRADING.

bubble policy *See* BUBBLE APPROACH.

bubnoff unit A standard measure for describing the rates of geologic and geomorphologic erosional processes. One bubnoff unit (B) is equal to the removal of one micrometre per year, or one millimetre of surface material per thousand years. The unit is named after the Russian-born German geologist Serge von Bubnoff (1888–1957).

bucolic Typical of a *rural or *pastoral life.

Budget Period *See* COMMITMENT PERIOD.

buffer 1. A solution that works to keep *pH levels fairly constant when acids or bases are added, effectively neutralizing them. **2.** *See* BUFFER STRIP.

buffer solution A solution that contains a *buffer and is thus able to oppose changes in *pH when small quantities of acid or base are added to it.

buffer species A non-game or undesirable species of animal that provides food for *predators and thus reduces the loss of *game or other desirable species.

buffer strip (buffer, buffer zone, filter strip) An area of land or water, usually around or beside a sensitive wildlife habitat (such as a *wetland), that contains undisturbed vegetation and is designed to minimize sharp changes in habitat, inhibit soil erosion, or prevent disturbance from surrounding land uses.

buffer zone *See* BUFFER STRIP.

buffering agent Anything that turns an acidic (*pH less than 7.0) or alkaline (pH greater than 7.0) solution neutral (pH 7.0). *See also* BUFFER SOLUTION.

buffering capacity (alkalinity, acid neutralizing capacity) The ability of a medium (such as soil or water) to resist rapid changes in *pH.

building code Local regulations that control the design, construction, and materials used in construction, usually based on health and safety standards.

building-related illness A discrete, identifiable disease or illness (such as legionnaire's disease) that can be linked to a specific pollutant or source within a building. *Contrast* SICK BUILDING SYNDROME. *See also* LEGIONELLA.

bulk density The mass or weight of unconsolidated material, such as soil, usually expressed in grams per millilitre (g ml^{-1}). Compaction (for example by recreational use, grazing animals, or logging equipment) increases bulk density.

bulky waste Large items of waste materials (such as appliances, furniture, large vehicle parts, trees, and stumps) that cannot be handled by normal procedures for processing *municipal solid waste.

bunchgrass A North American *grassland vegetation in which different types of native *perennial grass grow in tufts or clumps rather than forming a sod or mat. Dominant grasses include little bluestem (*Schizachyrium scoparium*) and buffalo grass (*Buchloe dactyloides*), which provide good *forage for grazing animals (such as cattle and buffalo). Common throughout the western states.

bund An artificial barrier on a slope, made, for example, from soil or agricultural waste, designed to reduce runoff and soil erosion.

buoyancy The force exerted on a body when it is immersed in a fluid, due to a difference in density between the body and the fluid. If the body is less dense than the fluid the force will act upward (positive buoyancy); if the body is denser than the fluid the force will act downward (negative buoyancy); and if the two densities are similar there will be no net force (neutral buoyancy).

Bureau of Land Management *See* US BUREAU OF LAND MANAGEMENT.

Bureau of Reclamation *See* US BUREAU OF RECLAMATION.

Burgess shale A layer of *Cambrian rocks in British Columbia, Canada. It contains *fossils of 140 species in 119 genera of soft-bodied animals that have not been found elsewhere. More than 30% are *arthropods, but among the other groups there are forms that appear bizarre.

burial ground (graveyard) **1.** A disposal site for unwanted radioactive materials, where earth or water are used as a shield. **2.** A piece of land where dead bodies are buried.

burn **1.** A land management technique that involves setting fire to vegetation to clear it, encourage new growth, and restore soil fertility. *See also* PRESCRIBED BURN. **2.** An area of land that has recently been burned. *See also* FIRE.

bush **1.** A low woody *perennial plant that has no distinct trunk but usually has several major branches. **2.** An area of dense vegetation dominated by stunted trees or bushes.

bush encroachment The unplanned conversion of vegetation dominated by grassland to one dominated by woody species, often as a result of *overgrazing or invasion by *aliens.

bush fallow The natural vegetation that grows on land that is left uncultivated for some time, and includes small trees, shrubs, grasses, sedges, and herbaceous plants. *See also* ENRICHED FALLOW; FALLOW; SHIFTING CULTIVATION.

bush land An open area with tall, scattered *bushes covering at least 40% of the area.

business-as-usual scenario A scenario for future patterns of activity which assumes that there will be no significant change in people's attitudes and priorities, or no major changes in technology, economics, or policies, so that normal circumstances can be expected to continue unchanged.

butadiene A *hydrocarbon ($CH_2CHCHCH_2$) that is a major raw material for the production of synthetic rubbers, water-based latex paints, certain plastics, etc. At room temperature it is a heavy, colourless gas, but it liquefies at $-4.4°C$ and at $25°C$ under 0.28 megapascals pressure. It is highly reactive, making it difficult and hazardous to handle.

butane (C_4H_{10}) A gaseous *hydrocarbon that is extracted from *natural gas or refinery gas, and is used as household fuel, a propellant, and a refrigerant.

butte A narrow flat-topped hill of resistant rock with very steep sides, found in an arid area where there is little vegetation. It is formed by the erosion of horizontal *strata where remnants of a resistant layer protect the softer rocks underneath.

butterfly effect A metaphor to explain how a small difference in initial conditions can cause two complex systems to develop in very different ways. This is often summarized in the suggestion that a butterfly flapping its wings in Brazil might trigger a tornado in Texas.

butyric fermentation The *decomposition of various types of organic matter by chemical reaction. One of the many forms of *fermentation involved in *putrefaction.

buy-back centre A facility where individuals or groups take *recyclable material in return for payment.

Buys Ballot's law A law named after the Dutch meteorologist H. D. Buys Ballot (1817–90), who in 1857 defined the relationship between the *pressure gradient and the *Coriolis effect. The simple rule of thumb is: in the northern hemisphere, if you stand with the wind blowing into your back, low pressure is always to your left and high pressure is always to your right; in the southern hemisphere the pattern is reversed, and low pressure is on your right and high pressure on your left.

BWR *See* BOILING WATER REACTOR.

bycatch (incidental catch, incidental take) Fish and other marine life that is caught incidentally while fishing for something else. Un-

wanted bycatch is normally thrown back into the sea as a waste product, even if it is commercially valuable. *See also* LONGLINE; NON-TARGET SPECIES.

bypass A route or road that passes around a *city or other congested area.

byproduct Any material, other than the principal product, that is generated as a consequence of an industrial or biological process, and for which there is often no commercial market.

C$_3$ plants Plants that utilize the most common pathway of carbon fixation in *photosynthesis, in which the first product of carboxylation is 3-phosphoglycerate, a compound with three carbon atoms. Most broadleaved plants and plants of temperate climates use the C$_3$ pathway.

C$_4$ plants Plants that utilize a pathway of carbon fixation in *photosynthesis, in which the first product of carboxylation is the four-carbon compound oxaloacetate. Most C$_4$ plants occur in low latitudes and are adapted to high temperatures and high light intensities. Many are grasses, including maize (*Zea mays*) and sugar cane (*Saccharum officinarum*).

C:N ratio *See* CARBON: NITROGEN RATIO.

cable logging A method of *logging in which timber is dragged by cable from where it is cut to a collecting point. *See also* GROUND-LEAD LOGGING; HIGH-LEAD LOGGING.

cadmium (Cd) A naturally occurring, soft, bluish trace *heavy metal that accumulates in the environment. Sources include smelter fumes and dust, some incineration products, *phosphate fertilizer, municipal wastewater, and sludge discharges. It is also an industrial *byproduct of the manufacture of *zinc, *copper, and *lead. It corrodes galvanized pipes, and can be extremely toxic to humans and aquatic life. *See also* ITAI-ITAI DISEASE.

caesium (Cs) A silver-white, soft *ductile element, part of the *alkali metal group. Used in *photoelectric cells. The naturally occurring *isotope is ^{133}Cs but there are 15 other radioactive isotopes.

CAFE *See* CORPORATE AVERAGE FUEL ECONOMY.

CAFO *See* CONCENTRATED ANIMAL FEEDING OPERATION.

Cainozoic *See* CENOZOIC.

Cairo Conference *See* INTERNATIONAL CONFERENCE ON POPULATION AND DEVELOPMENT.

calcareous **1.** A substance that is composed of, or contains, *calcium carbonate, which typically causes an *alkaline reaction (*pH greater than 7.0). **2.** A species that accumulates *calcium carbonate in its tissues.

calcicole A plant that is adapted to growing on *limestone or on soils that are derived from limestone and have a high *calcium content.

calcification **1.** A *soil forming process in which *calcium carbonate accumulates in the lower *horizons. This occurs mainly under grass or *xerophytic shrub in subhumid, semiarid, and arid climates and produces neutral or *basic soils. **2.** Replacement of the hard body parts of an organism by *calcium carbonate (for example in the form of a shell).

calcifuge Applied to a plant that is seldom found on soil containing free calcium carbonate. *Compare* CALCICOLE.

calcisols Soils that have, within 125 cm of the surface, a mineral *soil horizon with evidence of secondary deposition of calcium carbonate that is more than 15 cm thick, contains more than 15% calcium carbonate by weight, and has 5% more carbonate than the parent material or the horizons below it. Calcisols are a reference soil group in the *World Soil Classification.

calcite A common rock-forming *mineral of *calcium carbonate. It is crystalline, stable, one of the most common minerals, and a main ingredient of *limestone.

calcium (Ca) An *alkaline metal that occurs naturally in the *environment and accounts for 3.63% of the Earth's *crust. It readily forms salts with various *metals and *halogens, and is an *essential element (a *minor element) for animals and humans.

calcium carbonate (CaCO$_3$) A *chemical precipitate which is formed from the skeletons of corals and the shells of molluscs, and occurs as *calcite, *chalk, and *limestone. It dissolves in water and so affects *salinity and *alkalinity, and at high concentrations it can make water hard. It is usually white, colourless, or light shades of grey, yellow, and blue, and is used in polishes and the manufacture of lime and cement.

calcrete *See* CALICHE.

caldera A large, steep-sided, circular depression formed by the collapse of the roof of a volcanic *magma chamber. The caldera is usually much larger than the original *vent of the volcano and has a relatively flat floor.

caliche (calcrete) A layer of *calcium carbonate that has been deposited on or near the surface of a stony soil in an *arid or *semi-arid area, by the *evaporation of moisture in the soil.

California grassland A North American native *grassland vegetation common throughout California, which was originally a mixture of short and tall bunch grasses. Much of the habitat has been lost through development and conversion, and in the areas that remain many of the native *perennials have been replaced by introduced *annuals.

calm Undisturbed air in which there is no apparent motion. The lowest force on the *Beaufort scale.

calorie A measure of energy. One calorie is equal to the total amount of heat that is required to raise the temperature of one gram of water by $1°C$; 1 cal. = 4.128 joules. The Calorie, used to measure food values, is 1000 calories.

calorific value The amount of heat that is liberated when a unit weight of a substance is burned in oxygen and the residue comprises oxygen, carbon dioxide, sulphur dioxide, nitrogen, water, and ash. Traditionally it was expressed in *calories (c) or kilocalories (C) per gram dry weight or ash-free dry weight; it is now more often expressed in *joules.

calving The process of forming *icebergs, in which pieces of a *glacier or *ice sheet break off when the ice meets the ocean.

CAM *See* CRASSULACEAN ACID METABOLISM.

cambisols Soils that have a weakly developed mineral horizon or a dark surface horizon containing at least 1% (dry weight) organic matter or 0.6% carbon above a B *soil horizon with a *base saturation lower than 50% in the upper 100 cm, or a horizon with weathered volcanic

material, clayey material, or volcanic glass with an upper boundary 25–100 cm below the surface. Cambisols are a reference soil group in the *World Soil Classification.

cambium A single layer of cells between the *xylem and *phloem of a woody plant, where *secondary thickening takes place. This growth is visible as the growth rings that can be counted to determine the age of a tree. *See also* DENDRO-CHRONOLOGY.

Cambrian The first geological period of the *Palaeozoic era, ranging from 542 to 488.3 million years ago, during which marine life (particularly invertebrates) evolved and spread widely. The oldest *fossils of organisms with mineralized skeletons date from the Cambrian. *See also* BURGESS SHALE.

( ) SEE WEB LINKS

• The Cambrian period of the Paleozoic era.

Cambrian Explosion The common name for the huge increase in the number and diversity of life forms in the Earth's oceans that started during the *Cambrian period.

camouflage The disguise that a species of animal develops (through *natural selection) that enables individuals to hide from predators by blending in with their surroundings, usually through the colour and pattern of their skin or fur. *See also* COUNTERSHADING; CRYPTIC COLORATION.

Campbell–Stokes sunshine recorder An instrument for measuring how long the Sun shines at a particular place, based on a glass sphere which focuses the Sun's rays to burn a hole through a graduated card. It is the most common sunshine recorder in use outside the United States.

canal An artificial waterway that has been built for navigation, water supply, land irrigation, or drainage.

canalization Engineering works that straighten and/or deepen a natural channel to improve navigability, or that artificially force a river to flow along a particular course (often within a concrete channel) to speed the flow and/or reduce flooding.

cancer A group of more than 120 different diseases in which abnormal cells divide and grow rapidly and uncontrollably, producing tumours that can be malignant and often invade surrounding cell tissue. *See also* CARCINOMA.

candidate species Species of plants and animals that are considered (by the *US Fish and Wildlife Service or the National Marine Fisheries Service) to be candidates for listing (and thus protecting) under the *Endangered Species Act.

cannel coal *Coal containing finely divided plant material rich in *kerogen. It burns brightly and leaves little ash.

canopy The roof-like cover formed by the leafy upper branches and *crowns of the tallest trees in a *forest. In tropical forests, the canopy may be 50 m or more above the ground. *See also* OVERSTOREY.

canopy closure The progressive reduction of space between the *crowns of trees in a *forest as they spread laterally, increasing *canopy cover.

cantharophily *Pollination by beetles.

canyon A large, narrow valley or *gorge with deep sides that is cut by a river.

CAP *See* COMMON AGRICULTURAL POLICY.

cap (cover material) 1. A layer of *clay or other impermeable material that is spread over the top of a closed *landfill or *hazardous waste site in order to seal it, and thus prevent the *infiltration of rainwater and minimize the *leaching of *pollutants into adjacent soil and rock. **2.** A thin, impermeable layer covering the soil surface caused by the impact of rain on bare ground. **3.** *See* CAP ROCK.

cap and trade An approach to *air pollution control, introduced in the *Kyoto Protocol, that is based on the trading of emissions allowances between countries, within a total allowance that is strictly limited or capped. *See also* EMISSIONS ALLOWANCE; EMISSIONS TRADING.

cap rock The hard, impervious layer of rock that overlies and seals a source of water, crude oil, or natural gas.

capability, land The suitability of a particular area of land for a given type and intensity of use, without permanent damage, which reflects factors such as site conditions (particularly climate, soils, geology, broader socioeconomic factors (including political, social, and economic constraints), and land management practices.

capacity The total amount of *sediment that a *river can transport, which is determined by both discharge and particle size.

Cape floral region A region synonymous with R. Good's South African kingdom (*The Geography of the Flowering Plants*, 1974), and in relation to its size one that has perhaps the most remarkable and richest flora in the world. There are about 2500 *species, and an unusually high proportion of the genera and species (e.g. 520 species of *Erica*) are *endemic. Many well-known garden plants and greenhouse succulents originated in this floral region (e.g. many pelargoniums).

capillary action The process by which water moves through very small spaces between particles in *soil. It is caused by attraction (capillary forces) between the liquid and the particles. This process allows water to be drawn upwards in the soil.

capillary fringe In *rock or *soil, the zone of porous material just above the *water table that remains more or less saturated with water, because of *capillary action.

capillary water Water that is held within a *soil by *surface tension in and on soil particles, and in the pore spaces between particles. It can move in any direction within the soil, by *capillary action. *See also* FIELD CAPACITY.

capital Any form of wealth, resources, or knowledge that is available for use in the production of more wealth.

capital cost The total investment that is needed to complete a project and make it commercially operable, such as the cost of building a new factory or engineering scheme.

capitalism (capitalist economy) An economic system that is based on private enterprise, in which the means of production are owned privately and resources are exchanged through market processes. *Contrast* MARXISM; SOCIALISM. *See also* MARKET ECONOMY.

capitalist economy *See* CAPITALISM.

captive breeding The breeding and raising of *endangered species of animals in captivity (for example, in a *zoo), where they can be protected and cared for, as part of a *living collection, before being released into the wild in an attempt to prevent their extinction. *See also* SELECTIVE BREEDING; REINTRODUCTION.

captive conservation Keeping small numbers of animals in protective isolation, to ensure that they breed successfully before being released.

capture–recapture method (mark–recapture) A procedure for estimating the size of a biological population, based on the distinctive marking and subsequent recapture or sighting of individuals.

carapace The hard case or shell that covers the body of animals such as turtles or crabs. *Contrast* PLASTRON.

carbamate A class of *insecticides derived from carbamic acid, which is less *toxic and more *biodegradable than many *organophosphate insecticides.

carbamate herbicide A group of *herbicides that inhibit cell division and the formation and arrangement of microtubules in cells. Carbetamide, chlorpropham, and propham are carbamate herbicides.

carbaryl A contact insecticide of the *carbamate group that resembles *acetylcholine but kills insects by inhibiting the *enzyme cholinesterase. Marketed as sevin, it is used to kill malaria-carrying mosquitoes, earthworms in turf, and winter moth caterpillars and earwigs. It is harmful to non-target insects (e.g. honeybees), crustaceans, and fish, and toxic to humans. Its use is banned in the UK, Angola, Austria, Denmark, Germany, and Sweden.

carbendazim A broad-spectrum, systemic, carbamate fungicide that controls a number of fungal diseases of crop plants including black spot, mildew, and blight. It is toxic to some fish. Although it is of low toxicity to mammals and birds, it is suspected of being an *endocrine disruptor.

carbohydrate An *organic chemical compound that contains only *carbon, *hydrogen, and *oxygen and supplies energy to organisms. Examples include *starch, *glucose, and *cellulose.

carbon (C) A non-metallic *element that occurs in many *inorganic compounds and all *organic compounds, and is one of the most widely distributed elements on Earth. There are five *allotropes: diamond, graphite, carbon black, buckminsterfullerene, and graphene. Carbon occurs in combination with other elements in all plants and animals, and is a basic building block of life. It is also found as *calcium carbonate in *carbonaceous rocks such as *chalk and *limestone, as *carbon dioxide in the atmosphere, and as *hydrocarbons in *fossil fuels.

carbon-14 (^{14}C) A naturally occurring *carbon *isotope that is produced in the atmosphere by cosmic ray bombardment and has a half-life of 5700 years. It is useful for the *absolute dating of samples up to 40000 years old. *See also* RADIOCARBON DATING.

carbon absorber An *air pollution control device that uses *activated carbon to absorb *volatile organic compounds from a stream of gas, which are later recovered from the carbon.

carbon adsorption A water treatment system that removes *contaminants from groundwater or surface water by *adsorption, by forcing the water through tanks that contain *activated carbon, which attracts the contaminants.

carbon assimilation The process by which plants take in (assimilate) *carbon dioxide.

carbon budget The balance of the exchanges (incomes and losses) of carbon between different reservoirs of *carbon in the *carbon cycle, which shows whether particular reservoirs (such as oceans or forests) are operating as *sources or *sinks for *carbon dioxide.

carbon credit In *greenhouse gas *emissions trading, a credit granted to a particular country that counts towards their emission targets as agreed in the *Kyoto Protocol.

carbon dating (radiocarbon dating) A method of dating *organic material that is applicable to material of up to at least 40000 years old. It uses the known rate of disintegration of the *carbon-14 atom as a basis for determining the age of a sample, based on the principle that the ratio of ^{14}C/^{12}C is directly related to the age of the sample.

carbon dioxide (CO_2) A naturally occurring, heavy, colourless, odourless gas, which is a part of the *ambient air, accounting for 0.035% of the Earth's *atmosphere, by volume. It is produced by *respiration, decomposition of organic substances, and the combustion of *fossil fuels and *biomass (particularly forest fires). It dissolves in water to form *carbonic acid, is the principal *greenhouse gas (it accounts for 80% of all greenhouse gas emissions), and persists in the air for more than 100 years. More than 90% comes from natural sources, the rest from human activities (particularly from the burning of fossil fuels to run vehicles, heat buildings, and power factories). Roughly half of the CO_2 that is released is soon absorbed by the oceans or by increased plant *photosynthesis, but the other half remains in the atmosphere for many decades. Concentrations of carbon dioxide in the atmosphere have risen by about a quarter since the *Industrial Revolution. Analysis of *ice cores from *Antarctica shows that natural background levels of atmospheric CO_2 are in the order of 200 parts per million by volume (ppmv) during *glacial periods, rising to around 280 ppmv during warmer *interglacials. In 1958 the atmospheric concentration was measured at 315 ppmv, and by the early 1990s it had risen to more than 350 ppmv. By 1997 the concentration stood at more than 360 ppmv, the highest level in 160 000 years. It is predicted to continue rising at a rate of 0.4% a year, and to rise above 600 ppmv over coming decades. *Industrialized countries produce much more than their fair share of CO_2; for example the USA houses 5% of the world's population but produces 25% of the CO_2. *Per capita emissions of CO_2 are much lower amongst *developing countries, largely because per capita energy use is much lower.

carbon dioxide equivalent *See* GLOBAL WARMING POTENTIAL.

carbon dioxide fertilization The increased plant growth or rise in *net primary production in natural or agricultural systems that occurs when the atmospheric concentration of *carbon dioxide increases.

carbon fixation A chemical process by which *carbon from the atmosphere is assimilated into *organic compounds and made available to *organisms through *food chains. *See also* PHOTOSYNTHESIS.

carbon flux The rate of movement of *carbon between different pools or reservoirs in the *carbon cycle.

carbon footprint a measure of the *environmental impact of a particular human activities, based on the amount of *natural resources they consume and the amount of *greenhouse gases they produce. It is measured in units of *carbon dioxide such as tons per year, for comparative purposes.

carbon isotope There are three naturally occurring *isotopes of carbon: ^{12}C or carbon-12 (which accounts for 98.9 of all the carbon), ^{13}C or carbon-13 (about 1.1%) and ^{14}C or carbon-14 (negligible amount). Changes through time in the absolute and relative amounts of the carbon isotopes can be measured in *ice cores and lake sediments, and these provide *indicators or *proxy measures of long-term climate change.

carbon management An approach to limiting the emission of *carbon dioxide that is based on storing it (for example in *carbon sinks), or using it in ways that prevent its release into the air.

carbon monoxide (CO) A colourless, odourless, non-irritating but highly *toxic gas that is produced by the incomplete combustion of *hydrocarbon fuels, incineration of *biomass or solid waste, or partially *anaerobic *decomposition of organic material. Much comes from vehicle exhausts. It is a *criteria pollutant which affects human health by interfering with the ability of blood to carry oxygen to cells, tissues, and organs in the body, and exposure to high

---

CARBON CYCLE

The natural *biogeochemical cycle through which *carbon circulates through the *biosphere, *atmosphere, and *hydrosphere (see Fig. 3). This involves *abiotic and *biotic parts of interconnected cycles on land, sea, and the atmosphere. In the atmosphere carbon is found as *carbon dioxide (CO_2), which plants use in the process of *photosynthesis to manufacture *carbohydrates. Plants can then be consumed by *herbivores and the carbon is passed along *food chains, as these animals are then eaten by *carnivores. Some of the carbon is returned to the atmosphere when these animals respire or when they die and decay through the respiration of decomposing bacteria. If plants are not eaten the carbon contained in them may become fossilized as fuels such as oil and coal, or it may return to the atmosphere as CO_2 by the decay of the plant matter. Plants may also return carbon to the atmosphere by the process of *respiration. The carbon cycle is also being disrupted by changes in land use, particularly the removal of natural vegetation. Natural *sinks of atmospheric CO_2 are decreasing as a direct result of vegetation clearance and changing land use. Levels of carbon dioxide are building up in the atmosphere as a result, thus contributing to the *greenhouse effect.

Fig. 3 Carbon cycle

levels is harmful to people, but particularly to those with diseases of the heart, lung, and circulatory system.

carbon: nitrogen ratio (C:N ratio) The ratio between the amount of *carbon and *nitrogen in a particular soil or organic material, which affects *fertility and suitability for *composting.

carbon offset *See* OFFSET.

carbon pool The total amount of *carbon that is stored, cycling, or otherwise available for use in *biogeochemical cycles.

carbon reservoir Any of the locations within the *carbon cycle at which carbon compounds are stored, including the atmosphere, oceans, vegetation and soils, and reservoirs of fossil fuels.

carbon sequestration The long-term natural storage of *carbon in forests, soils, oceans, or underground in oil and gas reservoirs and coal seams. There have been initiatives to reduce the amount of carbon that is in the atmosphere by increasing the number and size of *carbon sinks, in order to slow down *global warming.

carbon sink A *geochemical reservoir (*sink) that can absorb or *sequester *carbon which has been released from another part of the *carbon cycle, thus removing it from the flowing part of the cycle for a period of time. Examples include *soils, *peat, large *forests (which store organic carbon), and ocean sediments (which store *calcium carbonate). One of the *flexibility measures introduced in the *Kyoto Protocol for

dealing with *air pollution by *greenhouse gases is to increase carbon sinks by *afforestation or other means.

carbon source Any part or reservoir of the *carbon cycle that releases carbon to some other part of the cycle. Examples include the burning of *fossil fuels, *decomposition of *organic waste, and burning of trees or other vegetation.

carbon stock The *carbon that is naturally stored in vegetation, decomposing organic matter, soils, and wood products.

carbon tax A tax or surcharge on the sale of *fossil fuels (oil, coal, and gas) that varies according to the carbon content of each fuel, and is designed to discourage the use of fossil fuels and reduce emissions of *carbon dioxide.

carbon tetrachloride (tetrachloromethane, CCl₄) A colourless, non-flammable, *toxic liquid compound that was once widely used as an industrial raw material, as a solvent, and in the production of *CFCs. It is highly *carcinogenic, and its use has been banned or strictly regulated in most countries since 1995, under the *Montreal Protocol.

carbonaceous A rock, sediment, or aerosol that contains *carbon.

carbonate A mineral that is mostly found in limestones and dolomites (such as *calcite). The term is also used to describe sedimentary rocks that are largely composed of carbonate minerals.

carbonate hardness The hardness in water that is caused by *bicarbonates and *carbonates of *calcium and *magnesium. *See also* HARD WATER.

carbonation A chemical *weathering process in which dilute carbonic acid, derived from the solution in water of free atmospheric and soil-air carbon dioxide, reacts with a mineral. The best-known example is the reaction between limestone (calcium carbonate) and carbonated water (carbonic acid) which yields calcium and bicarbonate ions in solution: $CaCO_3 + H^+ + HCO_3^- \rightarrow Ca^{2+} + 2HCO_3^-$.

carbon-based resource The amount of recoverable *fossil fuel and *biomass that can be used to produce *fuel.

carbonic acid (H_2CO_3) The weak *acid that is formed when *carbon dioxide (CO_2) is dissolved in water.

Carboniferous The penultimate period of the *Palaeozoic era, preceded by the *Devonian and followed by the *Permian. It began about 359.2 million years ago and ended about 299 million years ago. North American geologists subdivide the Carboniferous System into two periods or subperiods. Of these the lower (359.2–318.1 million years ago) is called the Mississippian and the upper period, the Pennsylvanian (318.1–299 million years ago). During the Carboniferous very lush, swamp forests dominated the landscape in low-lying areas, where minor changes in sea level alternately exposed forested land then inundated and buried the vegetation. The climate was very humid until the end of the period, when it became arid, conditions then selecting against seed-bearing plants. The buried vegetation was compressed and changed through time to form the rich coal measures of southern Wales, England, Scotland, the USA, and many other areas worldwide, in which recognizable seed plants are common fossils. The first tetrapods (e.g. the amphibian *Ichthyostega*) appeared very early in the Carboniferous.

 SEE WEB LINKS

• The Carboniferous period of the Paleozoic era.

Carboxyl The group COOH, which forms part of many organic molecules.

carcinogen Any substance that produces *cancer, by causing changes in the *DNA of cells. *See also* MUTAGEN; TERATOGEN.

carcinogenic *Cancer causing.

carcinoma A type of *cancer that occurs in particular types of tissue.

cardenolide A *toxic material that certain plants are able to produce as a defence against their own predators.

Caribbean floral region Part of R. Good's *Neotropical floral kingdom (*The Geography of the Flowering Plants*, 1974). It comprises isthmian America and the West Indies. There are thought to be well in excess of 500 *endemic genera and many thousands of endemic *species. Some of the most diverse floras in the world are found here; for example, Cuba alone has roughly 8000 species, many of which are endemic. A very large number of valuable economic plants and some garden plants are from this region.

Caring for the Earth A strategy for *sustainable development that was published in 1991 by the *IUCN, jointly with the *United Nations Environment Programme and the *World Wide Fund for Nature.

carnivore A flesh-eating animal (*predator or *carrion eater).

carnivorous Meat-eating.

Carolina parakeet A species of parrot (*Conuropsis carolinensis*) that was the only parrot species *native to the eastern USA. It lived in old forests along rivers, and was found from the Ohio Valley to the Gulf of Mexico. By the early 1890s it had become *extinct as a result of shooting by farmers (who saw it as a *pest), over-collecting (for its colourful feathers), and destruction of its native *habitat.

car-pooling Sharing a car to a destination in order to reduce fuel use, pollution, and travel costs.

carr Wet *woodland that grows on soils with permanently high water levels and is usually dominated by alder or willow trees.

carrier A person or animal that carries a specific infectious *agent and is a potential source of infection. *See also* DISEASE VECTOR.

carrion The decaying flesh of a dead animal that is used as food by animals that *scavenge.

carrying capacity (ecological limit, environmental capacity) The maximum number of individuals (people or animals) that can be supported by a particular *ecosystem (or area) on a *sustainable basis without degrading it. Global carrying capacity refers to the total number of people which the Earth and its environmental systems can support on a sustainable basis. There are no clear-cut answers to the question of what the Earth's carrying capacity really is; published values range between about three billion and 14 billion people. Experts expect there to be natural limits, but there is no consensus over precisely what those limits are likely to be. *See also* MALTHUS; TRAGEDY OF THE COMMONS.

Carson, Rachel (1907–64) An American biologist and writer whose polemical book *Silent Spring* (1962) warned of the dangers of the over-use of *insecticides. *See also* BIOACCU-MULATION.

Cartagena Protocol on Biosafety An international agreement arising from the *United Nations Framework Convention on Biological Diversity, that came into force in January 2000, and is designed to protect *biodiversity from the potential risks posed by *living modified organisms that result from *biotechnology. *See also* BIOSAFETY.

cartel A consortium of producers of a single product who agree to limit production to keep the price of the product high.

cartography The construction and study of maps.

cascade 1. A small waterfall or series of small waterfalls. 2. A sudden downpour.

cash crop Any crop that is grown for sale in a market, to agents, or directly from the farm. *See also* SUBSISTENCE FARMING.

casing The pipe that provides the walls of oil, gas, or water wells.

cask (coffin) A thick-walled container, usually made from lead, that is used to transport *radioactive material.

casualty Any person suffering physical and/or psychological damage that kills, injures, or leads to material loss.

CAT *See* CLEAR AIR TURBULENCE.

catabolism (destructive metabolism) The process by which a living cell or organism breaks down complex *organic molecules to smaller ones, producing energy and waste matter. *See also* METABOLISM.

catadromous Applied to the behaviour of fish that spend most of their lives in fresh water but migrate to the sea to breed, e.g.

common eel (*Anguilla anguilla*). *Compare* AMPHIDROMOUS; ANADROMOUS; DIADROMOUS; POTAMODROMOUS.

catalysis Increasing the rate of a chemical or biochemical reaction by the addition of a *catalyst.

catalyst An *inorganic substance that increases the rate of a chemical or biochemical reaction without being consumed or chemically changed in the process.

catalytic converter A device fitted to the exhaust systems of motor vehicles which uses a catalytic agent (tiny quantities of metals such as platinum) to stimulate chemical reactions that remove pollutants from the exhaust gases. The process reduces emissions of noxious gases such as *nitrogen oxides, unburnt *hydrocarbons, and *carbon monoxide and replaces them with less harmful emissions, either by *oxidizing them into *carbon dioxide and water or reducing them to *nitrogen. *See also* END-OF-THE-PIPE.

catalytic incinerator A pollution control device that *oxidizes *volatile organic compounds by using a *catalyst to promote the combustion process.

catastrophe (disaster) A sudden, severe event that causes unusually large-scale losses (including deaths, injuries, damage to property, and financial loss), beyond normal expectation. Examples include extensive damage caused by flooding, hurricanes, or large fires. *See also* EMERGENCY.

catastrophism An interpretation of features of the Earth's surface (including rocks, fossils, and landforms) as the product of sudden, cataclysmic upheavals, particularly caused by major floods (*neptunianism) or volcanic activity (*vulcanism). This view was popular during the 19th century, but it was challenged and eventually replaced by *uniformitarianism, although many modern geologists would describe themselves as neocatastrophists, following the discovery of evidence of an asteroid collision that caused a mass extinction at the end of the *Cretaceous.

catch basin A sedimentation area that is designed to remove pollutants from *runoff before it is discharged into a stream or pond.

catchment *See* DRAINAGE BASIN.

catena 1. (toposequence) A sequence of soils in a landscape that are of similar age and have developed from similar parent material in the same climate, but which have different properties because of variations in relief and in drainage. **2.** A series of volcanic *craters.

cation An ion that has a positive charge. *See also* ANION.

cation adsorption capacity *See* CATION EXCHANGE CAPACITY.

cation exchange The chemical exchange of *cations that takes place between plant roots and the water, minerals, and organic matter within a soil.

cation exchange capacity (CEC) A measure of the ability of the *colloids in a soil to attract and retain *cations, which is usually expressed in terms of milliequivalents per 100 grams of soil (mEq $100g^{-1}$). This capacity is highest in soils that contain a lot of *humus and *clay.

Cato Institute A US non-profit *anti-environmental *think-tank based in Washington, DC that seeks to promote traditional American principles of limited government, individual liberty, free markets, and peace within public policy debates.

catotelm *See* ACROTELM.

cauliflory The growth of flowers on the large branches and trunk of a tree.

caustic Burning or corrosive.

caustic scrubbing A process for removing *sulphur dioxide from *flue gases by passing the gases through a solution of *caustic soda. The resulting reaction yields sodium sulphite and sodium bisulphite, and the addition of calcium carbonate causes the precipitation of calcium sulphate (gypsum), leaving the water enriched in sodium carbonate, which is harmless.

caustic soda Sodium hydroxide. A strongly *alkaline substance that is used in the manufacture of soap, paper, *aluminium, and a range of sodium compounds.

caution A warning against danger. *See also* ADVISORY.

cave A hollow chamber in rock, which is accessible from the surface, is large enough for a person to enter, and has usually been formed by natural processes.

cavernicolous Living in caves.

cavity Any hollow or hole, such as a hole in a tree, that is regularly used by species of wildlife (particularly birds) for nesting, roosting, and reproduction.

cavity tree *See* DEN TREE.

cay A small, flat, marine island formed from coral-reef material or sand. The term is applied, for example, to the low-lying, sparsely vegetated islands off the coast of southern Florida.

CBD *See* BERYLLIOSIS.

CBNRM *See* COMMUNITY BASED NATURAL RESOURCE MANAGEMENT.

CDC *See* CONSERVATION DATA CENTER.

CDM *See* CLEAN DEVELOPMENT MECHANISM.

CEC *See* CATION EXCHANGE CAPACITY.

ceiling In the *atmosphere, the height of the lowest layer of *clouds when the sky is broken or overcast.

celerity Speed, swiftness of motion.

celestial Of or relating to the sky or outer space.

celestial equator The projection onto the sky of the Earth's *equator, which is 90° from each of the Earth's *celestial poles.

celestial pole The points in the sky that are above the Earth's North and South poles.

cell The smallest unit of living matter that is able to grow and reproduce independently, of which all living organisms are composed. Cells contain *DNA (information store), ribosomes (protein synthesis), and mechanisms for converting energy into usable forms. There are two main types of cell, *prokaryotic and *eukaryotic. *See also* CYTOPLASM; GENOME; NUCLEUS.

cell division The process by which two identical *cells are formed from one.

cell fusion A technique of joining two *cells from different *species to create one hybrid cell, in order to combine some of the genetic characteristics of each original.

cell membrane The outer *membrane of a *cell, which separates it from the surrounding environment. The term is used particularly to refer to the *plasma membrane.

cell wall A tough *permeable layer that surrounds the *cells of a plant.

cellular respiration The process by which a *cell breaks down *organic compounds (such as sugar) in order to release the energy it needs to perform work. This process may be *aerobic or *anaerobic, depending on the availability of *oxygen.

cellulose ($C_6 H_{10}O_5$) A colourless, solid *carbohydrate *polymer that is made from the simple sugar *glucose, and is the most abundant compound on Earth that is manufactured by living things.

Celsius (°C) A temperature scale that is used internationally and was devised by the Swedish astronomer Anders Celsius (1701–44). In it water freezes at 0°C and boils at 100°C. The equation for converting temperature from *Fahrenheit to Celsius is °C = 5/9 (°F − 32), so that 100°C is equal to 212°F. Previously known as **Centigrade**.

cement 1. To bind or join together. **2.** Any material that hardens to act as an adhesive. **3.** A building material made of *limestone and *clay, which is mixed with water and sand or gravel to make concrete and mortar.

cemented The grains of a *sedimentary rock that have been bonded together by substances such as *calcium carbonate, *silica, oxides of iron and aluminium, or *humus.

Cenozoic The current geological era, after the *Mesozoic era, from 65.5 million years ago to the present, during which the modern continents formed and modern animals and plants evolved. The Cenozoic is subdivided into the *Palaeogene, *Neogene, and *Quaternary periods.

((⊕)) SEE WEB LINKS

• The Cenozoic era of the Phanerozoic eon.

census 1. A count of all of the individuals in a specified area over a specified time interval or at a particular point in time. **2.** The act or process of counting all individuals within a specified area and estimating population density or a total population for that area.

Centigrade See CELSIUS.

Central Australian floral region Part of R. Good's Australian kingdom (*The Geography of the Flowering Plants*, 1974), which accounts for most of the Australian continent, including all the central parts. The flora is imperfectly known, although the great majority of it is likely to be *endemic. Ecologically it coincides with extensive *thorn forest, with much *Acacia aneura* (mulga), *A. harpophylla* (brigalow), and *Eucalyptus hemiphloia* (mallee). The flora is poor, partly because of the extensive deserts and semi-deserts that account for most of the region, and partly because central Australia was submerged for much of the *Palaeogene and *Neogene periods.

Central European Sea See PARATETHYS.

centrally planned economy An economic system (like those in former communist countries) in which investment and production are coordinated by a central government body rather than by market forces.

centre of diversity A geographical area that has high levels of genetic or species diversity. See also BIODIVERSITY.

centre of endemism A geographical area that has a relatively high number of locally *endemic species.

centre of origin A geographical area in which a *taxon originated, which may or may not correspond with the *centre of diversity for that taxon.

centrifugal force The apparent force that causes a body moving in a curve to move away from the centre of the curve. It results from the balance between the tendency of a moving body to continue in a straight line and the *centripetal force acting towards the centre of rotation.

centripetal drainage pattern A *drainage pattern that is the opposite of a *radial drainage pattern, in which the rivers drain in towards the centre of a basin, like the spokes of a wheel.

centripetal force The force that causes a moving object to follow a curved path rather than continue on a straight line. The force is directed towards the centre of the curve. *Contrast* CENTRIFUGAL FORCE.

century A period of a hundred years.

cephalopod A squid, octopus, cuttlefish, or nautilus, which are *molluscs of the class Cephalopoda, literally meaning 'head-foot'. Cephalopods are exclusively marine, most are active predators, and all have prehensile tentacles. They move by a form of jet propulsion by forcing water through a muscular funnel.

CEQ See COUNCIL ON ENVIRONMENTAL QUALITY.

CERCLA *See* COMPREHENSIVE ENVIRONMENTAL RESPONSE COMPENSATION, AND LIABILITY ACT.

CERCLIS *See* COMPREHENSIVE ENVIRONMENTAL RESPONSE, COMPENSATION, AND LIABILITY INFORMATION SYSTEM.

cereal A plant in the grass family Poaceae, which produces edible seeds (*grain) These include wheat, oats, barley, rye, rice, maize, sorghum, millet, triticale, buckwheat, and quinoa.

CERFA *See* COMMUNITY ENVIRONMENTAL RESPONSE FACILITATION ACT.

certification Part of the *Clean Development Mechanism agreed by the *Kyoto Protocol by which an accredited body gives written assurance of the emission reductions that have been achieved, which can be confirmed by independent third parties, and which then allows the emissions reduction to become a separate commodity for *emissions trading.

certified emissions reduction A unit of *greenhouse gas reductions that has been achieved and has been subjected to *certification under the *Clean Development Mechanism agreed by the *Kyoto Protocol. *See also* CREDIT; EMISSIONS REDUCTION UNIT.

cesspit/cesspool A covered container, hole, or pit in which untreated *sewage is stored.

cetacean Any member of the order of marine *mammals that includes whales, dolphins, and porpoises.

cetane ($C_{15}H_{34}$) A colourless, liquid *hydrocarbon that is found in *petroleum and is used as an indicator of fuel efficiency for diesel oils.

CFCs *See* CHLOROFLUOROCARBONS.

CGIAR *See* CONSULTATIVE GROUP FOR INTERNATIONAL AGRICULTURAL RESEARCH.

chain reaction 1. A general term for any self-sustaining process. **2.** A nuclear reaction in which the fission of nuclei produces *neutrons that then split other nuclei and the process becomes self-sustaining.

chalk A porous, fine-grained, sedimentary rock made of *calcium carbonate derived predominantly from the shells and skeletons of marine organisms.

chalk grassland A type of *grassland that grows in thin *calcareous soils over *chalk bedrock.

channel 1. (watercourse) A waterway, such as a *stream, *river, or *canal, that contains moving water (continuously or periodically) and has a definite bed and banks. **2.** A narrow seaway, such as the English Channel.

channel bar A ridge of coarse *gravel that is deposited on the bed of rivers with steep slopes, where *flow velocity decreases, for example where a steep *tributary stream flows into the main river.

channel fill The sediment infill of a *channel, produced either by the accretion of sediment transported by water flowing through the channel, or by the infilling of an abandoned channel.

channel improvement (channelization) An engineering scheme that is designed to stabilize a river channel to increase flow speeds, reduce *bank erosion, and/or protect against flooding. This might involve decreasing channel roughness (e.g. by lining the channel with smooth artificial bed and banks), widening and/or deepening the channel (by *dredging), or shortening the channel (by straightening it and cutting off *meander bends).

channel pattern The shape of a river *channel when viewed from above or on a map. There are three main patterns, which are straight, *meandering, and *braided.

channel storage The volume of water that is temporarily stored in a river *channel and its *floodplain while it flows towards an outlet (such as a *lake, *reservoir, or *estuary).

channelization *See* CHANNEL IMPROVEMENT.

chaos The breakdown of predictability, or a state of disorder in a complex system in which patterns exist but they are complicated, not truly *random, and difficult to discover.

chaos theory The mathematical study of complex systems governed by non-linear equations where a small change in one variable produces a large change in another, with the result that the development of the system is acutely sensitive to small variations in starting conditions. Complex systems exhibit discontinuous change that is only partially predictable.

chaparral An *arid *biome in California that is dominated by *broadleaved, *evergreen, drought-resistant *shrub, associated with the climate of hot dry summers and mild wet winters.

char A solid, carbonaceous residue, of high calorific value, derived from incomplete burning of organic material. It may be formed into briquettes and burned for fuel; if pure it can be used as a filter medium. Charcoal is made from wood or bone; coke, another char, is derived from *coal.

character Any recognizable trait, feature, or property of an organism.

character displacement An ecological pattern in which two closely related *species differ more when they live together than when they live apart. The difference is usually morphological (such as head size) and is caused by competition and adaptation to local conditions (such as the size of available *prey).

character type An area of land that has relatively uniform vegetation, geology, hydrology, and topography.

characteristic Any one of the four categories that are used to define *hazardous waste in North America: *corrosivity, *ignitability, *reactivity, and *toxicity.

characteristic diversity The natural pattern of distribution and abundance of *populations, *species, and *habitats in the absence of human impact.

characteristic species *Species that are special to or especially abundant in a particular situation or *biotope, which can usually be easily identified.

characterization The process of determining the scale and nature of a release of a *pollutant, which helps to determine appropriate ways of dealing with it and cleaning it up.

charcoal A very dark grey porous form of *carbon that is made by incomplete burning of wood or bone.

charge An excess or deficiency of *electrons in an *atom.

chattermark *See* STRIATION.

chelate 1. A ring structure comprising a metal ion enclosed within a carbon-based substance. *Haemoglobin and *chlorophyll are chelate compounds in which the metals are iron and magnesium, respectively. **2.** Claw-like or pincer-like.

chelation A reaction in which a metal *ion combines with an organic molecule with more than one bond. Chelation is used to increase

*absorption of mineral *nutrients (such as *calcium and *magnesium), to remove toxic substances (such as *lead and *arsenic), and to prevent the precipitation of metals (*copper).

chemical Any *element, *chemical compound, or mixture of elements and/or compounds.

chemical agent A *chemical that is used for some purpose, particularly to reduce or remove *pollutants from water.

chemical bond The force that holds atoms together in a molecule or crystal.

chemical compound The combination of two or more *elements in defined amounts.

chemical control Using *pesticides and *herbicides to control *pests and unwanted plant species.

chemical decomposition *See* CHEMICAL WEATHERING.

chemical element *See* ELEMENT.

chemical emergency An *emergency created by an accidental release or spill of *hazardous chemicals that threatens the safety of workers, residents, the environment, or property.

chemical energy Energy that is stored in *chemical compounds and released as a result of *chemical reactions.

chemical equilibrium A stable chemical reaction or series of reactions in which the concentrations of all substances remain constant through time.

chemical fixation *See* SOLIDIFICATION.

chemical of concern (COC) In *risk assessment, particularly in the USA, these are particular *chemicals that are identified for evaluation, to determine whether they pose a risk to people or the environment.

chemical of potential concern (COPC) In *risk assessment, particularly in the USA, these are *chemicals identified as possibly posing a risk to people and the environment, which are further investigated.

chemical oxygen demand (COD) A measure of the amount of *oxygen that is required to oxidize all of the *organic and *inorganic compounds in a particular *waterbody. *Biological oxygen demand only measures the oxygen used in breaking down the biodegradable material. *See also* BIOCHEMICAL OXYGEN DEMAND.

chemical partitioning The separation of a *chemical into different media or states. Many metals, for example, are more likely to partition to *sediments than remain in *groundwater.

chemical pollution The introduction of chemical contaminants into air, water, or soil.

chemical precipitate *See* EVAPORITE.

chemical reaction A change in one or more chemical elements or compounds which results in a new compound.

chemical stress The result of a *chemical reaction between two or more materials, such as corrosive materials attacking a metal.

chemical stressor Any *chemical that is released into the environment through human activities (such as industrial waste, vehicle emissions, and pesticides) that can damage or kill plants and animals.

chemical symbol A shorthand way of representing an element, using a one- or two-letter symbol. For example, sodium chloride is represented in chemical symbols as NaCl (Na is sodium and Cl is chlorine).

chemical synthesis The production of complex chemical compounds from simpler ones, for commercial or research purposes.

chemical treatment 1. The use of *chemicals or chemical processes to treat waste materials. **2.** The use of chemicals to control unwanted vegetation. *See also* HERBICIDE.

chemical warfare The use of *chemical agents to kill, injure, or incapacitate the enemy, or to destroy the enemy's crops or vegetation providing cover, during a conflict.

chemical weapon Any chemical substance that can be used to kill or injure people, animals, and plants. A *weapon of mass destruction.

chemical weathering The breaking down of rocks and minerals as a result of *chemical reactions with the surrounding air and water. The most common processes are *oxidation, *carbonation, and *hydrolysis, and decomposition is usually fastest in hot, humid climates. *Contrast* MECHANICAL WEATHERING. *See also* WEATHERING.

chemistry The study of the properties, composition, and structure of matter.

chemoautotroph An organism that uses *inorganic *carbon (*carbon dioxide or *carbonates) as a source of energy for the synthesis of organic matter. *See also* AUTOTROPH; PHOTOAUTOTROPH.

chemoreception The ability to sense changes in the concentration of chemicals in the environment.

chemoreceptor A sense organ that responds to chemical stimuli.

chemosynthesis The process in which chemical energy is used to make *organic compounds from *inorganic compounds, such as the *oxidation of *ammonia to nitrite by *nitrifying bacteria. *Compare* PHOTOSYNTHESIS.

chemotroph An *autotrophic *organism (such as certain *bacteria and cyanobacteria) that obtains energy from *inorganic substances by *oxidation.

chernozem (dark earth) A dark-coloured *soil that is common under *grassland in cool, temperate climates. It is a productive, well-developed soil with a thick *A-horizon which is rich in *organic matter and exchangeable *calcium, and a zone of *calcium carbonate accumulation beneath it.

chert A hard, fine grained siliceous *sedimentary rock that varies in colour between white, pink, brown, and grey.

chestnut blight A disease of American chestnut trees (*Castanea dentata*) caused by a *fungus (*Endothia parasitica*) that was accidentally introduced to the USA around 1900–1908, either in imported chestnut lumber or in imported chestnut trees. By 1940 the disease had made the American chestnut virtually *extinct.

chestnut soil A type of *soil that has a relatively thick, dark brown *A-horizon over a lighter coloured *B-horizon.

Chihuahuan Desert A North American hot *desert, which is located mostly in Mexico but extends into southern New Mexico and Western Texas.

chimney A vertical *flue or *stack.

china clay (kaolin) A fine, pure *clay which is non-plastic and takes the form of a white

CHERNOBYL

A *nuclear power plant in the Ukraine (former Soviet Union) that was the site of the world's worst nuclear power accident in 1986. One of the four *nuclear reactors at the plant was badly damaged by a chemical explosion after it seriously overheated and went out of control. Highly *radioactive and dangerous *fission products poured out uncontrollably into the atmosphere over a period of ten days while the struggle was underway to plug the leak. This material created an invisible radiation cloud which blew over much of Western Europe within days, and many areas were contaminated by dry *fallout (of particles and dust) and when rain washed the material back to the ground. More than 1000 people in the area were injured, 31 were killed, and 135000 people were evacuated from surrounding towns and villages. Up to 100 million people across Europe received some exposure to low levels of radiation (particularly *iodine-131 and *caesium-137) from the accident. The whole world is believed to have received a *radiation dose equivalent to all previous years' fallout from *nuclear weapons, and some individual doses in Britain were equivalent to one year of natural background radiation. In the area around Chernobyl there has since been a dramatic rise in the incidence of thyroid diseases, *anaemia, *cancer, and symptoms of *radiation sickness (including fatigue, loss of vision, and appetite) amongst humans, and some major birth defects among livestock.

powdery material made by the chemical decomposition of *feldspar in *granite.

China Syndrome Non-scientific expression for the meltdown of a nuclear reactor, based on the (impossible) science-fiction idea that an immensely hot damaged reactor could vaporize (melt) its way through the centre of the Earth from the USA to China.

chinook A warm, dry *adiabatic wind that blows down the eastern slopes of the Rocky Mountains in North America. *See also* FOEHN; SANTA ANNA.

Chipko Movement A local *environmental movement that began in India in the early 1980s, when a group of village women engaged in *direct action to save the forest on which their livelihoods depended by literally hugging the trees in order to prevent *deforestation. *See also* ECO-ACTIVISM.

chitin A long chain of *carbohydrates (a polysaccharide) that is used for structural support in *invertebrates, for example in insect *cuticle.

chitin inhibitor An *insecticide that works by stopping the formation of *chitin, so that when the insect starts to moult it dies.

chloramquat A plant growth regulator that is applied to *cereal crops prior to harvest to shorten and strengthen the straw.

chlordane A persistent, broad-spectrum, contact, *organochlorine insecticide that was formerly used on a wide range of crops, and also to kill termites and, in Britain, to kill earth-

worms in turf. Its use is now banned or severely restricted in most countries.

chlormequat A plant growth regulator that inhibits cell elongation and is used to improve resistance to *lodging in *cereals.

chlorides (Cl⁻) 1. The *anions that are formed when the element *chlorine gains an electron. 2. The salts of hydrochloric acid that contain chloride ions.

chlorinated hydrocarbon *See* ORGANO-CHLORINE.

chlorinated solvent An organic solvent that contains *chlorine atoms. Such solvents are used in aerosol spray containers, highway paint, and dry cleaning fluids.

chlorination 1. The addition of *chlorine to drinking water, *sewage, or industrial waste in order to disinfect it or to *oxidize unwanted compounds within it. 2. The addition of *chlorine atoms to compounds by chemical reactions.

chlorine (Cl) A highly reactive *halogen gas that is added to drinking water to kill *bacteria and *algae, and used as a raw material for products such as plastics, pharmaceuticals, and *pesticides. It is a very *toxic *biocide, poisonous to fish and invertebrates, persistent in the environment, and important in the destruction of *ozone.

chlorine demand The quantity of *chlorine that is required to kill all the *pathogens in a sample of water.

chlorocarbon A compound (such as *carbon tetrachloride) that contains *carbon and *chlorine and destroys *ozone.

chlorofluorocarbons (CFCs) A group of odourless, inert, synthetic, non-toxic, and easily liquefied chemical compounds consisting of *chlorine, *fluorine, and *carbon. They are very long-lasting (50 to 200 years) and very efficient absorbers of *infrared radiation. Until the early 1990s CFCs were widely used as propellants in aerosol cans, as refrigerants in refrigerators and air conditioners, and in the manufacture of foam boxes for take-away food cartons. CFCs are important *greenhouse gases that are broken down by strong *ultraviolet light in the *stratosphere and release chlorine atoms that then deplete *ozone. Since the early 1990s most industrial countries (including the USA and UK) agreed under the *Montreal Protocol to phase out production of CFCs and a range of other ozone-depleting chemicals by the year 2000. There are a number of important species of CFC, including CFC-11 and CFC-12 which remain active in the atmosphere for 50 to 100 years. The concentration of all CFCs is now decreasing.

chloroform (trichloromethane) An *organochlorine ($CHCl_3$) used as an industrial solvent and raw material in the manufacture of plastics, refrigerants, synthetic rubber, and resins. Its former use as an anaesthetic was abandoned because the difference between an anaesthetizing dose and a fatal one is small, and exposure to chloroform can cause liver damage and possibly cancer. Chloroform is produced naturally by several species of seaweed.

chloromethane (methyl chloride) A highly flammable, colourless gas (CH_3CL) with a mildly sweet odour that several fungal species and marine *phytoplankton produce naturally; chlorine from this source is a major contributor to free *chlorine in the *stratosphere. It is synthesized industrially for use in the manufacture of silicone polymers, synthetic rubber, and in *petroleum refining. Its former use as a refrigerant was abandoned because of its flammability and toxicity.

chloronicotinyl A systemic form of *insecticide that works by disrupting the central nervous system of an insect.

chlorophyll A green pigment found in plants that absorbs light energy, releasing electrons that provide the energy for *photosynthesis.

chloroplast A structure that is found in some cells of plants and contains *chlorophyll.

chlorosis A discoloration of plant leaves from green to pale green or yellow, where production of *chlorophyll is prevented. It is caused by disease, lack of essential nutrients, or exposure to various air pollutants.

chlorpropham A *carbamate *herbicide that is used to prevent sprouting in stored potatoes and to control germinating weeds.

chlorthiamid A *soil-acting *herbicide that inhibits the formation of cell walls. It is used for total weed control on land and in still or slow-moving water.

CHM *See* CLEARING-HOUSE MECHANISM.

cholera An acute infectious *disease caused by a *bacterium that is transmitted in drinking water contaminated by faeces. It causes severe vomiting and diarrhoea, leading to dehydration and death if left untreated.

chordate A member of the phylum Chordata comprising animals that possess a rod of flexible tissue (notochord) that in many groups is protected by a vertebral column. Tunicates, amphioxus, fish, amphibians, reptiles, birds, and mammals are chordates.

C-horizon The mineral layer beneath the *B-horizon within a *soil profile, which is relatively unaffected by biological activity and is composed of only partially weathered material. *See also* SOIL HORIZON; A-HORIZON.

choropleth map A map showing discrete areas, such as counties, soil units, and vegetation types. Uniform conditions are assured within each map unit.

chromatography An analytical technique that is used for the chemical separation of mixtures and substances.

chromium (Cr) A naturally occurring, hard, brittle, greyish, non-toxic *heavy metal, that is resistant to corrosion and tarnishing. It enters surface waters in wastewater from electroplating operations, leather tanning industries, and textile manufacturing, and is harmful to aquatic organisms. One of eleven *pollutants of concern, it is corrosive to skin and *carcinogenic in humans.

chromosome A package of *genes in the nucleus of a *cell, composed of *DNA and *proteins, which contains the genetic information for that cell. Humans have 46 chromosomes in

23 pairs, and children receive half of their chromosomes from each parent.

chronic Long-lasting or taking a long time to manifest itself. *Contrast* ACUTE.

chronic beryllium disease *See* BERYLLIOSIS.

chronic effect A long-lasting adverse effect on a human or animal (e.g. of exposure to a *toxin) that can result from either one *acute exposure or a period of continuous, low-level exposure.

chronic exposure Continuous or repeated exposure of a human or animal to a hazardous substance over a long period of time, usually at least seven years. *Contrast* ACUTE EXPOSURE.

chronic respiratory disease A persistent or long-lasting intermittent disease of the respiratory tract.

chronic toxicity The effects of repeated or long-term exposure to a *toxic substance, which can often become apparent only after many years. *Contrast* ACUTE TOXICITY.

chronology The order of events according to time. *See also* ABSOLUTE CHRONOLOGY; RELATIVE CHRONOLOGY.

chronosequence A sequence of related *soils that differ because of differences in their ages.

chronostratigraphy The organization of layers of *rock or *sediment into units, based on age or time.

chrysalis The *pupa of a butterfly or moth, which is not covered in silk. *Contrast* COCOON.

CI *See* CONSERVATION INTERNATIONAL.

cinder cone A steep-sided conical hill that is built of coarse *ash material thrown out of a volcano by escaping gases.

circadian rhythm Biological activity that occurs at 24-hour (circa diem) intervals, related to sleep cycles. *See also* DIURNAL.

circle of influence The circular outer edge of a depression in the surface of a *water table that is caused by pumping water from a well. *See also* CONE OF INFLUENCE; CONE OF DEPRESSION.

circle of life The idea that all livings things need other living things to exist and prosper, and so they are all linked together.

circumboreal Found throughout the high latitudes of the northern hemisphere.

circumpolar Found in an area around either the *North Pole or the *South Pole.

cirque Bowl-shaped depression in an upland area, that has been eroded by glacial *quarrying processes at the head of valleys in which *glaciers form. There are many regional names for a cirque, including corrie (Scotland) and cwm (Wales).

cirque glacier A small *glacier within a *cirque.

cirriform High-altitude ice clouds that appear very thin and wispy.

cirrocumulus (Cc) A genus of high *cloud composed entirely of ice crystals that appears as small white patches or sheets arranged in patterns resembling ripples on a beach or, more rarely, in groups or lines. Cirrocumulus forms at 3–8 km and often marks the leading edge of an approaching *cold front.

cirrostratus (Cs) A thin, white *cloud, composed entirely of ice crystals, that looks like a flat sheet. Sometimes it covers the whole sky and is so thin it can hardly be seen. The sun and moon are clearly visible through it, although it can form haloes. These clouds are high, forming between 3 and 8 km, and often indicate the approach of a *warm front.

cirrus (Ci) High, thin, wispy, feather-like *clouds composed entirely of ice crystals that form between 3 and 8 km. Cirrus always has a fibrous appearance.

cistern A small tank that is used to store water for a home or farm, and is often used to store rain water.

CITES *See* CONVENTION ON INTERNATIONAL TRADE IN ENDANGERED SPECIES.

CITES species *Species that are listed under the 1975 *Convention on International Trade in Endangered Species, which cannot be commercially traded as live specimens or wildlife products because they are *endangered or threatened with *extinction.

city A large, densely populated *urban settlement, larger than a *town, which can include two or more independent administrative districts within it and usually has *suburbs.

city planning *See* URBAN PLANNING.

CJD *See* CREUTZFELDT–JAKOB DISEASE.

clade A group of *species which are all descended from a single common ancestor.

cladistic species concept (phylogenetic species concept) The definition of *species as a lineage of populations between two *speciation events (*phylogenetic branch points), based on the branch points not on how much change has occurred between them. *See also* BIOLOGICAL SPECIES CONCEPT; ECOLOGICAL SPECIES CONCEPT; PHENETIC SPECIES CONCEPT; RECOGNITION SPECIES CONCEPT.

cladistics (phylogenetic systematics) A method of classifying *organisms into groups (*taxa) that is based on order of evolutionary branching rather than on present similarities and differences.

cladogenesis The development of a new *clade by the splitting of a single lineage into two distinct lineages which are *taxonomically different. *See also* ADAPTIVE RADIATION; SPECIATION.

cladogram A branching tree diagram, based on *cladistics, that shows the apparent sequence of branching by which individual *clades have come into being and charts the emergence of a particular *taxon or taxa. It shows the sequence but ignores the time-scale of evolutionary divergence.

clarification The clearing action that happens during water treatment when solids settle out. It can be speeded up by *centrifugal action and chemically induced *coagulation.

clarifier (settling basin, sedimentation basin) A tank, used in water treatment, in which solids settle to the bottom and are removed as sludge.

clarity The degree of transparency of a liquid such as water.

Clarke-McNary Act (1924) US legislation that authorized technical and financial assistance to states for forest fire control and for production and distribution of forest tree seedlings. Some sections of the act were repealed by the *Cooperative Forestry Assistance Act (1978).

class 1. In *taxonomy, a group of related and similar orders. It is the category above an *order and below a *phylum, so each phylum may comprise more than one class, and each class may comprise more than one order. **2.** A person's ranking in a social hierarchy, largely based on access to wealth and influence.

class action suit A North American term for a lawsuit in which one or more parties file a complaint seeking damages for injury or loss on behalf of themselves and all other people that have an identical interest in the alleged wrong doing.

Class I area A geographical area designated by the US *Clean Air Act where only a small amount of deterioration, or a small increase in deterioration, of air quality is permitted. Examples include national parks, wilderness areas, monuments, and other areas of special national and cultural significance.

Class I Substance One of several groups of chemicals that have a *global warming potential of 0.2 or higher, including *chlorofluorocarbons and *halons.

Class II Substance A substance that has a *global warming potential of less than 0.2, including *hydrofluorocarbons.

classical economics An economic theory based on the principles that both individuals and society prosper most with a minimum of political intervention, and that the allocation of a scarce resource is best decided through competition for supply and demand of goods and services in the marketplace. This is the foundation of modern, western economic theory and the basis for *capitalism. *Compare* ECOLOGICAL ECONOMICS; ENVIRONMENTAL ECONOMICS. *See also* ECONOMICS.

classification, biological *See* BIOLOGICAL CLASSIFICATION.

clast An individual mineral grain, constituent, or fragment of broken down rock.

clastic Applied to the texture of fragmentary sedimentary rocks.

Claus kiln A device used to recover sulphur from gases rich in hydrogen sulphide (H_2S) by burning the gas in a restricted air supply, giving the reaction $O_2 + 2H_2S \rightarrow 2H_2O + 2S$. The kiln is 95–97% efficient.

clay A fine-grained mineral *soil or *sediment with a *particle size of less than 0.002 mm (greater than 9.0 on the *phi (ϕ) scale).

clay pan A highly compacted *clay soil horizon. *See also* HARDPAN.

clay soil Any soil material that contains more than 40% *clay, less than 45% *sand, and less than 40% *silt.

Clean Air Act (1956, 1968) UK legislation introduced following the first *Great London Smog incident in 1952 in which 4000 people died. The 1956 act identified smokeless zones in which only smokeless fuels could be burned. The 1968 act introduced the use of tall chimneys to disperse pollutants. Both acts were repealed in 1993 and replaced by updated legislation.

Clean Air Act (1963) US legislation that gave the *Environmental Protection Agency authority to set standards for air quality and to control the *emission of *air pollutants from industries, power plants, and cars, in order to protect public health. The act was passed in 1963 and revised in 1970 and 1990. See also ACID RAIN PROGRAM; PREVENTION OF SIGNIFICANT DETERIORATION; NATIONAL EMISSIONS STANDARDS FOR HAZARDOUS AIR POLLUTANTS.

Clean Air Act Amendments (1970) US legislation that built on the *Clean Air Act (1963) and expanded the federal role in setting and enforcing ambient *air quality standards, including regulating land management practices to achieve and maintain such standards. It set *emissions standards for stationary sources (such as factories and power plants), motor vehicles (automobiles and trucks), *criteria pollutants (including *lead, *ozone, *carbon monoxide, *sulphur dioxide, *nitrogen oxides, and *particulate matter), and *toxic pollutants.

Clean Air Act Amendments (1977) US legislation that amended the *Clean Air Act (1963) by establishing the national goal of preventing any future reduction of visibility of Class I federal areas (which include all International Parks, all National Wilderness Areas that exceed 5000 acres, all National Memorial Parks that exceed 5000 acres, and all National Parks that exceed 6000 acres) from *air pollution caused by humans.

Clean Air Act Amendments (1990) US legislation that builds on the *Clean Air Act Amendments (1977) in an attempt to reduce *smog and *air pollution, particularly by dealing with problems such as *acid rain and *ozone depletion. The law allows the *Environment Protection Agency to set limits on how much of a particular pollutant can be in the air anywhere in the USA, but it allows individual states to have stronger pollution controls, and requires them to develop state implementation plans

which detail how they aim to achieve the national targets.

Clean Development Mechanism (CDM) One of the *flexibility mechanisms defined in the *Kyoto Protocol for dealing with *air pollution by *greenhouse gases. This involves a project between a developed country and a developing county in which the former is helped to comply with its *emissions reduction commitments in return for providing the latter with financing and technology to help with sustainable development. See also EMISSIONS TRADING; BUBBLE.

clean fuel *Alternative fuels such as *gasohol, *natural gas, and *liquefied petroleum gas, which emit less pollution than conventional fuels such as *gasoline and *diesel.

Clean Water Act (1972) US legislation that regulates water pollution. It gave the *Environment Protection Agency the right to set and enforce uniform national standards of water quality in order to restore and maintain the chemical, physical, and biological integrity of US surface waters.

cleanup The treatment or *remediation of an area of material that has been contaminated with a hazardous substance. See also CORRECTIVE ACTION; ENVIRONMENTAL RESTORATION.

clear A sky condition of less than one-tenth cloud cover.

clear air turbulence (CAT) Vertical air currents in unstable air that is unsaturated and, therefore, free from cloud (clear). There are several causes, the commonest being *wind shear associated with the *jet stream. Occasionally CAT can cause violent shaking of aircraft.

Clear Skies Initiative (2002) An initiative from US President George Bush designed to create a mandatory programme that would dramatically reduce emissions of *sulphur dioxide (SO_2), *nitrogen oxides (NO_x), and *mercury from *power plants, by setting a national limit on each *pollutant.

clear well A reservoir for the storage of previously treated *potable water, before it is distributed to users.

clearance A patch of land that has been cleared of vegetation in order to prevent the spread of *wildfires.

clearcut 1. A forest management technique in which all or most of the trees are felled and removed at one time. **2.** A previously forested area after all or most of the trees have been removed by *clearcutting.

clearcutting The practice of felling and removing most or all of the trees in a stand of *forest at the same time. *See also* DEFORESTATION.

clearing 1. A relatively small treeless area in the middle of a *wood or *forest. **2.** The process of disposing of undergrowth and debris left after trees have been felled and trimmed, usually by burning it.

clearing index *See* VENTILATION INDEX.

clearing-house A service or organization associated with an exchange between a large number of traders, where trades are confirmed, matched, and settled.

Clearing-House Mechanism (CHM) An international network of agencies that work together to implement the *United Nations Framework Convention on Biological Diversity by compiling and exchanging information on biodiversity around the world, and by promoting technical and scientific cooperation at all levels.

cleavage The ability of a *mineral or rock to split (cleave) along planes of weakness.

cleavage plane The smooth flat surface along which *minerals or rocks tend to break (*cleavage).

cleptobiosis (lestobiosis) An association between *species that is found in some social organisms, in which one species steals food from the stores of another species but does not live or nest close to it.

cliff A very steep, high face of rock, sediment, or soil, which might be vertical or even overhanging.

CLIMAP *See* CLIMATE, LONG RANGE INVESTIGATION, MAPPING AND PREDICTION PROJECT.

climate The long-term average *weather conditions of a place, in terms of *precipitation, *temperature, *humidity, sunshine, and *wind velocity and phenomena such as *fog, *frost, and *hail storms. These are determined by factors that are fixed through time, such as latitude, position relative to oceans or continents, and altitude. Climate changes from place to place, but much more slowly than weather because *climate zones are usually quite large. It also changes through time, again much

more slowly than weather, over decades rather than days.

climate change Any natural or induced change in *climate, either globally or in a particular area. Examples include the natural climate change that has caused *ice ages in the past, and *global warming that many believe is now being caused by rising concentrations of *greenhouse gases in the *atmosphere. By AD 1700 most of the standard *meteorological instruments that are used to measure *temperature, *precipitation, and other climate variables had been invented (they have since been greatly improved), although good quality records going back centuries are available for only a few sites. Direct measurements of *weather have been collected regularly only since about the 1850s, and many parts of the world (particularly in the tropics and southern hemisphere) only have records covering much shorter periods available. Long-term changes in climate can be reconstructed using historical evidence, and geological and biological *proxy indicators which include analysis of *ice cores, oxygen *isotope analysis, *pollen analysis, and *dendroclimatology.

Climate Change Convention *See* UNITED NATIONS FRAMEWORK CONVENTION ON CLIMATE CHANGE.

Climate Change Levy A tax on the use of energy in industry, commerce, and the public sector in the UK, which is designed to encourage these sectors to make more efficient use of energy and to assist the UK to meet its reduced *greenhouse gas emissions commitments under the *Kyoto Protocol. There are different rates of levy for electricity generated from gas, coal, and liquefied petroleum gas. The levy came into effect on 1 April 2001 and is a key part of the UK Government's overall climate change programme. It is expected to lead to reductions in *carbon dioxide emissions of at least 2.5 million tonnes of carbon a year by 2010.

Climate Change Protocol A series of international meetings held in Bonn, Germany between 1995 and 1997 to decide how best to address the problems associated with *greenhouse gas emissions and *global warming. It led to the *Kyoto Protocol.

climate lag The delay or time it takes for any factor that promotes *climate change (such as an increase or decrease in *greenhouse gas emissions) to produce a change that can be measured. Delay is often caused by *adjustment and *feedback in complex *environmental systems.

climate model A simulation of how the *climate system works, usually using large and complex computer programs that are based on mathematical equations derived from knowledge of the physics that governs the Earth–atmosphere system. *See also* GENERAL CIRCULATION MODEL.

climate modification Changes of the climate that can occur as a result of either natural processes (such as *volcanic eruptions, *El Niño–Southern Oscillation events, or *sunspot activity) or human activities (such as the effects of *pollution and *deforestation). *See also* CLIMATE CHANGE.

climate normal Weather conditions averaged over a period, usually 30 years, to yield a description of the *climate of a particular place, region, or the world.

climate sensitivity A measure of how rapidly and strongly the Earth's climate is likely to react to increases or decreases in radiation (*radiative forcing), such as those caused by the greenhouse effect, and reach a new *equilibrium state. *See also* SENSITIVITY.

climate system The five interacting environmental systems (*atmosphere, *hydrosphere, *cryosphere, *lithosphere, and *biosphere) that are responsible for the climate and its variations.

climate zone An area with generally consistent climatic characteristics. From the equator towards the poles there are the *tropical, *mid-latitude, *subpolar, and *arctic climates.

Climate, Long Range Investigation, Mapping and Prediction project (CLI-MAP) An international research project during the 1970s and 1980s that reconstructed the Earth's climate over the last million years and produced maps of sea-surface temperature at various periods, based on analysis of *proxy data from ocean sediment cores.

Climategate A scandal that began in November 2009 when more than 1000 emails together with more than 3000 text files, data processing programs, and other documents from the Climatic Research Unit (CRU) of the University of East Anglia, UK, were released on to the World Wide Web. Written over a period of 13 years, the information revealed the tactics climate modellers used to avoid releasing their data to outsiders under freedom of information laws, even to the extent of deleting data rather than releasing it, the contempt they showed for those who disagreed with them, and their willingness to discredit and attempt to boycott journals that published papers by their opponents. They also appeared to show that the scientists were prepared to select and modify data to make it support their global-warming theory. A second, larger batch of emails was released in 2011, adding further details.

climatic analogue A climatic event or situation from the past that displays similar characteristics to one occurring in the present. Comparing the two is often helpful in projecting how the present event might develop in the future. *See also* ANALOGUE.

climatic anomaly The deviation or departure of a particular climatic variable from the norm, as defined over a specified period of time.

climatic climax *See* CLIMAX COMMUNITY.

Climatic Optimum (Atlantic Period) The warm, moist, climatic phase during the *Holocene, between about 7500 and 5200 years ago, when average global temperatures were 1–2°C warmer than they are today, glaciers and ice sheets receded greatly from their post-glacial maximum, and the *meltwater raised sea level by about three metres. *See also* ALTITHERMAL; HYPSITHERMAL.

climatology The study of *climate, climate processes, and *climate change.

climax community (climatic climax, climax vegetation) The natural vegetation that exists in an area at the end of a *succession. This develops over a long enough period of time without major environmental change or human interference, for example *woodland in a *temperate area. Climax is indicated by a *community of vegetation that is stable, self-maintaining, self-reproducing, and in *equilibrium with its environment. Its species composition is stable through time, so long as its environment remains unchanged, because the growth of other species is inhibited by competition for food, energy, *nutrients, and space. It would normally take a long time to re-establish a climax community if it is destroyed or seriously damaged. *See also* BIOME; FIRE-CLIMAX COMMUNITY.

climax forest A forest *community that represents the final stage (*climax community) of natural forest *succession for its *environment.

climax vegetation *See* CLIMAX COMMUNITY.

climber A vine or climbing plant that grows up surrounding structures such as the branches of trees and shrubs for support and in order to raise its foliage and flowers above the ground.

cline A gradual change in a population of a species over a geographical area. It is genetically based and shows *adaptation to an *environmental gradient.

clint A flat surface in a *limestone pavement. Clints are separated by widened fissures called grikes.

clique A group of species that has a similar diet but is different from other such groups.

clod A compact mass of *soil produced by disturbance such as digging or ploughing.

clone A genetically identical copy of an *organism, derived from creating or reproducing a group of *cells or *DNA molecules from a single parent or ancestor. Most *plants, *fungi, *algae, and many other organisms naturally reproduce by making clones of themselves.

cloning The process of making genetically identical copies (*clones) of a *gene or *organism. Cloning is an essential element in *genetic engineering and *biotechnology. Growing cuttings from a plant is a traditional form of cloning.

close management measure Any technique that is used to aid the *reintroduction and establishment of viable populations of a species into its natural *habitat, such as artificial nesting boxes.

closed area An area that is closed to people, where specified activities are temporarily restricted, or where resource extraction (including harvesting) is temporarily or permanently banned, except by special permit for specific purposes.

closed canopy The condition of a *woodland or *forest in which tree *crowns overlap, shading the forest floor. *See also* CROWN CLOSURE.

closed forest A forest with a *closed canopy.

closed season A specified period of time each year during which particular *game species (such as certain fish) cannot be legally caught.

closed system A *system that can exchange energy but not matter with its surroundings. The global *water cycle is a closed system because there is a fixed amount of material (water) within the system, and the circulation of water is maintained by energy from the Sun (which is imported across the system boundary). *Contrast* OPEN SYSTEM.

closed-loop recycling The reuse of *wastewater for purposes other than drinking in an enclosed process.

closure 1. Any structure that is designed to close off the opening of a container and prevent loss of its contents. **2.** In North America, the process of preparing a *landfill site for closure, which involves covering it with soil and vegetation such as grass.

CLOUD An experiment (Cosmics Leaving OUtdoor Droplets) conducted at the European Organization for Nuclear Research (CERN) to study the influence of galactic *cosmic radiation on the generation of *cloud condensation nuclei and, therefore, of clouds, and the resulting effect on the global climate. The first results showed that the presence of ammonia at concentrations of 100 parts per trillion or less increased the formation of sulphuric acid particles by more than 100–1000 times, and that cosmic radiation increases *aerosol formation in the mid troposphere, but is negligible near the surface. The experiment therefore supported, but did not prove, the hypothesis that changes in solar activity affecting the *solar wind and, through that, the intensity of cosmic radiation penetrating the atmosphere, may be responsible for *climate change, including the late 20th-century warming.

(🌐) SEE WEB LINKS

• CLOUD home page.

cloud A mass of water droplets and/or ice crystals in the air, formed by *condensation of *water vapour around nuclei such as dust, salt, and soil particles as a mass of air rises and cools. There are three main types of cloud: *stratus, *cumulus, and *cirrus.

cloud base The bottom of a cloud measured as its distance above sea level.

cloud condensation nuclei Aerosols (including sea salts and byproducts of combustion) on which water vapour condenses to form *cloud droplets.

cloud cover The extent of *cloud in the sky at a given place and time, which is usually measured in eighths. A coverage of four-eighths means that half the sky is covered by cloud.

cloud deck The top of a *cloud layer, usually viewed from an aircraft.

cloud droplet A particle of liquid water that is created by the *condensation of *water vapour onto a *cloud condensation nucleus. Cloud droplets are typically 10 micrometres in size, there are usually about 100 000 in every litre of air, and they fall at about 1 cm s^{-1}. An average raindrop comprises about one million cloud droplets.

cloud forest A high mountain forest in which the temperature remains uniformly cool and fog or mist keep vegetation permanently damp. It is covered in cloud for most of the day.

cloud seeding (artificial rain) The deliberate introduction of artificial substances (usually silver iodide or *dry ice) into a *cloud in order to change the way it develops or to increase *precipitation, as a form of *weather modification.

cloud street A row of *clouds that are aligned parallel to the wind.

cloud type A classification of clouds. Clouds are classified by height into low, middle, and high. Low clouds, with bases from ground level up to about 2000 m, are the genera *stratus, *cumulus, *cumulonimbus, and *stratocumulus. Middle clouds, with bases between 2000 and 8000 m, are the genera *nimbostratus, *altostratus, and *altocumulus. High clouds, which form between 3000 m and 8000 m, are the genera *cirrocumulus, *cirrostratus, and *cirrus. In addition, clouds are classified by their appearance into ten basic types or genera, the genera are divided into fourteen species and these into nine varieties, to which accessory clouds and supplementary cloud features may be joined.

cloudburst A sudden, heavy shower of rain, that is usually intense but short-lasting. It occurs when the warm updraughts sustaining a cumulonimbus cloud fail and the cloud releases all its moisture as it dissipates.

cloudy The state of the sky when nine-tenths or more is covered by *clouds.

Club of Rome A non-profit, non-governmental, global *think-tank that brings together scientists, business people, and bureaucrats who share an interest in tackling what the Club calls the *world problematique. One of its most famous reports is *Limits to Growth.

SEE WEB LINKS
• Club of Rome home page.

cluster zoning A type of *open space zoning that allows a developer to reduce the minimum residential lot size below that required in the *zoning ordinance, if the land so gained is preserved as permanent open space for the community.

clutch A number of birds that are hatched at the same time.

CNG See COMPRESSED NATURAL GAS.

cnidarian A member of the phylum (Cnidaria) that includes the sea anemones, jellyfish, and corals. These are radially symmetrical animals that have tentacles with which they capture food. All are aquatic and most are marine.

CO See CARBON MONOXIDE.

co-adaptation The evolution, by *natural selection, of characteristics in two or more *species that are to their mutual advantage.

coagulant Any chemical that helps *colloidal particles to group together irreversibly to form larger masses. For example, chemicals such as *lime, *alum, and iron salts are often added to *wastewater to help settle out impurities.

coagulation The process in which *colloidal particles group together irreversibly to form larger clusters.

coal A *carbonaceous deposit that forms from the remains of *fossil plants. The plants are deposited initially as *peat, which (after compaction and burial) undergoes physical and chemical changes and is progressively turned into coal, to produce the *coal series. Coal is the dirtiest of the *fossil fuels when burned, and it contributes to the atmosphere a significant amount of *particles and *aerosols, *greenhouse gases, and *sulphur dioxide. There are much bigger reserves of coal and *lignite in the world than there are of *oil and *natural gas. Roughly half (48%) of the world's known coal reserves are in the former Soviet Union, Eastern Europe, and China, and there are also sizeable reserves in Western Europe (9%), Africa (6%), North America (26%), and Australia and Asia (9%). Known reserves are thought to be large enough to meet projected world demand for up to the next 500 years, but the life expectancy will fall sharply if large amounts of coal are used to make synthetic liquid fuels as a substitute for oil. See also ANTHRACITE; BITUMINOUS COAL.

coal cleaning technology The physical or chemical treatment of *coal before it is burned, in order to remove some of its *sulphur content and thus help to reduce *sulphur dioxide emissions (to reduce *acid rain). *See also* COAL WASHING.

coal gasification The conversion, by heating and partial combustion, of *coal into gases such as *methane and *carbon monoxide. It is an efficient fuel that produces less *air pollution than burning unmodified coal. Coal gasification was a major energy source in the 19th and early 20th centuries but production declined after the availability of *natural gas increased in the 1970s. *Coal tar was a byproduct.

coal liquefaction The conversion of coal into a liquid *hydrocarbon fuel such as synthetic gasoline or methanol.

coal measures A *stratigraphic unit that usually contains coal, occurring in the upper *Carboniferous in Europe (the Pennsylvanian in North America).

coal seam gas Natural gas (mainly methane) that is held by *adsorption in the pores in coal seams, from which it is extracted by drilling into the seam, releasing the pressure under which the gas is held.

coal series The different types of *coal, ranging from *peat, through *bitumen and *lignite, to *anthracite. Successive coals in the series contains less *volatiles, fewer *volatiles, and more *carbon.

coal tar A thick black liquid *hydrocarbon that is distilled from *coal and contains organic chemicals. *See also* COAL GASIFICATION.

coal washing A *coal cleaning technology that involves crushing coal and washing soluble sulphur compounds out of it with water or other solvents.

Coalition for Vehicle Choice A US non-profit *anti-environmental *front group, based in Washington, DC, that was 'created to preserve the freedom of Americans to choose motor vehicles that meet their needs and their freedom to travel'. It claims a membership of more than 40000 state and local organizations and individuals, including vehicle and tyre manufacturers.

coarse filter approach An approach to the *conservation of *biodiversity that involves maintaining a diversity of structures within stands and a diversity of *ecosystems across the landscape, in order to meet most of the habitat requirements of most of the native species. *See also* FINE FILTER APPROACH.

coarse woody debris Bits of wood, including rotting logs and stumps, that provide *habitat for plants, animals, and insects, and *nutrients for soil development.

coarse-grained 1. A *rock that has large (5 mm to 3 cm) grains or crystals. **2.** Ecological processes or factors that occur in large patches relative to the activity patterns of an *organism. *See also* FINE-GRAINED.

coast The zone where the land meets the sea, which is the boundary between *terrestrial and *marine *environmental systems.

coastal defence (coastal protection) Any activity or structure that is designed to protect a coastal area from erosion and/or flooding. Examples include engineering schemes such as sea walls and embankments.

coastal flooding The flooding of coastal areas by seawater, usually caused by unusually high *tides and/or *storm surges.

coastal pelagic fish Fish (such as mackerel, anchovies, and sardines) that live in the sea at or near the surface of the water but remain relatively close to the coast.

coastal plain A low-lying, relatively flat area of land beside the sea.

coastal processes The action of natural forces on the *shore and the nearshore sea bed.

coastal protection *See* COASTAL DEFENCE.

coastal reef A *coral reef that is located close to the *coast. *Contrast* FRINGING REEF.

coastal upwelling A process driven by winds blowing from land to sea that occurs along many coasts, especially on the western sides of continents. The wind produces an *Ekman effect which causes cold water from the deep ocean to rise to the surface. This brings *nutrients (particularly *nitrates and *phosphates) to the surface, which sustain *plankton at the base of the marine *food chain.

coastal wetland A *wetland habitat (such as a *tidal marsh, *lagoon, *tidal flat, or *mangrove swamp) that is found along a coastline and is covered with saltwater from the ocean for all or part of the year.

coastal zone The shallow part of the ocean that extends from the high-tide mark on land to the edge of the *continental shelf, and in which *marine and *terrestrial *environmental systems interact with one another. *Contrast* OPEN SEA.

Coastal Zone Management Act (1972) (CZMA) US legislation designed to encourage 30 seacoast and Great Lakes states to develop coastal management programmes. The Act established a method for the federal government to approve states' plans and funding for approved plans, and it requires federal actions to be consistent with the states' plans.

coastline (shoreline) The boundary between the land and sea.

cobalt (Co) A magnetic metallic element that is soluble in water. It is one of eight *trace elements that plants and animals require, and an important *catalyst in *nitrogen fixation.

cobble A rock or particle of sediment that has a *particle size between 64 and 256 mm (−6.0 to −8.0 on the *phi (ϕ) scale).

COC *See* CHEMICAL OF CONCERN.

cocoon A covering that protects the eggs and larvae of many *insects, such as the spinning of a silk sheath by larvae of moths, in which pupae develop. *Contrast* CHRYSALIS.

COD *See* CHEMICAL OXYGEN DEMAND.

Codex Alimentarius Commission A body established in 1963 by the *FAO and *WHO that develops and publishes international standards, guidelines, and codes of practice to protect consumers and ensure fair practices in the food trade.

(⊕) SEE WEB LINKS

• Home page of the Codex Alimentarius Commission.

codominant 1. Trees or shrubs with *crowns that receive full light from above but relatively little from the sides, and whose crowns usually form the general level of the canopy. **2.** A heterozygote (*see* HETEROZYGOSITY) that shows the full phenotypic effects of both *alleles at a *gene *locus.

co-evolution *Evolution in two or more *species that interact, in which the adaptive changes of each species influence those of the other.

coffin (cask) A thick-walled container, usually made of lead, that is used for the safe transport of *radioactive materials.

cogeneration (combined heat and power) The generation of two different and useful forms of energy (usually electricity and heat as steam or hot water) at the same time, from a single fuel source.

cohesion The force of attraction which holds like molecules or soil particles together.

cohort A group of individuals of similar age.

cohort study *See* PROSPECTIVE STUDY.

coke A hard, dry *carbon substance that is produced by heating *coal to a very high temperature in the absence of air.

col 1. A notch or natural pass cut through a mountain ridge, usually by *glacial erosion, such as an *arête between two back-to-back *cirques. **2.** A region of low *atmospheric pressure that is found between two high-pressure or two low-pressure systems.

Colburn, Theo Senior scientist and director of the Wildlife and Contaminants project at the *World Wildlife Fund, pioneer of low-dose toxicity research, and co-author of the book *Our Stolen Future*. Regarded by some as a latter-day Rachel *Carson.

cold cloud A cloud that contains only ice crystals. *Compare* MIXED CLOUD; WARM CLOUD.

cold desert A *desert that is hot or warm in the summer and cold in the winter, such as the Gobi Desert. *Contrast* HOT DESERT.

cold front A frontal boundary between two *air masses that advances with the air behind the front cooler than the air ahead of the front. *Contrast* WARM FRONT. *See also* FRONT; FRONTAL LIFTING.

cold occlusion *See* OCCLUDED FRONT.

cold pole The place that has the lowest annual mean temperature in its *hemisphere. The cold pole in the southern hemisphere is at Vostok Station (78.46°S 106.87°E); the northern hemisphere cold pole is at Verkhoyansk, Siberia (67.57°N 133.85°E), with a second cold pole at Snag, Yukon (62.37°N 140.40°W).

cold sector The region of cold air that partially surrounds the *warm sector in a *depression.

cold-blooded Applied to an *ecotherm or *poikilotherm.

cold-water fishery A lake or stream that supports species of fish (such as salmon and trout) which are intolerant of sustained water temperatures higher than about 21°C in the summer.

coliform bacteria *Bacteria such as *E. coli and *Salmonella* that live in the gastrointestinal tracts of vertebrates and indicate the presence of *faeces in water, exposure to which causes diseases such as *cholera.

coliform index A measure of the purity of water based on a count of how many faecal bacteria are present within a given volume of it.

coliforms See COLIFORM BACTERIA.

Collection and Disposal of Waste Regulations 1988 In Britain, the legislation that defines categories of waste and stipulates licensing for the disposal of scrap metal and the recycling of solvents and waste oil.

colliery A coal mine and associated coal processing facilities.

collision theory 1. A theory of chemical reactivity. Collision theory assumes that, in order for reaction to occur, molecules must collide with at least some minimum energy and with proper orientation. 2. A description of the way raindrops form in *warm clouds, as descending large droplets coalesce with smaller droplets, which fall more slowly.

collision zone The zone along which adjacent convergent *crustal plates push into each other. See also PLATE TECTONICS.

colloid A suspension in a liquid of tiny particles, that neither dissolve nor settle.

colluvial Composed of or relating to *colluvium. Compare ALLUVIAL.

colluvial deposit See COLLUVIUM.

colluvium (colluvial deposit) Loosely compacted sediment that has moved downhill and accumulated on the lower slopes and at the bottom of a *hill, as a result of *weathering, *erosion, and *mass movement processes. Compare ALLUVIUM.

colonial Of or relating to a *colony.

colonization 1. The establishment of a new *colony. 2. The arrival and establishment of plants and animals on a new area of land. See also ISLAND BIOGEOGRAPHY; SUCCESSION.

colony 1. A group of organisms of the same *species that live together, such as *algae, sea-birds, or people. See also AGGREGATION. 2. A geographical area that is politically controlled by a distant country.

co-management An approach to the management of natural resources which is based on the sharing of authority, responsibility, and benefits on a cooperative basis, either informally or legally, between different stakeholders, such as local government and local communities.

combined heat and power See COGENERATION.

combined sewer A sewer system that carries both *sewage and storm-water *runoff.

combustion Burning (rapid *oxidation) of fuel, which releases energy in the form of heat and light, and also releases pollutants (such as *sulphur dioxide, *nitrogen oxides, and *particulates).

combustion chamber A place where *combustion takes place, for example in an *incinerator or an *internal combustion engine. See also FURNACE.

combustion nucleus A *condensation nucleus that is formed as a result of *combustion.

comet A small astronomical object similar to an *asteroid but made largely of ice.

command and control An approach to *environmental regulation that relies on the ability of the state to regulate (*control) the behaviour of individuals, companies, and other groups by setting and imposing controls, rather than by *market-based mechanisms. Control is usually exercised through *legislation, introduction of *regulations that require specific action, and setting targets and defining how to meet them, sometimes including what technologies to adopt (for example in order to regulate emissions of *pollutants). Contrast ALTERNATIVE COMPLIANCE.

commensal A *parasite that benefits from, but does not harm, its host.

commensalism A form of *symbiosis between two different species in which one benefits and the other neither benefits nor is harmed, e.g. when *epiphytes use other plants for support.

commensurable Values or benefits that can be measured by a common standard (for example in dollars or cubic metres) and objectively compared. *Contrast* INCOMMENSURABLE.

commercial forestland *See* TIMBERLAND.

commercial reactor A *nuclear reactor that is used for commercial purposes to generate electricity, rather than for military purposes or scientific research.

commercial sector Non-manufacturing parts of the *economy, which includes leisure and recreation, health, and education. *See also* INDUSTRIAL SECTOR; RESIDENTIAL SECTOR; TRANSPORTATION SECTOR.

commercial thinning In *forest management, cutting and selling trees that are large enough to be sold as products (for example as poles or fence posts), which thins the forest and helps to improve the health and rate of growth of the crop trees that remain.

commercial waste All *solid waste that is generated by businesses (which includes stores, markets, office buildings, restaurants, shopping centres, and theatres).

commercial waste management facility A facility that accepts waste (for treatment, storage, disposal, or transfer) from a variety of sources, unlike a private facility which usually manages waste that it generates itself.

commercial whaling The hunting of *whales in order to sell whale products.

commercial/industrial land A North American category of *land use that covers land used primarily for buying, selling, and processing goods and services. This includes sites for stores, factories, shopping centres, and industrial parks.

commingled recyclables Mixed waste materials that can be *recycled and are collected together.

comminution 1. The shredding or pulverizing of waste in order to reduce its size, as used in *solid waste management and *wastewater treatment. 2. The extraction of valuable *minerals from their *ores by crushing and grinding.

commission 1. The granting of authority to undertake certain functions (for example, to open and operate a *nuclear plant that has been built). *Contrast* DECOMMISSION. 2. A special group that has been set up and authorized to consider some particular matter, such as the

*Independent Commission on International Development and the *Commission on Sustainable Development.

Commission on Sustainable Development (CSD) *See* UNITED NATIONS COMMISSION ON SUSTAINABLE DEVELOPMENT.

commitment (environmental commitment) The *environmental change that will inevitably occur at some time in the future as a result of human activities that have already taken place because of lags (such as *climate lags) in *environmental systems, or that are likely to occur in a *business-as-usual scenario. *See also* EQUILIBRIUM WARMING COMMITMENT.

Commitment Period (Budget Period, Compliance Period) The period of time, defined in the *Kyoto Protocol, during which a country's average level of emissions of *greenhouse gases must be kept within the agreed emission targets. The first Commitment Period covered 2008–12.

commodity Any good that is traded (bought and sold).

Common Agricultural Policy (CAP) A set of regulations and practices, adopted by members states of the *European Union, designed to provide a common, unified policy framework for *agriculture. The overall aim is to increase farm productivity, stabilize markets, ensure a fair standard of living for farmers, guarantee regular supplies, and ensure reasonable prices for consumers. *See also* SET-ASIDE.

common ancestor A species from which two or more different species have evolved.

common law An unwritten body of *law that is based on general custom and usage, and which is recognized and enforced by the courts.

Common Market The original (pre-1994) name for the *European Union.

common name The familiar, non-scientific name for a species of plant or animal, which is widely used. This can vary within and between countries, so there may be many common names for a particular species. *Compare* LATIN NAME.

common property resource *See* COMMON RESOURCE.

common property resource management The management of a particular local *common resource (such as a forest or pasture) by a well-defined group of resource users who have the authority to regulate its use by members and outsiders.

common resource A resource (such as the air, migratory birds, fish in the oceans, and wilderness areas) which is not privately owned. Rights of use are communally shared, so it is freely available, at least in theory, to anybody who wants to use it. *See also* TRAGEDY OF THE COMMONS.

common variety mineral A natural material such as sand, stone, gravel, and clay that has no market value as a metal or for energy production, which is often extracted in large amounts and used by the construction industry.

Commoner, Barry US cellular biologist (born 1917), author of *Science and Survival*, proposer of the four *'laws of ecology', and an influential writer who helped to initiate the modern *environmental movement.

commons An area of open land in which certain persons (commoners) have specified rights, e.g. to pasture livestock, gather fuel, etc., the overall management of the commons being the responsibility of a committee of commoners. *See also* COMMON RESOURCE; TRAGEDY OF THE COMMONS.

communal resource management system Resources that are managed by a community for long-term sustainability.

community (ecological community) A group of plant and animal populations that live together in a given area, are adapted to local environmental conditions, and interact with each other. *See also* CLIMAX COMMUNITY.

community based conservation A bottom-up (*grassroots based) approach to conservation, usually within the context of *ecosystem management, that is based on two broad concepts—that people who participate in decision-making will be more inclined to implement agreed outcomes, and that people are quite capable of deciding for themselves what the most appropriate solutions should be, provided they are given sufficient information and support. *See also* COMMUNITY BASED NATURAL RESOURCE MANAGEMENT.

community based natural resource management (CBNRM) An approach to the management of *natural resources that is based on engagement with local communities, as a means of focusing attention on natural resource problems or opportunities that require action at community level or that involve the management of shared resources (such as land, forest, water resources, fisheries, and wildlife). *See also* COMMUNITY BASED CONSERVATION.

community based planning An approach to *urban planning which engages citizens and local communities as stakeholders in the development of comprehensive neighbourhood plans.

community ecology The study of the interactions between the populations of organisms within a particular *ecosystem.

Community Environmental Response Facilitation Act (CERFA) A 1992 law in the USA that requires the Federal Government to identify land that it owns that is not contaminated with *hazardous substances and that can be made available for public use with a minimum of *cleanup.

community forestry An approach to *forestry management that includes local people and takes their needs into account. It includes the establishment of village woodlots, *farm forestry, tree planting in private fields, and joint management of forests by communities and governments. *See also* SOCIAL FORESTRY.

community involvement An inclusive and democratic approach to planning and management that allows all *stakeholders to have their concerns heard and taken seriously, by giving them access to reliable and up-to-date information and allowing them to exercise their right to have their say and to protest against decisions they are unhappy with.

community right-to-know Making information about environmental threats (particularly toxic pollution) readily available to anyone who would like access to it.

Community-Right-To-Know Act (EPCRA) (1986) US legislation on community safety, which was designated to help local communities protect public health, safety, and the environment from chemical hazards. It is based on local emergency planning committees for each district which include representation by fire fighters, health officials, government and media representatives, community groups, industrial facilities, and emergency managers.

community services land A North American category of *land use that covers land used primarily for schools, hospitals, churches, libraries, sewerage and water treatment plants, sanitary land fills, public parking areas, and other community service facilities.

compaction Decrease in volume caused by *compression.

comparative risk assessment A comparison of the *risks associated with two or more *hazards, judged by experts using a common scale.

compartment A subdivision of a site or area, for example a particular part of a *forest or *nature reserve, that is recognized in management plans.

compatible Able to exist together harmoniously. *Contrast* INCOMPATIBLE.

compatible use Different uses of land or other resources which are harmonious and can exist together in the same area, so that one does not inhibit or adversely affect another. *Contrast* INCOMPATIBLE USE. *See also* COMPLEMENTARY USES.

compensation level/point The point within a *water column at which plant *photosynthesis just equals plant *respiration. It defines the lower boundary of the *euphotic zone.

compensatory restoration *See* MITIGATION.

competence The ability of water, ice, or air to carry particles of a given size. The competence value is defined by the *viscosity of the medium, so ice has the highest competence and wind the lowest.

competent authority A government agency that is responsible for regulating complex things such as *biotechnology, *biosafety, and *intellectual property rights.

competition Interaction between two or more organisms in the same space, where each requires the same resource (such as food, water, or space) which has a limited supply and where the presence of each is in some way harmful to the other(s). Competition can occur within (*intraspecific competition) and between species (*interspecific competition) and it is an important factor in *adaptation and *evolution by *natural selection.

competitive consumerism A competitive form of *consumerism, driven by the quest for unlimited control of *resources for personal use.

competitive exclusion principle (Gause's principle) The principle that two or more species that utilize the same resources in the same way and whose numbers are limited by resource availability cannot coexist in a stable environment, because one of the species will out-compete or otherwise eliminate the other(s).

complementary uses Different uses of land or other resources, each of which benefits from the other(s) where they exist together in the same area.

complex terrain Any highly variable land surface (*terrain), particularly mountains.

compliance coal (low sulphur coal) Any *coal that meets *sulphur dioxide emission standards for air quality without the need for *flue gas desulphurization.

compliance monitoring Monitoring that is done to ensure that statutory requirements (such as limits on the amount of a particular *pollutant that can be emitted) are met.

Compliance Period *See* COMMITMENT PERIOD.

compliance schedule An agreement that has been negotiated between a polluter and a government agency, which details dates and procedures by which *emissions will be reduced in order to comply with a regulation.

component An identifiable, functional part of a *system that is defined for a particular reason. Within an *ecosystem, for example, this could be a *species, a *habitat, an individual organism, or even part of an individual, depending on the purpose of the study.

composition The relative proportion of space or *biomass that is accounted for by each *species or system *component in a given area.

compost Completely or partly decayed *organic matter that is dark, odourless, and rich in nutrients. It results from the controlled biological decomposition of solid organic waste materials under *aerobic conditions by *bacteria, *fungi, and other micro-organisms, and is used to fertilize the soil and increase its *humus content.

compound A substance that is made from two or more *elements in fixed proportions.

Comprehensive Environmental Response, Compensation, and Liability Act (CERCLA) (1980) (Superfund) US legislation that provides for the *cleanup of *hazardous substances released to the environment, usually after the substances were disposed of improperly, by giving the

*Environmental Protection Agency the authority to clean up abandoned hazardous waste sites.

Comprehensive Environmental Response, Compensation, and Liability Information System (CERCLIS) A database and management system operated by the *Environmental Protection Agency that contains the official inventory of *Cercla sites in the USA.

comprehensive plan (general plan, master plan) An official plan, developed and adopted by local government, that contains a vision of how the local economy is expected to change and a set of plans and policies to guide *land use decisions.

Comprehensive Soil Classification System A system for classifying *soils that was developed by the US Department of Agriculture and is now widely used around the world. All soils are divided into 11 *soil orders, which in turn are subdivided into 47 suborders, 185 great soil groups, many subgroups, and a great many soil families and series. *See also* ALFISOL; ANDOSOLS; ARIDISOL; ENTISOL; HISTOSOL; INCEPTISOL; LATOSOL; OXISOL; ULTISOL; VERTISOL.

compressed natural gas (CNG) *Natural gas stored in a high-pressure container. It provides a clean alternative fuel for motor vehicles because it emits little *hydrocarbon or *ozone-producing material, but it does emit a significant quantity of *nitrogen oxides.

compression The process of becoming smaller or closer together, which increases density. Geological compression causes *folding in rocks.

computational biology *See* BIOINFORMATICS.

computer model A *model of a complex *environmental system that is based on known mathematical relationships between system components and uses a computer to do the complicated modelling, usually in order to predict future states or patterns. Examples include *Daisyworld, *general circulation models, and *Limits to Growth.

concentrated animal feeding operation (CAFO) An agricultural business in which animals are raised in confined situations and fed an unnatural diet, rather than allowing them to roam and graze freely.

concentrated recreation *Recreation activities associated with developed recreation

sites, such as campgrounds, picnic grounds, ski areas, fishing ramps, scenic viewpoints, and interpretive sites. *Contrast* DISPERSED RECREATION; INTENSIVE RECREATION.

concentration The amount of a particular substance that is contained or dissolved in a given amount of another substance or medium (such as air, water, or soil).

concession A defined area of *land that is licensed or leased to a company for a given period of time, for exploration and development of *natural resources (such as *logging) under specified terms and conditions.

concretion A small, hard, local mass of mineral matter (such as *calcite, *gypsum, *iron oxide, or aluminium oxide), often rounded, which is found in *sedimentary rock and often contains a *fossil nucleus. *See also* MANGANESE NODULE.

condensate The liquid that is produced when a vapour is cooled or *compressed, such as the liquid *hydrocarbons that are condensed from *natural gas and oil wells.

condensation The change of phase in which a gas becomes a liquid with the release of *latent heat. *Contrast* EVAPORATION.

condensation level *See* LIFTING CONDENSATION LEVEL.

condensation nuclei Minute particles in the air that are derived from *air pollution or from natural processes (such as pollen, salt from sea spray, and dust from volcanic eruptions), around which moisture can collect via the *condensation of *water vapour, to produce *precipitation. Many are *hygroscopic.

condensation point *See* DEW POINT.

condensation trail *See* CONTRAIL.

condition indicator *See* ECOLOGICAL INDICATOR.

conditional instability The condition of air in which the *environmental lapse rate (ELR) is greater than the *dry adiabatic lapse rate (DALR) but lower than the *saturated adiabatic lapse rate (SALR). Air that is forced to rise cools faster than the DALR and so remains stable (losing *buoyancy) until it reaches its *lifting condensation level, beyond which it becomes unstable, continuing to rise because it cools more slowly than the SALR, gaining buoyancy. Thus the air is stable unless it meets the condition of rising above its lifting condensation level.

conditionality A state of being conditional, or qualified by reservations. The granting of development assistant funds to a country might depend on it signing a climate change policy agreement, for example.

conditioned air (tempered air) Air that has been heated, cooled, humidified, or dehumidified to maintain comfort inside a building, vehicle, or other space.

conditioned response A response that is learned or altered by conditioning.

conductance *See* CONDUCTIVITY.

conduction The transfer of *heat within a substance or between substances that are in direct physical contact. *See also* ELECTRICAL CONDUCTION.

conductivity (conductance) A measure of the ability of a substance to conduct heat or an electrical current. In a sample of water, the electrical conductivity reflects the concentration of ionized substances (*dissolved solids) in the water.

conductor Any material that readily transmits (conducts) heat or electricity.

cone of depression A cone-shaped depression in the surface of a *water table, in the vicinity of a *well, that is caused by pumping. *See also* DRAW DOWN.

cone of influence The cone-shaped depression produced in a *water table by the pumping of water from a *well. The surface area included in the cone is known as the *circle of influence of the well.

confined aquifer An *aquifer that is sealed between two layers of impermeable material above and below.

confinement The act of confining or restraining, such as the techniques that are used to confine a release of hazardous material (such as a spill or leak) to a limited area, and prevent damage elsewhere.

confining unit A layer of rock that is less permeable than those above or below it, and which prevents or restricts the vertical movement of water.

confluence 1. A place where things merge or flow together (such as where a tributary flows into a river). 2. The process of *convergence.

conformable contact A boundary between two layers of rock that does not indicate a major change in sedimentary conditions.

congener A member of the same *species or *genus.

conglomerate A coarse-grained *clastic *sedimentary rock composed of large rounded clasts (*gravels, *cobbles, *boulders) which are cemented together in a matrix of fine materials.

Congressionally Reserved Area An area of land in the USA that has been reserved by an act of Congress for a specific purpose, such as a *wilderness area or a *wildlife refuge.

conifer A tree or shrub with leaves that are needle- or scale-like and that produces seeds in cones, e.g. pine, spruce, or fir. There are about 550 species of conifer; most are *evergreen, but a few (such as larch) are *deciduous. They usually grow faster and develop less dense wood (*softwood) than other trees, and are commercially important as a source of timber for the papermaking, building, and furniture industries.

coniferous forest A forest dominated by *conifer tree species. It occurs in climates with a pronounced dry season in winter, when the ground is frozen and water is not available, or in summer. The *boreal forest is of this type and it also grows in Mediterranean climates and in the south-eastern United States.

conk *See* FRUITING BODY.

connectedness The state of being connected. Used by ecologists to describe the networks of *corridors that link isolated patches of *habitat in an area. *See also* FRAGMENTATION; HABITAT CONNECTIVITY.

conservancy 1. An official term for *conservation of the environment and natural resources. 2. In the USA, a commission that has jurisdiction over fisheries and navigation in a port or river.

conservation assessment An evaluation of the natural *ecosystems and *biomes of a region, with a special focus on the need and potential for *nature conservation and protecting *biodiversity.

conservation biology The multidisciplinary science that deals with *biodiversity.

Conservation Data Center (CDC, Natural Heritage Program) In North America, an

C

CONSERVATION

The planned protection, maintenance, management, sustainable use, and restoration of natural resources and the environment, in order to secure their long-term survival. Conservation recognizes that natural communities of plants and animals are not static, and it involves preventing any development that would alter or destroy natural habitat but not interfering unduly with ecological changes that occur naturally. It differs from *preservation because of the emphasis on positive management, not simply preventing environmental change. Since the 1960s the word conservation has been used more widely to embrace the rational use of all types of natural resources (*biotic and *abiotic). This is a core belief of modern *ecology and central tenet of *sustainable development. There are many arguments in favour of conservation, including economic or utilitarian arguments (plant and animal resources provide the material basis for human life, and the genetic variation in plant and animal species provides the requisite materials for sustaining and improving farm production, forestry, animal husbandry, and fisheries), moral or ethical arguments (we owe it to future generations to leave an environmental heritage or estate for them; all species have a right to live), aesthetic arguments (wildlife is attractive and interesting, and it makes the world pleasurable, e.g. watching birds and butterflies, hearing birdsong, seeing wild flowers and natural forest), and environmental arguments (natural wildlife is important to *environmental systems such as *biogeochemical cycles, on which all life on Earth depends). *See also* EX SITU CONSERVATION; IN SITU CONSERVATION.

organization or government programme that compiles, maintains, and disseminates information about *biodiversity in the area it is responsible for.

conservation easement An *easement that restricts a landowner to use that particular land for functions that are compatible with long-term *conservation objectives (such as protecting wildlife habitat, agricultural lands, natural areas, scenic views, historic structures, or open spaces). It is a means by which the development rights to that land are secured (by the government), without buying the land itself.

conservation farming Farming practices that are designed to protect *wildlife and *habitats, for example by minimizing *soil erosion and the release of *pollutants.

Conservation Foundation A British charitable (non-profit) organization founded in 1982 to promote positive environmental news, awareness, and action.

(●)) SEE WEB LINKS
• Home page of the Conservation Foundation.

Conservation International (CI) A non-profit, US-based international organization whose mission is to conserve global *biodiversity and demonstrate that human societies are able to live harmoniously with *nature. It has headquarters in Washington, DC, and works in more than 40 countries on four continents. *See also* BIODIVERSITY HOTSPOT.

Conservation Reserve Program A long-range federal programme in the US, in which farmers voluntarily contract to take *cropland out of production for 10 to 15 years and to devote it to nature conservation uses.

conservation tillage The cultivation (*tillage) of soil with minimum disturbance (no ploughing), which leaves plant residues on the soil surface, controls soil erosion, and conserves soil moisture.

conservation zoning *Land use *zoning which limits the development of unsuitable areas such as steep slopes, scenic areas, and spaces with other natural values.

conservative margin *See* CONSERVATIVE PLATE BOUNDARY.

conservative plate boundary (conservative margin) A junction in the Earth's *crust between two *crustal plates that move past each other in opposite directions along a *transform fault, where crust is being neither created nor destroyed. *Contrast* CONSTRUCTIVE PLATE BOUNDARY.

conserve To save, use sustainably, avoid waste, and preserve for the future. For example, protecting a natural resource (such as *water or an *endangered species) through wise management and use.

consilience The view, put forward in the 1990s by biologist Edward O. Wilson, that everything in the world can be understood and explained through a small number of natural laws or principles, which apply across the sciences and the humanities, but which are based on physics and evolve according to the laws of evolution.

consolidated Tightly packed or composed of particles that are not easily separated. *See also* UNCONSOLIDATED.

consolidation Compression or compaction.

conspecific Belonging to the same *species.

conspicuous consumption Buying expensive services and products that are not really needed, in order to impress others.

constant level balloon A *weather balloon that is designed to rise to a predetermined height and remain at that level.

constructive margin *See* CONSTRUCTIVE PLATE BOUNDARY.

constructive metabolism *See* ANABOLISM.

constructive plate boundary (constructive margin) A divergent boundary between two *lithospheric plates that are moving apart, where new crustal rocks are being formed. For example, at *mid-ocean ridges associated with *sea-floor spreading. *See also* PLATE TECTONICS; DESTRUCTIVE PLATE BOUNDARY. *Contrast* CONSERVATIVE PLATE BOUNDARY.

Consultative Group for International Agricultural Research (CGIAR) The agency that aims to coordinate international agricultural research. It is sponsored by the *World Bank, *United Nations Food and Agriculture Organization, and the *United Nations Development Programme.

 SEE WEB LINKS

• CGIAR home page.

consumer An *organism (such as an *animal or a *parasitic plant) that obtains energy and nutrients by feeding on other organisms or their remains. There are several different kinds of consumers including *carnivores, *herbivores, and *detritivores. *Contrast* PRODUCER. *See also* HETEROTROPH.

consumerism A term used to describe the effects of equating personal happiness with purchasing material possessions and consumption.

consumption The process of using *resources to satisfy human wants or needs.

consumption residues Wastes that result from the final consumption of goods or services, in contrast to production residues, which are wastes resulting from their production and distribution.

consumptive use The use of *resources in ways that reduce supply. Examples include *mining and *grazing, or *hunting, *fishing, and *logging in a *forest. *Contrast* NON-CONSUMPTIVE USE.

consumptive wildlife Any *game and fur-bearing species of *wildlife that are harvested for sport, food, fur, study, or commerce.

contact herbicide A *herbicide that only kills the part of the plant it is sprayed on, not the root systems. *Contrast* SYSTEMIC HERBICIDE.

contact metamorphism The *metamorphism of rock that is caused mainly by heat and pressure from pockets of *magma, which bakes and hardens the surrounding pre-existing rocks. *Contrast* REGIONAL METAMORPHISM.

contact pesticide A *pesticide that kills *pests when it touches them, instead of when they eat it.

contagious Any disease that is easily spread between individuals by direct contact.

contained use Any activity involving organisms that limits their contact with people and the environment, by the use of a physical, chemical, or biological barrier.

containment Any method of enclosing or containing *hazardous substances in a structure, in order to prevent the release of *contaminants into the *environment. Examples include the shielding of a *nuclear reactor within a thick concrete structure and the containment of an *oil spill using a floating *boom.

contaminant Any substance that pollutes or *contaminates another. In particular any physical, chemical, biological, or radiological substance that causes an impurity in the environment (air, water, and soil) and/or which may be harmful to human health.

contaminant level A measure of how much of a *contaminant is present.

contaminate To pollute or make impure or unclean, either by contact or by mixture.

contaminated land Land which has had its quality and usefulness reduced by the presence of one or more *contaminants in the *soil and/ or *groundwater.

contaminated site Any site or land that contains harmful contaminants (particularly in its soil and water) because of previous *land use.

contamination 1. The act of polluting or contaminating. **2. (environmental contamination)** An increase in the background concentration of a chemical, micro-organism, or radionuclide.

contiguous Very close or connected without a break, sharing a common boundary or edge. For example, the contiguous states of the USA do not include Alaska and Hawaii.

contiguous zone A zone of the *high sea around each coastal state, that was established by the *Convention on the Territorial Sea and Contiguous Zone, and extends seaward up to 12 miles from the state's *territorial sea. A state has the authority within this zone to exercise the control necessary to prevent violations of regulations within its territories and territorial sea.

continent One of the seven major land areas on the Earth, which are North America, South America, Europe, Africa, Asia, Australia, and Antarctica.

continental Originating in an inland area, away from the coast.

continental air mass An *air mass that develops over a *continent.

continental climate A climate that is found in the interior of continents, having low humidity, low rainfall, and large diurnal variations in temperature compared with *maritime climates.

continental crust That part of the Earth's *crust that forms the continents and the *continental shelves. It is composed of rocks that are rich in *silica, and varies in thickness from 35 to 70 km. *Contrast* OCEANIC CRUST. *See also* CONTINENTAL PLATE; SIMA.

continental divide The line of high ground that separates *rivers that flow toward opposite sides of a *continent, usually into different *oceans.

continental drift A geological hypothesis, first proposed around 1910, that sought to explain the relative positions and shapes of *continents, and the relative movement of continents across the Earth's surface. It has been supplanted by the theories of *plate tectonics and *sea-floor spreading.

continental glaciation The formation of an *ice sheet over a large area of a *continent during a glacial period.

continental glacier *See* ICE SHEET.

continental margin The area between the *shoreline and the beginning of the *ocean floor, which includes the *continental shelf, *continental rise, and *continental slope.

continental plate A thick section of the Earth's *continental crust that is composed mainly of granite, floats on the *asthenosphere, and moves over the surface of the Earth.

continental polar air mass A dry, cold *air mass that develops over *continental areas at high latitudes in the *northern hemisphere, and is very cold in winter and mild in summer.

continental rise The part of the *ocean floor that extends from the *continental slope down to the *abyssal plain, with a gentle slope and a smooth bed.

continental shelf The gently sloping part of the *ocean floor that extends from the *shore of a continent down to the *continental slope, usually to a depth of about 200 m.

continental slope The relatively steep-sloping part of the *ocean floor that extends from the *continental shelf to the *continental rise or *ocean trench.

continental South-east Asia floral region Part of R. Good's *Palaeotropical floral kingdom (*The Geography of the Flowering Plants*, 1974), which lies within the Indo-Malaysian subkingdom. Floristically it is a poorly documented region, transitional between the rich floras of China to the north and Malaysia to the south. There are relatively few *endemic genera, probably around 250, although the proportion of endemic species is thought to be high. This region is very likely the source of such important crop plants as rice, tea, and citrus fruit.

continental tropical air mass A warm, dry *air mass that develops over subtropical *deserts and *continental areas at low latitudes. *Contrast* TROPICAL MARITIME AIR MASS.

continentality In climatology, the degree to which the climate of a place resembles that of the most extreme *continental climate. This is calculated from the average annual daytime temperature range and the latitude to give an index of continentality.

contingency plan A plan for action that is prepared in anticipation of an incident (such as a release of toxic chemicals, a fire, or an *earthquake), that clarifies responsibilities, resource requirements, and appropriate action. *See also* DISASTER PLAN.

contingent valuation method In *economic evaluation, a method of valuing *non-market uses of a *natural resource (such as clean air, wildlife, or an attractive view) by directly asking people how much they would be willing to pay for it under certain circumstances, or what sort of compensation they would regard as necessary if it were not available. *See also* NON-MARKET VALUES.

continuous cropping The growing of *crops each year in succession, without a period of *fallow, which allows *soil fertility to recover.

continuous discharge A permitted release of *pollutants into the *environment that occurs without interruption, except for infrequent shutdowns for things like maintenance.

continuous monitoring Monitoring of flows or processes that continues without interruption, normally using equipment that is fitted with a recording device.

continuous stocking Allowing grazing livestock unrestricted and uninterrupted access to a given area of land over the whole period when grazing is allowed.

contour *See* CONTOUR LINE.

contour cropping *See* CONTOUR FARMING.

contour farming (contour cropping, contour ploughing, contour tillage) Planting a *crop and ploughing in horizontal rows that follow the *contour lines of a hill, which minimizes *soil erosion.

contour hedge A type of *barrier hedge that is grown along contours to help prevent *runoff and *soil erosion from a field.

contour line (contour) A line drawn on a map that connects points of the same elevation.

contour map A *topographic map that shows relief by means of *contour lines.

contour mining (contour strip mining) A type of *strip mining in hilly areas where the *mineral is exposed at the surface at roughly the same height along the *hillside. It involves removing the *overburden from the mineral seam, starting at the *outcrop and proceeding around the hillside, so that the cut appears as a contour line.

contour ploughing *See* CONTOUR FARMING.

contour strip mining *See* CONTOUR MINING.

contour stripping A form of *strip mining used in areas of steep topography, where the mineral seam outcrops at roughly the same elevation along a hillside.

contour tillage *See* CONTOUR FARMING.

contraction limit *See* ATTERBERG LIMITS.

contrail The condensation trail from an aircraft's engine exhaust.

control 1. To manage or regulate. *See also* CONTROL MEASURE; COMMAND AND CONTROL. **2.** In a scientific experiment, a standard or baseline against which other conditions can be compared.

control measure An activity that is undertaken to ensure that a standard is maintained, or a risk or hazard is eliminated or reduced to an acceptable level. *See also* CONTROL TECHNOLOGY.

control rod A rod made of *cadmium or *boron (which absorb *neutrons) that is used to control the power in a *nuclear reactor. Large numbers of rods are lowered into or lifted from the reactor *core in order to control the number of neutrons that cause a *chain reaction.

control technology A *control measure that uses special equipment, for example in order to reduce air pollution. *See also* BEST AVAILABLE CONTROL TECHNOLOGY; BEST AVAILABLE CONTROL MEASURES; MAXIMUM ACHIEVABLE CONTROL TECHNOLOGY.

controlled burn *See* PRESCRIBED BURN.

conurbation An extensive *urban settlement that is formed when two or more *cities, which were originally separate, grow together to form a continuous metropolitan region or *megalopolis.

convection The vertical circulation of air, water, or molten rock within the Earth which is driven by density differences and results in heat transfer.

convection column A rising column of gases, smoke, ash, particulates, and other debris that is produced by a fire.

convection current A current that transfers material (such as air, water, or molten rock within the Earth) due to differences in density that result from differences in temperature. *See also* SEA-FLOOR SPREADING; TURNOVER.

convection rain A form of *rain that occurs when heated air rises and cools, so that air temperature drops to the *dew point and *condensation occurs.

convective instability (potential instability, static instability) Instability that is caused in stratified air by the rising of very dry air over warm, moist air below. Air in the lowest and highest layers cools at the *dry adiabatic lapse rate, while air in the middle layer cools at the *saturated adiabatic lapse rate (SALR), with the result that the lowest layer becomes saturated before the air above it. If the lapse rate in the rising air is greater than the SALR, air will continue to rise and the layers may overturn.

convention 1. (international convention) An international agreement that is usually legally binding between the states that sign up to it. **2.** A large formal assembly.

Convention Concerning the Protection of the World Cultural and Natural Heritage (1972) (World Heritage Convention) An international *convention that was adopted by *UNESCO in 1972, which aims to encourage the identification, protection, and preservation of cultural and natural heritage. It recognizes that nature and culture are complementary and that cultural identity is strongly related to the natural environment in which it develops, and provides for the protection of those cultural and natural 'properties' that are regarded as being of greatest value to humanity. It is not intended to protect all properties of great interest, importance, or value, but to protect a select list of the most outstanding of these from an international viewpoint. Cultural heritage refers to monuments, groups of buildings, and sites with historical, aesthetic, archaeological, scientific, ethnological, or anthropological value. Natural heritage covers outstanding physical, biological, and geological

formations, habitats of *threatened species, and areas with scientific, conservation, or aesthetic value. The level of *biodiversity within a given site is a key indicator of its importance as a natural property.

Convention for the Prevention of Marine Pollution by Dumping from Ships and Aircraft (1972) (Oslo Convention) A regional component of the *Convention on the Prevention of Marine Pollution by Dumping of Wastes and Other Matter, which applies to states bordering the north-east Atlantic Ocean, from Iceland to Spain.

Convention on International Trade in Endangered Species of Wild Fauna and Flora (CITES) An international agreement, launched under the auspices of the *IUCN in 1975, designed to regulate trade in *endangered wildlife and thus help to conserve those *species. It has been signed by 175 nations, and protects nearly 90 species of plants and 400 species of animals which are listed as 'threatened with extinction'.

⊕ SEE WEB LINKS
• CITES home page.

Convention on the Conservation of Migratory Species of Wild Animals *See* BONN CONVENTION.

Convention on the Prevention of Marine Pollution by Dumping of Wastes and Other Matter (1972) (London Convention) An international *convention that prohibits the dumping at sea of certain *hazardous materials, requires a prior special permit for the dumping of a number of other identified materials, and a prior general permit for other wastes or matter.

Convention on the Territorial Sea and Contiguous Zone A United Nations convention that came into force in 1958 and defines the *territorial sea and the *contiguous zone for each coastal state.

conventional agriculture *Farming practices that involve the use of chemical *fertilizers, *pesticides, and machinery. *Contrast* ALTERNATIVE AGRICULTURE.

conventional pollutant *See* CRITERIA POLLUTANT.

convergence Coming together or *confluence. *Contrast* DIVERGENCE. **1.** The process by which a similar character evolves independently in two species. *See also* CONVERGENT EVOLUTION. **2.** The flowing together of air masses or ocean currents. **3.** The coming together of plates in *plate tectonics.

convergent evolution (convergence) The development of similar features in species that are unrelated except through a very distant ancestor as each species adapts to similar environmental conditions. The similarities between sharks (fish), dolphins (mammals), and ichthyosaurs (reptiles) result from convergent evolution, as do the wings of birds and bats, which in both cases are modified forelimbs. *Contrast* DIVERGENT EVOLUTION.

convergent margin *See* CONVERGENT PLATE BOUNDARY.

convergent plate boundary (convergent margin) A junction between two *lithospheric plates on the Earth's *crust that are moving towards each other, which forces one plate down beneath the other into the *mantle (where it melts), by the process of *subduction.

conversion The change of one form of energy into another, for example converting the chemical (potential) energy of a fuel (such as gasoline, coal, or *biomass) into heat or electricity (both of which are varieties of kinetic energy).

conveyance loss The loss of water from a pipe or *canal that is caused by leakage, seepage, *evaporation, or *evapotranspiration.

convivium A population within a *species which is isolated geographically and different from others within the same species, usually a *subspecies or *ecotype.

coolant A liquid or gas that is used to cool a machine, including the liquid or gas used to transfer heat from the *core of a *nuclear reactor to the steam generators or directly to the turbines.

cooling tower A structure that helps to remove heat from water that has been used as a *coolant (for example in an electric power generating plant) by direct contact (*evaporation) between the warm water and cooler atmospheric air.

Cooperative Forest Management Act (1950) US legislation that authorized technical and financial assistance to states to enable them to provide technical assistance to private forest landowners and processors.

Cooperative Forestry Assistance Act (1978) US legislation that brought together authority from nine cooperative assistance programmes in forestry, expanded some of them, and authorized consolidated programmes to participating states. It built on the *Clarke-McNary Act (1924), the *Forest Pest Control Act (1947), and the *Agriculture and Consumer Protection Act (1973).

coordinate 1. To bring order and organization to. *See also* COORDINATION. **2.** A number that identifies a location relative to two or more axes, on a graph or map.

Co-ordinated Information on the Environment in the European Community *See* CORINE PROJECT.

coordination The planned collaboration of individuals and organizations, and their resources, in order to achieve a common goal.

COPC *See* CHEMICAL OF POTENTIAL CONCERN.

copepod A member of a class (Copepoda) of small (up to several millimeters) aquatic *crustaceans with more than 7500 species. Most are marine, but some inhabit fresh water and others live in the films of water between soil particles and in mosses. Some are *ectoparasites of fish and whales, and many are planktonic (*zooplankton).

copper (Cu) A metallic *trace element that occurs naturally in rock, soil, water, sediment, plants, and animals. It is a good conductor of heat and electricity and is used in making brass, copper alloys, and electrical conductors, in agriculture (to treat plant diseases), for water treatment, and as a preservative for wood, leather, and fabrics. In high concentrations copper can be *toxic to plants.

copper acetoarsenite (Paris Green) An *arsenic-based *insecticide that is *toxic by ingestion. It is also used as a wood preservative and has an emerald green colour.

coppice A traditional form of *woodland management in which multiple stems (poles) are allowed to grow up from the base of a felled *tree. The poles are then cut every few years to provide fuel and wood for making tool handles, fencing, and charcoal. *Contrast* HIGH FOREST. *See also* POLLARD.

coprolite Fossilized excrement or *faeces.

coprophage An organism (such as a dung beetle) that feeds on *faeces.

copse A small group of *trees.

coral Small *colonial invertebrates (*polyps) that live in shallow seas found in the *coastal zones of warm tropical and subtropical oceans. The coral can be white, red, or black in colour. When they die, their vacant protective skeletons (also called coral) form layers on which other corals build, and this creates a *coral reef.

coral bleaching The whitening of a *coral colony, indicative of environmental stress. This occurs when the coral *polyp expels symbiotic algal cells (*zooxanthellae), which contain photosynthetic pigments, from its body. The *coral reef appears bleached because most reef-building corals have white *calcium carbonate skeletons, and these show through the tissue of the corals. When the stress is removed most corals recover by recruiting different species of zooxanthellae and evidence indicates that bleaching is an adaptive response to an environmental change.

coral budding The way in which a *coral colony expands in size, by forming an offshoot. A new individual *polyp develops inside an adult polyp, producing a swelling that eventually detaches.

coral reef A *reef made by colonies of stony *coral invertebrates (*polyps), together with algal and mineral components, which through time have been *consolidated into *limestone. Coral reefs are found only in shallow regions of tropical oceans. See also ATOLL; COASTAL REEF; FRINGING REEF; LAGOON.

corbiculum See POLLEN BASKET.

cordwood Small-diameter and/or low-quality wood that is suitable for pulp, woodchips, or firewood, but not for *sawlogs.

core 1. The central part of the *Earth's interior, which is composed mainly of *nickel and *iron, divided into a relatively small inner core and a much thicker outer core, and surrounded by the *mantle. The inner core has a radius of about 1255 km (about 20% of the total radius of the Earth). It is solid, and made up mainly of iron molecules with some nickel and possibly some *silicon and *sulphur. This material is extremely dense (more than thirteen times the density of surface water), extremely hot (temperatures are estimated at between 4500 and 5500°C, almost as hot as the surface of the Sun), and under extremely high pressure (estimated at 3.5 million times atmospheric pressure). These extreme conditions mean that the iron material

in the inner core behaves rather differently than it would at the Earth's surface. The outer core is about 2220 km thick. This layer is also made up mostly of *iron and *nickel, but this material is *molten. With increasing distance from the inner core temperature drops from around 4500°C to less than 2000°C, pressure drops by half, and the density of material also decreases. **2.** See REACTOR CORE. **3.** See CORE AREA.

core area 1. (core) The inner area of a *biosphere reserve which is legally protected and where only the minimum amount of human activity is allowed, to enable plants and animals to thrive without disturbance from people. Often surrounded by a *buffer zone. **2.** The part of its range in which a group of animals may rest securely and raise young, and where food may be carried to be eaten.

CORINE project A project (Co-ordinated Information on the Environment in the European Community) that is designed to build a common environmental database for the *European Union, using *geographical information systems.

Coriolis effect The tendency for air above the *Earth, and for ocean currents, to appear to be deflected to the right (in the northern hemisphere) or the left (in the south) because of the rotation of the Earth. See also GEOSTROPHIC WIND.

cornucopian A view that natural resources are unlimited and perpetual economic growth is not only possible but essential. See also OPTIMIST, ENVIRONMENTAL.

corona A series of coloured rings in the sky that surround the Sun or Moon, caused by the diffraction of light by small water droplets.

Corporate Average Fuel Economy (CAFE) (1975) A US approach to reducing energy consumption by increasing the fuel economy of cars and light trucks, based on calculating the sales weighted average *fuel economy, expressed in miles per gallon (mpg), of a manufacturer's fleet of passenger cars or light trucks manufactured for sale in the USA for any given model year.

corporate social responsibility Awareness, acceptance, and management of the implications and effects of all corporate decision-making, taking particular account of community investment, human rights, and employee relations, environmental practices, and ethical conduct.

corrasion *See* ABRASION.

corrective action The adoption of solutions that result in the reduction or elimination of an identified problem. For example, the *cleanup of *hazardous waste contamination at particular sites.

correlation 1. A measure of the association between two or more variables. 2. The matching of sedimentary deposits (for example on a lake bed or in a rock) that are of similar age but in different places.

corridor (buffer, buffer strip, buffer zone, greenway, migration corridor) A strip of natural *habitat that connects two or more larger areas of natural habitat (or *nature reserves) surrounded by developed land, which allows the *migration of *organisms from one place to another.

corrie *See* CIRQUE.

corrosion A process in which a metal is attacked in a chemical reaction. *See also* RUSTING.

corrosive A liquid or solid that destroys metals and other materials or burns the skin.

corrosivity The ability to dissolve or break down certain substances, particularly metals. This is one of the four *characteristics that is used to define *hazardous waste in North America.

cosmic radiation A variety of high-energy particles (mainly *protons (92%) and *alpha particles (6%)) that bombard the Earth from outer space.

cosmology The study of the origin and nature of the *universe.

cosmopolitan Widely distributed across the globe, as opposed to local or regional.

cost The quantity of resources that are required in order to achieve a desired end, usually expressed in monetary terms.

cost effective Achieving specified objectives under given conditions, for relatively little expenditure or at equal or lower cost than current practice.

cost recovery A legal process in the USA that allows the government to recover the cost of *cleanup at hazardous (*Superfund) waste

sites from those who cause the contamination. *See also* COST SHARING.

cost sharing Sharing the costs of a project between different people or agencies. For example, the government might share the cost of a *cleanup operation with those who caused the pollution. *See also* COST RECOVERY.

cost–benefit analysis A formal quantitative assessment of the short-term and long-term social and financial costs (losses) and benefits (gains) that arise from an economic decision, for example about investing in a major project which may have social as well as economic outcomes. Financial values are assigned to each cost and benefit, and the decision whether or not to proceed with the project is made based on the comparison of anticipated costs and benefits. The technique is widely used but has some inherent difficulties, including how to assign monetary values to intangible things (such as *aesthetics), and how to take into account future conditions (*discounting) and externalities (such as the generation of *pollution). This approach assumes that everything has a monetary value, and that this value is more important than any ecological, health, or environmental issues involved which have not been costed. It cannot include political judgements about what is acceptable at a particular point in time, and moral judgements about what is right and wrong and who should decide these issues, and it does not distinguish between who may or should benefit from a proposed scheme, and who may or should pay the costs. *See also* FULL COST PRICING.

coulee A long, deep, winding channel formed by water erosion (probably by *glacial meltwater at the end of the *Pleistocene), which is often dry or carries intermittent flow, and might have an *underfit stream flowing through it.

Council of Ministers The Council of the *European Union which directly represents the Member Governments, and is the principal decision-making body that acts on proposals from the *European Commission.

Council on Environmental Quality (CEQ) An advisory council to the President of the USA that was established by the 1969 *National Environmental Policy Act and reviews federal programmes for their effect on the environment, conducts environmental studies, and advises the President on environmental matters.

countershading A form of *camouflage in some birds and aquatic organisms, that are dark coloured on top but light coloured underneath.

countries with economies in transition Those Central and East European countries and former republics of the Soviet Union that are in transition to a *market economy.

country 1. Short for *countryside. 2. The land occupied by a nation.

country breeze A light *breeze that blows into a city from the surrounding countryside, and is most obvious on clear nights when the *urban heat island is strongest.

country park In Britain, an area of land, or of land and water, in the countryside that offers the public opportunities for recreation. Country parks are usually not less than 10 ha in area and charge may be made for access, although most are free.

country rock The rock into which *igneous rock has intruded or by which it is surrounded.

country sports *See* FIELD SPORT.

countryside The land and scenery of a *rural area.

Countryside Agency A statutory agency that was established in the UK in 1999 and is now called *Natural England.

Countryside and Rights of Way Act 2000 UK legislation, affecting England and Wales, that contains provisions for access in the countryside and for protection of *Sites of Special Scientific Interest.

(⊕) SEE WEB LINKS

• Countryside and Rights of Way Act 2000.

covalent bond The linkage of two *atoms that share a pair of *electrons. *See also* IONIC BOND.

cover 1. The percentage of ground that is covered by living or organic material. *See also* GROUND COVER. 2. (covert, escape cover, shelter) Any feature that conceals wildlife or fish and allows them to escape from predators, rest, or feed.

cover crop Plants, such as rye, *alfalfa, or clover, that are planted in between the main crop in order to maintain a plant cover on the

land after harvest, and thus reduce erosion and *leaching.

cover forage ratio The ratio between hiding *cover and *forage area for wildlife, in a given area of land.

cover material *See* CAP.

cover type The dominant vegetation in an area.

covert A covering that helps to conceal, such as *cover for wildlife (usually *game).

covert release A release of a biological agent that is unannounced and causes illness. *Contrast* OVERT RELEASE.

covey A small flock of *game birds such as grouse or partridge.

cowboy economy General term to describe an economy that behaves as if *natural resources are infinite in supply and nature can absorb all *wastes.

CPM *See* CRITICAL PATH METHOD.

cracking An oil-refining process that breaks large *hydrocarbon molecules into smaller ones.

cradle-to-grave system (manifest system) A procedure used in North America in which *hazardous materials are identified and tracked as they are produced, treated, transported, and disposed of by a series of permanent, linkable, descriptive documents (manifests).

crag A steep rocky cliff.

crag-and-tail *Landform created by glacial *scour and (like a *rôche moutonnée) formed around resistant rock underneath moving ice, which has a rocky, angular upstream (crag) side and a gently sloping downstream (tail) side.

crassulacean acid metabolism (CAM) A method of carbon dioxide fixation that conserves water in certain succulent, drought-resistant plants. At night, when the external temperature and therefore the evaporation rate are low, the leaf stomata open allowing carbon dioxide to enter leaf cells where it is incorporated in an organic acid. During the day the stomata remain closed, conserving moisture, while the acids are decarboxylated and the carbon dioxide is used for the *dark reactions of *photosynthesis. This pathway of carbon fixation was first observed in members of the Crassulaceae (stonecrops and house-leeks), hence the name.

- 'Crassulacean acid metabolism: A plastic photosynthetic adaptation to arid environments'.

crater 1. The bowl-shaped *vent at the top of a *volcano. **2.** The approximately circular depression caused by the impact of an extraterrestrial body.

craton (shield) A very large, ancient, stable core area within the *continental crust, made of highly deformed *metamorphic rocks, which are effectively the roots of the continents.

created opening An opening in a forest that is created by the application of *even-aged *silviculture practices. *See also* CLEARCUT.

creationism The doctrine that all of the universe (including each species of organism) was created separately, in much its present form, by a supreme being or deity.

Creative Act (1891) US legislation that authorized the President of the USA to set aside public lands as public reservations.

creature A living organism.

credit In the politics of climate change, an amount by which a particular country has actually reduced its pollution emissions, particularly of *greenhouse gases, beyond the agreed or required amount. *See also* CERTIFIED EMISSIONS REDUCTION; EMISSIONS REDUCTION UNIT.

creek A small natural *stream, smaller than a *river.

creep 1. (soil creep) The extremely slow, continuous movement of *unconsolidated soil or rock debris down a slope in response to gravity. A very slow form of *mass movement. **2.** *See* GLACIER CREEP.

creeper Any plant (such as ivy) that grows by sending out a shoot that grows along the ground, rooting all along its length. The term is also applied to a tight-clinging vine.

crest The high point of a *wave.

Crenarchaeota *See* ARCHAEA.

Cretaceous The final geological period of the *Mesozoic era that began 145.5 million years ago and ended 65.5 million years ago, during which flowering plants expanded to grow over a wide area and shallow seas submerged much of the surface of the Earth. Dinosaurs became *extinct in the *mass extinction that marks the end of the Cretaceous.

- The Cretaceous.

Creutzfeldt-Jakob disease A rare brain disease in humans, which usually affects in middle age, is usually fatal, is characterized by progressive dementia and gradual loss of muscle control, and is caused by a *prion protein. *See also* BOVINE SPONGIFORM ENCEPHALOPATHY.

crevasse A deep crack in the ice of a *glacier or *ice sheet that is caused by ice movement.

crisis management 1. Management of a crisis: measures that are taken to identify, acquire, and plan the use of resources to anticipate, prevent, and/or resolve a threat (for example to public safety arising from terrorism). **2.** Management in a crisis: decision-making based on a seat-of-the-pants response to the immediate issue, with little if any consideration of longer-term effects.

criteria pollutant (conventional pollutant) A group of common *air pollutants (*sulphur dioxide, *carbon monoxide, *particulates, *hydrocarbons, *nitrogen oxides, *photochemical oxidants, and *lead) that pose the greatest threat to human health and are regulated in the USA by the *Environmental Protection Agency. *See also* DESIGNATED POLLUTANT; HAZARDOUS AIR POLLUTANT.

critical factor The environmental factor that is closest to a *tolerance limit for a given species at a given time. *See also* LIMITING FACTOR.

critical habitat An area that has been designated (usually by government) as critical for the survival and recovery of *threatened or *endangered species.

critical load The maximum amount of a particular *pollutant that an *environment or *ecosystem can tolerate without suffering long-term damage.

critical path method (CPM, programme evaluation and review technique) In *project management, a technique that is used to plan and control the activities in a project, based on identifying the series of successive activities which take up most time (the 'critical path'). This determines the total lead time of the project.

critical wildlife habitat A *habitat that is vital to the health and survival of one or more *species, because it provides such features as nesting sites, food sources, and *breeding grounds.

critically endangered A *species which, according to the *IUCN *Red List, faces an extremely high risk of *extinction in the wild in the immediate future. See also EXTINCT; ENDANGERED; VULNERABLE SPECIES.

croft Scottish name for a small tenanted *farm, generally run on a *subsistence basis.

Cromerian A northern European *interglacial stage dating from about 0.8 to 0.5 million years ago.

crop 1. A plant (such as cereals, vegetables, or fruit plants) that is cultivated and harvested for use by people or livestock. See also COMPANION CROP. **2.** See CROP YIELD.

crop dusting The application of *pesticides to plants by a low-flying plane.

crop productivity A measure of efficiency, that is, output (production) per unit of input over time; for example grams of biomass per square metre per day, or crop yield expressed in tonnes per hectare per season. Can also be expressed in terms of labour or financial inputs, solar energy inputs, and so forth.

crop residue The portion of a plant or crop that is left in the field after *harvest.

crop rooting zone The depth of soil in which crop roots are found.

crop rotation The practice of planting an area with different crops from year to year, in order to maintain soil fertility and organic matter content, and reduce *soil erosion. Most rotations include *legume-type crops to rebuild stores of *nitrogen in the soil. See also ROTATION PASTURE.

crop yield (crop) The amount of a crop that is harvested from a given area of land (such as a field) in a single *growing season, usually expressed as yield per unit area (for example, tonnes per hectare). See also HARVEST.

cropland Land that is used for the production of cultivated crops for harvest, either alone or in rotation with grasses and *legumes.

cropping pattern The layout of crops and fallow in a given area of land, and how these vary through the year.

cropping regime The way in which crops are grown. See also CROP ROTATION.

cropping season See GROWING SEASON.

cropping system A subsystem of the farming system, or a unit of land use, that comprises the soils and plants, water, nutrients, labour, and other inputs that are used to produce food, feed, fuel, and fibre.

crossbreeding (crossing) The production (*breeding) of a *hybrid plant or animal by deliberately mixing different *species, *breeds, or *varieties.

cross-contamination 1. The transfer of micro-organisms from one place or food to another, usually by direct contact. **2.** The movement of underground contaminants from one level or area to another.

crossing See CROSSBREEDING.

cross-pollination The fertilization of a flower by pollen from a different plant of the same species, which creates an offspring with a different genetic makeup from either of the parent plants. See also CROSSBREEDING.

cross-section A view or representation of the interior of an object, viewed along a plane.

crown The top or highest part of a tree and the *canopy in a forest, made of branches and *foliage. See also OVERSTOREY.

crown class A classification of individual *trees in a *forest, based on dominance relative to adjacent trees, which reflects position in the *canopy and amount of sunlight received. The four classes, in descending order of crown height and size, are *dominant, *codominant, *intermediate, and *suppressed.

crown closure The growth of the crowns of trees in a *forest so that they touch and effectively block out sunlight from the area below. See also CLOSED CANOPY.

crown density The amount of *foliage in the crown of a tree.

crown fire An intense forest fire that burns the top of living trees as well as the plants below it.

crown height The distance from the ground to the base of the crown in a tree.

crude birth rate The number of live births in a given year, per thousand individuals in that *population.

crude death rate (crude mortality rate) The number of individuals who die in a given year, per thousand individuals in that *population.

crude mortality rate *See* CRUDE DEATH RATE.

crude oil *See* PETROLEUM.

crust The outer layer of the *Earth, which varies in thickness between 5 and 60 km, and floats on and surrounds the *mantle. It comprises *oceanic crust and *continental crust, and the thick continental crust and much thinner oceanic crust are separated from the mantle below by the *Mohorovičić discontinuity. The crust is made largely of *oxygen (47%) and *silicon (28%), with much smaller amounts of *aluminium (8%), *iron (5%), *calcium (4%), *sodium (3%), *potassium (3%), and *magnesium (2%). It is effectively the Earth's outer skin, occupying much less than 1% of the volume of the planet. All of the Earth's *landforms (mountains, plains, and plateaux) are contained within it, along with the oceans and seas. Whilst the crust appears to be solid, it is subject to repeated movement (including bending, folding, and breaking) associated with the movement of material on the mantle below.

crustaceans *Arthropods of the class Crustacea that have two pairs of antennae, one pair of *mandibles, and limbs adapted for a wide range of functions. Most of the 31 400 species are marine, but there are also freshwater and a few terrestrial species, and the class also includes parasites of other crustaceans and one group (whale lice) that parasitizes whales. Examples include shrimps, crabs, lobsters, crayfish, barnacles, slaters, and woodlice.

crustal deformation The bending up or down of rocks in the Earth's *crust that is caused by pressure, either from within the Earth (for example by mountain building) or from on top of it (for example by *crustal subsidence or *crustal rebound). Deformation includes *faulting, *folding, *shearing, *compression, and extension caused by *tectonic forces.

crustal plate (plate, tectonic plate) One of the large sections or blocks of the Earth's *crust, which are curved to the spherical shape of the Earth and fit together like a jigsaw. There are seven major plates (the North American, South American, African, Eurasian, Indo-Australian, Pacific, and Antarctic plates) and at least twelve minor plates. These plates float on the *asthenosphere, allowing them to move relative to one another, driven by *sea-floor spreading, giving rise to *plate tectonics.

crustal rebound The raising of part of the Earth's *crust after the melting of heavy continental *ice sheets.

crustal subsidence The depression of part of the Earth's *crust that is caused by the immense weight of continental *ice sheets.

cryogenic storage *See* CRYOPRESERVATION.

cryogenics 1. The branch of physics that studies the production and effects of very low temperatures. **2.** The preservation of living organisms in a dormant state by freezing, drying, or both.

cryophyte A plant, commonly *algae and *mosses, or *fungus that grows on the surface of snow or ice.

cryopreservation (cryogenic storage) The *in vitro* preservation of organic material (such as embryos, sperm, or eggs) by freezing, usually in liquid nitrogen.

cryosols Soils that have a *permafrost layer within 100 cm of the surface. Cryosols are a reference soil group in the *World Soil Classification.

cryosphere The frozen part of the Earth's surface, which includes the polar *ice caps, continental *ice sheets, mountain *glaciers, sea ice, snow cover, lake and river ice, and *permafrost.

crypsis *See* CRYPTIC COLORATION.

cryptic Behaviour or coloration that helps to conceal an animal. *See also* CRYPTIC COLORATION.

cryptic coloration (crypsis) A form of *camouflage, in which an animal has colouring and/or markings that make it difficult to detect against the background, as a protection against *predators. *See also* CRYPTIC.

cryptogams Non-vascular plants such as fungi, mosses, lichens, and liverworts.

cryptosporidium A single-celled microorganism (*Protozoa) that is commonly found in lakes and rivers, is highly resistant to disinfection, and causes acute diarrhoea, abdominal pain, vomiting, and fever in humans.

crystal A homogeneous regularly shaped solid with flat surfaces (faces) and specific angles between the faces. The crystal form varies from one substance to another, reflecting the atomic, molecular, or ionic structure of the crystal.

CSD *See* COMMISSION ON SUSTAINABLE DEVELOPMENT.

cuesta *See* ESCARPMENT.

cull 1. An organism or other object that is rejected or set aside because it is of inferior quality. **2.** The process of killing designated animals in a particular place, as part of a management plan, in order to reduce the number of individuals within the population.

culling *See* ROGUING.

cultivar (cultivated species) A domesticated variety of plant that has been cultivated by *selective breeding and is not normally found in wild populations.

cultivate 1. To prepare and use land for growing crops. **2.** To adapt a wild plant to a new environment. *See also* DOMESTICATE.

cultivated species *See* CULTIVAR; DOMESTICATED SPECIES.

cultural eutrophication *Eutrophication caused by human activities.

cultural extinction The accelerated *extinction of *species that is caused by human activities such as the over-hunting of animals, over-collection of plants, introduction of non-native species, removal of habitat, and induced environmental change (for example, related to *pollution).

cultural landscape Natural *landscape that has been modified (both by accident and by design) by humans.

cultural resource The physical remains (including *artefacts, objects, and structures) of past human activities. *Contrast* AESTHETIC RESOURCE. *See also* RESOURCE.

culture 1. The growth of cells or an organism in a prepared medium, under laboratory conditions. **2.** A set of beliefs, attitudes, and rules for behaviour that are commonly held in a particular society.

culvert A drain or pipe that carries surface water under a built structure such as a road or railway.

cumulative effect Effects that result from separate, individual actions that collectively become significant over time.

cumulative exposure The sum of exposures that an *organism has to a *pollutant over a period of time.

cumuliform Having the appearance or character of *cumulus clouds.

cumulonimbus (Cb) A *cumuliform *cloud with a low base but with a top sometimes reaching an altitude of 9000 m, formed in turbulent, rising air. They are usually grey or dark grey due to the amount of sunlight they reflect. Their tops may be smooth or striated or be flattened into an anvil shape, and they often bring heavy *rain or *hail (formed in the strong vertical uplift). They are often associated with *thunderstorms and occasionally they trigger *tornadoes.

cumulus (Cu) A type of *cloud that is associated with rising air currents, usually below about 2400 m. In Latin *cumulus* means heap. They are dense, well-defined mounds with dark bases and white, rounded upper regions. Relatively thin cumulus clouds, which are common on warm summer afternoons in middle latitudes, indicate fair weather and relatively stable conditions.

cup anemometer An instrument used to monitor wind speed, via the rotation of cups by the movement of air.

curie An obsolete measure of radioactivity, equal to 3.7×10^{10} (37000000000) nuclear disintegrations per second. Replaced by the *becquerel.

current 1. A horizontal movement of water, for example along a stream or through an ocean. **2.** The movement or flow of electricity. **3.** Occurring in or belonging to the present time.

Current Warm Period (CWP) The period of relatively warm climate that developed during the 20th century.

cursorial Adapted for running.

cuticle 1. A waxy film made of *cutin that covers the external surface of the stems and leaves of plants, which helps to prevent water loss. **2.** The *exoskeleton made of *chitin that is secreted by *invertebrates.

cutin A waxy substance that, together with *cellulose, forms the outer layer of the skin (*cuticle) of many plants.

cut-off *See* OX-BOW LAKE.

cutting A part (stem, leaf, or root) that is removed from a plant and is capable of developing into a new plant through rooting or grafting.

Cuyahoga River A river in northeast Ohio, USA, into which industries around Cleveland dumped oily wastes, and which caught fire on numerous occasions. The most serious fire occurred on 23 June 1969, and that event triggered a series of important pollution control initiatives including the *Clean Water Act (1972) and the *Great Lakes water quality agreement, and the creation of federal and state *environmental protection agencies.

cwm *See* CIRQUE.

CWP *See* CURRENT WARM PERIOD.

cyanides A group of inorganic salts that contain the cyanide ion (CN⁻). They are highly poisonous and are used in ore processing to extract *gold and *silver from crushed rock.

cyanobacteria A large and varied group of *bacteria, formerly known as blue green algae, that contain *chlorophyll and can *photosynthesize. Some can form large coloured mats on the surface of lakes and rivers. One species causes a *red tide.

cybernetic A *system that continuously changes in response to *feedback.

cycle of erosion (geomorphic cycle) A hypothetical model of how *landscapes evolve through a progressive sequence of stages, starting from an uplifted surface dissected by some rivers, through a youthful landscape with steep valley sides and steep long profiles, to a mature landscape dominated by low hills and low river slopes, to the gentle undulating or flat landscape of old age.

cyclic/cyclical Recurring in cycles.

cyclodiene insecticides A subgroup of the *organochlorine insectides that includes *aldrin, *chlordane, dieldrin, and *endrin.

cyclogenesis The development of low-pressure systems (*depressions) in the atmosphere. *See also* FRONTOGENESIS.

cyclone 1. The name for a *hurricane in the northern Indian Ocean. **2.** *See* DEPRESSION. **3.** *See* TORNADO.

cyclone collector A device with no moving parts that removes dust from waste gases. The velocity of an input gas stream is transformed into a confined vortex, and dust particles are driven centrifugally to the wall of the cyclone body, from where they are collected.

cyclonic circulation The movement of air around a *depression. In the northern hemisphere the flow is anti-clockwise, and in the southern hemisphere it is clockwise.

cyclonic rain (frontal rain) *Rain that occurs in a *depression, when warm air rises above cold air and cools *adiabatically, causing the *condensation of *water vapour and the formation of *raindrops.

cytoplasm The contents of a *cell, other than the *nucleus. *See also* PROTOPLASM.

CZMA *See* COASTAL ZONE MANAGEMENT ACT.

D

dairy Relating to the production of milk or milk products, such as butter and cheese.

dairy farm A farm where *dairy products are produced.

Daisyworld A *computer model developed by *James Lovelock to illustrate his *Gaia hypothesis on any planet that supports life, based on how black and white daisies adapt to changes in *radiation and temperature.

dalapon A selective *herbicide and plant growth regulator that is used to control annual and perennial grasses, and the growth of reeds and sedges in water. It is used on a range of crop plants either before or after emergence.

DALR *See* DRY ADIABATIC LAPSE RATE.

Dalton minimum A period of low solar activity that lasted from about 1790 to 1830 during which temperatures fell, at Oberlach Station, Germany, by 2°C over 20 years. It is named after the English meteorologist and chemist John Dalton (1766–1844). *See also* MAUNDER MINIMUM; SPÖRER MINIMUM.

dam An artificial barrier constructed across a river or valley, usually for flood control, *irrigation, and/or power generation. *See also* RESERVOIR.

damage assessment Evaluation of the magnitude, physical extent, and types of damage that a biological or physical *resource experiences as a result of an event such as a *natural hazard.

daminozide *See* ALAR.

danger The condition of being susceptible to harm or injury, for example as a result of exposure to a *natural hazard.

Dark Ages Cool Period (European Migration Period) A period from about 300–800 CE, when the average global temperature was up to 0.5°C lower than the 1961–90 mean. The Black Sea froze in 800 and in 829 the Nile froze. The alternative name refers to the extensive migration that occurred in Europe as people moved southwards, seeking warmer climes.

dark earth *See* CHERNOZEM.

Darling, Sir Frank Fraser (1903–79) A British ecologist and animal geneticist whose 1969 Reith Lectures for the BBC, 'Wilderness and Plenty' (published in 1970 with the same title) was influential in drawing attention to the relationship between humans and the natural environment. Darling was knighted in 1970 and served on the Royal Commission on Environmental Pollution from 1970 to 1973.

Darwin, Charles Robert (1809–82) The British naturalist who is widely considered to be the father of the theory of *evolution. In his landmark work, *On the Origin of Species by Means of Natural Selection*, published in 1859, he presented compelling evidence for evolution by means of *natural selection.

Darwin Day An international celebration of science and humanity that is held on 12 February each year, to celebrate the birth of Charles *Darwin in 1809.

Darwin Declaration An international agreement reached in Darwin, Australia in 1988, in response to the *United Nations Framework Convention on Biological Diversity, that countries should work together to improve knowledge and understanding of the world's biological diversity.

Darwinism The theory put forward by Charles *Darwin that *species originate and develop by evolution from simpler species, and that evolution is driven mainly by *natural selection.

data (*sing.* datum) A collection of facts (usually created by measurement) from which conclusions may be drawn. *See also* INFORMATION.

data mining The processing of large amounts of data in order to extract new kinds of useful information from them, based on patterns and relationships. *See also* INFORMATICS.

dating *See* ABSOLUTE DATING; RELATIVE DATING.

datum level A reference (such as mean *sea level) against which to measure heights or depths.

daughter product *See* DECAY PRODUCT.

dawn (daybreak) The first light of day, in the eastern sky before sunrise. *See also* DUSK.

day 1. A 24-hour period of time that begins at midnight and ends the following midnight, during which the *Earth makes a complete rotation on its axis with reference to the Sun. 2. The time between *sunrise and *sunset, when it is light outside. *Contrast* NIGHT.

day degrees The departure of the average daily temperature from a defined base (e.g. the minimum recognized temperature for the growth of a plant species). The number of day degrees may be totalled to assess the accumulated warmth of a particular year's growing season for crops.

day length The number of hours between *sunrise and *sunset.

daybreak *See* DAWN.

daylight Light that is received from the Sun and the sky, during the daytime.

daylighting 1. Using sunlight to provide supplementary lighting for the interior of a building. 2. The act of cutting back vegetation bordering a road, in order to encourage the growth of new herbs and shrubs.

DCMU *See* DIURON.

DDT A colourless *insecticide (dichlorodiphenyltrichloroethane), which is persistent and can collect in the fatty tissues of certain animals. It was used during the Second World War to control the spread of typhus and malaria by insects, and was widely used as an agricultural *pesticide during the 1950s and 1960s. It has been banned in the US since 1973 as a result of growing public concern because of its persistence in the environment and accumulation in the *food chain. It particularly damaged the peregrine falcon, whose numbers declined rapidly because DDT was causing the birds' egg shells to become thin and the eggs to break before hatching.

death rate (fatality rate, mortality) The number of individuals in a population who die in a given year, usually expressed as a ratio (number of deaths per year per 1000 individuals).

debris Dead organic material (leaves, twigs, etc.) and sediment.

debris flow (flow) A type of overland or submarine *mass movement involving a downslope flow of a saturated mass of soil and rock debris, with more than half of the material being particles larger than *sand size. Slower than a *debris slide.

debris slide (slide) A rapid downslope movement of an *unconsolidated mass of mud, sediment, and rock. Faster than a *debris flow.

debt-for-nature swap An emerging approach to the *conservation of *wildlife, which involves conservation organizations (usually from developed countries) acquiring part of the international debt of a particular developing country at an agreed discount price. The organization then redeems the debt in local currency, and uses it to fund conservation activities such as the setting up and running of *nature reserves and *national parks. Supporters of such schemes claim that there are no losers and few financial risks in this innovative form of international financial transaction, and for this reason it is an ideal way of raising the financial resources required for major conservation initiatives. The debt-for-nature swap mechanism also helps to break down some of the persistent barriers that inhibit collaborative policies in a world of sovereign states—including lack of co-operation, different agendas and different objectives, short-term perspectives, and inward-looking and territorially defined concerns.

decade A period of ten years.

Decade of the Environment The 1970s, when a large number of the most important US policies towards the environment were passed because of greater public engagement, broader support for environmental policies in Congress, pro-environmental leadership from Republican and Democratic presidents, and favourable interpretations of statutory laws by key US courts (particularly the Supreme Court).

decant To pour or draw off the upper layer of liquid after the heavier material has settled. For example, drawing off water after a solid pollutant has settled out, as a means of cleaning up polluted water.

decay To graduate decrease or decompose. **1.** The breakdown of *organic matter by *micro-organisms. **2.** The decrease of a radioactive substance because of nuclear emission of alpha or beta particles, or gamma rays. Each *radionuclide has a specific *half-life and *decay constant.

decay constant The rate of *radioactive decay, which is characteristic of the given nuclide. The decay constant is the probability that an atom of the *radionuclide will decay within a stated time (it is measured in units of reciprocal time).

decay product (daughter product) An element that is formed by the *radioactive decay of another element. The decay product may be stable, or radioactive and subject to further decay.

decay series The sequence of radioactive daughter nuclides formed by the decay of a parent nuclide to a final, stable daughter nuclide. For example, uranium has three naturally occurring isotopes, ^{238}U, ^{235}U, and ^{234}U, all of which are radioactive. Decay of ^{238}U gives rise to the uranium series, which includes ^{234}U as an intermediate daughter and ends in stable ^{206}Pb. The decay of ^{235}U gives rise to the actinium series, which ends in stable ^{207}Pb.

dechlorination The partial or complete removal of chlorine from a substance, for example by using *activated carbon and *sulphur dioxide.

decibel (dB) A unit that measures the intensity or loudness of sound.

deciduous Applied to a tree or plant that sheds its leaves at the end of the growing season (autumn) each year (e.g. ash, beech, hickory, maple, and oak, *compare* EVERGREEN), or to any part of an animal that is shed seasonally (e.g. deer antlers).

deciduous forest A *temperate or *tropical forest in which the *deciduous trees shed their leaves during either cold or dry seasons. It is relatively fertile (because of the abundant leaf litter), plant biodiversity is high, and typical trees include oak, hickory, maple, ash, and beech. Found in areas with moderate rainfall and marked seasons.

deciduous summer forest One of the two kinds of broadleaved forest in the middle latitudes, the other being broadleaved and *evergreen forest. The deciduous summer forest is by far the more important of the two in the north-ern hemisphere, and is absent from the southern hemisphere. The deciduous nature of the forest is believed to be principally an adaptation to drought in winter, when the soil is frozen.

decision-making The process of acting upon the best information available in order to determine the most appropriate course of action.

declination 1. A downward slope or bend. **2.** Angular distance north or south of the *celestial equator. **3.** The angle between *magnetic north and geographical north.

decommission To permanently shut down a facility (such as a *nuclear reactor or *power plant) or withdraw it from service or active use *Contrast* COMMISSION.

decommissioning waste The waste materials that are produced when a facility (such as a nuclear *power plant) is *decommissioned.

decomposer *See* DETRITIVORE.

decomposition 1. The breakdown of *organic matter into smaller particles by organisms such as bacteria and fungi, releasing simple organic material (such as sugars and proteins) and inorganic compounds (*nutrients) back into the environment where they become available to *plants. **2.** The *chemical weathering of *rock.

decontamination Removal of harmful substances (such as chemicals, bacteria, or radioactive material) from exposed individuals, rooms, and furnishings in buildings or from the exterior environment.

deduction *See* DEDUCTIVE REASONING.

deductive reasoning (deduction) Reasoning from the general to the particular, for example by developing a hypothesis based on theory and then testing it from an examination of facts. *Compare* INDUCTIVE REASONING.

deep ecology A *worldview or set of beliefs that calls for a major shift in human attitudes, values, and behaviour that rejects *anthropocentrism and directs personal action to protect *nature and improve the *environment. *Contrast* SHALLOW ECOLOGY. *See also* ECOCENTRIC; RADICAL ECOLOGY.

deep ocean Areas of the *oceans that are seaward of the *continental shelf.

deep-scattering layer A well-defined layer in the *ocean that reflects *sonar and indicates the presence of fish, squid, or other large marine organisms.

deepwater habitat Any area of open water that is deeper than two metres or covers the deepest emerging vegetation.

Deepwater Horizon An oil exploration rig that sank in the Gulf of Mexico on 22 April 2010, following an explosion and fire, releasing an estimated 4.9 million barrels of oil and causing the most serious oil spill in US history. Water movements in the gulf accelerated the break-up of the oil and the effects on wildlife were smaller than many had feared.

deep-well injection Disposal of waste fluid (particularly *hazardous waste) by pumping it into a deep well, where it is stored underground in permeable rock surrounded by impermeable layers.

deflation The removal of *clay and dust from dry soil by wind. *See also* DESERT PAVEMENT.

deflocculate The breakdown of clusters of soil particles. The term is usually applied to *clay soils.

defluoridation The removal of excess *fluoride in drinking water in order to protect teeth from damage or staining.

defoliant A chemical herbicide that causes the leaves to fall from trees and growing plants. *See also* AGENT ORANGE.

defoliate To remove the leaves from plants, trees, or shrubs.

deforestation (forest clearance) The permanent clearance of a *forest, usually rapidly by cutting or burning over a large area, without replanting or natural *regeneration. *Contrast* AFFORESTATION.

deformation A change in the original shape of a material, such as a layer of *sedimentary rock that has been affected by *folding. *See also* CRUSTAL DEFORMATION.

DEFRA In the UK, the Department for Environment, Food and Rural Affairs, formerly *MAFF.

degasification The removal of dissolved gases from water in order to purify it.

deglaciation The melting (*ablation) and receding of *ice sheets and *glaciers, which uncovers the land beneath. *Contrast* GLACIATION.

degradable Able to be broken down or separated into a simpler form, using chemical, physical, or biological means. *See also* BIODEGRADABLE.

degradation 1. The chemical or biological breakdown of a complex compound into simpler compounds. **2.** General lowering of land surfaces by *erosion. *Contrast* AGGRADATION.

degree day *See* ACCUMULATED TEMPERATURE.

DEIS *See* DRAFT ENVIRONMENTAL IMPACT STATEMENT.

delist The process of changing the designated status of a particular resource, such as removing a species of animal or plant from the *IUCN *Red List, or removing a *Superfund waste site from the *National Priorities List in the USA.

dell A small wooded hollow.

Delphi method A method of long-term forecasting or *decision-making based on expert judgement. It involves a number of stages: experts are interviewed anonymously and separately, in order to gain their views on a particular issue or problem; the results are combined and fed back to the experts as a group; each expert is then interviewed again, in the light of peer group opinion. In theory, the process continues until consensus emerges within the group.

delta A fan-shaped *alluvial deposit at the mouth of a *river, built up by the deposition of successive layers of fine-grained *sediment due to a reduction in velocity of the current so that the sediment settles out.

deluge A heavy downpour of *rain, or a heavy *flood.

demand The ability and desire to buy goods and services, or the quantity of a good or service that is needed in order to meet the requirements of the user. *See also* MARKET EQUILIBRIUM; SUPPLY.

demand management (demand-side management) An approach to the allocation of scarce *resources that is based on minimizing wastage, restricting supply, and educating people to use less of the resource and use it more carefully.

demand schedule The relationship between price and quantity demanded of a good or service, which shows how much would be bought or consumed at various prices at a particular time.

demand species *Native and desired *non-native species of plants and animals that have a high social, cultural, or economic value.

demand-side management *See* DEMAND MANAGEMENT.

demersal Applied to fish and other *aquatic animals that live at or near the bottom of a *sea or *lake.

demersal fish *See* GROUNDFISH.

demetron-S-methyl A *systemic *insecticide and *acaricide used to control aphids and red spider mites in agricultural and horticultural crops. It is flammable and toxic to vertebrates.

demineralization The removal of dissolved minerals and mineral salts from a liquid, particularly water.

demographic Relating to *population *statistics, changes, and trends based on measures of *fertility, *mortality, and *migration.

demographic balancing equation An equation that is used to calculate *population changes from one year to the next in a given area, based on the number of *births, *deaths, and *migrations. The general form of the equation is a *mass balance equation, in which end population = starting population ± natural increase ± net migration, where natural increase = births – deaths, and net migration = immigrants – emigrants. At the global scale there is no net migration (unless the Earth is invaded by aliens from another planet, or people permanently leave the Earth to set up home in space), so the balancing equation is then simply end population = starting population ± natural increase.

demographic force Any of the three factors (*fertility, *mortality, and *migration) that determine the level, composition, and distribution of population in a particular place or area. *See also* DEMOGRAPHIC BALANCING EQUATION; DEMOGRAPHIC TRANSITION MODEL.

demographic transition The growth pattern that many human *populations go through as countries develop, undergo *industrialization and *urbanization, and improve their *standard of living. Birth and death rates converge and *zero population growth is achieved.

demographic transition model A four-stage model that shows how *birth rates and *death rates change through time in a particular country or area, giving rise to phases of population stability and change. During stage one the death rate is usually very high because of poor health and difficult living conditions, *life expectancy at birth is less than 30 years, but birth rates are also high and so *population growth rate is zero or close to zero. Stage two begins when the death rate begins to fall (usually because of improved living conditions, better food supplies, and better health practices such as immunization). The birth rate remains high, and may even increase because women are healthier. A high population growth rate is triggered by the excess of births over deaths. It takes time, sometimes generations, for social attitudes (such as the high value attached to having children) to change, so during this phase birth rates remain high. In stage three the birth rate declines (because of better education, better family planning, more career options for women, and reduced *infant mortality), and it eventually catches up with the death rate. Population growth remains relatively high during the early part of this stage, but it falls close to zero towards the end of the stage. By stage four the birth rate and the death rate have converged, and they oscillate around a relatively low level. The population growth rate is once again zero or close to zero during this phase, in which birth rates and death rates are once again similar but now both low. By the year 2000 most *developed countries had completed all four stages, whilst most *developing countries lagged behind at stage two or early in stage three.

demographics *Statistics that describe the characteristics of a *population, such as age, sex, race, family size, income, and location of residence.

demography The statistical study of the characteristics of *populations, including distribution, age structure and composition, and patterns of *fertility, *mortality, and *migration.

den A rain-proof, weather-tight cavity in a tree or a space dug by animals among rocks or in soil. *See also* DEN TREE.

den tree (cavity tree) A tree with cavities in which birds, mammals, or insects (such as bees) can nest.

denaturing Making reversible or irreversible alterations to the biological activity of *proteins or *nucleic acids, through changes in their molecular structure that do not involve breaking the primary bonds between *amino acids or *nucleotides in the chain. This may be accomplished by changes of solvent, *pH, or temperature, or through the physical abuse of the molecules.

dendritic A type of *drainage pattern that develops as a random network and has branches like a tree.

dendroarchaeology The use of *growth rings in trees to date when timber was felled, transported, processed, and used for construction.

dendrochronology A dating technique based on the analysis of *growth rings in trees. The number of rings indicates age, and the width of individual rings indicates climatic conditions at the time of growth and is used in *dendroclimatology. *See also* TREE RING.

dendroclimatology A technique used to reconstruct past *climate, based on analysis of *growth rings in trees, as *proxy climate indicators. Ring width reflects the climatic conditions (temperature and/or precipitation) during the growing season (but also the level of disease and predation), and rings can be counted to give ages. *See also* TREE RING.

dendrogram A branching, tree-like diagram, which usually has a single source, and shows relationships produced by *classification. *See also* CLADOGRAM.

dendrology The study of the identification, habits, and distribution of *trees. *See also* SILVI-CULTURE.

denitrification The biological process in which *nitrates are reduced to *nitrogen gas, by *denitrifying bacteria, in soil under *anaerobic conditions. *Contrast* NITRIFICATION.

denitrifying bacteria Free-living *bacteria in soil that convert *nitrates to gaseous *nitrogen and *nitrous oxide.

dense fog A *cloud with its base on the ground surface, that reduces *visibility to 0.5 km or less.

dense non-aqueous phase liquid (DNAPL) A liquid that does not dissolve in water, and which is also denser than water so it sinks. Many *chlorinated solvents are DNAPLs.

density 1. The mass of a substance per unit volume (kilograms per cubic metre, kg m^{-3}). **2.** The number of *individuals of a defined group that are present in a given area at a particular time. *See also* FREQUENCY; POPULATION DENSITY.

density current A *current in water that flows because of differences in *density. For example density currents in the *ocean are caused by differences in *temperature, *salinity, and *turbidity.

density stratification The creation of layers in a water body due to differences in *density, which may be caused by differences in *temperature and in concentrations of *dissolved solids and *suspended solids.

density-dependent The regulation of the size of a population by mechanisms that are controlled by *population density (such as the availability of *resources, or the incidence of *contagious disease), and that become more effective as density increases. *Contrast* DENSITY-INDEPENDENT.

density-independent A factor that influences the individuals in a population in ways that do not vary with *population density. *Contrast* DENSITY-DEPENDENT.

denudation The wearing down of the land surface by natural geological processes, which involves *weathering, *mass movement, and *erosion.

denudation chronology The long-term history of *landscape development by *denudation. *See also* CYCLE OF EROSION; EROSION SURFACE.

denuded Laid bare, stripped of all *vegetation cover, often as a result of a disturbance such as a *landslide.

deoxygenation The consumption of *oxygen in water by aquatic organisms, as they decompose (*oxidize) organic materials.

deoxyribonucleic acid *See* DNA.

dependency In *conservation assessment, the reliance of a *species, *community, or ecological process on a particular location (such as a *feeding ground or a *migration corridor) or structure (such as a *coniferous forest) for survival.

dependency ratio In a given human population, the number of economically dependent, non-working members (who are younger than 15 or older than 65) compared with the number of productive, working members (aged 15 to 64).

dependency theory A theory that the relationships between advanced *capitalist societies and less developed, poor countries has always been exploitative. Development of the former has resulted in underdevelopment of the latter; the latter are kept dependent on the former by the capitalist system, and as a result the former continue to exploit the latter for their own gain.

depensation In some animal species (e.g. whales) an increase in *parasitism and *predation that occurs when the size of a *population falls below a threshold. This further depletes the population, reducing the likelihood that it will recover.

depletable resource *See* NON-RENEWABLE RESOURCE.

depletion Decline in availability that results from using *abiotic (*non-renewable) resources, or from using *biotic (*renewable) resources faster than they can be renewed.

depletion time The time it takes to use up a *non-renewable resource.

deposit 1. An accumulation of *sediment, minerals, and precipitated substances. *See also* ALLUVIUM; COLLUVIUM; BOULDER CLAY. **2.** A facility where things can be stored for safekeeping.

deposit feeder *See* DETRITIVORE.

deposition 1. The accumulation or laying down of *sediment. **2.** The conversion of *water vapour directly into *ice, without first becoming a liquid. In chemistry this is known as sublimation.

deposition nuclei (ice nuclei) Tiny particles in the atmosphere on which ice crystals can grow by the process of *deposition.

depositional environment Any part of the *environment in which *sediment is deposited, such as a *lake, *coast, or *river.

depression A midlatitude frontal *cyclone, often associated with overcast skies and persistent precipitation.

depression storage *See* DETENTION STORAGE.

deranged drainage pattern A *drainage system having no obvious pattern. Sometimes found in areas of low relief, low slope, and large sediment loads, and typical of recently glaciated areas.

derelict land Land that has been so damaged by extractive or other industrial activity, or by prolonged neglect, that it is unsightly and incapable of *beneficial use without remedial treatment.

derived character (advanced character, apomorphic character) In *cladistics, a feature that is shared among members of smaller groups or *clades and is believed to have evolved at a later date than primitive features.

derived demand The *demand for a particular *resource (such as bricks) that is created by the desire to satisfy the demand for some other resource (such as houses).

dermal exposure Contact between a gas, liquid, or solid (such as a *pollutant) and the skin.

dermal toxicity The ability of a *pesticide or *toxic chemical to poison an organism (including people and animals) by contact with the skin.

DES *See* DIETHYLSTILBESTROL.

desalination The removal of *salt from water, usually by *distillation, *freezing, *electrodialysis, or *reverse osmosis.

desalting The process of removing *salt from *crude oil.

descendant A person who is descended from a particular ancestor or race, as an *offspring.

desert A dry *biome that is common in the *subtropics, the interior of continents, and in polar regions, and that supports plants and animals adapted to extreme water shortage. It is created by an *arid climate in which, averaged over the year, *evaporation exceeds *precipitation, and precipitation is infrequent and unpredictable. Desert is likely to develop anywhere that receives less than 25 cm of rain a year. *See also* TROPICAL DESERT; TEMPERATE DESERT; COLD DESERT; SAND DESERT.

desert climate Different climates produce *tropical deserts, *temperate deserts, and *cold deserts, but they have in common wide *diurnal variations in *temperature, low *relative humidity, limited *precipitation, more or less continuous sunshine throughout the year, little *cloud cover and clear skies, and occasional intense local convectional showers. Middle-latitude deserts are cooler than the low-latitude deserts and they receive low and unreliable rainfall. Most are located in the dry *rain shadows *leeward of topographic barriers, or in the interior of large land masses far from *maritime sources of moisture. Such deserts have much less extreme climates than low-latitude deserts and are much less inhospitable to people.

desert crust A hard surface layer that develops in a *desert climate, caused by the *evaporation of water from the ground which leaves *calcium carbonate, *gypsum, or other cementing materials as a *precipitate. *Contrast* DESERT PAVEMENT.

desert grassland A North American *grassland vegetation that grows in semi-arid climates on *bajadas and in valley bottoms where clay-rich soils prevent water from draining. It is often dominated by bunch grasses or (where disturbed) various shrubs.

desert lake basin A depression in a hot *desert that receives drainage from inflowing streams, forming an *exorheic lake which is often salty.

desert pavement Gravel and stones left after wind and water erosion have removed finer material from a desert floor. *Contrast* DESERT CRUST.

desert province A region of the Earth in which deserts are found. There are five main desert provinces: the Sahara, southern Africa, South America, North America, and Australia. There are also deserts in central Asia, central Greenland, and Antarctica.

Desert Solitaire A book by *Edward Abbey who regarded the *wilderness as a place where people can separate themselves from society but from which they need to return to society refreshed and ready to deal with the problems of society. Regarded by some as a latter-day *Walden.

desert varnish A dark, hard, shiny coating of *iron and *manganese oxides that is found on *rocks in *arid regions.

desert wind A hot, dry, dusty wind that blows outwards from the semi-permanent *anticyclones centred on the subtropical *deserts. The wind is hot in summer and cold in winter.

desiccant Any material (such as a chemical) that absorbs moisture.

desiccation 1. A long-term loss of water associated with a change in regional climate. *See also* EXSICCATION. **2.** The drying-out of an organism that is exposed to the air.

design capacity The maximum volume of flow that an engineering structure is designed to handle, such as the number of vehicles using a road per day or the average daily flow of material into a water treatment plant.

designated pollutant An *air pollutant (such as *acid mist or *fluorides) which is not defined in the US *Clean Air Act as either a *criteria pollutant or a *hazardous air pollutant, but for which *emission standards exist for new sources.

DESERTIFICATION

The spread of desert-like conditions in *semi-arid regions due to human activities (including *overgrazing, *deforestation, or *soil erosion), prolonged *drought, and/or climatic change (*global warming), which cause long-term changes in the soil, climate, and plants and animals of an area. The term was originally used to mean the spread of *desert conditions over adjacent areas as a result of climatic factors and/or use of resources by humans, but it is now used more broadly to describe a range of processes occurring in many arid and semi-arid areas. An estimated 135 million people are directly affected by desertification, mainly in Africa, the Indian subcontinent, and South America. But the problems are not confined to the particular places where desert expansion, and soil degradation are concentrated. On a global scale the major impacts include stress on food producing capacity, reduction in *biodiversity, and modification of climate. In 1977 the *United Nations Conference on Desertification (**UNCOD**) concluded that desertification was then one of the most serious environmental problems in the world. UNCOD data suggest that about 6000 km^2 of land are turned into desert each year, and that the productive capacity of a further 210 000 km^2 is ruined each year, making it unprofitable for farmers to use. More recent data suggest that over 3.1 million km^2 of the world's rangelands (80% of the total), 3.35 million km^2 of rain-fed cropland (60% of the total), and 0.4 million km^2 of irrigated *drylands (30% of the total) are threatened by moderate to severe desertification.

designated use Uses for water that are identified in state water quality standards in the USA for which water quality must be protected. These include *hydroelectric power generation, navigation, public water supply, fisheries, and recreation (such as swimming, boating, and fishing).

designer bug A common term for *microbes that are developed through *biotechnology and can degrade specific *toxic chemicals in toxic waste dumps or in *groundwater.

desired condition The future condition of a particular resource (such as a forest or grassland) that is expected to result if the goals and objectives of resource management are fully achieved.

desired plant community The plant *community that best meets the agreed objectives for a particular site, as defined in a *land use or management plan.

desorption The release of atoms, molecules, or ions that are attached to solid surfaces. *Contrast* ABSORPTION.

destratification The mixing of water within a *lake or *reservoir in order to reduce or remove separate layers (for example of *temperature or *aquatic organisms). *Contrast* STRATIFICATION.

destructive distillation The decomposition of organic material by heating it in the absence of air. Destructive distillation of *coal yields *coke and *coal tar. Solid domestic refuse can be processed in this way by heating it to 500–1000°C; this reduces its mass by about 90%. Destructive distillation produces combustible gases, volatile liquids, tar, and *charcoal that can be recycled; the useless residue can be disposed of by *landfill.

destructive margin *See* DESTRUCTIVE PLATE BOUNDARY.

destructive metabolism *See* CATABOLISM.

destructive plate boundary (destructive margin) A convergent boundary between adjacent *crustal plates that are moving towards each other, where crust is being destroyed by *subduction. Usually associated with *volcanoes and *earthquake activity. *See also* PLATE TECTONICS; CONSTRUCTIVE PLATE BOUNDARY.

desulphurization (fuel desulphurization) The reduction or removal of the *sulphur content of *fuel in order to reduce *air pollution.

detention storage (depression storage) The temporary storage of surface water in low areas such as puddles, *bogs, *ponds, and *wetlands, from which it evaporates or flows overland towards a stream channel.

detention time The period of time for which a particular material is stored temporarily in a particular way, such as the storage of water in a reservoir before being used, or in a *settling basin.

detergent A synthetic cleansing agent that, when added to water, helps to remove oil and dirt. *See also* SURFACTANT.

deterministic A process or event that is predictable because it is governed by definite rules of system behaviour which produce the same results each time. *Contrast* RANDOM; STOCHASTIC.

detoxify To remove a poison or render safe through removal of a poison.

detrital carbonate Crystalline *calcium carbonate that is found in ocean sediments and is usually derived from the *weathering of carbonate rock.

detrital food chain *See* DETRITAL PATHWAY.

detrital pathway (detrital food chain) A food chain in which the primary producers (green plants) form litter (*detritus) on which decomposers (micro-organisms) and *detritivores feed, with the subsequent transfer of energy to various levels of *carnivore, e.g. leaf litter → earthworm → blackbird → sparrowhawk). Detritus from organisms at higher *trophic levels may also form the basis for a detrital pathway. *Compare* GRAZING PATHWAY.

detrital sediment A sediment (such as *detrital carbonate) that is produced by the mechanical breakdown of rock by *weathering and *erosion.

detritivore (decomposer, deposit feeder, detritus feeder) An animal (such as an earthworm, maggot, or woodlouse) that feeds on dead and decaying *organic matter from plants and animals. *See also* DECOMPOSITION.

detritus 1. *Organic debris from dead *organisms, which is often an important source of *nutrients in a *food web. **2.** Loose, *unconsolidated particles or sediments that are formed by the *weathering of rocks.

detritus feeder *See* DETRITIVORE.

deuterium (D) An *isotope of *hydrogen that contains one *proton and one *neutron in its *nucleus.

developed country A country that has evolved through the *demographic transition and is technologically advanced, capital-intensive, highly urbanized, and wealthy. These are usually industrialized countries such as European countries, Canada, the USA, Australia, Japan, New Zealand, and Russia. *Compare* DEVELOPING COUNTRY; MORE DEVELOPED COUNTRY; TRANSITIONAL NATION. *See also* ANNEX I COUNTRIES; ANNEX B COUNTRIES.

developed land Any land that has been built on or substantially altered to benefit people, including development of settlements, factories, and roads.

developed recreation Any form of recreation requiring facilities that, in turn, result in concentrated use of the area. Examples include skiing (that requires ski lifts, car parks, buildings, and roads) and campgrounds (that require roads, picnic tables, and toilet facilities). *Contrast* DISPERSED RECREATION; INFORMAL OUTDOOR RECREATION.

developing country (less developed country) A low-income country with an economy that is largely based on agriculture and/or the extraction and export of minerals, which may be going through the *demographic transition, is often in the process of industrialization, and usually has few resources to spare to solve its own socio-economic and environmental problems. Most developing countries are in the southern hemisphere. They were formerly known as Third World countries. *Compare* DEVELOPED COUNTRY; TRANSITIONAL NATION.

development A process in which something changes by degrees to a different stage, particularly a more advanced stage. **1.** The process by which a living organism is produced and matures from a single cell. **2.** Conversion of land into *developed land. **3.** Conversion of a *developing country/nation into a *developed country/nation.

development control The statutory process *land use planning system in the UK, through which a local authority determines whether a proposal for a large-scale building development should be granted planning permission, and whether any particular conditions or restrictions should apply.

development rights The rights to develop land, as distinguished from ownership of it. *Compare* CONSERVATION EASEMENT.

development well A *well that is drilled with the intent of producing *oil or *gas from a reservoir that is known to be productive.

Devensian The most recent *continental glaciation, known as the Devensian in Britain and the Wisconsinian in North America, which began about 70000 years ago, reached a peak about 18000 years ago, and ended about 10000 years ago. *Ice sheets covered much of North America and Europe/Asia and sea surface temperatures were about 2–2.5°C below present ones.

Devonian A period of geological time in the *Palaeozoic era, dating from 416.0 to 359.2 million years ago, during which *fish were dominant and the first *trees, *insects, and *vertebrates appeared.

(((⊕))) SEE WEB LINKS
• The Devonian period of the Palaeozoic era.

dew Small drops of moisture that form on cool surfaces at night, caused by the *condensation of *water vapour from the air on to surfaces that have radiated away the heat they absorbed by day.

dew point (condensation point, isobaric saturation point) The temperature at which *water vapour in air will condense on a cool surface and form drops (*dew). This is the temperature at which a parcel of air would become saturated if it were cooled with no change in the amount of moisture it contained or in the atmospheric pressure.

dewater 1. To remove some of the water in a *sludge or *slurry, in order to dry the sludge so that it can be handled and disposed. **2.** To drain water from a tank or trench. **3.** To extract groundwater by wells, *electro-osmosis, *sumps and drains, or by exclusion.

D-horizon (R-horizon) The unweathered *bedrock beneath the soil in a *soil profile. *See also* SOIL HORIZON.

diabatic The direct transfer of heat energy. Examples include *condensation, *evaporation, *solar radiation, and the release of *latent heat. *Contrast* ADIABATIC.

diadromous Applied to fish that regularly migrate between the sea and freshwater systems. *Compare* AMPHIDROMOUS; ANADROMOUS; CATADROMOUS; POTAMODROMOUS.

diagenesis The processes that take place at low temperature and pressure in a sediment after *deposition. These include *compaction, cementation (*lithification), *dissolution, and recrystallization.

diagnostic horizon A soil layer that contains a combination of characteristics typical of that kind of soil.

diallate A *soil-acting *thiocarbamate herbicide used to control weed grasses, especially in brassica and beet crops. It can cause skin irritation and is harmful to fish.

diamicton A general term for unsorted, unstratified rock debris that is composed of a wide range of particle sizes and could be formed by a variety of different processes.

diamide insecticides A small group of *insecticides used to control lepidopteran pests.

diamond A crystalline *allotrope of *carbon that is very hard (the hardest known substance) and durable. It is valued as a precious gem when it is cut and polished.

diapause A period of dormancy in insects and other *invertebrates, during which growth or development is suspended. Roughly equivalent to *hibernation.

diapir A dome-like intrusion of a light rock, e.g. salt, granite, into an overlying denser rock. Diapirs form where a system is disturbed, e.g. by an earthquake, and the denser material sinks, fracturing as it does so, around the lighter material.

diastrophism The deformation of the Earth's *crust by *tectonic forces, which gives rise to continents, *mountains, and major geological features such as *folds and *faults, through the processes of *warping, *folding, and *faulting.

diatom Microscopic single-celled *algae that grow in both fresh and saltwater. They produce *silica skeletons that are often preserved in lake or marine sediments after death and are studied in *palaeolimnology. There are more than 11500 different species of diatoms, and they are a common form of marine *phytoplankton and a primary food source for aquatic animals, especially *filter-feeding shellfish. Diatoms belong to the division (phylum) Bacillariophyta.

diatom ooze A fine muddy deep sea *sediment that is formed mainly from the hard *silica remains of *diatoms.

diatomaceous earth *See* DIATOMITE.

diatomite (diatomaceous earth) A light, easily crumbled, *silica-rich material that is formed mainly from *diatom remains and is used to filter out solid waste in *wastewater treatment plants.

dichlobenil A *soil-acting *herbicide that is used for total weed control on land not intended for cropping and for selective weed control in orchards and forests. It is also used to kill submerged and floating plants in still or slow-moving water.

dichlorodiphenyltrichloroethane *See* DDT.

2-4-dichlorophenoxyacetic acid (2-4-D) *See* AUXIN.

dichlorprop A *systemic herbicide that interferes with plant growth. It is used to kill post-emergent broadleaved annual and perennial weeds in lawns and other turf, on roadsides, and in forests, but not on agricultural crops. It can cause eye irritation but is of low toxicity.

dichlorvos An *organophosphate *insecticide and *acaricide of short persistence that is used to kill crawling and flying insects in private homes, in glasshouses, and outdoors on fruit and vegetables where it achieves a rapid kill shortly before harvest. Traces rarely appear in food products. It has been withdrawn from domestic use in the UK.

dicotyledon A flowering plant of the *angiosperm group, which has a seed usually with two seed leaves (cotyledons).

dieback *See* POPULATION CRASH.

diesel engine *See* INTERNAL COMBUSTION ENGINE.

diesel oil A form of *petroleum that is used to fuel *internal combustion engines. *See* CLEAN FUEL.

diet The usual food and drink that an organism consumes.

diethylstilbestrol (DES) A synthetic oestrogen drug that was once widely prescribed to prevent miscarriages, and was used in feed for livestock and poultry.

differentiation 1. The process by which cells grow to become more specialized. **2.** In tackling climate change under the *Kyoto Protocol, the setting of different *emissions reduction targets and timetables for individual countries, to allow for differing national circumstances.

diffraction The bending of light around objects (such as cloud and fog droplets) which produces fringes of light and dark or coloured bands.

diffuse radiation *Radiation within the *atmosphere that is scattered by tiny particles and travels in all directions, rather than travelling in a beam.

diffused air A method of *aeration that forces *oxygen into *sewage by pumping air through perforated pipes inside a *holding tank.

diffusion The random movement of atoms, molecules, or ions from areas of higher to lower *solute concentration, which tends to distribute them more uniformly.

digester An enclosed *composting system that includes a device to mix and aerate the waste materials in order to speed *decomposition by *aerobic bacteria.

digestion The biochemical *decomposition of *organic matter into mineral compounds and simple organic compounds that can be absorbed into the body of an *organism or excreted from it. *Bacteria decompose *sewage in this way.

dike *See* DYKE.

diluent A fluid that is used to *dilute a substance.

dilute To become weaker in strength or affect, for example thinning out a solution or making it less concentrated by adding a liquid, usually water.

dilution The process of reducing the concentration of a *solute in solution, usually by mixing it with more *solvent.

dilution ratio The ratio between the concentrations of a *solute in a solution before and after *dilution.

dimethoate A widely used systemic *organophosphate *insecticide and *acaricide that kills a wide range of insects and mites on fruit and vegetable crops. It does not persist in the environment, but is moderately toxic to humans.

dimethyl sulphide (DMS) A molecular gas that is produced by *phytoplankton in the surface waters of the *ocean and escapes into the *atmosphere. Oxidation of DMS creates a *sulphate-based *aerosol that acts as *cloud condensation nuclei, and DMS is a major source of such nuclei over the open oceans, far from land.

dimictic A *freshwater lake or reservoir that has two mixing periods (*turnovers) a year, usually in spring and autumn. *See also* MIXING CYCLE.

diminishing returns A situation in any *open system (such as a company or the economy) in which continually increasing the input of a particular resource, with other inputs fixed, results in smaller and smaller returns for each increment.

dinitro pesticides Chemical compounds that contain a dinitro group, i.e. two nitrogen atoms, and that are used as contact *herbicides, *fungicides, and *insecticides. They are very effective against their targets, but highly toxic to mammals.

dinitro-*ortho*-cresol *See* DNOC.

dinitrophenol pesticide (DNP) A compound that was used as a dieting aid in the 1930s, but was then banned due to its side-effects. It is used industrially and as a *fungicide on fences, pilings, etc. to prevent wood rot, as an *acaricide inside buildings, and outdoors as an insecticide targeting mosquitoes. Its acute toxicity to humans is uncertain.

dinocap (DNOPC) A dinitro *fungicide and *acaricide (2,6-dinitro-octylphenyl crotonates) used on fruit, vegetable, and ornamental crops. It is slightly to moderately toxic to humans but very toxic to fish.

dinoflagellates Microscopic, single-celled marine organisms which are usually classified as *algae (division Dinophyta) because some contain *chlorophyll, but sometimes as *protozoa because they possess flagella (*See* FLAGELLUM) Many emit light. Most are *planktonic in marine and freshwater environment, but some live in *symbiotic associations with animals. *See also* RED TIDE.

dinosaur An ancient terrestrial *reptile that stood upright on its legs, did not fly or swim, and could be either carnivorous or herbivorous. Dinosaurs became *extinct at the end of the *Cretaceous Period, 65 million years ago. *See also* K–T BOUNDARY.

dinoseb (DNBP, DNSBP, DNOSPB) A dinitrophenol herbicide (2-*sec*-butyl-4,6-dinitrophenol) used for the selective control of grass and broadleaved weeds on fruit, vegetable, and a number of field crops. It causes eye, respiratory, and skin irritation and is highly toxic by ingestion. It is also toxic to birds, fish, and bees. Its use is banned in the EU, USA, Canada, and many other countries.

dioxin A group of about 300 different *chlorinated hydrocarbon compounds that are created in the production of *pesticides by the incomplete incineration of chlorinated hydrocarbons, especially *polychlorinated biphenyls, at temperatures below about 1200°C, and in volcanic eruptions and forest fires. They have no industrial use, are persistent, and at high doses are very *toxic and *carcinogenic to humans. Exposure to dioxins affects humans in various ways, including disfiguring skin complaints, birth defects, miscarriages, and *cancer. Recent European Union directives have significantly decreased dioxin emissions from large incinerators. More dramatic and concentrated releases occur from time to time, particularly in chemical accidents. The 1976 accident at a chemical plant in *Seveso, Italy, spread dioxins over a wide area and contamination only came to light slowly as animals died and people showed signs of dioxin exposure.

(((◉))) SEE WEB LINKS

• Dioxins and their effects on human health.

dip The angle between a geological surface in *rock (such as a *bedding plane or a *fault) and the horizontal. *See also* INCLINATION.

diploid Having a full set of genetic material consisting of paired *chromosomes, one from each parent.

dip-slope fault A geological *fault that involves vertical movement up and down the *dip of the *fault line.

Diptera A large order of *insects with two wings, which includes flies, gnats, midges, and mosquitoes. More than 85 000 species have been described.

diquat A non-selective contact herbicide that destroys those parts of the plant that it touches. It is used to control broadleaved weeds in many situations, to control weeds in still and slow-moving water, and to dry foliage to facilitate harvesting of potatoes. It breaks down rapidly

after application. It may be fatal if ingested but is otherwise moderately toxic to mammals.

direct action Protective action by a particular group of people, that is based on non-violent, passive resistance (for example, using protest marches, picketing a site, or blocking roads) which forces opponents to defend their position. *See also* CHIPKO MOVEMENT; ECO-ACTIVISM.

direct circulation Any form of air circulation (such as a *land breeze) that is driven mainly by warm air rising and cold air sinking.

direct effect (primary effect) An effect that occurs at the same time and place as the initial cause, without any other cause or factor being involved. *Contrast* INDIRECT EFFECT.

direct filtration A method of treating *wastewater that involves adding chemicals but not using *sedimentation.

direct insolation *See* DIRECT RADIATION.

direct radiation (direct insolation) *Radiation within the *atmosphere that reaches the ground surface directly from the Sun, without being deflected or scattered. *See also* DIFFUSE RADIATION.

direct runoff Water that flows through or over the ground directly into streams, rivers, and lakes.

direct use value Economic values that are associated with the direct use of a natural resource.

directional selection Preferential selection that leads to a consistent change in how a particular character of a population changes through time, such as selection for larger eggs. *Compare* NATURAL SELECTION.

directive An instruction that defines what is to be done or achieved, without necessarily specifying how. *See also* REGULATION.

disaster A *hazard event (natural or induced) that seriously disrupts the normal functions of society and causes widespread human, material, or environmental losses which exceed the ability of the affected society to cope using only its own resources. *See also* CATASTROPHE.

disaster management (emergency management) A comprehensive approach to reducing the adverse impacts of particular *disasters (natural or otherwise) that brings together in a *disaster plan all of the actions that need to be taken before, during, immediately after, and well after the disaster event. These include *mitigation, *preparedness, *emergency response, *recovery, *rehabilitation, and *reconstruction.

disaster plan (contingency plan) A formal record of agreed roles, responsibilities, strategies, systems, and arrangements for managing a particular type of disaster in a particular place.

disaster risk management An approach to *disaster management that is based on reducing the likelihood of situations or events that lead to disasters, and increasing the capacity to deal with disasters effectively should they arise.

disaster vulnerability A measure of the ability of a community to cope with the effects of a severe *disaster and to recover afterwards.

discharge 1. The rate of flow of surface water in a *stream or *canal, or of groundwater from an *artesian well, a ditch, or a *spring. Usually expressed in cubic metres per second ($m^3 s^{-1}$) (cumecs) or litres per second ($l s^{-1}$). 2. Any substance (a gas, liquid or solid, or a *microorganism) that is emitted, deposited, or allowed to escape from any activity. 3. To remove the electrical energy from something.

discharge consent Approval to *discharge an agreed amount of a substance into the *environment, such as a *pollutant released into the air or into a stream.

discharge hydrograph *See* HYDROGRAPH.

discing *See* HARROWING.

disclimax community *See* EQUILIBRIUM COMMUNITY.

discontinuity A major interruption or break in continuity. In geology, a sudden change in the physical properties of rocks within the Earth.

discontinuous distribution *See* DISJUNCT DISTRIBUTION.

discordant Not in agreement. 1. In geology, applied to a body (such as a *dike or *vein) that cuts across primary rock structures (such as bedding). 2. In ecology, applied to a set of individuals that display different traits.

discount The difference between present and future value.

discount rate A rate that is used to convert future costs or benefits to their present value,

based on assumptions about how to *discount or reduce the value of each in the future. *See also* COST–BENEFIT ANALYSIS.

disease Any disorder in the normal function of an *organism, which can be genetic but is often caused by *pathogenic *bacteria, *fungi, or *viruses.

disease agent A physical, chemical, or biological factor that causes disease. *See also* PATHOGEN.

disease host The individual who contracts a particular *disease.

disease reservoir Any source that harbours disease-causing organisms and could thus cause an outbreak of that *disease. *See also* DISEASE VECTOR.

disease transmission chain The routes by which a particular *disease is transmitted and spread, including direct contact, indirect contact, via droplets, orally, and by *vectors.

disease vector An organism that transmits a *disease or a *parasite without necessarily being affected itself. *See also* CARRIER; VECTOR.

disinfect To kill all *pathogenic *micro-organisms.

disinfectant A chemical or physical substance or process that kills *pathogenic organisms in water, air, or on surfaces. Examples are *chlorine and *ozone that are used to disinfect water supplies, wells, swimming pools, and effluent from *sewage treatment.

disinfection *See* STERILIZATION.

disjunct distribution (discontinuous distribution) The occurrence of *populations of closely related species in locations that are separated from one another by oceans.

dispersal 1. The movement of *organisms away from the places where they were born (*natal dispersion) or where they breed (*breeding-dispersal). 2. An approach to containing *oil spills, in which chemical *detergents are used to break up the slick.

dispersant A chemical agent that is used to break up concentrations of organic material, such as spilled oil.

dispersed recreation Forms of recreation (such as hunting, fishing, backpacking, or scenic driving) that are usually low-density and take place without facilities, not in a developed recreation site. *Contrast* DEVELOPED RECREA-TION; INFORMAL RECREATION; CONCENTRATED RECREATION.

dispersed settlement Scattered individual homesteads in the *countryside. A dispersed form of *rural settlement.

dispersion Scattering or spreading widely. *See also* DISPERSAL.

dispersion model A computer model that is used to predict how *pollutants disperse across an area, based on local environmental factors. *See also* POINT SOURCE.

disphotic zone *See* APHOTIC.

disposable Designed to be thrown away after use.

disposables Common term for consumer products and packaging that are used once or a few times and then thrown away.

disposal 1. To get rid of something. **2.** The final placement or destruction of toxic, radioactive, or other wastes. *See also* WASTE DISPOSAL.

disposal charge (throughput tax) A fee or tax that is paid by a producer of waste materials, which reflects the *social cost of the pollution.

disposal facility Equipment and land that is used to receive waste and dispose of it, including *landfills, *surface impoundments, *land farming, *deep-well injection, *ocean dumping, or *incineration.

disposal well A *well that is used for the disposal of waste into rocks beneath the ground surface.

disruptive coloration A form of *camouflage in which colours and patterns disrupt the body shape and outline of an individual.

dissolution The dissolving of a substance in a solvent.

dissolved load (dissolved solids, solution load, total dissolved solids) The fraction of a river's load that is carried in solution. It is made up for the most part of ions of *chloride, *sulphate, *bicarbonates, *sodium, and *calcium. It is estimated by measuring *electrical conductivity and provides an indicator of *salinity or *hardness. Excessive amounts make water unfit to drink or use in industrial processes.

dissolved oxygen Oxygen that is dissolved in water. The amount of oxygen a given volume of water holds at a given temperature and *at-mospheric pressure is usually expressed in milligrams per litre (mg l^{-1}), parts per million (ppm), or per cent of saturation. It is a widely used *indicator of *water quality, and adequate levels are necessary for fish and other aquatic life. *Secondary wastewater treatment and *advanced wastewater treatment are usually designed to ensure adequate level of dissolved oxygen in waterbodies that receive *wastewater. *See also* BIOLOGICAL OXYGEN DEMAND.

dissolved solids *See* DISSOLVED LOAD.

distillation A process that is used to separate the components of a liquid mixture, by boiling the liquid and then condensing the *vapour. It is used to purify water by removing *inorganic contaminants, and in *desalination to remove salt from water.

distribution area *See* RANGE.

disturbance Any activity or event (such as a forest fire or change in land use) that disrupts natural environmental systems and processes.

disulfoton A selective, *systemic *organophosphate insecticide and *acaricide that is used to control sucking insects, e.g. aphids, leafhoppers, thrips, and red spider mite. It is highly toxic to all mammals, birds, and aquatic animals.

diurnal 1. Active during daylight hours. **2.** Recurring every day or having a daily cycle. *See also* CIRCADIAN RHYTHM.

diuron (DCMU, DMU) A *soil-acting *urea herbicide (3-(3,4-dichlorophenyl)-1,1-dimethylurea) that inhibits *photosynthesis. It is used for total weed control on land that is not intended for cropping and for selective control of annual weeds in fruit crops and tree nurseries. It can be irritating to the eyes and is harmful to fish.

divergence Movement or flow in different directions, such as winds or ocean currents. *Contrast* CONVERGENCE.

divergent evolution The evolution of two or more *species from a common ancestral species that become increasingly different in successive generations. *Contrast* CONVERGENT EVOLUTION.

divergent margin *See* DIVERGENT PLATE BOUNDARY.

divergent plate boundary (divergent margin, constructive margin, constructive plate boundary) A boundary between adjacent *lithospheric *plates that are being pulled or pushed apart, and where new lithosphere is created, such as at *mid-oceanic ridges.

diversification The process of increasing *diversity or variety.

diversion A change in direction. Planned diversions are used, for example, to direct part of a stream flow into a *water supply system and to control the spread of *hazardous material in order to contain risk.

diversion ditch An artificial channel that intercepts and transports water from one place to another.

diversion rate The percentage of waste materials that are diverted from traditional disposal (such as *landfill or *incineration) to be *recycled, *composted, or *reused.

Diversitas An international partnership of intergovernmental and *non-governmental organizations that was formed in 1991 to promote and facilitate scientific research on *biodiversity.

 SEE WEB LINKS

• Diversitas home page.

diversity Variety, the presence of a wide range of variation in the qualities or attributes of the thing under discussion. See also BIODIVERSITY.

divide See DRAINAGE DIVIDE.

diving A method of marine *fishing in which some species (such as octopus, sea urchins, and sea cucumbers) are handpicked by divers, brought to the surface, placed in boats, and taken ashore for processing.

division One of the major subgroups within the *plant kingdom, comprising a number of similar *classes of plants. Plant divisions are often called phyla, with which they are equivalent. See also BIOLOGICAL CLASSIFICATION.

DMS See DIMETHYL SULPHIDE.

DMU See DIURON.

DNA Deoxyribonucleic acid, the genetic material that is found in all living organisms. It is the long molecule composed of *carbon, *nitrogen, and *phosphorus that is in the *nucleus of every *cell, *mitochondrion, ribosome, and *chloroplast. It controls inheritance, and directs the development and functioning of all cells. The strand or string of DNA has a *double helix structure so that the genetic instructions (*gene code) of the *cell are passed on when the cell divides (in one of the split pairs of the helix, which then builds its own matching helix), to produce a perfect copy. See also CHROMOSOME; GENE; RECOMBINANT DNA.

DNA bank The storage of *DNA, for example to assist future medical research, allow individuals to trace the pattern of *diseases in families, or create an archive of the genetic material of different organisms.

DNA fingerprinting Techniques that are used to detect the unique patterns in *DNA, which operate like a genetic bar-code and can be used to indicate the presence of a *gene associated with a given trait. This has applications in forensic science, and in selecting breeding stock with favourable characteristics (such as disease resistance or rapid growth).

DNA replication The duplication of a *DNA molecule by itself, in order to create new strands of DNA.

DNAPL See DENSE NON-AQUEOUS PHASE LIQUID.

DNOC (dinitro-*ortho*-cresol) A contact dinotro herbicide, *insecticide, and *acaricide (See DINITRO PESTICIDES) that was used to control broadleaved weeds and the overwintering stages of many insect and mite pests. It is highly toxic by inhalation, ingestion, and skin contact. Its use is banned in the EU, USA, and many other countries.

DNOPC See DINOCAP.

DNP See DINITROPHENOL PESTICIDE.

Dobson unit (DU) A unit that is used to measure the amount of any gas in the *atmosphere, but usually applied to *ozone, based on the thickness of the layer that gas would form if all other gases were removed and the gas subjected to sea-level pressure. 100 DU of ozone would form a layer 1 mm thick.

dodo Common name for the Mauritius dodo (*Raphus cucullatus*), a flightless bird that lived on the island of Mauritius and has been extinct since about 1660 because of over-killing. It was about 1 m high, lived on fruit, nested on the ground, and was captured and eaten by visiting sailors.

DOI See US DEPARTMENT OF THE INTERIOR.

doldrums Regions inside the *Intertropical Convergence Zone where the winds are light and variable and sailing ships were liable to be becalmed. The extent of the doldrums varies with the seasons.

doline *See* SINKHOLE.

dolomite 1. A common rock-forming *mineral, composed of calcium–magnesium carbonate, that is crystalline and forms extensive beds as a compact *limestone. *See also* KARST. **2.** A term also often used to refer to the *sedimentary rock dolostone, but strictly speaking it applies only to those dolostones that contain more than 90% dolomite.

domain The highest taxonomic category in a classification system based on comparisons of ribosomal RNA. There are three domains: *Archaea; *Bacteria; and *Eukarya. Each domain comprises organisms that are not closely related genetically to members of either of the other domains.

dome 1. The high, stable central part of an *ice sheet, with low rates of accumulation and slow ice movement. **2.** A round *anticline from which the ground slopes downward in all directions.

domestic sewage Organic waste and wastewater that is produced by a household and discharged from it.

domestic use Applied to water that is used for *household purposes such as washing laundry, food preparation, and bathing.

domestic waste *See* HOUSEHOLD WASTE.

domesticate To *breed a *species for specific characteristics that humans value, or the species that is so bred. *See also* CULTIVATE.

domesticated species (cultivated species) A species in which the evolutionary process has been deliberately influenced by humans to meet their needs.

dominance The extent to which a particular species or organism exerts the most influence in a *community because of its size, abundance, or cover.

dominant plant/species/tree The tallest individuals or species in a stand of vegetation (such as a forest), which receive the greatest amount of sunlight.

dominant social paradigm (DSP) The view that humans are superior to other all other *species, the Earth provides unlimited *resources for humans, and that progress is an inherent part of human history. *Contrast* NEW ENVIRONMENTAL PARADIGM.

dominant use An approach to *resource management in which land and water are the main type of land use, and others are treated as of secondary importance.

dominant use management An approach to *resource management that is based on the idea that although a given area of land may be capable of many uses, it will provide for one use better than any other, so the land is managed for the single purpose of maximizing that use to the exclusion of other uses where conflicts exist.

do-no-harm principle *See* PRECAUTIONARY PRINCIPLE.

donor site The site from which individuals of an *introduced species are taken in order to be introduced to another place (the *receptor site).

Donora A small town in Pennsylvania that in October 1948 suffered USA's first major pollution incident. Fog formed beneath a *temperature inversion and mixed with smoke from coal fires and fumes from an iron works and a zinc works to form smog. Approximately 6000 people, almost half the population, fell ill and 19 died.

Doppler effect The rise in pitch of a sound from a source that is approaching rapidly and the fall in pitch of a sound from a retreating source. This also occurs with any form of wave radiation. It was first described in 1842 by the Austrian physicist Christian Andreas Doppler (1803–53).

Doppler radar A type of weather radar that determines whether precipitation (and thus weather) is moving toward or away from the radar.

dormant Temporarily inactive, such as a volcano that is no longer active but not known to be extinct. *See also* QUIESCENCE; TORPOR.

dosage *See* DOSE RATE.

dose The quantity of a chemical that is given to an organism or to which it is exposed, or the amount of ionizing radiation that someone or something has been exposed to. *See also* ABSORBED DOSE; ADMINISTERED DOSE; APPLIED DOSE; HUMAN EQUIVALENT DOSE; LD50; POTENTIAL DOSE.

dose effect *See* DOSE RESPONSE.

dose equivalent A measure of the amount of ionizing *radiation that an individual person receives, which is based on the type of radiation, the amount of the body exposed, and the risk of exposure. Expressed in *rem.

dose rate (dosage) A measure of the *dose that is received per unit of time, expressed for example in milligrams per day (mg day $^{-1}$).

dose response (dose effect) An indication of how an individual, or a population, is likely to be affected by a change in the amount, intensity, or duration of an exposure.

dose-response assessment An estimation of the potency of a chemical.

dose–response relationship The quantitative relationship between the amount of exposure to a substance and the extent of *toxic injury or *disease that is produced in response to that exposure.

dosimeter An instrument that is used for measuring and registering the *radiation dose a person has received or that something has absorbed.

double helix The twisted-ladder shape that two linear strands of *nucleotides assume when they are bonded together via their *base pairs to form *DNA.

doubling time The time it takes, usually expressed in years, for a quantity to double in size if it is increasing at a constant *exponential rate. A population growing at 5% a year would double in 14 years, whilst a population growing at 1% a year would double in 70 years. Doubling time can be estimated by dividing the annual percentage growth rate (r) into 70, i.e. doubling time = $70/r$. The importance of doubling time as an indicator of rate of change is that it shows very clearly how quickly a quantity increases as the growth rate changes by even a relatively small amount. This is because the change involves *geometric growth rather than *arithmetic growth, in the same way that money accumulates in a bank savings account with compound interest. Population cannot double if the *growth rate is zero (there is no growth) or negative (population is declining, but also exponentially, so the equivalent measure is the halving time).

downburst A *downdraft from a *cumulonimbus cloud that reaches the surface and spreads to the sides producing strong gusts and wind shear. Downbursts have been known to generate gusts of more than 120 km h^{-1}. *See also* MACROBURST; MICROBURST.

downdraught A current of air descending through a *cumulonimbus cloud, usually at less than 20 km h^{-1}, although downdrafts can be much stronger in a *supercell cloud.

downpour Heavy *rainfall.

downstream In the same direction as the current or stream. *Contrast* UPSTREAM.

downwarping The *warping or bending downwards of the Earth's *crust.

downwelling The process by which surface water in the sea increases in density and sinks, usually along a *coastline or where water masses converge in the oceans. *Contrast* UPWELLING.

downwind In the direction that the wind is blowing, with the wind. *Contrast* UPWIND.

downy mildews *See* OOMYCETES.

draa A high (more than 300 m) sand ridge or chain of *dunes in the Sahara, lying about 0.5–5 km from its nearest neighbour and moving at 2–5 cm per year. It is the largest land-form of the *erg or sand desert. A star-shaped dune, or rhourd, is developed at the site where two draa chains cross.

draft environmental impact statement (DEIS) The draft version of an *environmental impact statement that is made available to the public and other agencies for review and comment.

dragline An excavating machine that uses a bucket operated and suspended by means of cables, which allow the bucket to be dragged toward the machine for loading.

drain An open channel (*drainage ditch) or pipe that is used to move water such as surface runoff or wastewater from a factory *downstream.

drainage 1. A method of improving land quality by removing excess water from the soil, which decreases *waterlogging. *See also* SUBSURFACE DRAINAGE; SURFACE DRAINAGE. **2.** The removal of water from land by streams and rivers, as part of the local *water cycle.

drainage area The area of land that is drained by a particular river within a *drainage basin, defined by the *drainage divide.

drainage basin (basin, catchment, water catchment, watershed, river basin) The area of land that is drained by a *river and its *tributaries. The boundary of a basin is defined by the *drainage divide, and the area within the divide is the *drainage area. In US usage, a drainage basin is usually known as a catchment.

drainage density The length of river channel per unit of *drainage area measured in kilometres per square kilometre (km km^{-2}). It provides a measure of the concentration of streams in an area and thus a measure of the amount of dissection of the land surface. *Contrast* STREAM FREQUENCY.

drainage ditch A ditch or open *channel that is used to carry excess water or sewage downstream. *See also* SURFACE DRAINAGE.

drainage divide (divide, hydrographic divide, interfluve, watershed) A ridge of land that separates adjacent *drainage networks.

drainage network (river network) The network of *river channels and *tributaries that forms within a *drainage basin.

drainage pattern The pattern displayed by a *river network, as seen from the air or on a map, which is usually controlled by *geology. The most common ones are *dendritic, *trellis, *rectangular, *annular, *radial, *centripetal, *parallel, and *deranged (see Fig. 4).

drainage system A network formed by a main *river and its *tributaries.

drainage tile *See* FIELD TILE.

drainage wind *See* KATABATIC WIND.

drainfield 1. An area of land that is used as a filter for *wastewater. 2. The part of a *septic system where the wastewater is released into the *soil.

draw down To decrease water level, such as in a storage tank or *reservoir, or in groundwater around a well, by the *extraction of water. *See also* CONE OF DEPRESSION.

dredge 1. A device used to scoop or scrape sediment from the seabed in order to keep navigable channels open. 2. An item of fishing equipment comprising a scoop made from chains that is dragged behind a vessel in order to scrape the bottom, usually to catch shellfish.

dredgeate The material that is excavated during *dredging.

dredging The process of excavating, creating, or altering a water body such as a *river,

Dendritic

Rectangular

Radial

Fig. 4 Drainage patterns

*lake, or *estuary, by scooping or sucking up sediment from the bed in order to deepen it.

drift 1. Sprayed or dusted material that does not settle on the target area but blows further away. 2. Sediment created by glacial activity, such as *boulder clay or till. 3. Material that is transported by wind and deposited in heaps, such as snowdrift. 4. A horizontal tunnel in an underground *mine. 5. *See* GENETIC DRIFT.

drift current A broad and slow-moving type of *ocean current.

drift net A fishing net that can be several kilometres long and is suspended vertically from floats at a specific depth in the water. It is left to drift freely with the current to catch fish.

driftwood Wood that is floating on the sea or has been washed ashore.

drill seeding Sowing seed in rows in the soil. *Contrast* BROADCAST SEEDING.

drinking water *See* POTABLE WATER.

drinking water supply Any source of raw or treated water that is, or may be, used by a public water system, or as *drinking water by one or more individuals.

drip irrigation (trickle irrigation) A form of *irrigation that uses a perforated pipe to deliver water directly to the soil around the roots of each plant, in order to minimize losses by evaporation and to eliminate *runoff and *soil erosion.

drizzle Very light *rain composed of very fine droplets, less than 0.5 mm in diameter, that falls from *stratus clouds.

drop-off A method of collecting *recyclable materials in which individuals take them to a designated collection site.

drumlin A long, elliptical hill usually composed of glacial *till (but occasionally composed of solid rock), streamlined in the direction of ice movement, that was deposited beneath an advancing *glacier. Usually found in a cluster (*drumlin field).

drumlin field (drumlin swarm) A group of *drumlins that are aligned more or less parallel to one another (in the direction of ice movement).

drumlin swarm *See* DRUMLIN FIELD.

dry adiabatic lapse rate (DALR) The rate (9.8°C per km) at which a rising parcel of dry air cools, by *adiabatic expansion, and at which a sinking parcel of dry air warms. *Contrast* SATURATED ADIABATIC LAPSE RATE. *See also* LAPSE RATE.

dry alkali injection A method of controlling *emission of *air pollutants by spraying dry sodium bicarbonate into *flue gas in order to absorb and neutralize *acidic *sulphur compounds.

dry deposition The *fallout of gases, aerosols, and fine particles with no associated *precipitation. This usually occurs relatively close to the emission sources of the gases. An important process in the formation of *acid deposition.

dry farming A method of *farming in *arid and *semi-arid areas without using *irrigation, which relies on treating the land in ways that conserve moisture (including using a *mulch).

dry ice Frozen *carbon dioxide. At sea-level pressure it sublimes at –78.5°C.

dry impingement A process for pollution control in which particulate matter carried in a gas stream is pushed against a retaining surface which may be coated with an adhesive.

dry prairie A type of *prairie that occurs on slopes and well-drained uplands, and is often interspersed with areas of *mesic prairie in valleys.

DROUGHT

A prolonged, continuous but temporary period of very dry *weather compared with the long-term average for that place. A drought is different from a dry climate, which is usually associated with a region that is normally, or at least seasonally, dry. A drought is also drier and lasts much longer than a dry spell, which is usually defined as more than 14 days with no significant *precipitation causing a relatively short period of moisture deficiency. Droughts often last for months or even years. Direct impacts of drought include decreased biological productivity (and thus lower yields) in cropland, rangeland, and forest land; increased fire hazard; reduced water levels; increased mortality rates amongst livestock and wildlife; and damage to fish and wildlife habitats. There are four main types of droughts: meteorological drought (usually defined by rainfall deficit or the degree of dryness compared with the average amount), hydrological drought (usually defined by river flow deficit), agricultural drought (usually defined by soil moisture deficit), and famine drought (usually defined by food deficit). Drought severity is usually gauged by a number of factors, the most important of which are the degree of moisture deficiency (the greater the deficiency, the worse the drought), the duration of the deficiency (the longer it lasts, the worse the drought), the size of the area affected (the bigger the area, the worse the drought), and the number of people affected (the greater the number, the worse the drought). *See also* DUST BOWL.

dry rock geothermal energy A method of extracting *geothermal heat from the Earth based on pumping water through hot rocks.

dry valley A valley that has no river flowing through it. It would have been formed under a climate that is very different from today's (for example by *meltwater at the end of the *Pleistocene) and indicates previous erosion by water.

dry wash The dry bed of an *intermittent stream.

Dryas Part of the characteristic three-fold late-glacial sequence of climatic change and associated deposits following the last ice advance and prior to the onset of the markedly warmer conditions of the current *interglacial. The colder Dryas phases mark times of cold, *tundra-like conditions throughout what is now temperate Europe. The Older Dryas lasted from about 14 000–13 500 years ago and the Younger Dryas from 12 700–12 000 years ago. The Dryas episodes were identified by the presence of pollen from an alpine plant, *Dryas octopetala* (mountain avens).

dryfall The delivery to surface communities of nutrients in the form of molecules or particles deposited on to surfaces from dry air. *Compare* WETFALL.

dryland An area with an *arid climate, with low precipitation and rainfall mainly in localized, brief, high-intensity storms.

drystone wall A stone wall that is built without mortar.

dry-summer subtropical climate *See* MEDITERRANEAN CLIMATE.

DSP *See* DOMINANT SOCIAL PARADIGM.

DU *See* DOBSON UNIT.

Ducks Unlimited A US-based non-profit conservation organization which is committed to conserving, restoring, and managing the country's *wetlands, *waterfowl, and *wildlife.

 SEE WEB LINKS
• Ducks Unlimited home page.

ductile The physical property of being able to sustain large *plastic *deformations without fracture, as occurs in metals that are capable of being hammered thin without breaking, or drawn into a thin shape such as a wire. *See also* MALLEABLE.

duff A North American term for *organic material (such as dead grass, leaves, conifer needles, and other plant parts) that is in various stages of *decomposition on the floor of a *forest.

dulosis Enslavement, usually of worker ants by a rival species.

dump An uncontrolled area where *solid wastes have been left on or in the ground, sometimes illegally, without environmental controls. *See also* LANDFILL.

dune 1. A *bedform in an *alluvial channel that forms at higher *flow velocity than a *ripple and which gradually moves downstream along the bed of the channel, much more slowly than the water flows. **2. (sand dune)** A mound of sand that is built up by prevailing winds, in a *desert or on a sandy *beach.

dune form The shape assumed by a sand *dune, which depends on wind speed and direction, and the availability of sand. Examples include crescent-shaped dunes (*barchans), *seif dunes, and star-shaped dunes.

dung Animal manure. *See also* FARMYARD MANURE.

duricrust A weathered soil deposit, found especially in subtropical environments, which may ultimately develop into a hardened mass. A range of types occurs, each distinguished by a dominant mineral. *See also* DURIPAN.

duripan A mineral *diagnostic horizon that is cemented by *silica and so will not slake or fall apart in water or hydrochloric acid. It may contain secondary cement (e.g. carbonates and iron oxide). Where duripans are exposed on the soil surface, they are called *duricrust. *Compare* CALICHE.

durisols Soils that have a *soil horizon containing cemented *silica within 100 cm of the surface. Durisols are a reference soil group in the *World Soil Classification.

dusk (twilight) The period of declining daylight between sunset and dark. *See also* DAWN.

dust General term for fine *particles that are light enough to be suspended in *air.

dust devil A strong miniature whirlwind that develops best on clear, dry, hot afternoons and throws up dust, litter, and leaves into the air.

dust storm A strong wind that blows fine dust across the surface of a *desert, which can

DUST BOWL

An area in the *Great Plains region of the USA that experienced prolonged *drought and *soil erosion in the late 1920s and 1930s, partly caused by dry weather but aggravated by over-intensive farming practices. The area—which includes parts of Kansas, Oklahoma, Texas, New Mexico, and Colorado—has a long history of persistent droughts and had a natural vegetation of grass which protected the fine-grained soils from *wind erosion. Between about 1885 and 1915 many people moved into the area to settle, many new farms were established, and large areas were given over to wheat and crops and to cattle grazing. The *marginal land was unsuited to intensive agricultural use and serious soil erosion began in the early 1930s when a period of severe droughts affected the area. Up to 10 cm of valuable *topsoil (including *organic matter, *clay, and *silt) was blown from some places, removing the very resource on which farming was dependent, and it drifted against fences and buildings in other areas. Thousands of families migrated westward, abandoning their farms, and up to a third of the families who stayed behind survived only with the aid of government relief. Farm incomes were seriously depressed during the drought in the 1930s and they also suffered badly during a drought in the 1950s. From 1942 onwards concerted efforts were made by federal and state governments to develop programmes for soil conservation and for rehabilitation of the Dust Bowl region. These included seeding large areas with grass, introducing 3-year *crop rotations, and use of *contour ploughing, *terracing, strip planting, and shelter belts. Whilst these measures have protected much of the remaining soils in the region, droughts in the 1950s, 1960s, and late 1970s caused further wind erosion and reinforced the need for more sustainable use of resources in this marginal area.

significantly reduce *visibility and adversely affect communications and agriculture. *Contrast* SAND STORM. *See also* HABOOB.

dust veil Fine particles of *ash, dust, and *sulphur dioxide that are thrown up into the *stratosphere by a volcanic eruption, and which can serve as *condensation nuclei for the formation of sulphate *aerosols.

dust whirl *See* DUST DEVIL.

Dutch elm disease A disease of elm trees that is caused by a *fungus (*Ceratocystis ulmi*) which is spread by a bark-beetle. The disease is usually fatal, was first introduced to the UK in the 1930s, and since the 1960s has devastated the elm population of the UK.

duty of care The obligation to avoid negligence, particularly to take reasonable care not to cause physical, economic, or emotional loss or harm to others.

dyke 1. An embankment made of earth and rock, for example to prevent a spill from spreading or to prevent flooding. **2.** A steeply inclined layer of *intrusive *igneous rock, formed from cooling *magma, that is relatively resistant to

*erosion and is *discordant and cuts across existing layers.

dynamic equilibrium A form of *equilibrium in which short-term changes are superimposed on a background state which is itself changing, which allows open systems to remain stable over long periods of time.

dynamics The study of the relationships between motion and the forces that affect motion.

dysgenic The creation of low-quality offspring, for example by harvesting the best individuals and leaving poorer ones to reproduce. *Contrast* EUGENIC.

dysphotic zone The region of the *photic zone that lies below the *compensation level, and within which light penetration is such that oxygen production by *photosynthesis is exceeded by oxygen consumption by *respiration. *Compare* EUPHOTIC ZONE.

dystrophic Applied to a shallow lake that contains much *organic matter, but has a low *pH, few available nutrients, and high oxygen demand. It is almost *eutrophic, and supports many plants but few fish.

E

E. coli A species of *bacteria (*Escherichia coli*) of the coliform type that are found in the intestine and indicate *faecal contamination of water. *See also* COLIFORM BACTERIA.

early action The technical term for taking steps to reduce *air pollution by *greenhouse gases before the start of the *Kyoto *Commitment Period, by reducing *emissions, investing in *Clean Development Mechanism projects, *Joint Implementation, or *emissions trading.

early forest succession The *community of plants and animals that develops first after the removal or destruction of vegetation in an area. An early stage in *succession. *Contrast* LATE FOREST SUCCESSION.

earlywood (springwood) The light-coloured wood cells within the annual *growth ring of a tree that are formed at the beginning of the *growing season. *Contrast* LATEWOOD.

Earth Charter An international initiative that was formed in 1994 in response to the *World Commission on Environment and Development, in order to 'establish a sound ethical foundation for the emerging global society and to help build a sustainable world based on respect for nature, universal human rights, economic justice, and a culture of peace'.

Earth Council Alliance An international *non-governmental organization that was created in September 1992 to promote and advance the implementation of the agreements reached at the *United Nations Conference on Environment and Development.

(⊕) SEE WEB LINKS

• Earth Council Alliance home page.

Earth Day An event that was established in 1970, is supported by the United Nations, and is held every year on 22 April in many countries in order to raise environmental awareness.

Earth Liberation Front (ELF) A North American radical, underground environmental movement that has no leadership, membership, or official spokesperson but is a loose coalition of individuals and groups engaged in radical *environmental activism.

Earth Observing System (EOS) A *remote sensing programme developed by NASA in 1998, as part of *Mission to Planet Earth, which uses a series of *satellites to monitor long-term global *environmental change.

Earth Resources Technology Satellite (ERTS) A *satellite that was launched by NASA in 1972 and used for *remote sensing of land

---

EARTH

Our home planet, the fifth largest of the nine planets within the *solar system. It rotates around its axis (once every 24 hours), orbits around the *Sun 150 million km away (once a year), and the *Moon orbits around it 385000 km away (once every 27 days 7 hours and 43 minutes). These rhythmic motions create night and day and the seasons of the year. Although we can't feel it, the Earth is moving through space at great speed. Planetary movement is far from random and chaotic, and the order and pattern within it are vital for life on Earth. The Earth moves within the solar system, and the solar system itself is moving through the vastness of space. By planetary standards the Earth is relatively small; it has a surface area of 510 million km^2 and a mean radius of 6371 km. The Earth is almost but not entirely spherical; it is an oblate spheroid. The circumference around the equator is 40077 km, compared with 40009 km around the poles. (See Fig. 5.)

Fig. 5 Earth's interior

resources on Earth. In 1975 the name was changed to *Landsat.

Earth Summit *See* UNITED NATIONS CONFERENCE ON ENVIRONMENT AND DEVELOPMENT.

EarthFirst! A radical activist movement within the broader *environmental movement, based on local or regional groups who take *direct action to try to prevent activities (such as highway construction or airport developments), that would cause environmental damage and *ecosystem changes. *See also* ENVIRONMENTAL ACTIVISM; MONKEY-WRENCHING.

earthflow A flow of unconsolidated material down a hill-slope, normally resulting from an increase in pore-water pressure, which reduces the friction between particles. Flow velocities vary from slow, when behaviour is plastic, to rapid, when behaviour is more liquid, and reflect variations in water content. Dry flows may occur when an earthquake shock breaks intergranular bonds.

earthquake Shaking and vibration of the surface of the Earth that is caused by the release of stress accumulated along a *fault or by *volcanic activity, usually associated with *plate tectonics. As *seismic energy accumulates in rocks subjected to *strain, they bend slowly until they can no longer withstand the strain. They then split apart along a fault. The sudden failure and displacement produces an earthquake which might vary in intensity from barely detectable trembling to violent and damaging shaking of the ground. As the stressed area ruptures, this relieves the strain and causes a sudden ground movement on one or both sides of the fault. *Aftershocks occur as the fault settles back, and as slower-moving seismic waves affect the area. Stress builds up through time, and the greater the accumulated stress released, the larger the earthquake. The *focus is the centre of the earthquake underground and the *epicentre is found on the ground surface directly above the focus. Earthquakes often trigger other geological hazards too, including *landslides and *liquefaction. Submarine earthquakes can cause *tsunamis. *See also* MERCALLI SCALE; RICHTER SCALE.

earthquake intensity *See* MERCALLI SCALE.

earthquake magnitude *See* RICHTER SCALE.

Earthwatch Popular name for a programme (United Nations System-wide Earthwatch) that was established in 1973 as part of the *United Nations Environment Programme, through which UN agencies work together on global environmental issues by exchanging and sharing environmental data and information.

earthworks The disturbance of land by moving, loosening, depositing, shaping, compacting, and stabilizing *soil and *rock.

easement A North American term for a voluntary binding agreement that allows the right to use someone else's land for a specific purpose, such as for a right-of-way or for a utility company to build a power line. *See also* CONSERVATION EASEMENT.

east The compass point that is at 90° from north.

East African steppe floral region Part of R. Good's African subkingdom (*The Geography of the Flowering Plants*, 1974), which lies within his *Palaeotropical floral kingdom. The flora includes about 150 *endemic genera, nearly all of which are small. They include *Saintpaulia*, one species of which, *S. ionantha* (African violet), is now a popular houseplant.

easterlies *Winds that blow from the east, for example in equatorial regions (trade wind region) and polar regions (polar easterlies).

easterly wave (African wave, tropical wave) A long, weak, low-pressure *trough aligned north–south that emerges from an intense storm over West Africa and travels in a westerly direction (i.e. from the east, hence the name) past Cape Verde and across the Atlantic. If it intensifies over the ocean it may develop into a *tropical cyclone. The most severe hurricanes begin in this way.

ebb current *The tidal current that flows away from the shore, or down a *tidal river or *estuary.

ebb tide (falling tide) The part of the *tide cycle between high water and the following low water, during which the water level is falling.

EC *See* EUROPEAN COMMUNITY.

eccentricity A measure of how much an ellipse or elliptical planetary orbit departs from a perfect circle, which has an eccentricity of zero. If the geometric centre of the ellipse is C and the principal focus or focus of the orbit is F_1, the distance between C and F_1 is the linear eccentricity, le. The location of the second focus, F_2, is at the centre of the major axis, α, measured from C to the point at which the orbit is farthest from F_1. Eccentricity, e, is then given by: $e = le/\alpha$. The present eccentricity of Earth's orbit is 0.017.

ecdysis Shedding of the skin by *arthropods and *reptiles.

ecdysone The moulting hormone of insects and *arthropods, which causes them to *moult.

ecesis The ability of a plant or animal to become established in a new *habitat. *See also* SUCCESSION.

ECHA *See* EUROPEAN CHEMICALS AGENCY.

echinoderm A member of the phylum Echinodermata, comprising brittle-stars, starfish, sea cucumbers, sea lilies, and sea urchins. All are marine. They have a skeleton of *calcite plates covered by tube-feet that resemble spines (the phylum derives its name from the Greek *ekhinos*, 'hedgehog', and *derma*, 'skin').

echo-sounder An instrument that measures the depth of a body of water by emitting pulses of sound into it and measuring the time it takes them to return.

ecliptic The plane of the *Earth's orbit about the *Sun, which defines the apparent annual movement of the Sun among the stars.

eclosion The emergence of an insect *larva from the egg or an adult insect from the *pupa.

eco- A prefix derived from the Greek word for house.

eco-activism *Direct action designed to raise awareness of, lobby against, or stop particular activities that damage the environment, often at a particular site (such as a planned new road site). *See also* CHIPKO MOVEMENT; ECODEFENCE; ECO-EXTREMISM.

ecocatastrophe An ecological or environmental *catastrophe, or a situation or event that causes major ecological or environmental change.

ecocentric (biocentric) Nature-centred. Based on the belief that all living organisms are equally important, that the environment exists for the benefit of all of nature and not just people, and that nature has rights. *Contrast* ANTHROPOCENTRIC; TECHNOCENTRIC.

ecocentrism (biocentrism) A *worldview that sees all of nature as having inherent value, and is centred on nature rather than on humans. *See* ANTHROPOCENTRISM.

ecocide A planned effort to eliminate all or part of an *ecosystem.

ecocline A gradient of gradual and continuous geographical change in the environmental conditions of an *ecosystem or *community.

ecodefence The use of non-violence, civil disobedience, and *direct action to prevent damage or destruction of ecological resources. A form of *eco-activism.

ecodevelopment An *environment-friendly approach to *sustainable development that seeks to include social balance, ecological balance, economic efficiency, respect of cultural identity, and harmonious regional development.

ecodoom pessimist *See* PESSIMIST, ENVIRONMENTAL.

eco-efficiency A management process that is designed to reduce the *environmental impact of producing goods and services, for example by increasing mineral recovery, using fewer inputs (such as energy and water), *recycling more, and reducing *emissions.

eco-extremism Extreme and often aggressive forms of *eco-activism, including *ecotage, *ecoterrorism, and *monkey-wrenching.

ecofarming An ecological approach to *farming that is designed to *conserve *biodiversity and *natural resources, for example by using organic rather than chemical *fertilizers and *pesticides. *See also* ALTERNATIVE AGRICULTURE.

ecofascism The insistence by some extreme *environmentalists that everyone should adopt *environment-friendly lifestyles, irrespective of their personal wishes, preferences, or needs.

ecofeminism A philosophy of respect for nature that is based on feminist philosophies of justice, egalitarianism, cooperation, and non-aggressive behaviour. It reflects a convergence of the *radical ecology movement and feminism, and seeks to transform the traditional patriarchal socio-economic system which is based on male domination and emphasizes competition, dominance, and individualism.

ecoforestry A passive approach to *forest management that is *ecocentric and based on the values of *deep ecology.

ecogeographical rule A so-called 'rule' (in reality a general statement), proposed by 19th-century naturalists, that describes the association between climate and the morphology of warm-blooded animals (mammals and birds). *See also* ALLEN'S RULE; BERGMANN'S RULE; GLOGER'S RULE.

Ecoglasnost An *non-governmental environmental organization that was established in Bulgaria in 1989.

ecohouse An *environment-friendly house that is designed to be *sustainable, and built and operated to reduce environmental impacts to a minimum.

eco-label A label that is attached to products (such as paper products, textiles, detergents, paints, and electrical appliances such as refrigerators or dishwashers) that produce fewer *environmental impacts than other competing products, to help consumers make informed choices. *See also* ENVIRONMENTAL LABELLING.

ecological Relating to the interrelationships between *organisms and their *environment.

ecological amplitude The range of one or more environmental conditions in which an *organism or a process can function. *See also* TOLERANCE.

ecological approach An approach to the management of *natural resources that considers the relationships among all organisms (including humans) and their *environment.

ecological assessment An evaluation of how a *chemical of concern does or might affect plants and animals other than people and domestic species.

ecological balance A state of *dynamic equilibrium within a *community of organisms, in which *diversity (genetic, species, and ecosystem) remains relatively stable but can change gradually through natural *succession.

ecological community *See* COMMUNITY.

ecological development 1. A gradual process of environmental modification by organisms. 2. An approach to development that takes into account ecological factors and the need to conserve *biodiversity and protect *ecological systems. *See also* SUSTAINABLE DEVELOPMENT.

ecological economics A branch of *economics that takes into account ecological principles and examines the economic values of *non-market ecological products and services. *See also* ENVIRONMENTAL ECONOMICS.

ecological efficiency The ratio between the *productivity at successive *trophic levels within a *food web, which is usually expressed as a percentage.

ecological energetics The study of how *energy is used within an *ecosystem, particularly by tracing the movement of energy through a *food web.

ecological entity Any particular part of an *ecosystem, including a *species, a group of species, an ecosystem function or characteristic, or a specific *habitat or *biome.

ecological equivalent Different species that occupy similar *niches in similar *ecosystems in different places.

ecological evaluation Determining the value of the functions of an *ecosystem that are provided by natural ecosystems, in monetary or other terms, to guide the planning and management of *nature conservation.

ecological exposure The exposure of a non-human organism to a chemical, radiological, or biological *agent.

ecological fallacy The mistake of assuming that a relationship that is found between variables based on aggregate or grouped data will also be found or will apply between individuals.

ecological footprint (footprint) A measure of the amount of space or *environment that is necessary in order to produce the goods and services that are required to support a particular lifestyle. See also CARBON FOOTPRINT.

ecological impact The effect that an activity (natural or otherwise) has on living *organisms and their *abiotic environment.

ecological indicator A characteristic of the *environment that can be measured and indicates the current state of ecological resources, or an ecological response to exposure to an *agent.

ecological integrity See ECOSYSTEM INTEGRITY.

ecological introduction See INTRODUCED SPECIES.

ecological isolation The separation of groups of organisms as a result of changes in their *ecology or in the environment in which they live. This is one of the processes leading to *speciation, since there will be a restriction in the movement of *genes between groups thus separated, and changes in gene frequencies may occur, owing to local selection or *genetic drift, until eventually the groups may be so divergent that reproductive barriers exist.

ecological land type A North American term for an area of land that has a distinct combination of natural, physical, chemical, and biological properties, which cause it to respond in a predictable way to particular *management practices.

ecological limit See CARRYING CAPACITY.

ecological management unit A North American term for an area of land that contains *soils with similar characteristics, enabling it to be managed as a single body.

ecological modernization The belief that *economic development and *environmental protection are compatible, that industrial economies can be reconciled with nature by means of markets, politics, and cultures, and that a sustainable balance can be achieved through *environmental management, environmental policy, cleaner technologies, and the 'greening' of institutions. See also SUSTAINABLE DEVELOPMENT.

ecological niche See NICHE.

ecological pyramid A diagram that shows the number of *organisms (*pyramid of numbers), total *biomass (*pyramid of biomass), or energy (*pyramid of energy), at each *trophic level within a *food chain.

ecological quality The quality of an *ecological system, in terms of biological, physical, and chemical conditions and of *environmental integrity.

ecological quality objective The desired level of the *ecological quality that is defined in a *management plan or policy.

ecological range See NATURAL RANGE.

ecological resilience See RESILIENCE.

ecological restoration The recovery of a damaged *ecosystem, either naturally or as a result of management that is designed to re-establish its structure and function. See also RESTORATION; REHABILITATION.

ecological risk See ENVIRONMENTAL RISK.

ecological risk assessment A formal process that evaluates the likelihood of adverse ecological effects as a result of *exposure to one or more *agents.

ecological risk characterization A process that evaluates the risk posed to a *population or *ecosystem by an *agent, based on results from studies of *exposure and *resilience.

ecological services See ECOSYSTEM SERVICES.

ecological species concept A definition of *species as a set of *organisms that is adapted to a particular set of resources (*niche) in the environment, which explains differences in form and behaviour between species as *adaptations to resource availability. *Compare* BIOLOGICAL SPECIES CONCEPT; CLADISTIC SPECIES CONCEPT; PHENETIC SPECIES CONCEPT; RECOGNITION SPECIES CONCEPT.

ecological sustainability The maintenance or restoration of the composition, structure, and processes of *ecosystems. *See also* SUSTAINABILITY; SUSTAINABLE DEVELOPMENT.

ecological system *See* ECOSYSTEM.

ecological trap theory A proposed situation in which organisms may be induced to settle in a low-quality *habitat. It is assumed that organisms will ordinarily prefer to settle in a high-quality habitat, providing abundant resources, and that they receive cues by which they identify such habitats. If it should happen that changes in either the quality of the habitat or the cues decouple the two, so the cues are no longer a reliable indication of habitat quality, organisms may be misled, or trapped, into settling in an apparently attractive but in fact low-quality habitat.

ecologically and scientifically significant natural area A North American term for land and water that retains most but not necessarily all of its natural character, which is significant for historical, scientific, palaeontological, or natural features.

ecologically sustainable use The use of a *species or *ecosystem within its natural ability for renewal or *regeneration, or its *carrying capacity.

ecologism 1. The use of ecological terminology or simplistic interpretations of ecological concepts in support of political or moral arguments. 2. Any supposedly ecological expression that is so used.

ecology The study of the interrelationships between *organisms and their *environment, including all *biotic and *abiotic components. The term was first used in 1866 by the biologist Ernst Haeckel. More recently it is generally taken to mean the study of the structure and function of *nature. Core themes in modern ecology include: the relationship between *habitat stability, rate and direction of *evolution, and changes in *biodiversity; the relationship between environmental changes caused by human activities and by *extinction; the importance of diversity as an attribute of ecosystems and of the *biosphere, and the significance of losses of diversity; *carrying capacity and the extent to which useful productivity can be enhanced and sustained; and *resilience, the extent to which nature can restore itself.

Eco-Management and Audit Scheme (EMAS) A *European Union regulation that came into force in 1995 and is designed to promote continuous improvement in the environmental performance of industrial activities by allowing companies and services to certify that they have an appropriate *environmental management system (under *ISO 14001).

econometrics The application of mathematical and statistical models to economic theories and problems.

economic analysis Study of the economic effects of a particular activity or decision.

economic depletion The use of 80% or more of a *non-renewable resource.

economic development The historical process whereby the economic base of a country changes from a reliance on agriculture, forestry, and the provision of raw materials (primary industries) to the industrial processing of raw materials, then to the provision of services, and finally to reliance on high-technology industries and the obtaining, processing, and dissemination of information. In a less developed economy primary industries are likely to provide at least 50% of all employment and 70% of all export earnings. In a developed economy primary industries are likely to provide 20% or less of all employment and a very small proportion of export earnings. *See also* ECOLOGICAL MODERNIZATION; ECONOMIC GROWTH; SUSTAINABLE DEVELOPMENT.

economic entomology The study of insects (entomology) with particular reference to agricultural pests and the control of their populations.

(SEE WEB LINKS)

• *Journal of Economic Entomology*.

economic evaluation Comparative analysis of alternative courses of action in terms of both their costs and consequences. *See also* CONTINGENT VALUATION METHOD; COST–BENEFIT ANALYSIS; HEDONIC PRICING; TRAVEL COST METHOD.

economic growth An increase in the amount of economic activity in a country, often expressed in terms of *gross national product.

economic impact The *impact or effect on an economy (of a place, region, or country) of a particular activity, project, or programme.

economic injury level (EIL) The level of pest infestation below which the cost of reducing the pest population further exceeds the benefits that such reduction would achieve. In the case of *vectors of life-threatening diseases, the value of saving one human life may be thought to exceed the (probably very high) cost of eliminating the vector totally. This is rarely the case where the damage is purely economic (e.g. to a farm crop or stored goods). If the benefits under consideration are social (e.g. relative freedom from clouds of insects which are a nuisance but otherwise harmless) EIL is known as the aesthetic injury level.

economic life The period of time over which an asset (such as a facility, structure, or source of resources) will have economic value and be usable.

economic scarcity The shortage of a marketable good or service, for which the price will rise so long as there is demand for it. *See also* RESOURCE SCARCITY.

economic system How a particular society distributes its resources in order to produce goods and services.

economics The study of the production, distribution, and consumption of resources, and the management of state income and expenditure. *See also* CLASSICAL ECONOMICS; ECOLOGICAL ECONOMICS; ENVIRONMENTAL ECONOMICS; MACROECONOMICS; MICROECONOMICS.

economies in transition (EIT) The Central European, Baltic, and former Soviet countries during their transition from centrally planned economies to market-based economies, which involves both political and economic reform.

economy The organized system for the production, distribution, and consumption or use of material goods and services.

ecophysiology The scientific study of the physiological adaptation of *species to their environments.

ecopiracy *See* BIOPIRACY.

ecoregion Part of an *ecozone that has distinctive *climate, *physiography, *vegetation, *soil, water, and animals, and is defined by environmental, geological, and geographical factors. *Contrast* NATURAL REGION. *See also* BIOREGION.

ecosophy A philosophy of ecological harmony or equilibrium that was proposed by Arne *Næss, who stressed the need to consider ethics and values as well as the physical symptoms of environmental change.

ecosphere *See* BIOSPHERE.

ecosystem (biocoenosis, holocoen) Short for ecological system, meaning the natural interacting *biotic and *abiotic system in a given area, which includes all of the *organisms (plants, animals, fungi, and micro-organisms) that live in particular *habitat, along with their immediate physical environment (see Fig. 6). Examples include a *lake, *forest, or *drainage basin. The term was first used by British ecologist Arthur Tansley in 1935, who visualized ecosystems as being composed of two parts, the *biome and the habitat. In Tansley's view 'all parts of such an ecosystem—organic and inorganic, biome and habitat—may be regarded as interacting factors which, in a mature ecosystem, are in approximate equilibrium; it is through their interactions that the whole system is maintained'. Many ecologists regard ecosystems as the basic units of *ecology because they are complex, interdependent, and highly organized, and because they are the basic building blocks of the *biosphere.

ecosystem approach *See* ECOSYSTEM MANAGEMENT.

ecosystem diversity The variety of unique biological *communities or *ecosystems, in terms of species composition, physical structure, and processes. This is the highest level of *biodiversity. *Compare* SPECIES DIVERSITY; GENETIC DIVERSITY.

ecosystem dynamics The processes and adjustments that take place within an *ecosystem, including energy flow, *nutrient cycling, and vegetation *succession.

ecosystem integrity (ecological integrity) The ability of an *ecosystem to function healthily, continue to provide natural goods and services, and maintain *biodiversity.

ecosystem management An integrated approach to the management of *ecosystems and *natural resources that seeks to balance ecological, economic, and social goals in a sustainable way, by respecting and protecting the

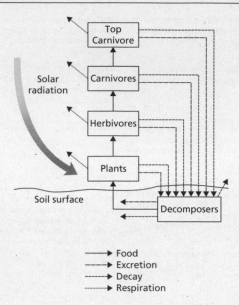

Fig. 6 Ecosystem

natural integrity and processes of ecosystems, and through deliberate manipulation of ecosystem structure and/or function, and/or regulation of human uses of ecological systems. *Natural resource management up to the 1960s relied heavily on managing parts of ecosystems as more or less independent units. Thus, for example, *forest management, wildlife management, and water and soil resource management were widely practised, but as largely separate activities; integrated management of ecosystems was rare. One important development since the early 1970s has been the widespread adoption of an integrated ecosystems framework and perspective in natural resource management, for example for planning and managing protected areas such as *national parks and *wilderness areas.

ecosystem rehabilitation *See* ECOSYSTEM RESTORATION.

ecosystem restoration The process of re-establishing, to as near its natural condition as possible, the structure, function, and composition of an *ecosystem.

ecosystem services (ecological services) Processes or materials such as clean water, energy, climate regulation, and *nutrient cycling that are naturally provided by *ecosystems.

ecosystem structure The *biotic and *abiotic elements of an *ecosystem, and the relationships between them, particularly in terms of *trophic levels.

ecotage Ecological sabotage, in the form of direct action or sabotage in defence of nature. An aggressive form of *eco-activism. *See also* ECOTERRORISM; MONKEY-WRENCHING.

ecoterrorism (bioterrorism) An aggressive or violent form of *eco-activism that involves the use of terrorism. *See also* ECO-EXTREMISM; MONKEY-WRENCHING.

ecotone A transitional area between two adjacent *communities, *ecosystems, or *habitats; the boundary or border zone which contains *species from both ecological communities. Ecotones are far from fixed, and they can change location as the species in adjacent *biomes adjust to *environmental change. Ecologists believe that many of the ecotones we see today are still in the process of adjusting to *post-glacial climate change. It is possible, for example, that the northern edge of the *taiga is still advancing northwards as climate warms from the *Pleistocene ice age. Human factors can also cause shifts in the boundaries between plant communities. Over the last two centuries, for example, the boundary between short grass (in the east) and tall grass (in the west) in the Central Plains of North America has moved progressively westwards, partly in response to *grazing and other human pressures. *See also* EDGE.

ecotope (biotope) An area that has uniform environmental conditions and characteristic plants and animals.

ecotourism Nature-based tourism that is ecologically sustainable, environmentally sensitive, and often involves adventure travel, environmental education, and cultural exploration.

ecotoxicity The ability of a substance to have a long-term, *toxic effect on living *species and *ecosystems.

ecotoxicology The application of *toxicology to the natural environment.

ecotype A local *population of a widespread *species, that has adapted to a particular set of environmental factors.

ecowarrior Short for ecological warrior, someone engaged in extreme forms of *eco-activism.

ecozone A large area in which there are distinctive climate patterns, ocean conditions, types of landscapes, and species of plants and animals. *See also* ECOREGION.

ectocrine *See* ENVIRONMENTAL HORMONE.

ectoparasite A *parasite that lives on the outside of the host's body. *Contrast* ENDOPARASITE.

ectotherm An animal that maintains a fairly internal constant body temperature by behavioural means, e.g. basking or seeking shade. Reptiles are ectotherms. *Compare* POIKILOTHERM.

ecumene All of the parts of the world that are inhabited or habitable by people.

edaphic Of or having to do with *soil.

edaphic factor Any property of *soil that influences the types of *plants that grow in an area, such as lack of *nutrients, presence of *toxic contaminants, *waterlogging, or moisture deficiency.

eddy A circular movement of water or air opposing the main direction of fluid flow. An eddy is formed, for example, where currents pass obstructions or between two currents that are flowing in opposite directions. *See also* MECHANICAL TURBULENCE.

eddy mixing Mixing of air or water that is caused by eddies.

EDF *See* ENVIRONMENTAL DEFENCE FUND.

edge A border or boundary between two different *ecosystems or *communities of plants or animals. *See also* ECOTONE.

edge effect The change in the number of species in the zone where two *habitats adjoin. This zone may contain species from both habitats as well as some unique to the zone itself, but although the zone may be rich in species, these are poorly adapted to one or both of the adjacent habitats. Predation and local extinction rates are both high. Ecologists regard the edge effect as indicating ecological deterioration. Fragmentation of habitats increases edge areas, but also decreases the interior areas of *ecosystems, leading eventually to a loss of species from those ecosystems and an increase in edge species, which are usually commonplace.

edge species Species that prefer the greater diversity of *habitat factors that occurs at the boundary between adjacent *ecosystems.

EEA *See* EUROPEAN ENVIRONMENT AGENCY.

EEC *See* EUROPEAN ECONOMIC COMMUNITY.

Eemian An *interglacial optimum period between about 130 000 and 110 000 years ago. Part of the Pleistocene, when temperatures were warmer than today.

EEZ *See* EXCLUSIVE ECONOMIC ZONE.

effect *See* IMPACT.

effective height of emission (effective stack height) The height above ground at which a *plume of waste gases begins to move horizontally after emerging from a *stack.

effective precipitation Net *precipitation after losses by *evaporation. An index of effective precipitation derived from a temperature : precipitation ratio has been used as a criterion for some systems of climate classification (e.g. those of *Köppen in 1936 and *Thornthwaite in 1948).

effective stack height *See* EFFECTIVE HEIGHT OF EMISSION.

efficacy A measure of effectiveness, or the ability to achieve a desired effect.

efficiency The ratio of the output to the input of any *system, usually expressed as a percentage.

efficient An activity that is performed successfully with a minimum of waste or unnecessary effort, or that produces a high ratio of results to resources.

effluent A waste product (such as water that contains *pollutants) that is released or discharged into the *environment. Means literally 'flowing out'. *Contrast* INFLUENT.

effluent based standard A *standard that sets the amount of *effluent that can be legally discharged into a *waterbody.

effluent fee A fee or tax that is paid by a polluter in exchange for the right to discharge an agreed amount of noxious *emissions into the air and water.

effluent limitation (effluent standard) A restriction on the quantity, rate, and *concentration of a particular pollutant from a *point source that can be legally discharged into a waterbody.

effluent standard *See* EFFLUENT LIMITATION.

Ehrlich, Paul US entomologist (born 1932) who is best known as a researcher and author on the subject of human overpopulation. He co-wrote the book *The *Population Bomb* in 1968 and was a co-founder of the group *Zero Population Growth in 1968.

EIA *See* ENVIRONMENTAL IMPACT ASSESSMENT.

EIL *See* ECONOMIC INJURY LEVEL.

EIS *See* ENVIRONMENTAL IMPACT STATEMENT; ENVIRONMENTAL INFORMATION SYSTEM.

EIT *See* ECONOMIES IN TRANSITION.

Ekman effect The change in wind direction with increasing height above the ground, or change in the direction of *ocean currents with depth, that is determined by the *Coriolis force.

elastic limit The maximum *stress that a material can withstand without causing permanent *strain or deformation.

elasticity 1. The ability of a material to return to its original shape after it has been stretched or compressed. **2.** In *economics, a measure of responsiveness of the quantity of a good or service that is demanded or supplied, to changes in price.

ELCI *See* ENVIRONMENT LIAISON CENTER INTERNATIONAL.

electric current A flow of electric charge through a wire or other material.

electric motor An engine that uses *electricity for doing work.

electric potential The difference in electrical charge between two points in a circuit, which can effectively push electric charges to different locations. Usually expressed in volts.

electric power The rate of energy transfer of *electricity.

electrical conduction The passage of a charge in an electric field.

electrical conductivity *See* CONDUCTIVITY.

electrical energy The energy that is produced by flow of electric charge in an electric field.

electricity A source of *energy that is made available by the flow of electric charge (*electrons) through a conductor.

electricity generation The process of producing *electricity or transforming other forms of energy into electricity. *See also* POWER PLANT.

electrode potential *See* REDUCTION POTENTIAL.

electrodialysis A method for *desalination of water that involves passing an electric current through the *saline water in a container, in order to remove minerals from water.

electrolyte A non-metallic substance that conducts an *electric current in solution, (such as many *acids, *bases, and *salts) due to the presence of positive and negative ions.

electromagnetic radiation The energy that is transmitted through space in the form of *electromagnetic waves, which include light, radio waves, X-rays, and gamma rays. *See also* RADIATION.

electromagnetic spectrum The range of *electromagnetic radiation, characterized by *wavelength or frequency, that extends from *gamma rays (10^{-8}-10^{-4} micrometres (μm); 300-30 exahertz (EHz)), *X-rays (10^{-5}-10^{-3} μm; 3 EHz-300 petahertz (PHz)), *ultraviolet (4-400 nanometres (nm); 30-3 PHz), visible light (400-700 nm; 405 terahertz (THz)-790 THz), and *infrared (0.74-300 μm; 1-400 THz) to microwaves (1 mm-1 m; 300 gigahertz (GHz)-300 megahertz (MHz)) and radio waves (1-100 km; 300 MHz-3 kilohertz (kHz)). Different wavelengths have different properties and they affect people and *environmental systems in different ways. Long wavelengths have a low frequency and thus a relatively low energy, and as a result they are less damaging to people's health. Short wavelengths, on the other hand, have a high frequency, high energy, and are damaging to people's health.

electromagnetic wave A wave that is partly electric and partly magnetic, is emitted by vibrating electric charges, carries energy, and can travel through a vacuum (such as light waves, radio waves, and microwaves).

electron A negatively charged subatomic particle that orbits around the *nucleus of an *atom. *See also* PROTON; NEUTRON.

electro-osmosis The movement of liquid in a porous medium that is caused by differences in *electric potential.

electroplating The process of coating base metal with a thin layer of another metal by passing an *electric current through it.

electrostatic precipitator An electrical device used in *air cleaning, that removes *fly ash from *flue gas before it is released into the atmosphere from the stack/chimney in a *power plant. *See also* ADVANCED AIR EMISSION CONTROL DEVICE.

element One of more than a hundred known substances (92 of which occur naturally) that cannot be chemically changed or broken down, and that singly or in combination make up all matter. *See also* MACROELEMENT; MICRO-ELEMENT.

elevation *See* ALTITUDE.

ELF *See* EARTH LIBERATION FRONT.

elfin woodland A type of tropical upper *montane or subalpine forest, with dwarfed and gnarled trees, which grows on extreme and exposed sites. The term is sometimes applied outside the tropics, although in this context it is more usual to apply the name kampfzone or krummholz.

eligibility criteria The criteria that must be met by an *emissions reduction project, under the *Kyoto Protocol, in order to produce reductions which can be banked, traded, or offset against emissions.

elm decline The sharp decrease in the amount of elm (*Ulmus*) pollen that occurs throughout north-western Europe in soil horizons radiocarbon-dated within 100-200 years of 5000 BP. It has been suggested that the decline is linked to the activities of early farmers, but it may have been caused by *Dutch elm disease.

elutriation A method of analysing the size of grains, in which the finer particles are separated from coarser and heavier ones by the use of a rising current of air or water. This carries the light particles upwards and allows the heavier grains to sink. By controlling the velocity of the flow, grains of different sizes can be separated.

eluvial horizon A *horizon in a *soil profile from which material has been removed, either in solution or suspension.

eluviation A *soil-forming process that involves the removal of fine particles of material in solution or suspension, usually from the *A-horizon. The material is usually deposited in an *illuvial horizon below.

EMAP *See* ENVIRONMENTAL MONITORING AND ASSESSMENT PROGRAM.

EMAS *See* ECO-MANAGEMENT AND AUDIT SCHEME.

embryo 1. An unborn or unhatched organism, the earliest stages of development until hatching or birth. **2.** In cloud physics, a tiny ice crystal that grows in size and becomes an ice nucleus.

emergence The act of emerging or coming out, such as the appearance of a *plant above ground after *germination in the soil.

emergence marsh The upper zone of a *saltmarsh, from the general mean high-water level to the mean high-water level of *spring tides. Typically it has fewer than 360 submergences per annum, often with less than an hour of submergence daily during sunlight. The minimum period of continuous exposure may exceed ten days. *Compare* SUBMERGENCE MARSH.

emergency A crisis that develops suddenly and unexpectedly, that usually involves danger, and that requires immediate action to prevent loss of life. Examples include *hurricanes,

EL NIÑO–SOUTHERN OSCILLATION (ENSO)

A climatic phenomenon that occurs roughly every three to seven years, lasts between six and 18 months, and peaks around Christmas time (El Niño means 'boy child') in the surface oceans of the equatorial South Pacific, linked to changes in the distribution of surface pressure between Tahiti and Darwin, Australia, known as the Southern Oscillation. It involves weakening of easterly *trade winds and, consequently, of the wind-driven South Equatorial Current that carries warm surface water westward, where ordinarily it forms a deep pool around Indonesia. This allows warm water to accumulate on the eastern side of the ocean, off the coasts of Peru and Ecuador. El Niño events usually affect only the Pacific region, although major events can disrupt weather patterns over a much wider region, and it has been linked to colder, wetter winters in parts of the USA, drier, hotter summers in South America and Europe, and drought in Africa. Recent El Niño disturbances occurred in 1953, 1957-8, 1972-3, 1976-7, 1982-3, 1986-7, and 1997-8. In the years between ENSO events, the *trade winds are stronger, the South Equatorial Current is stronger, and the ocean surface waters off South America remain relatively cool. El Niño regularly brings heavy rain to the coast of Peru, because the weakening easterly winds and increased evaporation from the warm surface water allow moist air to bring rain to the ordinarily parched coastal regions of South America. Torrential rains across Peru are not uncommon during El Niño, and they can trigger landslides and flash floods in the Andes. Farmers benefit from El Niño because it waters their grazing land (sometimes bringing an *año de abundancia*, year of abundance). But El Niño causes great hardship for the fishing people of Peru, because the deepening of the warm layer suppresses the normal *upwellings in the cold water of the Peru Current which sustains the anchovy fishing industry by increasing nutrient supplies close to the surface. Fish catches decline dramatically during ENSO events, with consequent impacts on food supplies and regional economies. When the El Niño flow pattern changes, the ENSO events can have widespread impacts on climatic and environmental systems. These impacts are not confined to the South Pacific, because they can be transferred around the world by adjustments to global climatic and environmental systems via so-called *teleconnections. Historical records of large-scale droughts and floods in India, Africa, Indonesia, and parts of China show close correlations with the chronology of El Niño events in South America at least as far back as 1750 and there is evidence of El Niño events over thousands of years. *See also* LA NIÑA.

*tornados, *storms, *floods, *tidal waves, *tsunamis,*earthquakes, *volcanic eruptions, *landslides, *fires, and *nuclear accidents. *See also* CHEMICAL EMERGENCY; DISASTER.

emergency management *See* DISASTER MANAGEMENT.

Emergency Planning and Community Right-to-Know Act (EPCRA) A federal law (also known as SARA) that was enacted in the USA in 1986, requiring federal, state, and local governments and industry that are involved in either emergency planning and/or reporting of *hazardous chemicals to allow public access to information about the presence of hazardous chemicals in the community and releases of such substances into the environment.

emergency response Actions that are taken during and immediately following a *disaster, in order to minimize serious harm to people or the environment. Examples include search and rescue, relief services, and restora-tion of power, water, and telephone services. *See also* DISASTER MANAGEMENT.

emergent vegetation Aquatic plants that grow with their roots under water but their leaves and stems above the surface of the water.

emergent wetland A type of *wetland (such as a *marsh) that is dominated by grasses, sedges, rushes, forbs, and other rooted, water-loving *herbaceous plants that emerge from the surface of water or soil.

Emerson, Ralph Waldo US writer, leading exponent of *Transcendentalism (1803–82), and one of America's most influential thinkers and writers. Many of his core ideas are contained in the essay *Nature*. He inspired many other writers, including Henry David *Thoreau.

emigration The movement of individuals out of a country or area; the opposite of *immigration.

emission The release or discharge into the *environment of a substance, particularly an *air pollutant.

emission factor The relationship between the amount of *raw material that is processed or burned and the amount of *pollution it produces, which is used in preparing an *emissions inventory.

emission permit A non-transferable, non-tradable permission that is granted by a government to an individual firm, which allows it to emit a defined amount of a *pollutant in a given period of time. *See also* PERMIT.

emission rate The amount of a particular *pollutant that is discharged or emitted within a defined period of time.

emission source The place from which a particular *pollutant is released or emitted into the *environment. *See also* AREA SOURCE; NON-POINT SOURCE; POINT SOURCE.

emission standard The maximum amount of air pollutant (such as *carbon monoxide, *sulphur dioxide, or *particulates) that can be legally discharged from a single mobile or stationary *emission source.

emission tax A tax or surcharge (such as a *carbon tax) that is imposed on *emission sources, to provide incentives to firms and households to reduce their emissions, in order to control pollution.

emissions allocation (emissions target) An approach to the control of *greenhouse gas emissions, under the *Kyoto Protocol, that is based on allocating permits to an emissions source (such as a company with net emissions) by a regulatory body during a specific *Commitment Period. Permits are allocated mainly through *grandfathering or *auctioning.

emissions allowance (emissions quota) An approach to the control of *greenhouse gas emissions, under the *Kyoto Protocol, that divides the total permitted quantity of emissions of a particular gas into allowances that grant the holder the right to emit a specified amount of *pollution over a given period of time (for example 1 tonne a year). Allowances can be traded but the overall amount remains controlled. At the end of each *Commitment Period each holder must surrender sufficient allowances to cover their emissions during that period; if they produce less pollution than they are permitted to, they can trade or sell some of their emissions

allowance, but if they produce more pollution they must trade or buy some allowance from another holder. *See also* EMISSIONS CAP.

emissions auctioning An approach to the control of *greenhouse gas emissions, under the *Kyoto Protocol, that is based on the trading of *emissions allowances by allowing *emission permits to be issued to polluters within a country, based on their willingness to pay for the permits. It may be combined with *grandfathering.

emissions banking Part of the *emissions trading procedures for *greenhouse gases that were agreed under the *Kyoto Protocol, in which *emissions allowances for future consumption or trading can be saved by holding reductions within a *Commitment Period, applying reductions earned from one period to another, or applying reductions earned before the first *Compliance Period via the *Clean Development Mechanism. *See also* FUTURES.

emissions borrowing An approach to the control of *greenhouse gas emissions, under the *Kyoto Protocol, that is based on borrowing from the future, by using *emissions reductions from future *Commitment Periods in order to meet current *emissions targets.

emissions bubble An approach to the control of *greenhouse gas emissions, under the *Kyoto Protocol, that treats two or more *emission sources as if they were one single source (the *bubble). This allows flexibility in applying pollution control technologies to whichever source within the bubble offers the most *cost-effective pollution control options, while ensuring that the total amount of emissions within the bubble does not exceed environmental requirements. *See also* EU BUBBLE.

emissions budget *See* ASSIGNED AMOUNT.

emissions buyer In *greenhouse gas *emissions trading, under the *Kyoto Protocol, a legally recognized entity (individual, corporation, not-for-profit organization, or government) that acquires credits, reductions, or allowances from another legally recognized entity, through a purchase, lease, trade, or other forms of transfer.

emissions cap A regulatory device that defines the maximum amount of emissions of *greenhouse gases that can be released into the *atmosphere within a given period of time, under the *Kyoto Protocol. A cap is a national *emissions allowance.

e

emissions inventory A list of the amounts of *air pollutants that are emitted by each particular source within a given area, which is used to establish *emission standards. The need for such inventories became obvious at the 1992 *Rio Earth Summit and during debate leading to the 1997 *Kyoto Protocol. An emissions inventory would usually include information on the chemical or physical identity of the pollutants included, the geographical area covered, the institutional entities covered, the time period over which the emissions are estimated, and the types of activities that cause emissions. Emission inventories are used in various ways. For example, they provide valuable inputs to air quality models, allow the success of air quality policies and standards to be evaluated, and enable regulatory agencies to establish compliance records with allowable emission rates.

emissions leakage The offsetting of emission reductions in one location (such as an *Annex I country) by an increase in emissions in another location (such as a non-Annex I country), under the *Kyoto Protocol.

emissions offset *See* OFFSET.

emissions quota *See* EMISSIONS ALLOWANCE.

emissions reduction Any decrease in the release of a *pollutant into the *environment. Usually used to refer to a decrease in emission of *greenhouse gases into the atmosphere in order to control *climate change and *global warming.

emissions reduction unit (ERU) A specified amount of *emissions reduction of *greenhouse gas that has been achieved and is used for *Joint Implementation, under the *Kyoto Protocol. *See also* CREDIT; CERTIFIED EMISSIONS REDUCTION.

emissions target *See* EMISSIONS ALLOCATION.

emissions trading A general term for the *flexibility mechanisms that were agreed under the *Kyoto Protocol and are designed to reduce *emissions of *greenhouse gases. It is a market-based system that allows polluters the flexibility to select cost-effective solutions to achieve the agreed emission goals, in which polluters that produce fewer emissions than they are allowed can sell or trade their excess capacity to others who do not, within the *bubble in which total approved emissions cannot be exceeded. *See*

EMISSIONS AUCTIONING; GRANDFATHERING; INTERNATIONAL EMISSIONS TRADING.

emissivity The amount of *radiation a body emits, compared with the radiation at the same wavelength that a *black body would emit at the same temperature. The emissivity of solid bodies is fairly constant but that of gases varies with wavelength.

emittance The amount of *radiant energy that a surface emits.

empirical A result based on experience, experiment, or observation, rather than on theory. *Contrast* THEORETICAL.

empowerment To increase the ability of an individual or community to do things for itself.

EMS *See* ENVIRONMENTAL MANAGEMENT SYSTEM.

emulsion A *colloid in which very small droplets of one liquid are suspended in another (such as oil in water), although the two liquids do not actually combine.

encapsulation The process in which *nutrients are wrapped in a *membrane to turn them into small pellets, for example to feed some larvae.

encephalitis Inflammation of the brain. *See also* SLEEPING SICKNESS.

enclosure An area of land that is walled or fenced.

end moraine (terminal moraine) A *moraine in the form of a ridge of *till that is deposited at or near the edge of a *glacier. A recessional moraine is similar, but is deposited during a period when a long period of glacial retreat is interrupted and the glacial terminus remains stationary.

endangered Applied to a *species that will be in danger of *extinction if existing pressures on it (such as over-harvesting or habitat change) continue, and which is therefore likely to disappear if it is not offered adequate protection. A *threatened category defined by the *IUCN *Red Data Book. *Contrast* EXTINCT; EXTIRPATATION; THREATENED; VULNERABLE SPECIES.

Endangered Species Act (1973) US legislation that established a federal programme for the protection and *conservation of *threatened and *endangered species of fish, wildlife, and plants.

Endangered Species List A list of species that are considered to be in imminent danger of *extinction, and are protected under the US *Endangered Species Act.

endangerment assessment A study that is designed to determine the nature and extent of *contamination at a site on the *National Priorities List in the USA, under *CERCLA or *RCRA, and the risks that contamination poses for public health or the environment.

endemic *Native to or confined to a certain region.

endemic species A species whose distribution is restricted to a certain area. A *native species found only within a given area.

endocrine Any gland that introduces *hormones directly into the blood.

endocrine disruptor (hormone disruptor, environmental hormone) A chemical (such as *DDT and other *chlorinated hydrocarbon compounds) that disrupts the natural *hormones and thus disturbs the *endocrine system of an animal.

end-of-the-pipe Technologies that reduce *emissions of pollutants after they have formed, such as *scrubbers on smokestacks and *catalytic converters on vehicle exhausts.

endogenous Internal, arising from within. *Contrast* EXOGENOUS.

endolithic Applied to organisms that grow within or between stones (e.g. the thalli of certain *lichens).

endoparasite A *parasite that lives inside the body of its host. *Contrast* ECTOPARASITE.

endophyte An organism that lives at least part of its life cycle within a host plant, in a *parasitic or *symbiotic relationship.

Endopterygota Insects that undergo complete metamorphosis. Their larvae are physically different from the adults and lack wings. Wings then develop internally. *Contrast* EXOPTERYGOTA.

 SEE WEB LINKS

• Endopterygota.

endorheic Applied to a lake from which no outlet stream flows, so that the lake loses water only by evaporation. *Compare* EXORHEIC.

endoskeleton A skeleton or support structure that is inside the body of the organism. *Contrast* EXOSKELETON.

endosulfan An organochlorine *insecticide and *acaricide that was used formerly to control aphids, leafhoppers, Colorado beetles, and lepidopteran larvae. Its production and use are being phased out owing to its toxicity and capacity for *bioaccumulation, and because it is an *endocrine disruptor.

endotherm An animal that maintains a body temperature that varies only within narrow limits by means of internal mechanisms, e.g. dilation or contraction of blood vessels, sweating, shivering, panting, etc. Birds and mammals are endotherms.

endothermic Applied to a *chemical reaction that absorbs heat from its surroundings. *Contrast* EXOTHERMIC.

endrin A *pesticide that is *toxic to freshwater and marine aquatic life, and can affect human health via domestic water supplies.

energetics The study of how *energy is transferred and used in a *system, such as an *ecosystem.

energy Usable *power, or the capacity to do work, measured by the capability to do work (*potential energy) or the conversion of this capability into motion (*kinetic energy).

energy balance The balance between the total energy that enters, leaves, and accumulates within a system (such as an *ecosystem). Based on the *first law of thermodynamics, which says that energy may be transformed, but cannot be created or destroyed.

energy budget A description of the overall *energy balance for a system (such as an *ecosystem), and of the components within it.

energy conservation Saving energy by eliminating wasteful use, making more efficient use of it, or reducing total use.

energy efficiency (fuel efficiency) The amount of energy output (work done) relative to the amount of energy input (fuel consumed). *See also* ENERGY INTENSITY.

energy farm (energy plantation) A farm that grows crops which provide fuel (such as fast-growing tree species).

energy flow The movement and loss of *energy through a *community or *ecosystem, via the *food web.

energy flux A measure of *energy flow, expressed as the amount of energy that moves through a given area in a unit of time.

energy intensity (fuel intensity) The amount of *energy used per unit of activity, such as litres of fuel per passenger-mile, or energy consumption per pound/dollar of *gross domestic product.

energy plantation *See* ENERGY FARM.

energy pyramid *See* PYRAMID OF ENERGY.

energy recovery The process of extracting useful *energy from *waste, such as the heat produced by *incineration or by harnessing *methane gas from *landfills.

energy resource *See* ENERGY SOURCE.

energy source (energy resource) Any material that is used to produce *energy, including fossil fuels (*peat, *coal, *oil, *gas), *nuclear (*fission and *fusion), and *renewables (*solar, *wind, *geothermal, *biomass, *hydroelectric).

energy type The form in which energy is available, such as *chemical energy, *electrical energy, or *heat energy, all of which are varieties of *kinetic or *potential energy.

enforcement Legal methods that are used to obtain compliance with environmental laws, rules, regulations, or agreements and/or deal with violations.

engineering The application of science to the design, creation, and function of machines and structures.

englacial Within ice, usually inside a *glacier or *ice sheet. *Contrast* SUBGLACIAL; SUPRAGLACIAL.

englacial stream A *meltwater *river that flows inside a *glacier or *ice sheet.

enhanced greenhouse effect The increase in the strength of the natural *greenhouse effect that is caused by human activities, particularly the emission into the *atmosphere of large amounts of *greenhouse gases. *See also* GLOBAL WARMING.

enhancement An improvement, or increase in quality or value.

Enlightenment (Age of Reason) A broad intellectual movement in 18th-century Europe that advocated the use of reason in the re-evaluation of accepted ideas. *See also* TRANSCENDENTALISM.

enriched fallow A form of *agroforestry in which useful woody species (such as fruits, bamboos, and rattans) are sown or planted before or when cultivation ceases, so that products are available for household use or market. *See also* BUSH FALLOW; FALLOW.

enrichment The process of increasing concentration, such as the addition of *nutrients from sewage effluent or agricultural runoff to surface water (which causes *eutrophication) or the process of increasing the proportion of uranium-235 in *nuclear fuel.

ENSO *See* EL NIÑO–SOUTHERN OSCILLATION.

enteric Relating to the intestines.

enteric bacteria *Bacteria that originate in the intestines of *warm-blooded animals.

enthalpy A measurement of the *energy content of a system.

entisols An *order of soils, that has no (or only poorly developed) soil *horizons. It often forms in recent *floodplains, under recent volcanic *ash and as wind-blown *sand.

entomology The study of insects.

entrain **1.** To set in motion (for example, particles of *sediment). **2.** To trap particles, gases, or liquid droplets in moving fluids, either mechanically (through turbulence) or chemically (through a reaction).

entropy A measure of the amount of disorder in a *system. A well-ordered and efficiently functioning system has a low level of entropy.

environment **1.** All of the external *abiotic and *biotic factors, conditions, and influences that affect the life, development, and survival of an *organism or a *community. **2.** The natural world in which we live.

Environment Agency The public body (*statutory agency) that is responsible for protecting and improving the *environment in England and Wales.

Environment Liaison Center International (ELCI) A coalition of more than 800 *non-governmental organizations, working in more than 80 countries, that aims to strengthen cooperation between member organizations, local communities, and the *United Nations Environment Programme. It was established in 1974 and its headquarters are in Nairobi, Kenya.

 SEE WEB LINKS

• ELCI organizational profile.

environmental accounting (natural resource accounting) An approach to *accounting that includes measures of the *environmental impacts and resource use of economic activities, as well as financial measures.

environmental activism (activism) Any form of activity by *environmentalists that is designed to raise public awareness of environmental issues. Extreme forms of activism include *monkey-wrenching and *EarthFirst, and more common forms include *lobbying and joining *pressure groups. See GRASSROOTS ACTIVISM.

environmental agent See AGENT.

environmental analysis Assessment of the predictable long- and short-term environmental effects of a proposed action, and of reasonable alternatives to that action. See also ENVIRONMENTAL ASSESSMENT; ENVIRONMENTAL IMPACT ASSESSMENT.

environmental assessment An *environmental analysis that is required in the USA under the *National Environmental Policy Act, which analyses a proposed federal action for the possibility of significant *environmental impacts. If the environmental impacts are likely to be significant, the federal agency must then prepare a more detailed *environmental impact statement. See also FINDING OF NO SIGNIFICANT IMPACT.

environmental audit A formal independent evaluation (*audit) of compliance (by a company, plant, or agency) with environmental regulations, standards, and policies, or an assessment of the management of any impact on the environment. For example, pollution prevention initiatives require an audit to determine where wastes may be reduced or eliminated or where energy can be conserved.

environmental balance sheet A method of *environmental assessment that analyses the *life cycle of a product or process.

environmental capacity See CARRYING CAPACITY.

environmental capital See NATURAL CAPITAL.

environmental change Any alteration to the *environment or to an *environmental system.

environmental commitment See COMMITMENT.

environmental contamination See CONTAMINATION.

Environmental Defense Fund (EDF) A leading US-based non-profit organization, founded in 1967, that is passionate in advocating environmentalist policies and objectives. It seeks innovative, equitable, and cost-effective solutions to serious environmental problems through a combination of science, economics, and law. It is committed to protecting the environmental rights of all people, including future generations, which includes the right to clean air, clean water, healthy food, and healthy *ecosystems.

 SEE WEB LINKS

• EDF home page.

environmental degradation Depletion or destruction of a potentially *renewable resource such as *air, *water, *soil, *forest, or *wildlife, by using it at a rate faster than it can be naturally renewed. See also SUSTAINABLE YIELD.

environmental determinism The view that was popular at the start of the 20th century, but is now regarded as too simplistic, that the most important control on human activities is the *environment.

environmental economics A branch of *economics that takes into account the current and future monetary costs and benefits of *environmental systems, human welfare, and *biodiversity. See also COST–BENEFIT ANALYSIS; ECOLOGICAL ECONOMICS; EXTERNALITY.

environmental education Formal and informal activities that are designed to promote people's understanding of, appreciation of, and care for the natural environment.

environmental effect See ENVIRONMENTAL IMPACT.

environmental equity (environmental justice) The extent to which all groups of people in a region or country (regardless of race, ethnicity, economic status, or income) receive

ENVIRONMENTAL CRISIS

A term that is used to describe the sum of the environmental problems that we face today. Key contemporary environmental problems include the *greenhouse effect and *global warming, the hole in the *ozone layer, *acid rain, and *tropical forest clearance. New dimensions to the environmental crisis include emerging threats and the global nature, rapid build-up, and persistence of the problems. Whilst the problems appear to be largely physical (environmental), the causes and solutions lie much more in people's attitudes, values, and expectations. A number of factors have helped to create these problems, including developments in technology, which have given people a greater ability to use the *environment and its *natural resources for their own ends (particularly since the *Industrial Revolution); the rapid increase in human *population in recent centuries, which has significantly increased population densities in many countries and led to a significant rise in human use of natural resources; the emergence of *free market economies, in which economic factors play a central role in decision-making about production, consumption, use of resources, and treatment of *wastes; attitudes towards the environment, particularly amongst western cultures, which regard it as freely available for people to do whatever they like with; and the short-term time horizon over which many people, companies, and countries make decisions, which means that short-term maximization of *profit has generally been taken more seriously than long-term *sustainable use of the environment. There are many symptoms of the so-called 'crisis'. According to the *UNEP *Global Environment Outlook 2000* report: there will be a billion cars by 2025, up from 40 million since 1945; a quarter of the world's 4630 types of *mammals and 11% of the 9675 species of *bird are at serious risk of *extinction; more than half of the world's *coral is at risk from *dredging, diving, and global warming; 80% of *forests have been cleared; a billion city dwellers are exposed to levels of *air pollution that threaten human *health; the global population will reach 8.9 billion in 2050, up from 6 billion in the year 2000; global warming will raise temperatures by up to 3.6°C, triggering a 'devastating' rise in *sea level and more severe *natural disasters; and global use of *pesticides is causing up to five million acute poisoning incidents each year.

equal treatment and protection under environmental statutes, regulations, and practices. Unlike *environmental racism, equity also considers the disproportionate burden of risk that any group of people (defined by gender, age, income, or race) is exposed to. *See* EQUITY.

environmental ethics A search for moral values and ethical principles in human relations with the natural world. *See also* ETHICS; LAND ETHCS; STEWARDSHIP.

environmental exposure The *exposure of people to particular *pollutants.

environmental fate The destiny of a chemical or biological *pollutant after it has been released into the environment.

environmental geology The study of the problems resulting from natural hazards and from human exploitation of the natural environment. The geologic techniques used include those of engineering geology, economic geology, hydrogeology, etc., as applied to waste disposal, water resources, transport, building, mining, and general land use.

environmental gradient A continuum of environmental conditions, such as the progressive change in climate with increasing latitude.

environmental group Any group of people who voluntarily join together to pursue an environmental objective. Examples include the *Worldwide Fund for Nature and *EarthFirst.

environmental hazard *See* NATURAL HAZARD.

environmental heterogeneity The patchiness of the environment, from the scale of an individual plant to the pattern of vegetation across a region.

environmental history The history of natural and induced environmental change in a particular area.

environmental hormone *See* ENDOCRINE DISRUPTOR.

environmental impact (environmental effect) Any *impact or effect (positive or negative) that an activity has on an *environmental system, *environmental quality, or *natural resources.

environmental impact assessment (EIA) A formal assessment of the *environmental impacts that are likely to arise from major activities such as new legislation or a new policy, programme, or project. The results of the assessment are reported in the *environmental impact statement. EIA was first introduced in the USA in 1969 and has since been widely applied. It is being adopted in one form or another in an increasing number of countries as a basis for making informed and rational judgements about what sorts of developments are environmentally acceptable. *Strategic environmental assessment has developed out of EIA.

environmental impact statement (EIS) A detailed written statement that describes the results of an *environmental impact assessment of a proposed large-scale project, which usually includes a description of the project and of the environment that would be affected, an assessment of the important effects of the project on environment, a justification of the project, and a non-technical summary. An EIS is required for all major federal projects in the USA under the *National Environmental Policy Act, and for all major projects in the *European Union under a 1988 directive.

environmental indicator A measurement or statistic that provides evidence of environmental quality, such as which *threshold concentrations of different *air pollutants are relevant to *human health and to *environmental stability, how best to measure the *biodiversity of species of *wildlife within *natural habitats, and how to express *land use change in the most useful ways. See also BIOINDICATOR; CORINE; EXPOSURE INDICATOR.

environmental informatics The use of computers and statistical methods in the classification, storage, retrieval, and analysis of environmental information. See also INFORMATICS.

environmental information See Appendix 1 for a list of useful online sources of information and data on particular environmental issues.

environmental information system (EIS) The storage and analysis of environmental data using a computer, which might include use of *geographical information systems (GIS), *remote sensing, and *simulation, which make it much easier to simulate how the environment works and how it might respond to different management *scenarios. Such analyses rely heavily on powerful computers that are used to store and manipulate databases and to run complex predictive *models. As computers become more and more powerful (between 1950 and 1990, for example, computers increased in speed by a factor of ten roughly every five years) it becomes possible to analyse bigger and bigger data sets and run more complex models in more sophisticated ways.

environmental justice See ENVIRONMENTAL EQUITY.

environmental labelling Attaching labels to products which advise consumers about environmental aspects of the production, use, or disposal of that product, such as the extent to which it is *biodegradable, can be *recycled, produces damaging *ozone, is *organic, is *toxic, and is based on *renewable materials. See also ECO-LABEL.

environmental lapse rate The rate at which *temperature decreases with increasing *altitude in the *troposphere, as measured at a particular time and place.

environmental law The body of official legal rules, decisions, and actions that relate to *environmental quality, *natural resources, and *ecological sustainability.

environmental literacy The level of understanding that an individual, group, or population has of ecological principles and the interrelationships between people and *environment.

environmental management The deliberate *management and control of the *environment and of *natural resources systems, designed to ensure the long-term sustainability of development efforts.

environmental management system (EMS) A method or tool for systematically addressing environmental issues within an organization, which includes concrete objectives, plans of action, and responsibility for dealing with environmental matters. See also ECO-MANAGEMENT AND AUDIT SCHEME.

environmental monitoring Technologies, procedures, and protocols for collecting, analysing, interpreting, and reporting *environmental information, including the use of *continuous monitoring, *remote sensing and *satellites, *geographical information systems, and *environmental informatics. Great improvements have been made since the early 1990s in harmonizing practices and standards between countries, so that it is now becoming both possible and meaningful to collate national statistics into global summaries. A useful product of this new interest in producing and interpreting environmental information is the *state of the environment reports that many countries now produce regularly. Monitoring provides the data that are needed to facilitate the development, testing, and operation of complex *global models. It also provides *baselines against which to evaluate rates and patterns of *environmental change, and which can be used to give early indications of natural environmental adjustments and possible risks. The *United Nations Environment Programme (UNEP) is responsible for coordinating the monitoring networks that provide invaluable information about the global environment. The data are collected mainly from surface stations around the world as part of the *Global Environmental Monitoring System (GEMS).

Environmental Monitoring and Assessment Program (EMAP) An *environmental monitoring system developed by the US *Environmental Protection Agency (EPA).

environmental movement A political movement that focuses on protecting the *environment, reducing environmental damage (such as *pollution), and reducing unsustainable use of *natural resources. See also ENVIRONMENTALISM.

environmental pathway Any route through the *environment along which *pollutants can move, such as air, water, and soil.

environmental philosophy See PHILOSOPHY.

environmental planning All planning activities that have the objective of preserving or enhancing environmental values or resources.

environmental policy 1. The official rules and regulations relating to the *environment that are adopted, implemented, and enforced by a government agency. 2. A statement by an organization of its intentions and principles with respect to environmental performance, which provides a framework for action and for the setting of environmental objectives and targets.

environmental politics See POLITICS.

environmental pollution See POLLUTION.

environmental protection Practices and procedures that are designed to avoid, minimize, eliminate, or reverse damage to the *environment and to *environmental systems. See

also ECOLOGICAL MODERNIZATION; ENVIRONMENTAL IMPACT; SUSTAINABLE DEVELOPMENT.

Environmental Protection Agency (EPA) The federal agency in the USA that was created in 1970 and is responsible for efforts to protect human health and to control air and water *pollution, *radiation and *pesticide hazards, ecological research, and the disposal of *solid waste.

environmental quality The state of the *environment, generally in a particular place, defined either objectively (for example by the use of *environmental indicators) or subjectively (in terms of attributes such as beauty and attractiveness).

environmental racism Intentional or unintentional racial discrimination in environmental policy-making, enforcement of regulations and laws, and targeting of communities for the disposal of *toxic waste and siting of polluting industries. See also ENVIRONMENTAL EQUITY.

environmental refugee A migrant from an area that is threatened with or damaged by a major *natural hazard or *disaster. Under international law, people who flee their own country to escape from persecution, armed conflict, or violence can be granted refugee status, but those forced to leave for social or environmental reasons do not qualify.

environmental regime The *regime for managing the environment, either globally or at a national level, which includes environmental *regulations and *conventions, and the institutions through which they are managed.

environmental regulation The management of activities that affect the environment, through such means as *command and control and *market-based mechanisms.

environmental regulator An agency (such as national or local government) that oversees and applies the legislation and regulations governing the *environment.

environmental reporting The release of environmental statements by businesses that usually contain information on *environmental impacts, *environmental management initiatives, and plans for future activities.

environmental resistance The sum total of the environmental *limiting factors, both *biotic and *abiotic, which together act to prevent the *biotic potential of an organism from being realized. Such factors include the availability of essential resources (e.g. food and water), *predation, disease, the accumulation of toxic metabolic wastes, and, in some species, behavioural changes due to stress caused by overcrowding.

environmental resource See NATURAL RESOURCE.

environmental restoration The *cleanup and *restoration of sites that have been contaminated with *hazardous substances.

environmental review Study of a company's processes and procedures, to assess compliance with environmental laws and regulations and to review its environmental policy and best practice.

environmental risk Any source of harm or danger in the *environment, for example from *natural hazards, *pollution, or depletion of *natural resources.

environmental science The interdisciplinary study of *cnvironmental systems, how they operate, how they interact with people, and how people interact with them.

environmental security The impact on security of the links between *environmental stress and violent conflict, particularly in *developing countries, caused, for example, by competition for scarce resources or exposure to serious natural hazards.

environmental site assessment The process of determining whether a particular plot of land has been contaminated.

environmental standard A limiting condition of *environmental quality, that is often expressed in numerical terms, has legal standing, and is designed to protect human health and well-being.

environmental stress Any form or level of *environmental change which particular organisms (including humans) find it difficult to adjust to.

environmental sustainability The long-term maintenance of *ecosystems and other *environmental systems for the benefit of future generations. See also SUSTAINABLE DEVELOPMENT; SUSTAINABILITY.

environmental system A *system that is based on the natural environment and includes *biotic and *abiotic components which interact. The major environmental systems are the *atmosphere (air), *biosphere (living organisms), *hydrosphere (water), *cryosphere (ice), *pedosphere (soil), and *lithosphere (rock). An *ecosystem is the term for a local environmental system.

environmental technology Any technology that is designed to control *pollution, treat or store waste materials, or cleanup contaminated sites. Examples include wet *scrubbers (air), soil washing (soil), granulated *activated carbon unit (water), and filtration (air, water). Contrast ALTERNATIVE TECHNOLOGY.

environmental toxicology The branch of toxicology (the study of poisons) that deals with the toxic effects on individual organisms of naturally occurring or synthetic substances present in the environment. Compare ECOTOXICOLOGY.

environmental treaty Any *treaty that deals with the *environment or with *natural resources. Appendix 2 contains a summary of international environmental treaties.

environmentalism 1. The beliefs behind an organized social movement of people who share a concern about solving problems of environmental *pollution and *natural resources. Environmental concern is reflected in a number of different ways, including membership of environmental *pressure groups and campaigning organizations (such as *Friends of the Earth and *Greenpeace), sympathy for and engagement with environmental *politics, *green consumerism, local *environmental activism, and adoption of *lifestyles that are *environment-friendly. Western environmentalism can be traced back to the emergence of concern about *nature and *natural landscape in the USA towards the close of the 19th century. The modern *environmental movement emerged during the 1960s, first in the USA and then in Britain. A number of books were particularly influential in orienting people's views and attitudes during this formative period, including *Silent Spring, *Blueprint for Survival, and *Limits to Growth. Environmentalism is founded on a number of concerns, including a reaction against *technocracy, a concern about the *welfare of deprived groups of people (particularly in *developing countries), a concern for wider issues of *equity and *justice, and a sense of personal responsibility to leave a worthwhile *environmental heritage for future generations. **2.** The belief that *environment is more important than *heredity in determining intellectual growth in humans.

environmentalist A person who works or engages in activities that are designed to protect the *environment from destruction or *pollution.

Environmentally Sensitive Area (ESA) An area of land, designated by the UK government under *EU regulations, where landowners and tenants are eligible to claim for subsidies for certain types of management that will benefit *landscape or *wildlife features within the ESA. *See also* MANAGEMENT AGREEMENT.

environment-friendly (green) Applied to activities, products, or *lifestyles that are designed to have a small *environmental impact, such as restricting family size to a maximum of two children, using public rather than private transport, using renewable materials wherever possible, and engaging in *green consumerism.

enzyme A *protein that catalyses a biochemical reaction.

Eocene The second of the three *epochs of the *Palaeogene period, from 55.8 to 33.9 million years ago, when the climate was significantly warmer, commencing in the *Palaeocene–Eocene thermal maximum, seas extended much further than today, and the first modern *mammals appeared.

(⊕) SEE WEB LINKS

• Eocene epoch.

eocyte hypothesis A proposed taxonomic system in which all organisms are placed in two *domains, *Bacteria and *Archaea, the *Eukarya being contained within the Archaea.

eolian *See* AEOLIAN.

eolithic The earliest part of the *Stone Age, in which the earliest signs of human culture appear.

EOS *See* EARTH OBSERVATION SATELLITE.

EPA *See* ENVIRONMENTAL PROTECTION AGENCY.

EPCRA *See* COMMUNITY-RIGHT-TO-KNOW ACT.

ephemeral Transitory, *episodic, lasting for only a short period of time.

ephemeral flow Flow in a *river or *stream that only occurs during and immediately after *rain. *Contrast* INTERMITTENT FLOW; PERENNIAL FLOW.

ephemeral plant An *annual plant with a very short lifespan (a few weeks or a very few months), which is common in *desert climates.

ephemeral stream A stream or river that has no permanent flow, but flows only as the direct result of *rainfall or *snow melt.

ephemeral wetland A *wetland that fills with water in the *spring but is dry by the end of the *summer.

epibenthos All of the *organisms that live on the surface of the bottom of a *waterbody, such as the *sea-bed. *See also* EPIFAUNA; EPIFLORA.

epicentre The centre of an *earthquake, located on the ground surface directly above the *focus, where the most severe shock waves are usually experienced.

epidemic A widespread outbreak of an infectious *disease.

epidemiology The study of the *incidence, distribution, and control of *disease in a *population.

epidermis The outer layer of *cells on *plants and *animals which covers and protects the underlying dermis.

epifauna Animals that live on the floor of a *waterbody, such as the *sea-bed.

epiflora Plants that live on the floor of a waterbody, such as the sea-bed.

epigene Produced or occurring at the Earth's surface, especially in relation to the processes of *weathering, *erosion, and sediment *deposition. 'Epigenetic drainage' is sometimes used as a synonym for 'superimposed drainage' (*See* SUPERIMPOSED RIVER).

epigenetic drainage *See* EPIGENE; SUPERIMPOSED RIVER.

epilimnion The top layer of water in a *lake or *reservoir, which has the warmest water and a relatively uniform temperature, and which is mixed by the *wind.

epilithic Growing on stone or on rock surfaces.

epipelagic Applied to the top 200 m of the ocean, seas, and lakes.

epipelagic zone *See* PHOTIC ZONE.

epipelic At the *interface between sediment and water.

epiphyte A plant which does not root in *soil but uses the trunk or stem of another plant for support as it grows. It draws no nutrients from its *host plant, but gets its moisture and nutrients from the air, rainwater, and organic debris. This is a form of *commensalism and an example of *symbiosis.

epipsammic Attached to *sand particles.

episode *See* POLLUTION EPISODE.

episodic *See* INTERMITTENT.

epizoic Growing or living on the exterior of a living animal, as a non-parasitic organism.

epoch A subdivision of geological time that is shorter than a period. For example, the *Quaternary period is divided into the *Holocene epoch and *Pleistocene epoch.

equality The state of being the same in terms of quantity, value, or status. *Contrast* INEQUALITY.

equator An imaginary circle around the Earth that is equally distant from the North and South poles and defines the latitude 0°.

equatorial forest *See* TROPICAL RAINFOREST.

equatorial low *See* DOLDRUMS.

equatorial trough A shallow zone of low surface atmospheric pressure around the equator, where the *trade-wind systems tend to converge. *See also* DOLDRUMS; INTERTROPICAL CONVERGENCE ZONE.

equatorial wet climate zone A hot, wet *tropical climate zone, with high temperatures (usually around 30°C) through the year, *precipitation (at least 60mm of rainfall) every month, and *cloud cover on most days. *Rainforest is the typical natural vegetation.

equifinality A state or condition of a *system that can be created in more than one way, so it is often difficult to work out cause-and-effect associations between the many parts of a system.

equilibrium A state of balance in a *system that is produced and maintained by a variety of forces which may increase or decrease but they always cancel each other out, producing a *steady state. *See also* CHEMICAL EQUILIBRIUM.

equilibrium community 1. A *community of *organisms that are able to co-exist indefin-

itely. 2. A community that is able to return to its former state following a disturbance.

equilibrium line The boundary in a *glacier between the *accumulation zone and the *ablation zone.

equilibrium response The anticipated change in *climate that would result from a change in *radiative forcing.

equilibrium species A *species whose *population exists in *equilibrium with available *resources, at a stable *density.

equilibrium state *See* STEADY STATE.

equilibrium theory A theory in *island biogeography that greater numbers of species are found on larger islands because the populations on smaller islands are more vulnerable to *extinction.

equilibrium warming commitment The increase in *temperature that would result at some point in the future if atmospheric concentrations of *greenhouse gases remained constant at the levels of a particular year. *See also* COMMITMENT.

equinox Either of the days each year when the noonday Sun is directly overhead at the *equator and daylight and darkness are of equal length. These are 20–21 March and 22–23 September. *See also* WINTER; SPRING; SUMMER; AUTUMN/FALL. *Compare* SOLSTICE.

equitability *See* EVENNESS.

equitable That which is fair, impartial, and just, and which provides equal opportunity for all. *Contrast* INEQUITABLE.

equity Fairness arising from the equal use and allocation of resources. *See also* ENVIRONMENTAL EQUITY. *Contrast* INEQUITY.

era A unit of geological time that is longer than a *period. Examples include the *Paleozoic era, the *Mesozoic era and the *Cenozoic era.

eradication The removal from the *environment of all units of an infecting *agent or *pathogen.

erg 1. A *desert surface that is covered by *sand dunes. 2. The work done by a force of one dyne (10^{-7} *joules) acting over a distance of one centimetre.

ergot A *fungus (*Claviceps purpurea*) that affects *cereal plants, replacing grains with resting bodies containing *alkaloids that can cause severe poisoning or even death in mammals including humans.

Ericaceae A family comprising 124 genera and about 4050 species of shrubs and small trees, including 665 species of heathers.

erode To wear away by the process of *erosion. For example the effect of wind, water, and movement of *glaciers in moving material from the ground surface, which is then transported and deposited elsewhere. *See also* SOIL ERO-SION.

erodibility The ease with which a soil or rock can be *eroded.

erosion A group of natural *geological processes by which soil and rock material are loosened (*weathering) or dissolved (*solution) and then moved (*transportation) from their original location. The processes involve transporting agents such as running water, moving ice, or blowing wind, which are active within *rivers, *coasts and *oceans, *glaciers and *periglacial areas, and *deserts and semi-arid areas. Approximately 10 million tonnes of *sediment is eroded from the world's continents each year, the vast majority (nearly 95%) transported by rivers. Much smaller quantities are eroded by wind and ice. Rates of erosion vary a great deal from place to place, reflecting variations in key controlling factors such as *climate (particularly temperature and rainfall), vegetation cover, changes in *land use, geology, and soil type, and *topography (particularly the steepness and uniformity of a hillslope). Human activities can significantly alter the pace and pattern of erosion. The *United Nations Environment Programme estimates that, as a result of human activities world-wide, some 10 930 million km^2 of land have been seriously damaged by *water erosion, 9.2 million km^2 by *sheet and *slope erosion, and 1.73 million km^2 by the development of *rills and *gullies. The main causes are clearance of natural vegetation and forest (43%), overgrazing (29%), poor farming practices such as cultivation of steep slopes (24%), and over-exploitation of natural vegetation (4%). *See also* ACCELERATED EROSION; NAT-URAL EROSION.

erosion surface 1. (planation surface) A gently undulating land surface that cuts across underlying geological features and is the result of a long period of *erosion. **2.** An irregular surface that has been shaped by erosion. *See also* CYCLE OF EROSION.

erosivity The ability of *rainfall to cause *erosion, which depends on rainfall intensity and drop size, as well as the material it lands on.

erratic (exotic) A large particle of *rock that has been transported by a *glacier away from its source and deposited in a region of different rock.

ERS *See* EUROPEAN REMOTE SENSING SATEL-LITE.

ERTS *See* EARTH RESOURCES TECHNOLOGY SAT-ELLITE.

ERU *See* EMISSIONS REDUCTION UNIT.

ESA *See* ENVIRONMENTALLY SENSITIVE AREA.

escape cover *See* COVER.

escape hypothesis *See* JANZEN–CONNELL ESCAPE HYPOTHESIS.

escapement 1. The number or proportion of elk or other *wildlife that survive the hunting season. **2.** The number or proportion of fish that avoid or escape from *fisheries and move offshore, where they eventually spawn.

escarpment (cuesta, scarp) A long cliff or relatively steep slope that faces in one direction, separating two generally level surfaces, often produced by *faulting or *erosion.

esker A sinuous ridge of coarse gravel that is deposited by a *meltwater stream beneath a *glacier. *Contrast* KAME.

essential element A *chemical element that is required by all living organisms for normal growth. This includes the primary essential elements (*carbon, *hydrogen, *oxygen, *nitrogen, *phosphorus, and *potassium), secondary essential elements (*sulphur, *calcium, *sodium, *chlorine, and *magnesium), and the *trace elements (*iron, *boron, *manganese, *copper, *zinc, *iodine, *cobalt, *selenium, *chromium, *silicon, and *molybdenum).

Esso Bernicia A British oil tanker that collided with a jetty at the Sullom Voe oil terminal, Shetland Islands, on 1 January 1979, releasing more than 1100 tonnes of heavy fuel oil. The release caused severe contamination. About 3700 seabirds and 50 sheep were killed and 2000 sheep were badly oiled.

establishment The successful growth and reproduction of plants and/or animals in a site that provides them with favourable conditions.

estate 1. An extensive tract of land, particularly in the country, that is owned and retained by the owner for his/her own use. **2.** All of a person's assets and liabilities; everything they own.

ester A compound that is formed as the condensation product (i.e. water is removed) of an acid and an alcohol; water is formed from the OH of the acid and the H of the alcohol. Replacing the H in an organic acid by an organic radical converts the acid to its ester (e.g. acetic acid (CH_3COOH) becomes ethyl acetate (the ethyl ester $CH_3COOC_2H_5$). Many esters are liquid with pleasant smells and are used to flavour food, and many vegetable and animal fats are esters.

estivation *See* AESTIVATION.

estuarine Of or relating to an *estuary.

estuarine flow The seaward flow of freshwater over a deeper layer of seawater with higher *salinity, within an *estuary.

estuarine subtidal A *habitat of open water within an *estuary that is continuously covered by seawater.

estuarine wetland A *tidal *wetland within an *estuary.

estuary The wide mouth of a *river where it flows into the sea, in which fresh (river) water meets and mixes with salt (sea) water, and which is *tidal.

ethanal *See* ACETALDEHYDE.

ethane (ethylene, C_2H_6) A colourless, odourless *hydrocarbon gas that is extracted mainly from *natural gas and is used as a *fuel.

ethanoic acid *See* ACETIC ACID.

ethanol (fuel ethanol, C_2H_5OH) A colourless, flammable liquid produced by *fermentation of sugars (derived from agricultural products such as corn, grain, and sugar cane) which is used as an *alternative fuel and a fuel additive. It is the most widely used renewable *biofuel.

ethical values Statements of ethical principle that inform the private and social valuation of *environmental resources.

ethics The philosophical study of moral values and rules, that inform decisions about wrong and right. *See also* ENVIRONMENTAL ETHICS.

Ethiopian faunal region An area that corresponds with sub-Saharan Africa, although it is not completely separated from the neighbouring faunal regions; generally it is taken to include the south-west corner of the Arabian peninsula. Varied game animals are found there, and there are a number of *endemic families, including various rodents and shrews, giraffe, hippopotamus, aardvark, tenrec, and lemurs.

ethnobotany The study of what plants people use and how they use them.

ethnography The study of culture (including behaviour, beliefs, and attitudes), based on observation of and interaction with living people. *See also* ANTHROPOLOGY.

ethnozoology The study of the uses to which animals and animal products are put by people of different cultures.

ethyne *See* ACETYLENE.

EU *See* EUROPEAN UNION.

EU Bubble A *greenhouse gas *emissions bubble in which member states of the *European Union have accepted an aggregated emissions reduction target and arrangements that allow the target to be shared among all of the countries within the *bubble.

EU Directive A legal *directive from the *European Union that is binding on member states but leaves the method of implementation for national governments to decide.

EU Habitats Directive *See* HABITATS DIRECTIVE.

EU Life Programme *See* LIFE PROGRAMME.

Eubacteria In the widely used five-kingdom system of *taxonomy, one of the subkingdoms in the *kingdom *Bacteria, containing organisms that need to be distinguished from members of the other subkingdom, the *Archaea. In the three-*domain classification system, one of the three domains, containing the single kingdom Bacteria. In an alternative two-domain system proposed by the *eocyte hypothesis, one of the two domains.

eugenic Applied to the creation of high-quality offspring. *Contrast* DYSGENIC.

eugenics The study of hereditary improvement amongst humans by controlled *selective breeding.

euhaline Fully saline; seawater with a *salinity of greater than 30 parts per thousand.

Eukarya (Eukaryota) In *taxonomy, the group that includes all *eukaryotes. In the widely used five-kingdom classification system, the Eukarya is ranked as a superkingdom containing the kingdoms Protoctista, Animalia, Fungi, and Plantae. In the three-domain classification system, Eukarya is the *domain containing the kingdoms Protista, Animalia, Fungi, and Plantae.

Eukaryota *See* EUKARYA.

eukaryote An organism with cells that have a distinct *nucleus (i.e. all protists, fungi, plants, and animals). The first eukaryotes were almost certainly green *algae (Chlorophyta) and what appear to be their microscopic remains occur in *Precambrian sediments dating from a little less than 1500 million years ago. *Compare* PROKARYOTE.

eulittoral The intertidal zone.

euphotic zone (photic zone, epipelagic zone) The layer of water in a lake or sea (usually the top 80 m) where sunlight is sufficient for *photosynthesis to occur.

European Chemicals Agency (ECHA) The principal regulatory authority responsible for implementing European Union chemicals legislation. The ECHA helps companies comply with the legislation, promotes the safe use of chemicals, provides information about chemicals, and draws attention to chemicals that cause concern.

(⊕) SEE WEB LINKS

• Home page of the ECHA.

European Commission The administrative and executive institution of the *European Union, which is responsible for initiating proposals for legislation, ensuring the implementation of treaties to which the EU is party, executing EU policies, and representing the EU in trade negotiations with non-member countries. *See also* COUNCIL OF MINISTERS.

European Community (EC) A regional organization created by the Treaty of Rome (1957), which provided for the gradual elimination of customs duties and other interregional trade barriers between member states in Europe. In 1993, with establishment of the *European Union (EU), the EC became the customs union component of the EU.

European Economic Community (EEC, Common Market) An economic union that was established in 1958 to promote trade in Western Europe by merging separate national markets into a single market that ensures the free movement of goods, people, capital, and services. Renamed *European Union in 1994.

European Environment Agency (EEA) The body of the *European Union that is responsible for supporting *sustainable development and helping to achieve significant and measurable improvement in Europe's *environment through the provision of timely, targeted, relevant, and reliable information to policy-making agents and the public.

European Migration Period *See* DARK AGES COOL PERIOD.

European Remote Sensing (ERS) satellite Two radar satellites launched by the European Space Agency in 1991 and 1995. They collected data on land surfaces, oceans, and polar caps until ERS-1 failed in March 2000 and ERS-2 was retired in July 2011.

European Union (EU) An economic association of European countries that was founded by the Treaty of Rome in 1957 and was known as the European Community before 1993. Its goals are a single market for goods and services without any economic barriers and a common currency with one monetary authority. In March 2012 the EU had 27 member states—Austria, Belgium, Bulgaria, Cyprus (Greek part), Czech Republic, Denmark, Estonia, Finland, France, Germany, Greece, Hungary, Ireland, Italy, Latvia, Lithuania, Luxembourg, Malta, Netherlands, Poland, Portugal, Romania, Slovakia, Slovenia, Spain, Sweden, and the United Kingdom. *See also* COUNCIL OF MINISTERS; EUROPEAN COMMISSION.

(⊕) SEE WEB LINKS

• EU official website.

Eurosiberian floral region Part of R. Good's Boreal Realm (*The Geography of the Flowering Plants*, 1974): an extensive region in which the flora of the western part is richer than that of the eastern part. Whereas Europe has roughly 150 *endemic genera, Siberia apparently has only about twelve, almost all of which are *monotypic. The contrast between the two subregions reflects primarily the different climatic regimes.

eury- A prefix denoting the ability of an *organism to tolerate a wide range of environmental conditions, such as *eurythermal. *Contrast* STENO-.

Euryarchaeota *See* ARCHAEA.

euryhaline Able to live in environments with a wide range of *salinity.

eurythermal Able to live in environments with a wide range of temperature.

eustasy Global position changes in *sea level due to tectonic movements or *glacio-eustasy.

eustatic Pertaining to *eustasy. *Contrast* ISO-STATIC ADJUSTMENT.

eutherians The placental mammals, comprising an infraclass of the class Mammalia.

eutrophic Enriched in *nutrients. A body of water which has a high concentration of dissolved nutrients, is very biologically productive, and has large amounts of *algae, low water transparency, and low *dissolved oxygen. *Contrast* OLIGOTROPHIC. *See also* DYSTROPHIC; EUTROPHICATION.

eutrophication (nutrient enrichment) A common form of *water pollution which involves the *enrichment of a body of *freshwater with *nutrients such as *nitrate *fertilizers (washed from the soil by rain) and *phosphates (from fertilizers and *detergents in *municipal sewage). The pollution enriches the waterbody, and this encourages the rapid growth of aquatic plants and can cause excessive growth of *algae (*bloom) and vascular plants. This in turn reduces the availability of light and the *aerobic decomposition of dead algae reduces dissolved oxygen, making the water uninhabitable for some species. Some of the algae and *bacteria produce relatively large amounts of *toxins, which further disrupt the aquatic ecosystem. Since the early 20th century such blooms have been a regular occurrence in the most heavily polluted parts of the *Great Lakes in North America, but they have declined as *water quality has improved as a result of improved pollution control and water quality management strategies. Lakes can be classified according to their nutrient content as *oligotrophic (nutrient poor), *mesotrophic (moderately productive), or *eutrophic (very productive and fertile).

euxinic Applied to an aquatic environment in which the circulation of water is restricted, leading to reduced oxygen levels or anaerobic conditions. Such conditions may develop in swamps, barred basins, stratified lakes, and *fjords. Euxinic sediments are those deposited in such conditions, and are usually black and organic-rich.

evacuation A prolonged precautionary stay away from an area that is affected by a *hazardous material or a *natural hazard.

evaluation An examination or judgement about the worth, quality, significance, amount, degree, or condition of a project or object.

evaporation The process by which a liquid changes into a *vapour with the absorption of energy (*latent heat). *Contrast* CONDENSATION.

evaporation fog 1. (mixing fog) *Fog that forms when very moist air mixes with cooler, relatively drier air. **2. (frontal fog, precipitation fog)** Fog that forms when *raindrops falling from warm air evaporate into cooler air beneath the *front, eventually saturating the cool air, causing *condensation.

evaporation pond 1. An area where *sewage sludge is dumped and dried by *evaporation. **2.** An enclosed body of sea water that is allowed to evaporate in order to obtain the salts that crystallize from it.

evaporite A type of *sedimentary rock that is formed by the *precipitation of minerals dissolved in water as a result of *evaporation. Examples include *rock salt and *gypsum.

evapotranspiration The process by which *water vapour is released to the atmosphere from surface water, soils, and plants through the combined effects of *evaporation and *transpiration.

even-aged stand A group of trees that are essentially the same age. *Contrast* ALL-AGED STAND; UNEVEN-AGED STAND.

evenness (equitability) The quality of uniformity and lack of variation. For example, the degree to which all species in an area are equal in abundance and not dominated by one or a few species.

Everglades A large natural *freshwater *marsh which covers nearly 13 000 square kilometres of southern Florida in the USA. The wetland was created by regular overflowing from Lake Okeechobee during the wet season, which flooded the Everglades up to one metre deep in water. Most of the area is a wilderness of *swamp, *savanna, and *primary forest and it contains a rich diversity of wildlife, much of which is protected within the Everglades National Park (which covers 6100 square kilometres). The marsh is covered with dense saw grass which rises up to three metres above the water level, making access difficult in many places. Many small islands covered with thick bushes and trees (including cypress, mangrove, and palms) are scattered throughout the marsh, all of which are less than two metres above sea level.

(⊕) SEE WEB LINKS

• Everglades National Park home page.

evergreen Applied to shrubs and trees with persistent leaves that are not all shed at the same time of year, so the crown is never completely bare. *See also* CONIFEROUS. *Contrast* DECIDUOUS.

evergreen forest A forest in which there is no complete, seasonal loss of leaves (i.e. trees shed old leaves and produce new ones partially, and sometimes throughout the year, rather than during particular periods). The trees may be softwood conifers or broadleaved *hardwoods. The distribution of these forests ranges through *boreal, middle, and tropical latitudes. Evergreen coniferous forests predominate where the growing season is less than half the year; *broadleaved evergreen forest is found in regions that lack a prolonged dry season.

evergreen mixed forest A forest in which the dominant trees are both *evergreen broadleaved *hardwoods and *conifers. Such forests are particularly well developed in the southern hemisphere, in South Africa, Tasmania, New Zealand, and Chile. In the northern hemisphere, eastern Asia and the Mediterranean

basin once contained large tracts of such forest, but most of it has long been cleared.

evolutionary change Progressive modification that occurs in a *species from generation to generation.

evolutionary classification A *classification of *organisms that is based on their relationships through shared ancestry.

ex situ (off-site) Outside, off site, or away from the natural location. For example, biological material which is in a laboratory, collection, *botanical garden, *zoo, or *aquarium. *Contrast* IN SITU.

ex situ conservation An approach to the *conservation of *biodiversity that is based on keeping organisms and species alive by the deliberate removal of biological resources (seed, pollen, sperm, individual organisms) from their original habitat or natural environment, and protecting them elsewhere under controlled conditions. *Contrast* IN SITU CONSERVATION. *See also* GENE BANK.

exaptation A characteristic that opens up a previously unavailable *niche to its possessor. The characteristic may have originated as an *adaptation to some other niche (e.g. it is proposed that feathers were an adaptation to thermoregulation, but opened up the possibility of flight to their possessors), or as a neutral *mutation.

exceedance A measured level of a particular *pollutant that is higher than the *ambient air quality standard.

EVOLUTION

Heritable change in successive generations of *organisms, described by Charles *Darwin as 'descent with modification'. The modern scientific theory of evolution is derived from Darwin's *On the Origin of Species by Means of Natural Selection* (1859). Darwin argued that: (*a*) the individuals of a species show variation; (*b*) on average, more offspring are produced than are needed to replace their parents; (*c*) populations cannot increase indefinitely and mainly they remain stable; (*d*) therefore, there must be competition for survival; and (*e*) those variants that are best adapted to their environmental conditions (the fittest) survive. The fittest succeed by gaining greater access to resources than their competitors and, therefore, by raising more offspring. Thus the successful features are preserved in succeeding generations and less successful features are removed as the organisms possessing them fail to reproduce, in a process called *natural selection that is analogous to the breeding programmes by which plant and animal breeders develop new varieties or breeds. The Darwinian theory has been modified by the addition of information from genetics and the mechanisms of inheritance. *Contrast* EXTINCTION. *See also* ADAPTATION; ADAPTIVE RADIATION; ARTIFICIAL SELECTION; SPECIATION; INDUSTRIAL MELANISM; PUNCTUATED EQUILIBRIUM.

exception In land *zoning, the granting of a special permit for a use which is outside of those normally approved for that type of zone.

exchange capacity A measure of the surface charge of a substance that is capable of absorbing ions. *See also* CATION EXCHANGE CAPACITY.

exclusion principle A principle introduced in 1934 by the Russian ecologist G. F. Gause (1910–86), that two *species with identical ecological requirements cannot coexist in the same locality.

exclusion zone (hot zone) The area surrounding an operation which may threaten human health or well-being, from which non-essential personnel are kept out.

Exclusive Economic Zone (EEZ) A zone of the oceans over which a particular nation has claims or exclusive rights to explore, exploit, conserve, and manage *natural resources, as defined in the 1982 *United Nations Convention on the Law of the Sea.

exclusive use zoning A *zoning regulation that allows only one type of land use in a particular established zone or district.

exfoliation A *weathering process in which thin layers of rock peel off from the surface, which is often caused by the heating of the rock surface during the day and cooling at night leading to alternate expansion and contraction. It can also be caused by the release of pressure when previously covered rocks are exposed, for example by weathering and *erosion.

exhaust ventilation The mechanical removal of air from part of a building.

exhaustible resource Any *non-renewable resource (such as *minerals, non-mineral resources, and *fossil fuels) that are present in fixed amounts in the *environment. Over-exploitation of a *renewable resource may convert it to an exhaustible resource.

exine The resistant outer shell of a spore or *pollen grain that can be preserved in *sediments and which can be identified in *pollen analysis.

existence value *See* NON-CONSUMPTIVE VALUE.

exobiology The study of life outside the *Earth.

exogenous External, arising from outside. *Contrast* ENDOGENOUS.

Exopterygota Insects in which the wings develop externally and the young, known as nymphs, undergo no pupal stage or rapid metamorphosis. *Contrast* ENDOPTERYGOTA.

exorheic Applied to a lake that has one or more outflow streams. *Compare* ENDORHEIC.

exoskeleton The horny outer covering that encloses the body of all *arthropods. *Contrast* ENDOSKELETON.

exosphere The outermost part of the *atmosphere that lies beyond the *thermosphere, its base 250–500 km above the surface, where atomic *oxygen, *helium, and *hydrogen are the predominant gases. The exosphere has no clearly defined outer limit, but an upper boundary can be said to exist at about 190 000 km, which is halfway to the Moon.

exothermic Applied to a chemical reaction which gives off heat. *Contrast* ENDOTHERMIC.

exotic (alien) Not naturally occurring in a particular area. *Contrast* INDIGENOUS; NATIVE. *See also* ERRATIC.

exotic species *See* INTRODUCED SPECIES.

exploitation 1. The killing, capture, or collection of *wild organisms for human use. 2. The use of a *natural resource for profit or benefit to humans.

exploitation competition Competition between two or more *organisms for the same limited *resource. *See also* INTERFERENCE COMPETITION.

exploratory well A *well that is drilled to find and produce oil or gas in an unproved area, to find a new reservoir of oil or gas in a field previously found to be productive, or to extend the limit of a known oil or gas reservoir.

exponential growth Growth at a constant rate of increase per unit of time, which can be expressed as a constant fraction or exponent and graphed as a *J-curve. *Contrast* ARITHMETIC GROWTH; GEOMETRIC GROWTH.

export To transport a commodity to another area, such as the transport of *municipal solid waste and *recyclables outside the locality where they originated.

exposed Visibly unprotected. In terms of wave *exposure, an open coast that is facing away from prevailing winds but has a long *fetch, where strong winds are common.

exposed group The members of a *population who have been exposed to a *pollutant or other *agent.

exposure 1. Contact between an *organism and a chemical or physical *agent, by swallowing, breathing, or direct contact (such as through the skin or eyes). Exposure may be either short term (*acute) or long term (*chronic). **2.** The degree of wave action on an open shore, which is determined by the *fetch and the strength and duration of *winds. *Compare* EXPOSED; EXTREMELY EXPOSED; SHELTERED; ULTRASHELTERED; VERY EXPOSED; VERY SHELTERED.

exposure assessment An estimation of the magnitude, frequency, duration, route, and extent (number of people) of exposure to a chemical or physical *agent.

exposure event An incident of contact with a chemical or physical *agent.

exposure indicator An *environmental indicator that provides evidence of exposure to a chemical or biological *agent.

exposure level The amount or concentration of a chemical or biological *agent that is measured in or on an *organism.

exposure limit The regulated level of exposure of a chemical or biological *agent that should not be exceeded in order to protect human health and well-being.

exposure pathway The route that a particular *pollutant takes from its source to people or other organisms, via, soil, water, or food. *See also* EXPOSURE ROUTE; INDIRECT EXPOSURE PATHWAY.

exposure–response relationship The relationship between *exposure level and incidence of *adverse effects.

exposure route The way that a chemical or pollutant enters an organism after contact (by ingestion, inhalation, or absorption through skin). *See also* EXPOSURE PATHWAY.

exsiccation Dehydration of an area by a process (e.g. drainage) in the absence of changes in precipitation levels. Draining of marshlands and deforestation are examples of processes that can lead to exsiccation. *See also* DESICCATION.

extant Existing or surviving, still living at the present time. *Contrast* EXTINCT.

extended outlook A basic forecast of general weather conditions three to five days in the future.

extensive recreation *See* DISPERSED RECREATION.

extent In *conservation assessment, the size of site that is required to ensure that the unit to be managed is viable.

external cost *See* EXTERNALITY.

external forcing *See* RADIATIVE FORCING.

externality (externalization of production costs, social cost) A consequence or impact of a decision about *resources that is not directly accounted for in the price paid for the resource, such as *pollution, loss of *wilderness, or *environmental change. *See also* ENVIRONMENTAL ECONOMICS; INTERNALIZATION; MARKET FAILURE.

externalization of production costs *See* EXTERNALITY.

extinct No longer living anywhere. A *species for which there is no reasonable doubt that the last individual has died. A *threatened category defined by the *IUCN *Red Data Book. *Contrast* ENDANGERED; EXTIRPATION; THREATENED; VULNERABLE.

extirpated Locally extinct.

extirpation (local extinction) The disappearance of a *population or *species from an island, area, or region. *Contrast* EXTINCTION.

extract To remove or take out.

extraction (abstraction) The act of removing a resource, such as felled timber from a forest or *groundwater from an *aquifer.

extractive reserve A *conservation area in which certain kinds of *resource harvesting on a *sustainable basis are permitted.

extrapolation Estimating a value by projecting or extending known values, for example in order to predict outside a range of known conditions (such as predicting future values). *Contrast* INTERPOLATION.

extraterrestrial shortwave radiation The *radiation from the Sun that reaches the top of the Earth's *atmosphere. *See also* SOLAR CONSTANT.

extratropical Occurring outside the *tropics.

extreme environment Any *environment that has extremes in growth conditions for

EXTINCTION

The permanent disappearance of a *species throughout its entire range, caused by the failure
to reproduce and the death of all remaining members. Extinction has occurred throughout
Earth history for entirely natural reasons, either because of major *catastrophes (such as
meteorite impacts) or because species were unable to adapt quickly enough to natural
*environmental change. Most recent extinctions are the result of *human impacts, amongst
the most important of which are *habitat alterations, hunting, and the introduction of alien
species. Extinction is final, because once a species has become extinct its genetic composition
is lost and cannot be replaced naturally, so it is lost to present and future generations. Since
1600 some 485 species of animals and 584 species of plants have become extinct, largely if not
entirely as a result of human activities. More than a tenth of the world's plant species are
heading towards extinction according to the first fully comprehensive study. The 1998 IUCN
*Red List of threatened plants includes 33 798 species, of which 380 are extinct in the wild, 371
may be extinct, 6522 are endangered, and the rest are vulnerable or rare. Around 90% of the
species listed are *endemic to just one country, and those growing on isolated islands are
especially vulnerable because they can be displaced by plants and animals introduced by
humans. Ecologists fear that human activities could trigger another of the *mass extinctions
that have occurred several times during the Earth's history. If this happened the
consequences could be catastrophic, because environmental change is too rapid and time too
short to allow natural rapid speciation. *Contrast* EVOLUTION; EXTIRPATION. *See also*
BACKGROUND EXTINCTION; MASS EXTINCTION.

plants, including *temperature, *salinity, *pH, and *water availability.

extremely exposed In terms of wave *exposure, an open coastline which faces into the prevailing wind, is directly affected by both wind-driven *waves and ocean *swell, and has deep water close to the shore.

extremely hazardous substance Any of more than 400 *chemicals that are classified as *toxic by the *Environmental Protection Agency and listed under *SARA.

extremely sheltered In terms of wave *exposure, a fully enclosed *coast with a *fetch of no more than about three km.

extremophile A *micro-organism (domain *Archaea) that thrives under conditions of extreme *acidity or alkalinity, *salinity, *temperature, or *pressure.

extrinsic External, coming from outside. *Contrast* INTRINSIC.

extrinsic resource A *natural resource that has been adapted or modified by people in order to provide additional values, particularly for *recreation. Examples include historic sites and archaeological sites.

extrinsic value Value in terms of what something means to people. *Contrast* INTRINSIC VALUE.

extrusive Applied to rock formed from lava that rose above the surface during a volcanic eruption. *Contrast* INTRUSIVE.

exurbia The region surrounding a *city and its *suburbs where wealthier families tend to live.

Exxon Valdez An *oil tanker that ran aground, spilling 300 000 barrels of oil in Prince William Sound in Alaska on 24 March 1989, creating an *oil slick that covered 12 400 km^2 and polluting at least 1100 km of coastline. Damage was extensive, partly because the area is ecologically sensitive and thus not able to withstand great stress. The problem was made worse by a lack of *disaster preparation and an inability to use containment methods, so large amounts of damaging *detergents were used to try to disperse the oil. The oil spill caused extensive damage to the ecology of the area.

eye The warm calm area at the centre of a *tropical cyclone, where the winds are light and skies are clear or partly cloudy.

eye wall The zone of powerful *updraft around the *eye of a *tropical cyclone, which has the heaviest *rain, strongest *winds, and worst *turbulence and causes a ring of heavy *thunderstorms.

eyrie The nest of a bird of prey, such as a hawk or eagle, which is usually built high in a tree.

F scale *See* FUJITA SCALE.

fabric The way in which particles and minerals are arranged in a rock, sediment, or soil. *See also* IMBRICATION.

facies The characteristics of a *sediment or *sedimentary rock unit, such as *mineralogy, colour, *texture, and *fossil content, which are indicative of the conditions when the rock formed.

facility A building or place that provides a particular service or is used for a particular activity.

factory farming Large-scale, industrialized *agriculture, especially with reference to live-stock farming.

factory ship A ship that is equipped to process large quantities of fish or whale products at sea.

facultative Having the ability to live under different conditions, either with or without a particular environmental factor such as *oxygen.

facultative aerobe An *aerobe that is capable of growing under either *aerobic or *anaerobic conditions.

facultative mutualist A beneficial *symbiont that associates with its *host but is also able to live apart from it. *Contrast* OBLIGATE MUTUALIST.

faecal Relating to *faeces.

faeces Solid unabsorbed residue (waste matter) that is passed out of the digestive tract of an animal, though its anus. *See also* COLIFORM BACTERIA.

Fahrenheit (°F) A *temperature scale in which the freezing point of water is 32°F and the boiling point is 212°F at sea level atmospheric pressure. 32°F is equal to 0° *Celsius, and $°C = (°F-32) \times 5/9$. This scale is widely used in the USA.

fair A *weather condition in which there is less than four-tenths opaque cloud cover, no *precipitation, and no extremes in *temperature, *visibility, or *wind.

fall 1. A *season between *summer and *winter, that is known as *autumn in most of the English-speaking world beyond North America. 2. A rapid process of *mass movement on a *hillslope. 3. Another name for *waterfall.

fall line The line of steepest descent on a slope.

fall wind *See* KATABATIC WIND.

falling tide *See* EBB TIDE.

fallout Solid material that falls to the ground from the sky, including *radioactive debris that falls after a nuclear explosion, and volcanic *ash that falls after a *volcanic eruption.

fallow The practice of leaving a patch of land idle and uncropped, either tilled or untilled, during much or all of a *growing season, in order to accumulate moisture, improve *soil structure, or restore nutrient content.

fallstreak *See* VIRGA.

family 1. A social unit, including parents and children, which lives together and may include relatives. 2. The fifth highest (of seven) category in the scientific system of classification for organisms (*taxonomy), below *order and above *genus. Each order comprises more than one family, and each family comprises more than one genus. 3. A category in the *Comprehensive Soil Classification System that is intermediate between *great soil group and *soil series.

family planning A system of limiting family size and the frequency of childbearing by the appropriate use of *birth control.

famine An acute shortage of food that leads to malnutrition and starvation.

fan A wedge-shaped body of sediment (usually sand and gravel), such as an *alluvial fan.

fanning The pattern made by a chimney *plume when the gases and particles travel downwind smoothly and horizontally, without dispersing.

FAO *See* UNITED NATIONS FOOD AND AGRICULTURE ORGANIZATION.

FAO–UNESCO Classification *See* WORLD SOIL CLASSIFICATION.

farinose Floury or powdery in appearance or texture.

farm Buildings and associated land that are used for *agriculture.

farm forestry *See* TREE FARMING.

farming *See* AGRICULTURE.

farmland *Arable land that is worked for *farming by ploughing, sowing, and raising crops.

farmstead Land that is occupied by the dwellings, barns, pens, corrals, gardens, and similar associated with an operating *farm.

farmyard manure The partly decomposed excreta of domestic animals mixed with straw or other litter. *See also* DUNG; SLURRY.

fast breeder *See* BREEDER REACTOR.

fast ice Ice in a lake, river, or the sea that is permanently attached to a *glacier or to the shore, the bottom, or in shallow water.

fatal accident An *accident that causes death.

fatality A death that is caused by an *accident or a *disaster.

fatality rate *See* DEATH RATE.

fathom A unit of water-depth measurement, originally 6 feet, equal to 1.83 m.

fault A large-scale linear fracture at the Earth's *crust, along which the rocks on either side have been displaced as a result of pressure in the adjacent bodies of rock. The displacement can be vertical, horizontal, or both at the same time. There are four common types of faults (*normal fault, *reverse fault, *strike-slip fault, and *thrust fault), which are produced in different ways and produce different landscapes. Distinctive large-scale *landforms (*graben and *horst) are created when two or more fault systems intersect one another. *See also* EARTHQUAKE.

fault line The contact zone between two sides of a *fault, along which the rocks on either side move.

fault plane/zone The part of the Earth's crust that is affected by *faulting. *Faults occur where such a zone intersects the ground surface.

fault-block mountain *See* HORST.

faulting A fracturing of the rocks on the Earth's *crust that produces a line (*fault line) along which significant movement takes place, which causes rocks on either side to be displaced vertically or horizontally relative to each other.

fauna **1.** All forms of animal life that live in a region, period, or special environment. **2.** A record or book of animals.

Fauna and Flora International The world's longest-established international conservation body, founded in 1903, and one of only a few whose mission is to protect the entire spectrum of *endangered species of animals and plants world-wide. In 2012 it had more than 100 projects in nearly 40 countries.

(((●))) **SEE WEB LINKS**

• Fauna and Flora International home page.

faunal province *See* FAUNAL REGION.

faunal realm *See* FAUNAL REGION.

faunal region (**faunal province, faunal realm, faunal zoogeographic kingdom**) A biological division of the Earth's surface (i.e. a large geographical area) that contains a fauna more or less peculiar to it. The degree of distinctiveness varies with the region concerned and reflects partly climate and partly the existence of barriers to migration. The number of regions recognized varies from one authority to another, but a minimum of six are recognized: *Australian, *Ethiopian, *Nearctic, *Neotropical, *Oriental, and *Palaearctic. In defining a region, greatest emphasis is given to mammals.

faunal zoographical kingdom *See* FAUNAL REGION.

favourable condition The desirable state for a site to be in for *conservation purposes.

favourable status The desirable status of a *population for *conservation purposes.

FC *See* FLUOROCARBON.

feasibility study 1. An investigation to establish whether a project will work and achieve the desired results. **2.** A study to evaluate alternative *remedial actions from a technical, environmental, and cost perspective, which normally recommends selection of a cost-effective alternative.

fecundity The state of being fertile; capable of producing offspring. *See also* FERTILITY.

Federal Emergency Management Agency (FEMA) The leading federal emergency planning agency in the USA that seeks to reduce the loss of life and protect property against all types of *hazards (including *disasters and urban riots) through a comprehensive, risk-based *emergency management programme.

federal land Land that is owned and managed by the US government, including *National Parks and *National Forests.

Federal Land Policy Management Act (FLPMA) (1976) US legislation that governs how the *US Bureau of Land Management manages, protects, develops, and enhances public lands. It specifically requires the Bureau to manage public lands for multiple use and sustained yield, for the benefit of both present and future generations. This act triggered the *Sagebrush Rebellion. It was partly replaced by the *Public Rangelands Improvement Act (1978).

Federal Water Pollution Control Act Amendments (1972) US legislation that established as a national objective the restoration and maintenance of the chemical, physical, and biological integrity of the nation's water, and required area-wide planning to prevent future *water pollution that could be associated with growth, development, and land use, including timber management.

feed Ground or processed grains that are fed to animals, including hay such as *alfalfa or *silage.

feedback An internal adjustment within a *system, where once a component reaches a certain level it inhibits (*negative feedback) or promotes (*positive feedback) further action. For example, a thermostat signals a boiler to turn on or off according to room temperature. *See also* HOMEOSTASIS.

feeding ground A place where animals feed naturally.

feedlot A confined area for the controlled feeding of large numbers of animals, which produces large amounts of animal waste that can flow into and pollute nearby *waterbodies.

feldspar A group of common *aluminium silicate minerals (the most common minerals in the world) that contain *potassium, *sodium, or *calcium, and that form rocks.

fell 1. To cut down standing vegetation, such as a tree. **2.** Traditional British name for open *moorland.

felling Cutting down trees. *See also* CLEARING.

felsic Applied to light-coloured *igneous minerals (such as *quartz and *feldspars), and rocks rich in those minerals. Felsic rocks are a major component of the Earth's *continental crust. *Contrast* MAFIC.

FEMA *See* FEDERAL EMERGENCY MANAGEMENT AGENCY.

female In organisms with separate sexes, the one which is capable of giving birth or laying eggs. *Contrast* MALE.

feminism *See* ECOFEMINSM.

fen A type of *wetland dominated by *marshlike vegetation, which receives water both from rainfall and from *groundwater, and in which in summer the *water table is at or below the surface of the upper layer of sediment. It is a *peat-forming environment. *Bogs have similar types of vegetation but are fed only by rainwater.

fen peat *Peat that is *alkaline or non-acidic because of the presence of *calcium carbonate.

fencerow A row of *trees, *conifer, *shrubs, or groundcover plants that provides food and cover for *wildlife.

fenitrothion An *organophosphorus *insecticide and *acaricide that is used to control aphids and caterpillars in fruit crops, moths and weevils in peas, leatherjackets in cereals, and beetles in grain stores. It is of low toxicity.

fentins A group of three moderately toxic compounds containing tin that are used as *fungicides and *molluscicides.

feral Describes a *domesticated *animal that has adapted to living in the *wild.

fermentation A type of *anaerobic respiration by a living agent (such as yeast, *bacteria, or *mould), which breaks down complex *organic compounds into simple ones. For example, yeast converts sugar into alcohol and carbon dioxide. In *biotechnology, fermentation is the process of growing *microbes to produce chemical or pharmaceutical compounds.

ferrallization Part of the *leaching process found in tropical soils, by which large amounts of iron and aluminium oxides accumulate in the B *soil horizon.

ferralsols Soils that have an iron-rich B *soil horizon with distinctive red mottling that is more than 15 cm deep. This horizon is highly weathered (*see* WEATHERING) and contains high concentrations of iron and aluminium. Ferralsols are a reference soil group in the *World Soil Classification.

Ferrel cell In the *three-cell model of atmospheric circulation, the cell that lies between the *Hadley and *polar cells and is driven by them. Air rises at the polar front, moves towards the equator at high altitude, subsides in the subtropics, and moves away from the equator at low level. The cell was discovered by the American climatologist William Ferrel (1817–91).

ferric/ferrous Composed of and/or containing *iron.

fertility rate The number of live births per female within a population during her reproductive life, which is always lower than *fecundity. In the first decade of the 21st century, based on United Nations figures, the global average fertility rate was about 2.55 children per woman; the average in the USA was 2.05, the average in Italy was 1.38, in Spain 1.41, in the United Kingdom 1.82, and in the West African state of Niger (the world's highest) it was 7.19. A population stops growing when it reaches the *replacement-level fertility, but this requires a *total fertility rate (TFR) higher than 2 mainly because some children die before they grow up to have their own children. The critical TFR is around 2.1 in a country with low mortality (such as the USA), but it can be higher than 3 in a country with high mortality (such as Sierra Leone).

fertilization 1. The union of male and female cells (sperm and egg; *gametes) to form a new individual. 2. Adding *nutrients to soil or plants to stimulate growth.

fertilizer A substance (such as animal *manure or an artificial chemical, particularly one that contains *nitrogen, *phosphorus, and *potassium) that is added to *soil in order to increase its productivity for crops.

fetch The distance of open sea over which the *wind may blow to generate *waves until it meets a coastline.

fetus *See* FOETUS.

field A cultivated area of land that is usually enclosed by a *hedge, wall, or fence, and is used for a particular crop or cropping sequence.

field capacity (field moisture capacity) The amount of water that a particular *soil retains after excess water has drained away. This is mostly *capillary water, measured as a percentage of the weight or volume of oven-dried soil.

field layer The vegetation at ground level in a *forest or *woodland.

field moisture capacity *See* FIELD CAPACITY.

field sport (country sports, game sport) The pursuit, capture, and killing of *wildlife for entertainment. *See also* BIG GAME; FISHING; GAME; HUNTING; SHOOTING.

field tile (drainage tile) A perforated pipe, usually made from plastic or clay, that is buried under the surface of the ground to improve soil *drainage.

fill Soil or sediment that is added to change the height of the land, for example to fill in a hole or to build an embankment.

filter A porous mesh that allows air or liquid to pass through but holds back solid particles.

filter feeder (suspension feeder) An *organism that filters out food particles (such as *plankton, *bacteria, or *detritus) from *freshwater or *seawater.

filter strip *See* BUFFER STRIP.

filtration The process of removing *particulate matter from water by passing it through a porous medium such as sand or a *filter. Filtration does not remove *dissolved salts or *organic contaminants. *See also* DIRECT FILTRATION; FLOCCULENT.

final cut Cutting of the few original trees that remain in a *shelterwood cut, once new trees have been established.

final deal In *greenhouse gas *emissions trading, the fully matched and negotiated bids/offers that are under contract for delivery.

Finding of No Significant Impact (FNSI) A document prepared by a federal agency in the USA, based on the results of an *environmental assessment, that shows why a proposed action would not have a significant impact on the environment and would thus not require preparation of an *environmental impact statement.

fine filter approach An approach to the *conservation of *biodiversity that is directed toward particular habitats or species that may be *threatened or *endangered and might fall through the *coarse filter.

fine textured Having a smooth, *fine-grained structure.

fine-grained A *soil, *sediment, or *rock in which the grains or crystals are too small to be seen with the naked eye.

finished water (product water) *Water that has passed through all the processes in a *water treatment plant and is ready to be delivered to consumers.

fipronil A type of *insecticide that works by disrupting normal nerve functions in the insect.

fire The rapid oxidation of a *fuel that results in the release of heat, light, and other *byproducts.

fire line *See* FIREBREAK.

fire management All activities that are associated with the management of fire-prone land, including the use of *fire to meet land management goals and objectives. *See also* FUEL BREAK; PRESCRIBED FIRE.

fire regime The role that *fire plays in an *ecosystem, which depends on the frequency and scale of fires, and may include proposals for the controlled use of fire in a given area. *See also* PRESCRIBED FIRE.

fire season The period(s) of the year during which fires are likely to occur, spread, and cause enough damage to require organized fire control.

firebreak (fire line) A barrier, usually either a natural *clearing or one created by removing vegetation (*fuel break), that is designed to prevent or slow the spread of *fire.

fire-climax community A *climax community of vegetation that is maintained by periodic *fires. Examples include *grasslands, *chaparral shrubland, and some pine forests.

firestorm A raging *fire of great intensity that spreads rapidly.

firn (granular snow, névé) *Snow on the surface of a *glacier that has remained from the previous year, which may be compact but not yet turned into ice. A transitional stage between snow and ice.

firn limit The dividing line between old ice and new snow on a *glacier, at the end of the melting season.

firn line The zone on a *glacier that separates the (upper) *accumulation area from the (lower) *ablation area.

first draw The *water that comes out when a tap is first opened, which is likely to contain the highest level of *lead contamination from plumbing materials.

First Nation *See* NATIVE AMERICAN.

First World A term introduced in the 1940s to describe the *capitalist or *market economy countries of Western Europe, North America, Japan, Australia, and New Zealand that were the first to industrialize. The term is no longer used. *See also* SECOND WORLD; THIRD WORLD.

fish A *poikilothermic, legless, *vertebrate animal that lives in water and breathes through gills, has a two-chambered heart, no internal nostrils, and at least one fin in addition to the tail fin. *See also* GAME FISH; ROUGH FISH.

Fish and Wildlife Service *See* US FISH AND WILDLIFE SERVICE.

fish farm A place where aquatic plants or animals are grown commercially, in ponds, pens, tanks, or other containers. *See also* AQUACULTURE.

fish farming *See* AQUACULTURE.

fish kill The sudden death of most if not all of the *fish in a waterbody, caused by the introduction of *pollutants or a reduction in *dissolved oxygen concentration.

fish ranching A form of *aquaculture in which a *population of a *fish species (such as salmon) is held in captivity for the first stage of their lives, then released, and later harvested as adults when they return from the sea to their freshwater birthplace to *spawn.

fish trapping 1. A method of small-scale *fishing in which a trap inserted into flowing water is used to catch fish. 2. **(beach seining)** A method of small-scale *fishing in which a *seine net is operated from the shore.

fisheries habitat Any stream, lake, or reservoir that supports *fish, or has the potential to support fish.

fishery A place where *fish are caught and processed and sold.

Fishery Conservation and Management Act (1976) (Magnuson Fishery Conservation and Management Act) US legislation that provided for the conservation and management of fisheries, which established a 200 mile fishery conservation zone and Regional Fishery Management Councils comprising federal and state officials, including the *US Fish and Wildlife Service.

fishing Catching fish, for food or as a *field sport, in freshwater or at sea.

fissile 1. The ability of certain rocks to be split along *bedding planes. 2. *See* FISSIONABLE.

fission 1. The nuclear process in which the *nucleus of a particular *isotope splits into (usually) two nuclei of lighter elements, releasing great amounts of energy at the same time. This process is exploited in the *thermal reactor. *Contrast* FUSION. 2. Division of a cell into two cells by splitting.

fissionable (fissile) The property of the nucleus of some atoms that allows them to split into smaller particles, and so be capable of sustaining a chain reaction of nuclear *fission.

fissionable isotope An *isotope that can undergo nuclear *fission when it is hit by a *neutron at the right speed. Examples include uranium-235 and plutonium-239.

fissure A long, deep, narrow opening in a *rock or *glacier (*crevasse), or an opening in a *volcano through which volcanic products can erupt.

fitness Adaptedness, or the ability of an *organism to survive and flourish in its current *environment, relative to the other organisms that are also there, which is measured ultimately by reproductive success.

fix To convert *carbon dioxide to carbohydrate (*carbon fixation), or *nitrogen dioxide to *ammonia (*nitrogen fixation).

fixed dune A sand *dune that has become stabilized by vegetation and is therefore largely protected from further *erosion and movement by the wind.

fjord A long, deep, steep-sided valley with a *U-shaped profile, that was formed by *glacial erosion and is now flooded by the sea.

flagellate Applied to a *micro-organism that has one or more hair-like projections (*see* FLAGELLUM) on the cell surface, which it uses for locomotion or food gathering.

flagellate protozoa *Protozoa that have *flagella.

flagellum (*pl.* **flagella**) A thin, whip-like appendage on a *motile cell, which is used for locomotion or food gathering.

flagship species A small number of globally important *endangered species (including the giant panda, tiger, marine turtles, great apes, whales, elephants, and rhinos) which are well known and attract public interest in *conservation efforts both for themselves and other *species at risk.

flammable Capable of igniting easily and burning rapidly.

Flandrian *See* HOLOCENE.

flare 1. A sudden burst of flame. 2. A device that burns gases (such as *methane gas in a *landfill) to prevent them from being released into the *environment.

flaring The controlled burning of waste gases (for example, through a *chimney) before releasing them to the air.

flash flood A localized *flood that rises and falls quite rapidly with little or no advance warning, usually as the result of heavy rainfall on to saturated ground over a relatively small area.

flatworms A phylum (Platyhelminthes) of unsegmented worms that are bilaterally symmetrical and lack a coelom (internal, fluid-filled cavity). Many are *parasites.

fledgling A young bird that has grown feathers.

flexibility mechanism (Kyoto mechanism) The three cooperative mechanisms for reducing *greenhouse gas emissions that were agreed under the *Kyoto Protocol, namely *Joint Implementation, *emissions trading, and the *Clean Development Mechanism. *See also* FUNGIBILITY.

flint A type of *chert that is found as *nodules or bands in *chalk and *limestone.

floc A collection of smaller particles that have come together into larger particles, such as the solids that are formed in *sewage as a result of biological or chemical action.

flocculation Chemical processes in which salts (*flocculent) are added to water to make *colloids aggregate into larger masses that are too heavy to remain suspended.

flocculent 1. A substance that is added to water to make particles clump together, in order to produce more effective *filtration. **2.** The particles that clump together in this way.

flock (*noun*) A group of *birds, sheep, or goats with a social organization. (*verb*) To form a flock.

flood To fill to beyond capacity, so that the fluid spills out. In a *river, it means a high flow that overflows from the *channel and inundates the *floodplain, which is normally dry. On a coast, it means seawater flowing over low-lying land that is normally dry. *See also* FLASH FLOOD; INUNDATION.

flood basin *See* FLOODPLAIN.

flood control An engineering scheme that is designed to protect areas of land from being flooded. Options include the construction of embankments (*levees and *dykes) and walls, *channel improvement, detaining part of the flood flow in a reservoir, and diverting some of the water into a bypass or *floodway.

flood conveyance The transport of floodwaters downstream, with little if any damage.

flood current The onshore movement of a *tidal stream, toward the *shore or up a *tidal river or *estuary.

flood damage The economic loss that is caused by a *flood, which includes direct damage due to *inundation, *erosion, and *sediment deposition, as well as emergency costs and business or financial losses.

flood forecast (flood prediction) A prediction of the likely height, timing, and duration of a *flood, particularly the peak *discharge at a specified point on a stream, based on

information about precipitation and/or snowmelt and the form of the drainage area. *See also* FORECAST.

flood frequency The probability (likelihood) that a *flood of a certain size will occur in a given year in a particular river or part of a river. *See also* RECURRENCE INTERVAL.

flood frequency analysis Analysis of *hydrograph records of *river flow to determine the *flood frequency at a particular location within a river system, based on either the *annual maximum series or the *partial duration series.

flood irrigation A method of *irrigation in which entire *fields are occasionally deliberately flooded.

flood peak (peak discharge) The highest *stage (largest *discharge) reached during a particular *flood at a given point on a river.

flood prediction *See* FLOOD FORECAST.

flood protection *See* FLOOD CONTROL.

flood stage The water level (*stage) in a river or stream beyond which the flow starts to *flood adjacent land. *See also* BANKFULL.

flood tide (rising tide) The portion of the *tide cycle between low water and the following high water, during which the water is rising or levelling off.

floodplain (alluvial plain, flood basin) An area of flat, low-lying land adjacent to a *river, that is composed of *alluvium. It is normally dry but is covered by water during a *flood. It is formed from relatively coarse material deposited as *meanders migrate across it and finer material deposited during occasional floods.

floodplain management A coordinated approach to the reduction of flood damage that usually includes emergency and contingency plans, *flood control works, and regulations to control current and future development in the flood plain.

floodplain zoning A type of *natural resource zoning that prohibits and restricts development within *floodplains, in order to prevent damage to property and risks to people. *See also* PROHIBITION ZONING.

floodproofing The process of protecting a building from *flood damage, for example by raising it above the ground, building a wall round it to keep out flood water, or using lower floors for activities that can tolerate *inundation.

floodway The *river channel and parts of the adjacent *floodplain that are required to carry flood water and must therefore not be built on or restricted.

flora 1. All forms of plant life that live in a region, period, or special environment. **2.** A record or book of plants.

floral region A large area that has a distinctive *vegetation.

floristic Referring to plants.

flow 1. The movement of a liquid or a gas. *See also* FLOW RATE. **2.** Rapid *mass movement of any *unconsolidated material. *See also* DEBRIS FLOW.

flow augmentation The addition of water to a stream from a storage reservoir in order to enhance flow, particularly to help fish migration.

flow duration The percentage of time that *discharge in a river exceeds a particular level, averaged over a number of years.

flow hydrograph *See* HYDROGRAPH.

flow meter A device that is used for measuring the flow or quantity of a moving fluid.

flow rate *See* VELOCITY.

flow regime The annual pattern of variations in *discharge in a river.

flow resource A *natural resource that is simultaneously used and replaced, which includes all *perpetual resources and *renewable resources.

flow velocity *See* VELOCITY.

flower 1. A *plant that is cultivated for its blooms or blossoms, its colours, and/or its scent. **2.** The reproductive part of a plant.

flowing well An *artesian well in which the pressure is large enough to make water flow out onto the land surface.

FLPMA *See* FEDERAL LAND POLICY MANAGEMENT ACT.

flue A vent or *chimney for a combustion device, through which smoke, gas, and fumes rise.

flue gas The air that is released by a *flue or *stack after combustion in the burner it is venting, which can contain *nitrogen oxides, *carbon oxides, *water vapour, *sulphur oxides, *particles, and many chemical *pollutants.

flue gas desulphurization (flue gas scrubbing) A method of reducing the *sulphur content of *fossil fuels at combustion, in order to reduce *air pollution, which involves passing the *flue gas through a mixture of crushed *limestone and water. *See also* SCRUBBING.

flue gas scrubbing *See* FLUE GAS DESULPHURIZATION.

fluid Any gas or liquid that can flow freely.

fluidization Making particles float in a gas or fluid that is blowing upwards.

fluidized bed combustion (fluidized bed technology) A method of reducing the *sulphur content of *fossil fuels at combustion, in order to reduce *air pollution, which involves burning the fuel in a special furnace that lifts it in a stream of air and passes air through it while it burns.

fluidized bed technology *See* FLUIDIZED BED COMBUSTION.

flume A natural or man-made structure that conveys *water.

fluorescence The property of absorbing light of a particular *wavelength and then emitting light of a different colour and wavelength.

fluoridation The addition of a *fluoride to the water supply, usually in order to prevent dental decay.

fluoride A compound that contains *fluorine.

fluorine (F) A non-metallic element, the lightest of the *halogens, usually in the form of a yellow, irritating, flammable gas which is one of the 100 most toxic substances known, and is persistent in the environment. Used commercially in the form of sodium fluoride.

fluorine insecticide Sulfuryl fluoride (SO_2F_2), a gas used as an insecticide and rodenticide to fumigate closed structures and their contents to kill termites, beetles, clothes moths, bedbugs, cockroaches, rodents, etc. Although it is only mildly toxic if inhaled, it is classed as hazardous because it is colourless and odourless.

fluorocarbon (FC) A compound that contains *fluorine and *carbon, including those which are chlorinated (*CFCs) and those which are brominated (*halons). They are inert and highly stable, and are used in refrigerators and aerosols.

fluorosis A disease caused by the over-consumption of *fluoride that produces spots of brown, yellow, or white discolouration on the teeth and, in more severe cases, deformations in tooth enamel. Fluorides entering the air as an industrial pollutant may be deposited on vegetation that is then grazed by ruminant animals, in which the consumption of high levels of fluoride may cause thickening of the bones as well as mottling and weakening of the teeth.

flurry A sudden, brief, light *snowfall or gust of *wind.

flush 1. A sudden, rapid flow of water. **2.** A type of *fen that is irrigated by a *spring or soakway.

flushing rate *See* RETENTION TIME.

fluvent A *floodplain *soil, that usually has buried *horizons and amounts of *organic matter that decrease irregularly with depth.

fluvial Of or relating to *rivers.

fluvial process Geological work (*erosion, *transport, and *deposition of sediment) that is done by a *river.

fluvioglacial *See* GLACIOFLUVIAL.

fluvisols Soils that have formed on recent *alluvial deposits and have a *soil horizon that is dark in colour and usually rich in pyroclastic material (*see* PYROCLAST) extending from 25 cm below the surface to a depth exceeding 50 cm. Fluvisols are a reference soil group in the *World Soil Classification.

flux Flow of energy, fluid, or particles per unit of area per unit of time.

fly ash Fine particles of *ash that are made from the burning of *coal or other material, released in *flue gas, and carried in suspension in the air. Fly ash may be mixed with incompletely burned fuel and other pollutants.

flyway A seasonal *migration route along which waterfowl travel between wintering grounds and nesting/breeding grounds.

FMD *See* FOOT AND MOUTH DISEASE.

FNSI *See* FINDING OF NO SIGNIFICANT IMPACT.

focal species A *species that is the focus of a *conservation effort.

focus (hypocentre) The point within the Earth's *crust at which an *earthquake originates, which is located directly below the *epicentre.

fodder Coarse food that is composed of entire *plants or the leaves and stalks of a *cereal crop, and is fed to cattle and horses.

FOE *See* FRIENDS OF THE EARTH.

foehn (föhn) A warm, dry *adiabatic *wind which blows downslope on the *lee side of mountains. The term was originally applied only in the European Alps, but it is now used for all similar winds. *See also* CHINOOK; SANTA ANA.

foetus The *embryo of a mammal (including humans) when the main adult features have developed.

fog A *cloud of tiny water droplets that is suspended in the lower atmosphere, produced by the cooling of moist air near the ground, which condenses to create a *visibility of 1 km or less.

fog bank A dense mass of *fog surrounded by clearer air, often as viewed from a distance at *sea.

fogging A method of applying a *pesticide by rapidly heating the liquid chemical so that it forms very fine droplets like *smoke or *fog and is used to destroy mosquitoes, black flies, and similar pests.

fold A curve or bend in *stratified rocks that is usually caused by *compression pressure. The line along which a bed of rock folds is called its axis, and the *limbs of the fold are the tilted beds that extend outwards from the axis. The fold can be upwards (*anticline) or downwards (*syncline).

fold mountain A *mountain or *mountain range (such as the Alps and the Himalayas) that is formed as a result of intense *folding of material within the Earth's *crust.

folding The process by which layered *sedimentary rocks in the Earth's *crust bend and buckle in response to *compressional forces, often caused by the convergence of two adjacent *tectonic plates.

foliage The leaves that are growing on a *tree or *plant.

foliation The banding or *lamination seen in *metamorphic rocks, which is caused by the arrangement of *minerals in parallel, sheet-like layers as a result of *compression.

foliose Bearing leaves or resembling a leaf, particularly leaves or plants that are thin, flattened, and lobe-like.

Food and Agriculture Organization *See* UNITED NATIONS FOOD AND AGRICULTURE ORGANIZATION.

food chain The transfer of food energy from plants through *herbivores to *carnivores. *Primary producers capture energy from the environment through *photosynthesis or *chemosynthesis, and they form the base of the food chain. Energy is then passed to *primary consumers (herbivores) and on to *secondary consumers (carnivores) and *tertiary consumers (top carnivores). For example, in a marine food chain *phytoplankton (primary producers) are eaten by *zooplankton (primary consumers), which are eaten by herring (secondary consumers), which are eaten by killer whales (tertiary consumers). Once they die, all of these organisms are in turn consumed and their energy transferred to *detrivores and *decomposers. *Compare* FOOD WEB.

Food Quality Protection Act (1996) US legislation that governs how the *Environmental Protection Agency regulates *pesticides, including a requirement that a safety standard (reasonable certainty of no harm) must be applied to all pesticides used on foods.

food waste Food that is discarded from kitchens, including restaurants, grocery stores, and homes.

food web A group of interconnecting *food chains within an ecosystem, which often has numerous organisms at each level (see Fig. 7).

food-chain efficiency The ratio between the energy value (the nutritional value, discounting indigestible parts such as hair or feathers) of prey consumed by a *predator and the energy value of the food eaten by that prey. Maximum food-chain efficiency (gross ecological efficiency) occurs when the yield of prey to the predator is such that the surviving prey just consume all the available food: this implies that the food of the prey is being exploited to the best advantage by the predator.

foot and mouth disease (FMD) A severe disease that affects *ungulate *ruminant animals, particularly cattle, and is spread by a virus. Symptoms include fever, blisters, and damage to the animal's mouth and hooves, and it causes serious loss of production of meat and milk.

footprint *See* ECOLOGICAL FOOTPRINT; CARBON FOOTPRINT.

forage 1. Grasses, herbs, and small shrubs that can be used as feed for livestock or wildlife. 2. The act of searching for food and provisions. *See also* FORAGING.

forage crop A crop of *cultivated plants that is grown to be grazed or harvested for use as *feed for livestock.

forage production *See* FORAGE YIELD.

forage yield (forage production) The weight of *forage that is produced within a particular area, per year.

foraging Searching or hunting for food, rather than growing food.

foraminifera (forams) An order or subclass (depending on the classification) of marine amoeba-like *protozoa in which the single cell

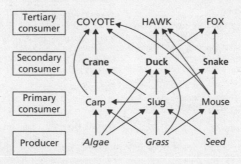

Fig 7. Food web

is enclosed in a test (shell) comprising one to many chambers. The composition and structure of the test is important in classifying foraminifera. Tests may consist of a wall of a substance resembling *chitin (which may form the inner layer in other types of test); or may be made from sedimentary particles cemented together; or the test may be fully mineralized and made from *calcareous or *siliceous material. Aragonite and *calcite (both made from calcium carbonate) tests are the most common, and form an important ingredient of *chalk.

foraminiferal ooze A *calcareous sediment composed of the shells of dead *foraminifera. See also PELAGIC SEDIMENT.

forams See FORAMINIFERA.

forb A *broadleaved *plant (such as a *wildflower) that has a soft rather than a woody stem, and is not a *grass or grass-like plant. See also HERB.

Forbes band See OGIVE.

forcing See RADIATIVE FORCING.

forecast To predict or estimate a future event or trend. See also FLOOD FORECAST; WEATHER FORECAST.

foreground The part of a scene or *landscape that is closest to the viewer. See also BACKGROUND; MIDDLEGROUND.

foreshore The lower zone of a *beach, that lies between *low water *spring tide level and *high water spring tide level.

forest An *ecosystem that is dominated by *trees, the crowns of which touch to form a continuous canopy, or the trees that comprise such an ecosystem. See also CONIFEROUS FOREST; DECIDUOUS FOREST; THORN FOREST; TROPICAL RAINFOREST.

Forest and Rangeland Renewable Resources Planning Act (1974) US legislation that provided for continuing assessment and long-range planning of the nation's *forest and *rangeland *renewable resources, under the jurisdiction of the Secretary of Agriculture.

Forest and Rangeland Renewable Resources Research Act (1978) US legislation that authorized more research on *renewable resources in *forest and *rangeland.

Forest and Rangeland Resources Extension Act (1978) US legislation that built upon the *McSweeny-McNary Act (1928) and

authorized expanding the portion of the extension education programme that is dedicated to *renewable resources in *forest and *rangeland.

forest certification A process of labelling wood that has been harvested from a *forest that is responsibly managed.

forest clearance See DEFORESTATION.

forest conservation The deliberate *management of forests in order to conserve the *habitat and *natural resources. Strategies listed in *Agenda 21 include: planting new forests; increasing practical knowledge on the state of forests; increasing research into *forest products such as wood, fruits, nuts, *dyes, medicines, gums, etc.; replanting damaged areas of woodland; breeding trees that are more resistant to environmental pressures; encouraging local business people to set up small forest enterprises; limiting and aiming to stop *slash and burn farming methods (the basis of *subsistence-level *shifting cultivation); keeping wood waste to a minimum; finding ways of using trees that have been burnt or thrown out; and increasing tree planting in urban areas.

forest cover A *forest stand that consists of a *plant community made up of trees and other woody vegetation which are growing together.

forest death See TREE DIEBACK.

forest ecology The relationships between *forest *organisms and their *environment.

forest fire An unplanned and uncontrolled *fire in an area of *forest.

forest floor The ground surface and *ground layer beneath a *forest *canopy, which often contains layers of fresh leaf and needle *litter, moderately decomposed organic matter, and well-decomposed organic residue (*humus).

forest fragmentation Isolated patches of forest *habitat that survive when the intervening forest has been removed, either naturally (for example through *forest fires) or by clearance (*felling). See also FRAGMENTATION; HABITAT CONNECTIVITY.

forest grazing The combined use of a *forest or wood for both wood production and animal production by grazing of *forage shrubs.

forest health A measure of the resilience of a *forest to damage, reflected, for example, through its *biodiversity, its sustained provision of *natural resources for people to use, and its natural flows of *water and *nutrients.

forest litter The freshly fallen or only slightly decomposed plant material on the floor of a *forest, which includes foliage, bark fragments, twigs, flowers, and fruit. *See also* LITTER.

forest management The *management of *forest resources for specified purposes, which might include *nature conservation, *timber yield, or scenic variety.

Forest Pest Control Act (1947) US legislation that established a programme to protect forestlands under all ownerships from destructive forest insect and disease pests. This Act was repealed and replaced by provisions of the *Co-operative Forestry Assistance Act (1978).

forest plan A long-range plan for the management of particular *forestlands. *See also* NATIONAL FOREST LAND AND RESOURCE MANAGEMENT PLAN.

forest product All usable raw materials that a *forest makes available, including major products (such as *poles and *roundwood) and minor products (such as medicinals, gums, resins, oils, fungi, honey).

forest range (grazable woodland) *Forestland that has a *herbaceous or *shrubby *understorey that provides *forage for grazing or browsing animals.

forest resource The *natural resources and values associated with forestland, which includes *forest products and associated water, fish, game, scenic, historical, recreational, and geological resources.

forest sequestration The growth and use of *forests to remove *greenhouse gases from the atmosphere. *See also* SEQUESTRATION.

Forest Service *See* US FOREST SERVICE.

forest stand An area of forest.

Forest Stewardship Council (FSC) An independent, non-profit, *non-governmental organization, with international members from all areas of *forest management, whose aim is to ensure the sustainable management of global forestry reserves.

(⊕) SEE WEB LINKS

• Forest Stewardship Council home page.

forest type A way of categorizing *forest that is usually defined by its *vegetation, particularly the *dominant tree *species, e.g. oak–beech forest, pine–birch forest, etc.

forest use zoning A type of *natural resource zoning that restricts land uses to *forestry and related uses, such as timber production, *watershed protection, and *recreation.

forestation *See* AFFORESTATION.

forested wetland An area of tall woody vegetation in which the soil is at least periodically covered by water.

forestland A *land use category in the USA that includes *grassland, *shrubland, treeland, *wetland, and/or *barren land.

forestry The management of trees, forests, and associated resources, on a *sustainable basis, for particular purposes such as commercial timber production. *See also* SILVICULTURE.

formaldehyde (CH_2O) A colourless, strong smelling gas that is used in solution as a *disinfectant and *preservative.

formamidine A type of *insecticide which works by causing tremors, convulsions, and loss of appetite, suppressing reproduction, and disturbing insect flight.

formation 1. The basic unit for the naming of rocks in *stratigraphy, based on *lithology. **2. (plant formation)** A unit of classification that describes a group of *communities of plants that have a similar form and structure, but may differ in the species they contain. *See also* BIOME.

forward contract (forward settlement, spot forward) In *greenhouse gas *emissions trading, under the *Kyoto Protocol, an agreement to buy or sell an *emissions allowance at a certain time in the future for a certain price.

forward settlement *See* FORWARD CONTRACT.

fossil The remains or traces of an organism that lived long ago; no age is specified provided the material is ancient. Most fossils are hardened (*lithified) and found embedded in rock, but insect and plant fragments encased in *amber and the bodies of woolly mammoths buried in *permafrost are also fossils.

fossil air A sample of *air (e.g. in the bubbles trapped in an *ice core) that preserves the composition of the atmosphere at the time it was deposited.

fossil fuel A naturally occurring *hydrocarbon *fuel (such as *coal, *oil, and *natural gas) in the form of an *organic sedimentary deposit or produced by the *decomposition of fossilized remains of plants and animals, which can be burned to supply heat or power. Fossil fuels emit *carbon dioxide into the air when they are burned, which contributes to the *greenhouse effect and *global warming. They are *non-renewable resources, because we use them much faster than they form naturally. Substitutes and alternative forms of energy are being actively sought and developed as a matter of urgency, before fossil fuel supplies run out completely or before they become so scarce that price rises make them non-viable as a major energy source. Recent assessments of shale oil, *shale gas, coal-seam gas, and methane hydrates indicate, however, that fossil fuel reserves may be sufficient to last more than a century. *Contrast* ALTERNATIVE ENERGY.

fossil fuel reserve The quantity of a particular *fossil fuel that is known to exist (based on geological and engineering evidence) and that can be recovered under current economic conditions and with available technology.

fossorial Adapted for burrowing or digging.

fouling community *Benthic organisms that are attached to submerged objects which have some economic importance, such as pilings or boats.

founder effect The development of a new population derived from a single individual or limited number of immigrants, e.g. to an island. The founder(s) represent only a small sample of the *gene pool to which they belonged and the operation of *natural selection on this restricted genetic variety yields gene combinations that are markedly different from those found in the ancestral population. *See also* GENETIC DRIFT.

(((●))) SEE WEB LINKS

• Small population size effects.

Fourth World Very poor nations that have neither market economies nor central planning, and are developing very slowly if at all. The term is no longer used. *See* FIRST WORLD; SECOND WORLD; THIRD WORLD.

fowl A *domesticated bird (such as a chicken) that is kept for its eggs or meat.

fracking *See* HYDRAULIC FRACTURING.

fractional cloud cover The relative amount of *cloud cover at site, usually expressed in amounts from 0 to 1 in increments of 0.1. *See* OKTA.

fracture Any break in a rock including cracks, *joints, and *faults.

Fragile or Historic Lands Areas where uncontrolled or incompatible development could result in irreversible damage to important historic, cultural, scientific, or aesthetic values or natural systems which are of more than local significance. An *area of critical environmental concern in the USA.

fragility *See* VULNERABILITY.

fragipan A soil *horizon that is loamy, weakly cemented, has low permeability and high density, is compact and brittle, and is hard when dry.

fragment A small mass of *soil or piece of broken *rock.

fragmentation 1. The breakup of large *habitats into smaller, isolated fragments, which may or may not be connected by *corridors. *See also* CONNECTEDNESS; FOREST FRAGMENTATION; HABITAT CONNECTIVITY; SLOSS PRINCIPLE. **2.** A type of asexual reproduction, in which a plant or *fungus breaks into pieces, each of which is capable of forming a new organism.

Framework Convention on Biological Diversity *See* UNITED NATIONS FRAMEWORK CONVENTION ON BIOLOGICAL DIVERSITY.

Framework Convention on Climate Change *See* UNITED NATIONS FRAMEWORK CONVENTION ON CLIMATE CHANGE.

frass The fine powdery material to which *phytophagous insects reduce plant parts; it is the faeces left by the insects.

free acceleration test A test for measuring vehicle exhaust emissions in which the engine is accelerated rapidly in neutral gear and the exhaust gases are fed through a smoke meter, which analyses them.

free air wind (general wind) A *synoptic-scale *wind.

free atmosphere The part of the *atmosphere that lies above the planetary *boundary layer.

free convection *Convection of air that is triggered by heating of the Earth's surface.

free draining Applied to a *soil or deposit that allows water to *percolate freely through it.

free enterprise system *See* MARKET ECONOMY.

free growth The ability of a tree or other plant to grow relatively free from *competition from adjacent vegetation.

free market A market in which buyers and sellers can exchange goods or services by competitive bidding which is open to all, without constraint. *See also* MARKET EQUILIBRIUM; MARKET ECONOMY.

free market environmentalism An ideology based on the belief that the *free market is the most effective means of preserving the health and sustainability of the environment, rather than relying on government intervention.

free product A *hazardous substance that exists as a separate liquid phase which is not dissolved in water, and which has been released into the *environment.

free trade Trade amongst countries that is free of such government interference as quotas, subsidies, and tariffs.

free-living Applied to an organism that lives independently, as opposed to a *parasite or an organism in a *symbiotic relationship.

free-range Describing a management system in which livestock are allowed to *graze or *forage, rather than being confined to a cage, barn, or *feedlot.

freeze 1. To change *phase from a liquid to a solid. 2. Informal term for a spell of weather that is cold enough to cause *freezing over a wide area. *See also* HARD FREEZE.

freeze–thaw Process (particularly *weathering process) associated with daily and seasonal cycles of freezing and melting.

freezing The *phase change in a substance from a liquid to a solid. *See also* FREEZING POINT.

freezing condensation A cloud process in which *supercooled water droplets evaporate and the water vapour is deposited on to ice crystals, which grow larger and heavier until they begin to fall as *snow (which may melt at a lower level).

freezing drizzle *See* FREEZING RAIN.

freezing fog *Fog, comprising *supercooled droplets, that forms when the air temperature and surfaces exposed to the air are below freezing. The fog droplets freeze instantly on contact with surfaces.

freezing level The *altitude at which the air temperature is 0°C (*freezing point).

freezing nuclei Tiny particles that promote the freezing of *supercooled liquid droplets.

freezing point The temperature at which a substance changes from a liquid to a solid state. For pure water, the freezing point at sea-level pressure is 0°C or 32°F.

freezing rain *Rain that falls as *supercooled droplets which freeze instantly into *glaze on contact with the ground. *See also* ICE STORM.

frequency The number of occurrences within a given period of time or a given area. *See also* DENSITY.

freshet 1. The annual rise of streams in cold climates that is caused by *snow melt during the late winter or spring. 2. A flood that is caused by rain or melting snow.

freshwater Water that contains little or no chlorine. According to the *Venice system for classifying *brackish water, freshwater contains 0.5% of salt or less, or 0.03% or less of chlorine. Freshwater streams, rivers, lakes, ponds, and *wetlands cover about 2% of the surface of the Earth. *See also* SALINITY; WATER RESOURCE.

friable Applied to *soil that is easily crumbled into small fragments or powder under hand pressure.

friction The force that resists the relative motion between bodies that are in contact with each other.

friction layer An alternative name for the planetary *boundary layer, in which air is affected by *friction with the Earth's surface.

Friends of the Earth (FOE) An international network of *grassroots environmental groups in 70 countries, which was founded in San Francisco in 1969 by David *Brower, and runs high-profile campaigns designed to raise public awareness of environmental issues. *See also* ENVIRONMENTALISM; PRESSURE GROUP.

fringing reef *Coral reef that is directly attached to the *shore, or separated from it by a shallow, narrow *lagoon. *Contrast* COASTAL REEF.

frog An *amphibian that has moist skin, a stout body, and long legs for jumping. *Contrast* TOAD.

frond A large compound leaf, such as those of ferns and palms, or the leaf-like blade of a *kelp plant or other seaweed.

front The boundary between two *air masses.

front group A *pressure group that is structured to look like a voluntary association, but may in reality be controlled by a particular interest (such as a company, industry, or political party), and which may give the appearance of being set up to do one thing but actually be set up to do something else on behalf of its parent group. Examples of US environmental front groups include the *Coalition for Vehicle Choice, *National Wetlands Coalition, and the *Wise Use Movement.

frontal fog See EVAPORATION FOG.

frontal inversion A temperature *inversion that develops above a *front when warm air lies above cold air, the front forming a barrier preventing the air below from rising by *convection.

frontal lifting The forced ascent of warmer air over cooler, denser air. Frontal lifting occurs at a *front when cold air pushes under a warmer air mass at a *cold front, or when warm air flows over a *warm front with colder air below.

frontal rain See CYCLONIC RAIN.

frontal system A *warm front, *cold front, and *occlusion as these are depicted on a weather map.

frontal thunderstorm A *thunderstorm that develops in response to forced *convection along a *front. Contrast AIR MASS THUNDERSTORM.

frontal zone The part of a weather *front where the temperature gradient is strongest. It is 100–200 km wide in both *warm fronts and *cold fronts.

frontogenesis The process by which a *front forms and develops. Contrast FRONTOLYSIS. See also CYCLOGENESIS.

frontolysis The process by which a *front weakens and subsides. Contrast FRONTOGENESIS.

frost A white deposit of ice crystals that forms on exposed surfaces when the temperature falls below *freezing point.

frost heave (frost weathering) A process by which the soil surface is pushed up by the accumulation of ice in the soil below. A form of *mechanical weathering that occurs in cold climates and *periglacial environments.

frost hollow A low-lying area (e.g. a valley bottom or a smaller hollow) that is very liable to severe and frequent frosts as a result of dense, cold air moving down-slope (*katabatic wind) and collecting there under conditions of radiation cooling (e.g. at night).

frost point The temperature at which air reaches saturation with respect to *snow or *frost. As the temperature falls below the frost point, water vapour turns directly to ice; as temperature rises above it, ice sublimes. See also DEW POINT.

frost table See TJAELE.

frost weathering See FROST HEAVE.

frost wedging The process in which rocks are forced apart by the expansion of water as it freezes in fractures and pore spaces.

frostbite Human tissue damage, especially in the feet, face, and hands, that is caused by exposure to extreme cold.

frugivore An animal that eats fruit.

fruit The part of a plant that contains seeds, such as a berry or pod.

fruiting body The reproductive part of a *fungus (such as a mushroom) that produces, contains, and releases *spores. Foresters and wood-cutters describe the fruiting body of certain wood-rotting fungi as a conk.

fry Newly hatched fish.

fuel Any material (such as *wood, *coal, *oil, or *gas) that can be burned to produce heat or light. See also FOSSIL FUEL.

fuel assembly A bundle of hollow, metal rods (fuel rods) that contain pellets of uranium oxide, used to fuel a *nuclear reactor.

fuel break A strip of land where the native vegetation has been permanently modified or replaced to assist *fire management. See also FIREBREAK.

fuel cell A mechanical device that uses *hydrogen or hydrogen-based *fuel (such as *methane) to produce an electric current. Fuel cells are clean, quiet, and very efficient sources of *electricity.

fuel cycle The stages in the total life of a fuel. For example, the fuel cycle of coal is extraction, transportation, combustion, air emissions, ash removal, transportation, and disposal. *See also* NUCLEAR FUEL CYCLE.

fuel desulphurization *See* DESULPHURIZATION.

fuel economy US term for the average mileage travelled by an automobile per gallon of gasoline (or equivalent amount of other fuel) consumed, measured in accordance with the testing and evaluation protocol set forth by the *Environmental Protection Agency. *See also* CORPORATE AVERAGE FUEL ECONOMY.

fuel efficiency *See* ENERGY EFFICIENCY.

fuel ethanol *See* ETHANOL.

fuel intensity *See* ENERGY INTENSITY.

fuel management Any planned activity (including cutting *firebreaks or starting *prescribed fires) that changes vegetation in order to reduce fire risk.

fuel rod *See* FUEL ASSEMBLY.

fuel switching A change from using one *fuel to another, usually in order to decrease emissions of *greenhouse gases or other *pollutants.

fuelwood Wood (including sawn branches, twigs, logs, and wood chips) that is harvested for use as *fuel.

fugitive dust Dust that comes from *non-point sources (such as open fields and roads) not from *point sources (such as industrial smokestacks).

fugitive emission The uncontrolled escape of a gas, liquid, solid, vapour, fume, mist, fog, or dust from process equipment, without going through a *smokestack.

fugitive species (opportunist species) A species of plant or animal that is adapted to rapidly colonize newly disturbed habitats. It is typical of unstable or periodically extreme habitats (e.g. deserts, ephemeral ponds).

Fujita scale A system that classifies *tornadoes based on wind damage. The scale is from F-0 for weak tornadoes (light damage caused by winds up to 32 m s^{-1}) to F-5 for the strongest tornadoes (heavy damage from winds 116 m s^{-1}). The scale is given in Appendix 5.

full cost pricing The pricing of commercial goods (such as electric power) in a way that includes not just the cost of production but also the cost of *externalities created by their production and use (which includes *pollution, *waste management, and environmental damage).

fumarole A vent on the side of a *volcano from which *volcanic steam and gases emerge.

fume A cloud of gas, smoke, or vapour that is suspended in a gas.

fumigant A chemical *pesticide that forms vapours (gases) that are used to destroy *weeds, plant *pathogens, insects, or other pests.

fumigation The destruction of any unwanted organisms by exposure to a poisonous gas or smoke.

fundamental niche The total range of environmental conditions that are suitable for the existence of a species, without effects of interspecific *competition and *predation. *See also* NICHE; POTENTIAL NICHE; REALIZED NICHE.

fungibility Interchangeability, such as the *flexibility mechanisms for reducing *greenhouse gas emissions that were agreed under the *Kyoto Protocol.

fungicide (fungistat) A chemical *pesticide that is used to control or kill *fungus.

fungistat *See* FUNGICIDE.

fungus An organism belonging to the kingdom Fungi. It is *eukaryotic, non-photosynthesizing, and obtains nutrients by absorbing them from its surroundings. Most fungi have cell walls containing *chitin. They may be single-celled, filamentous, or form plasmodia, and live as *saprotrophs, *symbionts, *parasitically, etc. Some can cause disease. The fungi include yeasts, moulds, and mildews, and some are known by the fruiting bodies, e.g. mushrooms and toadstools.

 SEE WEB LINKS

• Fungi Online.

funnel cloud A rotating column of cloud beneath a *cumulonimbus cloud, which does not reach the ground.

furan (furfuran) The simplest (C_4H_4O) of a group of compounds related to *dioxin, some of which are manufactured for industrial use as solvents and raw materials. It is toxic to humans, causing irritation to the eyes, skin, respiratory tract, and digestive tract.

furbearer Any mammal species or individual that is valued and sought for its pelt or fur.

furfural A compound ($C_5H_4O_2$) that occurs naturally in tea, coffee, cocoa, and many fruits, and is produced industrially from *cellulose in agricultural wastes. It can be used as a *biofuel and is also used in the manufacture of perfumes and flavourings, and as a *nematicide and *fungicide.

furfuran See FURAN.

furnace A *combustion chamber or an enclosed structure in which *fuel is burned.

furrow A long, narrow, shallow trench carved in the ground by a plough or other agricultural implement.

furrow irrigation A form of *irrigation in which water is allowed to flow along the *furrows between rows of crops.

fusion **1.** The act of fusing or melting together. **2.** The process in which *nuclei are joined together under intense heat to form a heavier nucleus, at the same time releasing great amounts of energy. *Contrast* FISSION.

fusion reactor A *nuclear reactor in which atoms of *deuterium, tritium, lithium, or some combination of these are made to fuse to form *helium with the release of neutrons and energy. The operating temperature is approximately 100×10^6 degrees C.

futures A contract to buy or sell a specified resource at a fixed price at some agreed time in the future. *See also* EMISSIONS BANKING.

futurity In the future, yet to come.

FWS *See* US FISH AND WILDLIFE SERVICE.

G7 *See* GROUP OF 7.

G8 *See* GROUP OF 8.

G10 *See* GROUP OF 10.

G15 *See* GROUP OF 15.

G77 *See* GROUP OF 77.

gabbro A coarse-grained *intrusive volcanic rock that is formed at great depth within the *Earth from the slow crystallization of *magma.

gaging station A particular site on a river where variations in stage or *discharge are measured systematically, usually continuously.

gale A sustained strong wind, between a strong breeze and a storm, moving at speeds of between 28 and 55 knots (32 to 63 miles per hour or 51 to 101 km per hour), which is force 7 to 10 on the *Beaufort scale.

gallery forest *See* RIPARIAN FOREST.

gallon A unit of liquid capacity. A British imperial gallon is 4.545 litres and a US gallon is 3.785 litres.

galvanize To coat a metal (especially iron or steel) with zinc in order to prevent *corrosion.

game Animals (mammals, birds, or fish) that are hunted for food or sport. *See also* BIG GAME.

game bag The record of game taken from a particular place over a given period of time.

game cropping The culling or husbanding of game animals for meat and other products, usually for human consumption. Game

---

GAIA HYPOTHESIS

The idea that the *Earth should be viewed and treated as a living organism, which was first suggested by James *Lovelock in 1979 who named it after the Greek Earth goddess Gaea. This perspective assumes that the living (biotic) and non-living (abiotic) parts of the Earth *system are mutually interdependent, both having been influenced by the other, with the survival of each dependent on the survival of the other. According to the Gaia hypothesis, as life evolved on Earth it both created and was created by biological processes that have radically altered the chemistry of the planet and its *environment, in ways that promoted further biological *evolution of plants and animals on land and in the sea. This planetary *positive feedback gave rise to large-scale *dynamic equilibrium between life and the planet. There are a number of interesting implications of the Gaia hypothesis. For example: the whole system matters much more than its component parts; complexity in the environment is inevitable and fundamental, and much of it we simply do not understand; feedback links in environmental systems are critical, but whilst they are not always fully understood, they should form the basis of any human intervention (deliberate or accidental) in environmental systems; biotic and abiotic aspects of the environment affect each other, and the symbiosis is important but easy to disturb or destroy; the stability of global environmental systems has evolved over long periods of time; short-term changes must be seen against a background of long-term geological change and progression; it is unwise to radically modify global environmental systems and equilibrium, because we can't always properly predict the outcomes and consequences; the Earth has a great natural capacity to look after itself (self-repair), so long as change remains within critical limits (thresholds), many of which we simply don't know enough about; the Earth will probably survive, no matter what humans do to it, but its survival might not include humans. The hypothesis is scientifically useful, but its interpretation remains controversial.

cropping is often advocated as an ecologically sound method of farming the African *savanna and similar environments: it is argued that the wide variety of game animals, with their different food preferences, utilize the primary production more efficiently than cattle, and are generally better adapted to the environment. This gives added reason for conservation of the wild ungulate population. Other social, economic, and political difficulties mean that game cropping is practised less widely than may seem desirable.

((⨁)) SEE WEB LINKS

• Wildlife utilization and food security in Africa.

game fish (sport fish) Any species of *fish that is caught for sport. Examples include salmon, trout, black bass, and lake trout. *Contrast* ROUGH FISH.

game reserve An area of wildland that is set aside for the protection of *wildlife, usually for tourism or hunting purposes.

game species Any species of wild animal that people hunt or fish for sport, recreation, and food, and for which hunting seasons, *bag limits, and other laws and regulations have been prescribed.

game sport *See* FIELD SPORT.

gamekeeper A person who is employed to take care of *game and *wildlife.

gamete (germ cell) A reproductive cell, either an egg (female gamete) or a sperm (male gamete). *See also* FERTILIZATION; SEXUAL REPRODUCTION; ZYGOTE.

gamma diversity (regional diversity) Regional-scale *species diversity, expressed as the total number of species in the different *ecosystems within a region. A measure of *biodiversity. *See also* ALPHA DIVERSITY; BETA DIVERSITY.

gamma ray Very short wavelength (10^{-8}–10^{-4} μm) *electromagnetic radiation that can be produced by *radioactive decay. It travels in straight paths at the speed of light, and penetrates matter (including lead) but does not make the material *radioactive. *See also* ELECTROMAGNETIC SPECTRUM.

gap analysis The identification of *species and *classes of organisms that are not currently protected, to find out where they need protecting, on the basis of comparing the actual distri-

bution of species and vegetation classes with the areas that are preserved or managed for their protection.

gap dynamics The process of colonization and the development of vegetation within an opening in a forest.

gap formation The creation of a patch of *habitat that is different from the surrounding larger habitat, for example by *felling parts of a *forest.

gap phase In forestry, the *pioneer phase during which trees begin to colonize a site.

gap wind A strong *wind that blows through low passes or breaks in *mountain barriers, for example where coastal mountain ranges meet the sea.

garbage A North American term for food waste, or *refuse in general.

garden A plot of ground on which plants (flowers, vegetables, fruits, or herbs) are cultivated. *See also* HORTICULTURE; MARKET GARDEN.

garden city A new town that has been designed with a special emphasis on natural landscaping and retaining a rural atmosphere.

garigue *See* GARRIGUE.

garrigue (garigue) A low-growing, secondary vegetation that is widespread in the Mediterranean basin and is derived from the original *evergreen mixed forest. The dominant plants are aromatic herbs and prickly dwarf shrubs, with drought-resistant foliage, many of them legumes (Fabaceae) or belonging to the mint family (Lamiaceae). Garrigue is a degraded, fire-prone form of vegetation produced by intensive grazing and other human-based activities.

gas 1. A substance that is not a solid or a liquid; matter that occupies all of its container regardless of its amount. **2.** *See* NATURAL GAS. **3.** North American term for *petrol; short for *gasoline.

gas chromatography An analytical separation technique in which the minor ingredients in a mixture of gases are separated into their individual components. This involves entraining the mixture in a gas flow (usually helium) to move it over a solid adsorbent in a column; each gas is absorbed at a known rate.

gas chromatography–mass spectrometry An analytical technique for measuring the concentrations of various chemicals in samples of soil or water, by first separating them using *gas chromatography and then analysing them by *mass spectrometry.

gas solubility The ability of a gas to dissolve in another substance.

gas stripping The transfer of an undesirable gas from water to the *atmosphere.

gasification The conversion of solid or liquid *hydrocarbons (such as coal) into a *gas, for use as a *fuel.

gasohol A mixture of gasoline and *ethanol.

gasoline A liquid petroleum *fuel that is composed of a mixture of small, light *hydrocarbons, produced by refining *crude oil, and used mainly by cars, trucks, and other motor vehicles. Known as petrol in the UK.

gastropod A member of the Gastropoda class of molluscs, which includes snails and slugs. Gastropods have a head, unsegmented body, and a broad, flat foot.

GATT *See* GENERAL AGREEMENT ON TARIFFS AND TRADE.

Gause's principle *See* PRINCIPLE OF COMPETITIVE EXCLUSION.

Gaussian curve (normal distribution) A symmetrical bell-shaped curve representing the distribution of results from a normal sample population.

GCM *See* GENERAL CIRCULATION MODEL.

GDP *See* GROSS DOMESTIC PRODUCT.

GEF *See* GLOBAL ENVIRONMENTAL FACILITY.

Geiger counter An electrical device that measures *radioactivity.

gene A sequence of *DNA (or *RNA in some viruses) that is the basic unit of inheritance, coding for one or more related functions or proteins. In all plants and animals it forms part of a *chromosome.

gene bank A facility established for storage in a viable form of individuals, tissues, or reproductive cells of plants or animals, so that the material can be used in the future when required, as part of an *ex situ* conservation strategy.

gene fixation The condition in which a particular *allele becomes the only one that is present in a *population, because of either *natural selection or *genetic drift.

gene flow The movement of *genes from one population to another by movement of individuals, *gametes, or *spores.

gene frequency The relative occurrence of a particular *allele within a *population.

gene mapping Determination of the relative positions of *genes on a *chromosome and of the distance between them.

gene pool The stock of different *genes in an interbreeding *population at a given time.

gene splicing *See* GENETIC ENGINEERING.

gene therapy An approach to preventing and/or treating disease by replacing, removing, or introducing *genes or otherwise manipulating *genetic material.

genecology Study of the genetic variation among *populations of a *species, and its relationship with *environmental factors. *See also* AUTECOLOGY; SYNECOLOGY.

genera Plural of *genus.

General Agreement on Tariffs and Trade (GATT) A 1947 multilateral trade agreement that was designed to establish rules, reduce tariffs, and provide a setting for solutions to international trade problems. It was succeeded in 1994 by the *World Trade Organization.

general circulation The continuous circulation of *wind and *ocean currents that acts to control temperature differences between the *poles and the *equator.

general circulation model (GCM) A large, complex computer program of atmospheric behaviour that simulates the *global climate, based on mathematical equations derived from knowledge of the physics and chemistry that govern the Earth–atmosphere system. Such models are used to predict the likely speed and pattern of *climate change, given various assumptions and *scenarios.

general fertility rate The number of births per 1000 women of childbearing age (15–44) in a year, for an area, country, or the world.

g

General Mining Law (1872) US legislation that governs the mining of hardrock *minerals (*gold, *silver, *copper, platinum, *uranium, and others) on federal lands, and is still in effect.

general plan *See* COMPREHENSIVE PLAN.

general systems theory A way of looking at the world or any part of it as an interacting set of parts, as *systems.

general wind *See* FREE AIR WIND.

generalist A species that can live in many different habitats and can feed on a number of different organisms. *Compare* SPECIALIST.

generating capacity The capacity of a *power plant to generate *electricity, which is usually expressed in megawatts (MW).

generation 1. All of the people who are alive at the same time or who are of a similar age. 2. The production of heat or electricity.

generation time The average period of time between birth and reproduction in a given population.

generator A machine that produces electricity (*electrical energy) from mechanical energy.

genetic Relating to or carried by *genes; hereditary or inherited.

genetic analysis The study of how *traits, and the *genes that carry them, are passed from generation to generation, and how the interaction of genes and the *environment results in particular traits.

genetic assimilation The progressive disappearance of a *species as its genes are diluted through *crossbreeding with a closely related species. *See also* GENETIC DRIFT.

genetic base The total genetic variability that is available within a *cultivar or *species.

genetic code The set of correspondences between *base pair triplets in *DNA and the *amino acids in *proteins that determine the structure and functions of a living organism. For example, the triplet CAA (cytosine, adenine, adenine) codes for the amino acid valine.

genetic damage Damage that is caused to the *chromosomes in the *germ cells by environmental factors (for example *radiation). Such changes can be passed on to offspring. *Contrast* SOMATIC DAMAGE.

genetic distance A measure of the genetic similarity, and therefore relationship, between any pair of *populations, based on *phenotypic traits, *allele frequencies, or *DNA sequences.

genetic diversity The number of different types of *genes in a *species or *population, which is a measure of *biodiversity.

genetic drift Fluctuations in the frequencies of particular *genes within a *population over time that are caused by random events rather than by *natural selection, and can lead, over successive generations, to a progressive change in the genetic composition of the population. *See also* FOUNDER EFFECT; GENE FIXATION; GENETIC ASSIMILATION.

genetic effect A heritable effect, that is passed on to descendants via *genes.

genetic erosion The loss of genetic *diversity between and within populations of the same species over time, as a result of *environmental change or human impacts.

genetic manipulation *See* GENETIC ENGINEERING.

genetic material Any *organic material that contains functional units of *heredity.

genetic modification *See* GENETIC ENGINEERING.

genetic polymorphism The presence of two or more *genotypes (e.g. blue eyes versus brown eyes) within a population, which may be the result of chance processes, or may have been caused by external *agents (such as *viruses or *radiation).

genetic resource Genetic material of plants, animals, or micro-organisms that is of actual or potential value as a resource for humans. Examples include modern *cultivars and *breeds, primitive varieties and breeds, *landraces and wild/weedy relatives of *crop plants or *domesticated animals.

genetic use restriction technology (GURT) *See* TRAITOR TECHNOLOGY.

genetically engineered organism *See* GENETICALLY MODIFIED ORGANISM.

genetically modified organism (GMO, genetically engineered organism) An organism whose genetic makeup has been deliberately altered by inserting a modified *gene or a gene from another variety or species, in order

GENETIC ENGINEERING (GENE SPLICING, GENETIC MANIPULATION, GENETIC MODIFICATION, RECOMBINANT DNA TECHNOLOGY)

The selective, deliberate alteration of the genetic makeup (*DNA) of an organism by removing, modifying, or adding genes to a chromosome in order to change the information it contains, which enables cells or organisms to make new or different substances (*proteins) or perform new functions. Such manipulation is sometimes done for pure research purposes, to discover more about *genetics and the way it works. But, increasingly, the commercial benefits of genetic engineering are being exploited in the breeding of plants, animals, and bacteria for particular purposes which benefit humans (so-called 'designer breeding'). Such organisms with a foreign gene added are referred to as *transgenic. There are many potential applications of *biotechnology, including *hazardous waste disposal and the recovery and *recycling of natural resources. Some scientists fear that transgenic organisms could do more damage than good. There is also widespread public concern over the risk that new and harmful strains might be produced (accidentally or on purpose) when genes are transplanted between different types of bacteria. The release of such material into the environment could create a nightmare scenario. Genetically modified plants might breed with wild species, and thus spread their genes far and wide, although the burden of additional genes is likely to prove disadvantageous, causing such hybrids to die out rapidly. Cultural problems surrounding biotechnology have to be addressed too, including *technology transfer between the developed and developing worlds, although GM crops are widely grown by small farmers in some developing countries. There is also a clear need for internationally accepted mechanisms to ensure that all humankind will benefit. *See also* BIOTECHNOLOGY; HUMAN GENOME PROJECT.

to create or enhance desirable characteristics from the same or another species.

genetics The study of *genes, *inheritance, and variation in *organisms.

genome All of the *genetic information or hereditary material in the *chromosomes of a particular *organism.

genome project Scientific research that is designed to map and sequence the entire *genome of an organism, such as a human being.

genomics The study of *genes and their function.

genotype The genetic make-up or blueprint of an individual organism, the set of *genes that it possesses. *Contrast* PHENOTYPE.

genotypic adaptation A form of biological *adaptation that is genetically determined, occurs by *natural selection (because those individuals which have favourable genetically acquired traits tend to breed more successfully than those which lack these traits), and can be passed on to future generations. *See* ADAPTIVE STRATEGY.

genus The sixth highest (of seven) category in the scientific system of classification for organisms (*taxonomy), below *family and above *species. Thus each family comprises more

than one genus, and each genus comprises more than one closely related species. Scientists refer to living things by a combined genus and species name, using Latin terms. The genus name is always capitalized, and the species name is usually not; both are normally put in italics. For example, the proper name for humans is *Homo sapiens* where *Homo* is the genus. The plural of genus is genera.

geo- Relating to the *Earth.

geoarchaeology The study of sediments and deposits at *archaeological sites, in order to reconstruct local *environmental history.

geochemical Relating to the chemistry of rocks.

geochemistry The study of the chemical properties, abundance, and distribution of materials within the Earth's waters, *crust, and *atmosphere.

geochronology The science of *absolute and *relative dating of geological formations and events.

geocoordinates *See* GEOGRAPHICAL POSITION.

geodesic The shortest line connecting two points on the surface of a sphere, such as the *Earth.

geodesy The science of determining the size and shape of the *Earth, and the precise location of points on its surface.

geodetic Relating to or determined by *geodesy.

geodetic survey A precise survey of a large area of ground that takes into account the shape of the *Earth.

geographical information system (GIS) A computer system that is designed for the storage, manipulation, analysis, and display of large volumes of spatial data in a map format, with different characteristics (such as *soil type or *vegetation) stored as separate layers which can be combined to display interactions of characteristics. Often simply referred to as GIS.

geographical isolation The separation of a *population from the rest of its *species by a physical barrier such as a mountain range, ocean, or great distance.

geographical position (geocoordinates) The location of a point on the surface of the Earth, usually expressed in terms of *latitude and *longitude or as a grid reference. *See also* GLOBAL POSITIONING SYSTEM.

geographical range *See* NATURAL RANGE.

geographical variety A subdivision of a *species with distinct *morphology and a distinctive *geographical range, which is given a unique Latin name. A taxonomic variety is known by the first validly published name applied to it and that nomenclature tends to be stable. *See also* VARIETY.

geography The study of the Earth's surface and of the ways in which people, plants, and animals live on and use it.

geohydrology *See* HYDROGEOLOGY.

geoid The figure of the Earth assuming that its whole surface is at current sea level (that is, it ignores topography on land and below the sea), which provides the reference level for astronomic observations and for *geodetic surveying.

geoinformatics The use of computers and statistical methods in the classification, storage, retrieval, and analysis of information about the *Earth. *See also* INFORMATICS.

geological column The arrangement of *rock units in their proper chronological order, from youngest to oldest.

geological cycle *See* ROCK CYCLE.

geological erosion *See* NATURAL EROSION.

geological log A detailed description of all of the underground features (depth, thickness, and type of rock formations) that are discovered during the drilling of a *well.

geological process Any natural process that affects the surface or interior of the *Earth, including *erosion, *deposition, *folding, *faulting, *plate tectonics, and *sea-floor spreading. *See also* LANDFORM.

geology The study of the origin, history, and structure of the *Earth.

geomagnetic storm (magnetic storm) A worldwide disturbance of the Earth's *magnetic field which is created when particles travelling from the Sun in *solar flares are drawn towards the Earth by its magnetic field. It often coexists with an *aurora.

geometric growth A pattern of growth that increases at a constant geometric rate over a specified time period, such as 2, 4, 8, 16 (in which, in this example, each value is double the previous one). *Contrast* ARITHMETIC GROWTH; EXPONENTIAL GROWTH.

geomorphic cycle *See* CYCLE OF EROSION.

geomorphic process Processes that change the form or shape of the surface of the *Earth, including *desertification, *erosion, *fluvial processes, *glaciation, and *weathering.

geomorphology The study of *landforms and how they develop.

geophysics The study of the physical characteristics and properties of the *Earth, which includes *geodesy, *seismology, *meteorology, *oceanography, atmospheric electricity, terrestrial magnetism, and tidal phenomena.

geophyte A *perennial *herbaceous plant that reproduces by underground bulbs, tubers, or corms.

geopolitics The combination of geographical and political factors that affect a country or area.

geopotential height The height above sea level (in metres) that takes account of the increase in gravitational acceleration with latitude. It is the height at which the atmospheric pressure has a specified value.

georeferenced Describes data that are defined by *geographical position.

geoscience Study of the science of Earth systems.

geosphere The solid, *abiotic portion of the *Earth, excluding the *atmosphere, *hydrosphere, and *biosphere.

Geostationary Operational Environmental Satellite (GOES) A series of *geostationary satellites that were launched by the USA starting in 1968, and use a variety of *remote sensing devices for *weather forecasting and *environmental monitoring. GOES-E is positioned over the USA and South America, and GOES-W is positioned over the Pacific Ocean. Two GOES satellites are operational at any time and they all transmit data to the *NOAA receiving station at Wallops, Virginia.

(((•))) SEE WEB LINKS
• Office of Satellite Operations.

geostationary satellite A satellite that orbits the *Earth in the same direction and at the same rate that the Earth rotates and so remains over a fixed place above the *equator. It orbits at a height of about 36000 km.

geostrophic wind A wind that flows parallel to *isobars, which is produced when the *pressure gradient is balanced by the *Coriolis effect, usually at some height above the ground surface where *friction is reduced.

geosyncline A large *depositional basin on the ocean floor, usually close to a continental margin, in which *sediments accumulate to thicknesses of many kilometres.

geotactic Moving in response to the Earth's gravitational field.

geothermal Relating to or produced by the internal heat of the *Earth, which is generated by a number of processes, including *radioactive decay of rocks and *compression at great depth. *See also* HYDROTHERMAL.

geothermal belt An area where the *geothermal gradient is unusually steep, where *geothermal energy might be exploited.

geothermal energy 1. Heat energy that is derived from the Earth's interior, either through *geysers, *fumaroles, *hot springs, or other natural *geothermal features. **2.** The use of *geothermal heat to generate usable energy, for example through using heat from a subterra-

nean reservoir of water heated by contact with anomalously *hot rock, or by pumping water through fractures in hot rocks and recovering it as superheated water or steam to drive turbines and produce electricity. Hot water is pumped to the surface and converted to steam or run through a heat exchanger. Dry steam is pumped to the surface, and can then be directed through turbines to generate electricity. In volcanic regions such as New Zealand, Japan, and Iceland water heated beneath the ground may erupt at the surface as geysers, hot springs, or boiling mud. This heated material can sometimes be used directly, saving on the cost of pumping to the surface. By the early 1990s geothermal energy fields were being exploited in more than 20 countries, including New Zealand, Iceland, the USA, and the former Soviet Union. Geothermal energy is an important source of energy in some areas, particularly in Iceland and parts of New Zealand. Direct heat use of geothermal energy in the USA occurs mainly in the western States, particularly southern California. Geothermal power plants are usually relatively small, and serve local rather than regional or national needs. The fraction of total world energy needs that is provided by geothermal sources is currently very small, but rising rapidly. Over time, the extraction of heat cools the rocks, so the resource eventually depletes.

geothermal gradient The natural increase in rock temperature with increasing depth within the Earth's *crust, usually measured at depths below 200 m. Direct observation, in places such as deep mines and wells, has shown that this gradient varies from place to place, but the average is about 20–40°C for every kilometre of depth. In some places the geothermal gradient is much steeper than the norm, and this can be exploited as a source of *geothermal energy.

germ A *micro-organism that can cause *disease.

germ cell *See* GAMETE.

germicide A chemical *pesticide that is used to control or kill *germs or other *micro-organisms.

germination The initial stages in the growth of a *seed, *spore, *pollen grain, or other structure, usually following a period of dormancy and triggered by the return of favourable environmental conditions.

germplasm The hereditary *genetic material of which an organism is composed, which is transmitted from one generation to the next by the *gametes.

gestalt The perception of a pattern or structure as a whole, rather than as the sum of its constituent parts.

geyser A violent ejection of superheated water and steam from a hole in the ground. The underground reservoir consists of water-filled chambers that are connected by a central pipe. Heated by the surrounding rocks, water in the lower part of the pipe boils before water above, and rising bubbles expel water from the top of the pipe. That reduces pressure below, boiling recommences, and the process repeats until all the water has been expelled. *See also* GEOTHERMAL GRADIENT; HYDROTHERMAL ACTIVITY; HOT SPRING.

Giardia lamblia A *protozoan *micro-organism that is frequently found in rivers and lakes, which (if not treated properly) can cause diarrhoea, fatigue, and cramps in humans who ingest it.

gibberellins A group of plant hormones that stimulate the growth of leaves and shoots. Unlike *auxins, they tend to affect the whole plant and do not induce localized bending movements. They are thought to act either at a transcriptional level or as inducers of *enzymes.

gigahertz (GHz) A unit of *frequency that is equal to 1 billion hertz (Hz).

gigatonne (Gt) A unit of mass that is used for large quantities (such as the amount of *carbon dioxide in the Earth's atmosphere). 1 Gt = 1 billion tonnes = 10^{15} grams.

gill A respiratory organ in aquatic organisms (such as fish) that is used for obtaining oxygen which is dissolved in the water.

gillnet A net that is set upright in water in order to catch fish by entangling their *gills in its mesh.

girdling A method of killing a *tree by removing a strip of bark from around its trunk or a branch, which interrupts the flow of *nutrients between the leaves and the rest of the tree.

GIS *See* GEOGRAPHICAL INFORMATION SYSTEM.

glacial 1 Relating to a *glacier. **2** A period when *ice sheets expand, and global climate is colder and drier, i.e. an *ice age.

glacial breach A glacially eroded trough that cuts through a ridge and so breaches a former

*drainage divide. It is formed when the outflow of a *glacier (or ice sheet) is impeded, so that the thickness of the glacier consequently increases, and ultimately a higher escape route (the breach) is exploited. This process is called 'glacial diffluence' when a single glacier spills out of its valley, and 'glacial transfluence' when several breaches are formed, owing to the accumulation of a large ice sheet. The many breaches through the western Highlands of Scotland were caused by the accumulation of transfluent ice east of the main watershed.

glacial deposit *Sediment that is transported by a glacier and left behind as a deposit when the ice melts. *See also* BOULDER CLAY.

glacial diamicton *See* BOULDER CLAY.

glacial diffluence *See* GLACIAL BREACH.

glacial drift *See* BOULDER CLAY.

glacial epoch *See* ICE AGE.

glacial erosion The processes of *erosion that are associated with *glaciers and *ice sheets, which include *quarrying and *abrasion. *See also* U-SHAPED VALLEY.

glacial flour Very fine particles of rock that are carried by a *glacier and contribute to *abrasion processes and *glacial polish.

glacial ice A very dense form of *ice that is formed from the accumulation and recrystallization of *snow, is relatively impermeable, and is much harder than snow, *névé, or *firn.

glacial lake A natural lake that is formed by the damming of *meltwater by *glacial deposits in front of a *glacier.

glacial limit A line that marks the furthest extent of a former glacial advance. It may be identified on the ground through the recognition of features associated with glacial margins, including lateral and terminal *moraines, *outwash plains, marginal *meltwater channels, and *pro-glacial lakes.

glacial maximum The position or time of the greatest advance of a *glacier, before it starts to recede and melt. *See* LAST GLACIAL MAXIMUM.

glacial meltwater *See* MELTWATER.

glacial milk Glacial *meltwater which is light coloured and cloudy because of the large quantities of *clay-sized *sediment that are held in *suspension within it.

glacial outwash Well-sorted sand, or sand and gravel, that is deposited by a *meltwater stream in front of a *glacier.

glacial polish The smoothing of a *bedrock surface as a result of *abrasion by *sediment that is transported on the bottom of a *glacier.

glacial rebound (glacial uplift) The *isostatic adjustment of an area after the retreat of a *continental glacier.

glacial retreat The backward movement of the front of a *glacier, as the glacier melts and shrinks.

glacial surge A rapid forward movement of the front of a *glacier.

glacial transfluence *See* GLACIAL BREACH.

glacial trough *See* U-SHAPED VALLEY.

glacial uplift *See* GLACIAL REBOUND.

glacial valley A valley that is or was occupied and shaped by a *glacier. *See also* U-SHAPED VALLEY.

glaciation **1** The formation, movement, and recession of *glaciers or *ice sheets. **2** The geological processes of *glacial activity, including *erosion and *deposition, and the effects of such action on the Earth's surface. **3** The process by which cloud particles change from water drops to ice crystals.

glacier A large mass of ice that rests on or adjacent to a land surface and typically moves very slowly. *Ice caps and *ice sheets are glaciers; glaciers that flow down mountainsides are valley glaciers, e.g. *alpine glaciers. Valley glaciers may open at the foot into *piedmont glaciers.

glacier budget The *mass balance of a glacier, which takes into account inputs (new snow and ice) and outputs (including *evaporation and *meltwater). The larger the positive balance the faster the glacier grows; when the mass balance is negative, outputs exceed inputs and the glacier retreats.

glacier creep One of the mechanisms by which *glaciers flow, in which gravitational stress causes ice crystals to deform and slide across one another.

glacier flow (ice flow) The slow but continuous downward or outward movement of *ice in a *glacier that is driven by *gravity.

glacier wind A shallow downslope wind above the surface of a *glacier. Winds blowing outward from the dome of the East Antarctic ice sheet commonly blow at 65 km h^{-1} or more, but affect only the lowest 500 m of the atmosphere.

glacioeustasism *See* GLACIOEUSTASY.

glacioeustasy (glacioeustasism) The theory that sea levels rise and fall in response to the melting of ice during *interglacials and the accumulation of ice during *glaciations. A major glacioeustatic oscillation has an amplitude of some 100 m.

glaciofluvial (fluvioglacial) Relating to meltwater coming from a glacier, which creates such features as *eskers and *kames, *outwash plains, *pro-glacial lakes, and *meltwater channels.

glacioisostasy The adjustment of the *lithosphere following the melting of an *ice sheet. Some 1000 m of depression may have occurred in Scandinavia during the last ice age, where 520 m of recovery has subsequently been recorded. The process gives rise to warped shorelines.

glaciology The study of the formation, movement, and properties of *glaciers and *ice in general.

glade An open clearing in a *woodland or *forest.

glass A solid that results from cooling of *magma that is too fast to allow crystals to grow.

glassiness The amount of glass in an *igneous rock.

glaze A layer or coating of *ice that is generally smooth and clear, and forms on exposed objects by the freezing of *raindrops, *drizzle, or *fog. *See also* ICING.

gleization *See* GLEYING.

glen Scots word for a *valley.

gley A dark grey to black *soil, often mottled and with rust colours, that forms slowly in a waterlogged environment, has a thick *organic horizon over a horizon of chemically reduced *clay, and has low fertility.

gleying (gleization, gleyzation) The formation of *gley through the *reduction of iron in an *anaerobic environment, which creates grey or blue colours mixed with rusty colours in soils.

gleysols Soils with evidence of *gleying within 50 cm of the surface. Gleysols are a reference soil group in the *World Soil Classification.

gleyzation See GLEYING.

global Involving or relating to the whole world.

Global 200 An initiative of the *World wide Fund for Nature (WWF) which seeks to ensure that the full range of *ecosystems will be represented in regional *conservation and development strategies. WWF have identified 867 terrestrial *ecoregions, as well as freshwater and marine ecoregions, and selected 233 of them (136 terrestrial, 36 freshwater, and 61 marine) to represent the Global 200 network of ecoregions which are most crucial to the conservation of global *biodiversity. *Contrast* BIODIVERSITY HOTSPOT.

Global 2000 A report on global environmental trends that was commissioned by US President Carter in 1977 and published in 1980, which concluded that by the year 2000 the world would be more crowded, more polluted, and more fragile if global trends continued.

global biodiversity The number of different *species in the world at a particular point in time. *See also* BIODIVERSITY.

Global Climate Coalition A US non-profit *anti-environmental *front group comprising mainly US businesses that for reasons of self-interest oppose immediate action to reduce *greenhouse gas emissions. It disbanded in 2002 after losing most of its members.

global commons Natural systems and resources (such as the *atmosphere and the *oceans) that do not belong to any one country. *See also* COMMON RESOURCES; TRAGEDY OF THE COMMONS.

global dimming The supposed gradual reduction in the amount of *sunlight reaching the Earth's surface, based on studies suggesting the amount of *insolation in Israel decreased by 50% during the second half of the 20th century and globally by 1–2% per decade between 1950 and 1990 due to an increase of *aerosols and other *particulates in the *atmosphere. Later research showed that although dimming occurred between 1960 and 1990, after 1990 average insolation increased, possibly because of reduced pollution linked to industrial contraction in the former Soviet Union.

Global Environment Facility (GEF) An international fund set up in 1991 under the umbrella of the *United Nations Conference on Environment and Development, by the *World Bank, the *United Nations Development Programme (UNDP), and the *United Nations Environment Programme (UNEP) to help meet the costs of *Agenda 21.

Global Environmental Monitoring System (GEMS) A global *environmental monitoring system that was established in 1973 under the *United Nations Environment Programme, which collects data relating to *atmosphere, *climate, *pollution, and *renewable resources.

global environmental research Research into environmental issues at the global scale, which reflects growing interest in two sets of processes. First, there are the natural *environmental processes that are global in scale. These include *plate tectonics, *atmospheric circulation, *ocean currents, the *water cycle, and the *biogeochemical cycles. Second, there are induced environmental changes at local and regional scales which are becoming issues of global concern. Obvious examples include *air pollution, *climate change, *deforestation, *desertification, *ocean pollution, *ozone depletion, *soil erosion, and *tropical forest clearance.

Global Heritage Fund A private, non-profit, international funding organization, established in 2001, whose mission is the conservation of around 200 archaeological sites in the Americas, Asia, and the Pacific where the threats of neglect and destruction are most urgent, and which provide major opportunities for *sustainable tourism and development. *Contrast* WORLD HERITAGE FUND.

global positioning system (GPS) A navigation system that pinpoints a *geographical position precisely in all weathers. The user transmits a radio signal to several *satellites, which measure its direction and transmit the coordinates to the receiver.

global rank (G-rank) The global *conservation status rank of a species, subspecies, or variety of plant or animal, based largely on the total number of known sites occupied by it worldwide, and the degree to which they are potentially or actively threatened with destruction. *See also* PROVINCIAL RANK.

global scale (planetary scale) Large scale, at the scale of the whole world.

grade

Global Warming Policy Foundation (GWPF) A British non-governmental (non-profit) organization established in November 2009 that aims to inform the media, politicians, and the public on the costs and implications of official policies related to global warming, on the subject of global warming in general, and on the misinformation to which its target audience is frequently subjected. It has no view on the scientific merits of the case for global warming, although it recognizes that the issue remains far from settled. It is a registered education charity and accepts no funding from energy companies or from any individual with a significant interest in an energy company.

(∰) SEE WEB LINKS
• GWPF home page.

global warming potential (GWP, carbon dioxide equivalent) An index that allows for direct comparison of the various *greenhouse gases, based on the *radiative forcing (amount of *global warming) that results from the addition of 1 kilogram of a particular gas to the atmosphere compared with 1 kilogram of *carbon dioxide. Carbon dioxide has a GWP of 1, and *methane has a GWP of 25 (it produces 25 times as much warming as carbon dioxide). Nitrous oxide has a GWP of 310, CFC-11 has a GWP of 4750, and CFC-12 has a GWP of 10 900. Each of these values is for a period of 100 years; over 500 years the equivalent values are 7.6, 153, 1620, and 5200, respectively.

(∰) SEE WEB LINKS
• United Nations Framework Convention on Climate Change.

globalization Growth to a world-wide scale, the transition from national and regional economies to global economies.

globally rare A *native species that is both a *rare species and one that is found in only one or a few particular places.

globally threatened A *taxon that is threatened on a world-wide scale.

Gloger's rule An *ecogeographical rule, proposed by the German zoologist Constatin Wilhelm Lambert Gloger (1803–59), that the drier the climate, the lighter the colour of animals relative to closely related taxa of more humid regions. Thus, for example, yellows and light browns are dominant in arid regions, and dark browns and blacks in humid regions. This may be a camouflage adaptation, but there are many exceptions. *See also* BERGMANN'S RULE.

glucose A simple sugar that is a major energy source, and is made in plants by *photosynthesis and in animals from the *carbohydrates in food.

glyphosate A *systemic *organophosphate *herbicide that is widely used to control both broadleaved weeds and grasses. It is only mildly toxic to mammals.

GMO *See* GENETICALLY MODIFIED ORGANISM.

GMT *See* GREENWICH MEAN TIME.

gneiss A hard, coarse-grained, banded *metamorphic rock that is composed of *quartz, *feldspar, amphibole, and *mica.

GNP *See* GROSS NATIONAL PRODUCT.

GOES *See* GEOSTATIONARY OPERATIONAL ENVIRONMENTAL SATELLITE.

gold (Au) A bright, yellow, precious, transition element that occurs naturally in rock, is widely mined, and has many uses, including currency, jewellery, printed circuits, and semiconductors.

Gondwana A former supercontinent that was located mainly in the *southern hemisphere. It existed from about 510 million years ago to 180 million years ago and broke apart in the late *Palaeozoic to form what are today Africa, Australia, *Antarctica, South America, the Arabian Peninsula, and India. *See also* LAURASIA.

gonochorism Describing a sexually reproducing species in which individuals are distinctly male or female. *Contrast* HERMAPHRODITE.

gorge 1. A deep *ravine with a river running through it. **2.** A narrow pass between adjacent mountains. *See also* CANYON.

GPS *See* GLOBAL POSITIONING SYSTEM.

graben A *valley or *trough, often of considerable length, that is produced by the lowering of a block between two normal *faults or fault zones. *Contrast* HORST; INTERMONTANE BASIN.

grade 1. The slope of the surface of the Earth. **2.** Organisms that have the same morphological features but are not genetically related. **3.** The size range of *sediment. For example sand grade. **4.** Stream, or river grade is the balance between *erosion and *deposition. **5.** The grade of a mineral ore is a description of its quality. For example high-grade ore.

GLOBAL WARMING

An increase in the *temperature of the *troposphere, which has occurred frequently in the past as a result of natural processes but which many scientists believe is now accelerating as a result of increased *emissions of *greenhouse gases associated with the burning of *fossil fuels. Other scientists point out that although the global mean temperature rose by about 0.5°C between 1976 and 1997, the temperature then ceased to rise, and that the warming may be largely natural. Depending on the scale of the rise, scientists expect global warming to change world *climate in a number of ways. For example, cold seasons are likely to become shorter and warm ones to become longer. Northern latitudes are likely to have wetter autumns and winters, and drier springs and summers. There would be more rainfall in the *tropics, and *subtropical areas could become drier. Global warming is likely to cause shifts in the main *climate zones around the world. Some argue that this will probably bring a rise in the frequency and intensity of *floods, *droughts, *typhoons, *tornadoes, and *hurricanes in many areas, but so far this has not occurred. This would further aggravate the losses and hardships caused by *sea level rise. *IPCC scientists have predicted that if emissions of greenhouse gases continue at present rates, the Earth's temperatures will increase on average by about 2.5°C by the year 2050. Different *scenarios—low, middle, and high—put the likely increase as high as 4.5°C or as low as 1.5°C. This is very much a global average, and regional variations may be much higher than this, particularly in polar and near-polar regions, and other atmospheric scientists maintain that natural negative feedback will most probably restrict the warming to no more than about 1°C. Any rise approaching the higher estimates would far exceed natural temperature changes over the last 8000 years, which have been of the order of 1°C. Since the end of the *Little Ice Age (between about AD 1450 and AD 1850) temperatures have risen by about 0.8°C. Warming by as much as 5.0°C would be greater than the difference between the depth of the last *ice age (about 18 000 years ago) and today. Most experts agree that a rise of between 1°C and 2°C above the average pre-industrial temperature is probably the most the Earth can cope with without massive and widespread environmental damage and disruption. If warming does occur as predicted, it will be relatively rapid. Most computer forecasts are of the order of about 0.3°C per decade, which is three times faster than *ecosystems are believed to be capable of adjusting to. Even reducing emissions of *carbon dioxide today might not be enough to prevent widespread environmental disruption and damage. Recent studies have suggested that the warming is likely to occur more rapidly over land than over the oceans. A further complication is that rises in temperature tend to *lag behind increases in greenhouse gases. It is likely, therefore, that initially the cooler oceans will absorb much of the additional heat, which would serve to decrease the warming of the atmosphere. Only when the oceans reach *equilibrium with the higher level of CO_2 will the full atmospheric warming occur. Global warming can probably best be slowed down by a combination of steps based on two broad *strategies—reducing emissions of greenhouse gases, and enhancing the terrestrial *sinks and stores for greenhouse gases (for example by planting *forests to absorb carbon from the atmosphere). The long-term and global character of the climate change problem requires an international long-term *strategy based on internationally agreed principles such as *sustainable development and the *precautionary principle. The *Kyoto Protocol is designed to reduce overall emissions of greenhouse gases by setting targets and allowing countries to buy, sell, and exchange permits to pollute the atmosphere. *See also* CLIMATE CHANGE; INTERGOVERNMENTAL PANEL ON CLIMATE CHANGE; UNITED NATIONS FRAMEWORK CONVENTION ON CLIMATE CHANGE.

graded A measure of the variation of sizes in *soil or an *unconsolidated *sediment; well-graded materials have many sizes, whereas poorly graded materials are more uniform in size.

graded bedding A layer of *sediment in which the coarsest particles are concentrated at the bottom and particle size decreases upward into fine *silt.

graded stream A stream that maintains an *equilibrium between the processes of *erosion and *deposition, and thus between *aggradation and *degradation.

gradient 1. The *slope of a surface, usually expressed as a percentage. **2.** A variation in one quantity relative to another, such as a vertical temperature gradient (how temperature changes with *elevation).

gradient wind A theoretical *wind that blows parallel to the *isobars at a speed determined by the *pressure gradient force, *Coriolis effect, and *centripetal force.

grading 1. Sorting and evaluation of a natural resource, such as grading fish by size or timber by quality. **2.** Altering a land surface by cutting, filling, and/or smoothing in order to create a desired surface.

gradualism A model of *evolution that assumes slow, steady rates of change, such as *Darwin's concept of evolution by *natural selection. *Contrast* PUNCTUATED EQUILIBRIUM.

graft A transplant; a tissue or organ that is transferred from one individual plant or animal to another, or the process of transferring it.

grain 1. The dry, starchy seed that is produced by *cereal grasses. **2.** The texture of wood, which is determined by the type of *xylem cells that it contains.

gram A metric unit of weight equal to one-thousandth of a kilogram.

Gramineae *See* POACEAE.

graminoid Of *grasses (formerly Gramineae) and grass-like plants, including sedges and rushes (*marsh plants).

grandfathering In *greenhouse gas *emissions allocation, under the *Kyoto Protocol, an approach that allows existing emitters to continue their previous levels of emissions while new sources must meet new standards.

granite A hard, coarse-grained, light-coloured *intrusive *igneous rock containing at least 20% *quartz with alkali *feldspar, *mica, and other minerals, that accounts for nearly 15% of the rocks exposed at the *Earth's surface.

granivore An animal that lives on a diet of grain or seeds.

G-rank *See* GLOBAL RANK.

granular activated carbon treatment A *wastewater filtering system that is used in small water systems and individual homes, which uses *activated carbon to remove organics.

granular snow *See* FIRN.

grass A member of the *Poaceae family of flowering plants, which have long, narrow leaves and stems that are hollow or pithy in cross section.

grass heath *See* ACID GRASSLAND.

grass minimum temperature The lowest temperature recorded at night in open ground by a thermometer whose bulb is exposed over the tips of short grass.

grassland A plant *community dominated by various types of *grass, which is home to herds of *grazing animals. It is common in areas that are too dry during the summer months to support *forest or *shrubland. Temperate grassland vegetation in North America includes *bunchgrass, *California grassland, *desert grassland, *mixed grass, *Palouse prairie, *shortgrass, *sodgrass, and *tallgrass. Temperate grassland in South America is called pampa (plural pampas) and in Eurasia it is called steppe. Tropical grassland in Africa is called *savanna. *See also* RANGELAND.

grassroots Organizations or movements, people or society at a local level rather than at the centre of major political activity. Local, or person-to-person.

grassroots activism A form of *environmental activism that is local and based on *grassroots activities.

grassroots conservation *Conservation activities that are undertaken by individuals and citizen-based groups, usually on a voluntary basis.

graupel *See* SNOW PELLET.

gravel *Unconsolidated *sediment that is composed of particles of between 2 and 75 mm in diameter.

graveyard *See* BURIAL GROUND.

gravitational water *Water that sinks through the *soil by gravity, moves between the soil particles, and fills the pore spaces between them. It must be removed for the soil to reach *field capacity.

gravity The attractive force that acts between bodies and is proportional to their masses multiplied by the acceleration it produces, and that decreases with increasing distance between them.

gravity transfer *See* MASS MOVEMENT.

gravity wind *See* KATABATIC WIND.

gray (Gy) The SI unit for the *absorbed dose of *radiation. It replaced the *rad. 1 Gy = 100 rad.

gray water North American term for *sanitary water.

grazable woodland *See* FOREST RANGE.

graze To feed on vegetation, usually in a *field, *pasture, or *meadow.

grazer A *herbivore. *See also* PRIMARY CONSUMER.

grazing cycle The time elapsed between the beginning of one grazing period and the beginning of the next grazing period in the same paddock where the forage is regularly grazed and rested. One grazing cycle includes one grazing period plus one rest period.

grazing food chain *See* GRAZING PATHWAY.

grazing land Any land that is covered with vegetation and is suitable for *grazing by livestock.

grazing line *See* BROWSE LINE.

grazing pathway (grazing food chain) A *food chain in which the *primary producers (green plants) are eaten by grazing *herbivores, with subsequent energy transfer to various levels of *carnivore, e.g. plant (blackberry, *Rubus*) → herbivore (bank vole, *Clethrionomys glareolus*) → carnivore (tawny owl, *Strix aluco*). *Compare* DETRITAL PATHWAY.

grazing season The period of time during which *grazing can normally be practiced each year.

Great Barrier Reef A chain of *coral reefs nearly 2010 km long in the Coral Sea, off the north-eastern coast of Australia. This unique environment is the world's largest coral reef system, and it appears on the *Unesco World Heritage List. The reef is economically important to the state of Queensland and the country of Australia, because it supports significant tourism and fishing industries. Since the early 1960s the reef has suffered extensive damage, much of it caused by humans through intensive *recreational use, shipping accidents, *runoff from the mainland (which increases *turbidity, reduces *salinity, and introduces some *pollutants), and perhaps from *climate change (via sea level rise, ocean warming, and increased air temperatures), although coral reefs have survived past changes in temperature and grow upwards in response to rising sea level. The Great Barrier Reef Marine Park has been established to preserve the reef in perpetuity, and a comprehensive programme of *water quality management within the park is designed to protect the reef and the industries that depend on it.

Great Basin Desert A North American cold desert produced by the *rain shadow of the Sierra Nevada and Cascade Mountains, which has long, cold winters and much of its *precipitation falls as snow.

Great Conveyor *See* OCEANIC CONVEYOR BELT.

Great Lakes The five connected *lakes along the border of the USA and Canada which make up the world's largest body of *freshwater. They are Lakes Ontario, Erie, Superior, Michigan, and Huron.

Great London Smog Two episodes of unusually severe *smog that occurred in Greater London in December 1952 and December 1962. During the 1952 smog visibility was less than 10 m for 48 consecutive hours, and theatres and cinemas closed because audiences could not see the stage or screen. An estimated 4000 excess deaths resulted from the 1952 smog and 700 from the 1962 smog. The 1952 smog led directly to the 1956 *Clean Air Act and the lower death toll in 1962 was attributed to the implementation of the act.

Great Plains A *prairie region in the western USA that extends from North Dakota south to Texas and from the Rocky Mountains east to western Minnesota and Missouri.

great soil group A broad group of *soils that share common characteristics which are usually associated with particular climates and vegetation types. The concept formed the basis of a soil classification devised in 1949 that divided soils into three orders: *zonal soils, *azonal soils, and *intrazonal soils. The orders were further divided into nine suborders and the suborders into the great soil groups. This classification is no longer used.

greater ecosystem An approach to *conservation in North America which is based on a *core protected area surrounded by a defined region of controlled development or some form of cooperative management. Examples include the Greater Yellowstone Ecosystem, the Greater Fundy Ecosystem, and the Greater Salt Lake Ecosystem.

green *See* ENVIRONMENT-FRIENDLY.

green consumerism Purchasing *environment-friendly products, such as electric or hybrid vehicles, wooden products that don't contain tropical hardwoods obtained from natural forests, and paper that has been recycled.

green design Products and services that have been specifically designed to cause less harm to the environment than those they replace.

green manure Any crop that is grown to be ploughed into the soil, in order to increase soil organic content and improve *soil quality.

Green Party An *environmentalist political party.

green plan An integrated environmental plan that is designed to reduce pollution and resource consumption, achieve *sustainable development, and *increase environmental restoration.

green politics An approach to politics in which environmental issues are given prority.

Green Revolution The informal name for a complex suite of agricultural development programmes devised by the *FAO and introduced in Latin America and Asia from the 1960s, centred on high-yielding hybrid varieties of wheat, rice, and corn (maize), along with an increased use of machines, fertilizer, pesticides, and irrigation. These developments resulted in dramatic increases in agricultural output. *See also* AGRICULTURAL REVOLUTION; INDUSTRIAL REVOLUTION.

((()) SEE WEB LINKS

• International Food Policy Research Institute.

green tax A tax or surcharge that is imposed on activities that pollute, deplete, or degrade the *environment.

greenbelt A *buffer zone that is designed to restrict development from particular areas.

Greenbelt Movement A tree-planting programme in Kenya that was initiated by Wangari *Maathai and the National Council of Women of Kenya (NCWK). It is based on turning small-scale farmers into *agroforesters, with a particular emphasis on training women to plant and cultivate seedlings in order to assist in *reforestation and generate a source of income for themselves.

greenfield Land in rural and urban areas that has not already been developed. *See also* BROWNFIELD.

greenhouse A building with glass walls and roof, in which plants are grown under controlled conditions. *See also* PASSIVE SOLAR HEATING.

greenhouse effect The mechanism in which radiation from the Earth's surface is absorbed and reradiated by *greenhouse gases, thereby warming the lower atmosphere (see Fig. 8). A *black body emits all the radiation it absorbs at a wavelength inversely proportional to its temperature. Consequently, the Earth's surface absorbs short-wave *insolation and emits radiation at a longer wavelength. Greenhouse gas molecules absorb long-wave radiation, immediately reradiating it in all directions. Eventually all of the radiation escapes into space, but while it remains it raises the temperature in the *troposphere 30–40°C above the temperature it would have if the atmosphere were transparent to radiation at all wavelengths. Despite the popular name, air inside a greenhouse warms because it is unable to leave the building, so the mechanism is quite different. The burning of *fossil fuels since the *Industrial Revolution has caused significant increases in atmospheric concentrations of the main *greenhouse gases (*carbon dioxide has risen by nearly 30%, *methane has more than doubled, and *nitrous oxide has risen by about 15%). This has enhanced the natural greenhouse effect and accelerated *global warming, although the extent to which an enhanced greenhouse effect accounts for the rise in global temperatures during the late 20th century is disputed.

greenhouse gas A gas that traps heat in the *atmosphere, by absorbing and immediately re-emitting radiation in wavelengths similar to those emitted by the Earth, which prevents excessive loss of terrestrial radiation and accompanying heat loss, and leads to *global warming. The most important greenhouse gases are *water vapour, *carbon dioxide, *methane, *nitrous oxide, and *CFCs. Others include *methyl chloroform and *carbon tetrachloride.

greenline park *See* NATIONAL PARK.

greenness The amount of living material (*biomass) in vegetation.

Greenpeace An international *non-government organization, founded in 1971 initially to oppose the atmospheric testing of nuclear weapons, that campaigns against whaling,

Fig. 8 Greenhouse effect

environmental pollution, and nuclear power, and for environmental *conservation and the preservation of *endangered species.

greens 1. Leafy plants or their leaves and stems which are eaten as vegetables. **2.** Individuals and political parties that have an environmental agenda.

greenspeak Environmental discourse. The term is most commonly used to describe the use of environmental terms and language by individuals or groups who are intent on portraying themselves and their causes as pro-environmental, even when they are not (*greenwash).

greenwash A term (combining green and whitewash) that *environmentalists use to describe the activity (for example by corporate lobby groups) of giving a positive public image to practices that are environmentally unsound. *See also* GREENSPEAK.

greenway *See* CORRIDOR.

Greenwich Mean Time (GMT, Z) The mean solar time at 0° *longitude that passes through Greenwich, England, and is used as the basis for standard time throughout the world. In 1928 the name was changed to Universal Time (**UT**) to avoid confusion. UT is counted from midnight.

Greenwich Meridian The Prime Meridian, which passes through the original site of the Royal Observatory at Greenwich, England and was adopted in 1884 by a conference of nations as the initial or zero of *longitude. It is the reference for *Greenwich Mean Time, and for all longitude measurements. *See also* INTERNATIONAL DATE LINE.

gregarious Sociable, living in groups or communities. *Contrast* SOLITARY.

greywacke A coarse-grained *sandstone that is *cemented by more than 15% *clay minerals. Fragments are rounded to subrounded.

grike *See* CLINT.

groin *See* GROYNE.

gross domestic product (GDP) The total monetary value of the goods and services that are produced by a country, within that country, over a given year.

gross national product (GNP) The total monetary value of all goods and services that are produced in a nation's economy over a given year. Unlike *gross domestic product, it includes goods and services produced abroad.

gross primary production The total amount or weight of organic matter that is created by *photosynthesis over a defined period of time.

gross primary productivity The total rate of *photosynthetic production of *biomass. *Contrast* NET PRIMARY PRODUCTIVITY.

ground cover Plants that are grown in order to protect the soil from *eroding. *See also* HERBACEOUS LAYER.

ground fire A fire that burns material on the ground such as *litter, grasses, and non-woody plants, and organic matter in the soil, but does not affect trees which have thick bark or high crowns.

ground flora (ground layer) Low plants (such as grasses and herbs) that grow at the lowest level of a plant community, such as on a forest floor.

ground fog (radiation fog) Any *fog that hides less than 60% of the sky.

ground game Rabbits and hares.

ground layer *See* GROUND FLORA.

ground moraine A thick layer of *till that has been deposited by a melting *glacier and often forms gently rolling ground.

ground truth The facts that are found when a location shown on a map, *air photograph, or *satellite image is checked on the ground, as *validation.

ground zero **1.** The point on or above the ground at which a nuclear weapon explodes. **2.** The common name for the site of the World Trade Center in New York after it was destroyed on 11 September 2001.

groundfish (bottom fish, demersal fish) A species or group of fish that lives most of its life on or near the sea bed.

ground-lead logging A method of *cable logging in which timber is dragged from where it is cut to a collecting point by a powered cable at or near ground level. *Contrast* HIGH-LEAD LOGGING.

groundwater Water that occupies pores, cracks, and crevices in *rocks underground, below the *water table. World-wide between about 10% and 30% of river flow is accounted for by groundwater, and groundwater provides about 6% of the water and around 50% of the dissolved sediment that rivers input into seas and oceans. *See also* AQUIFER.

groundwater abstraction The *extraction of *groundwater, pumped from underground *aquifers, as a source of *freshwater. In many aquifers the groundwater has to be pumped out through *boreholes or *wells. As water is abstracted the *water table is lowered around the borehole. If rates of abstraction exceed rates of *groundwater recharge within an aquifer, the water table can fall across a wide area. Borehole yields decline when this happens, and wells begin to dry up. Sometimes it is necessary to sink boreholes deeper into the aquifer, which further lowers the water table. *Groundwater depletion follows, and water supplies are threatened if not reduced.

groundwater contamination *See* GROUNDWATER POLLUTION.

groundwater depletion A decline in the level of the *water table and availability of *groundwater within an *aquifer, often as a result of excessive *groundwater abstraction.

groundwater discharge North American term for *groundwater that enters coastal waters, having been contaminated by *landfill leachates, *hazardous wastes, and *septic tanks.

groundwater flow The movement of *groundwater through openings in *sediment and *rock within the zone of *saturation.

groundwater mining *See* AQUIFER DEPLETION.

groundwater pollution The *pollution of *groundwater, for example by *intrusion of water into coastal *aquifers, or by leakage from *landfill sites or underground long-term storage of high-level *nuclear waste.

groundwater recharge The natural replenishment of *groundwater by the *water cycle, which raises the *water table.

groundwater remediation The treatment of *groundwater in order to remove *pollutants.

groundwater runoff *Groundwater that is discharged into a stream or river channel as spring water or *seepage water.

Group of 7 (G7) Seven of the largest industrialized countries (Canada, France, Germany, Italy, Japan, UK, and USA) whose leaders meet regularly in economic summit meetings.

Group of 8 (G8) A group that has replaced the *Group of 7, by also including the *European Union and Russia (which does not participate in all events). It holds an annual economic and political summit (the G8 Summit), comprising heads of government and international officials.

Group of 10 (G10) The ten most influential environmental *non-government organizations in the USA, which are the Environmental Defense Fund, Wilderness Society, Sierra Club, National Audubon Society, National Parks and Conservation Association, Natural Resources Defense Council, Defenders of Wildlife, Environmental Policy Institute, National Wildlife Federation, and Izaak Walton League of America.

Group of 15 (G15) A group of fifteen *developing countries that meet to discuss issues relating to the *Third World.

Group of 77 (G77) A group of *developing countries that negotiate collectively on some international economic issues and political concerns about climate change and development, which was founded in 1964 under the auspices of the *United Nations Conference on Trade and Development (UNCTAD), with 77 initial members. The group now has 130 members.

group selection 1. A method of tree harvesting in which patches of selected trees are cut in order to create a mosaic of openings in the forest *canopy and to encourage the growth of *uneven-aged stands. **2.** A type of selection that favours behaviour that is advantageous to a population rather than individuals.

grouting Injecting liquid cement or a chemical into the ground, where it sets and subsequently impedes or prevents the flow of water by sealing pore spaces and fractures in the subsurface rock.

grove A small *wood or group of trees that has no *undergrowth. *See also* COPPICE.

growing season (cropping season) The period of the year during which temperature remains high enough to allow plant growth, which is usually between the average date of the last *frost in *spring and the first frost in *autumn. *See also* HARVEST.

grow-out The process of growing a plant in order to produce fresh viable *seed which can be used to evaluate the characteristics of its varieties.

growth band The annual growth pattern found in many organisms, such as snails. In *coral the band is caused by the secretion of *calcium carbonate. One yearly growth band contains two smaller bands, which represent winter growth and summer growth.

growth form The physical appearance and structure of an *organism.

growth rate The percentage rate at which something (such as an organism, population, or economy) is growing per unit time (normally a year). *See also* DOUBLING TIME.

growth retardant A synthetic compound that reduces stem elongation in plants. An important agricultural use is in the prevention of *lodging in cereals. In horticulture retardants are used to produce more compact plants. Some of these compounds inhibit *gibberellin synthesis.

growth ring (annual ring) The layer of wood growth that is formed by a tree during a single growing season, which includes both the *earlywood (which forms in spring) and the *latewood (which forms in autumn).

growth substance A naturally occurring compound, other than a nutrient, which promotes, inhibits, or otherwise modifies the growth of a plant.

groyne (groin) A narrow protective structure that is built out into the sea from the land, in order to restore an eroding beach by intercepting *longshore drift and trapping sand.

guano The accumulated droppings of birds, bats, or seals, found at sites where large colonies of these animals occur. Guano is rich in plant nutrients, especially calcium phosphate (bird guano is richer than bat or seal guano). Such deposits are found particularly on arid oceanic islands and in caves. Guano is worked industrially as a *phosphate resource.

guild A group of species whose members exploit similar resources in a similar manner.

Guinea zone The wettest and most wooded *savanna zone in West Africa in the classic threefold model of savanna vegetation. These are the *Sahel zone, consisting of dry scrub with occasional grasses and patches of bare earth; typical grassy savanna; and the wetter, semi-wooded Guinea zone.

Gulf Stream A narrow, fast-flowing warm ocean *current which forms the North Atlantic *gyre. It starts in the Gulf of Mexico around the Caribbean as the Florida Current, and (driven by the westerly winds and deflected by the *Coriolis effect) flows north-eastwards across the Atlantic and warms the climate of the east coast of the USA. The current divides around the latitude of Spain and part of it flows south as the cool Canary Current, eventually rejoining the Equatorial Current. Part of the current continues to flow towards the north-east, as the North Atlantic Drift, and it brings relatively mild climatic conditions to Britain and north-west Europe.

gully A deep ditch caused by the *erosion of *soil on a *hillslope by running water.

gumbotill Glacial *till that is highly weathered, has a high *clay content, and becomes sticky and *plastic when wet.

Günz The first of four periods of *Pleistocene *glaciation in Europe, named after an alpine river and approximately equivalent to the *Nebraskan in North America.

GURT *See* GENETIC USE RESTRICTION TECHNOLOGY.

gust A sudden, brief increase in wind speed, generally lasting less than 20 seconds.

guyot *See* SEAMOUNT.

GWP *See* GLOBAL WARMING POTENTIAL.

GWPF *See* GLOBAL WARMING POLICY FOUNDATION.

gymnosperm A non-flowering seed plant in which the ovules are carried naked on the cone scales rather than being enclosed in an ovary as in *angiosperms.

gypcrete A soil profile rich in *gypsum ($CaSO_4$) that is developed in arid regions. Gypcretes are formed by the precipitation of gypsum from saline waters drawn to the surface by *capillary action.

gypsisols Soils that have, within 100 cm of the surface, a *soil horizon more than 150 mm thick in which gypsum ($CaSO_4$) has accumulated so it contains at least 5% more gypsum than the underlying horizon, or more than 15% gypsum below 100 cm. Gypsisols are a reference soil group in the *World Soil Classification.

gypsum An *evaporite mineral, calcium sulphate ($CaSO_4 \cdot 2H_2O$), that is formed by the *evaporation of saltwater, and is used in making plasters and cements.

gypsy moth A European moth (*Lymantria dispar*) that was introduced into North America in 1869 and is a serious *defoliating *pest of *hardwood shade trees.

gyre A permanent large-scale circulation cell of water in the open *ocean, which is driven by prevailing *winds and the *Coriolis effect.

gyttja *Freshwater *anaerobic mud that contains abundant *organic matter.

Haber-Bosch process An industrial process for synthesizing ammonia (NH_3) from atmospheric nitrogen (N) and hydrogen (H) from a *hydrocarbon source by passing the gases at high temperature and pressure through a bed containing a *catalyst. The gases combine: $N_2 + 3H_2 \rightarrow 2NH_3$. The process was developed in Germany during the 1914–18 war, under the pressure of an acute ammonia shortage, by Fritz Haber (1868–1934), for which he received the 1918 Nobel Prize for Chemistry; it was adapted for industrial application by Karl Bosch (1874–1940).

habit The typical form or shape of a *plant, e.g. creeping plants, trees, shrubs, and vines.

habitat The place or set of environmental conditions (*abiotic and *biotic) in which a *plant or *animal normally lives. Areas within a habitat that are occupied by a particular species or community are described as *microhabitats.

habitat action plan (habitat conservation plan) A *management plan that defines objectives and targets for the maintenance or enhancement of a particular habitat, and the actions that are regarded as necessary to achieve them.

habitat connectivity The network of *corridors that links isolated *patches of *habitat, which allows organisms to move through an area. *See also* FRAGMENTATION.

habitat conservation plan *See* HABITAT ACTION PLAN.

habitat enhancement Any managed change to a *habitat that improves its value and increases its ability to meet the particular needs of one or more *species.

habitat fragmentation The break-up of a large *habitat into a number of separate, smaller remnants, for example because of *land use change. *See also* CORRIDOR.

habitat indicator Any physical attribute of the environment (such as soil *pH or the *salinity of a water body) that can be measured to characterize the conditions necessary to support an *organism, *population, or *community in the absence of *pollutants.

habitat loss The disappearance or conversion of natural *habitat, often as a result of human actions.

habitat patch An area of *habitat that differs from the surrounding area, and meets particular needs for particular *organisms.

habitat restoration Restoring a *habitat to its original *community structure, by removing *exotic species and/or reintroducing *native species. *See also* ACTIVE RESTORATION; NATURAL PROCESS RESTORATION.

habitat type An area of land that is capable of supporting a particular *climax plant *association.

Habitats Directive A major initiative of the *European Union that is designed to protect *biodiversity through the conservation of natural *habitats and *wild plants and animals, and the creation of a network of protected areas across the EU to be known as *Natura 2000 sites.

haboob A *dust storm or *sandstorm in southern Sudan that is caused by cold *downdrafts from a *thunderstorm which turbulently lift dust and sand into the air. Haboobs occur most often late in the day in summer.

hadal zone The deepest part of the *ocean, at depths greater than the *abyssal zone or more than six kilometres, which includes the lower levels of *ocean trenches.

Hadean The oldest eon of geological time, extending from the origin of the Earth about 4.567 billion years ago until the date of the oldest known rocks, about 3.8 billion years ago (the start of the *Archaean). There are no rocks on Earth this old.

• The Hadean eon of Precambrian time.

Hadley cell One of the most fundamental divisions of the global wind circulation, comprising the net ascent of air by convection over equatorial latitudes, the compensatory downward motion in the subtropical *anticyclone belt, and the resulting *trade winds which blow towards the meteorological equator (the *intertropical convergence zone). It is named after the English meteorologist George Hadley (1685–1768), who in 1735, seeking to account for the trade winds, proposed a single, large-scale convective cell representing a thermally driven, low-latitude atmospheric circulation.

haemoglobin A protein found in the red blood cells of mammals and other animals that carries *oxygen round the body.

hail Solid *precipitation that falls as ice particles from *cumulonimbus clouds. Individual particles are called hailstones, and the storm is called a hailstorm.

Haines index See LOWER ATMOSPHERE STABILITY INDEX.

half-life **1.** The time required for half of the *atoms of a *radionuclide to decay, which is specific to each nuclide. *Radon-222 has a very short half-life of 3.82 days, compared with radium-226 (half-life of 1622 years) or *thorium-232 (half-life of 14 million years), so radon gas disappears very quickly. **2.** The time required for a *pollutant to decrease in concentration by half. For example, the half-life of *DDT in the *environment is 15 years. **3. (biological half-life)** The time required for the elimination of half a total *dose of a substance from a body.

half-tide level See MEAN TIDE LEVEL.

haline Pertaining to chloride. See also SALINE.

halite See ROCK SALT.

halo A circle of white light around the Sun or Moon, subtending an angle of 22° or, less commonly, 46° to the observer, that is caused by the *refraction or *reflection of light by the ice crystals in *cirrostratus clouds.

halocarbon A compound that contains *carbon and at least one *halogen, and sometimes *hydrogen. *Chlorofluorocarbons (CFCs) are halocarbons.

halocline A layer in a body of water at which *salinity and thus *density change sharply.

halogen Any of a group of five chemically related, non-metallic elements (*bromine, *fluorine, *chlorine, *iodine, and astatine) that can combine with metals to form salts or substitute for *hydrogen in many *organic compounds.

halogenated A compound in which a *halogen atom has been introduced, via a chemical reaction.

halomorphic soil A *soil that contains a significant proportion of soluble salts.

halon A synthetic *halogenated *hydrocarbon compound that consists of *bromine and other *halogens (which could include *fluorine and/or *chlorine). It is used as a fire extinguishing agent, and persists in the atmosphere for a long time. Halons are much more effective in terms of *ozone destruction than *CFCs. See also OZONE DEPLETION POTENTIAL.

halophile An *extremophile that is adapted to live in extremely saline environments.

halophyte A plant that is adapted to grow in salty soil and air.

halving time See DOUBLING TIME.

hamlet A *rural settlement that is smaller than a *village and contains a few houses.

hammada A surface of stones (pebbles, gravel, or boulders) on a *desert, that is formed by the washing or blowing away of the finer material.

hand-lining (jigging) A traditional method of *fishing, using a line with many hooks which is held down in the water with a weight and pulled up by hand or with pulleys.

Hanford Nuclear Reservation The site of a nuclear facility in south-central Washington, USA which was established in 1943 (during World War II) as part of the Manhattan Project, to provide the *plutonium necessary for the development of nuclear weapons.

hanging valley A former *glacial *tributary valley that enters a larger glacial valley above the floor of the larger valley, high up on the valley wall (see Fig. 9). Waterfalls (such as Bridal Veil Falls in Yosemite) are common features of hanging valleys.

HAP See HAZARDOUS AIR POLLUTANT.

haploid The number of *chromosomes in a *gamete (*n*). In sexual reproduction body cells

Fig. 9 Hanging valley

acquire chromosomes from both parents, so the *nucleus of each body cell contains two sets of chromosomes and is diploid (2*n*). In the course of their life cycles, all plants and many *fungi alternate between the haploid and diploid (often polyploidy) condition; this is known as the alternation of generations.

hard energy path An approach to *economic development that relies on conventional sources of *energy, including *fossil fuels and *nuclear energy, which create environmental problems including *pollution and *waste management. *Contrast* SOFT ENERGY PATH.

hard freeze A *freeze in which vegetation is killed and the ground surface is frozen solid.

hard mast The fruit or nuts of trees such as oak, beech, and walnut.

hard water *Alkaline water that contains dissolved mineral salts (particularly calcium and magnesium *bicarbonates), which reduces the cleansing power of soap and produces *limescale in hot water appliances. Dissolved calcium and magnesium sulphate or chloride causes permanent hardness; bicarbonate causes temporary hardness. *See also* ION EXCHANGE TREATMENT.

hardboard A board-like building material that is made from wood fibre.

hardness 1. A measure of the amount of dissolved salts (particularly *calcium carbonate) in *alkaline water. *See* HARD WATER. **2.** The degree of resistance of a *mineral to scratching, which is usually measured on the *Mohs's hardness scale.

hardpan A hard, relatively impervious, layer of soil in the lower *A-horizon or in the *B-horizon. It is difficult for plant roots to penetrate and is caused by cementation of soil particles with *organic matter or with materials such as *clay or *calcium carbonate. *See also* IMPEDED DRAINAGE; INDURATED; IRON PAN; PAN.

hardwood The wood of *angiosperm trees. The use of the term is entirely arbitrary; balsa wood is a hardwood, while wood from paraña pine, which is used to make staircases and furniture, is a softwood because the tree is a *gymnosperm.

harmattan A dry *desert wind that blows southwards from the *Sahara across West Africa between November and March. It blows only during the day.

harpoon A spear with a barbed point and a strong line attached to it, which is used for catching large fish (such as giant tuna and swordfish) or whales.

harrow Farm equipment that is used to break up clumps of *soil on heavy ground. There are many types of harrow. Most comprise a rigid frame holding tines mounted vertically which is dragged over the ground. Others utilize rows of sharp-edged wheels (discs) mounted on bars that cut into the ground.

harrowing A technique that breaks up the *soil in preparation for planting. Harrowing with a disc harrow is sometimes called discing.

harvest 1. The act of gathering a ripened *crop. **2.** The season in which a crop is gathered. *See also* CROPPING SEASON. **3.** The yield from plants in a single growing season. *See also* CROP YIELD.

harvest cut The removal of mature trees from a *forest. *Contrast* INTERMEDIATE CUT.

harvesting The gathering of a ripened *crop or the felling and removal of trees.

haustellate Relating to the mouthparts of an insect that are modified for sucking.

Hawaiian floral region Part of R. Good's *Polynesian floral subkingdom (*The Geography of the Flowering Plants*, 1974), which falls within his *Palaeotropical floral kingdom. This is the most isolated floral region, which accounts for its great distinctiveness. About 20% of the genera and over 90% of the *species are *endemic. No valuable economic or horticultural plants belong to this region.

hay Grass that has been mowed and dried for use as *fodder.

hay meadow A *field of *grass which is cut two or three times in the summer to produce a crop of *hay for feeding to *livestock.

hazard A source of danger or disruption. *See also* NATURAL HAZARD.

hazard assessment (hazards analysis, hazard evaluation) The analysis and evaluation of the physical, chemical, and biological properties of a particular hazard. The term, as used in North America, is usually applied to human exposure to particular *agents such as *toxic substances.

hazard evaluation *See* HAZARD ASSESSMENT.

hazard identification The process of determining whether exposure to a particular *agent might affect human health.

hazard index The sum of all *hazard quotients for a specific pathway or *scenario, which takes into account the presence of multiple substances at one site, or exposures to the same chemicals through multiple media and pathways.

hazard mapping The process of establishing where and to what extent particular *hazards are likely to pose a threat to people, property, and the environment.

hazard quotient A measure of the health risk of exposure to a particular *toxic material, expressed as the ratio between average daily *dose and a reference dose defined from *toxicity tests.

Hazard Ranking System (HRS) A method used in the USA by the *Environmental Protection Agency for evaluating potential relative risks to public health and the environment from abandoned or uncontrolled *hazardous waste sites. The scale runs from 0 to 100; if a site scores 28.5 or more it is placed on the *National Priorities List. *See also* NATIONAL OIL AND HAZARDOUS SUBSTANCES CONTINGENCY PLAN; SITE INSPECTION.

hazardous air pollutant (HAP) Any *air pollutant that in the USA is not covered by *ambient air quality standards but which (as defined in the *Clean Air Act) may reasonably be expected to cause or contribute to irreversible illness or death. Examples include *asbestos, *mercury, *radionuclides, and vinyl chloride.

hazardous chemical Any chemical whose presence or use is a physical hazard or a health hazard. Examples include *flammables, explosives, and *acids.

hazardous material *See* HAZARDOUS SUB-STANCE.

hazardous substance (hazardous materi-al) Any substance that, because of its quantity, concentration, or physical, chemical, or infectious characteristics, has the potential to cause a physical or health hazard.

hazardous waste *Waste material that is reactive, *toxic, *corrosive, or otherwise poses a hazard to human health and the *environment. *Contrast* TOXIC WASTE.

hazardous waste landfill A *landfill site in which *hazardous waste is deposited and covered.

hazardous waste minimization Reducing the amount of *hazardous waste that is produced by a facility, via *source reduction or environmentally-sound *recycling.

hazards analysis *See* HAZARD ASSESSMENT.

haze A reduction in *visibility, but not to less than 2 km, that is caused by the absorption and scattering of sunlight by particles of *dust and other *aerosols.

HCFC *See* HYDROCHLOROFLUOROCARBON.

HDGCP *See* HUMAN DIMENSION OF GLOBAL CHANGE PROGRAMME.

head 1. (headwater) The source of water from which a *stream arises. **2.** The elevation of a water surface above a particular point, such as the height of water in a *reservoir above the turbine that is used for generating *hydroelectricity. **3.** Unsorted angular rock debris.

headcut *See* KNICK-POINT.

headland 1. A rocky *promontory that sticks out into the sea. **2.** A strip of unploughed land at the end of a set of *furrows or along a fence.

headwall A steep slope at the head of a *valley, such as the rock cliff at the back of a *cirque.

headwater *See* HEAD.

health A state of complete physical, mental, and social well-being and not merely the absence of *disease or infirmity.

health assessment The process of collecting, analysing, and disseminating information on health status and health risks, which is used in prioritizing and managing public health problems.

health hazard A *chemical, a mixture of chemicals, or a *pathogen for which there is statistically significant evidence that *acute or *chronic effects may occur in any people who are exposed to it.

Healthy Forest Initiative (2003) An initiative from US President George Bush that is designed to improve regulatory processes to reduce the risk of catastrophic *wildfires and restore forest health.

Heartland Institute A US non-profit *think-tank that was founded in Chicago, Illinois in 1984 and whose mission is to help build social movements in support of ideas that empower people. Such ideas include *market-based approaches to environmental protection, privatization of public services, and deregulation in areas where property rights and markets do a better job than government bureaucracies.

(⊕) SEE WEB LINKS

• The Heartland Institute home page.

heartwood The wood in the centre of a tree that is composed of non-living cells and is usually darker than the *sapwood.

heat A form of *energy that is transferred from one body to another body at a lower *temperature (i.e. possessing lower *kinetic energy) by *conduction, *convection, and *radiation.

heat capacity (thermal capacity) The amount of heat energy that is required to raise the temperature of a substance, usually expressed in *Joules per *Kelvin ($J K^{-1}$). It is measured in respect of a unit mass of the substance, when it is known as the specific heat capacity, or to a unit amount of the substance, when it is known as the molar heat capacity. *See also* BRITISH THERMAL UNIT; CALORIE; SPECIFIC HEAT.

heat engine Any *engine that makes use of *heat to do mechanical work.

heat exchanger A device for transferring heat from one fluid to another, e.g. a coiled pipe carrying hot water through a tank of cooler water to warm one, cool the other, or both.

heat exhaustion A mild form of *heat stroke that causes faintness, dizziness, and heavy sweating in humans.

heat flux (thermal flux) The amount of *heat that is transferred across a surface of given area in a given amount of time.

heat index (HI) The apparent *temperature that is created by the combined effect of high air temperatures and high *humidity levels.

heat island *See* URBAN HEAT ISLAND.

heat of transformation *See* LATENT HEAT.

heat recovery 1. The transfer of heat from a substance that has been heated during an industrial process to a substance that is about to be treated, thereby reducing the amount of energy required. **2.** The use of waste heat for another purpose, e.g. using hot water from power generation to provide district heating.

heat stroke A condition that results from excessive exposure to intense *heat, causing high fever, collapse, and sometimes convulsions or coma in humans. It can be fatal.

heat wave A continuous period, usually lasting several days or weeks, of unusually hot weather.

heath A plant *community that is dominated by low-growing shrubs with woody stems and narrow leaves (members of the *Ericaceae or *heather family), which often grow on acidic or upland soils.

heath forest A distinctive kind of tropical *rainforest, with *sclerophyllous, microphyllous leaves, found in south-eastern Asia, South America, and on a small area of the coast of Gabon, central Africa.

heather A low shrub (*Erica* species) with small evergreen leaves and clusters of pink flowers, which was traditionally used in Britain to make brooms, thatch, and bedding, and for heating ovens. There are 665 species, of which 520 are *endemic to the Southern Cape, South Africa. Ling (*Calluna vulgaris*) is very similar.

heathland A lowland community dominated by *heather and *heath growing on *acidic, nutrient-poor, sandy soils.

heavy metal A *metallic element that has a high atomic weight, is often *toxic, and tends to accumulate in the *food chain. Examples include *cadmium, *chromium, *lead, and *mercury. *See also* BIOACCUMULATION.

heavy water *Deuterium oxide (D_2O), water in which *hydrogen is replaced by deuterium, which is used as a *moderator in some *nuclear reactors.

heavy water reactor A nuclear *fission reactor that uses *heavy water to *moderate the fission reaction.

heavy-metal tolerance A biochemical and physiological adaptation to heavy metals (i.e. metals, e.g. copper and zinc, that have a density greater than 5 g cm^{-3}) shown by plant *species or *genotypes: such plants may therefore be found growing successfully on soils contaminated by metals, where other species or genotypes would fail. Many common grasses (e.g. *Agrostis tenuis* and *Festuca ovina*) have developed strains that are naturally tolerant of heavy metals on soils derived from geological strata rich in heavy metals. Seeds from these genotypes are used commercially in revegetating spoil contaminated by metals.

hectare A unit of area that is equal to 10000 m^2 or 2.47 acres.

hedge A living fence that is created by a row of closely planted shrubs or bushes.

hedgerow A *hedge or barrier of bushes, shrubs, or small trees that are growing close together in a line, which creates a natural growing fence and provides *cover and a *corridor for *wildlife. *See also* LIVE FENCE.

hedonic pricing A method of *economic evaluation, based on the premise that the price of a good is partly determined by its characteristics or the services it provides. The approach seeks to value the individual characteristics of that good by studying how the price people are willing to pay for it changes when the characteristics change. It is widely used to explain variations in house prices in terms of variations in environmental quality (such as air pollution, water pollution, or noise) and environmental amenities (such as attractive views or access to recreational sites). *See also* TRAVEL COST METHOD.

heliosis *See* SOLARIZATION.

helitanker A helicopter equipped with a tank for transporting fire suppressants or retardants and that drops them on to *wildfires.

helium A natural, inert gas that is colourless, non-toxic, non-combustible, and lighter than air. It is the second lightest and second most abundant element. Roughly 25% of the Sun is helium, but it accounts for only 0.0005% of the Earth's *atmosphere. *See also* HIGH TEMPERATURE GAS-COOLED REACTOR.

hemimetabolism Incomplete or partial *metamorphosis in insects. *Contrast* HOLOMETABOLISM.

hemipelagic sediment A deep-sea *sediment that accumulates near the *continental margin, and is composed of material that comes from both land and sea.

hemisphere Half of the *Earth, defined either in terms of north and south of the *equator, or east and west of the *Greenwich Meridian.

HEP *See* HUMAN EXCEPTIONALISM PARADIGM; HYDROELECTRIC POWER.

heptachlor An *organochlorine insecticide that was used in the 1960s and 1970s domestically to kill termites and agriculturally to protect crops, especially maize (corn). On exposure to oxygen heptachlor changes to heptachlor epoxide, which is persistent and toxic. Heptachlor is no longer manufactured or used.

herb Any small, non-woody *vascular plant, such as *grass or *forbs, in which the aerial parts die back at the end of each season.

herbaceous Applied to non-woody vegetation that dies back each season.

herbaceous layer (ground cover) The vegetation in the *understorey in a *forest that consists mainly of non-woody plants.

herbage The edible *biomass of *herbaceous plants, on which grazing animals feed.

herbarium 1. A collection of dried, pressed, or preserved plant specimens (leaves, flowers, seeds, and stems). **2.** The kitchen garden of an abbey or monastery.

herbicide A chemical *pesticide that is used to control or kill specific unwanted plants, particularly *weeds. *See also* CONTACT HERBICIDE; SYSTEMIC HERBICIDE.

herbivore An *organism that eats only *plants. *Granivores and *frugivores are special types of herbivores. *See also* PRIMARY CONSUMER.

herd 1. A group of *domesticated mammals (such as cattle or sheep) that are kept together and looked after by humans. **2.** A group of wild animals of one species that remain together in a *colony, such as antelope, elephants, seals, or whales.

heredity The passing on of characteristics from one generation to another, which in organisms takes place via *genes. *See also* INHERIT.

heritability 1. A measure of the extent to which a phenotype is influenced genetically and can be modified by *natural selection. **2.** The fraction of the total variance in a phenotype that remains once variance due to environmental effects is excluded.

heritable Something which can be *inherited.

heritage 1. Anything that is *inherited from an ancestor. **2.** The overall natural and cultural inheritance of a country, including important natural or archaeological sites, historic buildings, customs, and traditions.

Heritage Foundation A US non-profit *think-tank that was established in 1973 and whose mission is to promote conservative public policies based on the principles of free enterprise, limited government, individual freedom, traditional American values, and a strong national defence.

hermaphrodite An individual that possesses both male and female sex organs. *See also* ANDROGENY.

hermatypic Applied to a *reef-building *coral that contains *zooxanthellae.

herpetofauna *Reptiles (such as snakes, turtles, and lizards) and *amphibians (such as frogs, toads, and salamanders).

herpetology The study of *reptiles and *amphibians.

hertz (Hz) An *SI measure of frequency (number of cycles per second).

heterogeneity Variety or diversity, lack of uniformity; the variety of qualities found in an environment (*habitat patches) or a population (*genotypic variation). *Contrast* HOMOGENEITY.

heterogeneous Varied, not uniform. *Contrast* HOMOGENEOUS.

heterotroph (consumer) An *organism that is unable to synthesize organic compounds from simple chemical compounds and therefore feeds upon other living or dead *organisms. There are three types of heterotroph: *saprophytes, *parasites, and *holozoic organisms. *Contrast* AUTOTROPH.

heterozygosity A measure of the genetic variation in an individual or population.

heterozygous Applied to an organism or cell that has different *alleles (forms) of a particular *gene at a particular *locus.

HFC *See* HYDROFLUOROCARBON.

HI *See* HEAT INDEX.

hibernacula Secure places (such as *caves or *dens) where animals *hibernate during the winter in order to conserve energy.

hibernation A long-term, deep sleep during which some animals' heartbeat and respiration rates slow down to allow them to survive the winter cold period when there is little food available.

hide 1. The skin of a large, mature *animal. **2.** A hut or tent that allows observers of *wildlife to conceal themselves.

hierarchy A series of ordered groupings of things within a system.

high *See* ANTICYCLONE.

high forest *Woodland that is managed to allow the majority of trees to reach maturity. *Contrast* COPPICE.

high latitude Towards the *poles, away from the *equator. *Contrast* LOW LATITUDE.

high occupancy vehicle (HOV) A passenger vehicle that carries more than a specified minimum number of passengers, such as a bus or a car used within a carpool. *Contrast* LOW OCCUPANCY VEHICLE.

high risk community A community of people which is located close to numerous potential environmental and health hazards, which may result in high levels of *exposure to *contaminants or *pollutants.

high sea General term for international areas of the *oceans that lie beyond the legal control of any nation. Similar to *open sea.

high sulphur coal *See* NON-COMPLIANCE COAL.

high temperature gas-cooled reactor (HTGCR) A nuclear *fission reactor that uses *helium gas to transfer heat from the *core to a steam generator, and that operates at about 1000°C. It uses enriched *uranium fuel made into particles coated in carbon and silicon dioxide, and graphite as a *moderator.

high tide *High water. The highest level to which the *tide rises within the daily tidal cycle. *Contrast* LOW TIDE.

high water The maximum height or stage that is reached by rising water, such as a rising *tide at the *coast or a *flood in a *river.

high water mark The line along the coast to which the sea rises at *high tide. *Contrast* LOW WATER MARK.

high wind Sustained *winds of 64 km/h or greater which last for an hour or more, and/or *gusts of greater than 93 km/h.

high yield variety A variety of *crop plant that produces a high *yield relative to other varieties. *See also* GREEN REVOLUTION.

high-density planting Closely planted *crops or *trees.

high-grading A method of *harvesting *natural resources that removes the biggest and best of a species (e.g. of trees in a forest, or fish in the sea) and ignores the rest.

highland *See* UPLAND.

high-lead logging A method of *cable logging in which timber is dragged from where it is cut to a collecting point by a powered cable above ground level. *Contrast* GROUND-LEAD LOGGING.

high-level waste The longest-lasting and most dangerous of all the *radioactive waste produced by the nuclear industry, which contains highly *radioactive, short-lived *fission products, *hazardous chemicals, and *toxic *heavy metals. *Contrast* LOW-LEVEL WASTE; INTERMEDIATE-LEVEL WASTE.

high-level waste facility A *facility that is designed to handle the safe disposal of spent *nuclear fuel, high-level *radioactive waste, and *plutonium waste.

high-level waste repository A place where highly *radioactive wastes can be buried and stored safely for tens of thousands of years, unexposed to *groundwater and *earthquakes. *See also* YUCCA MOUNTAIN.

hill A local, well-defined elevated area of land with a rounded top, smaller than a *mountain. *See also* HILLSLOPE.

hill farming *Farming in an *upland environment, where the land is sloping, *fields are often relatively small, *soil erosion is a common problem, and *yield is often relatively low because of harsh *climate and poor *soils.

hill prairie A type of dry *prairie that is found in well-drained sites at the tops of hills, bluffs, and ridges, and on steep slopes.

hillside *See* HILLSLOPE.

hillslope (hillside) The side or slope of a *hill. *See also* COLLUVIUM.

hinterland The area that is *tributary to a place and linked to it by economic activities.

HIS *See* INTERNATIONAL HUMAN SUFFERING INDEX.

historic 1. Related to the known or recorded past, in times of written history. *See also* PRE-HISTORIC. **2.** Important or famous in history.

Historic District A land *zoning category in the USA that applies to an area in which the buildings have particular *historic, architectural, or cultural significance.

historic ecosystem The natural *ecosystem that currently exists or is known to have existed in the past, which guides *restoration activities.

historic land *See* FRAGILE OR HISTORIC LANDS.

historic range The *natural range or geographical areas that a particular *species was known or believed to occupy in the past.

historic range of variability *See* RANGE OF VARIABILITY.

history The study of past events within the *historic period.

histosols An order of wet, organic soils found in *bogs, *swamps, and *wetlands, which contains a large amount (usually more than 30%) of *organic material. They are a reference soil group in the *World Soil Classification.

HNS Protocol *See* PROTOCOL ON PREPAREDNESS, RESPONSE AND CO-OPERATION TO POLLUTION INCIDENTS BY HAZARDOUS AND NOXIOUS SUBSTANCES (2000).

hoar (white frost) *Frost that consists of a thin layer of needle-like soft ice crystals on vegetation, the ground, or other exposed surfaces. It forms by direct *deposition on to surfaces at temperatures below *freezing.

hobby farming *See* AMENITY HORTICULTURE.

hockey stick A graph published in *Nature* on 23 April 1998 (Mann, M. E., Bradley, R. S., and Hughes, M. K., 'Global-scale temperature patterns and climate forcing over the past six centuries,' *Nature*, 1998; 392: 779–87) that showed global temperatures fluctuating but with no overall rise or fall from 1400 until the 20th century, when they rise sharply, the complete curve resembling an ice-hockey stick. The graph purported to show temperatures rising at an unprecedented rate during the latter part of the 20th century and was used widely by the *Intergovernmental Panel on Climate Change as evidence of *anthropogenic global warming. Critics subsequently exposed flaws in the methods used to construct the graph and comprehensively discredited it. *See* THE HOCKEY STICK ILLUSION.

Hockey Stick Illusion, The A book by A. W. Montford (Stacey International, London, 2010), subtitled *Climategate and the Corruption of Science*, that describes the work of those who exposed the errors in the data and statistical methods behind the *hockey stick graph, thereby discrediting it, and also the significance of *'Climategate'.

hogback A narrow ridge of *hills. *See also* ESCARPMENT.

Holarctica A biogeographic region, embracing what are now North America, Europe, and Asia, that was once unified as *Laurasia. The legacy of this region is attested to by the great floral and faunal similarities between the three northern continents.

holding pond A *pond or *reservoir that is usually made of soil or sediment, and is designed to store *polluted *runoff.

holding tank A container where *wastewater is stored before it is removed for treatment or disposal.

holding time The maximum amount of time that a sample (for example, of soil or polluted water) can be stored before analysis.

holism The idea that the whole is greater than the sum of the parts, so that studying a whole *system and its interrelationships is better than studying isolated parts of it. *Contrast* REDUCTIONISM.

holistic An explanation that attempts to explain complex phenomena in terms of the properties of the *system as a whole. *See also* HOLISM.

holistic management A *holistic approach to the management of natural resources, that takes into account interrelationships between people, the environment, and *ecosystems.

Holocene The *post-glacial epoch. The most recent phase of geological time within the *Quaternary, which began 10000 years ago, after the end of the *Pleistocene ice age when glaciers retreated and sea level rose because of a warmer global climate. Climatic change in the northern hemisphere through the Holocene includes the *Climatic Optimum, the *Medieval Warm Period, and the *Little Ice Age.

holocoen *See* ECOSYSTEM.

holometabolism Complete *metamorphosis in insects. *Contrast* HEMIMETABOLISM.

holoplankton *Zooplankton organisms that remain planktonic throughout the whole of their life cycles. *Compare* MEROPLANKTON.

holozoic organism A *heterotrophic *organism that ingests complex organic matter, and can absorb large particles of undissolved food and soluble compounds. All animals (including humans) are holozoic.

home range An area in which an *animal normally lives, and where it obtains its food. Depending on the species, the boundaries may be marked by scent or defended. *Contrast* TERRITORY.

homeland The country in which someone was born.

homeostasis The process of self-regulation which maintains *steady state within *environmental systems through *adjustment and *feedback.

homeotherm A *warm-blooded organism (such as a bird or mammal) that regulates its body temperature independently of changes in the temperature of its environment. *Contrast* ECTOTHERM; POIKILOTHERM. *See also* ENDOTHERM.

homestead The home and adjacent land that is occupied by a family.

hominid A primate of the family *Hominidae, which includes *Homo sapiens as well as extinct human ancestors.

Hominidae The *Primate family that includes modern humans and their extinct immediate ancestors as well as, in some interpretations, bonobos, chimpanzees, gorillas, and perhaps orang-utans.

Homo erectus (**Homo ergaster**) A species of *hominid that lived between 1.89 million and 143000 years ago, stood upright, had a brain slightly smaller than that of modern humans, and was the first *Homo species to migrate beyond Africa. It was the first human to possess body proportions similar to those of modern humans.

(((●))) **SEE WEB LINKS**
• What does it mean to be human?

Homo ergaster *See* HOMO ERECTUS.

Homo habilis A species of *hominid that lived in Eastern and Southern Africa between 2.4 and 1.4 million years ago. *Homo habilis* was once believed to be the first hominid to make and use tools; its name means 'handy man'. Tools predating *Homo* have since been discovered.

(((●))) **SEE WEB LINKS**
• What does it mean to be human?

Homo neanderthalensis A species of *hominid that lived between 20000 and 28000 years ago (the Middle *Palaeolithic) in Europe, southwestern, and Central Asia. Once thought to be a geographical variant of *Homo sapiens* it is now recognized as a distinct species.

(((●))) **SEE WEB LINKS**
• What does it mean to be human?

Homo sapiens Modern humans, who appeared in the fossil record about 200000 years ago.

homocentric A view of nature that considers only human, rather than plant or animal, needs. *Contrast* ECOCENTRIC. *See also* ANTHROPOCENTRIC.

homochromy Induced colour change in an organism based on perception of the background against which they are cultured.

homogeneity Uniformity. *Contrast* HETEROGENEITY.

homogeneous Uniform. *Contrast* HETEROGENEOUS.

homosphere The lower part of the *Earth's *atmosphere in which the chemical composition is *homogeneous, consisting of the *troposphere, *stratosphere, and *mesosphere.

Hooke's law The physical principle that the *stress within a solid is proportional to the *strain, so that the movement of an object is proportional to the pressure that is applied to it.

hoop-net A device used in small-scale *fishing, comprising a net that is suspended from a hoop on a pole.

horizon 1. The line where the visible edge of the Earth's surface meets the sky. 2. A surface that separates two adjacent *beds in *sedimentary rocks. 3. *See* SOIL HORIZON.

hormesis The benefit to health or stimulus to growth or reproduction which results from exposure to small doses of substances that are toxic in larger doses.

hormone A chemical substance that is produced in the body by an *endocrine gland, is carried around the body in the bloodstream, and regulates the activity of other organs or cells in particular ways.

hormone disruptor *See* ENDOCRINE DISRUPTOR.

horn 1. A sharp-edged mountain peak (such as the Matterhorn) that is formed by *glacial erosion when *cirques erode simultaneously on more than two sides of a mountain. *See also* ARÊTE. 2. A pointed projection from the head of an animal. In mammals it consists of a bone core covered in fibrous proteins including keratin.

horse latitudes The subtropical region at latitudes 30° to 35° in both hemispheres, where winds are mainly light and variable. Sailing ships could become becalmed there and when water supplies ran low horses carried as cargo sometimes died and were thrown overboard.

horst An upthrown block of the Earth's *crust that is bounded by steep-angled *faults and has been uplifted by *tectonic forces. If it is separated from other high ground by basins or troughs it is known as a fault-block mountain.

horticulture The cultivation of plants, particularly fruit, flowers, ornamental plants and vegetables, usually for sale, either in *gardens and *smallholdings or on general farms.

host An animal or plant that supports a *parasite, although the host does not benefit and is often harmed by the association.

host country The country where the reduction, avoidance, or *sequestration of *greenhouse gas *emissions takes place.

host preference The extent to which a *herbivore feeds on a host plant when it is offered a choice of host plants, either simultaneously or sequentially.

hot air In the context of *climate change negotiations, a broad term for reductions in *greenhouse gas emissions (for example, in the former Soviet Union) that are caused by economic crisis rather than intentional efforts to reduce emissions.

hot desert A *desert (such as the *Sahara in North Africa) that is located between about 20° and 30° north and south of the *equator, where temperatures can be very high. Desert surfaces heat up rapidly during the day (daytime temperatures of up to 55°C in the shade are not uncommon) and lose heat rapidly at night by radiation back to the overlying air. Night-time temperatures can fall close to freezing. Hot *deserts make up about 20% of the Earth's land surface in two subtropical belts. These are bordered by *semi-arid belts. Together they form a third of the Earth's land area and are home to nearly 1000 million people. *Contrast* COLD DESERT.

hot dry rock system An approach to the exploitation of *geothermal energy, in which cold water is pumped through fractured hot dry rock deep underground, is heated by contact with the rock, and is then extracted and used for heating and electricity generation.

hot rock An area of the Earth's *crust where there is an anomalously high *geothermal gradient close to the surface, which provides a source of *geothermal energy.

hot spring A natural *spring of hot mineral water, associated with *hot rock. *See also* GEYSER; HYDROTHERMAL ACTIVITY.

hot zone *See* EXCLUSION ZONE.

hotspot An area that has an unusually high level of some particular quality or activity, such as *air pollution, *biodiversity, or *volcanic activity. *See also* BIODIVERSITY HOTSPOT.

household A group of people who live together.

household waste (domestic waste, residential waste) *Solid waste that originates in a private home or apartment.

HOV *See* HIGH OCCUPANCY VEHICLE.

HRS *See* HAZARD RANKING SYSTEM.

HTGCR *See* HIGH TEMPERATURE GAS-COOLED REACTOR.

Human Dimension of Global Change Programme (HDGCP) A large-scale international social science research programme that ran through the 1990s, and sought to obtain a better understanding of the human causes of *global environmental change, and to formulate appropriate responses for reconciling *economic development and the maintenance of *environmental quality.

human ecology The study of the interactions between humans and the environment.

human equivalent dose A *dose which, when given to humans, produces an effect equal to that which is produced by a dose in *animals.

human exceptionalism paradigm (HEP) The view (*paradigm) that humans are different from all other organisms, all human behaviour is controlled by culture and free will, and all problems can be solved by human ingenuity and technology. *See also* ANTHROPOCENTRISM.

human exposure evaluation A description of the nature and size of the population that is exposed to a particular substance, and the magnitude and duration of *exposure.

human genome The complete *DNA sequence (*genome) for a human; all of the genetic materials that make up a human being.

Human Genome Initiative The original name for what became the *Human Genome Project.

Human Genome Project A major international research project that was established in 1990 (originally called the Human Genome Initiative) to study differences in the genetic make-up of ethnic groups and to sample DNA from populations around the world. It seeks to identify the 60000 to 80000 *genes that are carried by humans, and help to find genetic causes and possible treatments of disease. *See also* GENETIC ENGINEERING; GENOME.

(((●))) SEE WEB LINKS

• About the Human Genome Project.

human health risk The probability that a particular *exposure or series of exposures may

have damaged, or will damage, the health of individual people.

human impact The result or *impact of human activities. *See also* ENVIRONMENTAL IMPACT.

humanitarian Devoted to the promotion of human welfare.

humic Relating to or derived from *humus.

humic acid A dark brown *organic substance which is the main constituent of *humus, and is soluble in water only at *pH values greater than 2.0.

humid Moist, damp.

humid continental climate A quite severe climate, with harsh winters, average temperatures below freezing ($0°C$) in several months, mild to warm summers, and adequate annual precipitation, which is found in mid-latitude continental areas of the northern hemisphere, between about $40°$ and $60°$.

humid continental mixed forest A *temperate *forest *biome found in middle latitudes where *precipitation is greater than about 750 mm a year, and droughts and drying winds are rare. The natural *climax vegetation is *deciduous *broadleaved trees, including oak, maple, beech, hickory, and elm in the USA.

humid subtropical climate A mid-latitude *climate that is dominated by hot, humid summers and cool winters, and is often found on the eastern side of a *continent.

humid subtropical forest A *forest *biome of the *humid subtropical climate zone, which is dominated by *coniferous trees, has a dense *undergrowth and many climbing plants. Its *habitats support a wide variety of animals (particularly reptiles, mammals, and birds) and insects.

humid tropics Those parts of the *tropics that receive a lot of *rainfall during part of the year, and that have temperatures which are generally suitable for year-round *crop production.

humidification The addition of *water vapour to *air in order to increase its *humidity.

humidity The amount of *water vapour in the air, which can be expressed as *absolute humidity, *mixing ratio, *specific humidity, or *relative humidity.

humification The *decomposition of *organic material in the *soil into *humus, by *biochemical and *abiotic processes.

humus 1. Decomposed *organic matter within a *soil, that increases fertility and water retention in the soil, and improves soil texture. The decomposing humus is usually dark coloured (dark brown or black), so the uppermost *horizon of the soil (*A-horizon) where it accumulates is generally darker than the soil below. **2. (soil organic matter)** In *horticulture, any surface organic matter in the soil.

hunt To pursue, kill, or capture wild animals for food, *pelts, or as a sport.

hunter-gatherer A person in a society that obtains food by *hunting (fish and wild animals) and gathering (wild berries, fruits, fungi, nuts, leaves, and edible roots) rather than raising livestock or crops (*agriculture).

hunting The activity of finding and killing or capturing wild animals for food, *pelts, or as a *field sport.

hurricane 1. Originally, a *tropical cyclone that develops over the North Atlantic and Caribbean. The term is now often applied to all tropical cyclones, regardless of where they develop. **2.** Any storm with sustained winds of more than 120 km/h, which is force 12 on the *Beaufort scale.

hurricane track The course followed by a *hurricane as it moves across the land and/or sea.

hurricane warning A formal alert that is issued when a *hurricane is approaching and is likely to make landfall in a specified area within 24 hours or less.

hybrid An *organism that is the offspring of two different *genotypes, i.e. *varieties, *breeds, or *species. Hybrids may be fertile or sterile and so unable to reproduce, depending on the extent to which the parental *genomes differ. For example a mule is the hybrid of a male donkey and a female horse. *See also* CROSSBREEDING.

hybridization The process of crossing individuals from *strains, *populations, or *species that are genetically different, which is usually done on purpose as part of a *selective breeding programme in order to produce *hybrids.

hydrarch succession *See* HYDROSERE.

hydration The chemical combination of *water with a *solute.

hydraulic boundary Within a *groundwater system, the interface between regions of different hydraulic characteristics, e.g. where an *aquifer abuts an *aquiclude.

hydraulic conductivity The rate at which water can move through a *permeable medium, such as soil. *See also* PERMEABILITY.

hydraulic fracturing (fracking) The propagation of fractures in rocks by the injection of pressurized fluids followed by sand to keep the fractures open, in order to extract natural gas (methane), coal seam gas (methane), or petroleum.

hydraulic geometry In a *river, the relationship between *discharge and channel width, depth, and velocity as discharge varies through time either at a particular site (the at-a-station hydraulic geometry) or in a downstream direction (the downstream hydraulic geometry), which can be shown in graphs and as equations.

hydraulic gradient The slope of the *water table, which determines the direction and rate of *groundwater flow.

hydraulic head The elevation of a water body above a particular datum level. Specifically, it is the energy possessed by a unit weight of water at any particular point. It consists of three parts: the elevation head, defined with reference to a standard level or datum; the pressure head, defined with reference to atmospheric pressure; and the velocity head. Water invariably flows from points of larger hydraulic head to points of lower head down the *hydraulic gradient.

hydraulic jump A rapid change in the flow depth of water in a *stream, which creates a *standing wave on the water surface.

hydraulic mining A form of *placer mining in which water under pressure is used to break down *placer deposits (such as *china clay). *See also* PLACER MINING.

hydraulics 1. The study of the mechanical properties of liquids. **2.** A movement or action that results from the flow of a liquid.

hydric Having or requiring an abundant supply of water. Applied to an environment that is extremely wet.

hydric soil A *soil that is saturated with water long enough during the plant *growing season to become *anaerobic, and that supports *wetland vegetation.

hydro- Related to or produced by *water or the movement of water, as in *hydroelectricity.

hydrocarbon A naturally occurring compound of *hydrogen and *carbon. There are many different types of hydrocarbon, which can take the form of a gas, liquid, or solid; examples include *natural gas, *bitumen, and *petroleum. A *conventional or criteria pollutant. *See also* FOSSIL FUEL.

hydrochloric acid (HCl) An *aqueous solution of hydrogen chloride gas that is a strongly corrosive acid and is widely used in metal cleaning and electroplating.

hydrochlorofluorocarbon (HCFC) A partly *halogenated *chlorofluorocarbon compound that consists of *hydrogen, *chlorine, *fluorine, and *carbon. HCFCs are a replacement for *CFCs, but they are also *greenhouse gases that contain *chlorine and deplete stratospheric *ozone, but to a much lesser extent than CFCs. *See also* OZONE DEPLETION POTENTIAL.

hydrodynamic A body shape that is streamlined to allow easy movement through a liquid such as water. *Compare* AERODYNAMIC.

hydrodynamics The study of the motion of liquids.

hydroelectric power (HEP) Electricity that is generated by the passage of water through a *turbine, usually at a dam. Traditional HEP schemes make use of natural slopes and *topography to create a *head of water. In a typical scheme water is stored in a *reservoir, from where it drops under the influence of gravity down pipes into water turbines which are coupled to electricity generators. Steep mountain rivers with high *discharges provide ideal sites for hydropower developments. In 2010 HEP provided about 16% of the world's electricity, and it is now the largest renewable source of electricity around the world. Capacity has increased by 14-fold since 1950, but the spread between countries is very uneven; Paraguay generates 100% of its electrical power from hydroelectric dams, compared with 7.2% for Japan and 5.7% for the USA. It is estimated that about a quarter of the world's HEP potential had been exploited by the mid-1990s. Large-scale growth of hydropower is unlikely to continue significantly in the future, partly because of the lack of suitable sites and the environmental and social impacts of such schemes. The high *capital cost per unit of electricity produced is a further constraint. Small-scale local hydropower schemes appear to have much greater potential,

particularly in developing countries, because they are cheaper, quicker to install, easier to maintain, and cause less damage. This is a form of *hydropower that is *renewable, reliable, *sustainable, pollution-free, and environmentally sound. *See also* PUMPED STORAGE SCHEME.

hydroelectricity Electricity that is generated from flowing water via *turbines; a form of *renewable energy.

hydrofluorocarbon (HFC) A compound that consists of *hydrogen, *fluorine, and *carbon. A *fluorocarbon that is emitted as a *by-product of industrial manufacturing, is used as a *solvent and cleaner in the semiconductor industry, is an alternative to *CFCs, does not contain *chlorine or *bromine, and does not deplete the *ozone layer. HFCs are powerful *greenhouse gases, with *global warming potentials of between 140 and 12100. *See also* OZONE DEPLETION POTENTIAL.

hydrogen (H) A colourless, odourless, tasteless, flammable gas that is the simplest, lightest, and most abundant of the elements, but is found only in trace quantities (about 0.00005% by volume) in the Earth's *atmosphere. It combines with oxygen to form water and forms organic compounds (*hydrocarbons) with *carbon. In the form of *amino acids, *carbohydrates, and fats hydrogen is a macronutrient essential for animal growth and health.

hydrogen sulphide (H_2S) A colourless, flammable, toxic natural gas that smells like rotten eggs and is emitted during organic *decomposition and produced as a *by-product of oil refining and burning. It is also found in North Sea gas and in volcanic emissions.

hydrogenation 1. A method of converting liquid fats to solid fats, by adding *hydrogen gas to a *hydrocarbon. **2.** A method of converting coal to oil.

hydrogeological cycle *See* WATER CYCLE.

hydrogeology (geohydrology) The study of the chemistry and movement of *groundwater.

hydrograph A graph that shows variations in river level through time (called a stage hydrograph), or the water level in a *borehole above a datum point. A unit hydrograph converts the data to stream flow and a discharge hydrograph shows the flow rate in a body that is discharging. A storm hydrograph shows the response to the rainfall input by an individual storm event.

hydrographic divide *See* DRAINAGE DIVIDE.

hydrography The study of large bodies of water on the *Earth. *See also* HYDROLOGY.

hydrological Relating to water flow.

hydrological budget An account of the inflow to, storage in, and outflow from a *hydrological unit over a given period of time, such as a year.

hydrological cycle *See* WATER CYCLE.

hydrological unit A *drainage basin or a subdivision of one, such as an *aquifer, soil zone, *lake, *reservoir, or *irrigation project.

hydrology The study of the properties, distribution, and circulation of *water on, over, and through the *Earth. *See also* HYDROGRAPHY.

hydrolysis The *decomposition of a chemical compound by reaction with *water, as in the *chemical weathering of *rocks. For example, in *granite the *feldspar minerals break down into clay minerals like *kaolinite.

hydrometeor Any condensed water particle in the atmosphere, including *rain, ice crystals, *hail, *fog, or *cloud.

hydrometer An instrument that is used for measuring the *specific gravity or density of a liquid.

hydromorphic soil *Soil that has developed under *waterlogged conditions.

hydrophilic Applied to a surface or molecule that can be wetted or solvated. *Contrast* HYDROPHOBIC.

hydrophobic Water-avoiding, water-repelling, or non-soluble. *Contrast* HYDROPHILIC.

hydrophyte (phreatophyte) A plant that is adapted to grow in or under the surface of water. *Contrast* MESOPHYTE; XEROPHYTE.

hydropolitics The politics of allocating and managing *water resources, particularly between countries.

hydroponics A method of growing plants, especially vegetables, in water that contains essential mineral *nutrients, without the use of *soil.

hydropower *Electricity or *power that is generated from the movement of *water; a *renewable source of *energy that emits no *greenhouse gases. Examples include *water mills, *hydroelectric power schemes, and *tidal power.

hydrosere (hydrarch succession) A vegetation *succession from open water to *mire and *bog at the edge of a *lake.

hydrosphere The water on or around the surface of the Earth, which includes *oceans, *seas, *lakes, *rivers, *groundwater, and atmospheric moisture, and is cycled through the *water cycle. It is a major *environmental system that interacts with the *lithosphere, the *atmosphere, and the *biosphere.

hydrostatic Relating to the pressure or forces exerted by fluids in equilibrium.

hydrostatic equation An equation that represents the balance between *gravity and the vertical *pressure gradient force. If these forces are equal, there is *hydrostatic equilibrium and thus no vertical motion.

hydrostatic equilibrium A balanced state in which the outward pressure of a fluid is balanced by the inward force of *gravity. In the atmosphere, the condition in which the weight of a *parcel of air is balanced by the upward pressure at the base of the parcel.

(((⊕))) SEE WEB LINKS

• Hydrostatic equilibrium and the homogeneous atmosphere.

hydrostatic pressure The pressure that is exerted on a fluid at rest. In *groundwater, it is the pressure at a specific elevation that is caused by the weight of water at higher levels in the same *zone of saturation. In the atmosphere it is the weight of the column of overlying air at a specific altitude. *See also* ARTESIAN WELL.

hydrothermal Relating to the hot water and steam that are generated by *igneous activity, trapped in fractured or porous rocks within the *Earth, and which contain dissolved *minerals. *See also* GEOTHERMAL.

hydrothermal activity A range of geological processes that involve the movement of hot *groundwater and steam, particularly the alteration and emplacement of minerals and the formation of *hot springs and *geysers. *See also* GEOTHERMAL.

hydrothermal mineral A *mineral that is precipitated from a *hydrothermal fluid.

hydrothermal vein A layer of *minerals that has been precipitated from a *hydrothermal fluid between layers of rock underground.

hydrothermal vent A fissure in a *mid-ocean ridge on the deep ocean floor that is created by *sea-floor spreading, where hot, *sulphur-rich water is released from rock that is heated by *geothermal activity.

hydroxide An ion (OH⁻) that is ionically bonded with a negative charge. It also forms compounds of an *oxide with water.

hydroxyl Alcoholic group (–OH) that consists of *hydrogen and *oxygen in a compound which is covalently bonded (so it has no charge).

hygrometer An instrument that is used to measure the amount of *water vapour (*humidity) in the *atmosphere.

hygroscopic Capable of absorbing and retaining *moisture, for example from *water vapour in the air.

hygroscopic nuclei See CONDENSATION NUCLEI.

hygroscopic water Water that is *adsorbed onto a surface from the *atmosphere. In soil, for example, this water is tightly held as a very thin layer around each individual particle of soil; it is not accessible to plants in amounts they need to survive, and at least some of it remains in the soil even after extreme *drought.

hypermetamorphosis A type of *metamorphosis that is typical of certain types of insects (such as some beetles), in which the larva changes into markedly different forms during its development.

hyperparasite A *parasite that attacks another parasite inside a host, not the host itself. If it kills the host it is often called a *parasitoid.

hyperplasia An abnormal increase in tissue growth that is caused by an increase in the number of cells, by cell division. *Contrast* HYPERTROPHY.

hypersaline Containing excessive *salts, having high *salinity (greater than 35 parts per thousand).

hypertrophic Containing excessive *nutrients.

hypertrophy An increase in the size of an organ that is caused by an increase in cell size. *Contrast* HYPERPLASIA.

hypoallergenic Not likely to cause an *allergic reaction.

hypocentre See FOCUS.

hypolimnion The bottom layer of water in a thermally stratified lake. It is the densest layer, is usually the coldest layer in summer and warmest in winter, usually lacks oxygen, and is too dark to support *photosynthesis.

hypothecation The pledge of property and assets as collateral in order to secure a loan, which does not transfer title but does provide the right to sell the hypothecated property in the event of default.

hypothermia Lowering of core body temperature to below 35°C as a result of exposure to extreme cold, causing rapid, progressive mental and physical collapse. *See also* WIND-CHILL.

hypothesis A statement of the expected relationship between things being studied, which is intended to explain certain facts or observations. An idea to be tested.

hypoxia Depletion of *dissolved oxygen in water and *sediments, relative to the needs of most *aerobic species.

hypoxic water Water which has a *dissolved oxygen concentrations of less than 2 parts per million (ppm), which makes it difficult for most aquatic life to survive and reproduce.

hypsithermal See ALTITHERMAL.

hypsometric curve A graph showing the proportion of a land surface that is higher or lower than a given level, *usually sea level.

IAEA *See* INTERNATIONAL ATOMIC ENERGY AGENCY.

IAM *See* INTEGRATED AREA MANAGEMENT.

IBI *See* INDEX OF BIOLOGICAL INTEGRITY.

ICDP *See* INTEGRATED CONSERVATION AND DEVELOPMENT PROGRAMME.

ice Frozen water.

ice age A time of widespread *glaciation. *See also* PLEISTOCENE.

ice cap A large mass of ice that covers an area of less than 50 000 km² but is deep enough to conceal the underlying topography. It comprises a central *ice dome with *outlet glaciers.

ice cliff (ice front) A wall of ice where a *glacier meets the sea, for example at the edge of an *ice shelf.

ice contact deposit Sediment that is deposited when *meltwater flows over, through, or under the stationary front of a melting *glacier. *See also* ESKER; KAME; KAME TERRACE.

ice core A column of ice that has been drilled from a *glacier or *ice sheet, and which can be used to reconstruct past changes in air chemistry and climate.

ice cover The extent (particularly the thickness) of ice on a land surface, or the proportion of a sea surface that is covered with sea ice.

ice dome A main component of an *ice sheet or *ice cap. It has a convex surface form, of parabolic shape, and tends to develop symmetrically over a landmass. Its thickness often exceeds 3000 m.

ice fall A steeply sloping part of a *glacier, where the ice tumbles down and is broken by *crevasses. *See also* OGIVE.

ice field A nearly level field of ice with an area ranging from about 5 km² to near continental size, which is formed when the land surface is sufficiently high or uniform for ice to accumulate. It differs from an *ice cap in that it is not domed and its flow is controlled by the underlying relief.

ice floe A large piece of floating ice. *See also* ICEBERG.

ice flow *See* GLACIER FLOW.

ice fog A type of *fog that is composed of minute ice particles, which occurs when warm water is suddenly released into very cold air and water vapour changes directly into ice crystals. It occurs under clear, calm conditions in polar latitudes, and can produce a *halo around the *Sun or *Moon.

ice front *See* ICE CLIFF.

ice jam An accumulation of floating *ice that dams a narrow river *channel, and can cause local *flooding during a thaw in late winter or early spring when the dam breaks.

ice nuclei *See* DEPOSITION NUCLEI.

ice pellet *See* SLEET.

ice sheet (continental glacier) A large, thick body of ice, typically more than 50 000 km² in extent and therefore larger than an *ice cap, that lies on land and is able to expand laterally because it is not confined by the underlying *topography. Examples include Greenland and *Antarctica today and much of North America and Northern Europe during the *Pleistocene *ice age.

ice shelf A sheet of very thick ice which has a more or less level surface, with one side attached to the land but most of it is floating over an *ocean or large *lake. It is the outer part of an *ice cap or *ice sheet. In Antarctica 7% of the total ice is held in ice shelves that are up to 200 m thick.

ice storm *Freezing rain that results in a thick accumulation of ice on trees, power lines, and roads.

ice stream The rapidly flowing body of ice within a valley *glacier, which does not mix with other ice streams it comes into contact with, and which often deposits *lateral moraine and/or *medial moraine at its sides.

iceberg A large piece of floating ice, most of which is below sea level, that has broken off a *glacier. Larger and deeper than an *ice floe.

Iceland low A low-pressure system in a region of the North Atlantic between Iceland and Greenland, centred between about 60° N and 65° N, in which such systems occur so frequently that the average atmospheric pressure is low. Any one of these systems may be called 'an Iceland low', but the term is used mostly to describe the general statistical or climatic feature. *See also* ALEUTIAN LOW.

ICES *See* INTERNATIONAL COUNCIL FOR THE EXPLORATION OF THE SEA.

ichthyofauna The fish population of a particular area or time.

icing The forming or deposition of ice (*glaze) on a solid object.

ICM *See* INTEGRATED CATCHMENT MANAGEMENT.

ICPD *See* INTERNATIONAL CONFERENCE ON POPULATION AND DEVELOPMENT.

ICSU *See* INTERNATIONAL COUNCIL OF SCIENTIFIC UNIONS.

identified resource Deposits of a specific mineral *ore or *fossil fuel whose location, quantity, and quality are known or have been estimated from direct geological evidence.

idiobiont An ectoparasitoid that parasitizes later *host stages, completely paralysing the host and terminating its development, and sucking nutrients through the host's *exoskeleton. *Contrast* KOINOBIONT.

( ) SEE WEB LINKS

• Parasitic wasps.

IDNDR *See* INTERNATIONAL DECADE FOR NATURAL DISASTER REDUCTION.

IEA *See* INTERNATIONAL ENERGY AGENCY.

IET *See* INTERNATIONAL EMISSIONS TRADING.

igapo *See* AMAZON FLORAL REGION.

IGBP *See* INTERNATIONAL GEOSPHERE-BIOSPHERE PROGRAMME.

igneous rock (primary rock, volcanic rock) A type of *rock that is formed when molten *magma cools and crystallizes, either underground or on the surface. Examples include *basalt, *rhyolite, *andesite, *lava, and *granite. *See also* ROCK CYCLE.

ignimbrite A *pyroclastic flow deposit that contains material varying in size from *ash to *pumice clasts; it may be *unconsolidated or *cemented.

ignitable Capable of burning or causing a fire.

IIASA *See* INTERNATIONAL INSTITUTE FOR APPLIED SYSTEMS ANALYSIS.

IISD *See* INTERNATIONAL INSTITUTE FOR SUSTAINABLE DEVELOPMENT.

IJC *See* INTERNATIONAL JOINT COMMISSION.

Illinoian The third (0.17–0.12 million years ago) of four *glacial stages recognized in North America. It is represented by deposits from ice moving from the north-east, and in formerly glaciated areas to the west pollen evidence suggests that mean annual temperatures were 2–3°C cooler than they are now.

illness The state of being sick, because of stress, *disease, *accident, or injury.

illuvial horizon A soil *horizon in which material that is transported downwards by *eluviation out of a horizon above, in solution or in suspension, has been deposited and accumulates. *See also* B-HORIZON.

illuviation A *soil-forming process that involves the movement of material (*humus, chemical substances, and fine *mineral particles), in solution or in suspension, down through the *soil profile from the *A-horizon and its deposition in the *B-horizon below. The term implies the inward movement of material.

imago The adult stage of *an insect.

imbrication The layering of inclined particles of *sediment or rock fragments against each other, resembling the way roof tiles overlap and lie parallel to one another. *See also* FABRIC.

immature soil A soil that lacks a well-developed *profile, usually because it has not had enough time for one to develop by normal *soil-forming processes.

immigration The movement of people or *organisms into a country or area; the opposite of *emigration.

imminent threat In *risk assessment, a high probability that exposure to an *agent is actually occurring or is likely to occur in the very near future.

immiscible Incapable of being mixed or blended together to form a *homogeneous mixture, such as oil and water. The opposite is *miscible.

immobilization 1. Preventing movement to allow natural healing to take place. 2. The conversion of an element from the *inorganic to the *organic form, in the tissues of *plants or *micro-organisms, which makes it unavailable to other plants.

immunity A natural or acquired resistance to a *pathogen or its products (e.g. to a particular *disease). See also NATURAL IMMUNITY.

immunization The process by which a susceptible individual is protected against the adverse effects of infection by a disease-causing *micro-organism, typically by the administration of a *vaccine.

immunology The scientific study of *immunity and the immune system.

immutability The ability to withstand change, or the quality of being incapable of *mutation.

IMO See INTERNATIONAL MARITIME ORGANISATION.

impact 1. (effect) The direct or indirect changes, whether beneficial or adverse, that result from a specific act or series of acts, or a project or programme. See also ECONOMIC IMPACT; ENVIRONMENTAL IMPACT; SOCIAL IMPACT. 2. The force of impression of one thing on another, such as a *meteorite hitting the surface of the *Earth.

impact assessment See ENVIRONMENTAL IMPACT ASSESSMENT.

impair To damage or make worse or less effective.

impairment Any adverse or damaging *impact on an *environment or *ecosystem which makes it less suitable for an intended use.

impeded drainage A restriction of the downward movement of water in *soil, which is usually caused either by *waterlogging or by the existence of a *hardpan.

imperilled species A general term used in North America which includes *endangered, *threatened, and *species at risk and *species of concern.

impermeable Not easily penetrated. An impermeable substance does not permit fluids to pass through it. Contrast PERMEABLE. See also IMPERVIOUS.

impervious A surface through which little or no water will move due to lack of pore space. Contrast PERVIOUS. See also IMPERMEABLE.

important species *Species or *biotopes which are rare, have a restricted distribution, and/or are in decline; species which are listed for protection on *statutes, *directives, and *conventions.

imports 1. Commodities (goods or services) that are bought from elsewhere (e.g. a foreign country). 2. *Solid waste materials and *recyclables that have been transported from where they originated to another place for processing or final disposal.

impoundment A body of water (such as a *reservoir) that is confined by a barrier such as a dam or floodgate.

improved grassland Grassland in which yield is deliberately increased by *drainage, application of *fertilizers and/or *herbicides, *ploughing, and reseeding with fast-growing *varieties.

in situ On site or in its natural location. Contrast EX SITU.

in situ conservation The *conservation of *species in their natural *habitat. Contrast EX SITU CONSERVATION.

in situ treatment The treatment of a particular *waste material on site, where it is generated, rather than transporting it elsewhere for treatment.

in vitro In an artificial environment outside a living *organism. Contrast IN VIVO. See also CRYOPRESERVATION.

in vivo Within a living *organism. Contrast IN VITRO.

inbred Produced by *inbreeding.

inbreeding The *mating of close relatives, i.e. individuals who are likely to share some of their *genes due to common ancestry, which reduces genetic diversity. *See also* BREEDING; OUTBREEDING.

inbreeding depression The accumulation of harmful genetic traits (through random *mutations and *natural selection) that results from *inbreeding in a small *population, and that decreases the viability and reproductive success of enough individuals to adversely affect the whole population.

in-bye Enclosed *grassland that is located close to a *farm.

incentive-based regulation A government *regulation (such as a tradable *emissions allowance) that is designed to induce changes in the behaviour of individuals or firms, in order to produce environmental, social, or economic benefits that would otherwise be prescribed by *legislation.

inceptisols An *order of young soils in the early stages of *pedogenesis, in which the *horizons are starting to develop.

incidence The frequency of new *occurrences of a condition (such as the number of new cases of a *disease) in a *population over a defined period of time. *Contrast* PREVALENCE.

incidence rate The ratio of new cases (for example, of a *disease) in a *population to the total population at risk over a defined period of time.

incidental catch/take *See* BYCATCH.

incineration The process of burning *solid waste and other material, under controlled conditions, to produce *ash. *See also* MASS BURN; WASTE DISPOSAL.

incineration at sea The disposal of *toxic waste by burning at sea using specially designed *incinerator ships.

incinerator A furnace or chamber in which waste material is destroyed by burning. *See also* AFTERBURNER.

inclination The degree of dip or tilt from the vertical. *See also* DIP.

inclusion *See* XENOLITH.

income The flow of money, goods, or services that is created by the productive use of assets.

incommensurable Values or benefits that are not measurable by a common standard (for example in dollars or cubic metres), and

thus cannot be objectively compared. *Contrast* COMMENSURABLE.

incompatible Not *compatible, unable to exist together harmoniously.

incompatible use Different uses of land or other resources which cannot exist together in the same area because one inhibits or adversely affects another. *Contrast* COMPATIBLE USE.

incompatible waste A *waste material that is unsuitable for mixing with another material because it may react to create a *hazard.

increment 1. An increase in quantity, by a factor of one unit. 2. The increase in diameter, height, volume, weight, or value of individual trees or crops over a defined period of time.

incrementalism An approach to decision-making which is based on making decisions one at a time, each one designed to deal with short-term imperfections in an existing policy, rather than establishing long-term future goals.

incubation period (latent period) The period of time between initial exposure to an infectious *agent and the appearance of the first sign or symptom of *disease.

Independent Commission on International Development A major international *commission, chaired by German Chancellor Willy Brandt, that examined the interrelationships between *environment and *development. It reported in 1980, coined the terms North (*developed countries) and South (*less developed countries), and called for the cancellation of old debts among countries of the *Third World.

indeterminacy Unpredictability in outcome, because a very large number of interrelated factors are involved and/or because understanding of the particular *system is still quite limited.

indeterminate species A *threatened category of species defined by the *IUCN *Red Data Book as 'taxa known to be *extinct, *endangered, *vulnerable, or *rare but there is not enough information to say which of the four categories is appropriate'.

index fossil (index species, zone fossil) A *fossil that is specific to one geographical area or geological time and so can be used to identify and date rocks.

index of abundance An estimate of the relative size of an animal *population calculated from counts of the number of individuals attracted to a standard bait or the number caught for each standardized unit of effort (e.g. of fishing effort, used in estimating the size of a fish stock).

Index of Biological Integrity (IBI) A measure of *biological integrity for a particular site that is based on integrating a number (usually at least seven) of *indices describing site conditions.

index of sustainable economic welfare A measure for assessing the strength of an *economy and human well-being within a country, which (unlike *gross national product and similar *indicators) includes measures of environmental damage and reductions in *environmental quality.

index species See INDEX FOSSIL; INDICATOR SPECIES.

index/indices A numerical scale (such as the *Celsius temperature scale) that is used to compare variables with one another or with a reference number.

Indian floral region Part of R. Good's Indo-Malaysian floral subkingdom within his *Palaeotropical floral kingdom (*The Geography of the Flowering Plants*, 1974), and more a region of floral mixing than a distinct entity, notwithstanding the extent of the subcontinent. There are only about 150 *endemic genera and most of these are monotypic.

Indian summer A period of unusually warm weather in mid to late autumn, with clear skies and cool nights, which usually follows a period of cool weather.

indicator 1. An *organism, *species, *community, or aspect of the environment whose characteristics show the presence of specific environmental conditions or *pollutants. *See also* BIOINDICATOR; ENVIRONMENTAL INDICATOR; POLLUTION INDICATOR; PROXY INDICATOR. **2.** A substance that shows a visible change, usually of colour, at a known point in a chemical reaction.

indicator species (index species, management indicator species) A *species whose presence or absence is an *indicator of environmental conditions in a *habitat or *community.

indigenous Naturally occurring in a particular area. *Contrast* EXOTIC. *See also* NATIVE.

indigenous knowledge *See* TRADITIONAL KNOWLEDGE.

indigenous peoples (aborigines, native peoples, tribal peoples) The original or natural inhabitants of a country. For example, Native Americans (First Nation) are the indigenous peoples of the USA (and Canada).

indigenous species *See* NATIVE SPECIES.

indirect competition The use of a *resource by one individual in such a way that it reduces the availability of that resource to others.

indirect discharge The introduction of *pollutants into a *municipal waste treatment system from any non-domestic source, such as an industrial or commercial *facility.

indirect effect A secondary effect or *impact which occurs elsewhere and/or after the initial action. Examples include *acid rain, *bioaccumulation, and *global warming.

indirect exposure pathway An *exposure pathway that contains at least one intermediate release to any media between the source and the point of exposure. For example, *chemicals of concern can be transported by water from the *soil through *groundwater to the point of exposure.

individual risk The probability that a particular *individual within a *population will experience an adverse effect.

individual variation The diversity of *phenotypes within a *population.

Indomalayan realm A *biogeographical realm that is almost entirely *tropical forest, throughout much of South East Asia.

indoor air The breathable air within a building or structure.

indoor air pollution *Pollution of *indoor air by chemical, biological, or physical *contaminants, such as *radon gas, *carbon monoxide, or tobacco smoke.

indoor climate The temperature, humidity, lighting, air flow, and noise levels inside a building or structure.

induced recharge Replenishing a waterbody or *aquifer using water from somewhere else.

induction *See* INDUCTIVE REASONING.

inductive reasoning (induction) Inferring general principles from specific examples. *Compare* DEDUCTIVE REASONING.

indurated A *soil or *sedimentary rock which has become hardened or *cemented, and will not soften when wetted. *See also* HARDPAN; IRON PAN.

industrial biocatalyst A *biocatalyst (particularly an *enzyme) that is used in industrial processes.

industrial biotechnology The application of *biotechnology to create new and alternative products for consumers, such as chemicals, textiles, food and animal feed, pulp and paper, energy, metals, and minerals.

industrial chemical Any *chemical that is used in industrial processes, including *pharmaceuticals, *plastics, and *enzymes.

industrial ecology A framework by which industry and organizations can reduce their *environmental impacts by treating their operations as *ecosystems and monitoring and reducing the flow of materials and energy between different parts of their operation. This is designed to use materials more efficiently, reduce *waste, and prevent *pollution.

industrial forestry Large-scale, commercial tree planting in order to produce *timber and other wood products (such as wood chips).

industrial melanism The progressive *adaptation of a species, over a number of generations, to changing environmental factors. The classic example is the adaptation of the peppered moth (*Biston betularia*) to increased sooty *air pollution in Manchester between 1848 and 1895; white moths on dark surfaces were eaten by *predators, so darker moths became more common. *See also* EVOLUTION; MELANISM; NATURAL SELECTION.

industrial process waste Waste materials that are produced during manufacturing operations.

Industrial Revolution The rapid development of industry that began in Britain in the late 18th and early 19th centuries, assisted by the introduction of machinery and the development of a market economy, and which spread to other countries.

industrial sector That part of the *economy that is based on manufacturing industries, mining, construction, agriculture, fisheries, and forestry. *See also* COMMERCIAL SECTOR; RESIDENTIAL SECTOR; TRANSPORTATION SECTOR.

industrial sludge A semi-liquid residue or *slurry that remains after the treatment of *industrial water and *wastewater.

industrial source reduction Measures and equipment that reduce the amount of a *hazardous substance, *pollutant, or *contaminant that is produced by industry and enters any waste stream or is released into the *environment, in order to protect the environment and *public health.

industrial timber Trees grown for wood that is used for *lumber, plywood, veneer, particleboard, chipboard, and paper.

industrial waste Any unwanted materials from an industrial operation or activity, which includes liquid, *sludge, and solid and *hazardous waste.

industrialization The development of *industry on a large scale. A stage in the development of the *economy and *society in a particular country during which manufacturing replaces agriculture, forestry, and mineral extraction as the primary economic activity. *See also* DEMOGRAPHIC TRANSITION.

industrialized countries Nations (such as the USA, Japan, and the countries of Europe) which have economies based on industrial production and which use large amounts of energy (particularly *fossil fuels and *nuclear power).

industry The organized process of *manufacturing goods for sale.

inequality The state of being different in terms of quantity, value, or status. *Contrast* EQUALITY.

inequitable That which is unfair, partial, and unjust, and which does not provide equal opportunity for all. *Contrast* EQUITABLE.

inequity Unfairness arising from the unequal use and allocation of resources. *Contrast* EQUITY.

inert Applied to a substance that is chemically very stable and does not react readily with other substances.

inert gas (noble gas, rare gas) Any one of six gases (*helium, *neon, *argon, *krypton, *xenon, and *radon) that are almost completely chemically inactive.

inertia The tendency of an object to remain at rest or moving in a straight line at a constant speed unless a force acts on it.

inerts A collective term for *non-biodegradable products (such as *glass or *plastics) that are contained in wastes.

infant mortality The number of infants who die within the first year of life, per 1000 live births.

infanticide The intentional killing of a child that is less than 12 months old.

infauna *Benthic organisms that live below the surface of the *sediment on the floor of a waterbody such as a lake or sea.

infection The invasion of a living organism by a *pathogen that becomes established, multiplies within the host, and causes symptoms.

infectious agent Any *pathogenic microorganism (e.g. *virus, *parasite, or *bacterium) that is capable of causing *infection.

infectious disease A *disease that is caused by *pathogenic organisms.

infectious waste (red bag waste) *Hazardous waste that is capable of causing *infections in humans. This includes contaminated animal waste, human blood and blood products, isolation waste, and pathological waste and discarded syringes, needles, and blades.

inference A conclusion that is drawn logically from premises that are known or assumed to be true.

infest 1. To occupy in large numbers. 2. To live on a host. See also PARASITE.

infestation A troublesome invasion by *parasites or *pests.

infill The process of developing open zones within an established area (such as *brownfield sites within a town) before developing outside the established area (such as on *greenfield sites).

infiltration The movement of water from the ground surface into a *soil or into a *porous *rock or *sediment. Contrast PERCOLATION.

infiltration capacity The maximum rate at which water can enter the soil at a particular point, under a given set of conditions.

infiltration rate The amount of water that enters the soil at a particular point in a given period of time.

inflation The average rate at which the general price of goods and services increases through time.

inflow 1. The natural flow of water into a *lake or *reservoir from upstream *tributaries. 2. The flow of rainwater into a *sewer system from drains and sewers.

influent 1. A stream that enters a large or larger river. 2. A waste product (such as water that contains *pollutants) that enters a particular part of the environment, often accidentally. Means literally 'flowing in'. Contrast EFFLUENT.

informal outdoor recreation *Recreation activities that take place outside and are not directly managed. See also DISPERSED RECREATION; DEVELOPED RECREATION.

informal settlement Houses (for temporary or permanent use) which have been built on land without formal planning approval.

informatics The scientific study of *information, its storage, and its processing. See also BIOINFORMATICS; DATA MINING; GEOINFORMATICS.

information *Data that have been transformed through analysis and interpretation into a form which is useful for drawing conclusions and making decisions. See also MANAGEMENT INFORMATION.

information management The administration, use, and transmission of information and the use of theories and methods of *information science to create, modify, or improve systems for handling information. See also KNOWLEDGE MANAGEMENT.

information science The study of the creation, use, and management of information.

infrared (IR, thermal radiation, longwave radiation) *Radiant energy that has a *wavelength of 7 nm^{-1} mm within the *electromagnetic spectrum, between *visible light and *microwaves. Most of the energy that is radiated by the Earth and its atmosphere is infrared. Gases such as *water vapour, *carbon dioxide, and *ozone absorb infrared radiation, which creates the *greenhouse effect.

infrastructure The basic services and facilities (such as roads and sewers) that are needed for the development and growth of an area or activity.

ingestion Taking material into the body, usually via the mouth, after which it is swallowed. *Contrast* ABSORPTION.

inhalation Breathing in.

inherent *See* INTRINSIC.

inherent value *See* INTRINSIC VALUE.

inherit 1. To receive *genetic material from parents through biological processes. *See also* HEREDITY. **2.** To receive an item from a previous owner (often a relative) upon their death. *See also* LEGACY.

inholding General term for private land within public parks, forests, or wildlife refuges.

injection well A *well that is used for injecting water or other fluid into a groundwater *aquifer, by pressure.

injection zone A geological formation that receives fluids through a *well.

inland waters Waterbodies (such as *lakes, *streams, *rivers, *canals, waterways, inlets, and bays) that have no direct access to the ocean.

inlet An entrance to a *waterbody, such as an *estuary or *bay.

inner core *See* CORE.

innovative treatment technology New methods to effectively treat *hazardous waste, which can offer cost-effective, long-term solutions to *cleanup problems, may provide an alternative to land disposal or incineration, and are often more acceptable to local communities than some established treatment technologies.

inoculation *See* VACCINATION.

inorganic A substance (such as *metals, *minerals, and *rocks) that does not contain *carbon and is not derived from biological material. *Contrast* ORGANIC.

inorganic chemistry The chemistry of substances that do not contain *carbon. *Contrast* ORGANIC CHEMISTRY.

inorganic compound Any compound that does not contain *carbon. *Contrast* ORGANIC COMPOUND.

inorganic nitrogen *Nitrogen which is in the *mineral state and can be readily used by plants. *Contrast* ORGANIC NITROGEN.

inorganic waste Waste (such as *sand, *glass, or any other *synthetic material) that consists of materials other than plant or animal matter.

input Energy, matter, or information that is put into a *system in order to achieve a result. *Contrast* OUTPUT.

INQUA *See* INTERNATIONAL UNION FOR QUATERNARY RESEARCH.

inquiline An *organism that lives on or in the body of another, or in its nest or abode, without benefit or damage to the other organism from which is gets shelter and sometimes food.

insect A member of the *arthropod class Insecta (Hexapoda) of *invertebrate animals that have three body parts, three pairs of jointed legs, and usually two pairs of wings borne on the thorax. Most insects have a single pair of antennae and compound eyes. There are more than 750 000 living species. Examples include beetles, flies, bees, ants, and moths.

insect growth regulator A chemical substance that interferes with the ability of an insect to moult its *exoskeleton. It may inhibit or mimic the hormones involved in moulting, causing larvae to moult prematurely, preventing the insect from maturing, or inhibit the formation of *chitin, from which the exoskeleton is made. Insect growth regulators may also sterilize insects and interfere with *diapause.

insecticidal oil A light-weight oil that smothers plants, insect eggs, and larvae on contact, which offers an environmentally sound means of controlling *insects.

insecticidal soap A *soap that is derived from fats or oils that have been treated with a specific kind of alkaline substance (such as *potash), which paralyses and eventually kills insect pests (such as aphids) when sprayed on them. A common form of *insecticide.

insecticide A chemical *pesticide that is used to control or kill *insects.

insecticide resistance *See* PESTICIDE RESISTANCE.

insectivorous Insect-eating, feeding largely or exclusively on *insects.

inselberg An isolated, steep-sided *hill composed mainly of hard rock, which rises sharply above a *plain in tropical and subtropical areas.

inshore Towards the *shore, or close to a shore, where wave characteristics are modified by interaction with the sea bed. *Contrast* OFF-SHORE.

insolation Incoming *solar radiation, the *radiation from the *Sun that enters the Earth's *atmosphere (see Fig. 10). Around a third is returned to *space (21% is reflected back into space from *clouds, 6% is reflected back from the ground, and 5% is scattered by tiny particles in the air as *diffuse radiation); half reaches the ground (30% by *direct radiation and 20% by diffuse radiation); and 18% is absorbed in the atmosphere (3% by clouds and 15% by *dust and the *ozone layer).

insolation weathering (thermoclastis) A type of *physical weathering which involves re-peated heating and cooling of rock over daily cycles, causing uneven expansion and contraction that progressively causes breaks between mineral grains that lead to failure of rocks.

insoluble Not capable of being dissolved. *Contrast* SOLUBLE.

instability A meteorological condition that exists when a rising *parcel of air continues to rise because at every height it is warmer, and thus less dense, than the air around it (the opposite of *stability). Instability may be absolute or conditional. *See* ABSOLUTE INSTABILITY; CONDITIONAL INSTABILITY.

instar An *insect larva that is between moults of its *exoskeleton, or between its final *ecdysis and emergence in its adult form.

Fig. 10 Insolation

institutional waste *Waste material that is generated at institutions such as schools, libraries, hospitals, and prisons.

instream flow The quantity of water that is required in a stream in order to meet the needs of fish, wildlife, and recreational users.

instream use (non-abstractive use) Water that is used within the *stream channel, for uses such as *hydroelectric power generation, navigation, *fish farming, and *recreation. *Contrast* OFFSTREAM USE.

instrumental value The *value or worth of objects that provide a means to some desirable end, thereby satisfying some human needs and wants. *See also* INTRINSIC VALUE.

insufficiently known species A category of species defined by the *IUCN *Red Data Book as taxa that are suspected but not definitely known to belong to any of the at-risk categories (*endangered, *extinct, *extirpated, *threatened, *vulnerable), because of lack of information. *See* UNKNOWN (THREAT) CATEGORY OF SPECIES.

intake 1. A structure through which water enters a *reservoir. 2. The process (*ingestion or *inhalation) by which a substance enters a body without being absorbed through its exterior. *See also* ADMINISTERED DOSE.

intangible Incapable of being touched or seen, having no physical or material presence.

intangible resource (intangibles) Assets such as open space, attractiveness, diversity, and satisfaction that are not material or physical.

intangibles *See* INTANGIBLE RESOURCE.

integrated area management (IAM) An approach to the management of *natural resources in which a specific area is zoned and regulated for a variety of uses (such as research, *conservation, tourism, harvesting, *hunting, or *fishing) that is compatible with the management goals for the area.

integrated assessment An assessment that brings together data about the past, current, and future condition of *ecosystems, the impact of humans on the ecosystems, and the effects of *environmental change on humans. This form of analysis is regularly carried out to predict the likely impact of environmental change (such as *global warming) and to evaluate policy responses to it. *See also* ENVIRONMENTAL ASSESSMENT.

integrated catchment management (ICM) A *systems approach to the management of *natural resources within a *drainage basin, which includes consideration of all environmental, economic, and social issues within an overall management plan. *See also* INTEGRATED WATER RESOURCE MANAGEMENT.

integrated conservation and development programme (ICDP) An approach to *environmental management that is based on linking nature conservation in *protected areas (such as *national parks) with local social and economic development, with a view to making *biodiversity conservation more effective, increasing local community participation in conservation and development, and increasing economic development for the rural poor.

integrated exposure assessment An estimate of the total *exposure of a person or population to a particular *toxic chemical, through all media, over a given period of time.

integrated pest management (IPM) An *ecological approach to the management of *pests that relies on natural mortality factors (such as natural enemies, weather, and cultural control methods) and carefully applied doses of *pesticides.

integrated pollution control (IPC) An approach to the control of *pollution by industry in the UK, in which any person who carries out a prescribed process must obtain authorization from the *environmental regulator, and must comply with conditions set by the environmental regulator. This has been replaced since 2000 by *Pollution Prevention and Control.

Integrated Pollution Prevention and Control (IPPC) Directive An *EU *directive that was introduced in 2008, which promotes an integrated approach to controlling the *environmental impacts of certain industrial activities, and involves determining the appropriate controls for industry to protect the environment through a single permit process. *See also* POLLUTION PREVENTION AND CONTROL.

(⊕) SEE WEB LINKS

• Europa: Summaries of EU legislation.

integrated resource management (integrated resource planning, multiple-use management) The comprehensive management of two or more *natural resources (including water, soil, timber, range, fish, wildlife, and recreation) in the same area, in order to optimize the overall benefits on a sustainable basis.

integrated resource planning See INTEGRATED RESOURCE MANAGEMENT.

integrated waste management (IWM) An approach to the *sustainable management of *waste, based on environmentally sound processes such as *source reduction, *recycling, *resource recovery, *incineration, and *landfill.

integrated water resource management (IWRM) An approach to the *sustainable management of *water resources in a *drainage basin which recognizes the need to preserve the integrity of the basin *water cycle, and respects the interrelationships between different parts of that cycle. See also INTEGRATED CATCHMENT MANAGEMENT; INTEGRATED RESOURCE MANAGEMENT.

integrity Completeness or totality, unmodified and not reduced. See also BIOLOGICAL INTEGRITY.

integumentary system In animals, the covering of skin (which includes hair, nails, scales, and feathers) which supports and protects the body.

intellectual capital The overall body of *knowledge that exists within an organization in terms of data, information, and wisdom, which is held in the minds and experience of people, creates intelligence, and helps to drive creativity and innovation.

intellectual property *Knowledge that stems from the exercise of the mind, is recognized and protected under law (for example by patent, trade mark, design, copyright, and plant breeder's rights), and can be given a monetary value and made subject to contractual agreements such as licensing.

intellectual property right (IPR) The major legal mechanisms by which *intellectual property is protected (particularly copyright, patent, and trademark), which enable owners to select who may access and use their property, and thus protect it from unauthorized use.

intensification In *synoptic meteorology, an increase in the *pressure gradient surrounding an *anticyclone. See also WEAKENING.

intensive agriculture *Agriculture which involves intensive management of land, designed to maximize output through the use of chemicals (*fertilizers) and machinery, the re-seeding of *grassland, clearance of unproductive areas (such as *hedges and small *copses), and drainage of wetland. See also AGRICULTURAL INTENSIFICATION.

intensive recreation High-density *concentrated recreation activities, such as developed campgrounds and picnic sites, swimming beaches, hiking trails that are major access routes into wilderness areas, and areas used by all-terrain vehicles. Contrast DISPERSED RECREATION.

interbasin transfer (trans-basin diversion) The diversion and conveyance of water from one *drainage basin to another, usually via pipes and *aqueducts.

interception 1. The catching of *precipitation by the leaves and other surfaces of plants, or of sunlight by objects that cast shadows. **2.** The abstraction of *groundwater that otherwise would flow into the sea.

intercropping (interplanting) Growing two or more crops in the same field at the same time, either mixed together or in alternating rows, in order to protect the soil and use land efficiently.

interdisciplinary Applying the knowledge and skills from different academic disciplines or subjects that are normally regarded as distinct, to the same task or project. See also MULTIDISCIPLINARY.

interest group See PRESSURE GROUP.

interface A shared *boundary, for example between liquids, solids, and gasses, or between two systems (for example where a river meets the sea).

interference competition *Competition in which one *species denies another access to a limiting *resource on which both species depend. See also EXPLOITATION COMPETITION.

interflow (throughflow) Water that moves laterally through the upper *soil horizons, usually following heavy rain. It may emerge above the surface at the foot of slopes.

interfluve See DRAINAGE DIVIDE.

intergenerational equity The principle that the present generation should pass on to future generations enough *natural resources and sufficient *environmental quality that they can enjoy at least a comparable quality of life, and inherit a healthy and sustainable *environmental heritage. It seeks a fair distribution of the costs and benefits of a long-term *environmental policy, when costs and benefits are borne by different generations. For example, the costs of policies designed to address the problem of *global warming by reducing *emissions of *greenhouse gases will be largely carried by the present and next few generations, whereas generations in the more distant future will enjoy the long-term benefits.

interglacial A period of increased temperatures between *ice ages, or between major phases of *glaciation or ice advance. The present *Holocene period is an interglacial. *See also* INTERSTADIAL.

Intergovernmental Panel on Climate Change (IPCC) An international institution, comprising climate and other scientists, many with links to environmental campaign groups, climate modellers, and government officials, whose participants study peer-reviewed scientific publications as well as non-scientific articles and reports in order to predict the extent and adverse consequences of *anthropogenic climate change (AGW). It was established in 1988 by the *World Meteorological Organization and the *United Nations Environment Programme and advises governments through the *United Nations Framework Convention on Climate Change. The IPCC has three working groups. Working Group I summarizes the scientific basis for AGW. Working Group II considers the economic, social, and environmental impacts of AGW. Working Group III considers ways to mitigate AGW and its effects, primarily through reducing emissions of *greenhouse gases. The IPPC issues its own publications, the most important of which are its assessment reports, issued every few years. The fourth assessment report (AR4) appeared in 2007 and AR5 is scheduled for publication in 2014.

Interior Department *See* US DEPARTMENT OF THE INTERIOR.

interior drainage A *drainage pattern in which streams converge in a closed *basin and evaporate without reaching the sea.

intermediate A *crown class of trees in a *forest.

intermediate cut The removal of immature trees from a *forest, often by thinning, before the major harvest, in order to improve the quality of the remaining forest stand. *Contrast* HARVEST CUT.

intermediate disturbance hypothesis The belief that, within a given *ecosystem, the highest species *diversity exists under conditions of intermediate disturbance because too much disturbance causes local extinction (*extirpation) and at low levels of disturbance competitive species exclude others.

intermediate rock *Igneous rocks that have a *silica content between the extremes of the *mafic and *felsic rocks, and weather down to produce quite fertile soils. Intermediate between *basic and *acidic rocks.

intermediate technology (appropriate technology) *Technology that can be made at an affordable price, by ordinary people in *developing countries, using local materials, in ways that minimize damage to the environment.

intermediate-level waste *Radioactive waste that contains higher levels of *radioactivity than *low-level waste, and less than *high-level waste.

intermittent (episodic) Occurring from time to time.

intermittent flow River flow that is irregular and occurs only after heavy rain or *snow melt. *Contrast* EPHEMERAL FLOW; PERENNIAL FLOW.

intermittent stream A *stream that flows only at certain times of the year when it receives water from upstream, from heavy rain or *snow melt.

Intermodal Surface Transportation Efficiency Act (ISTEA) (1991) US legislation that authorized funding for highways, highway safety, and mass transportation between 1991 and 1997, when it expired, but much of the programme was carried forward by the *Transportation Equity Act for the 21st Century.

intermontane basin A low-lying area (*basin) between mountain ranges that is being slowly filled with sediment eroded from the mountains.

internal combustion engine An engine in which the fuel burns inside the engine itself, as opposed to a steam engine in which fuel is burned in a separate furnace. Most vehicles powered by internal combustion engines use *gasoline as fuel, and emit *air pollutants such as *carbon monoxide, *nitrogen oxides, and reactive *hydrocarbons.

internal cost The direct cost (monetary or otherwise) that is met by those who use a resource.

internal dose *See* ABSORBED DOSE.

internal energy The *energy which a substance possesses because of the motion and configuration of its *atoms, *molecules, and *subatomic particles.

internal migration The movement (*migration) of people or animals within a country or defined region. *Contrast* INTERNATIONAL MIGRATION.

internal trading In *greenhouse gas *emissions trading, internal trading is trading within a company which allows the company to trade *emission permits between its business units in order to maximize cost-effective emission control.

internal waters Any body of surface water that is under the exclusive control of a coastal nation, including *bays, *estuaries, and *rivers. *Contrast* INTERNATIONAL WATERS; INTERSTATE WATERS.

internalization In *accounting, the process of including in financial balance sheets the cost factors which were previously either not calculated (for example the cost of *environmental damage) or met by society at large (for example the health costs associated with pollution). *See also* EXTERNALITY.

International Atomic Energy Agency (IAEA) A United Nations agency that was formed in 1957, is based in Vienna, Austria, and is responsible for supervising the use of nuclear material, developing safety standards, preventing the proliferation of *nuclear weapons, and promoting the peaceful use of *nuclear energy.

International Bank for Reconstruction and Development *See* WORLD BANK.

International Conference on Population and Development (ICPD), Cairo (1994) A major international conference organized by the *United Nations that met in Cairo, Egypt in September 1994, and discussed the global dimensions of *population growth and change. The conference agreed goals for 2015 that are designed to improve individual and family well-being and enhance the status of women. The goals include universal access to *family planning and primary school education, increased access by girls and women to secondary and higher education, and reductions in infant, child, and maternal mortality. The conference is widely credited as a major turning-point in establishing international consensus on effective ways of slowing the pace of population growth and improving *quality of life, by addressing root causes of unwanted *fertility.

International Conference on Population, Mexico City (1984) An international conference organized by the *United Nations which built on the success of the *World Population Conference in Bucharest 1974, was attended by representatives from 150 countries, provided a further impetus for the *World Population Plan of Action, and was a key milestone in the development of the 1994 *International Conference on Population and Development (ICPD) held in Cairo.

international convention *See* CONVENTION.

International Convention for the Prevention of Pollution from Ships (1973, 1978, MARPOL) An international *convention combining two treaties adopted in 1973 and 1978 that covers the prevention of pollution of the marine environment by ships, from operational or accidental causes. The convention was modified by protocols in 1978 and 1997.

(((⊕))) SEE WEB LINKS

• International Convention for the Prevention of Pollution from Ships.

International Convention for the Regulation of Whales (1946) An international *convention that was signed in Washington, DC in December 1946, and is designed to safeguard whale stocks for future generations. It set up the *International Whaling Commission and introduced regulations concerning: the conservation and utilization of whale resources, relating to protected and unprotected species; open and closed seasons; open and closed waters; the designation of sanctuary areas; size limits for each species; time, methods, and intensity of whaling (including the maximum catch of whales to be taken in any one season); types and specifications of gear and apparatus and appliances that may be used; methods of measurement; and catch returns and other statistical and biological records.

International Convention on Oil Pollution Preparedness, Response and Co-operation (1990) An international *convention that provides a global framework for international cooperation in combating major incidents or threats of marine *pollution.

International Convention on the Control of Harmful Anti-fouling Systems on Ships (2001) An international *convention that prohibits the use of harmful *organotins in antifouling paints used on ships, and establishes a mechanism to prevent the potential future use of other harmful substances in antifouling systems.

International Convention Relating to Intervention on the High Seas in Cases of Oil Pollution Casualties (1969) An international *convention that affirms the right of a coastal state to take such measures on the *high seas as may be necessary to prevent, mitigate, or eliminate danger to its coastline or related interests from pollution by oil or the threat of such pollution, after a maritime accident.

International Council for the Exploration of the Sea (ICES) An intergovernmental organization concerned with marine and fisheries science. It was established in Copenhagen in 1902 to promote the exchange of information on the sea and its living resources and to promote and coordinate marine research between member countries.

International Council of Scientific Unions (ICSU) A non-governmental organization that was founded in 1932 to bring together scientists in international scientific endeavours in order to help members address major international, interdisciplinary issues.

international credit (international permit) In *greenhouse gas *emissions trading, under the *Kyoto Protocol, a method by which emissions credits or permits can be transferred between countries through *Joint Implementation, *Clean Development Mechanisms, and *international emissions trading.

International Date Line A line of *longitude that lies generally 180° east and west of the prime meridian (*Greenwich Meridian); the date is one day earlier to the east of the line.

International Decade for Natural Disaster Reduction (IDNDR) An international programme of the *United Nations, between 1990 and 2000, that sought to harness the political resolve, experience, and expertise of each country in order to reduce the loss of life, human suffering, and economic losses caused by *natural hazards. Some scientists point out

that many of the IDNDR targets complement the objectives of *Agenda 21, although few planners and decision-makers yet build upon the links between successful *disaster management and *sustainable development.

international emissions trading (IET) The international trading of *greenhouse gas permits (*assigned amount units), under the *Kyoto Protocol, which allows developed countries to meet their assigned amounts. *See also* EMISSIONS TRADING.

International Energy Agency (IEA) An intergovernmental organization that was formed in 1973 by major oil-consuming nations in order to manage the security of *energy supply, *economic growth, and environmental *sustainability through energy.

International Geosphere-Biosphere Programme (IGBP) A major international programme of research that began in the early 1980s and was designed to describe and understand the interacting physical, chemical, and biological processes that regulate the Earth's *environmental systems. It was established by the *International Council of Scientific Unions (ICSU) in 1986, and its activities are focused on a series of core projects, which are the International Global Atmospheric Chemistry Project, Stratosphere–Troposphere Interactions and the Biosphere, the Joint Global Ocean Flux Study, the Global Ocean Euphotic Zone Study, Land–Ocean Interactions in the Coastal Zone, Biospheric Aspects of the Hydrological Cycle, Global Change and Terrestrial Ecosystems, Past Global Changes, and Global Analysis, Interpretation and Modelling. *Mission to Planet Earth is an important component of the IGBP.

International Human Suffering Index (HIS) A composite index of economic and social well-being that can be used to show changes in human well-being, based on a number of key variables including life expectancy, daily calorie intake, clean drinking water, infant immunization, secondary school enrolment, *GDP per capita, rate of inflation, communications technology, political freedom, and civil rights.

International Institute for Applied Systems Analysis (IIASA) A non-governmental research organization located near Vienna in Austria, that conducts *interdisciplinary scientific studies on environmental, economic, technological, and social issues in the context of the human dimensions of global change.

International Institute for Sustainable Development (IISD) A non-governmental organization based in Winnipeg, Canada, that advances policy recommendations on international trade, economic instruments, *climate change, and *natural resource management in order to make development *sustainable.

International Joint Commission (IJC) An independent binational organization established by the *Boundary Water Treaty of 1909, whose purpose is to help prevent and resolve disputes relating to the use and quality of *boundary water between Canada and the USA.

International Maritime Organisation (IMO) A United Nations specialized agency that is concerned with setting international *standards in the marine environment, particularly to improve maritime safety and to prevent marine *pollution. The IMO is responsible for a number of UN conventions on marine pollution—the *Convention on the Prevention of Marine Pollution by Dumping of Wastes and Other Matter (1972), the *International Convention for the Prevention of Pollution from Ships (1973, 1978), the *International Convention on the Control of Harmful Anti-fouling Systems on Ships (2001), the *International Convention on Oil Pollution Preparedness, Response and Co-operation (1990), the *International Convention Relating to Intervention on the High Seas in Cases of Oil Pollution Casualties (1969), and the *Protocol on Preparedness, Response and Co-operation to Pollution Incidents by Hazardous and Noxious Substances (2000).

SEE WEB LINKS
• Introduction to the IMO.

international migration The movement (*migration) of people or animals across a national border, from one country to another. *Contrast* INTERNAL MIGRATION.

International Organization for Standardization (ISO) A network of national standards institutes from 145 countries. *See also* ISO 9000; ISO 14001.

international permit *See* INTERNATIONAL CREDIT.

International Planned Parenthood Federation (IPPF) An international organization made up of autonomous family planning associations (FPAs) in over 180 countries

around the world, which are concerned with *family planning and sexual and reproductive health.

international pollution *See* TRANS-FRONTIER POLLUTION.

international regime An international agreement between countries.

International Seabed Authority An autonomous organization, established in November 1994 under the *United Nations Convention on the Law of the Sea, through which parties to the convention organize and control activities on and beneath the seabed and ocean floor in areas beyond the limits of national jurisdiction. The authority is based in Kingston, Jamaica.

SEE WEB LINKS
• Home page of the International Seabed Authority.

International Union for Conservation of Nature and Natural Resources (IUCN) *See* WORLD CONSERVATION UNION.

International Union for Quaternary Research (INQUA) An international scientific organization that was founded in 1928 for the study of *Quaternary geology, climate, biology, and anthropology.

international waters The open seas outside the territorial waters of any individual nation. *Contrast* INTERNAL WATERS; INTERSTATE WATERS.

International Whaling Commission (IWC) An international organization that was set up under the *International Convention for the Regulation of Whales in 1946 in order to regulate the whaling industry and conserve *whales.

interplanting *See* INTERCROPPING.

interpluvial A period during which the *climate is relatively dry, lasting for decades or longer, between *pluvials.

interpolation Estimating values between known numerical values, for example in order to draw an *isopleth. *Contrast* EXTRAPOLATION.

interpretation 1. An explanation of the meaning of data. 2. The provision of scientific and academic information about a site or area in formats (such as fixed signs) that are meaningful to non-specialists and help people to understand and appreciate the natural and cultural heritage.

interseeding Sowing seeds into existing vegetation.

interspecific competition *Competition for resources between individuals of different species in a given *community. *Contrast* INTRA-SPECIFIC COMPETITION.

interstade (interstadial) A brief period of glacial retreat (*deglaciation), lasting 1000–2000 years, caused by warming within a glacial stage. *Contrast* STADE.

interstadial *See* INTERSTADE.

interstate pollution Pollution (such as *acid rain) that moves across the borders between states within a country. *Contrast* TRANS-FRONTIER POLLUTION.

interstate waters Bodies of *surface water that flow across or form part of state or international boundaries, such as the *Great Lakes and the Mississippi River. *Contrast* INTERNAL WATERS; INTERNATIONAL WATERS.

interstices The space between two or more objects, such as the *pore spaces between the individual grains in a *soil or *rock.

interstitial Relating to *interstices.

interstitial fauna Animals that live in the *interstices between sand grains. The term is often used synonymously with *mesofauna.

intertidal The zone of the *shore that lies between the *high and *low water marks, which is submerged at *high tide and exposed at *low tide.

Intertropical Convergence Zone (ITCZ) The zone of converging *trade winds along the *equator, which causes rising air currents, low surface *atmospheric pressure, and often a continuous band of *clouds or *thunderstorms. It provides the upward motion in the *Hadley cell.

intolerant In ecology, unable to withstand adverse environmental conditions such as shade or drought. *Contrast* TOLERANT.

intraspecific competition *Competition for *resources between members of the same *species within a *community. *Contrast* INTER-SPECIFIC COMPETITION.

intrazonal soil A *soil that is untypical of its *climate zone because it has been strongly affected by more local factors such as *topography and parent material. *Contrast* ZONAL SOIL; AZONAL SOIL. *See also* GREAT SOIL GROUP; SOIL ORDER.

intrinsic (inherent) Inside, or belonging to something by its very nature. *Contrast* EXTRIN-SIC.

intrinsic resource *See* NATURAL RESOURCE.

intrinsic value (inherent value) Ethical *values or rights that exist as an *intrinsic characteristic of a particular thing or class of things simply because of their existence. *Contrast* ACQUIRED VALUE; EXTRINSIC VALUE; INSTRU-MENTAL VALUE.

introduced species (alien, exotic species, non-native species) A *species that has been brought into an area where it does not naturally occur, outside its known *historic range, usually by humans, and which is able to survive and reproduce. *See also* INVASIVE SPECIES; NATIVE SPECIES.

intrusion (pluton) A body of *igneous rock that is formed by the injection of molten *magma into pre-existing rocks beneath the *Earth's surface.

intrusive (plutonic) Applied to rocks formed from molten *magma that is forced into cracks between layers of other rock. *Contrast* EXTRU-SIVE.

inundation The process of being covered with standing or slow-moving water. *See also* FLOOD.

invader *See* INVASIVE SPECIES.

invasive species (invader) An aggressive *introduced species which spreads and dominates its new location, competing with and often replacing *native species and proving difficult to remove. *See also* INTRODUCED SPECIES.

inventory A detailed list of items, such as the register of *sources and *sinks of *greenhouse gases in a particular country.

inversion (temperature inversion) An increase in air temperature with height, resulting in a layer of warm air lying above cooler air, thereby inhibiting *convection. An inversion often traps *pollutants beneath it and can cause an air *pollution episode. *See also* ADVEC-TION INVERSION.

invertebrate An animal that has no backbone or spinal column. Examples include *arthropods, *cnidarians, and *molluscs. *See also*

MACROINVERTEBRATE;   MICROINVERTEBRATE.
Contrast VERTEBRATE.

iodine (I) A non-metallic *halogen element
that is required by humans in small amounts
for healthy growth and development, and is
often used in medicine as an antiseptic. It kills
bacteria and prevents algal growth, is found
naturally in *seawater, and is necessary in
small quantities for reef invertebrates such as
*corals and clams.

ion An *atom or group of atoms that has acquired an electric charge by the loss or gain of
one or more *electrons.

ion exchange A reversible *chemical reaction between a solid and a solution by means
of which *ions of the same charge may be exchanged between the two.

ion exchange treatment A common
method for making *hard water softer, based
on adding calcium oxide or calcium hydroxide
which increases *pH to a level at which *metals
*precipitate out.

ionic bond A force that holds together two
electrically charged atoms (*ions).

ionic strength A measure of the concentration and charge of *ions in *solution, which
affects the *solubility of *compounds.

ionization The production of *ions.

ionizing radiation High-energy radiation
(with wavelengths shorter than those of visible
light, e.g. *gamma rays and *X-rays) that is capable of causing *ionization in the matter
through which it passes and can damage living
tissue. *See also* IRRADIATION.

ionosphere The outer part of the *atmosphere, between about 60 and 1000 km altitude,
lying above the *mesosphere. It is the region in
which high-energy *ultraviolet radiation ionizes
atmospheric gases.

IPAT An equation $(I = P \times A \times T)$ that was
developed by Paul *Ehrlich and John Holdren in
1972 to describe how impact (I) or *environmental change is a function of population size
(P), affluence (A), and *technology (T). Although the I = PAT formula is a useful way of
studying the relationship between factors that
govern environmental change, critics have
pointed to two important weaknesses in this
sort of approach. First, the factors contributing
to any particular impact can vary a great deal,
depending on the *environmental impact in

question (for example, different factors contribute to depletion of the *ozone layer and to loss
of *biodiversity). Secondly, the equation suggests that the three factors (P, A, and T) operate
independently, whilst in reality they may well
interact with each other.

IPC *See* INTEGRATED POLLUTION CONTROL.

IPCC *See* INTERGOVERNMENTAL PANEL ON CLI-
MATE CHANGE.

IPM *See* INTEGRATED PEST MANAGEMENT.

IPPF *See* INTERNATIONAL PLANNED PARENT-
HOOD FEDERATION.

IPR *See* INTELLECTUAL PROPERTY RIGHTS.

Ipswichian The temperate, last *Pleistocene
*interglacial, named after Ipswich, Suffolk,
England, and the associated Late Pleistocene
deposits that occur in river valleys, often associated with *river terraces. It began about 130
000 years ago and ended about 114 000 years
ago. Pollen diagrams compiled from them indicate that the climate was 2–3°C warmer than
that of the present day. Hippopotamus, woolly
mammoth, rhinoceros, and the straight-tusked
elephant (*Elephas antiquus*) were present as far
north as the Thames and Rhine. The Ipswichian
is the British equivalent of the *Eemian in northern Europe and the Sangamonian in North
America.

IR *See* INFRARED.

IRA Inventoried roadless area in US *national
forest lands, defined under the *Roadless Area
Review and Evaluation survey.

iridescence Shimmering spots or borders of
colours (most often red and green) which are
caused by *diffraction of light by oil molecules,
small water droplets, and ice particles of approximately equal size. The effect can sometimes be seen in high- or medium-level
*clouds (particularly in thin *cirrus clouds),
known as iridescent clouds.

iridescent clouds *See* IRIDESCENCE.

iron (Fe) A *malleable metal that occurs naturally and is the fourth most abundant *element
in the Earth's *crust. It is a *trace element (*micronutrient) for plants and an essential *nutrient for humans.

Iron Age The *prehistoric period of human
culture which began in Europe around 1000
BCE (after the *Bronze Age), during which

*iron was the principal material used for making tools and weapons.

iron formation A *sedimentary rock that has a high *iron content, usually more than 15%, as iron sulphide, oxide, carbonate, or silicate.

iron oxide (Fe₂O₃) A compound, whose proper name is iron (III) oxide, that consists of *iron combined with *oxygen, which forms the rust that is visible on iron or steel left exposed to oxygen and moisture in the air. *See also* LATERIZATION.

iron pan Soil in which *iron compounds have been washed from the upper *horizon and deposited as a *hardpan in a lower horizon. *See also* INDURATED.

iron triangle A US term for a close relationship between an agency, a congressional committee, and an interest group that can grow into a mutually advantageous alliance.

irradiated food Food that has been briefly exposed to *radioactivity (usually *gamma rays) on purpose, in order to kill *insects, *bacteria, and *mould, and to allow storage without refrigeration.

irradiation Exposure to *ionizing radiation for medical purposes, to sterilize milk or other foodstuffs, or to induce chemical changes (such as the vulcanization of rubber).

irreplaceability In *conservation assessment, *habitat features, *biotopes, or *species that cannot be replaced if they are destroyed or lost.

irretrievable Not retrievable, impossible to recover; a *natural resource (such as a *stream, *fishery, *wetland, or *wildlife habitat) which would be lost forever as a consequence of a particular activity. One of the categories of *impact that must be included in *environmental impact statements in the US under the *National Environmental Policy Act. The resource is irretrievable, but the action need not be *irreversible.

irreversible Not reversible; a category of *impact relating to non-renewable resources, or actions that can be renewed only after a long period of time (such as loss of soil productivity), that must be included in *environmental impact statements in the US under the *National Environmental Policy Act.

irrigation The application of *water to *land (by a sprinkler, ditch, or *canal), particularly in an *arid area, in order to augment the water supply to plants. By 2010 irrigation accounted for more than 70% of the total amount of water withdrawn on Earth, and 90% of the amount consumed. The total area irrigated was about 301 million hectares (ha); India had 39 million ha of irrigated land, China 19 million ha, and the USA 17 million ha. Of the total irrigated area, about 68% is located in Asia, 17% in America, 9% in Europe, and 1% in Oceania. The total area under irrigation increased by more than a third between 1970 and 1990, with most of the increase concentrated in developing countries. Output from irrigated land is more than double that from the same land unirrigated, and one-fifth of the world's food is grown on irrigated land. Two common problems created by irrigation are *waterlogging and *salinization of soils which result from supplying excessive water with inadequate drainage, and which cause a decline in *crop productivity and *yield.

irrigation efficiency The amount of *water that is stored in the crop *root zone of a soil, compared with the amount of *irrigation water that has been applied.

irrigation return flow Surface and subsurface water that leaves a *field after *irrigation water has been applied, and returns to the normal *water cycle.

irritant A *substance that produces an irritating effect when it comes into contact with the skin, eyes, nose, or respiratory system.

irruptive growth *See* MALTHUSIAN GROWTH.

island An area of land, smaller than a *continent, which is surrounded by water.

island arc A curved chain of *volcanic islands that develops between an *ocean trench and a continental *landmass, and forms above the *subduction zone at a *convergent plate boundary.

island biogeography The study of the relationship between the area of an island and the number of *species that live on it, based on the effect of factors such as rates of *colonization, *immigration, and *extinction, and size, shape, and distance from other inhabited regions. *See also* EQUILIBRIUM THEORY.

island hopping The colonization of an island or islands by plants and animals from an adjacent island or islands. Birds are particularly likely to hop from one island to another. Over geological time, islands move away from their areas of origin by *continental drift. The descendant biotas may maintain themselves in the ancestral environment by island hopping on to successively younger islands as these emerge.

ISO *See* INTERNATIONAL ORGANIZATION FOR STANDARDIZATION.

ISO 9000 A set of certification standards for quality management systems.

ISO 14001 The international standard for *environmental management systems and good environmental practices. *See also* ECO-MANAGEMENT AND AUDIT SCHEME.

isobar A line on a *weather map which connects points of equal *atmospheric pressure, measured in *millibars.

isobaric saturation point *See* DEW POINT.

isochron 1. A line on a map that connects points which have the same time or time interval. **2.** In geology, a line of equal age on a graph.

isohel A line drawn on a map that links places which experience an equal number of hours of sunshine.

isohyet A line on a *weather map which connects points of equal *rainfall over a given period of time.

isolated showers *Showers that cover less than 15% of an area.

isolated system A *system that has no exchange of *energy or *matter across its boundaries.

isoline *See* ISOPLETH.

isomer A chemical *compound that has the same number and kinds of *atoms as another compound, but a different structural arrangement of the atoms.

isopleth (isoline) A line on a map which connects points of a constant value, such as *isobar, *isochron, *isohel, *isohyet, *isopycnal, *isotach, or *isotherm.

isoprene A volatile *hydrocarbon compound (C_5H_8) that forms the structural base of many compounds synthesized by plants. Isoprene molecules form units that combine to make larger units, known as terpenes. Many plants, especially deciduous trees, emit both isoprenes and terpenes. These compounds are highly reactive and play a major role in the formation of

ozone in the lower atmosphere. Isoprene contributes to the formation of *photochemical smog and in rural areas it is the predominant hydrocarbon involved.

isopycnal A line on a map joining points of equal density within a water mass. A three-dimensional surface of equal density is called an isopycnal surface.

isostasy The mechanism by which the *lithosphere floats on the *asthenosphere, with *continents and *mountains supported by either low-density 'roots' within the Earth's *crust or lower-density surface rocks; changes such as loading and unloading by ice or water bodies, cause depression or rebound of the lithosphere. *See also* PLATE TECTONICS.

isostatic adjustment (isostatic rebound) The *warping of part of the Earth's *crust as a response to the redistribution of weight, for example associated with large-scale *glaciation and *deglaciation. *Contrast* EUSTATIC.

isostatic rebound *See* ISOSTATIC ADJUSTMENT.

isotach A line on a *weather map that connects points of equal *wind speed.

isotherm A line on a *weather map that connects points of equal *temperature.

isothermal At a constant *temperature, with height or through time.

isotonic Two *solutions, or a *cell and a surrounding solution, which contain the same *concentration of a *dissolved substance.

isotope One of two or more *atoms of the same *element that have the same number of *protons (and hence the same chemical properties) but a different number of *neutrons and thus different *atomic weights.

isotope analysis A technique that is used to reconstruct past *climate change, based on detailed analysis of the *oxygen isotope composition of *ice cores, the remains of marine organisms, and *calcite deposits in *caves.

isotropy Identical in all directions. *Contrast* ANISOTROPY.

ISTEA *See* INTERMODAL SURFACE TRANSPORTATION EFFICIENCY ACT.

Itai-Itai disease Health problems in humans occurring as a result of *cadmium poisoning, which causes softening of the bones and kidney failure. First observed in Japan in 1950.

ITCZ *See* INTERTROPICAL CONVERGENCE ZONE.

iteroparity The condition of an organism that has more than one reproductive cycle during its lifetime. *Compare* SEMELPARITY.

IUCN *See* WORLD CONSERVATION UNION.

IUCN management category Categories for the management of protected areas which were developed by the IUCN (*World Conservation Union) and are widely used around the world. The ten categories are: Category I, *Scientific Reserve/Strict Nature Reserve; Category II, *National Park; Category III, *Natural Monument/Natural Landmark; Category IV, *Managed Nature Reserve/Wildlife Sanctuary; Category V, *Protected Landscape or Seascape; Category VI, Resource Reserve; Category VII, *Natural Biotic Area/Anthropological Reserve; Category VIII, *Multiple-Use Management Area/Managed Resource Area; Category IX, *Biosphere Reserve; Category X, *World Heritage Site.

IWC *See* INTERNATIONAL WHALING COMMISSION.

IWM *See* INTEGRATED WASTE MANAGEMENT.

IWRM *See* INTEGRATED WATER RESOURCE MANAGEMENT.

Ixtoc I An oil well off the coast of Yucatán, Mexico, that blew out on 3 June 1979, releasing 30 000 bbl of oil a day into the Gulf of Mexico. The well was partially capped in October, but continued to leak until relief wells were drilled to release the pressure. The well was finally sealed in March 1980, by which time it had released about three million barrels.

Janzen–Connell escape hypothesis (escape hypothesis) The hypothesis that isolated individuals of a given plant *species will escape their specialist *herbivores and thus survive better than individuals growing together in clumps.

J-curve A growth curve that describes *exponential growth in a *population, so-called because of its shape. *Contrast* S-CURVE.

jet streak The region of fastest wind flow within the *jet stream.

jet stream A narrow, meandering band of very fast *wind in the *troposphere or lower *stratosphere, where temperature gradients are particularly strong (see Fig. 11). There are several jet streams. The polar and subtropical jet streams flow from west to east in both hemispheres. The easterly jet stream blows in summer from east to west across Asia and into north-eastern Africa.

JI *See* JOINT IMPLEMENTATION.

jigging *See* HAND-LINING.

joint A small-scale surface fracture or break within rocks which are subjected to *compression pressure or *tensional pressure beyond their *plastic limit, without movement (unlike a *fault).

joint and several liability A legal standard for the *cleanup of *Superfund sites in the USA, which makes all owners or users of a site potentially liable for cleaning up a site that has become contaminated over a number of years.

Joint Implementation (JI) A mechanism, established under the *Kyoto Protocol, which allows a *developed country to acquire emission credits to assist in meeting their assigned amounts (*emissions reduction unit) when it helps to finance projects that reduce net emissions in another developed country, including *countries with economies in transition. This allows industrialized countries to meet their obligations for reducing their *greenhouse gas emissions by receiving credits for investing in emissions reductions in *developing countries. *See also* ACTIVITIES IMPLEMENTED JOINTLY.

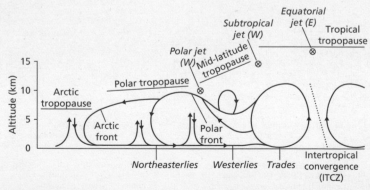

Fig. 11 Jet stream

jökulhlaup A destructive *flood caused by the sudden release of glacial *meltwater, often associated with a *subglacial *volcanic eruption.

joule (J) The derived *SI unit of energy; 1 joule is the work done when a force of 1 newton moves a point to which it was applied 1 metre in the direction in which the force is acting.

Juan Fernandez floral region Part of R. Good's *Neotropical floral kingdom (*The Geography of the Flowering Plants*, 1974), which corresponds geographically to the islands of Juan Fernandez and the Desventuradas Islands, 650–1000 km west of the coast of Chile. There is a remarkable degree of *endemism, including one family, 18 genera, and nearly 160 *species.

judicial precedent A previous decision set by a court, which can be reversed only by a higher court.

jungle Non-scientific name for impenetrable *rainforest.

Jurassic The middle *period of *geological time in the *Mesozoic era, between about 200 and 146 million years ago, named after the Jura Mountains between France and Switzerland. It is characterized by the existence of dinosaurs and the appearance of the earliest *mammals and *birds.

SEE WEB LINKS

• The Jurassic period of the Mesozoic era.

jurisdiction The territory within which legal power can be exercised.

Jusscannz A group of developed countries outside the *European Union, which share information and discuss matters of common interest (including the *Kyoto Protocol). It stands for Japan, the US, Switzerland, Canada, Australia, Norway, and New Zealand. Iceland, Mexico, the Republic of Korea and other invited countries may also attend meetings.

justice Fairness, the quality of being fair or just.

juvenile Youthful, before reaching sexual maturity at the adult stage.

juvenile gas Gas that comes to the surface of the Earth for the first time from deep inside.

juvenile hormone (neotenin) A natural *hormone that enables an insect larva to develop normally into an adult. An immature insect will not develop properly if it is exposed to synthetic juvenile hormones applied as a *pesticide. In adults, juvenile hormone has other functions, possibly related to the development of reproductive organs.

juvenile hormone analogue A synthetic *juvenile hormone that is used as a *pesticide, which reduces the reproductive capacity of the insect population and results eventually in eradication.

juvenile water Original water, formed as a result of magmatic processes, which has never been in the atmosphere. Juvenile water can form in very large quantities. A magma body with a density of 2.5, an assumed water content of 5% by weight, a thickness of 1 km, and an area of 10 km^2 contains some 1.25×10^9 m^3 of water. *See also* GROUNDWATER.

K

kairomone A *semiochemical that is emitted by an *organism (such as a plant) and triggers a response in an individual of another species (such as an insect) which benefits the recipient. This may be disadvantageous to the emitter, for example by attracting insects that feed on it, but the kairomone may also attract predators of those insects. Certain prey species benefit by showing a fear response to kairomones emitted by predators. *Contrast* ALLOMONE.

kame An undulating, steep-sided mound of *sand and *gravel that has been deposited in an irregular pattern by *meltwater adjacent to a *glacier or *ice sheet. *Contrast* ESKER.

kame delta A ridge of *sediment in the form of a steep, flat topped hill, that is deposited by *meltwater in front of a retreating continental *glacier. *See also* KAME TERRACE.

kame terrace A continuous line of *kame that stretches along much of a valley side.

kampfzone *See* ELFIN WOODLAND.

Kansan The name formerly given to the third of the four North American *Pleistocene *glaciations that together comprise the pre-Illinoan (about 2.5 million to 500 000 years BP), and approximately equivalent to the *Gunz in Europe. North American *stratigraphy proved to be more complex than had once been supposed, and the name is no longer recognized.

kaolin See CHINA CLAY.

kaolinite A mineral that is produced by *chemical weathering of *feldspar and consists of aluminium silicate; the main source of kaolin/*china clay.

karst A type of *landscape that results from the *chemical weathering and collapse of *carbonate rocks (such as *limestone and *dolomite), which creates such features as *sinkholes, *caves, and underground drainage. *See also* DOLINE.

karyotype The entire *chromosome complement of an individual organism or cell.

kastanozems Soils that have a dark-coloured surface *soil horizon containing at least 1% organic carbon or 0.6% organic carbon that is more than 20 cm deep, and that also has concentrations of calcium compounds within 100 cm of the surface. Kastanozems are a reference soil group in the *World Soil Classification.

katabatic wind (air drainage wind, fall wind, gravity wind, mountain breeze) Cool dense air driven downslope by gravity beneath warmer lighter air. *Contrast* ANABATIC WIND.

kata-front A weather *front at which air in the *warm sector is subsiding in relation to the cooler air on either side of the front. *Contrast* ANA-FRONT.

Keeling curve (Mauna Loa record) A record of measurements of atmospheric *carbon dioxide concentrations which has been collected by scientists at the Mauna Loa Observatory on *Mauna Loa in Hawaii since March 1958. This is the longest reliable daily record of atmospheric carbon dioxide measurements in the world. The technique for measuring atmospheric CO_2 in the middle *troposphere by its absorption of *infrared radiation was devised by the American geochemist Charles David Keeling (1928–2005).

(((∰))) SEE WEB LINKS

• About the Keeling curve.

kelp Any of a variety of brown seaweeds which contain *trace minerals, *vitamins, and *micronutrients. They are used in Japanese cookery, and can be ground up and used to enrich poor soil.

kelp forest A *marine *ecosystem that is dominated by large *kelps. These forests are restricted to cold and temperate waters, and are most commonly found along the western coasts of *continents.

Kelvin (K) The *SI unit of temperature which is equal in magnitude to a degree *Celsius; temperature expressed in Kelvin is the temperature in °C + 273.15. The temperature of absolute zero is 0 K. Note that degree symbols (°) are not used in the Kelvin scale. The Kelvin scale is used at extremely low temperatures, mostly by physicists, including atmospheric physicists, but rarely by climatologists or meteorologists.

kerbside collection The collection of *compostable or *recyclable material and/or trash at individual homes and businesses, which is then taken to a waste processing facility.

kerbside recycling scheme A *recycling scheme that involves collecting, sorting, and processing *solid waste material (such as glass, paper, *aluminium, and some plastics) which households have left in special containers by the side of the road adjacent to their properties.

kerogen The solid, *bituminous, waxy substance in *oil shales which can be extracted to produce *shale oil.

ketones Organic compounds that contain a ketone group ($>C=O$).

kettle hole An enclosed depression that is created by the melting of a mass of ice trapped in *glacial deposits, and which is often occupied by a *lake.

key facility A term used in the USA to describe public facilities which tend to trigger *development and *urban development. Examples include major airports, road interchanges and highways, recreational lands, and energy production facilities such as major power-plants, transmission lines, oil and gas pipelines, and refineries.

key species In land or conservation management, the major plant or animal *species that should be taken into account.

keystone species A *species that interacts with many other species in a *community, and whose loss would cause a greater than average change in the *populations of other species or in *ecosystem processes.

Kilauea One of the world's most active *volcanoes, located in Hawaii, whose quiet non-explosive eruptions are increasing the size of the island as the *lava descends to the sea.

kilobar (kb) A unit of *pressure equal to 1000 *bars (1 kb = 100 megapascals). *See also* MILLIBAR.

kilometre (km) A metric unit of distance equal to 1000 m or 0.62 miles.

kilowatt (kW) A unit of electrical power equal to 1000 watts (roughly 1.341 horsepower).

kilowatt hour (kWh) The work performed by 1 *kilowatt of power applied for 1 hour.

kinetic energy *Energy which is possessed by a body because of its motion, such as a rock rolling down a hill, the wind blowing through the trees, or water flowing over a dam. It is defined as the amount of work a moving body could do if it were brought to rest, and it is equal to ½ mv^2, where m is the mass of the moving body and v is its speed. For a rotating body it is equal to ½ $I\Omega^2$, where Ω is the angular velocity and I is the moment of inertia.

kingdom One of the major categories in the scientific system of classification for organisms (*taxonomy). In the five-kingdom system of classification the kingdoms are: *Bacteria, *Protoctista, *Fungi, *Plantae, and *Animalia; Bacteria are sometimes divided into two groups within the kingdom *Monera. In the three-domain classification and the two-domain *eocyte hypothesis kingdoms are ranked below *domains. *See also* BIOLOGICAL CLASSIFICATION.

kitchen garden A small *garden in which vegetables are grown.

kleptoparasitism *Parasitism that is based upon the theft of food from other organisms. Skuas practise this form of parasitism upon gulls and terns. Ants often attempt this parasitism upon carnivorous plants, robbing them of their insect prey. One estimate suggests that carnivorous plants may lose as much as 50% of their prey to kleptoparasites.

knick-point (headcut) A discontinuity in the *long profile of a *river, which usually develops where downcutting is inhibited by an *outcrop of resistant *rock, causing a step in the long profile which through time will move upstream as it erodes. (See Fig. 12.)

knoll 1. A small natural *hill. **2.** A small *reef within a *lagoon.

knot A measure of speed, usually applied to wind or to a ship or aircraft, which is equal to one *nautical mile per hour (= 1.15 mph; 0.51 metres per second, m s^{-1}).

knowledge Information, gathered from experience and reasoning, that has been interpreted and can be used.

Fig. 12 Knick-point

knowledge management The systematic management and use of the *knowledge (collective data, information, and body of experience) within an organization, to enhance the performance of the organization.

knowledge transfer The effective sharing of ideas, *knowledge, or experience between people, companies, or organizations.

known resource A *natural resource (such as a *mineral deposit) that has been located but not yet fully mapped, but which is likely to become economically viable in the foreseeable future. *See also* RESERVE.

koinobiont A *parasitoid that does not kill its host immediately. The host is temporarily paralysed, but recovers, and both host and parasitoid continue to develop until the parasitoid matures, at which stage it kills the host. *Contrast* IDIOBIONT.

Köppen classification system A system for classifying *climates, and defining *climate zones, that was developed by W. P. Köppen (1846–1940) between 1918 and 1936. In this system climates are divided into six broad groups, each with several subgroups, according to the types of vegetation associated with them, which is largely determined by the annual and monthly averages of *temperature and *precipitation.

Krakatoa A small, steep, forested, uninhabited *volcanic island in Indonesia (Indonesian name Krakatau), between Java and Sumatra, which erupted suddenly and violently in 1883, throwing an estimated 17 km^3 of rock, *ash, and *pumice high into the *atmosphere (which shaded out the Sun in many places for months afterwards), and triggering a catastrophic *tsunami, up to 40 m high, that flooded coastal towns and villages on the nearby coasts and drowned 36 000 people.

(((●))) **SEE WEB LINKS**

• How volcanoes work.

krill Small shrimp-like *planktonic *crustaceans, up to 5 cm long, that occur in large swarms and form an important part of the *food chain in *Antarctic waters.

krummholz *See* ELFIN WOODLAND.

krypton (Kr) An *inert, colourless, non-toxic *gas that occurs naturally in the Earth's *atmosphere in trace quantities. It is one of the six inert gases, and is used for insulating windows.

K-selection *Natural selection that favours species that are adapted to the maximum survival of individuals, at the expense of species with a high reproductive capacity. Typically it occurs in stable environments and selects for low birth rates, high survival rates for offspring, and prolonged development of young. Species with this type of life cycle are said to have evolved a K-strategy. *Contrast* R-SELECTION.

K-strategy *See* K-SELECTION.

K–T boundary In geology, the boundary between the rocks of the *Cretaceous and the *Tertiary periods 65 million years ago, indicated by a layer of clays enriched in iridium, which marks the time of a *meteorite impact on Earth, which caused *mass extinction of species including the *dinosaurs.

Kuznets curve A bell-shaped curve that shows the relationship between *development and *environmental degradation, which has *per capita income as the horizontal axis (x), and per capita pollution as the vertical axis (y). As per capita income rises per capita pollution also increases, but as people gain the disposable income that is necessary to value such things as clean air and water, per capita pollution peaks and then reduces as per capita income continues to rise.

KYOTO PROTOCOL

An international agreement that sets limits on the *emission of *greenhouse gases into the *atmosphere, in order to reduce the threat of *global warming by *air pollution. It was drawn up under the *United Nations Framework Convention on Climate Change (UNFCCC), drafted during the *Berlin Mandate process and agreed in Kyoto, Japan, on 11 December 1997 by the signatory countries to the UNFCCC. The protocol specifies targets for the level of emission reductions, the methodologies, and the deadlines that signatory countries have to achieve. The main components of the agreement are that *developed countries should commit to reducing their emissions of six key greenhouse gases by an average of at least 5%, national *emissions targets must be achieved by 2008–12, and countries must have some flexibility in how to reduce their emissions through a *Clean Development Mechanism, *international emissions trading, and *Joint Implementation. Some flexibility was agreed that would allow countries to emit more *greenhouse gases if they planted more trees (that act as *carbon sinks), or could demonstrate that they had reduced pollution in other countries (joint implementation, for example through *emissions trading). Under the Kyoto Protocol, rich industrial *developed countries agreed to reduce their emissions of greenhouse gases by an average of 5.2% by 2010. *Developing countries were not set formal emission limits, partly because to do so would unfairly inhibit their pursuit of *economic growth.

k-value The 'killing power' of an environment, calculated as the number of individuals lost from a specified stage in the life cycle of a *species and expressed logarithmically ($k = \log_{10} a_x - \log_{10} a_{x+1}$, where a_x is the number of individuals at the start of the stage, time x, and a_{x+1} is the number at the end of the stage, time $x + 1$).

Kyoto mechanism *See* FLEXIBILITY MECHANISM.

La Niña The opposite of *El Niño, when a major cooling occurs in the equatorial waters in the Pacific Ocean and causes shifts in normal *weather patterns. The *trade winds and South Equatorial Current strengthen, the pool of warm water close to Indonesia deepens, rainfall increases in south-eastern Asia, and aridity increases in western South America. There are also effects in the wider world and, often, a slight drop in global temperatures. La Niña means 'the little girl'.

LA21 *See* LOCAL AGENDA 21.

laccolith A large lens-shaped mass of *igneous *intrusive rock that has pushed up the overlying rocks; similar in form to but much smaller than a *batholith.

lacustrine Of or relating to a *lake.

lacustrine deposit *Sediment that has been deposited in a *lake.

ladder fuel *Vegetation (including shrubs and small trees) that is located below the *crown level of *forest trees, which can spread *fire from the forest floor to tree crowns.

lag (lag time) The period of time that elapses between the occurrence of an event and its resulting impact.

lag time *See* LAG.

lagoon A body of shallow water with access to a larger body (such as the *ocean) that is restricted by a *coral reef or *sandbar.

lahar A *mudflow or lubricated *landslide of volcanic debris, caused when melting snow, rain, or water from a volcanic steam or a crater lake mix with ash or volcanic fragments on the sides of a *volcano.

LAI *See* LEAF AREA INDEX.

lair A place where wild animals live.

lake A body of (usually fresh) *water that is entirely or nearly entirely surrounded by land.

lake breeze A convective *wind that blows onshore bringing cool, moist air from the surface of a large *lake. It is caused by the difference in the rates of heating of water and land.

lake forest A forest dominated by *conifers, which occurs in the eastern half of North America, in Minnesota, Michigan, northern Pennsylvania, southern Ontario, and northern New England. Although a distinct formation it is in many respects transitional between *boreal coniferous forest and southern *deciduous forest. Very little lake forest survives, having been cut in the latter part of the 19th century.

Lake Nyos A lake in the volcanic crater Iwi at Nyos in Cameroon, where a sudden release of *toxic *volcanic gas occurred on the night of 21 August 1986. More than 1700 people and all animal life within 14 km of the lake were killed, but plant life was mostly unaffected. Survivors suffered symptoms compatible with an asphyxiant gas like *carbon dioxide. Two different explanations have been offered for this extremely rare type of event: that it was the result of a *phreatic eruption of *groundwater that was exceptionally rich in CO_2 or it was a result of *overturn of water in the 220 m deep lake.

(((•))) **SEE WEB LINKS**

• The Lake Nyos disaster.

lake-effect storm A heavy localized snowstorm that can form on the lee side of a large lake (such as the *Great Lakes) in late *autumn/fall and early *winter, before the lake has frozen. Water evaporates into the air moving over the surface. On the lee side, where the mild, moist air crosses very cold ground, the moisture condenses and snow falls.

Lamarck, Jean-Baptiste Pierre Antoine de Monet, chevalier de A French naturalist (1744–1829) who proposed in 1809 that the *evolution of *species may be caused by the *inheritance of *acquired traits. His central point was that evolution is directional, with life climbing from simple to more complex forms, but that this process is diverted as organisms respond to the requirements of their environments, e.g. with cacti acquiring reduced leaves and giraffes developing long necks.

Lamb's dust veil index An index of the amount of finely divided material that remains suspended in the atmosphere after great volcanic eruptions, and of the duration of an effective veil intercepting the Sun's radiation. It can be calculated from estimates of the amount of solid matter thrown up, from the reduction of intensity of the solar beam, or from the reduction of temperatures prevailing at the surface of the Earth. The latitude of the volcano also affects the index values, because the maximum extent of the veil over the Earth varies, being greatest after eruptions in low latitudes. (The great eruption of *Krakatoa in Indonesia in 1883, which ejected about 17 km^3 of particulate matter into the atmosphere, where it remained for three years, gave an index value of 1000.) The index was devised by H. H. Lamb (1913–97).

lamina *See* LEAF.

laminar flow A type of fluid *flow that involves smooth movement without any turbulence; the fluid forms sheets that lie parallel to each other. *Contrast* TURBULENT FLOW.

lamination A structure in which material (e.g. sediment, flowing fluid) is layered or in layers. *See also* STRATIFICATION.

lamp shells *See* BRACHIOPODS.

land The solid, dry surface of the Earth, or any part of it. *Contrast* OCEAN.

land application The discharge of *wastewater onto the ground, for treatment or reuse. *See also* IRRIGATION.

land ban The phasing out of disposal on land of most untreated *hazardous wastes, as required by *legislation.

land breeze (offshore breeze) A coastal *breeze that blows from land to sea at night. A type of *local convective wind caused by the fact that at night land cools more rapidly than water. *Contrast* SEA BREEZE.

land bridge A natural connection between two land masses (for example, between Alaska and Siberia across the Bering Strait, or between France and England across the English Channel) that has been removed by *sea level rise,

crustal *warping, or the movement of *crustal plates.

land capability The inherent ability of *land to be used for agriculture without permanent damage (such as *soil erosion).

land capability classification A way of grouping *soils according to their suitability for intensive use (growing *crops and *pasture plants) on a *sustainable basis. *See also* LAND EVALUATION.

land capability map A map, produced from a *land capability classification, which shows the distribution of *land capability units.

land capability unit A group of *soils that are very similar in their inherent suitability for intensive use and in their responses to soil management.

land class A way of grouping areas of land on the basis of slope. For example, the US Forest Service uses three classes: 0–35%, 36–55%, and greater than 55%.

land classification A way of grouping areas of land on the basis of physical characteristics (including vegetation) without an explicit assessment of *land capability.

land cover *See* LAND USE.

land cover change Converting land from one use to another (such as from *grassland to *cropland), or changing the condition within a particular land use (such as thinning the trees in a *forest).

land development The process of improving an area of land and making it more useful, by installing streets, sewers, utilities, and other infrastructure.

land disposal restriction The requirement that *hazardous wastes must be treated before disposal on land, in order to prevent the *contamination of *soil and *groundwater by hazardous materials.

land ethic The principles and values that guide the *sustainable use and treatment of *land and other *natural resources. *See also* ENVIRONMENTAL ETHICS; STEWARDSHIP.

land evaluation (terrain evaluation) The formal assessment of the suitability of land for different types of use (for example for *agriculture, *forestry, or *recreation).

land farming A process of *waste disposal and *bioremediation in which *hazardous wastes are deposited on or in *soil and allowed to *decompose naturally by the action of *microbes.

land management The intentional process of planning and managing the activities that affect *land use, in order to achieve stated objectives.

land reclamation The process of creating new dry land (for example from the *sea-bed), or of restoring *productivity to land that has been damaged (for example by *erosion or *mining activities). *See also* RECLAMATION.

land reform The redistribution of land by the government, from rich land owners to the people who actually work the land, in order to improve the distribution of income and promote *sustainable *rural development.

land tenure The right to own land, or to occupy and use exclusively a particular piece of land.

land use (land cover, land utilization) The purpose for which an area of land is being used, such as residential, agricultural, commercial, retail, or industrial.

land use allocation Committing a particular area of land to one or more specific uses, for example for *residential development or as a *nature reserve.

land use capability An assessment of the ability of a particular area of land to sustain a range of *land uses.

land use change Converting an area of land from one *land use to another, usually on purpose.

land use plan A plan which outlines proposed future *land uses and their distribution in a particular area.

land use planning Local development of a plan, usually by a local government, for the use and development of land within its boundaries, taking into account existing *land use, *land capability, and local policies and strategic objectives.

land use survey A systematic survey of land use in a particular area, usually shown both in map form and statistically.

land utilization *See* LAND USE.

land value An assessment of the worth of a piece of land, expressed either in terms of money or more broadly in terms of factors such as *environmental quality, or *amenity or *heritage interest.

landfill A place or a process for the disposal of non-hazardous *waste, based on burying it in depressions in the ground then compacting it to reduce the volume and finally covering it with soil and landscaping it to look like part of the surrounding land. *See also* SANITARY LANDFILL; SECURE LANDFILL.

landfill gas Gas that is produced in *landfill sites by the anaerobic decomposition of *cellulose (mainly paper). The gas consists principally of *methane and may be hazardous if it seeps from the site and accumulates. In some sites it is tapped and used as fuel.

landform A natural feature of the surface of the land that has been created by *geological processes, which can vary in scale from the continental (for example the Andes *mountain chain which runs through South America) to the local (for example a *hillslope, river *meander, or *beach). *See also* GEOMORPHOLOGY.

landing In *forest management, a place where cut *timber is collected before being transported away from the forest.

landings The number of *fish that are landed (caught and brought back to the docks and marketed), either in a particular place or for an entire country.

landline A property boundary in the USA, for example for *National Forest land.

landlocked Applied to an area that is totally enclosed by land, with no direct access to the sea.

landmark Any readily identifiable structure or *landform (such as a particular building or mountain) on land that can be used in determining a location or direction, or that commemorates a historic event or achievement (such as the Statue of Liberty in New York).

landmass A large continuous area of land, such as a *continent or large *island.

landnám A local phase of *forest clearance by humans during *prehistory, detected in *pollen diagrams, and indicating brief agricultural use which was often followed by abandonment and then natural regeneration of *secondary woodland.

landrace A primitive variety of crop (*cultivar) or animal (*breed) that through time has been genetically improved by traditional agriculturalists to make it better adapted to local environmental conditions, but has not been influenced by modern breeding practices.

Landsat Land Remote-Sensing Satellite, a US *satellite programme used for *remote sensing of *natural resources on Earth, originally called *Earth Resources Technology Satellite (ERTS). The first satellite was launched in 1972 and the name was changed to Landsat in 1975. It uses two sensors: the *multispectral scanner (MSS) and the *thematic mapper (TM).

landscape *Scenery, either natural (*natural landscape) or modified by human activities (*cultural landscape); often used to refer to the expanse of scenery that can be seen from a single *viewpoint. *See also* SEASCAPE; SOUNDSCAPE; TOWNSCAPE; WILDSCAPE; WOODSCAPE.

landscape architecture Arranging and designing land and buildings, to optimize human benefit.

landscape ecology Principles and theories for understanding the structure, functioning, and change of *landscapes and *ecosystems over time.

landscape evaluation The assessment of a landscape as a scenic resource. It is controversial, since concepts such as 'scenic beauty' are neither generally agreed nor readily quantifiable. Nevertheless evaluations are vital for the conservation of high-quality and/or traditional landscapes, especially in densely populated, developed regions.

landscape indicator An index or measurement of some aspect of the *landscape of a particular place (such as extent of *forest cover), based on mapped or remotely sensed data, that can be used to describe *land use and monitor *environmental change.

landscape planning Part of the *land use planning process which seeks to balance decisions relating to large-scale physical factors (such as *ecosystems and *drainage basins) and broader aesthetic and cultural values (such as historical importance and *amenity value).

landscaped Deliberately improved by gardening or by *landscape architecture (landscaping). Improving the appearance of an area of land by planting (including lawns, trees, and shrubs), adding decorative features (such as structures or buildings), and/or altering the level or shape of the ground.

landscaping *See* LANDSCAPED.

landslide (slide, landslip) A sudden, rapid *mass movement of material down a *hillslope, often after heavy *rain or as a result of an *earthquake; slower than an *avalanche, but often equally destructive.

landslip *See* LANDSLIDE.

landspout (non-supercell tornado) A weak *tornado that develops in a *cumulonimbus cloud that does not contain a *mesocyclone or *supercell.

landward Towards *land. *Contrast* SEAWARD.

lapilli Cinders or small lumps of *lava, 2–64 mm in size, that are thrown up by a *volcanic eruption.

lapse rate The rate at which a rising *parcel of air cools with increasing altitude due to *adiabatic expansion. The average lapse rate is about $6.5°C \ km^{-1}$. *See also* DRY ADIABATIC LAPSE RATE; ENVIRONMENTAL LAPSE RATE; SATURATED ADIABATIC LAPSE RATE.

large woody debris Part of a *tree (either dead or alive), including branches and roots, usually longer than one metre, which rests in a *stream or on a *forest floor.

large-lot zoning A type of *open space zoning which prohibits the subdivision of land into individual plots smaller than a defined size (usually an acre or more).

larva The young, immature stage in the life cycle of some animals, such as insects, fish, and *amphibians. Larvae develop into the adult form by *metamorphosis; for example caterpillar larvae turn into butterflies.

larval paedogenesis Reproduction by larvae.

Last Glacial Maximum (LGM) The time, approximately 21 000 years ago, when the most recent *ice age reached its greatest intensity. The *ice sheets were then at their largest, the global mean temperature was about 5°C lower than today, and climates everywhere were drier.

late forest succession The stage of *succession in a forest in which most of the trees are mature, for example in *old growth forest. *Contrast* EARLY FOREST SUCCESSION.

late successional reserve (LSR) North American name for an *old growth forest or old *clearcut that has been set aside as a wildlife habitat, in which *logging is permitted only if it will help the reserve to reach old growth characteristics more quickly.

late-glacial The final part of the last *glacial stage, between about 16000 and 11500 years ago.

latency The period of time between first exposure to an *agent (such as something that causes a *disease) and the appearance of a health effect.

latent 1. Hidden, concealed. **2.** Potentially existing, but not currently active.

latent heat (heat of transformation) The heat energy that is absorbed or released when a substance changes state between *gas, *liquid, and solid.

latent heat flux The transfer of *latent heat energy via the global circulation of air and water, and through the processes of *evaporation and *condensation.

latent heat of fusion (latent heat of melting) The amount of *heat energy that is required to change a substance from solid to liquid at constant temperature.

latent heat of melting *See* HEAT OF FUSION.

latent heat of vaporization The amount of *heat energy that is required to change a substance from liquid to gas at constant temperature.

latent period *See* INCUBATION PERIOD.

lateral Sideways, as opposed to up and down (*vertical).

lateral accretion *Deposition by a *river on the inside corner of *meander bends, which creates *point bars and helps to build the *floodplain.

lateral moraine A type of *moraine that is deposited at the side of a valley *glacier, often composed of rock particles that have fallen off the sidewalls of the valley as a result of *frost wedging.

laterite A hard subsurface deposit (*hardpan) of oxides of *aluminium and *iron that is found in tropical soils where the *water table

fluctuates with seasonal changes in precipitation.

laterization A *soil-forming process that involves the deposition of a *hardpan made of metallic oxides (*laterite) in the *A-horizon, which most commonly occurs in humid tropical and subtropical areas, where precipitation is high.

latewood The portion of the annual *growth ring of a tree that is formed when growth slows down (during late summer and autumn or during the dry season), after the *earlywood formation has ceased. It is usually denser and darker than earlywood.

latex A white, milky, sticky fluid that is produced by specialized cells within certain plants. Latex from the rubber tree (*Hevea brasiliensis*) is processed to make rubber.

Latin American mammal region The area extending from Tierra del Fuego to just across the southern borders of the United States. The biogeographer Charles H. Smith (Western Kentucky University) considers these to be more appropriate boundaries in respect of mammals than those of the *Neotropical faunal region.

Latin name (binomial nomenclature, scientific name, species name) The name for a *species of plant or animal that is used around the world. The naming system, developed in the mid-1700s by *Linnaeus, uses Latin and has two parts; the first part, which is capitalized, is the *genus or generic name, and the second part is the name of the species (specific or trivial name). Both parts are usually written in italics. For example, the beech tree is *Fagus sylvatica*. *Compare* COMMON NAME.

latitude Distance on the Earth, measured in degrees, north or south of the *equator (0°); the *poles are at 90°N and 90°S.

latosol An *order of *zonal soil that develops under forested, tropical, humid conditions. It is usually red in colour, contains a *hardpan of *laterite, and has a deeply weathered *profile and relatively low mineral content, and thus low fertility.

Laurasia A large former continent in the northern hemisphere that formed in the early *Mesozoic through the rifting of the *Pangaea supercontinent. It comprised modern-day North America, Greenland, Europe, and Asia. *See also* GONDWANALAND.

Laurentide ice sheet An area of continental ice that lay over the eastern part of Canada during the *Pleistocene glaciations. The centre of the ice mass may have originated in or near northern Quebec, Labrador, and Newfoundland, and spread out to the south and west. At its maximum spread it may have covered an area of 1.3×10^6 km^2.

lava Molten rock that is erupted by a *volcano through *volcanic vents and fissures, and which then cools and solidifies into hard *igneous rock.

lava flow A stream of molten *lava that flows from a volcanic *vent.

law 1. A collection of rules, imposed by government, which govern a particular type of activity and apply over a certain territory (such as a country). *See also* COMMON LAW. 2. A general principle or description of how a natural phenomenon will occur under certain circumstances.

law of conservation of energy *See* THERMODYNAMICS, FIRST LAW.

law of the minimum The concept first stated by J. von *Liebig in 1840, that the rate of growth of a plant, the size to which it grows, and its overall health depend on the amount of the scarcest of its essential nutrients that is available to it. This concept is now broadened into a general model of *limiting factors for all organisms, including the limiting effects of excesses of chemical nutrients and other environmental factors.

lawn A patch of grass that has been cultivated and is regularly mowed.

laws of ecology Four so-called laws (which are really general principles) proposed by Barry *Commoner in the book *The Closing Circle: Nature, Man, and Technology* (1971). They are: everything is connected to everything else; everything must go somewhere; nature knows best; there is no such thing as a free lunch.

LBAP *See* LOCAL BIODIVERSITY ACTION PLAN.

LC50 (lethal concentration fifty) The concentration of a given substance in air that will kill 50% of a group of test animals with a single *exposure (usually 1–4 hours). *See also* LD50.

LCL *See* LIFTING CONDENSATION LEVEL.

LD50 (lethal dose fifty, median lethal dose) The size of the single *dose of a given substance that causes the death of 50% of an animal population from exposure by any route other than *inhalation, within a given period of time; the lower the LD50, the more *toxic the substance.

LDC *See* LESS-DEVELOPED COUNTRY.

leach To remove *soluble components from a solid by *infiltration of a *solvent. For example, to leach *salts from *soil by dissolving them in water, which *percolates through soil.

leachate A solution formed by *leaching.

leachate collection system A system that gathers *leachate (usually from *landfill) and pumps it to the surface for treatment, in order to prevent the spread of *contamination.

leaching The process by which *soluble *minerals (*humus and *inorganic *nutrients) in soil are dissolved in percolating water, and can be washed out from the *A-horizon and transferred within the soil. *See also* HARDPAN.

lead (Pb) A naturally occurring, grey-white *metal that is soft, *malleable, *ductile, and resistant to *corrosion. It was used in *gasoline, is still used in paints and plumbing compounds, and is both a *criteria air pollutant and a *toxic air contaminant. Human exposure to it can damage the brain and nervous system, especially in children. *See also* LEAD POISONING.

lead agency The agency that is identified as having primary responsibility for responding to a particular *disaster.

lead poisoning Damage to the body (specifically the brain) that is caused by breathing or swallowing substances that contain *lead, or by absorbing lead through the skin.

lead time The period of time between the start and end of an activity, such as the interval between introducing pollution control legislation and a reduction in pollution being observed.

leaded fuel *Petrol to which lead has been added in order to raise the octane level. *Contrast* UNLEADED FUEL.

leaf The flat, thin, usually green expanded organ that grows from a node on the stem of a *plant, in which *photosynthesis and *transpiration take place. It typically comprises a stalk (petiole) and blade (lamina).

leaf area index (LAI) The total leaf area of a plant that is exposed to sunlight in relation to the ground surface area beneath the plant (e.g.

an LAI of 5 means the leaf area is five times larger than the ground area beneath the plant).

leaf litter The accumulation of dead leaves on a *soil surface or *forest floor.

League of Conservation Voters (LCV) A US-based non-profit lobby group that was founded in 1970 by leaders of the *environmental movement following the first *Earth Day, and which is devoted to making the Congress and the White House more pro-environmental. It holds Congress and the Administration accountable for their actions on the environment through the *National Environmental Scorecard.

leaking underground storage tank (LUST) A US term for any underground container that is used to store chemicals (such as *gasoline, diesel fuel, or home heating oil) and which is damaged and leaking its contents into the ground; these may *contaminate *groundwater.

Le Chatelier's principle When an external force is applied to a *system in *equilibrium, the system will undergo *adjustment in order to minimize the effect of the force.

(( )) SEE WEB LINKS

• Le Chatelier's principle.

lectin A generic term for *proteins that bind to sugars produced by both plants (especially *legumes) and some *mollusks and fish. They are able to bind to the outside of a cell and cause *biochemical changes within it.

lee The side of something that is sheltered from the wind or water.

lee wave (mountain wave, standing wave) A wave that develops in stable air on the *lee side of a *mountain range when air is lifted over the range.

leeward In a downstream or downwind direction. *Contrast* WINDWARD.

legacy Something that is passed down in a will, or left behind from the past. *See also* INHERIT.

Legionella A type of *bacterium that thrives in central heating and air conditioning systems and can cause legionnaires' disease.

legislate To make *laws, or bring into effect by *legislation.

legislation The process by which government makes *laws.

legume A plant (such as peas, beans, alfalfa, soybeans, and clover, family Fabaceae) or its fruit, which usually comprises pods containing one or more seeds (e.g. peas, beans). Edible legume seeds are known as pulses. The plant also has *nitrogen-fixing *bacteria in its roots. These increase the nitrogen content of *soil and thus increase soil *fertility, which is why legumes are a common component of crop *rotation.

leisure Spare time that is available for relaxation or activities not related to work or obtaining necessities.

lek An area within which a number of males occupy very small territories where they display in order to attract the attention of females for the purpose of mating. The area each male occupies is thus a mating station and it is defended against rivals. The males remain at the lek throughout the breeding season. Females, whose breeding activity is not synchronized, visit the lek when they are ready to mate, select a male for the quality of his display, and leave immediately after mating. Since there are always more males than females present at the lek, competition among the males is intense and as well as display performance this translates into competition for the best stations. In many species females find the territories near the centre of the lek especially attractive and these are occupied by the most dominant and successful males. Lekking has been observed among insects, fish, and mammals, but has been studied in most detail in birds.

lentic water A standing or non-flowing body of water, such as a *lake, *reservoir, *pond, or *swamp.

lenticular In the shape of a lens.

Leopold, Aldo US ecologist, forester, and environmentalist (1887–1948) who many people regard as the father of wildlife ecology. He was a gifted writer, and is best known as author of the book *A *Sand County Almanac* (1948), in which he outlined his philosophy (*land ethic) of living in harmony with the land and with nature.

leptosols Soils in which there is hard rock within 25 cm of the surface, or that overlie material containing more than 40% calcium carbonate within 25 cm of the surface, or that have less than 10% fine-grained material to a depth of 75 cm. These are weakly developed soils. Leptosols are a reference soil group in the *World Soil Classification.

less developed country (LDC) See DEVEL-OPING COUNTRY.

lestobiosis See CLEPTOBIOSIS.

lethal concentration fifty See LC50.

lethal dose fifty See LD50.

leukaemia A *cancer of the blood-forming cells in bone marrow, which causes excessive production of white blood cells and weakens the body's immune system.

levee 1. A raised embankment of fine *alluvium that is deposited on a *floodplain beside the *channel by a river under *flood conditions. **2.** An artificial embankment constructed alongside a river (such as much of the lower Mississippi) designed to contain flood flows and reduce *flooding.

level of concern (LOC) The *threshold concentration in air of an extremely *hazardous substance, above which even a single short exposure can kill or seriously injure humans. See also VULNERABLE ZONE.

ley An area of temporary *grassland that is sown with *grass and/or *herbs to produce grazing and *hay or *silage, usually for a period of up to ten years, before being ploughed and cropped as part of a *crop rotation.

LGM See LAST GLACIAL MAXIMUM.

LIA See LITTLE ICE AGE.

liana (liane) A woody-stemmed vine-like climbing *plant which roots in the ground and grows by supporting itself on *trees or *shrubs.

liane See LIANA.

lichen A composite *plant that is made up of an *alga or *cyanobacterium and a *fungus growing together in a *symbiotic relationship. Lichen grows in patches on tree trunks, bare ground, rocks, and walls, and can be a sensitive *indicator of *pollution.

lichen zone An area with a characteristic *lichen flora ranging from complete absence to a full complement of foliose and fruticose species, depending on the level and type of air pollution present in the area. The standardized lichen zones for England and Wales range from zone 0 (complete absence) typical of heavily polluted industrial areas, to zone 10 in which bearded

lichens (e.g *Usnea* and *Ramalina* species) are present in association with many other species. Zone 10 is typical of unpolluted areas in which virtually no sulphur dioxide, fluorine compounds, or other air pollutants are present.

(⊕) SEE WEB LINKS
• Air quality and lichens.

Liebig, Baron Justus von (1803–73) A German chemist who contributed much to the systematization of organic chemistry, the early development of biochemistry, and agricultural chemistry. In 1840 he published *Die organische Chemie in ihrer Anwendung auf Agrikulturchemie und Physiologie* ('Organic Chemistry in its Application to Agricultural Chemistry and Physiology'), in which he showed that plants take up nutrients in simple chemical form and that nutrient deficiencies in soils may be remedied by the application of mineral fertilizers. He maintained that plant growth is limited by the availability of the scarcest essential nutrient (see LAW OF THE MINIMUM). Others expanded on this work later to produce a broader appreciation of the *limits of tolerance, recognizing that maximum as well as minimum thresholds exist for all commodities (not only chemicals) that are essential to plant and animal growth.

life cycle 1. The stages through which an *organism passes during its existence, from birth to death. See also LIFE HISTORY. **2.** Stages in the total life of a product, from raw materials, design, and manufacture to use, disposal, or *recycling.

life cycle analysis A process for evaluating and reducing the inputs and outputs of material and energy at each stage in the *life cycle of a product, from raw material to final disposal.

life cycle cost The total cost of a good or service over its entire *life cycle, including the cost of disposal.

LIFE Environment Part of the *LIFE Programme that is sponsored by the *European Union, which includes actions designed to implement EU *environmental policy and legislation, and to demonstrate and develop new methods for the *protection and the enhancement of the *environment.

life expectancy The length of time that an individual *organism (such as a person) is expected to live. See also LIFESPAN.

life form The characteristic structure of a *plant or *animal in a particular *environment. *Contrast* GROWTH FORM.

LIFE Fund A *European Union (EU) fund that has been established to assist the development and implementation of the EU's *environmental policies.

life history A descriptive account of the complete *life cycle of an *organism.

LIFE Nature Part of the *LIFE Programme sponsored by the *European Union. It includes actions which are aimed at the *conservation of natural *habitats and the wild *fauna and *flora of EU interest, and supports implementation of the EU *nature conservation policy and the *Natura 2000 network.

LIFE Programme A major initiative (L'instrument Financier pour l'Environnement) which is part of *European Union *environmental policy and finances project in three areas: *LIFE Nature, *LIFE Environment, and *LIFE Third Countries.

(((( )))) SEE WEB LINKS

• LIFE Programme home page.

life table A statistical table that summarizes the *mortality and *survivorship characteristics of a given population, broken down by *age class.

LIFE Third Countries Part of the *LIFE Programme sponsored by the *European Union, which includes actions that provide technical assistance for promoting *sustainable development in third countries.

life zone A region or belt that is defined by climate, altitude, or latitude, in which plants and animals are well adapted to the *environment and across which the *species composition and *biodiversity are relatively uniform.

lifespan The theoretical maximum number of years that the most healthy individuals within a *species can be expected to live. *Life expectancy in humans is lower than this because it reflects the real-life conditions within a population, which includes stresses such as *disease, *malnutrition, *environmental risk, and social tension. *See also* LONGEVITY.

lifestyle The mode or pattern of living that is adopted by an individual, which is reflected in that person's activities, interests, and opinions.

lifetime The period of time during which something is functional, such as between birth and death in a person, plant, or animal. *See also* RESIDENCE TIME.

lifetime exposure The total amount of *exposure to a particular substance that a human is likely to receive in a lifetime (usually taken as 70 years).

lifting condensation level (LCL, condensation level) The level to which a parcel of dry air must be lifted before it cools *adiabatically to its *dew point temperature.

light *Radiant energy with a *wavelength of 400–700 nm, which is visible to humans.

light non-aqueous phase liquid (LNAPL) Undissolved chemicals, such as petroleum products (*hydrocarbon fuels and lubricating oils), which float on the surface of *groundwater and do not mix with it.

light pollution High levels of artificial light that prevent viewing of the night sky.

light wave *Radiation in the middle part of the *electromagnetic spectrum, between shortwave (X-rays) and longwave (radio waves). This includes *ultraviolet (4 to 400 nanometres (nm)), visible light (400 to 750 nm), and *infrared (750 to 1 million nm).

lightning An electrical discharge between regions of separated charge that has accumulated within a *cumulonimbus cloud. The discharge is visible as a flash of light within a cloud, between *clouds, or between a cloud and the ground, and is accompanied by *thunder. From a distance, the lightning is seen before the thunder is heard because light travels faster than sound. Lightning that flashes within or behind cloud is seen from the ground as a general flash of light (*sheet lightning).

light-water reactor (LWR) A type of *nuclear power plant that uses ordinary water as the cooling medium and *moderator and slightly enriched *uranium as a fuel. The *boiling water reactor and the *pressurized water reactor, the most common types of commercial reactor used in the USA, are light-water reactors.

lignified Applied to plant cells that contain a large amount of *lignin in their walls, making them rigid and woody.

lignin A naturally occurring cross-linked polymer found in the *cell walls of many *plants, which gives strength and rigidity to the plant.

lignite A soft, brownish, low-grade *coal with a visibly woody structure that is formed during the middle stages of the *coal cycle. It is between *peat and *bituminous coal in rank and burns with a smoky flame.

limb 1. A main branch that grows from the trunk or a bough of a tree. **2.** A jointed appendage of an animal (such as an arm, leg, or flipper), that is used for locomotion or grasping. **3.** The tilted beds of a *fold in rock that extend outwards from the axis.

lime 1. A small, green, tart fruit, and the tree (*Citrus aurantiifolia*) on which it grows. **2. (linden)** The common name for trees of the genus *Tilia*. **3.** A common name for calcium oxide (CaO, quicklime); it is made from heating calcium carbonate ($CaCO_3$) and is used to make calcium hydroxide ($Ca(OH)_2$, slaked lime) for neutralizing *acidic soil.

limescale The hard, white, chalky deposit that is often found in kettles, hot water boilers, and old pipes where *hard water has evaporated, precipitating *calcium carbonate.

limestone A *carbonate *sedimentary rock, composed mainly of *calcium carbonate and smaller amounts of magnesium carbonate, usually in the form of the mineral *calcite and/or *dolomite. Commonly used as a building stone.

limestone pavement A flat, bare area of *limestone that has been smoothed by *glacial action, and has deep fissures crossing the surface in both directions.

limestone scrubbing (scrubbing) An *air pollution control process in which *sulphur gases are passed through a *slurry of *limestone and water, before being released into the *atmosphere through a *smokestack, in order to reduce the sulphur content.

limit of detection The level below which a test (or *assay) cannot measure the presence of a *substance.

limiting factor An environmental factor (such as the availability of the *nutrient *nitrogen in a particular *soil) that limits the growth and survival of a *species. *See also* PRINCIPLE OF LIMITING FACTORS; TOLERANCE LIMIT.

limits of tolerance The upper and lower limits to the range of particular environmental factors (e.g. light, temperature, availability of water) within which an organism can survive. Organisms with a wide range of tolerance are usually distributed widely, while those with a

narrow range have a more restricted distribution.

Limits to Growth A report written on behalf of the *Club of Rome by Dennis and *Donella Meadows, Jørgen Randers, and William Behrens III, as part of the Predicament of Mankind project, and published in 1971. Using dynamic computer models of various possible future *scenarios for world growth, it predicted that serious *natural resource scarcity would follow, probably within a century, if world *population and resource use continued to grow at the rate then evident, and if pollution increased in proportion to industrial activity. It had a significant impact on attitudes towards the *environment, and on the development of modern *environmentalism. *See also* NEO-MALTHUSIAN; SUSTAINABLE DEVELOPMENT.

limnetic Of or relating to deep open waters, such as large *lakes.

limnetic zone (sublittoral zone) In a freshwater lake, the open water zone to the depth of effective light penetration.

limnology The study of the physical, chemical, hydrological, and biological properties of freshwater.

lindane An *organochlorine *pesticide that is slowly *biodegradable, can be distributed through domestic water supplies, damages human *health, and is *toxic to *freshwater fish and *aquatic life.

linden *See* LIME.

line *See* LINEAGE.

line thinning The act of removing (*thinning) particular rows of *trees in a *forest or *plantation, for example every fifth row. *See also* MECHANICAL THINNING; SELECTIVE THINNING.

lineage (line) The *offspring or *descendants of one *individual.

liner A protective layer, often made of plastic or dense *clay, that is installed along the bottom and sides of a *landfill in order to prevent or reduce the flow of *leachate into the environment.

ling *See* HEATHER.

Linnaean classification A hierarchical method (developed by *Linnaeus) for naming *organisms in which each individual is assigned to a *species, *genus, *family, *order, *class, *phylum, and *kingdom, and some intermediate classificatory levels. *See also* LATIN NAME; TAXONOMY.

Linnaeus, Carolus A Swedish botanist (1707–78) who developed the hierarchical system of *biological classification that groups similar-looking *species into *genera, genera into *families, families into *orders, and so on. He also established the *Latin name system for giving *species names which is used around the world.

linuron A *systemic herbicide of the *urea group that is applied to soils prior to plant emergence and also around growing crops, mainly to control grasses and other weeds in cereal crops and vegetables. It is toxic to aquatic organisms and in high doses possibly to other wildlife, and causes eye and skin irritation in humans.

lipid solubility The maximum concentration of a *chemical that will dissolve in fatty substances, and that can disperse through the *environment via uptake in living tissue. .

lipids A group of *organic substances (such as fats and steroids) that are insoluble in water but soluble in solvents such as alcohol and ether.

liquefaction The process by which *soil or *sediment is transformed temporarily from a solid into a fluid state, when the *cohesion of *particles is lost, for example during and immediately after an *earthquake.

liquefied natural gas (LNG) *Natural gas (usually *methane) that has been converted to a liquid state, either by refrigeration or by pressure, in order to reduce its volume and thus make it easier to store or transport.

liquefied petroleum gas (LPG) A mixture of light *hydrocarbons (such as *propane and *butane) that has been converted to a liquid state, either by refrigeration or by pressure, in order to reduce its volume and thus make it easier to store or transport.

liquid A fluid whose shape alters to that of the container it is in, but whose volume does not expand to fill the container.

liquid limit *See* ATTERBERG LIMITS.

listed species Any *species of fish, *wildlife, or *plant that has been officially designated by an agency (such as a government department) as being *endangered or *threatened, and is therefore given enhanced protection.

listed waste In the USA, *wastes that are listed by the *Environmental Protection Agency as *hazardous by definition, even if they do not always exhibit the defined characteristics of hazardous waste.

listing The formal process by which an agency adds *species to the list of *endangered and *threatened wildlife and plants. .

lithic Made of stone.

lithification The *cementation of *sediment after deposition. *See also* DIAGENESIS.

lithologic trap *See* STRATIGRAPHIC TRAP.

lithology The description of the *mineral composition and *texture of *rocks and *sediments.

lithosphere The outer, solid part of the *Earth, including the *continental crust, *oceanic crust, and uppermost *mantle, which is generally around 100 km thick and is where *faulting and *earthquakes occur.

lithostratigraphy The organization of *rock or *sediment *strata into units based on their *lithology and *stratigraphic position relative to other units. *Contrast* BIOSTRATIGRAPHY.

lithotroph An *organism that synthesizes all of its *organic molecules from inorganic sources, such as *carbon dioxide or *bicarbonate. *Compare* ORGANOTROPH.

litre A unit of volume that is equal to one cubic decimetre, roughly 1.76 pints.

litter *Organic matter in the form of plant debris such as leaves and twigs that falls off living and dead plants, accumulates on the *soil surface, and is broken down by soil organisms to become *humus within the soil. *See also* DECOMPOSITION.

litterfall Leaves, twigs, and other plant material that falls to the ground and contributes to the *litter layer.

Little Climatic Optimum *See* MEDIEVAL WARM PERIOD.

Little Ice Age (LIA) A period of very cold climate that lasted from about AD 1550 to about 1850 throughout the world, as the global climate became much cooler after the *Medieval Warm Period. During this period, global temperatures were at their coldest since the beginning of the *Holocene, *valley glaciers grew rapidly, and there was renewed *periglacial activity, especially in the Alps, Scandinavia, and Greenland. The coldest conditions of the last 560 years were between 1570 and 1730 and in the 1800s. The LIA seems to have been associated with longer, more severe winters. In the late 1600s the River Thames completely froze over in London during some particularly cold winters, allowing Frost Fairs to be held on the ice. Tree rings in the southeastern USA preserve evidence of the LIA there, too. The cold conditions did not exist only in the northern hemisphere. In southern South America tree-ring evidence indicates a long, cold, moist period from AD 1270 to 1660, which was most pronounced between 1340 and 1640, and glaciers in many places advanced between the late 1600s and early 1800s. The climate was much warmer during the 20th century, partly due to recovery from the LIA.

littoral Of or relating to the side of a waterbody, such as a *lake or the *intertidal zone. *See also* SHORE.

littoral drift The movement of *sand and other material along the *shoreline, in the *littoral zone, under the influence of waves and currents.

littoral zone 1. The margin of a freshwater body, extending out from the shore to the limit of attached or rooted plants, where light can penetrate to the bottom. 2. (intertidal zone) The area between the high- and low-water marks on the seashore.

live fence (living fence) A *field *boundary formed by planting a line of closely spaced trees or shrubs. *See also* HEDGE; HEDGEROW.

livestock *Domesticated animals (such as beef cattle, dairy cows, goats, sheep, pigs, chickens, and turkeys) that are kept for meat or dairy production, usually on a *farm or *smallholding.

livestock unit (animal unit) A method for describing different types and age groups of *livestock, based on energy requirements, using standard ratios; one livestock unit is equal to one Friesian dairy cow weighing about 450 kilograms: 1 cow = 1 horse, 1 mule, 5 sheep, 5 pigs, or 6 goats.

living collection An approach to the *conservation of *biodiversity that is based on using off-site methods (such as *zoos, *botanical gardens, *arboretums, and *captive breeding programmes) to protect and maintain biodiversity.

living fence *See* LIVE FENCE.

living landscape A *landscape that changes with the changing needs of people and *wildlife for space and resources.

living modified organism (LMO) Any *genetically modified organism that has been produced through the use of *recombinant DNA technology, whose genetic material does not occur naturally by mating or natural recombination.

lixisols All soils that have an *illuvial horizon rich in silicate *clays within 100–200 cm of the surface, apart from *acrisols, *albeluvisols, *alisols, and *luvisols. Lixisols are a reference soil group in the *World Soil Classification.

LLRW *See* LOW-LEVEL RADIOACTIVE WASTE.

LMO *See* LIVING MODIFIED ORGANISM.

LNAPL *See* LIGHT NON-AQUEOUS PHASE LIQUID.

LNG *See* LIQUEFIED NATURAL GAS.

LNR *See* LOCAL NATURE RESERVE.

load on top A method for reducing the pollution caused when oil tankers wash out their empty tanks. In one of the tanks (the slop tank) the cargo floats on top of water. After the cargo has been unloaded, water from the slop tank is used to wash out the other tanks and residues from the ballast water are added to it. The oil floating on top of this water can be recovered and refined.

loading rate The rate at which materials (such as *suspended sediment, *nutrients, or *contaminants) are transported into a waterbody.

LOAEL *See* LOWEST OBSERVED ADVERSE EFFECT LEVEL.

loam A loose, *permeable *soil composed of *clay, *sand, and *silt, that is often very *fertile and good for growing most crops.

lobbying Activities engaged in by individuals or organizations which are designed to influence the thinking and voting of legislators or other public officials for or against a specific cause. *See also* ENVIRONMENTAL ACTIVISM.

LOC *See* LEVEL OF CONCERN.

Local Agenda 21 (LA21) A programme of action by *local government in the United Kingdom that is designed to promote *sustainable development at a local community level, under *Agenda 21.

local authority An administrative unit of *local government in the United Kingdom that governs local services such as education, housing, and social services.

local biodiversity The number of different *species in a particular area at a particular point in time. *See also* BIODIVERSITY.

Local Biodiversity Action Plan (LBAP) A *biodiversity action plan (BAP) that is produced for an area, within an overall national BAP.

local convective wind A local, *diurnal, thermally driven *wind that is generated over a relatively small area and is influenced by local terrain. Examples include *sea breezes and *land breezes, lake breezes, diurnal mountain wind systems, and *convection currents.

local diversity *See* ALPHA DIVERSITY.

local extinction *See* EXTIRPATION.

local government The administrative functions of regional areas which are carried out by locally elected political bodies, under the overall authority of central (national) government.

Local Nature Reserve (LNR) A *nature reserve in the United Kingdom which has been designated by a *local authority under the National Parks and Access to the Countryside Act (1949).

Local Plan A detailed *land use plan that is prepared and adopted by a local planning authority in the United Kingdom, in accordance with the policies of a *Structure Plan.

local wind A *wind that blows over a relatively small area, often caused by factors such as mountain barriers or large *waterbodies.

loch Scottish word for a *freshwater *lake, or a long narrow *inlet of the *sea.

Loch Lomond stadial A relatively cold period, equivalent to the Younger *Dryas *stadial, that occurred towards the end of the *Devensian glaciation in Scotland. The event took place about 11 000–10 000 radiocarbon years BP. It is characterized by the development of small *ice caps and *cirque glaciers in the Highlands.

locus The position of a *gene on a *chromosome.

lode (mining lode) A clearly defined mineral vein of rich *ore within a *rock formation, which extends through a continuous zone or belt. *See also* MOTHER LODE.

lode mining The *mining of a valuable mineral *lode which is found between other distinct mineral or rock units, and consists of several *veins that are spaced closely enough together so that all of them, together with the intervening rock, can be mined as a single unit.

lodging In plants, the permanent bending of the stem of a stem-crop plant (e.g. wheat, barley) from its upright position. This can reduce yield considerably. Normally, lodging results from storm damage, but rots, insects, or excess nitrogen may also cause it.

loess A *soil or *deposit composed of small *silt-sized particles that were transported by the *wind to their present location, for example after a *glacial period. *See also* AEOLIAN.

log 1. A cut segment of the trunk of a *tree. **2.** A record, for example a daily record of a ship's speed and progress or a record of *geological data collected in a *borehole.

logged-over forest A North American term for a *forest in which most or all of the commercially valuable *timber has been removed.

logging 1. Cutting down *trees for *timber. *See also* AERIAL LOGGING; CABLE LOGGING; GROUND-LEAD LOGGING; HIGH-LEAD LOGGING; SKYLINE LOGGING; TRACTOR LOGGING. **2.** Storing information about events, or storing the record of a *log.

logging concession A *concession of land for *logging operations.

logging debris *See* LOGGING RESIDUE.

logging residue (logging debris, slash) The material that is left on the ground after timber cutting, which includes unused logs, uprooted stumps, broken branches, bark, and leaves.

logistic growth Growth rates that are regulated by internal and external factors which establish an *equilibrium with *environmental resources. *See also* S-CURVE. *Contrast* J-CURVE.

London Convention *See* CONVENTION ON THE PREVENTION OF MARINE POLLUTION BY DUMPING OF WASTES AND OTHER MATTER (1972).

long profile (longitudinal profile) A section along a river *channel which shows how the *slope of the river changes downstream. Many rivers have concave long profiles because headwaters are steep and slope decreases downstream. *See also* BASE LEVEL; WATERFALL.

long term An extended period of time; in environmental terms often defined as of the order of 10–15 years. *Contrast* MEDIUM TERM; SHORT TERM. *See also* LONG-RANGE PLANNING.

Long Term Ecological Research Network (LTER) A collaborative scientific programme in the USA, funded by the National Science Foundation, which brings together scientists and students who are studying *ecological processes over long time and broad geographical scales.

longevity The *lifespan of an *organism, or age at death. *See also* SURVIVORSHIP.

longitude Distance on the Earth's surface east or west from a reference line (usually the *Greenwich Meridian), measured in degrees. The *International Date Line is longitude 180° east or west. *Contrast* LATITUDE.

longitudinal dune A long sand *dune that is aligned parallel to the direction of the prevailing *wind.

longitudinal profile *See* LONG PROFILE.

longleaf pine savanna A park-like type of vegetation, shaded by tall pines, kept open by frequent *wildfires, with a diverse layer of grasses and flowering plants including rare orchids, which was once common along the gulf coastal plain of Louisiana in the USA but has been reduced to isolated fragments as a result of *land use changes.

longline A long fishing line at sea, that stretches for tens of kilometres and is baited with hundreds of hooks and held by floats. This type of line often catches many *non-target species (such as tuna, sharks, and dolphins) so has a large unplanned *bycatch.

long-range navigation (LORAN) A system of navigation over long distances, in which *latitude and *longitude are determined from the time displacement of radio signals from two or more fixed transmitters.

long-range planning Strategic planning over an extended time period, usually at least 50 years. *Contrast* SHORT-RANGE PLANNING. *See also* LONG TERM.

Long-Range Transport of Air Pollutants (LRTAP) A major international research programme that was launched in 1972 by the *Organisation for Economic Co-operation and Development and is designed to measure air quality at 70 sites in order to develop a better understanding of the dispersion (particularly the *trans-frontier movement) of *air pollutants such as *acid rain.

longshore Along and parallel to the *coastline.

longshore bar A linear ridge of sand in which the long axis is parallel to the shore and which is in, or immediately seaward of, the intertidal zone (*see* LITTORAL ZONE).

longshore current A current that moves parallel to the *shore, and is formed from the momentum of breaking *waves that approach the shore at an angle.

longshore drift The processes by which *sediment is transported along the *coast by *wave action and *longshore currents. *See also* SPIT; TOMBOLO.

long-term effect An effect that generally occurs after a *lag of about 20 years.

long-term monitoring An *environmental monitoring system that is designed to continue over a period of decades.

longwave radiation *See* INFRARED.

loop highway A scenic drive which begins and ends at the same place, in the form of a circuit (which is not necessarily circular).

looping The pattern made by a chimney *plume that sinks towards the ground, then rises again, repeating this pattern until the gases, water droplets, and solid particles have dispersed.

lop To cut branches off a standing *tree.

LORAN *See* LONG-RANGE NAVIGATION.

Los Alamos A town in New Mexico, USA, which in 1942 was chosen as a *nuclear research site where the first atomic bombs were produced.

Los Angelization *See* SUBURBAN SPRAWL.

lot A North American term for a plot of land.

lotic Relating to flowing water such as rivers and streams. *See also* LENTIC WATER.

Love Canal An area near Niagara Falls, New York State, USA, which between 1920 and 1953 was used as a site to dump *hazardous wastes. In 1953, the canal area was covered with soil and presumed safe, but officials began to investigate the dumping of the hazardous wastes and local residents started to report serious health problems. The site was declared to be a health hazard, and the area was evacuated. Since then, the site has been cleaned up using the *Superfund, and people began moving back to live in the area in the early 1990s.

Lovelock, James The British atmospheric chemist and inventor (born 1919), who was the first to measure *DDT and *CFCs in the air at very low concentrations, and proposed the *Gaia hypothesis.

low (depression) The centre of an area of low pressure in the *atmosphere.

low flow Below-average depth or volume of water in a river, as occurs for example during a *drought or prolonged dry period.

low latitude Close to the *equator, away from the *poles. *Contrast* HIGH LATITUDE.

low pressure *See* DEPRESSION.

low risk (near threatened) Describes a *species that is regarded as having a relatively low risk of *extinction. *Contrast* ENDANGERED; VULNERABLE SPECIES; RARE.

low sulphur coal *See* COMPLIANCE COAL.

low tide Low water; the lowest level to which the *tide falls within the daily tidal cycle. *Contrast* HIGH TIDE.

low water mark The line along the coast to which the sea drops at *low tide. *Contrast* HIGH WATER MARK.

low-emission vehicle A vehicle which emits relatively little *air pollution compared with conventional *internal combustion engines.

lower atmosphere stability index (Haines index) A measure of the stability and dryness of the air, which is used to indicate the potential for wildfire to grow and spread through an area.

 SEE WEB LINKS

• Lower atmosphere stability index.

lowest achievable emission rate The lowest possible rate of *emission for a particular type of *facility and a specific *air pollutant.

lowest observed adverse effect level (LOAEL) The lowest *concentration of a *hazardous substance at which it is possible to detect a statistically or biologically significant increase in the frequency or severity of an *adverse effect between an *exposed population and a *control group.

lowland Low-level country. *Contrast* HIGHLAND; UPLAND.

low-level radioactive waste (LLRW, low-level waste) *Radioactive waste that is generated by hospitals, research labs, and some industries, and is less hazardous than *high-level radioactive wastes that are generated by *nuclear reactors.

low-level waste *See* LOW-LEVEL RADIOACTIVE WASTE.

LPG *See* LIQUEFIED PETROLEUM GAS.

LRTAP *See* LONG-RANGE TRANSPORT OF AIR POLLUTANTS.

LTER *See* LONG TERM ECOLOGICAL RESEARCH NETWORK.

LULU An acronym for Locally Unwanted Land Uses, such as toxic waste dumps, incinerators, smelters, airports, freeways, and other sources of environmental, economic, or social degradation. *See also* NIMBY.

lumber *See* TIMBER.

LUST *See* LEAKING UNDERGROUND STORAGE TANK.

lustre The way that *light is reflected from the surface of a *mineral. In mineralogy this may be described as adamantine, metallic (like polished metal), resinous, waxy, pearly, silky, greasy, vitreous (glassy), or earthy.

luvisols Soils that have an *illuvial horizon rich in silicate *clays with a *cation exchange capacity greater than 24 $cmol_c/kg$ (centimoles cation per kilogram). Luvisols are a reference soil group in the *World Soil Classification.

LWR *See* LIGHT-WATER REACTOR.

lysimeter A device for measuring potential and actual *evapotranspiration in a column of *soil.

maar A flat-bottomed *volcanic crater that was formed by an explosion that occurred when *magma encountered *groundwater. It is often filled with water forming a shallow lake.

Maathai, Wangari Muta Mary Jo (1940–2011) A Kenyan environmental and political activist, educated in the USA, who helped to establish the *Greenbelt Movement. She received the Right Livelihood Award in 1986 and in 2004 she became the first African woman to receive a Nobel Peace Prize for 'her contribution to sustainable development, democracy and peace'.

MAB *See* MAN AND THE BIOSPHERE PROGRAMME.

MAC *See* MARGINAL ABATEMENT COST, MAXIMUM ALLOWABLE CONCENTRATION.

Macaronesian floral region A region comprising the Canaries, Madeira, and the Azores, in which few genera are *endemic, perhaps fewer than 30; the most remote island group, the Azores, has no endemics. The flora of the Canaries displays a notably high frequency of succulents belonging to the Crassulaceae, in particular the genus *Sempervivum*.

macchia *See* MAQUIS.

Mach A measurement of speed relative to the speed of sound. Mach 1 is the speed of sound, which varies from about 1225 km h^{-1} in warm air at sea level to about 1060 km h^{-1} in very cold air at high altitude. It is named after the Austrian physicist Ernst Mach (1838–1916).

machair An area of low, undulating tracts, supporting stable, herb-rich grassland growing on shell sand, which has developed over a long period by the accumulation of blown sand behind coastal sand-dunes, occurring most typically in the Hebrides and along the north-west coast of Scotland.

mackerel sky An appearance of the sky in which units of *cirrocumulus cloud are swept into long, parallel rows, forming a pattern reminiscent of those on the back of a mackerel.

macro- Large. *Contrast* MESO-; MICRO-.

macrobenthos The larger organisms of the *benthos, generally longer than 0.5 mm. *Contrast* MEIOBENTHOS; MICROBENTHOS.

macroburst A strong *downburst of air from the base of a *cumulonimbus cloud, which usually lasts for 5–20 minutes and has a radius of more than four km. Strong macrobursts can cause damage similar to that of an F2 tornado on the *Fujita Scale. *Contrast* MICROBURST.

macroclimate The *climate of a large area such as a continent or the entire Earth, as distinguished from the smaller scale *microclimates and *mesoclimates within it.

macrocyclic lactone insecticides A group of about twelve *acaricides, *nematicides, and *insecticides that are used to control a wide range of crop pests and tsetse flies, and to treat parasitic worms in cattle, sheep, pigs, horses, dogs, and cats. The products are moderately toxic to humans.

macroeconomics The study and analysis of the whole *economy of a country or region, that considers issues such as *economic growth, inflation, unemployment, and economic fluctuations. *Contrast* MICROECONOMICS.

macroelement *See* MACRONUTRIENT.

macroevolution Biological *evolution above the species level, i.e. that results in the emergence of genera, families, orders, or higher *taxonomic groups.

macrofauna Small soil animals (such as earthworms and large *arthropods) that are longer than about 1 mm and can thus be seen with the naked eye. *Contrast* MESOFAUNA; MICROFAUNA.

macroinvertebrate Any *invertebrate that is large enough to be seen with the naked eye (with a body longer than 2 mm). This includes *crustaceans (such as crayfish), *insects, worms, etc. *Contrast* MICROINVERTEBRATE.

macroinvertebrate community index (MCI) A method for assessing the quality of a stream or river, based on the presence or absence of particular types of *invertebrate (*indicator species) on the stream bed, which have different abilities to tolerate *pollution.

macronutrient (macroelement, major element) A *nutrient or chemical element that is required in relatively large amounts by plants because it is vital for healthy plant growth. After *carbon, *hydrogen, and *oxygen the three most important ones are *nitrogen, *potassium, and *phosphorus, which are the usual ingredients of *fertilizers; others include *calcium, *magnesium, and *sulphur. Macronutrients essential for animals include *amino acids, *carbohydrates, and fats. *Contrast* MICRONUTRIENT. *See also* ESSENTIAL ELEMENT.

macroparasite A relatively large *parasite. *Contrast* MICROPARASITE.

macrophagous Applied to animals that feed on items that are large in relation to their own body size.

macrophyte An aquatic *plant that is large enough to be seen with the naked eye. The term is often applied to aquatic mosses, ferns, and rooted plants.

macroscopic Large enough to be visible to the naked eye, usually longer than about 1 mm. *Contrast* MICROSCOPIC.

MACT *See* MAXIMUM ACHIEVABLE CONTROL TECHNOLOGY.

Madagascan faunal subregion The strongly *endemic and insular fauna of Madagascar, which includes five orders found nowhere else. For example, four of the five families of lemurs survive only in Madagascar; and this is the only part of the African continent from which the more advanced apes and monkeys are entirely absent.

Madagascan floral region Part of R. Good's *Palaeotropical kingdom (*The Geography of the Flowering Plants*, 1974), which geographically includes Madagascar, the Seychelles, and the Mascarenes. A high proportion of the genera, perhaps exceeding 200, is *endemic and, depending on the taxonomic system adopted, there are two or three endemic families.

made ground (made land) An area of dry land that has been made by people, generally through the reclamation of marshes, lakes, or shorelines. An artificial fill (*landfill) is used, consisting of natural materials, refuse, etc.

made land *See* MADE GROUND.

Madrid Protocol on Environmental Protection to the Antarctic Treaty *See* ANTARCTIC TREATY.

MAFF In the UK, the former Ministry of Agriculture, Fisheries and Food, now replaced by *DEFRA.

mafic Applied to any dark-coloured *igneous rock (such as *basalt) that generally contains little *silica but a great deal of *magnesium and iron-rich minerals; found mainly in *oceanic crust. *Contrast* FELSIC.

magma Molten rock found beneath the Earth's crust from which *igneous rocks are formed, and which becomes *lava when it reaches the surface via a volcanic vent. It may contain some solid particles and gases.

magma chamber A chamber or large space within the *lithosphere in which *magma is stored.

magnesium (Mg) A silver-coloured, naturally occurring metallic element that is abundant in the environment (it accounts for 2.09% of the Earth's *crust, particularly the *oceanic crust), contributes to *hard water in high concentrations, is not generally considered toxic, and is a *macronutrient for animals and humans.

magnet Any material that has a permanent *magnetic field.

magnetic Capable of being magnetized, or having the properties of a *magnet.

magnetic anomaly Differences from place to place in the strength and direction of the *magnetic field, compared to the average.

magnetic field A field of force that is generated by electric currents. The Earth's magnetic field is believed to be generated by the rotation of the molten iron–nickel *outer core around the solid *inner core, like a dynamo. *See also* PALAEOMAGNETISM.

magnetic north The direction to which the needle of a magnetic compass points, which is towards the northern *pole of the Earth's *magnetic field rather than towards *true north.

magnetic polarity The direction, north (normal) or south (reversed), in which a magnetic compass needle points.

magnetic pole The end of a *magnet (or either end of the *Earth's *axis) where the strength of the *magnetic field is greatest.

magnetic reversal The process by which the *Earth's magnetic north pole and its magnetic south pole reverse their positions over time. *See also* PALAEOMAGNETISM.

magnetic separation The process of separating *ferrous materials from mixed *municipal waste streams using *magnets.

magnetic storm *See* GEOMAGNETIC STORM.

magnetic susceptibility The degree of magnetization of a material in response to a *magnetic field, which depends mostly on the concentration of ferromagnetic minerals within it.

magnetics The study of the properties of *magnets and *magnetic fields.

magnetometer An instrument for measuring the magnitude and direction of the Earth's *magnetic field.

magnetopause The boundary layer in space (about 63 000 km from Earth in the direction of the Sun), between *magnetosphere and the *solar wind, where the Earth's *magnetic field balances the pressure of the solar wind.

magnetosphere The region of space that exists above the *atmosphere and within the *magnetopause, that is under the direct influence of the Earth's *magnetic field.

magnetostratigraphy *See* PALAEOMAGNETISM.

magnox An *alloy of *magnesium oxide and *aluminium.

magnox reactor A redundant type of commercial *nuclear reactor that used *magnox as fuel cladding, uranium as fuel, carbon dioxide as a coolant, and graphite as a *moderator. It was designed in the UK, and was capable of producing *plutonium for nuclear weapons. A total of 26 were built in the UK. By 2012 all but one (Wylfa UK) had closed.

Magnuson Fishery Conservation and Management Act *See* FISHERY CONSERVATION AND MANAGEMENT ACT.

mainstream flow The portion of the flow in a fluid that is away from the surrounding surface, and thus not under the influence of the *boundary layer.

major element *See* MACRONUTRIENT.

major recreation facility A North American term for developed *recreation facilities that are costly to build and run, and are heavily used, such as campgrounds, picnic areas, swimming areas, boating sites, and *interpretation sites. *Contrast* MINOR RECREATION FACILITY.

malaria (marsh fever) An infectious *disease that is caused by a parasite (*Plasmodium*) transmitted by the bite of infected mosquitoes. It is common in hot countries, its symptoms include recurring chills, fever, and sweating, and it can be fatal.

malathion An *organophosphorus *insecticide and *acaricide that is used to control a range of pests including aphids, leafhoppers, codling moths, and mites. It is harmful to fish and bees, and *toxicity to *mammals is increased by prior exposure to *parathion.

Malaysian floral region Part of R. Good's Indo-Malaysian floral subkingdom within his *Palaeotropical floral kingdom (*The Geography of the Flowering Plants*, 1974), and including the Malay peninsula and archipelago of south-eastern Asia. The flora is one of the richest, if not the richest, in the world. It has yielded many plants of value to humans, of which bananas, nutmeg, cinnamon, and cloves are perhaps the best known.

male In organisms with separate sexes, the one which produces sperm. *Contrast* FEMALE.

maleic hydrazide A compound used as a growth regulator to control weeds on roadside verges and in amenity areas and to prevent sprouting in stored potatoes and onions. It has no harmful environmental effects and its toxicity to mammals is low.

Malesian flora The flora of the islands on and between the Sunda and Sahul shelves, covering an area comprising Malaysia, Papua New Guinea, and the islands of Indonesia, Brunei, and the Philippines. Malesia is sharply

m

delimited by major floristic changes at about the latitude of the Kra isthmus in the west and the Torres Strait in the south-east.

malformation Something abnormal; in humans, a structural defect that is present at birth, occurs infrequently, and is due to abnormal development.

malignant Cancerous; a growth in which cells reproduce faster than normal cells. *Contrast* BENIGN.

malleable Capable of being shaped or bent or drawn out. *See also* DUCTILE.

mallee An Australian name for grassy, open *scrub community, with plants up to 2–3 m high, which is found in many *semi-arid areas.

malnourishment *See* MALNUTRITION.

malnutrition (malnourishment) Undernourishment caused by insufficient food and/or a *diet that does not contain enough *protein, essential fats, vitamins, *minerals, and other *nutrients to ensure good health.

Malthus, Thomas An English economist (1766–1834) who argued, in *An Essay on the Principle of Population, as it affects the Future Improvement of Society* (1798), that increases in the human *population would outgrow increases in the resources available to support it, because populations increase *geometrically while food supplies increase *arithmetically, and that population is kept in check by a combination of war, *famine, and *disease. He assumed that if population growth continued unchecked, then population would outstrip the food available and this would cause widespread famine and death. He also described a *feedback mechanism: when the population became too large for the available food supply, increased mortality would reduce the population to the level that could be sustained by the amount of food produced. Providing assistance to the poor was, therefore, self-defeating.

Malthusian growth (irruptive growth) A pattern of growth in a *population (human or animal) in which a *population explosion is followed by a *population crash.

mammals A class (Mammalia) of *homeothermic, *vertebrate animals that breathe air, have hair, feed their young with the mother's milk secreted by mammae (giving the class its name), have four types of well-developed teeth, a four-chambered heart, a diaphragm separating the thorax and abdomen, and usually have four well-developed limbs with toes that have nails, claws, or hoofs.

Man and Nature A book by George Perkins *Marsh (1864) which described and illustrated many ways in which human activities change and damage environmental systems, and was a catalyst for the development of reforestation, watershed management, soil conservation, and nature conservation.

Man and the Biosphere Programme (MAB) An interdisciplinary programme of research and training, established by *UNESCO in 1971, designed to develop the basis for the *sustainable use and *conservation of biological diversity, and for the improvement of the global relationship between people and their environment.

managed burn *See* PRESCRIBED BURN.

Managed Nature Reserve/Wildlife Sanctuary An *IUCN Management Category (IV) for protected areas, designed to ensure the natural conditions necessary to protect nationally significant species, groups of species, biotic communities, or physical features of the environment.

Managed Resource Area *See* MULTIPLE-USE MANAGEMENT AREA/MANAGED RESOURCE AREA.

management The act of directing and controlling the affairs of a business, organization, or other body to ensure that they operate efficiently and effectively, in order to accomplish agreed objectives. *See also* RESOURCE MANAGEMENT.

management agreement An agreement between the owner of a property and the company or individual who is responsible for managing it. In the UK, it is a written contract agreement between an official body (such as *DEFRA) and landowners and tenants regarding their management of land, which is a prerequisite of certain incentive payments. *See also* ENVIRONMENTALLY SENSITIVE AREA.

management area An area of land, or a group of areas which are not necessarily contiguous, which have common *management objectives.

management indicator species (MIS) *See* INDICATOR SPECIES.

management information *Information that is required or useful for *management decision-making.

management information system (MIS) A system for collecting and analysing *information, usually computer-based, that is designed to help *management decision-making.

management objective A high-level statement of what is desired, or a description of an intended outcome, which is usually measurable, time limited, specific, and practical.

management plan A written plan that describes the overall guidelines within which an activity or project is organized, administered, and managed to ensure that agreed *management objectives are achieved in a timely manner.

management practice A specific action, measure, or treatment which is part of a *management plan and is designed to meet one or more stated *management objectives.

management prescription Definition of the most appropriate *management practices for use in a specific situation, or in a specific area, in order to achieve agreed *management objectives.

management programme The *management practices that are required to achieve agreed *management objectives within a management *plan.

management science *See* OPERATIONAL RESEARCH.

management unit (management zone) A defined area of land or water to which specific *management decisions apply.

management zone *See* MANAGEMENT UNIT.

management-by-objective An approach to *management (within an organization or agency) which involves the definition of goals and responsibilities, in terms of measurable results, and the use of these measures to guide the operation of the organization/agency and the assessment of the contribution of different parts of the organization/agency to meeting the specified goals.

managerialism Considering the behaviour of an organization or activity from the perspective of a manager responsible for delivering agreed *management objectives, with an emphasis on measuring performance, efficiency, and effectiveness against targets.

mandible 1. In *vertebrates, the lower jaw, which is used for biting or chewing. **2.** In birds, the lower jaw and bill, or the two parts of the bill (upper and lower mandibles). **3.** In *arthropods one of the pair of mouthparts that is most commonly used to seize and cut food.

maneb A dithiocarbamate (*see* CARBAMATE) fungicide used as a foliar spray to control diseases such as potato blight and tomato-leaf mould. It is of low mammalian toxicity but can cause eye and skin irritation.

manganese (Mn) A brittle, silvery *metal that is associated with iron *ores, is used in the manufacture of steel (to improve hardness and resistance to corrosion), and is an essential *element (*micronutrient) for plant and animal life.

manganese nodule A small, rounded *concretion that is found on the deep *ocean floor and may contain up to 20% *manganese and smaller amounts of *iron, *copper, and *nickel *oxides and *hydroxides.

mangel *See* MANGROVE FOREST.

mangrove A tropical *evergreen tree or shrub which grows in coastal areas, particularly on tidal flats and *estuaries. It has stilt-like roots which knit together to form dense thickets, which can trap coastal sediment and encourage coastal deposition, allowing the mangrove to extend further out from the shore. Mangrove swamps provide important habitats for aquatic and amphibious species.

mangrove forest (mangel, mangrove swamp) A *shoreline *ecosystem that is dominated by *mangrove trees, with associated *mud flats.

mangrove swamp *See* MANGROVE FOREST.

manifest system *See* CRADLE-TO-GRAVE SYSTEM.

man-induced turnover The additional flow of an element through the active part of a *biogeochemical cycle that results from human activity. For example, by burning fossil fuels humans add an extra 5 billion tonnes per year of carbon to the turnover of the carbon cycle, which is naturally about 75 billion tonnes per year.

man-made disaster *See* TECHNOLOGICAL DISASTER. *Contrast* NATURAL DISASTER.

mantle The hot, pliable zone within the *Earth's interior that surrounds the partially molten *core and underlies the thin, cool, outer *crust. The mantle is about 2900 km thick, and is made from rock that is relatively dense. It is often described as solid, but in reality it behaves like a *plastic and can flow. It is composed mainly of minerals that are *silicate compounds (combining silica and oxygen). *Iron is the main metal, but there is also a great deal of *magnesium. The composition and behaviour of material within the mantle varies with distance from the core (below) and crust (above), and two main zones can be distinguished within it: the *asthenospere and the *lithosphere. The sharp and well-defined junction between the mantle and the crust is called the *Mohorovičić discontinuity.

manual separation The sorting by hand of material in *waste that can be *recycled or turned into *compost.

manufacturing The conversion of raw materials into finished goods for sale.

manure The waste products of *animals that are sometimes used as a form of organic *fertilizer on *farms, *allotments, or *gardens. See also FARMYARD MANURE; GREEN MANURE.

maquis The name given to drought-resistant *scrub vegetation, consisting of *evergreen shrubs and isolated small trees with thick, leathery leaves, in the *arid region in France. This type of scrub is known as macchia in Italy and matorral in Spain.

marble A *metamorphic rock that is formed by applying great heat and pressure to *limestone.

mares' tails Long, white, hair-like wisps of *cirrus clouds, composed entirely of ice crystals. They taper and curl at the ends, resembling the tails of horses.

marginal abatement cost (MAC) The additional cost that is associated with reducing *emissions of a particular *pollutant by a set amount.

marginal cost The additional cost that is associated with producing one more unit of a particular good or service.

marginal land Land which barely pays the cost of working it because of physical limitations such as infertility, *drought, or shallow soils.

marginal value The additional value of a resource that is associated with an incremental change in the quantity of it that is available.

mariculture See AQUACULTURE.

marine (maritime) Of or relating to the *sea or *ocean.

marine ecosystem A *saltwater *aquatic *ecosystem that includes *estuaries and *coastal areas, along with the *open sea and *oceans.

marine intertidal A *coastal *saltwater *wetland *habitat that is flooded by *tidewaters.

Marine Mammal Protection Act (1972) US legislation that provides for the protection and *conservation of *marine *mammal species by prohibiting the taking (harassing, hunting, capturing, or killing) of marine mammals, and prohibiting the import of any marine mammal product or any fish that has been associated with the taking of marine mammals.

Marine Nature Reserve (MNR) A statutory marine protected area in Great Britain, declared under the Wildlife and Countryside Act 1981, which is designed to protect marine flora, fauna, or geological or *physiographic features in the area, and to provide opportunities for study and research.

marine pollution *Pollution of the seas and oceans.

Marine Protected Area (MPA) An area of land or sea that is dedicated to the protection and maintenance of *biodiversity, and of natural and cultural resources, and managed through legal or other effective means.

Marine Protection, Research, and Sanctuaries Act (1972) (Ocean Dumping Act) US legislation that regulates the dumping of any material in the ocean which might adversely affect human health, marine environments, or the economic potential of the ocean.

marine resource Any *natural resource that is found in, on, or under the *sea or *ocean, including fish and *minerals.

marine sanctuary A designated area of the sea or ocean that serves as a *nature reserve, which people can access. Non-extractive activities like boating, swimming, and snorkelling are allowed, but all types of fishing, including trawling, and all collecting and extractive activities are prohibited.

marine subarctic climate A cold *subpolar *climate, found in latitudes 50–60°N and 45–60°S in which temperatures remain cold throughout the year and precipitation is fairly heavy. Natural vegetation in this zone is either *tundra (where it is coldest) or *boreal forest (where it is milder).

marine system The open *ocean over the *continental shelf, where conditions are affected by *waves, *currents, and oceanic *tides.

marine west coast climate A *mid-latitude climate, found between latitudes 40° and 60° in both hemispheres, which is cloudy, with a small temperature range through the year. Precipitation is distributed fairly evenly through the year, but with a maximum in winter, and frontal storms are frequent. Forest cover often develops because of the heavy rainfall and moderate temperatures.

marine west coast forest A coniferous *temperate forest that is found along the west coasts of some continents, including the Pacific Northwest of North America, north-west Europe, southern Chile, and New Zealand. The forest often includes trees that are taller than 30 m, have diameters greater than two m, and are well over 1000 years old.

maritime *See* MARINE.

maritime air Air with a high moisture content, whose humid characteristics were developed over a large *sea or *ocean.

maritime climate (oceanic climate) A *climate that is produced by *maritime air and occurs in areas close to the *ocean, which keeps winters relatively mild and summers cool. Precipitation is fairly high.

maritime polar air mass A mass of cool, humid air that forms over the cold ocean waters of the North Pacific and North Atlantic, and over the northern part of the Southern Ocean. In North America maritime polar air from the Pacific brings mild, humid weather at all times of year, with showers in winter and more low cloud and drizzle in summer.

maritime tropical air mass A mass of warm, humid air that forms over *tropical and *subtropical oceans.

market barrier In *economics, any factor or condition that prevents or inhibits *market equilibrium. As applied to *air pollution control, for example, this includes policy and legal frameworks that prevent the adoption of cost-effective technologies or practices that could reduce *emissions of *greenhouse gases.

market cost The cost that a consumer pays to purchase a particular good or service, which usually fails to take into account *environmental degradation and other *externalities. *See also* TRUE COST.

market economy An *economy in which most goods and services are produced by the private sector rather than the public sector, and in which the prices of goods and services are determined by *supply and *demand, usually under *market equilibrium. *See also* MARKET-PLACE.

market equilibrium A situation in which the quantity of a particular good or service that people are willing to buy (*demand) equals the quantity that people are willing to sell (*supply). This is the basis of the *free market system, in which there are neither monopolies nor government interventions. *See also* MARKET ECONOMY.

market failure Any situation where a *free market fails to produce the best use of scarce *resources, which arises when *market prices are not equal to the *social cost of resources, because of *externalities. *See also* NON-MARKET DAMAGE.

market forces The interaction of *supply and *demand which determines *market equilibrium and shapes a *market economy.

market garden A plot of land on which fruit and vegetables are cultivated for sale. *See also* HORTICULTURE; SMALLHOLDING.

market price (market value) The price at which the buyers and sellers of a good or service in a *market economy are willing to do business with each other, when *supply and *demand are equal.

market value *See* MARKET PRICE.

market values Values that can be expressed in financial or monetary terms.

market-based incentive *See* MARKET-BASED MECHANISM.

market-based mechanism (market-based incentive) A mechanism (such as *command and control, and *environmental regulation) that is designed to influence *market forces in order to manipulate *market equilibrium, with a view to improving *environmental protection or reducing *environmental damage.

marketplace A situation (an actual place or any means of contact) in which two or more people agree to buy and sell a product or service. *See also* MARKET ECONOMY.

mark–recapture *See* CAPTURE–RECAPTURE METHOD.

marl An *alluvial *clay or *deposit that contains a relatively large amount of *calcium carbonate, and can be used as a *fertilizer on *soils that are deficient in *lime.

marl lake A *freshwater *lake in which the concentration of dissolved *calcium carbonate is greater than 100 milligrams per litre.

MARPOL *See* INTERNATIONAL CONVENTION FOR THE PREVENTION OF POLLUTION FROM SHIPS.

marram grass Two species of *Ammophila*, which are *grasses with an extensive, tightly knit underground root system which can survive in the relatively salty, nutrient-poor free-draining sand that is typical of *beach dunes. They are native to Europe and North Africa (but noxious weeds in California) and are used to stabilize dunes.

Marsh, George Perkins A US diplomat and classical scholar (1801–82) who published the influential book *Man and Nature* in 1864 and is regarded by some as the father of the *environmental movement.

marsh (marshland) A low-lying *wetland area with a *mineral soil supporting grassy vegetation, often close to a river or lake, that is frequently flooded to a shallow depth. Marshes can be *freshwater or *saltwater, tidal or non-tidal.

marsh fever *See* MALARIA.

marsh gas *See* METHANOGEN.

Marshall, Robert A US conservationist (1901–39) who founded the Wilderness Society. He was among the first to suggest that large tracts of Alaska be preserved, helped to shape the *US Forest Service's policy on *wilderness designation and management, and wrote with conviction on all aspects of *conservation and *preservation.

marshland *See* MARSH.

marsupial A *mammal (order Marsupialia) in which females produce a yolky egg with a thin shell. Within ten to twelve days of the shell breaking the embryo is born and crawls into a pouch (marsupium) where it attaches itself to a teat. It feeds in the pouch until it is weaned. There are about 250 species, e.g. opossums, kangaroos, and wombats.

Marxism The economic and political theories of Karl Marx (and Friedrich Engels), based on the belief that human actions and institutions are driven mainly by economic factors (particularly by a profit motive), that social change is driven mainly by class struggles, and that *socialism will ultimately replace *capitalism.

mass balance The relative balance between the *input and *output of material and processes within an *open system, such as the snow and ice within a *glacier, or the water or sediment moving through a *lake or *river.

mass burn The deliberate *incineration of unsorted *solid waste material.

mass extinction A catastrophic, widespread event in which a large proportion (up to 90%) of species become *extinct in a relatively short time compared with normal background extinction. There have been at least five such mass extinctions, including the wholesale extinction of the *dinosaurs, other big reptiles, and many marine invertebrates at the *K-T boundary. In the short term mass extinctions have a catastrophic impact on *biodiversity. But the long-term impact on biodiversity is generally limited, because mass extinctions have usually been followed by phases of rapid *speciation. Surviving species generally evolve rapidly, by *adaptive radiation, to occupy the *niches vacated by the species that became extinct.

mass mixing ratio *See* MIXING RATIO.

mass movement (mass wasting) The process by which unconsolidated material moves down *hillslopes in the form of a *flow, *slide, *fall, or *creep, as a result of *gravity. *See also* AVALANCHE; LANDSLIDE.

mass selection A method of plant *breeding in which seed from a number of individuals is selected to form the next generation, with selection criteria relaxed until later generations and crosses being created at random.

mass spectrometry A technique that is used to identify and measure the chemicals that are present in a substance by their mass and charge, based on very small samples. *See also* GAS CHROMATOGRAPHY–MASS SPECTROMETRY.

mass transit The US name for public transportation in which buses, trains, subways, trams, and other forms of transport are used to move large numbers of people efficiently, with reduced overall *environmental impacts.

mass wasting *See* MASS MOVEMENT.

massif A block of the Earth's *crust that is bounded by *faults and has been moved to create one or more peaks of a *mountain range. It is usually more rigid than surrounding rocks.

massive rock A solid mass of rock that is homogeneous, with no joints, cracks, *foliation, or bedding.

mast The *fruit and *seed of shrubs, woody vines, trees, cacti, and other non-herbaceous vegetation (including acorns, beechnuts, and chestnuts) that is available as food for *wildlife.

master plan *See* COMPREHENSIVE PLAN.

mating In animals, the act of pairing a male and female for sexual reproduction.

matorral *See* MAQUIS.

matrix In geology, the small-grained material that is found in the spaces between larger-grained materials in a rock.

matter Anything that takes up space and has mass.

mature soil A well-developed *soil that normally has a *soil profile with clearly defined *horizons.

mature timber (old growth, late successional) A stand of *trees that is fully grown, especially in height, and is in full seed production.

mature tree A *tree that has reached the desired size or age for its intended use, which varies from species to species.

maturity 1. Part of the *life cycle of an organism, when it has become adult, between *youth and *old age. **2.** The middle stage in the *cycle of erosion, in which the landscape has high relief and well-developed drainage. *Contrast* OLD AGE; YOUTH.

Mauna Loa A volcano in Hawaii which is one of the world's most active volcanoes. It has erupted 33 times since 1843 and last erupted in 1984.

Mauna Loa record *See* KEELING CURVE.

Maunder minimum The period from 1645 to 1715 when solar activity was very low and few *sunspots were observed. This period coincided with the coldest episode in the *Little Ice Age. It was detected by the English solar astronomer Edward Walter Maunder (1851–1928).

maximum achievable control technology (MACT) Emissions limitations based on the best demonstrated *control technology or practices, taking into account cost and technical feasibility, which produces a very high level of *pollution control.

maximum allowable concentration (MAC) The highest concentration of a particular *pollutant that workers can safely be in contact with in their work environment.

maximum contaminant level (MCL) The highest allowable concentration of a given *contaminant in *potable water.

maximum exposure limit (MEL) The highest level of exposure to a particular *pollutant to which a person may safely be exposed.

maximum permissible dose (MPD) The highest amount of *radiation to which a person may safely be exposed.

maximum residue level The upper limit permitted by law of a pesticide residue in food or animal feed, based on good agricultural practices and ensuring the lowest possible consumer exposure. Levels in the EU are set by the European Food Safety Authority (EFSA).

SEE WEB LINKS

• Home page of the European Food Safety Authority.

maximum sustainable yield (MSY) The maximum crop or *yield that can be taken on a sustained basis from a particular *population in a defined area (such as a portion of the *ocean) without driving it towards *extinction. *Contrast* OPTIMUM YIELD.

maximum tolerated dose (MTD) The highest dose of a drug, drug combination, or other treatment that an individual of a particular species of animal (including humans) can safely withstand over a major portion of its lifetime.

MCI *See* MACROINVERTEBRATE COMMUNITY INDEX.

McIntyre-Stennis Act (1962) US legislation that established a cooperative research

Fig. 13 Meander

programme in *forestry for state land-grant colleges and universities.

MCL *See* MAXIMUM CONTAMINANT LEVEL.

McMansion (starter castle) North American pejorative term for a large house built on a small plot of land, often constructed cheaply but including ostentatious traditional features.

MCPA A synthetic *auxin used as a *systemic herbicide to control a wide variety of broad-leaved weeds, both *monocotyledons and *dicotyledons, in cereal and grass crops. It is not persistent in the soil and is of low mammalian toxicity.

MCPP *See* MECOPROP.

McSweeney-McNary Act (1928) US legislation that authorized a comprehensive research programme for the *US Forest Service. This act was repealed and replaced by the Forest and Rangeland Renewable Resources Research Act (1978).

MDC *See* MORE DEVELOPED COUNTRY.

meadow A *field in which *grass or *alfalfa are grown to be used as *pasture or made into *hay. *See also* HAY MEADOW.

Meadows, Dennis US economist, co-author (with Donella Meadows) of the book *Limits to Growth*, and member of the *Club of Rome.

mean annual runoff The average amount of water that flows down a particular river, per year, expressed either as a depth (in millimetres) of water spread evenly across the entire *drainage basin, or as a volume (in cubic metres) of water flowing past a given point.

mean annual temperature The average *temperature of the air over a particular location, over the entire year.

mean daily temperature The average *temperature of the air over a particular place, over a 24-hour period.

mean low water The long-term average height of all low waters at a particular place.

mean sea level The long-term average height of the water level of the sea surface at a particular place.

mean tide level (half-tide level) The average of mean high water and mean low water.

meander A curve or bend in a *river channel, which forms naturally by *fluvial *erosion (see Fig. 13). *See also* FLOODPLAIN; OX-BOW LAKE.

measure 1. To determine the size of something. **2.** A reference point to which other things can be compared. **3.** An action that can be taken, for a defined purpose.

mechanical aeration The use of mechanical energy to inject air into water, to cause *waste material in the water to absorb *oxygen and *decompose.

mechanical separation The use of mechanical means to sort waste material into separate components.

mechanical site preparation Any activity that involves the use of machinery to prepare a site for other uses (including building).

mechanical thinning An approach to *thinning trees in a *forest which is based on removing an agreed proportion of the trees irrespective of tree size or quality, for example by removing every second tree. *See also* LINE THINNING; SELECTIVE THINNING.

mechanical turbulence Turbulent *eddy motions in the air which are caused by physical obstructions, such as trees, buildings, and mountains.

mechanical weathering (physical weathering) The process by which frost action, growth of salt crystals, absorption of water, and other physical processes break down rock into smaller fragments, without involving any chemical change. *Contrast* CHEMICAL WEATHERING. *See also* WEATHERING.

mecoprop (MCPP) A selective herbicide that is applied after plants have emerged to control broadleaved weeds in cereal crops, ornamental crops, turf, sites being prepared for *afforestation, and verges. It is not toxic to insects, aquatic life, birds, or mammals, and disappears from the soil in about two months.

media Plural of *medium.

medial moraine A type of *moraine that forms in the centre of a *glacier or *ice stream downstream from the confluence of neighbouring valleys, where adjacent *lateral moraines join together.

median lethal dose *See* LD50.

median tolerance limit The concentration of a particular *toxic substance at which 50% of the animals in a test are able to survive for a specified period of *exposure.

mediation An informal, voluntary process for resolving disputes, in which parties are encouraged to discuss issues openly, all decisions are reached by consensus, and any participant can withdraw at any time.

medical waste Any *solid waste that results from medical activity, including hospital waste. This includes human pathological wastes, human blood and blood products, used or unused sharps (syringes, needles, and blades), certain animal waste, and other waste that is contaminated with *infectious agents or *pathogens.

medicinal Something used to prevent or cure illnesses and diseases.

medicinal and aromatic plant material Whole plants and plant parts (including seeds and fruits) that are used primarily in pharmacy and in making perfumes.

medieval (Middle Ages) The period of history between the Fall of the Roman Empire (300 CE) and the Renaissance (1450) in Europe.

Medieval Warm Period (MWP, Little Climatic Optimum) A period of relatively mild, warm, dry climate between 900 CE and 1300 and the warmest period since the *Climatic Optimum. Vineyards flourished in England as far north as the Midlands and the seas around Iceland and Greenland were relatively ice-free. The MWP occurred throughout the world, bringing temperatures equal to, and in some places and times rather higher than, those of the *Current Warm Period.

mediterranean climate (dry-summer subtropical climate) A *climate that has mild, wet winters with frequent storms and warm to hot, dry summers with frequent droughts, and is found between *latitudes 30° and 45° in both hemispheres on the western side of *continents.

Mediterranean floral region Part of R. Good's *Boreal Realm (*The Geography of the Flowering Plants*, 1974), and geographically a relatively small region, being restricted to Iberia and the Mediterranean coast, but with an important extension northwards along the western coast of Europe. The vegetation is specialized, reflecting the distinctive climatic setting, and consequently contains a high proportion of *endemics. The Mediterranean has been called 'the cradle of civilization' and its long association with mankind has yielded many garden, horticultural, and agricultural plants, and has led to extensive and intensive human influence on the natural vegetation.

medium (*pl.* **media)** A substance through which something is transported, such as air or water, and through which *contaminants are distributed.

medium term A period of time, in environmental terms often defined as between about three and five years. *Contrast* LONG TERM; SHORT TERM.

megacity *See* MEGALOPOLIS.

megafauna Animals that are large enough to be seen with the naked eye. The term is often used of very large mammals and birds, i.e. those exceeding 50 kilograms in body weight.

megalopolis (megacity, supercity) The largest type of *urban settlement, with a population of more than 10 million inhabitants, which may contain some open land, and is formed when large *conurbations or *metropolises grow together and link up. In 1950 there were only two cities in the developing world with populations of more than five million each: Shanghai (China) and Buenos Aires (Argentina). If the definition is expanded to include urban agglomerations rather than metropolitan areas, in 2011 there were 26 megacities, 10 of them with more than 20 million inhabitants. The world's three largest cities were Tokyo (Japan), population 34.3 million, Guangzhou (China), population 25.2 million, and Seoul (South Korea), population 25.1 million. New York City was the eighth largest with 22 million people and London was 23rd, with 12.5 million.

megaplankton Large *planktonic organisms, at least two mm in size.

megatonne (Mt) A unit of weight equal to one million *tonnes.

megawatt (MW) A unit of electrical power equal to 1000 kilowatts (one million *watts).

meiobenthos Organisms of the *benthos which are between 0.1 and 0.5 mm in size. *Contrast* MACROBENTHOS; MICROBENTHOS.

meiofauna Members of the *microfauna that inhabit *algae, rock fissures, and the uppermost layers of mud on the seabed. The term is sometimes used synonymously with *interstitial fauna.

meioflora Plants which are between 0.1 and 0.5 mm in size and that inhabit the uppermost layers of mud on the seabed and the spaces between sand grains.

MEL *See* MAXIMUM EXPOSURE LIMIT.

Melaleuca tree An Australian shrub (*Melaleuca quinquenervia*), also known as the tea tree, whose extracted oil has antiseptic and healing properties. It has invaded *wetlands of south Florida, displacing *native species, reducing the quality of the wildlife *habitat, and changing local *hydrology, soils, and fire regimes.

Melanesian and Micronesian floral region Part of R. Good's *Polynesian floral subkingdom (*The Geography of the Flowering Plants*, 1974), within his *Palaeotropical floral kingdom, and geographically coinciding with Micronesia (Marianas, Carolines, Marshall, Kiribati, and Tuvalu) and Melanesia (New Guinea, Solomon Islands, Vanuatu, and Fiji, but not New Caledonia). The flora is not rich and although there is an appreciable *endemic component at the species level, most of the species belong to large, widespread genera. The status of the endemism is not high, therefore, and reflects the fact that the flora is largely derived from Malesia to the west (*see* MALESIAN FLORA).

melanin The dark pigment that gives colour to the skin, hair, and parts of the eye, and protects against the damaging effects of *ultraviolet radiation.

melanism The occurrence in an animal population of individuals that are black owing to the presence of an excess of *melanin. *See also* INDUSTRIAL MELANISM.

melanoma The most serious form of *cancer of the skin, which is highly malignant.

melittophily *Pollination by bees.

Mellanby, Kenneth (1908–93) A British ecologist who was one of the first scientists to warn of the harmful effects on wildlife of certain insecticides and who became a leading world authority on all forms of environmental pollution. Mellanby studied zoology and entomology at the University of Cambridge, conducted research in medical entomology, which he continued during the Second World War as a major in the Royal Army Medical Corps, and after the war was appointed principal, and professor of parasitology, at the University of Ibadan, Nigeria. In 1955 he became head of entomology at the Rothamsted Experimental Station and from 1961 to 1974 he was director of the Monks Wood Experimental Station (Nature Conservancy, later Institute of Terrestrial Ecology). It was there that major studies were conducted on the effect of toxic chemicals on wildlife. Despite his strong commitment to environmental improvement, he was scathing about the pessimism of many environmentalists. He was the author of several books, including *Pesticides and Pollution* (1967), *Can Britain Feed Itself?* (1975), *Waste and Pollution* (1992), and *The DDT Story* (1992).

meltdown In a *nuclear reactor, a situation in which uncontrolled nuclear chain reactions cause the *core to melt.

melting A *phase change from a solid to liquid.

melting point The *temperature at which a substance changes from a solid to a liquid state, by *melting.

meltwater Water that is produced by the melting ice of a *glacier or a *snowbank.

meltwater channel (overflow channel) A channel that is eroded by glacial *meltwater, either under the glacier or along its side.

membrane A thin film, usually *semi-permeable.

Mendes, Chico A Brazilian rubber tapper, trade unionist, and environmental activist (1944–88) whose full name was Francisco Alves Mendes Filho. He fought to stop the logging of the Amazon *rainforest to create land for cattle ranching, founded a national union of rubber tappers to try to preserve their profession and the rainforest that it relied upon, and was murdered in 1988 by ranchers opposed to his activism.

Mercalli scale A scale that is widely used to describe the intensity of *earthquakes. *See also* MODIFIED MERCALLI INTENSITY SCALE. *Compare* RICHTER SCALE. The scale is given in Appendix 7.

Mercator projection A projection of the *Earth onto a cylinder, in order to produce a flat map, in which areas appear greater the farther they are from the *equator. It is the most commonly used map projection in atlases.

merchantable timber Commercially valuable *timber, which can be sold at profit.

mercury (Hg) An element which is present in various *ores. It is a *heavy metal, and the only metal that is liquid at room temperature (it freezes at $-38.83°$C). Mercury is used as an industrial chemical in a range of processes (such as the production of *chlorine), in a number of scientific instruments, and it was formerly used in household and horticultural *thermometers and *barometers. Mercury and its compounds are very toxic and can be inhaled and absorbed through the skin.

mercury barometer A type of *barometer used for measuring atmospheric pressure in which mercury rises or falls in a graduated glass tube as the pressure of the atmosphere increases or decreases.

mercury poisoning A *toxic condition in humans that is caused by swallowing or inhaling *mercury or absorbing it through the skin, and can cause vomiting and diarrhea, kidney problems, and damage to the nervous system. Prolonged exposure may lead to death. *See also* MINAMATA DISEASE.

mere A shallow *freshwater *lake.

meridian A north–south line between the *North Pole and the *South Pole, at right angles to the *equator, which connects all places with a given *longitude.

meridional Along a meridian or line of longitude. *Contrast* ZONAL.

meromictic A permanently stratified lake in which complete mixing of the water does not naturally occur.

meroplankton *Organisms that live as *zooplankton for part of their lives, e.g. the larvae of other animals.

mesa A flat-topped, steep-sided hill capped with a protective layer of resistant rock, common in *semi-arid areas.

mesic A moderately moist *habitat.

mesic prairie A type of *prairie that is found on relatively well drained sites which have high moisture available through most of the growing season.

meso- Medium-scale. *Contrast* MACRO-; MICRO-.

Mesoarchaean The middle part of the *Archaean eon, lasting from 3200 to 2800 million years ago, during which the first *handed iron formations formed and from which there is the earliest accepted *fossil evidence for life.

mesobiota A general term for soil organisms of intermediate size. *Compare* MICROBIOTA.

mesoclimate The *climate of an area up to several square kilometres in area, e.g. a valley or town; larger than a *microclimate but smaller than a *macroclimate.

mesocyclone A mass of air that spirals upwards in the centre of a large *cumulonimbus cloud that has developed a *supercell. If the mesocyclone extends downwards through the base of the cloud it appears as a *funnel cloud which becomes a *tornado if it touches the ground.

mesofauna Small soil animals, such as worms and insects, which are bigger than *microfauna but smaller than *macrofauna.

mesoflora Small plants, which are bigger than *microflora but smaller than *macroflora.

mesohaline *Brackish water with a *salinity of between 5 and 18 parts per thousand (‰).

Mesolithic The middle *Stone Age, following the *Palaeolithic, which began in Europe about 8500 BCE, during which cultures were reliant on hunting, fishing, and gathering.

mesopause The upper boundary of the *mesosphere with the *thermosphere, at a height of 50–80 km above sea level.

mesopelagic The zone of *oceans and *seas between about 200 m and 700–1000 m below the surface, between the upper sunlit (*photic) zone above and the dark ocean depths below, where some light can still penetrate to allow limited *photosynthesis. It forms the upper part of the *aphotic zone.

mesophyte A plant that is adapted to grow in conditions that are neither very moist nor very dry. *Contrast* HYDROPHYTE; XEROPHYTE.

Mesoproterozoic The era of the *Proterozoic eon that began about 1600 million years ago and ended 1000 million years ago. *Eukaryotes became more complex during the Mesoproterozoic and *cyanobacteria were present.

(((⊕))) SEE WEB LINKS

• The Mesoproterozoic era of the Proterozoic eon.

mesoscale meteorology The study of weather systems that extend horizontally from 1 to 100 km. This includes local winds, *squall lines, *thunderstorms, and *tornadoes. *Contrast* SYNOPTIC METEOROLOGY. *See also* MESO-.

mesosphere 1. The layer within the upper *atmosphere that lies above the *stratopause, stretching from about 50–80 km above sea level, in which temperature decreases quite sharply with height to about -90°C in winter (but sometimes lower) and -30°C in summer. **2.** The name formerly given to the *mantle underlying the *asthenosphere within the Earth's *crust. The term is no longer used in this sense.

mesotrophic Applied to a moderately productive aquatic *habitat (such as a *lake or *reservoir) that has a moderate supply of *nutrients.

Contrast OLIGOTROPHIC; EUTROPHIC. *See also* EUTROPHICATION.

Mesozoic The middle *era of the *Phanerozoic eon of geological time, 251-65.5 million years ago when the *dinosaurs and marine reptiles became dominant, *mammals were small and mainly nocturnal, and flowering plants appeared. *Pangaea broke into *Gondwanaland and *Laurasia during the Mesozoic.

(((⊕))) SEE WEB LINKS

• The Mesozoic era of the Phanerozoic eon.

mesquite A small, thorny, leguminous (*see* LEGUME) tree (*Prosopis glandulosa*) that is found in arid parts of North America.

metabolic activity The chemical changes that occur in a living animal or plant as a result of *metabolism. In animals, this includes synthetic reactions (such as the manufacture of *proteins and *fats) and destructive reactions (such as the breakdown of sugars into *carbon dioxide and *water). In plants, it includes *photosynthesis.

metabolic engineering A process that is used to modify *organisms so they will produce particular molecules and chemicals, or *biochemicals.

metabolic rate The rate of *biochemical reactions within an *organism, which can be estimated by measuring food consumption, energy released as heat, or oxygen used in *metabolic activity. It is usually expressed as energy per unit surface area per unit time, e.g. kilojoules per square metre per hour ($kJ\ m^{-2}\ h^{-1}$).

metabolism The biochemical processes through which a living cell or organism converts food to energy and then eliminates waste products, thus allowing it to continue to function and grow. This involves *catabolism (the breakdown of complex substances into simple ones, which releases energy) and *anabolism (the building up of complex substances from simpler ones, which involves absorption or storage of energy).

metabolite A product of *metabolism, including intermediate and waste products, or something which takes part in the reactions.

metal A dense, opaque element that is usually a lustrous solid and is a good conductor of heat or electricity. Eighty per cent of the known elements are metals. Examples include *iron, *lead, *copper, *aluminium, *silver, and *gold.

metaldehyde An organic *molluscicide ($CH_3CHO)_4$ obtained from *acetaldehyde and the most widely used product for killing slugs and snails. It is moderately toxic to mammals and may kill dogs and cats if ingested.

metalimnion The layer of a lake or ocean where the *thermocline and *pycnocline are steepest. The term is sometimes used as a synonym of thermocline.

metamorphic rock Any *rock that has been altered by *metamorphism, involving heating and pressure. Also known as tertiary rock because metamorphic rock is derived from primary *igneous rocks and secondary *sedimentary rocks.

metamorphism Changes in the composition and texture of *rock which are caused by pressure, heat, and chemical reactions beneath the surface of the Earth, and result in a more compact and more highly *crystalline rock. See also CONTACT METAMORPHISM; REGIONAL METAMORPHISM.

metamorphosis 1. In general, a major change in appearance or character. **2.** In biology, a stage in the *life cycle of certain animals during which the *larva rapidly transforms into an adult, such as from a tadpole to a frog or from a caterpillar to a butterfly. See also HYPERMETAMORPHOSIS.

metapopulation A set of partially isolated *populations that belong to the same species, between which individuals can freely migrate.

metastable Applied to a situation or condition which is apparently stable but is capable of reaction if disturbed, usually because of the slowness of a system to attain equilibrium (e.g. a supersaturated solution).

meteor An extraterrestrial mass which has reached the Earth's *atmosphere from outer space and is heated to glowing hot by friction as it passes through the atmosphere. A meteor that reaches the Earth's surface is a *meteorite.

Meteor 3M(1) A joint US–Russian (NASA-Rosaviacosmos) *satellite remote sensing system launched on a three-year mission on 10 December 2001, which monitors the distribution and concentration of *aerosols and chemical compounds in the *atmosphere. It is in a polar orbit at an altitude of 1012 km.

meteorite An extraterrestrial mass which has reached the Earth from outer space, without burning up in the atmosphere. See also METEOR.

meteoric water Water of atmospheric origin that reaches the Earth's surface crust from above, either as rainfall or as seepage from surface-water bodies. See also GROUNDWATER.

meteorology The scientific study of the Earth's *atmosphere and of the processes that produce *weather, especially with reference to weather forecasting.

Meteosat A series of *geostationary weather satellites first launched by the USA in 1977 and now launched by the European Space Agency (ESA) and operated by Eumetsat. The first Meteosat Second Generation (MSG) satellite became operational on 29 January 2004 and a second was launched on 21 December 2005. These both return data on Europe, North Africa, and the North Atlantic. First-generation Meteosat-6, -7, and -8 are still operational, in orbit over Europe and Africa, and Meteosat-5 is operating over the Indian Ocean.

metham-sodium (metam-sodium) A soil *fumigant that is injected below the surface and migrates upwards as a gas. It is used to control *nematodes and a variety of disease fungi, weeds, and insect pests in root crops, vegetables and strawberries, ornamental crops, orchards, and vineyards. It can cause dermatitis and exacerbate respiratory ailments, and it is harmful to wildlife.

methane (CH_4, swamp gas) A colourless, non-poisonous, flammable *hydrocarbon gas created by *anaerobic *decomposition of organic compounds. It is the main component of *natural gas and can be used as a *fuel. The main sources of methane are natural gas fields including *shale gas and, potentially, methane hydrates, *landfills, coal *mines, rice paddy fields, and livestock (such as cows and sheep). Methane is a *greenhouse gas with a *global warming potential of 21 over 100 years. Concentrations of methane in the atmosphere rose steadily from the 1950s until peaking in the mid 1990s, then resumed their increase around 2000. Analysis of *ice cores reveals natural atmospheric concentrations of methane of about 0.3 ppmv (parts per million by volume) at the peak of glaciation. Current levels are around 1.8 ppmv, compared with around 350 ppmv for *carbon dioxide.

methane recovery The capture and reuse as fuel of *methane *emissions (particularly from animal wastes, *landfill sites, and coal *mines).

methanogen A single-celled organism that derives metabolic energy by using hydrogen to reduce carbon dioxide to *methane, emitting the methane as a by-product. Methanogens are *obligate *anaerobes found in *swamps and *marshes, and the methane they release bubbles to the surface as marsh gas.

methanol A colourless, nearly odourless, *volatile liquid *alcohol *fuel that is produced mainly from *natural gas and is used as an *alternative fuel or *biofuel, and as a fuel additive.

methoxyfenozide A type of *insecticide which works by accelerating the *moulting process.

methyl bromide (CH_3Br) A poisonous gas or liquid that contains carbon, hydrogen, and bromine, and is used as an effective pesticide. The bromine is an *ozone depleter which is harmful to the *stratospheric ozone layer.

methyl chloroform (CH_3CCl_3) An industrial chemical that contains *carbon, *hydrogen, and *chlorine, and is used as a solvent, aerosol propellant, *pesticide, and degreasing agent. It is a *greenhouse gas and *ozone depleter and production of it is now banned under the *Montreal Protocol.

methyl isocyanate (CH_3NCO) A persistent and particularly *toxic *gas which attacks many different organs in the human body. Ingestion, inhalation, and skin contact can be injurious at concentrations above 0.4 ppm, and exposure to more than 21 ppm can be fatal. It is an intermediate chemical formed in the production of *carbamate insecticides, and also in the manufacture of rubber and certain adhesives. Methyl isocyanate was the gas that killed and injured many people in the *Bhopal accident.

metric ton A tonne, equal to 1.1 US tons, 1.016 UK tons.

metropolis The largest *town or *city in a region or country, which dominates its economic and cultural life.

Meuse Valley A valley in Belgium that from 1–5 December 1930 became the site of the first modern major incident of air pollution. A spell of cold weather combined with a strong *katabatic wind produced a fog trapped beneath an *inversion where it mixed with coal smoke from many factories to produce a *smog that made many people ill and caused more than 60 deaths.

mica A member of a group of sheet *silicate *minerals that contain varying amounts of *aluminium, *potassium, *magnesium, *iron, and *water, and that split into thin, tough, smooth plates. They are common constituents of *igneous and *metamorphic rocks. *See also* VERMICULITE.

micro- Very small scale. *Contrast* MACRO; MESO-.

microbe *See* MICRO-ORGANISM.

microbenthos The smaller organisms of the *benthos, generally shorter than 0.1 mm. *Contrast* MACROBENTHOS; MEIOBENTHOS.

microbial Relating to microbes or *micro-organisms.

microbial contamination *Contamination of a *medium (such as a waterbody) by *pathogenic *micro-organisms. *See also* BIOLOGICAL CONTAMINANT.

microbial digestion The natural processes by which *micro-organisms break down and use a *substance.

microbial growth The activity and growth of *micro-organisms such as *bacteria, *algae, *diatoms, *plankton, and *fungi.

microbial pesticide A *micro-organism that is used to kill a particular *pest, to which it is *toxic, but which poses little health risk to humans.

microbiology The study of *micro-organisms.

microbiota (**microfauna, microflora**) The smallest soil organisms, comprising bacteria, fungi, algae, and protozoa.

microburst A small but strong *downdraught of wind that occurs below a weak *convection cell some distance from the centre of a *cumulonimbus cloud. It usually lasts for 5–15 minutes and has a radius of less than 4 km, but can generate winds of more than 160 km h^{-1}. *Contrast* MACROBURST.

microclimate The *climate of a small area (e.g. a building, city, or valley) that can be distinguished from the climate in the surrounding area (*mesoclimate) or region (*macroclimate).

microcosm (**micro-ecosystem**) A small-scale, simplified model *ecosystem that is used to study a natural ecosystem outside the laboratory.

microeconomics The study and analysis of the individual parts of the *market economy (such as companies or households), particularly in terms of the market process and how it works. *Contrast* MACROECONOMICS.

micro-ecosystem *See* MICROCOSM.

microelement *See* MICRONUTRIENT.

microenvironment *See* MICROHABITAT.

microevolution *Evolutionary changes on the small scale, such as changes in *gene frequencies within a population in response to changing local *environmental conditions. *Contrast* MACROEVOLUTION. *See also* ADAPTATION; EVOLUTION; NATURAL SELECTION.

microfauna Animals (less than 0.1 mm long) that are invisible to the naked eye and are visible only through a microscope; for example protozoa and nematodes. *See* MICROBIOTA. *Contrast* MACROFAUNA; MESOFAUNA.

microflora Small plants that are invisible to the naked eye and can be seen only through a microscope. *See* MICROBIOTA. *Contrast* MACROFLORA; MESOFLORA.

microhabitat (microenvironment, microsite) The immediate *environment in which an *organism lives, where factors such as moisture and light may be different from those in the surrounding area.

microinvertebrate Any *invertebrate organism that is too small to be seen with the naked eye (with a body length of less than 1 mm). *Contrast* MACROINVERTEBRATE.

micrometeorology The detailed study of weather within a *microclimate.

micrometre *See* MICRON.

micron (micrometer) A unit of length equal to one millionth (10^{-6}) of a metre.

micronutrient (microelement, essential element) A *nutrient or chemical *element that organisms require in very small amounts. These include *vitamins for animals. The micronutrients required for plant growth include *iron, *manganese, *zinc, *copper, *boron, *molybdenum, and *cobalt. *Contrast* MACRONUTRIENT.

micro-organism (microbe) Any living organism (including *bacteria, *viruses, *protozoa, and some types of *fungus and *algae) that is too small to be seen by the naked eye, and is only visible through a microscope.

microparasite A small *parasite. *Contrast* MACROPARASITE.

microphagous Applied to animals (e.g. baleen whales) that feed, usually almost continuously, on particles that are very small in relation to their own body size. *Compare* MACROPHAGOUS.

micropropagation The use of *biotechnology to grow large numbers of plants from very small pieces of plants, including single cells, tissues, and seeds by *in vitro methods.

microrelief (microtopography) Small-scale variations in the ground surface within a particular area.

microscopic Too small (usually smaller than about 1 mm) to be seen by the naked eye. *Contrast* MACROSCOPIC.

microseism A weak earthquake, measuring less than 2 on the *Richter scale.

microsite *See* MICROHABITAT.

microsporidia A phylum (Microsporidia) of single-celled *fungi that are important *obligate *parasites of *vertebrate and *invertebrate animals, and especially of insects. Several species are used in *biological control.

microtopography *See* MICRORELIEF.

microwave *Electromagnetic radiation which has a longer *wavelength (1 mm−1 m; frequency 300 GHz (gigahertz)–300 MHz (megahertz) within the *electromagnetic spectrum) than visible light, and is used in radar (longer waves) and in cooking (shorter waves).

Mid-Atlantic Ridge The *mid-ocean ridge that separates the North Atlantic and South Atlantic plates from the African and Eurasian plates. It is a slow-moving *sea-floor spreading zone. *See also* PLATE TECTONICS.

Middle Ages *See* MEDIEVAL.

middle latitudes *See* MID-LATITUDE.

middle term planning *See* MID-RANGE PLANNING.

middleground The part of the *scenery or *landscape that is mid-distance away from the viewer, further than the *foreground but closer than the *background.

mid-latitude (middle latitudes) The region of the world that lies between 30° and 50° *latitude.

mid-latitude climate The main *climate zones within the *mid-latitudes are the *mediterranean, *marine west coast, *humid subtropical, *humid continental, and the *mid-latitude steppe and desert.

mid-latitude steppe and desert climate zone A *mid-latitude *climate zone that is found in continental interiors, further from the coast than the *humid continental and *humid subtropical climates, and often cut off from maritime air masses by mountain ranges. The *climate is drier (particularly in winter) than in the tropics, and temperatures vary more throughout the year (temperatures below freezing are not uncommon in winter).

midnight dumping General term for the illegal disposal of *hazardous wastes in remote locations, often at night.

mid-ocean ridge An extensive *mountain chain that can rise thousands of metres above the surrounding *ocean floor, created by the rise of *magma along submarine *constructive plate boundaries, resulting in *sea-floor spreading. The ridges are part of a continuous system which runs for 60 000 km through all the oceans, and includes the *Mid-Atlantic Ridge. *See also* PLATE TECTONICS.

mid-range planning (middle term planning, mid-term planning) Planning over a period of between about 10 and 25 years into the future, which is intermediate between *short-range planning and *long-range planning.

mid-term planning See MID-RANGE PLANNING.

midwater The water that lies below the surface but above the bottom of a *waterbody.

Mie scattering The *scattering of incoming *solar radiation that interacts with particles similar in size to the wavelength of the radiation. The radiation is scattered predominantly forwards, and affects all wavelengths.

migmatite A coarse-grained rock that contains both *igneous and *metamorphic materials, that was formed under immense heat and pressure, and often contains large *mineral crystals.

migrate To move from one place to another and settle there, permanently, periodically or seasonally.

migration 1. The movement of people or animals, including *immigration, *emigration, *net migration, *internal migration, and *international migration. **2.** The stage in vegetation *succession at which the first plant seeds arrive on bare ground.

migration corridor *See* CORRIDOR.

migration pathway Any of the routes along which a *contaminant may move through the *environment, for example through *soil, in *groundwater, in surface water, and through the *air.

migratory Applied to the seasonal movement (*migration) of people, mammals, birds, or fish from one region to another.

migratory bird sanctuary In North America, a *nature reserve designed and set aside for the protection of *migratory birds.

Milankovitch cycles The cyclical changes in the orbit of the *Earth around the *Sun which are believed to cause long-term changes in the Earth's climate, according to the *Milankovitch theory. These are determined by variations in the elliptical shape of the Earth's orbit around the Sun (over a 100 000-year cycle), variations in the tilt of the Earth's axis of rotation (over a 42 000-year cycle), and variations in the time of year when the Earth is closest to the Sun (*perihelion) (over a 25 800-year cycle).

Milankovitch theory The theory, advanced by the Serbian mathematician and climatologist Milutin Milankovitch (1879-1958), that long-term changes in the Earth's *climate (e.g. *ice ages and *interglacials) are caused by variations in the amount of *solar radiation that is received at the Earth's surface, which are due to cyclical changes in the relationship between the *Earth and the *Sun. *See also* MILANKOVITCH CYCLE.

mill 1. Machinery (such as rotating *millstones) that grinds grain into flour or meal. **2.** Any machinery for manufacturing (e.g. papermill, sawmill, etc.). **3.** A building that contains such machinery.

millennium A period of 1000 years.

millibar (mb) A unit of atmospheric pressure that is equal to a thousandth of a *bar. Normal pressure at the Earth's surface is about 1013 mb. 1 mb = 100 pascals.

millstone One of a pair of heavy, flat, disc-shaped stones that are rotated against one another to grind grain in a *mill, or used separately for sharpening steel blades

millstone grit Coarse-grained *sedimentary rock, often comprising *sandstones, grits, and *conglomerates with alternate *shales, that can be used for making *millstones.

milpa *See* SLASH AND BURN.

mimicry The similarity (for example in appearance) of two *species, for evolutionary advantage. *See also* BATESIAN MIMICRY; MÜLLERIAN MIMICRY.

Minamata disease A crippling form of *mercury poisoning which was first detected among people who ate fish from the mercury-contaminated waters of Minamata Bay off Japan in the 1950s.

Mindel The second phase of *glaciation in Europe during the *Pleistocene *ice age, equivalent to the *Kansan in North America.

mine An underground excavation from which mineral or rock is extracted. *See also* MINING; QUARRY.

mine drainage Any water that is released from a mining operation. *See also* ACID MINE DRAINAGE.

mine spoils Mining waste from open-pit mining, rather than from hard rock mining. *See also* MINE TAILINGS.

mine tailings (mining refuse) The solid waste that is separated and left after raw minerals or *ore from hard rock mining have been processed. *Contrast* MINE SPOILS.

mined-land reclamation The return of *land to another use, often to the original pre-mining use, after *mining activities have ceased.

mineral **1.** A solid, naturally occurring, usually inorganic substance with a characteristic chemical composition, typically with a crystalline structure, and possessing physical properties of *hardness, *lustre, colour, *cleavage, relative density, and fracture. Rocks are composed of minerals. *See also* COMMON VARIETY MINERAL. **2.** Any organic substance that is obtained by mining (e.g. coal, oil, etc.).

mineral cycle *See* BIOGEOCHEMICAL CYCLE.

mineral oil (crude oil, petroleum) In general, any oil that is obtained by mining. Particularly, a thick, greenish-brown, flammable liquid that is found underground in permeable *organic *sedimentary rock, which can be refined to produce a number of valuable products including *oil and *petrol (gasoline).

mineral resource Any of the various naturally occurring substances such as coal, *mineral oil, *metals, *natural gas, *salt, *sand, *stone, and *water, which are extracted from the Earth's *crust and converted into products useful for humans. Mineral resources are normally classified as being either metallic (such as *iron and *aluminium ores) or *non-metallic (such as *fossil fuels, sand, and salt).

mineral rights The ownership of all rights to *gas, *oil, or other *minerals as they naturally occur at or below the surface of a particular area of land.

mineral soil Any *soil that is composed mainly of *inorganic material (such as weathered rock, or *sand, *silt, or *clay materials) rather than *organic matter.

mineralization **1.** The breakdown of *organic compounds to their *inorganic forms (e.g. proteins to nitrates and phosphates), as a result of *microbial *decomposition. **2.** In *fossil formation, the replacement of *organic parts by *inorganic materials.

mineralogy The study of the structure and properties of *minerals.

minerogenic Applied to any *clastic sediment which is composed of individual *mineral particles. They are usually classified according to grain size, such as *sand or *clay.

minimum acceptable flow In the UK, the minimum amount of water that should be allowed to flow down a particular *river in order to meet the requirements of existing lawful uses of the water (for *agriculture, industry, water supply, or other purposes) and the requirements of navigation, fisheries, or land drainage. Called minimum flow in the USA.

minimum flow The US name for *minimum acceptable flow.

minimum tillage An approach to the *conservation of *soil and *water resources in which the crop *residue or *stubble is left on the surface rather than ploughed under, in order to minimize the number of times that a field is tilled.

minimum viable population The smallest number of individuals of a *species in a particular locality that could reasonably be expected to survive in the long term.

mining The removal of *minerals from the ground. *See also* AREA MINING; AUGER MINING; CONTOUR MINING; LODE MINING; OPEN CAST MINING; PIT MINING; PLACER MINING; STRIP MINING.

mining debris (mining waste) Solid waste from mining activities, which includes the *overburden, *mining refuse, and *mining spoil.

mining lode *See* LODE.

mining refuse *See* MINE TAILINGS.

mining spoil The overlying material that is removed during *mining in order to gain access to the *ore within the *mineral material below.

mining waste *See* MINING DEBRIS.

Minoan Warm Period A period from about 1340 to 1120 BCE when global average temperatures were approximately 3°C warmer than those of the late 20th century.

minor element *See* MICRONUTRIENT.

minor recreation facility North American term for developed *recreation facilities that are relatively cheap to build and run, and are not heavily used, such as observation sites, playgrounds, fishing sites, trailheads, and minor *interpretation sites. *Contrast* MAJOR RECREATION FACILITY.

minority group Any group of people (often defined by race or ethnicity) whose members have significantly less control or power over their own lives than the members of a dominant or majority group have over theirs.

Miocene An *epoch of geological time comprising the first part of the *Neogene period, from 23.03 million to 5.332 million years ago, during which kelp forests and grasslands first appeared and *mammal diversity reached a peak.

(())) SEE WEB LINKS
• The Miocene epoch of the Neogene period.

mirage An optical illusion in which reflections of distant objects are distorted by atmospheric *refraction of light as it passes between layers of relatively warm and cool air.

mire A soft, wet *peatland plant community that develops on waterlogged land.

MIS *See* MANAGEMENT INFORMATION SYSTEM; MANAGEMENT INDICATOR SPECIES.

miscible Capable of being mixed or blended together to form a homogeneous mixture, such as water and *methanol. The opposite of miscible is *immiscible.

miserabilist *See* PESSIMIST, ENVIRONMENTAL.

misfit stream (underfit stream) A small, usually meandering *river within a larger meandering *valley which appears too big to have been formed by river erosion and may be *glacial in origin.

Mission to Planet Earth A coordinated international plan led by *NASA, as part of the *International Geosphere-Biosphere Programme (IGBP), to provide the *satellite platforms and instruments, data and information systems, and related scientific research which are necessary to support the programme. It examines critical interactions between the Earth's physical, chemical, biological, and social systems.

(())) SEE WEB LINKS
• Mission to Planet Earth.

mist A suspension of fine (0.005–0.05 mm) water droplets in the atmosphere that reduces horizontal visibility, but visibility remains more than 1 km. *Contrast* FOG.

mistral A strong, cold, dry, northerly, *katabatic wind which blows offshore along the north coast of the Mediterranean in winter.

mite A tiny *arachnid that may be a *parasite on plants and animals, and feeds on plants, other mites, or small insects.

mitigate To make less severe, or to lessen the seriousness or extent of.

mitigation Any actions that are taken to avoid or minimize negative *environmental impacts. This can take various forms, including avoiding the impact by not taking a certain action; minimizing impacts by limiting the scale of the action; rectifying the impact by repairing or restoring the affected environment; reducing the impact by taking protective steps; and compensating for the impact by replacing or providing substitute resources.

mitigation bank A site where *habitats (such as *wetlands) are restored, created, or preserved to serve as compensation for habitats that are going to be lost to *development elsewhere in a region.

mitochondrion (*pl.* mitochondria) An *organelle, about 2 micrometres long, that occurs in large numbers in all eukaryotic cells (*see* EUKARYOTE). It is the principal site of *aerobic respiration in cells. Mitochondria are semi-autonomous, containing their own *DNA, and are believed to have evolved from *symbiotic *bacteria.

mixed cloud A *cloud that contains both water droplets and *ice crystals. *Compare* COLD CLOUD; WARM CLOUD.

mixed cropping A *cropping system in which two or more *crops are grown on the same area of land at the same time, or with only a short interval between. *See also* INTERCROPPING; MULTIPLE CROPPING; RELAY CROPPING.

mixed farming Growing *crops and feed and *livestock on the same *farm at the same time.

mixed grass A North American native *prairie *grassland that is dominated by short and tall grass (including needle grasses and wheat grasses), with some tall shrubs and trees in moist areas and river valleys.

mixed layer 1. The upper part of a *waterbody, that is mixed by *wind and *wave action. 2. The layer of the *atmosphere that lies immediately above the ground, in which *air pollutants are well mixed by *turbulence.

mixed stand A *stand that contains two or more *species of *tree.

mixed waste A mixture of *radioactive waste and *hazardous waste.

mixed woodland A woodland in which the minority of trees, but amounting to not less than about 20%, are either coniferous or broadleaved.

mixing cycle The pattern of seasonal variations in temperature conditions and mixing status in a large body of *freshwater (such as a *lake or *reservoir), from *spring (mixed), through *summer (*stratified) and *autumn (*mixed), to *winter (stratified) pattern. *See also* MONOMICTIC; TURNOVER.

mixing depth The depth in a *waterbody, or height in the atmosphere, of the *mixed layer, in

which the water or air is evenly mixed by *wind action.

mixing fog *See* EVAPORATION FOG.

mixing ratio (mass mixing ratio) The ratio of the mass of a particular gas (such as *water vapour) present in the air to a unit mass of air without that gas. It is most often used to report *humidity and reported as grams $H_2O\ kg^{-1}$ air.

mixture An aggregate of two or more substances that are not chemically united.

MMI *See* MODIFIED MERCALLI INTENSITY SCALE.

MNC *See* MULTINATIONAL CORPORATION.

MNR *See* MARINE NATURE RESERVE.

mobile Capable of spontaneous movement, able to move freely.

mobile dune A coastal *sand dune that is becoming stabilized by the growth of *vegetation, but can still be affected by *wind erosion. *Contrast* FIXED DUNE.

mobile incinerator system A *hazardous waste *incinerator that can be transported from one site to another.

mobile source A pollution source (usually of *air pollutants) that moves. Mobile sources are divided into two groups: road vehicles, which includes cars, trucks, and buses, and non-road vehicles, which includes trains, planes, and lawn mowers.

mobility The ability of a *chemical element or *pollutant to move through the *environment, for example through a *food chain, or from a *waterbody into the *sediment beneath it.

mobility transition Change through time in the relative sizes of the rural-to-urban and urban-to-urban migration flows during the course of *urbanization within a country. *Contrast* DEMOGRAPHIC TRANSITION.

model A representation or description of a complex process or object, usually on a smaller scale and/or in a simplified form.

modelling The act of representing something, usually on a smaller scale, for example by use of statistical analysis, computer analysis, or a physical model.

moderate 1. Not extreme. 2. To lessen the intensity of, or slow down.

moderately exposed In terms of *wave exposure along a *coastline, coasts which face away from prevailing winds and do not have a long *fetch, but where strong *winds can be frequent.

moderately stratified estuary An *estuary in which the seaward flow of low-*salinity water and moderate vertical mixing result in a modest vertical gradient of salinity.

moderator 1. Material used to control the *fission reaction in *nuclear/thermal reactors by absorbing neutrons. **2.** A person who acts as a controlling influence during debates.

modern synthesis *See* NEO-DARWINISM.

modernization theory The theory that *less-developed countries will follow the course of industrial development experienced by the *developed countries.

modified Mercalli intensity scale (MMI) The most widely used form of the *Mercalli scale, devised by the Italian vulcanologist Giuseppe Mercalli (1850–1914) in 1884 and 1906, based on an earlier scale, and later developed further. It describes the *intensity of *earthquakes in a qualitative way, based on the relative amount of damage that structures undergo during an earthquake, using a scale from I (instrumental) to XII (cataclysmic). See Appendix 7.

Mohs's hardness scale A ten-point scale for measuring the *hardness of *minerals, devised in 1812 by the German mineralogist Friedrich Mohs (1773–1839), based on the ability of a specimen to scratch another specimen on the scale. The full scale is: talc 1 (softest), gypsum 2, calcite 3, fluorite 4, apatite 5, orthoclase 6, quartz 7, topaz 8, corundum 9, and diamond 10 (hardest). Diamond is about ten times harder than corundum.

Moho *See* MOHOROVIČIĆ DISCONTINUITY.

Mohorovičić discontinuity (Moho) The boundary between the Earth's *mantle and the *crust, named after Andrija Mohorovičić (1857–1936), the Croatian seismologist who first suspected its presence in 1909. It follows variations in the thickness of the crust, and is found roughly 32 km below the continents and about 10 km below the oceans. *Seismic waves speed up noticeably when they reach this junction.

moisture Wetness, for example as *water vapour in the *atmosphere or as a *condensed liquid on the surface of an object.

moisture content 1. The amount of *water that is present in the air, or in a material such as *wood or *soil, where it is usually expressed as a percentage of the oven dry weight of that material. **2.** The water equivalent of snow on the ground.

Mojave Desert A North American hot desert that occupies a significant portion of southern California and parts of Utah, Nevada, and Arizona, and has scattered creosote bushes, Joshua trees, and sagebrush.

mol *See* MOLE.

molar heat capacity *See* HEAT CAPACITY.

mole (mol) The SI (*Système Internationale) unit of amount of substance, equal to the amount of a substance that contains as many elementary units as there are atoms in 12g of ^{12}C. The elementary unit (atoms, molecules, ions, etc.) must be specified.

molecular biology The study of the structure, function, and composition of biological *molecules within *cells.

molecule A collection of two or more *atoms held together by chemical bonds.

mollisols A *soil order in the *Comprehensive Soil Classification System. These soils are dark coloured, have upper *horizons that are rich in *organic matter, and form mainly under *grassland.

mollusc A soft-bodied, aquatic (except for some snails) *invertebrate animal belonging to the phylum Mollusca, which is often protected by a calcium carbonate shell; in some molluscs the shell is modified to form an internal skeleton. Examples include the snail, clam, mussel, squid, and octopus. There are about 80 000 species.

molluscicide A chemical substance used to kill *molluscs.

molten In a liquid state, having been melted by heat.

molybdenum (Mo) A naturally occurring silvery-grey metallic *trace element, one of eight *micronutrients that are essential to plant health, and mined for use in hardening steel and cast iron.

moment magnitude scale (M_W) A scale for measuring the magnitude of an *earthquake in terms of the energy it releases, consisting of a dimensionless number calculated from the rigidity of the Earth multiplied by the average amount of movement on the *fault and the area affected.

momentum The product of the mass and velocity of a moving body.

monadnock An isolated *hill or *mountain that rises above a flat landscape or *peneplain.

Monera In some taxonomic schemes (*see* TAXONOMY), a *kingdom comprising the *prokaryotes *cyanobacteria and other bacteria in the group Schizomycophyta. In the three-*domain system the prokaryotes are placed in the more fundamental categories *Archaea and *Eubacteria.

monitor-and-modify approach *See* ADAPTIVE MANAGEMENT.

monitoring The collection and analysis of information on a regular basis in order to check performance against objectives, or compliance with a predetermined standard. *Contrast* SURVEILLANCE.

monitoring well A *well that is used to measure *groundwater levels or to collect samples of *water quality, for example at a *hazardous waste management *facility or a *Superfund site.

monkey-wrenching Popular name for environmental sabotage, involving such criminal activities as driving large spikes in trees to protect them from loggers, vandalizing construction equipment, pulling up survey stakes for unwanted developments, and destroying billboards. *See also* ECO-ACTIVISM; ECO-EXTREMISM; ECOTAGE; ECOTERRORISM.

monocline A one-sided *fold in *stratified rocks, caused by relatively weak *compression pressure, usually found on the outer edges of tightly folded areas like *fold mountains.

monocotyledon An *angiosperm (flowering *plant) which characteristically has a seed with a single seed-leaf (cotyledon), flower parts arranged in threes, and leaves with parallel veins. Examples include grasses, lilies, and palms.

monoculture *Crop cultivation in which a single *variety of plant is grown in a *field. *Contrast* POLYCULTURE.

monolectic Applied to a *pollinator which collects *pollen from only one species of plant. *Contrast* OLIGOLECTIC; POLYLECTIC.

monomictic Applied to a relatively deep *lake or *reservoir which undergoes a single *stratification and *mixing cycle during the year. In polar latitudes this occurs in summer and in warmer regions in winter.

monophagous Applied to an animal that feeds on or uses a single species or closely related species of *host plant or animal. *Contrast* POLYPHAGOUS.

monophyletic Applied to a group of *organisms originating from a single ancestor.

monotreme A *mammal belonging to the order Monotremata, comprising the duck-billed platypus (*Ornithorhynchus anatinus*) and five species of echidnas or spiny anteaters (*Tachyglossus aculeatus, Zaglossus attenboroughi, Z. bartoni, Z. bruijni, Z. hacketti* (known only from several bones), and *Z. robustus* (known only from a fossil skull)), as well as a small number of fossil species. The rectum and urinogenital system open to a common cloaca, hence the name from the Greek *monos* meaning 'alone' and *trema* meaning 'hole'. Young hatch from large, yolky eggs and are fed milk, which the female secretes from specialized sweat glands. Adults possess bills and lack teeth. Males have an erectile heel spur; in the platypus this can inject poison from a gland in the thigh. Platypus and echidnas locate prey by detecting weak electrical fields around the bill. Monotremes occur only in Australia and New Guinea.

monotypic Applied to any taxon that has only one immediately subordinate taxon. For example, a genus that contains only one species would be described as monotypic, as would a family containing only one genus. *Compare* POLYTYPIC.

monoxenous A *parasite that lives within a single host during its whole *life cycle. *Contrast* OLIGOXENOUS.

monsoon A large-scale seasonal reversal of *winds and air pressure systems that occurs in some *tropical areas (particularly southern Asia, but also in Africa) and is caused by the different rates at which the *oceans and *continents heat and cool. The wind blows from land to sea in the winter and from sea to land in the summer, producing two contrasting monsoons, the dry winter monsoon and wet summer monsoon. Monsoon circulations are associated with the movement of pressure cells and the intertropical front. When the *Intertropical Convergence Zone moves much further north of the equator during the northern hemisphere summer, it pulls the southeast *trade winds with it. These are deflected to the right by the *Coriolis effect as they cross the equator, turning them into southwesterly winds which blow across the Indian subcontinent, drawn in by an intense thermally induced *low pressure area across northwestern India and Pakistan (caused by rapid summer heating). Heavy rains during the monsoon often cause extensive and destructive *flooding, but farmers depend on them.

monsoon climate zone A *tropical climate zone, dominated by a winter–summer reversal of air flow (two *monsoon seasons, one dry the other wet) in the tropics, and best developed in South Asia. *Precipitation is less than 60 mm during at least one month in the year, *temperatures remain fairly high throughout the year, and there is pronounced seasonality (stormy, cloudy, wet summers, and dry winters).

monsoon forest Seasonal *forest that grows in the *tropics, adjacent to the tropical *rainforests in areas subject to a *monsoon climate. Most are in South East Asia, including northeastern India, Burma, Thailand, Cambodia, Laos, and Vietnam. Many species are found in both the monsoon forest and the tropical rainforest, but in the monsoon forest they have adapted by *natural selection to cope with *drought during the dry season. *Adaptations include a period of dormancy, shedding of leaves, and wider spacing between trees (which compete for water). Monsoon forests also have a much denser *ground layer of shrubs, because the wider spacing of trees allows more sunlight to reach the forest floor. There are fewer tree species in the monsoon forest than in the rainforest, and this makes commercial timber extraction easier and more cost-effective. Some of the rich teak forests in South East Asia are extensively worked, and in danger of disappearing altogether. Other monsoon forests (particularly in India) are being cleared to create land for agriculture and settlements, leaving small patches in remote areas.

monsoon season The rainy season in southern Asia and India, from about May to September, when the south-west *monsoon blows moisture-laden air from over the Indian Ocean, which brings heavy rains, and the dry season from October to April, when the northeast monsoon brings dry air from central Asia.

montane Relating to *mountains or mountainous country.

montane forest A forest type of vegetation in which the principal trees are *conifers (such as Ponderosa pine), which grows below the *alpine zone on mountains.

month A measure of time based on how long it takes the Moon to circle around the Earth, which is roughly 30 days. A calendar month varies between 28 and 31 days.

month degrees The excess of mean monthly temperatures above 6°C (43°F), added together and used as accumulated temperature (indicative of conditions for vegetation growth) in some climate classifications.

montmorillonite A very plastic *clay; an *aluminium *silicate which is the principal constituent of *bentonite. It can accommodate many water molecules in its structure, causing it to swell and shrink with variations in its moisture content.

Montreal Protocol *See* MONTREAL PROTOCOL ON SUBSTANCES THAT DEPLETE THE OZONE LAYER.

Montreal Protocol on Substances that Deplete the Ozone Layer (1987) (Montreal Protocol) An international *protocol that was drawn up in 1987 and came into force in 1989 to protect the *ozone layer in the *stratosphere from depletion. It built upon the *Vienna Convention for the Protection of the Ozone Layer (1985) and governs the phasing out of production and use of ozone-depleting substances such as *CFCs. The 39 signatory countries agreed to freeze production of *CFCs at 1986 levels, and to decrease production by 20% by 1993 and by half by 1999. The Montreal Protocol was widely welcomed, because it provided the international community with a mechanism for protecting the ozone layer that is effective (the measures are likely to work, particularly as substitutes for CFCs are developed and make it easier to reach the *emissions reduction targets), equitable (the measures share responsibility for solving the problem amongst all countries concerned), and dynamic (the measures get tougher through time, and can be further adapted if new scientific evidence comes to light).

moon A large body (natural *satellite) that orbits a *planet. The Moon is a natural satellite of the Earth. It has no atmosphere or free water (although there is believed to be some subsurface water). The Moon is much smaller than the Earth, barely a quarter of the size, with a diameter of 3476 km. Its surface gravity is only about one-sixth that of the Earth. The Moon orbits in a west–east direction, about 385000 km from the

Earth, and each orbit takes 27.32 days (a sidereal month) to complete. It also spins on its axis, with one face permanently turned towards the Earth. On Earth the *tides (cyclic rise and fall of sea level) are caused by the gravitational pull of the Moon and Sun, so the movements of the Moon affect the oceans which cover two-thirds of the Earth's surface. At intervals of 18.6 years the lunar orbit crosses the *ecliptic and research suggests that this cycle affects the periodic oscillations in Earth's climates (e.g. the *North Atlantic Oscillation).

moonlight The reflected light of the Earth's *Moon.

moor *See* MOORLAND.

moorland Unenclosed land in an *upland area that supports upland *heath, *blanket bog, and upland *grassland, with a moist peaty soil covered with *heather, *bracken, and *moss.

mor A layer of *organic matter that develops beneath *conifer forest and is associated with *acidic soils. *Contrast* MULL.

moraine The rocks, boulders, and debris that are carried and deposited by a *glacier or *ice sheet. The main types of moraines are *lateral moraine, *ground moraine, *medial moraine, and *terminal moraine.

moral Arising from a sense of right and wrong.

morality A recognized code of conduct or set of ethical principles that guide actions and relationships, based on the difference between right and wrong.

morals The ethics, values, principles, and customs of a person or society.

moratorium A temporary prohibition or suspension of a particular activity.

morbidity The rate of incidence of a particular *illness or *disease within a given *population.

more developed country (MDC) A highly industrialized country that has high *per capita incomes, low *birth rates and *death rates, low *population growth rates, and high levels of *industrialization and *urbanization. Examples include the USA, Canada, Japan, and many countries in Europe. *Contrast* LESS DEVELOPED COUNTRY.

morph A distinct, readily observable type of a particular *species.

morphactins A group of synthetic plant growth regulators that are used to inhibit seed germination, inhibit root and shoot growth in seedlings, cause dwarfing by inhibiting stem elongation, and increase branching and tillering by inhibiting apical dominance, prolonging bud dormancy, and altering the timing and sequence of flowering.

morphogenesis The evolution of form, such as the development of *landforms in a *landscape or the change in shape or structure of an *organism as it grows.

morphogenetic region A *region that has distinct *landscape characteristics which have been produced by dominant *geological processes which are determined by climatic conditions.

morphological map A map of variations in the structure and form of the land surface, and of the *landforms on it.

morphology The study of the structure and form of objects (such as *organisms and *landforms), without regard to function.

morphometry The quantitative expression of *morphology, for example by measuring the depth, surface area, and volume of a lake.

morphostratigraphy The organization of *rock or sediment *strata into units based on their surface morphology (*landforms).

mortality The *death rate of a population, normally expressed as the number of deaths per thousand per year. *Contrast* NATALITY.

mosaic 1. An interlocking group of *habitats that cover a particular area. **2.** A disease in plants, where patches of yellow develop on the leaves.

moss 1. Any of about 12 000 species of small, simple, flowerless green plants (*bryophytes), comprising the class Musci, which grow in moist places such as *moorland on rocks, tree bark, etc. **2.** Another term for *mossland.

moss animals *See* BRYOZOANS.

mossland (moss) A term used in northern England and Scotland to describe a lowland *raised bog habitat.

mossy forest A *tropical montane forest, typically with contorted trees no more than 10–15 m high with dense crowns, their trunks, boughs, and twigs being festooned with *mosses, *lichens, and liverworts. The growths of 'moss' are particularly luxuriant where mists prevail.

Mother Earth A general term that is widely used to refer to the Earth as our home planet, particularly by those who view it in a spiritual way.

mother lode The principal *lode of an *ore in a region.

mother-of-pearl cloud See NACREOUS CLOUD.

motile Able to move at will, self-propelled. *Contrast* SESSILE.

mottling The marble-like pattern that occurs in *soils as a result of periodic fluctuations in the *water table.

mould 1. The common name for a *fungus with a visible, woolly mycelium of fine fibres on which powdery spores can be seen. There are more than 20 000 species of mould. **2.** The impression of a *fossil in a deposit.

moulin A wide, vertical shaft in a *glacier, created by *meltwater, by which the meltwater enters the ice.

moult The seasonal or perodic shedding of old skin, feathers, or hair to allow new growth.

Mount Agung A *stratovolcano in Indonesia which erupted violently in March 1963, emitting large quantities of gases and ash. Sulphate particles rose to 22–23 km, spread throughout the world within about six months, remained aloft for several years, and produced spectacular twilight displays of colour. The temperature in the lower *stratosphere rose by 6–7°C shortly after the eruption and surface temperatures were depressed by 0.18–1.3°C for several years.

Mount Pinatubo A *volcano in the Philippines that erupted violently in June 1991, ejecting large amounts of gas and ash to a height of about 40 km. Sulphate particles spread over about 40% of the Earth's surface, reducing tropical surface temperatures by about 2.2°C and depressing global temperatures by 0.4–0.7°C in 1992 and 1993.

Mount St Helens A *volcano within the Cascade volcanic group in southern Washington State, USA, which had been *dormant since 1875 but erupted violently on 18 May 1980. Before the eruption *magma was pushed upwards beneath Mount St Helens, causing the mountain to bulge and the ground surface to tilt. The explosive eruption released pressure on the magma, causing a massive landslide and a

powerful lateral blast which deposited ash and blew down trees over a wide area.

Mount Tambora A *volcano in Indonesia that erupted in April 1815, ejecting an estimated 15 km³ of ash and sulphate *aerosol in what was one of the most violent eruptions for several thousand years. Temperatures fell by up to 1°C in many areas.

mountain A high area of land that rises steeply above its surroundings, usually has a sharply pointed top, and is larger than a *hill.

mountain breeze See KATABATIC WIND.

mountain chain See MOUNTAIN RANGE.

mountain glacier (alpine glacier, valley glacier) A *glacier which forms in an area of *mountains. *Contrast* ICE CAP; ICE SHEET.

mountain meteorology The study of *weather phenomena associated with *mountains or *topographically complex areas.

mountain range (mountain chain) A long chain of *mountains connected together by continuous high ground.

Mountain States Legal Foundation A US non-profit group public interest legal centre that is dedicated to individual liberty, the right to own and use property, and ethical government and the free enterprise system.

(((●))) SEE WEB LINKS

• Mountain States Legal Foundation home page.

mountain top removal A method of *mining which involves removing all of the *overburden covering a *coal seam, to allow all of the *mineral to be recovered. The *spoil is transported to a nearby hollow to create a valley fill. A form of *open cast mining.

mountain wave See LEE WAVE.

mountain wind system The system of *diurnal winds that forms in an area of complex terrain, consisting of mountain–plain, along-valley, cross-valley, and slope wind systems.

Mountains of California A book by John *Muir which was published in 1894 and describes the geology, landscape, and natural history of the Sierra Nevada mountains.

MPA See MARINE PROTECTED AREA.

MPD See MAXIMUM PERMISSIBLE DOSE.

MSS *See* MULTISPECTRAL SCANNER.

MSW *See* MUNICIPAL SOLID WASTE.

MSY *See* MAXIMUM SUSTAINABLE YIELD.

MTD *See* MAXIMUM TOLERATED DOSE.

muck 1. The general term (particularly in North America) for a highly decomposed layer of *organic material in a wet organic *soil. **2.** *Manure.

mud Soft wet *soil.

mud drape A layer of mud deposited over a pre-existing morphological feature.

muddling through *See* INCREMENTALISM.

mudflat A flat area along the coast or in an *estuary, that is covered with a thick layer of *mud or *sand, and is usually under water at *high tide.

mudflow A rapid *mass movement process in which *fine-grained *sediment (*clays) is saturated with water and moves downhill by *gravity. Common after prolonged or unusually heavy rain in areas with little or no protective vegetation cover.

mudslide A *landslide of *mud. Faster, more sudden, and more damaging than a *mudflow.

mudstone A fine-grained *clastic *sedimentary rock composed of compacted and hardened *clay, similar to *shale but with less developed *lamination.

Muir, John US naturalist, traveller, and writer (1838–1914) who was born in Scotland and became America's most famous and most influential conservationist. He lived in the Yosemite Valley in California and studied it in great detail and was the author of the book *The *Mountains of California*. He played a key role in the formation of Yellowstone and Yosemite National Parks and was one of the founders of the *Sierra Club, becoming a hero of the early American conservation movement.

mulch A protective covering for *soil; any natural or artificial substance that is spread or allowed to remain on the soil surface in order to conserve soil moisture, shield soil particles from *erosion, prevent freezing of plant roots, and control the growth of *weeds.

mulching The process of spreading a *mulch over a soil surface.

mull A type of *humus or layer of dark *organic matter that forms in freely drained, neutral to *alkaline *soils with good *aeration, mainly because of earthworm activity. *See also* MOR.

Müllerian mimicry A form of *mimicry, first described in 1879 by the German-Brazilian zoologist Fritz Müller (1821–97), in which two *species, both of which are unpalatable and have some form of defence mechanism (such as poisonous stingers), evolve to resemble each other. *Contrast* BATESIAN MIMICRY.

multicellular Composed of many *cells.

multidisciplinary The coordinated application of several academic disciplines or subjects, in order to achieve a common goal. *See also* INTERDISCIPLINARY.

multimedia approach An approach to *environmental management that is based on monitoring and managing several environmental *media (such as air, water, and land) at the same time.

multinational corporation (MNC) A company that operates, produces, and sells products in many countries, and is not wholly subject to the laws of any one nation. *Contrast* TRANSNATIONAL CORPORATION.

multiparasitism The process where by a *host is subjected to parasitism by more than one type of *parasite.

multiple cropping Growing more than one crop on the same piece of land. *See also* INTERCROPPING; MIXED CROPPING; SEQUENTIAL CROPPING.

multiple use The management and use of a *natural resource for more than one purpose. For example, using an area of land for the grazing of *livestock, protection of *watersheds, *conservation of *wildlife, *recreation, and timber production, or using a body of water for recreation, *fishing, and *water supply.

Multiple Use-Sustained Yield Act (1960) US legislation that declares that the purposes of the *National Forest System include outdoor recreation, range, timber, watershed, and fish and wildlife. The act directs the Secretary of Agriculture to administer national forest *renewable surface resources for *multiple use and *sustained yield.

multiple-use forestry (multipurpose forestry) Any forestry activity that is designed to meet two or more management objectives, including providing products, services, or other benefits.

multiple-use management *See* INTEGRATED RESOURCE MANAGEMENT.

Multiple-Use Management Area/Managed Resource Area An *IUCN Management Category (VIII) for protected areas, designed 'to provide for the sustained production of water, timber, wildlife, pasture, and outdoor recreation, with the conservation of nature primarily oriented to the support of economic activities (although specific zones may also be designed within these areas to achieve specific conservation objectives)'.

multipurpose forestry *See* MULTIPLE-USE FORESTRY.

multispectral scanner (MSS) A *radiation sensor system that is often carried in aeroplanes or *satellites (such as *Landsat), and records information about the same location in several *wavelength bands at the same time. This information shows the amount of energy reflected in particular wavelengths from specific ground locations, which can be decoded to indicate such things as land use, vegetation cover, crop growth, and health.

multistorey cropping The growing together of a number of different plant species (*annuals and *perennials) which are of different heights, so that several *canopy layers are formed. *See also* MULTIPLE CROPPING.

multivoltine Having many broods and generations in a year or season. *See also* VOLTINISM. *Contrast* BIVOLTINE; UNIVOLTINE.

municipal Belonging to or characteristic of a *municipality.

municipal discharge The discharge of *effluent from *wastewater treatment plants which receive wastewater from households, commercial establishments, and industries.

municipal sewage *Sewage that originates from households, commercial establishments, and industries.

municipal solid waste (MSW) Urban *refuse, including residential, industrial, and commercial wastes, that is collected for *landfill. It does not include agricultural and wood wastes or residues.

municipal waste combustor (waste-to-energy facility) A facility in which recovered *municipal solid waste is converted into a usable form of *energy, usually via *combustion.

municipality A *city, *town, or *village that enjoys self-government in local matters.

muskeg An ill-drained, often extensive, boggy tract, with at best sparse, stunted trees, which occurs within the *boreal forest. The vegetation is dominated by *Sphagnum* species (bog moss) and *Eriophorum* species (cotton sedge).

mutagen A substance that can induce *mutation. *See also* CARCINOGEN; TERATOGEN.

mutagenic Capable of causing *mutations in an organism. Mutagenic substances may also be *carcinogenic.

mutant A variant *organism that differs from its parent because of a change in its genetic material, caused by *mutation.

mutate To undergo *mutation and produce a *mutant.

mutation Any change in the *genotype of an *organism that is permanent and can be inherited by future generations, which occurs either by chance or a result of an external influence. *Contrast* IMMUTABILITY.

mutual recognition An agreement between two or more countries to permit goods originating in one country that meet mutually agreed standards to enter another country with minimal additional checks.

mutualism A mutually beneficial relationship (*symbiosis) between two different species, such as the *pollination of flowers by honey bees.

M$_W$ *See* MOMENT MAGNITUDE SCALE.

MWP *See* MEDIEVAL WARM PERIOD.

m.y. An abbreviation for million years.

mycelium A mass of thread-like filaments (hyphae) which makes up the vegetative state of many *fungi and actinomycete *bacteria.

mycorrhiza *Mutualism between a *fungus and the roots of a *plant, in which the fungus facilitates the uptake of *nutrients and water by the plant, so that both organisms benefit.

myiasis The *infestation of the living tissue of humans or animals by fly larvae.

myophily *Pollination by flies.

myrmecophily A relationship in which a plant possesses specialized structures in which it accommodates ants.

NAAQS *See* NATIONAL AMBIENT AIR QUALITY STANDARD.

nacreous cloud (mother-of-pearl cloud) White *cloud, often with a tinge of pink, that has a soft, pearly lustre and forms at altitudes of about 25 to 30 km above the Earth's surface. It is occasionally seen in high latitudes shortly before dawn or after sunset.

Næss, Arne (1912–2009) A Norwegian philosopher, alpine climber, and influential environmental thinker, who coined the term *deep ecology to express a vision of the world in which we protect the environment as a part of ourselves, never in opposition to humanity, based on a personal philosophy that he called *ecosophy.

nanometre A millionth of a millimetre (10^{-9} metres). *See also* ANGSTROM.

nanoscale On the scale of large molecules, measured in *nanometres.

nanotechnology Any *technology that is applied at the *nanoscale, particularly the development of new materials and processes (such as thin films, fine particles, or miniature machines) by manipulating molecular and atomic particles.

NAO *See* NORTH ATLANTIC OSCILLATION.

NAPL *See* NON-AQUEOUS PHASE LIQUID.

nappe A complex type of *fold in rock, in which an *overturned fold is detached and broken.

NASA The US National Aeronautics and Space Administration, which was created in 1958, and whose mission is to advance and communicate scientific knowledge and understanding of the Earth, the solar system, and the universe and use the environment of space for research.

 SEE WEB LINKS
• NASA home page.

natal dispersal The movement of *organisms away from the places where they were born. *See also* DISPERSAL.

natality The *birth rate of a population, normally expressed as the number of births per thousand per year. *Contrast* MORTALITY.

natatorial Specialized for swimming.

National Ambient Air Quality Standards (NAAQS) US *air quality standards, established by the *Environmental Protection Agency under the *Clean Air Act, that apply for outdoor air throughout the country.

National Audubon Society A society based in the USA with branches in every state which aims to conserve and restore natural *ecosystems, with particular focus on birds, other animals, and *habitats. The society was founded early in the 20th century and named after the American artist and naturalist John James Audubon (1785–1851).

SEE WEB LINKS
• National Audubon Society home page.

National Biodiversity Network (NBN) An initiative to set up a network of local record centres across Britain to collect and collate biological and geological observations and information from both amateur and professional naturalists, biologists, and ecologists.

SEE WEB LINKS
• NBN home page.

National Center for Atmospheric Research (NCAR) A federally funded research and development centre in the US, based in Boulder, Colorado, whose mission is to improve our understanding of *atmospheric systems.

national conservation strategy A plan that highlights country-level environmental priorities and opportunities for the sustainable management of *natural resources, following the example of the *World Conservation Strategy published by the *World Conservation Union (IUCN) in 1980.

National Contingency Plan (NCP) *See* NATIONAL OIL AND HAZARDOUS SUBSTANCES CONTINGENCY PLAN.

national delegation One or more officials who are empowered to represent and negotiate on behalf of their government in international discussions and at the drafting of international *conventions.

National Emissions Standards for Hazardous Air Pollutants (NESHAPS) The US *emissions standard, defined by the *Environmental Protection Agency, for an air pollutant that is not covered by *NAAQS but may cause an increase in fatalities or in serious, irreversible, or incapacitating illness. Primary standards are designed to protect human *health, secondary standards to protect public *welfare (including buildings, visibility, crops, and domestic animals).

National Environmental Policy Act (NEPA) (1969) US legislation that requires that environmental considerations be incorporated into all federal policies and activities, and requires all federal agencies to prepare *environmental impact statements for any actions significantly affecting the environment. It led to the setting up of the *Council on Environmental Quality.

National Environmental Scorecard A method of measuring the environmental actions of members of the US Congress that was developed in 1970 by the *League of Conservation Voters, and is based on the environmental voting records, based on a consensus of experts from 19 respected environmental and conservation organizations who selected the key votes on which Members of Congress should be graded.

National Estuary Program (NEP) A national programme that was established under the US *Clean Water Act Amendments of 1987 in order to develop and implement *conservation and *management plans to protect *estuaries, restore and maintain their chemical, physical, and biological integrity, and control pollution from *point sources and *non-point sources.

National Fire Danger Rating System A system for rating *fire danger in the USA, based on the environmental factors that affect the *moisture content of *fuels. Fire danger is

rated daily over large administrative areas, such as *National Forests.

National Fish and Wildlife Foundation (NFWF) A non-profit charitable organization in the USA which is dedicated to the *conservation and management of *fish, *wildlife, and *plant resources, and the *habitats on which they depend.

(globe icon) **SEE WEB LINKS**
• NFWF home page.

National Forest Public land (mostly *forest, *range, or *wildland) in the USA which is administered by the *Forest Service of the US Department of Agriculture, under a programme of multiple use and sustained yield for *timber harvesting, *grazing, *conservation of *wildlife, *watershed protection, and *outdoor recreation purposes. *Mining is also allowed within National Forests.

National Forest Land and Resource Management Plan (NFLRMP,forest plan) A plan that guides the management of a particular *National Forest and establishes management standards and guidelines for all lands of that National Forest.

National Forest Management Act (1976) US legislation that reorganized, expanded, and amended the *Forest and Rangeland Renewable Resources Planning Act (1974) and is the primary statute relating to the management of renewable resources on National Forest lands. It requires the Secretary of Agriculture to assess forest lands, develop a management programme based on *multiple-use, *sustained-yield principles, and implement a resource management plan for each unit of the *National Forest System.

National Forest System The national system of *forest land management in the USA, which includes all National Forest lands reserved or withdrawn from the public domain or acquired through purchase, exchange, donation, or other means, as well as other land that is administered by the Forest Service. The system includes state and private forestry programmes.

National Grassland An area or region of *grassland in the USA that has been designated for *conservation by the government.

National Historic Preservation Act (1966) US legislation that provides for managing *cultural resources on federal lands and that establishes procedures for determining relative significance among cultural resources.

National Monument An area in the USA that is owned by the federal government and administered by the *National Park Service, for the purpose of preserving and making available to the public objects of scientific and historical interest that are located on federal lands.

National Nature Reserve (NNR) A site in the United Kingdom that has been declared as a *nature reserve by *Natural England (or its predecessors or national equivalents) and is either owned or controlled by Natural England or held and managed by approved bodies such as wildlife trusts. The US equivalent is the national wildlife refuge.

National Oceanic and Atmospheric Administration (NOAA) A branch of the US Department of Commerce, established in 1970. NOAA is the parent organization of the *National Weather Service.

(((⊕))) SEE WEB LINKS
• NOAA home page.

National Oil and Hazardous Substances Contingency Plan (NOHSCP/ NCP, National Contingency Plan) The policy directive in the USA that guides the selection of sites to be cleaned up under the *Superfund Programme and the programme to prevent or control spills into surface waters or elsewhere. *See also* HAZARD RANKING SYSTEM.

National Park An *IUCN Management Category (II) for protected areas, designed 'to protect natural and scenic areas of national or international significance for scientific, educational and recreational use'. According to the IUCN, a national park is 'a relatively large area: (a) where one or several *ecosystems are not materially altered by human exploitation and occupation, where plant and animal species, *geomorphological sites and *habitats are of special scientific, educative, and recreational interest or which contain a natural landscape of great beauty; (b) where the highest competent authority of the country has taken steps to prevent or eliminate as soon as possible exploitation or occupation in the whole area and to enforce effectively the respect of ecological, geomorphological, or aesthetic features which have led to its establishment; and (c) where visitors are allowed to enter, under special conditions, for inspirational, cultural, and recreative purposes'. British national parks do not comply

strictly with the IUCN definition because they comprise areas that have been altered significantly over long periods of human occupation, are still actively farmed and occupied, and much of the land is owned privately. In Britain, national parks are designated to maintain long-established, cultural landscapes. Parks of this type are known in France as *parcs naturels et régionaux* and in the USA as greenline parks.

National Park Service (NPS) The agency of the US Department of the Interior which is responsible for the administration of *National Parks, *National Monuments, and historic sites.

National Parks and Access to the Countryside Act (1949) The national legislation under which Britain's first *National Parks were established.

National Priorities List (NPL) A formal list of the most serious uncontrolled or abandoned *hazardous waste sites in the USA that pose a serious threat to human health and/or the environment, which are candidates for long-term *cleanup using money from the *Superfund trust fund. The list is maintained by the *Environmental Protection Agency, is updated at least once a year, and contains about 1200 hazardous waste sites.

national rank (N-rank) A term used by *Conservation Data Centers in the USA, and by *NatureServe, to refer to the national *conservation status rank of a *species or *ecological community.

National Recreation Area An area of federal land in the USA that has been set aside by Congress for *recreational use by members of the public.

National Register of Historic Places A national list of districts, sites, buildings, structures, and objects that are significant in history, architecture, archaeology, engineering, and culture in the USA.

National Registry of Natural Landmarks A register of areas in the USA that possess such exceptional values or qualities for illustrating or interpreting the natural *heritage of the nation that they are considered to be of national significance.

National Response Center (NRC) The federal operations centre in the USA that receives notifications of all releases into the environment of *oil and *hazardous substances. It is operated by the US Coast Guard, which evaluates all reports and notifies the appropriate agency.

national sovereignty The right of individual nations to look after their own interests and to manage resources within their territorial borders to suit their own purposes.

national water quality standard The maximum allowable levels of *contamination in the USA for a range of *chemicals, *metals, and *bacteria, as defined by the US Safe Drinking Water Act.

National Weather Service (NWS) The branch of the *National Oceanic and Atmospheric Administration that is responsible for providing weather, hydrological, and climate forecasts and warnings for the USA and its territories.

 SEE WEB LINKS
• NWS home page.

National Wetlands Coalition A US non-profit *anti-environmental *front group that advocates a balanced federal policy for conserving and regulating the nation's *wetlands. Members of the coalition own or manage wetlands; they include local governments, ports, water agencies, developers, agriculture groups, electric utilities, oil and gas developers, producers, the mining industry, banks, environmental and engineering consulting firms, and Native American groups.

National Wild and Scenic Rivers System A series of *wild rivers and *scenic rivers in the USA that 'possess outstanding remarkable scenic, recreational, geologic, fish and wildlife, historic, cultural, or other similar values' and are protected 'for the benefit and enjoyment of present and future generations' under the *Wild and Scenic Rivers Act.

National Wilderness Preservation System A system of wild federal land and *National Forest land in the USA that was established by the *Wilderness Act (1964), which was to be managed 'for the use and enjoyment of the American people in such manner as will leave them unimpaired for future use and enjoyment as wilderness . . .'.

National Wildlife Federation (NWF) The largest and oldest protector of *wildlife in the USA, founded in 1936 as an environmental advocacy and educational group.

 SEE WEB LINKS
• NWF home page.

national wildlife refuge The US equivalent to a *National Nature Reserve in the United Kingdom.

National Wildlife Refuge System A national system of *nature reserves in the USA, which is managed by the *US Fish and Wildlife Service, and has the mission 'to administer a national network of lands and waters for the conservation, management, and where appropriate, restoration of the fish, wildlife, and plant resources and their habitats within the USA for the benefit of present and future generations of Americans'.

native (indigenous) Naturally occurring in a particular place; belonging there by birth or origin and not introduced deliberately or accidentally by humans.

Native American A tribe, people, or culture that is *native to the USA. In Canada the equivalent term is First Nation.

native element An *element (e.g. *sulphur) that occurs naturally in its free state, rather than in a compound.

native metal A *metal (e.g. *gold) that occurs naturally in its pure metallic form, i.e. it is not combined with other elements.

native pasture Land that is used for *grazing, on which the *climax plant community is *forest, but which is used and managed primarily to produce native or naturalized plants for *forage.

native peoples *See* INDIGENOUS PEOPLES.

native species (endemic species, indigenous species) A species that is within its known *natural range, and occurs naturally in a given area or habitat, as opposed to an *introduced species or *invasive species. *Contrast* NON-NATIVE SPECIES.

natron lake A saline lake, rich in the sodium carbonate salt natron ($Na_2CO_3.10H_2O$).

Natura 2000 A network of areas within the *European Community that is designed to conserve *natural habitats and *species of plants and animals which are *rare, *endangered, or *vulnerable. *See also* HABITATS DIRECTIVE.

 SEE WEB LINKS
• Natura 2000 Networking Programme.

natural Occurring in *nature; caused by *natural processes. *Contrast* SYNTHETIC.

natural air pollutant Any of a variety of substances that are released from *natural sources or processes, and which can locally overload the atmospheric system. These include *dust, *gases, and *aerosols from *volcanic eruptions and *forest fires and *sea spray.

Natural Area An area identified as having significant or unique natural *heritage features, with boundaries based upon the distribution of *wildlife and of natural features rather than administrative borders. The term is used in the UK, the USA, and Canada.

Natural Area Preserve (Natural Reserve) An area of land in the USA that is designated by a public or private agency specifically to preserve a representative sample of an *ecological community, primarily for scientific and educational purposes, in which commercial exploitation is generally not allowed and general public use is discouraged. *See also* RESEARCH NATURAL AREA.

natural barrier A natural feature, such as a dense *stand of trees, that will restrict the free movement of *animals.

Natural Biotic Area/Anthropological Reserve An *IUCN Management Category (VII) for protected areas, designed 'to allow the way of life of societies living in harmony with the environment to continue undisturbed by modern technology'.

natural capital (environmental capital) The stock of *natural resources and environmental assets within an area, country, or the world, which includes *water, *soil, *air, *plants, *animals, and *minerals.

natural community *See* ECOLOGICAL COMMUNITY.

natural disaster A disaster that is caused by a natural event. *See* NATURAL HAZARD. *Contrast* TECHNOLOGICAL DISASTER.

natural disturbance regime The historic patterns (frequency and extent) of natural processes such as fire, insects, wind, and *mass movement that affect the *ecosystems and *landscapes in a particular area. *See also* DISTURBANCE.

Natural England A public body, responsible to the Secretary of State for Environment, Food and Rural Affairs, charged with protecting and improving England's natural environment and encouraging people to enjoy it.

SEE WEB LINKS
• Natural England home page.

natural environment *See* ENVIRONMENT.

natural erosion (geological erosion) The gradual *erosion of the land surface under natural conditions, without any human activity or impact.

natural flow The flow of a *river as it would be under natural conditions, unaltered by upstream diversion, storage, import, export, or *consumptive use.

natural forest *See* PRIMARY FOREST.

natural gas A mixture of gaseous *hydrocarbons (*fossil fuel), chiefly *methane (CH_4), *ethane (C_2H_6), *propane (C_3H_8), and *butane (C_4H_{10}), which is trapped in porous rocks beneath the ground and is often found in association with reserves of *oil. It is a *clean fuel which burns without smoke or soot and has a high heat value, and is used as a fuel. It is now one of the world's three main fossil fuels, along with *coal and oil. Most is extracted from offshore wells (in the North Sea, for example) or from land-based wells in the USA and the Middle East. North America and the Middle East hold about 40% of the world's known recoverable gas resources, and the former Soviet Union holds a similar amount. It provides around a third of the energy used in the USA. *See also* SHALE GAS.

natural greenhouse effect *See* GREENHOUSE EFFECT.

natural habitat As defined by the EU *Habitats Directive 'natural habitats means terrestrial or aquatic areas distinguished by geographic, abiotic, and biotic features, whether entirely natural or semi-natural'.

natural hazard (environmental hazard) A process or event in the physical environment that occurs naturally, is usually not entirely predictable, and that is capable of injuring or killing people and damaging property. Examples include volcanic eruptions, *earthquakes, violent *storms (including *hurricanes and *tornadoes), river *flooding, *storm surges, *droughts, *avalanches and *landslides, and *sea level rise. Three trends have increased the problems of coping with natural hazards in recent decades: *population increase, *human impacts on *environmental systems, and *technological hazards. *See also* INTERNATIONAL DECADE FOR NATURAL DISASTER REDUCTION.

natural heritage All of the living *organisms, ecological *communities, *ecosystems, and natural areas that we inherit and leave to future generations.

Natural Heritage Network The network of *Conservation Data Centers and *Natural Heritage Programs throughout the Americas, which use the same methodology and database to monitor changes in *biodiversity in their jurisdictions.

Natural Heritage Program *See* CONSERVATION DATA CENTER.

natural history The systematic study of *nature, including animals, plants, minerals, and other natural objects.

natural immunity Inherited *immunity of an individual to a particular *disease.

natural increase The surplus of births over deaths in a *population over a given period of time (usually a year), normally calculated as crude *birth rate minus crude *death rate.

Natural Landmark *See* NATURAL MONUMENT/NATURAL LANDMARK.

natural landscape *Landscape that has not been modified by human activities. *Contrast* CULTURAL LANDSCAPE.

Natural Monument/Natural Landmark An *IUCN Management Category (III) for protected areas, designed 'to protect and preserve nationally significant natural features because of their special interest or unique characteristics'.

natural nidus The *niche of a disease.

natural process A process that results from natural forces rather than human activities.

natural process restoration The restoration of *habitat by natural processes (such as flooding or fire), which allows native vegetation to regenerate and inhibits the growth of *exotic plants.

natural range (ecological range, geographical range) The geographical area over which a *species has lived naturally in recent times (since about 5000 years before the present), excluding any changes to that range that result from human activities. *See also* HISTORIC RANGE; INTRODUCED SPECIES; NATIVE SPECIES.

natural range of variation *See* RANGE OF VARIABILITY.

natural regeneration The natural regrowth of vegetation (for example the renewal of a forest by natural seeding) without any human interference.

natural region An area of land that is defined by physical features (such as a surrounding mountain range) and contains similar plant and animal species. Natural regions and *ecoregions often overlap, but they are not the same.

Natural Reserve *See* NATURAL AREA PRESERVE.

natural resource (environmental resource, intrinsic resource) Any feature of the *natural environment that is of value in meeting human *needs, including *renewable resources (e.g. vegetation, water, soil, and wildlife) and *non-renewable resources (e.g. oil, natural gas, coal, and iron ore).

natural resource accounting *See* ENVIRONMENTAL ACCOUNTING.

natural resource accounts (NRAs) Published information about the level of *natural resource use, existing stocks of natural resources, and environmental degradation, within a region or country.

natural resource management The *management of *natural resources on a *sustainable basis, usually in ways that meet multiple objectives including the *conservation of *wildlife and *ecosystems, and the minimizing of *environmental impacts and *environmental change.

natural resource zoning All types of land use *zoning (such as *agricultural zoning, *floodplain zoning, and *forest use zoning) which restrict the uses that are made of *natural resource land, to protect the resource base.

Natural Resources Defense Council A US organization founded in 1970 to protect *natural resources.

natural sciences Those sciences that study the natural environment, including *astronomy, *biology, *chemistry, *geology, *physics, *oceanography, and *meteorology.

natural selection ('survival of the fittest') The complex process in which the environment selects those traits that are passed from one generation of organisms to the next. Those individuals that possess variations which equip them to find food, shelter, mates, or other resources better than individuals that lack them will tend to produce more surviving offspring. Those offspring will inherit their parents' advantageous traits and the traits will spread through the population. Over time, natural selection helps species become better adapted to their environment. It is the driving force behind the *evolution of species that was first suggested and illustrated by Charles *Darwin and Alfred Russel *Wallace.

natural turnover rate The normal rate of transfer of an element through the active part of a *biogeochemical cycle.

natural vegetation The natural state and *species composition of *vegetation in an area, as it is or would be if unmodified by human activities.

naturalized Applied to a *species that was originally imported from another country but now maintains itself without further human intervention, i.e. behaves like a native, and has invaded native communities.

naturally occurring background level *Ambient concentrations of *chemicals that are present in the *environment and have not been influenced by humans.

naturalness In *conservation assessment, the extent to which a location and its associated *biotopes are unaffected by human activities.

natural-technological disaster A *natural disaster that creates a technological emergency, such as an urban *fire that results from *seismic motion, or a chemical *spill that results from *flooding. *See also* DISASTER; TECHNOLOGICAL DISASTER.

Nature An essay published by Ralph Waldo *Emerson in 1836, in which he outlined his views of the links between people and nature.

nature The natural physical world including *plants, *animals, and *landscapes, particularly those parts that remain in a primitive state, unchanged by humans.

Nature Conservancy, The (TNC) A private, international *conservation group based in the USA which was established in 1951, whose mission is 'to preserve plants, animals, and natural communities that represent the diversity of life on earth by protecting the lands and waters they need to survive'.

((⊕)) SEE WEB LINKS
• Nature Conservancy home page.

nature conservation The *conservation of *wildlife, *biodiversity, and *natural ecosystems, by regulating the human use of ecosystems and *natural resources and promoting *sustainable development.

nature reserve An area of land that is set aside and managed in ways that benefit *nature conservation, usually with strong legal protection to restrict human access and prevent other uses. Nature reserves are usually much smaller than *National Parks or *Biosphere Reserves, and many *endangered species of plants and animals are protected inside them.

nature study The study of *plants and *animals in their natural *habitats.

NatureServe (Association for Biodiversity Information) A non-profit *conservation organization that provides the scientific information and tools needed to help guide effective conservation action throughout North America and the Caribbean, partly through an international network of natural heritage programmes which provide information about *rare and *endangered species and threatened *ecosystems.

((⊕)) SEE WEB LINKS
• NatureServe home page.

nautical mile (nm) The distance between each minute of *latitude, which is defined internationally as 1.852 km; 1 nm = 1.15 statute miles.

navigable waters *Waterways that are deep and wide enough to allow navigation by all or specified vessels.

NBN *See* NATIONAL BIODIVERSITY NETWORK.

NCAR *See* NATIONAL CENTER FOR ATMOSPHERIC RESEARCH.

NCP *See* NATIONAL CONTINGENCY PLAN.

Neanderthal A *hominid (*Homo neanderthalensis*), closely related to but distinct from modern humans, that lived in Europe and western Asia between about 150 000 and 30 000 years ago.

neap tide A *tide that occurs every 14 to 15 days, coincides with the first and last quarter of the Moon, and has a small tidal range. *Contrast* SPRING TIDE.

near infrared *Electromagnetic *radiation with a wavelength from 0.7–1 micrometres (μm) to 5 μm, which is associated with temperatures of 740 kelvin to 3000–5000 kelvin.

near threatened *See* LOW RISK.

Nearctic realm A *biogeographical realm that covers most of North America and contains a variety of *biomes including *tundra, *grassland, *deciduous forest, *coniferous forest, *chaparral, and *desert.

Nebraskan The earliest period of *Pleistocene glaciation in North America, lasting from about 1.8 million years ago to 1.65 million years ago and equivalent to the *Günz glaciation in Europe.

necrophage A *scavenger that feeds on animal carcasses (dead meat) rather than live *prey.

necrosis The death of plant or animal cells or tissues.

necrotic Dead and discoloured.

nectar The sweet, sugary liquid that many *flowers produce in order to attract the *insects that assist *pollination.

nectarivore An animal that eats *nectar.

needs The fundamental requirements of people, including basics such as food, clothing, shelter, drinkable water, and breathable air. Wants and desires go beyond the basics, and reflect taste and fashion as well as the need to survive.

negative charge An electrical charge that is created by having more *electrons than *protons.

negative feedback An interaction (*feedback) that reduces or dampens the response of a system to change. *Contrast* POSITIVE FEEDBACK.

nekton *Aquatic *organisms that swim and can move long distances to feed or breed (e.g. fish, amphibians, large aquatic insects). *Contrast* PLANKTON.

Nelson, Gaylord A US politician (1916–2005) who, in 1969 when he was a Senator from Wisconsin, proposed establishing *Earth Day.

nematicide A chemical substance that is used to control *nematodes (eelworms).

nematode A free-living, spindle-shaped worm (class Nematoda) that has an unsegmented body protected by a tough *cuticle. Nematodes are commonly found in *marine and *freshwater *habitats, in *soil, and as *parasites of plants and animals. Most are microscopically small, but some are up to 5 cm long.

Neoarchaean The final era of the *Archaean eon, lasting from 2800 to 2500 million years ago, during which most of the present continents formed and the earliest life was present.

neo-classical economics A branch of *economics that studies the allocation of scarce *resources between competing uses and users, based on principles of *market equilibrium and profit maximization.

neo-Darwinism (modern synthesis) The fusion of *Darwinian theory with genetics and molecular biology.

neoendemic Applied to a *species that has evolved relatively recently and is locally distributed, having not yet had time to expand its range.

Neogea A neotropical zoogeographical region that comprises Central and South America.

Neogene A period of geological time within the *Cenozoic era, between 23.03 and 2.588 m.y. ago, which comprises the *Miocene and *Pliocene epochs. The climate became cooler and drier during the Neogene. Grasses became widespread and grazing mammals thrived.

(((●))) SEE WEB LINKS

• The Neogene period of the Cenozoic era.

neoglaciation A series of relatively small *glacier advances in the *northern hemisphere during the last few thousand years of the *Holocene.

Neolithic The New *Stone Age, following the *Mesolithic, which began in the Near East around 8000 BCE and in Europe around 6000 BCE, and was characterized by the adoption of *agriculture, village life, and the use of pottery.

neo-Malthusian A *pessimist view of the relationship between *population, *economic growth, and *resources, based on the ideas of *Thomas Malthus, who argued that population growth and economic growth would eventually be checked by absolute limits on resources such as food, energy, or water. This viewpoint grew in popularity particularly between the 1940s and the 1960s, when population growth and economic development were particularly strong in many countries. Many experts concluded that rapid population growth would eventually be checked by some absolute limit on resources (such as food, energy, or water). There was mounting evidence, too, that continued population growth and the environmental stresses associated with economic development could cause irreversible damage to the environmental systems that support life. This school of thinking was widely promoted through books such as *Limits to Growth.*

neon (Ne) An element that is a colourless, *inert *gas which comprises 0.0012% of the Earth's *atmosphere. When an electric current is discharged through it, neon produces a reddish-orange glow. Neon is used in luminous tube signs and lights.

neonicotinoids A major class of *insecticides, chemically related to *nicotine, used to protect crops against piercing and sucking insects, and for flea control on cats and dogs. They have low toxicity to mammals, birds, and fish, but may harm bees.

Neoproterozoic The final era of the *Proterozoic eon, lasting from 1000 to 542 million years ago, during which there were between two and four major *glaciations. Eukaryotic organisms expanded during this era and multicelled organisms appeared in the Ediacaran period (630–542 million years ago).

(((⊕))) SEE WEB LINKS

• The Neoproterozoic era of the Proterozoic eon.

neotenin See JUVENILE HORMONE.

neoteny The retention of *juvenile body characters in the adult state.

Neotropical faunal region The region that includes South and Central America including southern Mexico, the West Indies, and the Galápagos Islands. Much of the area was isolated for the greater part of the *Palaeogene period, which explains the distinctiveness of the fauna and the survival of ancient forms of mammals, e.g. the *marsupials and edentates (sloths, armadillos, anteaters, etc.). *See also* LATIN AMERICAN MAMMAL REGION.

Neotropical floral kingdom One of the major floral subdivisions, covering Central and South America, with the exception of the southern tip, which is included in the Antarctic kingdom. The floristic distinctiveness results from the isolation of South America from other landmasses for much of *Cenozoic time.

Neotropical realm A *biogeographical realm that occupies Central and South America, and is dominated by *tropical forest, *savanna, and *desert.

neotropics The tropical parts of the New World (the Americas). *See also* PALAEOTROPICS.

NEP *See* NATIONAL ESTUARY PROGRAM.

NEPA *See* NATIONAL ENVIRONMENTAL POLICY ACT.

neptunism A geological explanation of the formation of the Earth, popular in the late 18th and early 19th centuries, according to which the oldest rocks crystallized from a primordial ocean. These rocks were later eroded and precipitated once more. *Contrast* UNIFORMITARIANISM. *See also* CATASTROPHISM.

nereistoxin analogue insecticides A group of natural neurotoxic products derived from the salivary glands of the marine annelid worm *Lumbriconereis heteropoda*, which are used to control beetles including Colorado beetle and caterpillars and other insect pests including rice stem borer and thrips. They are of low toxicity to non-target species.

neritic Applied to the relatively shallow waters within the *ocean over the *continental shelf, down to a depth of about 200 m. This *ecological zone is generally richer in *nutrients than deep ocean waters.

NESHAPS *See* NATIONAL EMISSION STANDARDS FOR HAZARDOUS AIR POLLUTANTS.

nest A structure in which animals (particularly *birds) lay eggs or give birth to their young.

nest box/structure An artificial box, platform, or other structure that enhances the reproductive habitat for target *species.

nest parasitism *See* BROOD PARASITISM.

nesting The nest-related activities of adult animals, including *nest building, egg laying, and departure of the young from the nest.

nesting cover Vegetation (including *grasses, low *shrubs, and *thickets) that protects nesting sites for quail, grouse, and many species of songbirds.

nestling 1. A young bird, before it leaves the nest. **2.** A mode of life adopted by certain bivalve *molluscs which live in crevices and depressions in hard substrates, which have not been excavated by the bivalve itself.

net economic welfare *Gross national product adjusted by subtracting the cost of problems such as *pollution and adding the value of beneficial, non-market activities such as leisure and *recreation.

net energy yield The total amount of useful *energy that is produced during the lifetime of an energy system, minus the energy that is used, lost, or wasted in making the useful energy available.

net migration The difference between the number of individuals who move in and the number who move out of a country or area within a specified period of time (normally one year). *Immigration minus *emigration.

net present value (NPV) The future stream of benefits and costs associated with a particular project or resource-using activity, converted into equivalent values today. This is estimated by assigning monetary values to benefits and costs, discounting future benefits and costs using an appropriate *discount rate, and subtracting the total discounted costs from the total discounted benefits. NPV is used in *cost-benefit analysis.

net primary productivity (NPP) See PRIMARY PRODUCTIVITY.

net radiation The balance between all incoming *energy and all outgoing energy carried by both *shortwave and *longwave radiation.

net radiative heating The net heating effect on the Earth of the *radiative forcing of climate, which can be positive or negative.

net reproduction rate The number of daughters that will be born to a woman during her lifetime if current birth and death rates continue.

net worth Net monetary value; total assets minus total liabilities.

netting In *greenhouse gas *emission control, the idea that all *emission sources in the same area that are owned or controlled by a single company can be treated as one large source, so an emission increase at one source can be offset with an emission reduction at another source in the same area. See also BUBBLE.

neurotoxin A *toxic substance, such as *lead or *mercury, that poisons nerve cells.

neustic community See NEUSTON.

neuston An *organism that rests or swims on the surface of a water body.

neutral Neither *acid nor *alkaline.

neutral soil A *soil solution with *pH of between 6.5 and 7.3.

neutral stability A stable atmospheric condition that exists in dry air when the *environmental lapse rate equals the *dry adiabatic rate, and in moist air when the environmental lapse rate equals the *saturated adiabatic rate.

neutralism A situation in which two *species *populations coexist, with neither population being affected by association with the other.

neutralize To decrease the *acidity or *alkalinity of a substance by adding alkaline or acidic materials, respectively, in order to make it *neutral.

neutron A subatomic particle that is found in all *atoms except normal hydrogen, and which has no electric charge. See also ELECTRON; PROTON.

neutron-activation analysis A method of identifying the *isotopes of an *element by bombarding them with *neutrons and observing the *radioactive decay products that are emitted.

névé See GRANULAR SNOW.

New Caledonian floral region Part of R. Good's *Polynesian floral subkingdom (*The Geography of the Flowering Plants*, 1974), within his *Palaeotropical floral kingdom, which also includes Lord Howe and Norfolk Islands. It has a remarkably rich flora, with a high degree of *endemism. Some of the endemic genera, of which there are well over 100, constitute separate families (or nearly so).

new environmental paradigm (NEP) The view that humans represent only one among many *species on Earth, that human activities are determined by the *environment as well as by social and cultural factors, and that humans are strongly dependent upon the environment and its resources. Contrast DOMINANT SOCIAL PARADIGM.

New International Economic Order (NIEO) The emergence of a new global political economy in the latter part of the 20th century, in response to powerful economic, political, and technological forces that have transformed the world. It is reflected, for example, in new attitudes towards economic growth and development, international aid, regionalism, *multinational corporations, national policies, and *sustainable development.

new social movement Any of a series of social movements that have emerged in recent decades (including the *environmental movement, the women's movement, and the gay rights movement), which have different origins, strategies, and goals from more traditional social movements based on class and economics.

new town A planned *urban community that is developed in a *rural area, and is designed to be largely self-sufficient with its own housing, education, commerce, and recreation.

New Urbanism A planning movement to promote cities and towns with planned growth that minimizes damage to the environment, through the restoration of *urban centres and towns, the reconfiguration of sprawling *suburbs into communities of neighbourhoods and districts, the conservation of natural environments, and the preservation of the built legacy.

New Zealand floral region Part of R. Good's Antarctic kingdom (*The Geography of the Flowering Plants*, 1974). Approximately 30 genera are known to be *endemic to it, but the surprisingly large number of endemic species (about 75% of the total) belong very largely to non-endemic genera.

newly industrializing country A country such as South Korea, Taiwan, and Singapore that has undergone major industrialization only in recent decades.

NFLRMP *See* NATIONAL FOREST LAND AND RESOURCE MANAGEMENT PLAN.

NFWF *See* NATIONAL FISH AND WILDLIFE FOUNDATION.

NGO *See* NON-GOVERNMENTAL ORGANIZATION.

niche overlap An overlap in resource requirements by two *species in the same *habitat or *ecosystem.

niche specialization The process by which a *species becomes better adapted, by *natural selection, to the specific characteristics of a particular *habitat.

nickel (Ni) A silver-white, hard, *malleable, *ductile *metal that can be highly polished, is resistant to corrosion, and is widely used in the manufacture of steel. It occurs naturally in all parts of the *environment, including plants and animals, is extremely persistent in soils, and is *carcinogenic to humans. *See also* OUTER CORE.

nicotine The main active ingredient of tobacco, which is addictive and extremely toxic to humans. It causes irritation of lung tissues, constriction of blood vessels, increased blood pressure and heart rate, and stimulation of the central nervous system. It is also used as an *insecticide.

nidiculous Applied to a young bird that stays in the nest until it is able to fly. Nidicolous young are usually naked and incapable of locomotion.

nidifugous Applied to a young bird that leaves the nest on hatching or soon after. Nidifugous young are down-covered and capable of locomotion.

NIEO *See* NEW INTERNATIONAL ECONOMIC ORDER.

night The time between *sunset and *sunrise, when it is dark outside. *Contrast* DAY.

nimbostratus (Ns) A genus of low, grey, uniform, and fairly featureless *clouds that often bring steady, continous rain or snow.

NIMBY *See* NOT IN MY BACKYARD.

NIREX An independent organization (the Nuclear Industry Radioactive Waste Executive) that was set up in the UK in 1982 to research, develop, and operate *radioactive waste disposal facilities on behalf of the *nuclear power industry. In 1985 it became a limited company whose mission is 'to provide the UK with safe, environmentally sound and publicly acceptable options for the long-term management of radioactive materials'. It advises the UK government and industry.

nitisols Soils that have a *clay-rich *soil horizon more than 39 cm deep, with a *cation-exchange capacity of less than 36 cmol$_c$/kg (centimoles cation per kilogram) and no evidence of clay *illuviation within 100 cm of the surface.

nitrate (NO$_3$) A naturally occurring salt that can exist in the atmosphere or dissolved in water, is a *nutrient for plants, and is widely used as a *fertilizer. It is produced naturally in septic systems, animal feed lots, industrial

NICHE (ECOLOGICAL NICHE)

The functional role and position of a *species within a *community or *ecosystem, which is defined by such things as what the species does, how it feeds, what and when it eats, when and for how long it is active, how it reproduces, how it behaves, what particular part of the habitat it uses, and how it responds to temperature and moisture. In most ecosystems a number of species could perform a particular role, but at any one point in time only one species actually does. In *grassland ecosystems, for example, bison (in North America), antelopes and zebras (in Africa), and kangaroos (in Australia) play more or less the same role in different places. Two species cannot live in the same *habitat on a sustainable basis if they occupy identical niches. There are four important implications of niches. First, many species have overlapping niches. Second, the greater the diversity of niches within an ecosystem, the greater the variety of energy flows and thus the more stable the ecosystem. Third, the introduction of *exotic species into an ecosystem, either deliberately or by accident, can create problems because they sometimes compete with native species for niches and food supplies, but in the absence of predation or other constraints on their expansion. Fourth, the removal of a species (or group of closely related species) can leave a niche empty and this can soon lead to reduced energy flow through the entire system, which can radically affect the structure and stability of the ecosystem overall. *See also* FUNDAMENTAL NICHE; POTENTIAL NICHE; REALIZED NICHE.

wastewaters, *sanitary landfills, and *garbage dumps.

nitrate-forming bacteria *See* NITRIFYING BACTERIA.

nitric acid (HNO$_3$) A colourless or yellowish *acid that is made by distilling a *nitrate with *sulphuric acid. It is used especially in the production of *fertilizers and explosives and rocket fuels. It is caustic and corrosive, is a component of *acid rain, and acute exposure to it can cause irritation to the lungs, nose, throat, and skin.

nitric oxide (NO) A colourless gas formed by the *oxidation of *nitrogen or *ammonia. It is the most common form of nitrogen emitted into the *atmosphere and is mainly released by burning fossil fuels and plant material. It is oxidized to *nitrogen dioxide in the atmosphere and is a precursor of *ozone and *photochemical smog.

nitrification The *oxidation of *ammonia to *nitrite and *nitrite to *nitrate by *micro-organisms. *Contrast* DENITRIFICATION.

nitrifying bacteria (nitrate-forming bacteria) *Bacteria that convert *nitrites into *nitrates that can be used by green plants to build *proteins. *See also* NITRITE-FORMING BACTERIA.

nitrite (NO$_2$) A *salt of nitrous acid that is commonly found in *soil, is produced by *nitrosifying bacteria, and is toxic to plants and animals at high concentrations. The second stage of the *nitrification process.

nitrite-forming bacteria (nitrosifying bacteria) *Bacteria that oxidize *ammonia (NH$_3$) to form *nitrites (NO$_2$), as part of the *nitrification process.

nitrogen (N) A colourless, tasteless, odourless, and relatively unreactive gas that makes up nearly four-fifths (78% by volume) of the *atmosphere. It is a *macronutrient, an essential component of *proteins and *nucleic acids in living organisms, occurs in nature in a variety of forms (*ammonia, *ammonium, *nitrate, *nitrite), and is a key ingredient in many commercial *fertilizers. Nitrogen availability controls plant growth and thus rates of photosynthesis in many terrestrial ecosystems. It can be a *pollutant when nitrogen compounds are mobilized in the environment, for example by *leaching from manured or fertilized fields, discharges from septic tanks or feedlots, or emissions from vehicle engines. *Nitrogen oxides and ammonia also affect atmospheric chemistry through their involvement in *acid rain and their reactivity with *ozone. Nitrogen can also affect *water quality. *See also* EUTROPHICATION.

nitrogen dioxide (NO$_2$) A reddish-brown *gas that is produced by combustion, when *nitric oxide emitted from power plants and vehicles, and from burning plant material, combines with *oxygen in the atmosphere. It is *toxic at high concentrations, reacts with *moisture in the air to form *nitric acid (which is highly corrosive to metals), and in the presence of sunlight and *volatile organic compounds it

NITROGEN CYCLE

The processes by which *nitrogen circulates in both *organic and *inorganic phases between the *atmosphere, the *soil, and the *biosphere (see Fig. 14). Compared with the other major *biogeochemical cycles it is relatively fast but also very complex. The atmosphere is composed mostly of nitrogen gas (N_2). This is chemically unreactive, which means that it cannot be used directly by plants. In order to make it available to plants, some of the nitrogen is oxidized by energy released in *lightning, and it then dissolves in raindrops to form *nitric acid (HNO_3). Most (more than 90%) of the nitrogen in soils is fixed biologically, and is thus available to plants. The nitrogen gas is used by soil bacteria (particularly the bacteria living in nodules attached to the roots of *legumes such as peas and beans as well as some non-leguminous plants) which convert it into *ammonia (NH_3). Inorganic *nitrate (NO_3^-) and ammonia in the soil are absorbed by plants (via their roots) and turned into organic compounds (such as *proteins) in plant tissue. A proportion of this nitrogen is eaten by *herbivores, which use nitrogen in the form of amino acids from which they synthesize proteins. Some of the nitrogen is passed on in the form of proteins to the *carnivores that feed on the grazing animals. The nitrogen is ultimately returned to the soil as waste products (in urine and faeces) and when organisms die and decompose. Bacteria convert the organic nitrogen into ammonia or *ammonium (NH_4^+) compounds. Other bacteria convert these into *nitrites (NO_2^-) and then into nitrates (NO_3^-) which can be taken up again by plants. Some of the nitrate and ammonia that is not absorbed by plants is leached (washed) from the soil into groundwater and surface water (lakes and rivers), where it provides nutrient supplies for aquatic plants. The oceans are also part of the nitrogen cycle. Some nitrogen accumulates as organic sediment which might through time be compacted and converted into sedimentary rock. The nitrogen can be released back into water by *weathering of the deposits and rocks. Ammonia (NH_3) evaporates quickly when it is released, thus recycling some nitrogen back into the atmosphere. From there it quickly dissolves in raindrops and is washed back to the ground. Special *denitrifying bacteria complete the cycle, converting nitrates to nitrite, nitrites to ammonia, and nitrates to gaseous nitrogen or nitrogen oxides. This effectively recycles all of the nitrogen compounds. The two most important ways in which human activities alter the natural nitrogen cycle are through the use in agriculture of *nitrogen fertilizers, and the release of *nitrogen oxides in *air pollution.

Fig. 14 Nitrogen cycle

can contribute to the formation of ground-level *ozone and *photochemical smog. It is also an important ingredient of *acid rain.

nitrogen fixation A chemical process by which *nitrogen in the atmosphere is assimilated into *organic compounds, by *nitrogen-fixing bacteria and made available to plants and from them to other *organisms through *food chains.

nitrogen oxides (NO$_x$) Any of the seven oxides of *nitrogen, but specifically *nitric oxide (NO) and *nitrogen dioxide (NO$_2$), which are produced directly or indirectly from the combustion of *fossil fuels and plant material, and from processes used in certain chemical plants. NO$_x$ catalyse the formation of ozone in the *troposphere and contribute to the formation of *photochemical smog, but they also destroy ozone in the *stratosphere. Nitrogen dioxide is a *criteria pollutant. All of the nitrogen oxides are *greenhouse gases.

nitrogen-fixing bacteria *Bacteria that convert *nitrogen from the atmosphere or soil into *ammonia, which can then be converted into plant *nutrients by *nitrite- and *nitrate-forming bacteria.

nitrogen-fixing plant A plant that has a *symbiotic association with *nitrogen-fixing bacteria.

nitrogenous waste Any animal or vegetable residues that contain significant amounts of *nitrogen.

nitrosifying bacteria See NITRITE-FORMING BACTERIA.

nitrous oxide (N$_2$O) A powerful and persistent *greenhouse gas, with a *global warming potential of 310 over a 100-year period. It is naturally created by *microbial activity in the *soils of wet tropical forests and dry *savanna grassland, and from the oceans, but its production is increased by soil cultivation practices (particularly rice paddies), the use of commercial and organic *fertilizers, combustion of *fossil fuels, production of *nitric acid, and burning of *biomass. Between them, tropical soils and the oceans account for 70% of the N$_2$O in the atmosphere.

NNR See NATIONAL NATURE RESERVE.

no longer threatened species *Species of plant and animal from which threats have declined, so their survival is not currently threatened.

no till (zero till) Planting a crop without preparing the ground in advance or working it afterwards.

NOAA See NATIONAL OCEANIC AND ATMOSPHERIC ADMINISTRATION.

noble gas See INERT GAS.

noble metal A *metal which is resistant to *corrosion or *oxidation. Ruthenium, rhodium, palladium, *gold, *silver, and platinum are noble metals and some authorities also include *mercury and rhenium. Because of their rarity, several of the noble metals are also precious metals.

noctilucent cloud A wavy, thin, bluish-white type of *cloud that forms at altitudes of 80–90 km, looks similar to *cirrus clouds, and is best seen at *twilight at high latitudes.

nocturnal Active only at night.

nocturnal inversion See RADIATION INVERSION.

node See STANDING WAVE.

nodule 1. A small lump, such as a small rounded lump of mineral substance (e.g. *chert) which is usually harder than the surrounding rock. **2.** A small growth on the roots of most *legumes and some other plants, which contains a colony of *nitrogen-fixing bacteria.

NOEL See NO-OBSERVED-EFFECT LEVEL.

NOHSCP See NATIONAL OIL AND HAZARDOUS SUBSTANCES CONTINGENCY PLAN.

noise 1. Unwanted or undesirable sound, particularly if it is loud and disturbs people's communication, sleep, study, or recreation. **2.** A signal that carries no useful information, e.g. background sounds that make it difficult to hear a conversation.

noise abatement Reducing or eliminating unwanted *noise.

noise pollution *Pollution that is caused by *noise, for example from heavy traffic, busy factories, or large gatherings of people.

nomad A person who lives in no fixed place but has a wandering lifestyle, moving about, often following traditional seasonal routes in search of food or grazing land for livestock.

nomadism The practice of living by moving from place to place, i.e. as a *nomad. Contrast* PASTORALISM; SEDENTISM; TRANSHUMANCE.

nomenclature Names or terms forming a set or a system.

non-abstractive use *See* INSTREAM USE.

Non-Annex 1 Countries Countries that are not included in Annex I of the *United Nations Framework Convention on Climate Change, and that therefore do not currently have binding *emission reduction targets.

Non-Annex B Countries Countries that are not included in Annex B of the *Kyoto Protocol, and that therefore do not currently have binding *emission reduction targets.

non-aqueous phase liquid (NAPL) Any *contaminant that remains undiluted as a bulk liquid in *groundwater, such as spilled liquid *petroleum products (like *gasoline) that are not mixed into groundwater but float as a layer in the rock above it.

non-attainment area An area that does not meet *ambient *air quality standards for a *criteria air pollutant.

non-biodegradable Materials (such as glass, *heavy metals, and most types of plastics) that cannot be broken down by livings things into simpler chemicals.

non-combustible Not capable of catching fire or burning.

non-commercial cutting A tree-felling activity which does not yield a net income, usually because the *trees that are cut are too small, are of poor quality, or are not marketable.

non-commercial vegetative treatment The removal of *trees for reasons other than *timber production.

non-compliance Not obeying all the federal and state regulations that apply.

non-compliance coal (high sulphur coal) A North American term for any coal that emits a relatively large amount of *sulphur dioxide (greater than 3.0 pounds per million *Btu) when burned.

non-consumptive use The use of *resources in ways that do not reduce supply. Examples include hiking, bird watching, and *nature study in a forest. *Contrast* CONSUMPTIVE USE.

non-consumptive value (non-use value, passive use value, existence value) The value of natural resources which are not diminished by their use, that do not require the valuer to have access to them or make active use of them. *Contrast* USE VALUE.

non-consumptive wildlife Any unharvested *wildlife that is valuable for observation, education, enjoyment, and as a natural member of an *ecological community.

non-consumptive wildlife use A general term for a variety of recreational activities related to wildlife. Primary non-consumptive uses include general wildlife observation, bird-watching, bird-feeding, and wildlife and bird photography. Secondary uses include nature walks, membership of wildlife organizations, ownership of wildlife pets, and visits to zoos.

non-conventional pollutant *See* NON-CRITERIA POLLUTANT.

non-criteria pollutant (non-conventional pollutant, unconventional pollutant) Any *pollutant (such as *asbestos, *benzene, *mercury, and *polychlorinated biphenyls) that is not a *criteria pollutant.

non-ferrous metal Any *metal other than *iron or an *alloy containing iron. Examples include *aluminium, *lead, and *copper.

non-forest land Land that is not used for *forestry or *timber production, but is used for other activities such as *farming, transport, industry, commerce, or housing.

non-game species *Wildlife species that are not hunted for *sport.

non-governmental organization (NGO) A non-profit group or association that is separate from government, and whose purpose is to pursue particular social objectives (such as *environmental protection) or to serve particular constituencies (such as *indigenous peoples). Examples include the *World Wide Fund for Nature and the Red Cross.

Nongovernmental International Panel on Climate Change (NIPCC) A panel of scientists and scholars who aim to understand the causes and consequences of climate change. Since they are not linked to governments and are not predisposed to believe greenhouse gas emissions by human activities are responsible for climate change they are able to examine evidence that the *Intergovernmental Panel on Climate Change ignores.

(⊕) SEE WEB LINKS

• NIPCC home page.

non-hydric soil A *soil that has developed mainly under *aerobic conditions.

non-ionizing electromagnetic radiation *Radiation (e.g. *visible light, *infrared, near *ultraviolet, *microwaves, *radio waves, and low-frequency *electromagnetic fields from high-voltage transmission lines) that does not *ionize atoms. Some forms of non-ionizing radiation heat tissue and may cause harmful biological effects.

non-market cost See SOCIAL COST. See also TRUE COST.

non-market damage Financial damages that are generated by *environmental change (such as *climate change), which cannot be evaluated in terms of *market failure because of a lack of information and/or an inability to act on the available information.

non-market values Estimated values for goods and services that are not traded for money but are valued in terms of what reasonable people should be willing to pay rather than go without them. Examples include fish and wildlife values and scenic quality values. Contrast MARKET VALUES. See also CONTINGENT VALUATION METHOD.

non-metallic Not containing, resembling, or having the properties of a *metal.

non-native See EXOTIC.

non-native species See INTRODUCED SPECIES.

non-permeable surface Any surface material that will not allow water to penetrate, such as roads and concrete.

non-persistent pesticide A *pesticide which has only short-lasting effects. Contrast PERSISTENT PESTICIDE.

non-point sources Scattered sources of *pollutants, such as runoff from *agriculture, *forestry, an *urban area, *mining, *construction, *dams, land disposal, and *saltwater intrusion. Contrast POINT SOURCE.

non-potable water Water that is unsafe or unpalatable to drink because it contains *pollu-tants, *contaminants, *minerals, or infectious *agents. Contrast POTABLE WATER.

non-renewable energy *Energy (such as the *fossil fuels: *oil, *natural gas, and *coal) that comes from a *natural resource which is not replaced, or is replaced only very slowly, by natural processes.

non-renewable resource (depletable resource, stock resource) A *natural resource (such as *oil) which cannot be replaced when it is used up. Contrast RENEWABLE RESOURCE.

non-silicate Rock forming minerals that do not contain *silicates.

non-statutory Not a legal requirement.

non-supercell tornado See LANDSPOUT.

non-target species 1. A *species that is not intentionally targeted for control by a *pesticide or *herbicide, but which may suffer damage because of exposure to it. 2. That part of a catch (e.g. of fish) which excludes the *target species but includes the *bycatch and *byproduct.

non-transmissable disease A *disease (such as *cancer and heart disease) that cannot be transmitted by a *micro-organism through human contact.

non-use value See NON-CONSUMPTIVE VALUE.

non-vascular plant A *bryophyte. Contrast VASCULAR PLANT.

no-observed-effect level (NOEL) The *exposure level at which no statistically or biological significant differences in the frequency or severity of any effect can be detected between an exposed and a control population.

noosphere The sphere of human thought, analogous to the atmosphere, biosphere, lithosphere, etc.

no-regrets policy 1. An approach to *environmental policy that is based on the idea that the problem of global *climate change is linked to other critically important problems of *environment and *development, the combined risks of which are serious enough, and the eventual benefits of action great enough, to require bold initiatives without delay, even if they impose great immediate cost. 2. An approach to *management that involves erring on the side of caution and planning well in advance. See also PRECAUTIONARY PRINCIPLE.

norm 1. Normal, average, or most common. **2.** An expected standard of behaviour and belief that is established and enforced by a group.

normal distribution *See* GAUSSIAN CURVE.

normal fault The simplest type of vertical displacement *fault, in which one side falls relative to the other. The higher side survives as a cliff-like *escarpment. Normal faults can develop from either *compression pressure or from *tension pressure.

north The compass point that is at 0° or 360°.

north/northern General term that is used to describe the *industrialized countries which are located mainly in the *northern hemisphere and are sometimes referred to as the *First World. This includes Canada, the USA, Western European countries, the former Soviet Union, Japan, Australia, and New Zealand. *Contrast* SOUTH.

North Atlantic Drift *See* GULF STREAM.

North Atlantic Oscillation (NAO) A periodic change in the distribution of surface atmospheric pressure between the regions around Iceland and the Azores, reported as an NAO index. When pressure is lower than average over Iceland and higher than average over the Azores the index is high; when pressure is relatively high over Iceland and low over the Azores the index is low. The NAO generates winds that drive weather systems in an easterly direction across the North Atlantic. When the index is high, increasing the pressure difference, the systems move rapidly; when it is low, reducing the difference, they move more slowly. These changes affect weather conditions on both sides of the ocean.

North Pole The most northerly point on Earth, at a latitude of 90°N in the *northern hemisphere; the northern end of the Earth's rotational axis. *Contrast* SOUTH POLE.

North–South divide The gap, particularly in financial well-being, between richer *developed countries and poorer *developing countries. The term is also used to describe socio-economic differences between northern and southern England.

north-east African highland-and-steppe floral region Part of R. Good's African subkingdom (*The Geography of the Flowering Plants*, 1974), within his *Palaeotropical floral kingdom. It contains about 50 *endemic

genera, although the island of Socotra off the Horn of Africa accounts for nearly half of these despite the fact that it is not notably isolated. *Coffea arabica* is native to this region.

northern hemisphere The half of the Earth that lies *north of the *equator. *Contrast* SOUTHERN HEMISPHERE.

northern lights *See* AURORA.

northern spotted owl A *threatened species of owl (*Strix occidentalis caurina*) which is nocturnal, feeds on small mammals and birds, and lives in *old growth forests of northern California and the Pacific Northwest of the USA and in southern parts of British Columbia, Canada. Its survival is under threat from the loss of old growth forest habitat, as a result of *logging and forest fragmentation, but also as a result of natural disasters such as fire, volcanic eruptions, and wind storms. The species is protected under the *Endangered Species Act and under *CITES.

not at risk A general term for a *species that has been evaluated and found not to be at risk of becoming *extinct or *extirpated.

not in my backyard (NIMBY) The belief that certain types of hazardous activities and substances may be needed or acceptable, but not round here. *See also* LULU.

not threatened category of species A category for *species under threat, developed as *IUCN Conservation (Red Data Book) Categories, and widely used around the world. The only category within this group is *safe.

no-take reserve A special type of *nature reserve in which, by law, no one is allowed to fish or collect biological specimens. Rules could apply to one or all species.

notice of intent A formal notice, published in the US federal register, of intent to prepare an *environmental impact statement on a proposed action.

notification The process of official designation of a protected area, such as the notification of a *Site of Special Scientific Interest in the UK.

Notogea The Australasian *faunal region, which possesses a very distinctive fauna. It comprises Australia, New Guinea, Tasmania, New Zealand, and the islands to the south and east of Wallace's line. It can be subdivided into the

Australian, Polynesian, and Hawaiian regions. *Compare* ARCTOGEA; NEOGEA.

nowcast A short-term *weather *forecast, generally for up to two hours.

noxious Irritating, unpleasant, or harmful to living *organisms.

noxious species Plant species that can be harmful or even fatal when eaten by animals.

NPK *Nitrogen (N), *phosphorus (P), and *potassium (K), which are common ingredients in commercial *fertilizers.

NPL *See* NATIONAL PRIORITIES LIST.

NPP *See* PRIMARY PRODUCTION.

NPS *See* NATIONAL PARK SERVICE.

NPV *See* NET PRESENT VALUE.

N-rank *See* NATIONAL RANK.

NRAs *See* NATURAL RESOURCE ACCOUNTS.

NRC *See* NATIONAL RESPONSE CENTER.

nuclear energy *Energy or *power that is produced by *nuclear reactions. Nuclear power currently uses only *nuclear fission.

nuclear fission (splitting the atom) A *nuclear reaction process in which *isotopes of certain heavy elements (such as *uranium and *plutonium) are bombarded with *neutrons, which atoms of the element absorb, rendering them unstable and causing each atom to divide into two smaller *atoms, with the release of a vast amount of *energy.

nuclear fuel *Fuel (such as *uranium) that can be used to generate electricity in a *nuclear reactor in a *nuclear power plant.

nuclear fuel cycle The sequence of processes that are associated with the use of *nuclear fuel, from initial mining and milling of the *ore, through conversion and *enrichment of the nuclear fuel, its use in *nuclear power plants, and the management of *nuclear waste.

nuclear fusion A *nuclear reaction process in which several light *nuclei are combined to make a heavier one whose mass is slightly less than the combined mass of the lighter nuclei, which releases energy. This is the reaction that fuels the Sun, where hydrogen nuclei are fused to form helium; it is also one source of power in

a *nuclear weapon and in the future it may be a source of energy for power generation.

(⊕) SEE WEB LINKS
• Nuclear fusion.

nuclear medicine A branch of medicine which uses *radioactive substances for the diagnosis and treatment of disease (such as *cancer).

nuclear pile US name for a *nuclear reactor.

nuclear power *See* NUCLEAR ENERGY.

nuclear power plant/station An electric power plant that converts *nuclear energy into *electrical energy. Heat that is generated by a *nuclear reaction is used to make steam, which drives a *turbine, which in turn drives an electric generator.

nuclear reaction A change in the composition of an atomic nucleus, caused by bombarding it with atomic or subatomic particles or very high energy radiation (e.g. in a *nuclear reactor). This process can form a new nucleus (*nuclear fusion) or split the original nucleus (*nuclear fission), and it releases a large amount of energy.

nuclear reactor A device in which *nuclear fission may be initiated, maintained, and controlled to produce energy, conduct research, or produce *fissile material for nuclear explosives. Known in the USA as a nuclear pile.

nuclear reactor and support facilities Facilities that are associated with the civilian use of *nuclear energy, including uranium mills, commercial power reactors, fuel reprocessing plants, and uranium *enrichment facilities.

nuclear test Military tests of *nuclear weapons that are carried out with government approval, in order to improve the design of nuclear weapons and to study the impacts and effects of nuclear explosions.

nuclear war Warfare that uses *nuclear weapons. *See also* NUCLEAR WINTER.

nuclear waste *See* RADIOACTIVE WASTE.

nuclear weapon (radiological weapon) A device that releases *nuclear energy from a *nuclear reaction in an explosive manner, in order to damage structures and materials and to kill or injure large numbers of people. A *weapon of mass destruction.

nuclear winter A long period of darkness and a drop in temperature of 20–40°C that a group of scientists predicted in 1983 would follow a full-scale *nuclear war, caused by the blocking out of sunlight by a layer of dust and smoke in the atmosphere, which few organisms could survive. Worst case scenarios predicted that nuclear war and nuclear winter would kill most plants and animals in the northern hemisphere and threaten the very survival of the human species. Subsequent climate models modified the original scenario and few climate scientists accept the nuclear winter theory.

nucleation The formation of a mineral or ice crystal or a water droplet around an initiating particle that acts as a nucleus. Water vapour requires a suitable surface on which to condense from saturated air; in clouds, water vapour condenses on to *cloud condensation nuclei. In the absence of *freezing nuclei water will remain in the gaseous *phase at temperatures as low as –40°C. See CONDENSATION; DEPOSITION; FREEZING.

nucleic acid A biological *molecule, composed of a long chain of *nucleotides, which controls activities in cells, helps in the synthesis of *proteins, and transmits *hereditary traits.

nucleotide The basic building block of *DNA, which consists of a sugar, a *phosphate, and an organic base that contains *nitrogen. Thousands of nucleotides are linked to form a *molecule of DNA or *RNA. See also NUCLEIC ACID.

nucleus 1. The centre of an *atom, which is composed of *protons and *neutrons. **2.** The part of a cell that contains the *chromosomes (*DNA). **3.** A particle (e.g. of dust or salt) on which water molecules or ice accumulate to form *raindrops, *snow, *hail, and other forms of *precipitation. See also CLOUD CONDENSATION NUCLEI.

nuclide Any species of *atom that exists for a measurable length of time, and is defined by the number of *protons and *neutrons in its *nucleus. A nuclide may be *radioactive.

nudation The creation of an area of bare land, either by natural events or by humans, which is the first stage in vegetation *succession.

nuée ardente A 'glowing cloud' that forms when a burning-hot ash, gas, steam, and rock emerges from a *volcano and flows downhill, burning everything in its path. Since the *pyroclastic flow behaves differently from the cloud of ash and gas above it, volcanologists tend to avoid using the term.

nuisance bloom A rapid increase of one or a few species of *phytoplankton in a water body, which discolours the surface water, often increases the concentration of *toxins, and reduces *water quality (particularly the concentration of *dissolved oxygen). See also ALGAL BLOOM.

nunatak A *mountain ridge that sticks up through an *ice sheet. They are usually angular with sharply defined ridges, caused by intense *freeze–thaw *weathering processes.

nuptial feeding Feeding of offspring by the male.

nurse tree A *tree that is grown to shelter and protect other young plants which are at a vulnerable stage of growth.

nursery A place where *plants are *propagated and grown to usable size, when they can be planted elsewhere.

nursery area An area (*range) that is used for *grazing during the summer months by a temporary social unit of *big game (cows and young calves).

nursery stock A *shrub or *tree species that is grown in a *nursery for subsequent planting out elsewhere.

nutrient Any chemical compound (such as *protein, fat, *carbohydrate, *vitamins, or *minerals) that provides the chemical energy (food) needed by living *organisms. See also MACRONUTRIENT; MICRONUTRIENT.

nutrient cycle The natural circulation of chemical elements (such as *carbon and *nitrogen) and compounds through specific pathways from the *abiotic parts of *ecosystems into the organic substances of the *biotic parts, and back again to the abiotic parts. A local example of the *biogeochemical cycle.

nutrient deficiency The lack of an adequate amount of a particular *nutrient which is important for the growth and health of plants and animals.

nutrient depletion A reduction in the level of *nutrients in a *habitat or *ecosystem, caused by uptake by plants, removal of plant residues, or *leaching, to a level at which they become unavailable for further uptake. The opposite of *nutrient enrichment.

nutrient enrichment An increase in the level of *nutrients in a *habitat or *ecosystem. The opposite of *nutrient depletion. *See also* EUTROPHICATION.

nutrient loading The quantity of *nutrients that is washed into a waterbody from its drain-age basin, usually expressed as mass per unit area per unit time (kilograms per hectare per year, kg ha^{-1} year^{-1}).

nutrient pollution *Contamination of *water resources by excessive inputs of *nutrients. *See also* EUTROPHICATION.

NWF *See* NATIONAL WILDLIFE FEDERATION.

NWS *See* NATIONAL WEATHER SERVICE.

oasis 1. In an arid region, an isolated area that supports plants throughout the year. Oases most commonly occur in depressions, where the *water table lies close enough to the surface to be within the reach of plant roots. The *groundwater supplying the vegetation is often enriched with salts and the vegetation can be zoned according to the concentration and type of salts present. **2.** By analogy, a small area supporting vegetation of one type (e.g. woodland) which is surrounded on all sides by a much larger area supporting vegetation of a quite different type (e.g. an arable field).

objective A high-level statement of what is desired in any project or activity, often expressed as a specific statement of the measurable results that are to be achieved within a stated time period.

obligate Without option; of a *species, restricted to specific environmental conditions and thus unable to change its mode of feeding or ecological relationships. *Compare* FACULTATIVE.

obligate mutualist A beneficial *symbiont that lives exclusively in the *host and depends on the host for survival. *Contrast* FACULTATIVE MUTUALIST.

obligation A legal responsibility.

oblique-slip fault A geological *fault that involves both vertical (*dip-slope) and horizontal (*strike-slip) movements.

obliquity The angle between the Earth's axis of rotation and a line passing through the centre of the Earth at right angles to the plane of the *ecliptic. The tilt varies over a cycle of about 42 000 years from 22.1° to 24.5°; at present it is 23.45°. This angle determines the latitude of the *tropics.

obsidian (volcanic glass) A black or dark green *extrusive *volcanic glass that is formed from fast-cooling *lava and has a similar chemical composition to *granite.

occidental From or relating to the western *hemisphere. *Contrast* ORIENTAL.

occluded front *See* OCCLUSION.

occlusion (occluded front) The final stage in the decay of a *depression, where the *cold front overtakes the *warm front of the depression, with cold air pushing under and lifting the warm sector completely clear of the ground surface. Occlusions are labelled warm or cold according to whether the air behind them is warmer or cooler than the air ahead. *See also* CYCLOGENESIS; FRONTOGENESIS.

occult precipitation *Precipitation arriving at a location by processes that would normally go unrecorded by a standard rain gauge, e.g. the condensation of *mist and *fog on foliage.

occupational exposure Exposure (for example to *pollutants and *toxic *agents) that people incur in the course of their work.

Occupational Safety and Health Act (OSHA) A federal law in the USA that defines minimum health and safety standards for the workplace.

occurrence In *epidemiology, the frequency of a *disease or event in a *population. *See also* INCIDENCE; PREVALENCE.

ocean The body of saltwater that surrounds the continents and covers two-thirds of the surface of Earth. The average depth of the ocean floor is more than 3790 m below sea level, and the total volume of the world's oceans is estimated at around 1370 million km^3.

ocean bed *See* OCEAN FLOOR.

ocean current The steady flow or circulation of surface water in a prevailing direction within the *ocean, as a non-tidal current. There are three types of oceanic currents: *drift currents, stream currents, and *upwelling currents. *See also* GULF STREAM.

ocean dumping The disposal of *hazardous wastes and other substances by dumping them in the deep waters of the *oceans. *See also* OFF-SHORE DUMPING.

Ocean Dumping Act *See* MARINE PROTECTION, RESEARCH, AND SANCTUARIES ACT (1972).

ocean energy sources Existing *marine sources of *renewable energy include ocean *thermal energy, *tidal power, *wave energy, and offshore *wind power stations. Future possibilities include exploitation of submarine *geothermal energy and marine *biogas energy, and energy generated by exploiting *salinity gradients within the oceans.

ocean floor (abyss, ocean bed) The *ecological zone that lies beyond the *continental shelf, *continental slope, and *continental rise; it underlies most of the major oceans, is often far from flat, and at depths greater than about 2000 m is largely covered by fine-textured sediment (*ooze) composed mostly of organic matter (see Fig. 15). It occupies approximately one-third of the floors of the Atlantic and Indian Oceans, and 75% of the Pacific floor.

ocean pollution *Pollution of ocean waters, both directly (such as by *oil spills) and indirectly via *rivers that flow into the sea.

ocean trench A deep, linear valley on the *ocean floor, which runs parallel to the *coast, and marks an active *subduction zone at the margins of one of the *continents, where one *crustal plate is pushed down beneath another at a *destructive plate boundary. The deepest known ocean trench is the Marianas Trench in the Pacific Ocean, which is 11 033 m below sea level.

Oceanian realm A *biogeographical realm that covers the Pacific Ocean and is dominated by *tropical forest.

oceanic Relating to or occurring in the open sea, beyond the *continental shelf.

oceanic climate *See* MARITIME CLIMATE.

oceanic conveyor belt (Atlantic conveyor, Great Conveyor) The closed loop of ocean currents that carries cold water away from the edge of the Arctic Circle in the North Atlantic and warm water from the Pacific through the Indian Ocean and into the Atlantic. Cold, saline water near the edge of the North Atlantic sea ice sinks beneath less dense water and flows southwards to the edge of the Circumpolar Current and from there into the Indian and Pacific Oceans, where it rises to become a system of surface currents. It forms the North Pacific gyre, flows westwards, and enters the South Atlantic, where it flows northwards and forms the North Atlantic gyre.

oceanic crust The part of the Earth's *crust that is formed at *mid-ocean ridges, underlies the *oceans, and is generally 5–10 km thick. Oceanic crust is thinner, denser, and heavier than *continental crust. It consists mostly of *basaltic types of rocks, and geologists formerly referred to this material as *sima. Because of the movements of *plate tectonics, the oceanic crust is nowhere older than about 200 million years. *Sea-floor spreading is continuously creating new oceanic crust, and *subduction is

Fig. 15 **Ocean floor**

continuously destroying existing crust, like some huge non-stop geological conveyor belt.

oceanic front A boundary that separates masses of water within the *ocean that have different temperatures and densities.

oceanic island An *island in the ocean, which will often support a distinctive *community of plants and animals, and may be a *centre of endemism. Such islands are formed in various ways, including by breaking away from a continental landmass, volcanic action, coral formation, or a combination of processes.

oceanic ridge One of a number of extensive, sinuous, underwater *mountain chains which are found on the *ocean floor, and which mark the boundaries of some *crustal plates.

oceanography The study of the *oceans, their origin, composition, history, and ecology.

octa See OKTA.

odour A smell.

odour threshold The lowest concentration of a chemical or *contaminant that can be smelled.

ODP See OZONE DEPLETION POTENTIAL.

Odum, Eugene Pleasants (1913–2002) An American ecologist who worked mainly at the University of Georgia. He pioneered the study of *ecosystems, *population dynamics, and *ecological energetics, and had a particular interest in wetland ecology, resource use, and ornithology. His *Fundamentals of Ecology* (first edition published in 1953) has been widely used for many years.

OECD See ORGANISATION FOR ECONOMIC CO-OPERATION AND DEVELOPMENT.

offer (ask) In *greenhouse gas *emissions trading, the price at which the owner of an emission reduction, credit, or allowance is willing to sell.

off-gas The *gas *effluent that is given off during any stage of an industrial process.

official development assistance Funding that is provided by the government of a *developed country to the governments of *developing countries, to pay for particular community, health, and commercial projects.

off-road vehicle (ORV) Any vehicle that is intended for use on unmade surfaces or rough terrain, including all-terrain vehicles,

mini-bikes, trail bikes, dirt bikes, dune buggies, and golf carts, but excluding snowmobiles.

offset A form of credit-based *emissions trading. An offset is created when a source reduces its *emissions by more than it is required to, on a voluntary, permanent basis. The source can then trade that offset (the extra emissions) to new sources to allow growth or relocation, with regulators approving each trade. See also BUBBLE; NETTING.

offset ratio In *greenhouse gas *emissions trading, the ratio between the amount by which on-site emissions are allowed to increase and the size of *offset that is purchased. In US domestic emission trading programmes, new sources must offset their emissions at a ratio greater than 1:1.

offshore All areas *seaward of the *coastline. *Contrast* INSHORE.

offshore breeze (land breeze) A light *wind that blows from the land out over the sea, usually late in the day when the land surface is cooling faster than the water. *Contrast* ONSHORE BREEZE; SEA BREEZE.

offshore dumping The disposal or dumping of waste material off or away from the shore. See also OCEAN DUMPING.

offshore facility Any facility (other than a vessel) that is located in, on, or under the water *offshore, and is subject to the *jurisdiction of a particular country.

offshore waters Ocean waters beyond the *inshore, between about 60 and 250 *nautical miles from land.

offshore zone The zone that extends seawards from the point of low tide to the depth of wave-base level, or to the outer edge of the *continental shelf.

off-site See EX SITU.

off-site facility A *facility for the treatment, storage, or disposal of *hazardous waste that is located away from the site where that material is created. *Contrast* ON-SITE FACILITY.

offspring Immediate *descendants.

offstream use (abstractive use) Water that is withdrawn from surface or *groundwater sources for use at another place, principally for domestic supply, industrial cooling and processes, *irrigation, livestock, power generation, and other uses, i.e. a use that does not return the water to the source from which it was taken (abstracted). *Contrast* INSTREAM USE.

ogive 1. (Forbes band) Alternating bands on the surface of a *glacier. These may be caused by variations in longitudinal pressure and often appear as bands of white and dark ice, containing many and few air bubbles, respectively. **2. (wave ogive)** Undulations in the glacier surface caused by ablation and plastic deformation as the glacier moves down an *ice fall.

O-horizon The layer rich in *organic matter within the *A-horizon of a *soil.

oil 1. In general, any viscous liquid, which includes natural plant and animals oils. **2.** A thick, black, sticky *hydrocarbon substance that is used to produce *fuel (petroleum) and materials (plastics). Oil is one of the world's principal *fossil fuel resources, and known reserves are fast being depleted. About two-thirds of the world's known *recoverable reserves are in the Middle East. Since the 1970s technology has allowed the pumping of oil from offshore fields (including the North Sea) and from the frozen north of Alaska. Exploitation and use of oil resources has a number of *environmental impacts, including *oil pollution. Burning of petroleum is a major cause of *air pollution, and the transport of oil (particularly at sea in large *oil tankers) has caused some major environmental disasters, including *oil spills.

oil desulphurization A method of reducing *sulphur dioxide emissions from *power plants that burn *oil, in which the oil is treated with hydrogen (forming *hydrogen sulphide gas and reducing the sulphur content of the oil) before combustion.

oil fingerprinting A method of identifying the chemical characteristics of a particular *oil, which allows *oil spills to be traced to their source.

oil pipeline A pipe along which *oil is transported from the *refinery to other places.

oil pollution *Pollution of soil and water as the result of an *oil spill.

oil rig A structure that stands on the *sea-bed over a submarine *oilfield, which provides a stable base above water for drilling *oil wells.

oil shale A dark grey or black *shale that contains organic substances that can be distilled to yield liquid *hydrocarbons, but does not contain free *petroleum.

oil slick A layer of *oil floating on an area of water, usually as a result of an *oil spill.

oil spill An accidental leakage of *oil from a container such as a storage tank, *oil tanker, or *oil pipeline, which causes *pollution of the surrounding area. Oil spills at sea can cause extensive ecological and environmental damage. Toxic chemicals leach out from the oil and contaminate the surrounding water, poisoning sea life around and below the spill. Light oils can float freely on the ocean surface, and be dispersed over a wide area, but they evaporate quickly. Heavy oils sometimes form globules (small spherical lumps) which sink to the sea-bed and poison plants and animals that live there. When an oil slick drifts or is blown towards the coast it can seriously pollute the shore, fouling beaches and killing all shore life. The oil clogs the feathers of birds, so that they lose their waterproofing quality and the birds ingest the oil trying to preen them. Most other coastal creatures are suffocated by the oil. Procedures that are used to control and remove oil slicks include *containment, *absorption, and *dispersal. *See also* EXXON VALDEZ.

oil tanker A cargo ship that is designed to carry *crude oil in bulk.

oil well A vertical shaft that is drilled through rock to reach and extract the *oil that is stored naturally in an *oilfield beneath. At sea, the well is sunk from an *oil rig.

oilfield An area where *oil is trapped in *porous rocks beneath the ground or the *sea-bed, from where it can be extracted via an *oil well.

okta (octa) The unit most often used to report the extent of cloud cover: 1 okta = one-eighth of the sky. Symbols for cloud cover are in oktas, but can be converted to tenths as: 1/8 = 1/10 or less; 2/8 = 2/10–3/10; 3/8 = 4/10; 4/8 = 5/10; 6/8 = 7/10–8/10; 7/8 = 9/10 or overcast but with gaps in the cloud cover.

old age 1. The latter part of the *life cycle of an organism, after *maturity. **2.** A late stage in the *cycle of erosion that is characterized by formation of a *peneplain near sea level. *Contrast* MATURITY; YOUTH.

old growth forest A North American term for an ecologically mature *forest that has not been significantly altered by humans for at least 120 years, and which contains old trees (more than 200 years old), fallen trees, trees with broken tops, and mature and dying trees. *See also* ANCIENT FOREST; OVERMATURE FOREST.

old-field ecosystem An *ecosystem that develops on abandoned farmland in a sequence known as old-field succession. The terms are most commonly used in the USA.

Oligocene An epoch of geological time within the *Paleogene period, extending from 33.9 to 23 million years ago. The Alps began to form as the African plate pushed northwards into the Eurasian plate.

(🌐) SEE WEB LINKS

• Oligocene.

oligohaline Relating to *brackish water, with a *salinity of between 0.5 and 5.0 parts per thousand (‰).

oligolectic Applied to a *pollinator which collects *pollen from a few species of plant. *Contrast* MONOLECTIC; POLYLECTIC.

oligomictic Applied to lakes that are thermally almost stable, mixing only rarely. This condition is characteristic of tropical lakes with very high (20–30°C) surface temperatures.

oligotrophic Deficient in the *nutrients that are needed for plant growth. The term is usually applied to water or soil. *Contrast* EUTROPHIC.

oligoxenous Applied to a *parasite that lives within more than one host during its *life cycle. *Contrast* MONOXENOUS.

olivine An olive-green, greyish-green, or brown *silicate mineral that contains *magnesium and *iron, and is common in *basalt and in some *meteorites.

ombrogenous bog A *peat-forming vegetation community lying above *groundwater level; it is separated from the ground flora and the mineral soil, and is thus dependent on rainwater for mineral nutrients. The resulting lack of dissolved bases gives strongly acidic conditions and only specialized vegetation, predominantly *Sphagnum* species (bog mosses), will grow. Two types of ombrogenous bogs are commonly distinguished: *raised bogs and *blanket bogs. *Compare* VALLEY BOG. The elevated bog forest found in the coastal regions of some of the islands of south-east Asia comprises a third type of ombrogenous bog. These bog forests form extensive domes, often more than 10 km in diameter, and their surfaces are elevated 5–10 m above the groundwater table.

ombrotrophic An *ecosystem (such as a raised *mire) that is entirely dependent on atmospheric sources (mainly *precipitation) for its supply of water and *nutrients.

omnivore An *organism (such as a human) that eats both plants and animals. *Contrast* HERBIVORE; CARNIVORE.

omnivorous Capable of eating plant and animal material.

onchocerciasis *See* RIVER BLINDNESS.

oncogenic Capable of producing tumours in animals, which can be either benign (non-cancerous) or malignant (cancerous).

oncology The study and treatment of cancer.

onion skin weathering *See* EXFOLIATION.

onshore On or towards the land.

onshore breeze *See* SEA BREEZE.

on-site facility A *facility for the treatment, storage, or disposal of *hazardous waste that is located on the site where that material is created. *Contrast* OFF-SITE FACILITY.

ontogenetic Of or relating to the origin and development of individual *organisms. *Contrast* PHYLOGENETIC.

ontogeny The history of the development and growth (*life cycle) of an individual.

ooid *See* OOLITIC LIMESTONE.

oolitic limestone A type of *limestone formed as a *chemical precipitate, and consisting of small spherical grains of *calcium carbonate (ooids) that have formed around tiny *nuclei.

oomycetes (water mould, downy mildews) A class (Oomycota) of fungus-like organisms that are single-celled, filamentous, and reproduce both sexually and asexually. Some oomycetes are serious *pathogens of plants and others infect fish. The serious plant pathogens include *Phytophthora*, the genus that causes dieback, sudden oak death, and late blight of potato.

ooze A fine-textured sediment that is formed from the remains of *pelagic organisms and is found on the *ocean floor.

opacity Lack of transparency, or the ability to keep light from passing through: for example, a glass window has almost 0% opacity, whereas a concrete wall has 100% opacity.

opaque Not allowing light to pass through.

opaque mineral A *mineral which transmits no light through a thin section under a microscope. Usually a *native metal, *sulphide, or metallic oxide mineral.

OPEC *See* ORGANIZATION OF PETROLEUM EXPORTING COUNTRIES.

open access system A *resource that is openly available to all users, without conditions or restrictions.

open burning The uncontrolled burning of *waste materials in the open, either in an outdoor *incinerator or an *open dump, either accidentally or on purpose.

open canopy forest *See* WOODLAND.

open cast mining (opencut mining, surface mining) The *mining of *minerals that occur near the surface, which are extracted through an open excavation. First the *overburden is removed, and then the mineral materials are broken up and removed. *See also* MOUNTAIN TOP REMOVAL; OPEN-PIT MINING.

open dump An uncovered *dump site in which *waste is left without environmental controls.

open forest *See* WOODLAND.

open range Unfenced, natural *grazing land, which includes *woodland as well as *grassland.

open sea That part of the ocean that lies beyond the *continental shelf. Similar to *high sea. *Contrast* COASTAL ZONE.

open space Public and private land that is undeveloped, which often retains its natural *vegetation, and is usually used for *recreation or as a reserve to protect natural areas.

open space zoning All types of land use *zoning (such as *large-lot zoning and *cluster zoning) which restrict land uses in order to preserve open space.

open system A *system that can exchange both matter and energy with its surrounding *environment. *Contrast* CLOSED SYSTEM.

open vegetation In *habitat evaluation, all *clearcuts, *meadows, and other openings.

opencut mining *See* OPEN CAST MINING.

open-pit mining A method of mineral or coal extraction that is used where the *overburden is limited and easily stripped, but where waste has to be transported to external dumps. It is generally used where deposits are limited laterally but are thicker than in *open cast mining.

operational research (management science) The use of analytical methods, usually with a computer, adopted from mathematics for solving operational problems.

opportunist species *See* FUGITIVE SPECIES.

opportunity cost The real cost of satisfying a want, expressed in terms of the cost of sacrificing an alternative. If capital or labour might earn a particular sum if engaged in some activity other than that in which it is presently engaged, then the forfeiture of that sum is the opportunity cost of the present activity. If the opportunity cost is less than the value of the present activity then the present activity can be justified economically. *See also* SOCIAL COST.

optimist, environmental (technological optimist) A person who is inclined to take a favourable view of the *environmental crisis and what can be done about it, for example by believing that the development of new *technology, better use of *environmental economics, and improvement in *resource management will further expand the Earth's *carrying capacity. *Contrast* PESSIMIST, ENVIRONMENTAL. *See also* SKEPTICAL ENVIRONMENTALIST.

optimization The process of making something as fully effective as possible, for example by selecting the most cost-effective combination of management practices.

optimum The most favourable condition under given circumstances.

optimum land use The *optimum use of available *land resources in a particular place or area, defined relative to stated management *objectives.

optimum yield The harvest level for a particular *species that achieves the greatest overall benefits, taking into account economic, social, and biological factors. This differs from *maximum sustainable yield, which considers only the biology of the *species.

option A right or agreement to buy or sell a specific commodity (including *emissions allowances) at a stipulated price and within a stated period of time. If the option is not exercised during that time, the money that has been paid for the option is forfeited.

option value The value that people place on having the option to enjoy something (such as the use of a particular *resource, or the ability to take part in a particular activity) in the future, even though they may not currently use it. The potential value of the resource for future (direct or indirect) use.

orchard A *plantation of fruit or nut trees that is managed to yield high quality produce on a *sustainable basis.

orchard heater (smudge pot) An oil heater that is placed in an *orchard in order to generate smoke and promote convective circulations to protect fruit trees from damaging low temperatures which result from the radiative cooling of the layer of air immediately above ground level.

order The fourth highest category (of seven) in the scientific system of classification for organisms (*taxonomy), below *class and above *family. Thus each class comprises more than one order, and each order comprises more than one family.

ordinance A regulation or statute (such as a local building code) that is enacted by a city government in the USA, under powers delegated to it by the state.

ordnance Military weapons and equipment.

Ordovician The second period of geological time in the *Palaeozoic era, dating from 488.3 to 443.7 million years ago, during which the first species of fish and fungi appear in one of the largest spurts of *adaptive radiation in history, and plants first move on to land.

(⊕) SEE WEB LINKS
• The Ordovician period of the Palaeozoic era.

ore Any naturally occurring *mineral or rock from which economically important constituents (such as *metals) can be extracted.

organelle A *cell structure that carries out a specialized function, such as *mitochondria.

organic Involving, related to, or derived from living matter or living organisms, including *compounds that contain *carbon.

Organic Administration Act (1897) US legislation that authorized the Secretary of Agriculture to manage the *National Forests to improve and protect the forests, to secure favourable conditions of water flow, and to furnish a continuous supply of timber.

organic agriculture (organic farming) The production of *crops without the use of *inorganic inputs (such as chemical *fertilizers and *pesticides). Fertilizer is derived from organic material such as animal *manure, *green manure, and *compost. *See also* ALTERNATIVE AGRICULTURE.

organic chemistry The chemistry of substances that contain *carbon. *Contrast* INORGANIC CHEMISTRY.

organic compound Any compound that contains *carbon which is chemically bound to *hydrogen. *Contrast* INORGANIC COMPOUND.

organic farming *See* ORGANIC AGRICULTURE.

organic matter Material in *soil that contains *carbon and is derived from living plants and animals. The organic matter breaks down by *decomposition to produce *humus.

organic nitrogen *Nitrogen that is bound to compounds (*amino acids and *proteins) which contain *carbon, and that must be subjected to *mineralization or *decomposition before it can be used by *plants. *Contrast* INORGANIC NITROGEN.

organic sedimentary rock A *sedimentary rock (such as *limestone, *chalk, *coal, and *oil shale) that is composed of the compacted decayed remains of plants and animals.

organic soil Any *soil that contains a high percentage (usually more than 25%) of *organic matter in the upper *horizons, where living roots are mostly found. *Contrast* MINERAL SOIL.

organic waste In general, any *waste that contains *carbon, which includes *paper, plastics, *wood, food waste, and *yard waste. The term is most often used to describe material that is directly derived from plant or animal sources, which can be decomposed by *microorganisms.

Organisation for Economic Co-operation and Development (OECD) A forum that was founded in 1961 for monitoring economic trends in its member countries from the free-market democracies of North America, Western Europe, and the Pacific.

organism An individual animal, plant, or single-celled life form that is able to grow and reproduce. There are two main types of organism that derive energy from different sources: *autotrophs that produce energy, and *heterotrophs that derive energy from consuming autotrophs.

Organization of Petroleum Exporting Countries (OPEC) An organization that was established in 1960, consisting of 13 countries which control 60% of the world's *oil reserves. OPEC negotiates with oil companies on matters of oil production, prices, and future concession rights.

organochlorine (chlorinated hydrocarbon) A synthetic *organic compound that contains *chlorine, is highly *toxic, and has a variety of forms and uses including aerosol propellants, plasticisers, transformer coolants, and food packaging. Its greatest use was in *pesticides, in the form of *DDT, *aldrin, and *lindane. Organochlorines accumulate in the fatty tissue of animals, and can reach toxic levels in *predators through *biomagnification in the *food chain. Most countries have banned or severely restricted their use as pesticides.

organomercury compounds A range of substances in which mercury is combined with carbon and hydrogen (e.g. a phenyl group, C_6H_5, or methyl group, CH_3), used as seed dressings, and sometimes applied to timber, to prevent fungal infestation. Dressed seed is dispersed widely, distributing the mercury present in the fungicide at concentrations well below those present naturally in most soils, but birds have been harmed by ingesting seed dressed with methylmercury compounds. Phenylmercury compounds are of low toxicity to vertebrates; methylmercury compounds are much more toxic.

organophosphate A synthetic *organic compound that contains *phosphate, and is used as a *pesticide that works by interfering with an insect's nervous system. Organophosphates are generally considered safer than *organochlorines because they break down rapidly in the environment and do not *bioaccumulate, but some are highly *toxic to mammals (including humans) and may be *carcinogenic.

organotin *See* TRIBUTYLTIN.

organotroph An organism that obtains energy from the metabolism of organic compounds, sometimes inaccurately used as a synonym of *heterotroph. *Compare* LITHOTROPH.

oriental From or relating to the eastern *hemisphere. *Contrast* OCCIDENTAL.

oriental faunal region The area that encompasses India and Asia south of the Himalayan–Tibetan mountain barrier, and the Australasian archipelago, excluding New Guinea and Sulawesi. There are marked similarities with the *Ethiopian faunal region (e.g. both have elephants and rhinoceroses) but there are *endemic groups (e.g. pandas and gibbons).

orientation Alignment, or relative direction.

ornamental A plant that is cultivated and prized for its beauty rather than for its produce (such as fruit). Such plants are often *exotic.

ornithology The study of birds.

orogen A belt of deformed rocks that make up the *continental crust around a *craton. Many have been deformed into *fold mountains.

orogenesis (orogeny) The formation of *mountain ranges by *tectonic processes, particularly large-scale compression and intense upward displacement.

orogenic belt A major range of *mountains on the continents that has been created by *folding and other deformation in a mountain-building episode.

orogeny *See* OROGENESIS.

orographic Relating to *mountains.

orographic precipitation *Precipitation (usually *rain or *snow) that results from the lifting of a moisture-bearing *air mass over a topographic barrier such as a mountain range. The *leeward slope, beyond the barrier, often lies in a *rain shadow and is dry.

orographic uplift The lifting of air over a topographic barrier such a *hill or *mountain.

orthodox seed *Seed that can be dried and stored long-term, at low *temperature and *humidity, and remain viable.

ORV *See* OFF-ROAD VEHICLE.

OSHA *See* OCCUPATIONAL SAFETY AND HEALTH ACT.

Oslo Convention *See* CONVENTION FOR THE PREVENTION OF MARINE POLLUTION BY DUMPING FROM SHIPS AND AIRCRAFT.

osmosis The process by which a *solvent can pass through a *semipermeable *membrane, from a dilute solution into a more concentrated solution.

ostracods (seed shrimps) A class (Ostracoda) of tiny marine and freshwater *crustaceans that have a shrimp-like body which is enclosed in a bivalve shell. The class includes *filter feeders, *carnivores, *herbivores, and *scavengers. There are more than 2000 species.

Our Common Future The title of the 1987 report of the *World Commission on Environment and Development, more commonly known as the *Brundtland Report, which defined *sustainable development.

Our Stolen Future A controversial book by *Theo Colborn, Dianne Dumanoski, and John Peterson Myers (1997), which outlined how *toxic pollutants such as chemical *pesticides cause birth defects, sexual abnormalities, and reproductive failures in wildlife. It built on Rachel *Carson's *Silent Spring*.

outbreeding (outcrossing) The *mating of individuals which are genetically unrelated. *See also* BREEDING; INBREEDING.

outcrop An exposure of *bedrock at the Earth's surface.

outcrossing *See* OUTBREEDING.

Outdoor Recreation and Wilderness System A system, managed by the US Department of Agriculture *Forest Service, that provides outdoor *recreation opportunities and *wilderness experiences within the USA.

outer core *See* CORE.

outfall The place where a *sewer, *drain, or *stream discharges.

outflow The flow of air out of a *thunderstorm, or of water out of a *lake or *reservoir.

outgassing The release of gas (such as *water vapour, *nitrogen, or *argon) from cooling *molten rock or the interior of the Earth.

outlet glacier A tongue of ice that extends radially from an *ice dome. Beneath the dome it forms a narrow *ice stream; beyond the dome it occupies a shallow, irregular depression.

output The energy, matter, or information that leaves a *system. *Contrast* INPUT.

outwash Sand and gravel that is deposited by *meltwater streams in the *pro-glacial environment, or beyond the margin of an active *glacier.

outwash plain The relatively flat area beyond the margins of a retreating *glacier,

where *meltwater streams draining from the ice deposit *sand, *gravel, and *mud washed out from the glacier. Most outwash plains are wide and extensive, but some (*valley trains) are confined within a narrow valley.

overbank deposition The deposition of *alluvial sediment on the surface of a *floodplain by a river under *flood (over the bank) conditions.

overbrowsing The *overgrazing of shrubs and trees by a large population of animals that *browse.

overburden The layer of *soil, *sediment, and *rock that covers a *mineral deposit (such as *coal), and must be removed to allow *surface mining.

overcast The sky condition when more than nine-tenths of the sky is covered by *clouds.

over-consumption The use of *renewable resources faster than natural processes can replace them, which is not *sustainable.

overcrowding effect The regulation of population growth by behavioural abnormalities caused by a malfunction of the endocrine glands, which themselves occur in response to overcrowding.

overdraft *See* AQUIFER DEPLETION.

overexploitation (overharvesting) The use or extraction of a *resource to the point of *depletion (for *inorganic resources) or *extinction (for *organic resources), or the reduction of a population to a level below the minimum needed for *sustainable yield. Activity that exceeds the *carrying capacity.

overfishing *Fishing beyond a *sustainable level, caused by harvesting so many fish (particularly immature individuals) of a particular species that the remaining *breeding stock is too small to replenish the species. *Overexploitation of fish populations.

overflow channel *See* MELTWATER CHANNEL.

overgrazing The damage or destruction of natural vegetation (particularly *grasses and *forbs) that is caused when too many *herbivores are allowed to *graze on it before it has a chance to recover from previous grazing. A form of *overexploitation.

overharvesting *See* OVEREXPLOITATION.

overland flow (sheet flow) The flow of water over the ground surface towards *stream channels.

overmature forest An *old growth forest in which tree growth has almost ceased, and decay and deterioration are increasing.

overpopulation (overshoot) A situation in which the *population of a *species exceeds the *carrying capacity of the *environment, and is likely to lead to a *population crash. *See also* MALTHUS, THOMAS.

overshoot *See* OVERPOPULATION.

overstocked A managed *forest in which the trees are so closely spaced that they compete for *resources, and grow more slowly as a result.

overstocking Allowing too many animals to *graze a particular area, usually for a short period of time. Continued overstocking will lead to *overgrazing.

overstorey The *crown or upper *canopy of branches and leaves in a stand of *stratified vegetation. *Contrast* UNDERSTOREY.

overt release An announced release of a biological *agent, by terrorists or others. *Contrast* COVERT RELEASE.

overtopped *See* SUPPRESSED.

overturn *See* TURNOVER.

overturned fold A type of *fold in rock, which is created where compressional forces are asymmetrical, so that one limb of the fold is pushed over the other limb and over-rides it. *See also* NAPPE.

overwinter To survive over the *winter period.

oviparous Egg laying; producing fertilized eggs that develop and hatch outside the female's body.

ovoviparous Applied to the method of animal reproduction in which young develop from eggs retained within the mother's body but separated from it by the egg membranes. The eggs contain considerable yolk, which provides nourishment for the developing embryo. Many insect groups, fish, and reptiles reproduce in this way. *Compare* OVIPAROUS; VIVIPAROUS.

ox-bow lake (cut-off) A *lake that is formed on the *floodplain of an *alluvial river when the river cuts through the narrow neck of a large *meander.

oxidant (oxidizer, oxidizing agent) A substance that causes *oxidation in other substances by undergoing *reduction itself.

oxidation **1.** A chemical process in which an element reacts with *oxygen, where oxygen is gained, or electrons are lost. **2.** A common form of *chemical weathering of *rocks, which involves the combination of rock materials (e.g. *silicates or *carbonates of *iron or *manganese) with oxygen and water.

oxidation pond (sewage lagoon) An artificial *pond or *lagoon that contains water in which *waste is consumed (oxidized) by *bacteria as part of a waste treatment process.

oxide A compound of *oxygen with another element or group. Examples include *sulphur dioxide and *nitrogen oxides.

oxidize To add *oxygen to or combine with oxygen, or to lose electrons.

oxidizer *See* OXIDANT.

oxidizing agent *See* OXIDANT.

oxisols A type (*soil order) of deeply weathered soils that contain *clays of *iron and *aluminium oxides, has low *fertility, and is *acidic. Oxisols occur widely in the humid *tropics, where they are usually heavily *leached as a result of tilling by hand, resulting in low fertility.

oxyfuel *See* OXYGENATED FUEL.

oxygen (O) An invisible, colourless, tasteless, odourless *gas that exists naturally in air (20.95% by volume), accounts for 46.6% of the Earth's *crust, and is the most abundant element on Earth. It is released by plants as a byproduct of *photosynthesis, and it is essential for *aerobic *respiration (it is breathed by humans and other animals). The Earth's early atmosphere probably contained little oxygen, but after the *evolution of the *cyanobacteria around 3.5 billion years ago the proportion of oxygen in the air began to increase. About 2.7 billion years ago certain cyanobacteria were incorporated into *eukaryotic cells, where they became *chloroplasts, and oxygen was accumulating in the atmosphere by about 2.3 billion years ago. Oxygen forms an average of 70% of the atoms in living matter and it is a basic building block of carbohydrates, fats, and proteins. It is chemically very active and combines with most elements to form oxides, such as *water, *carbon dioxide, and *silicon dioxide (*quartz). *Ozone (O_3) is an *allotrope of oxygen. The process of *oxidation speeds up *metabolic processes, and oxygen is essential for *combustion (which is a rapid oxidation process).

SEE WEB LINKS

• The atmosphere and the global ocean.

oxygen demand *See* BIOLOGICAL OXYGEN DEMAND; CHEMICAL OXYGEN DEMAND.

oxygen depletion (oxygen sag) A decrease followed by recovery in the concentration of *dissolved oxygen in a river downstream from a *point source of pollutants, which is caused by the uptake of *oxygen by *bacteria, *fungi, and *invertebrates in the water as they break down the pollutants by *aerobic *decomposition.

oxygen isotope Any of the oxygen *atoms that have the same atomic number (number of *protons) but different mass numbers (different numbers of *neutrons). The three stable *isotopes of oxygen are ^{16}O, ^{17}O, and ^{18}O, where ^{16}O is the most abundant (99.762% of all oxygen). In addition there are 17 short-lived radioactive isotopes.

oxygen isotope ratio The ratio between two of the stable *isotopes of oxygen (^{16}O and ^{18}O) in a sample such as old layers of ice or shells from ocean sediments. The ratio is temperature dependent and provides a reliable indicator (*proxy) of past climatic conditions. An increase in ^{18}O in calcium carbonate indicates climatic cooling and an increase in ^{18}O in ice indicates warming.

oxygen method An estimation of gross *primary productivity by monitoring rates of production of oxygen, the by-product of *photosynthesis. In field practice this principle is most often used for productivity measurement in aquatic *ecosystems.

oxygen minimum layer The level in a *waterbody, usually below the *thermocline, below which there is very little *dissolved oxygen.

oxygen sag *See* OXYGEN DEPLETION.

oxygen solubility The ability of oxygen *gas to dissolve into water.

oxygenated fuel (oxyfuel) *Gasoline that has been blended with *alcohols or ethers (which contain oxygen) in order to reduce emissions of *carbon monoxide and other *greenhouse gases.

ozonation The application of *ozone to water for purification purposes (as a *disinfectant, and to improve taste or control odour).

ozonator A mechanical device that creates *ozone, which is used to *oxidize water in order to eliminate *organic wastes.

ozone (O_3) A highly reactive *greenhouse gas, made of three atoms of *oxygen. Ozone comprises 0.00006% of the Earth's *atmosphere. It is formed when the molecule of the stable form of oxygen (O_2) is split by *ultraviolet *radiation or electrical discharge, for example when *lightning flashes through a cloud. There are two distinctly different ozone problems: depletion of *stratospheric ozone, and increasing concentrations of *low-level ozone in the *troposphere. The latter comes partly from natural sources, but most is produced by *pollution (particularly *photochemical reactions involving vehicle exhaust fumes). Ozone is a constituent of *photochemical smog, is at least partly responsible for some of the damage attributed to *acid rain, can damage plants, and causes respiratory problems (including asthma attacks) in people. It is *toxic to humans at a concentration as low as 1 part per million (ppm) in air. The US *Environmental Protection Agency recommends that people should not be exposed for more than 1 hour a day to ozone levels of 120 parts per billion (ppb), while the *World Health Organization recommends a lower limit of 76–100 ppb.

ozone depleter Any of a group of chemicals that destroy *ozone and attack the *ozone layer in the *stratosphere. Most are chemically stable compounds that contain *chlorine or *bromine, which remain unchanged long enough to drift up to the stratosphere. The best known are *chlorofluorocarbons (CFCs), but others include *halons (which are used in some fire extinguishers), *methyl chloroform and *carbon tetrachloride (solvents), some CFC substitutes, and the *pesticide *methyl bromide.

ozone depletion potential (ODP) A relative index of the extent to which a particular chemical may cause *ozone depletion, compared with CFC-11 and CFC-12 which have an OPD of 1.0. Other *CFCs and *HCFCs have ODPs that range between 0.016 and 1.0, *halons have ODPs ranging up to 10, and *HFCs have an ODP of 0 because they do not contain *chlorine.

ozone hole Popular name for an increase in the natural seasonal decrease in the concentration of ozone in the stratosphere that occurs over *Antarctica in the spring, which was first

OZONE DEPLETION (OZONE THINNING)

In 1985 British scientists J. C. Farman, B. G. Gardiner, and J. D. Shanklin discovered a marked increase (usually referred to as a hole) in the natural seasonal thinning of the *ozone layer over the *Antarctic. Field monitoring showed a 40% thinning in the ozone layer. Their evidence suggested that the hole was growing bigger through time, and *satellite surveillance confirmed the initial reports. The normal average thickness of the layer is 220–460 *Dobson units (DU) but the scientists found it was only slightly above 100 DU and in October 1993 it fell to its lowest value, 91 DU, due partly to sulphate particles from the eruption of *Mount Pinatubo. The main cause of the thinning was believed to be a three-fold increase in atmospheric *CFCs within 10 years. These and other *halons break down to release chlorine and bromine, which destroy *ozone molecules in the *stratosphere. From the mid-1980s onwards the issue of ozone depletion was taken seriously. In 1985 the *Vienna Convention for the Protection of the Ozone Layer was initially signed by 22 countries. Not all countries agreed on the urgency of the problem. Since 1987 the *Montreal Protocol was strengthened to work towards a faster phase-out of CFCs by 1996. By 1990 many European countries had made great progress in phasing out the use of CFCs. By the end of 1994 some *industrialized countries had already halted production of CFCs and others were well on target to meet the 1996 deadline. *Developing countries were given a 10-year extension. The ozone concentration appeared to stabilize in the late 1990s and by 2009 it was increasing by 0.8–1.4% per decade. Damage to the ozone layer would allow more UV radiation to pass through the atmosphere. This would have a variety of possible impacts, depending on the extent and location of the damage. Were the depletion to become established over middle latitudes, some agricultural crops would be harmed and yields would fall, marine *plankton would be affected, and human health would suffer, with more eye cataracts, more skin *cancer, and more problems arising from damage to people's immune systems. *See also* OZONE HOLE.

detected during the 1970s. *See also* MONTREAL PROTOCOL ON SUBSTANCES THAT DEPLETE THE OZONE LAYER; OZONE DEPLETION POTENTIAL.

ozone layer The layer of *ozone in the *stratosphere that is formed naturally by a *photochemical reaction with solar *ultraviolet *radiation. Ozone is constantly being formed, broken down, and re-formed above about 40 km, and it sinks and accumulates at the 20–30 km level. The ozone layer is not uniform around the world; it varies in density, being least dense over the equator, where ozone does not accumulate, and most dense over high latitudes (beyond 50°N and 50°S). In latitudes higher than 60° the ozone concentration decreases during winter, when fresh ozone is not being formed, but ozone carried from low latitudes by high-level winds prevents it from disappearing entirely. It reaches a natural minimum over polar regions in late winter and early spring.

The ozone layer absorbs some of the ultraviolet rays from the Sun, thereby reducing the amount of potentially harmful radiation that reaches the Earth's surface. *See also* MONTREAL PROTOCOL.

ozone monitoring Measurements of background levels of ozone that have been collected over 20 years at sites a long way from pollution sources (including the South Pole, Barrow in Alaska, and *Mauna Loa in Hawaii). These *baseline surveys show that ozone concentrations vary through the day and from season to season. Efforts are being made through the *International Geosphere-Biosphere Programme to collect more information on changing ozone levels in the atmosphere and on the ways these might promote other changes in atmospheric chemistry.

ozone thinning *See* OZONE DEPLETION.

PA *See* PRELIMINARY ASSESSMENT.

Pacific North American floral region
Part of R. Good's *Boreal Realm (*The Geography
of the Flowering Plants*, 1974), distinguished
by about 300 *endemic genera. Although the
flora as a whole has contributed few economic
plants, it has furnished numerous garden species. Like all floras of Mediterranean-type climates, the Californian part of this region
shows a marked degree of endemism, with 30–
50% of its species restricted to the state.

Pacific Ocean The largest *ocean in the
world, which covers a third of the Earth's surface, and contains about 25 000 *islands (more
than half of the global total). Its surface area is
165.2 km^2, but it is shrinking due to *plate tectonics; plate boundaries surround the ocean
with seismically active regions known as the
*Pacific Ring of Fire.

Pacific Rim General term for the 34 countries
and 23 island states that are situated in and
around the *Pacific Ocean and share similar
political, economic, and environmental interests.

Pacific Ring of Fire A *volcanic zone that
runs right around the edges of the *Pacific
Ocean, along a series of *subduction zones of
*convergent plate boundaries, where the moving
plates of the Pacific plunge beneath the confining
plates to the east, north, and west. It extends
through the Andes in South America, runs
through Central America and Mexico, along the
west coast of the USA into Alaska, across the
Aleutian Island chain, through the Kamchatka
Peninsula, through Japan and the Philippines,
and into New Zealand and the margins of Antarctica.

pack ice Seawater that is frozen into thick
blocks of *ice, under permanently cold conditions, such as those found around the *polar ice
caps. *See also* SEA ICE; ICE FLOE.

packaging Materials that are used for the
containment, protection, handling, delivery,
and presentation of goods.

packed tower *See* TRICKLING FILTER.

paddock An enclosed area of *grazing land
for animals, such as horses.

paedogenesis A form of reproduction in
*insects in which the larval stage reproduces
without maturing first. *See also* LARVAL PAEDO-
GENESIS; PUPAL PAEDOGENESIS.

paedomorphosis Evolutionary change that
results in the retention of juvenile characters
into adult life. It permits an 'escape' from specialization, and has been invoked to account for
the origin of many taxa, from subspecies to
phyla.

PAH *See* POLYCYCLIC AROMATIC HYDROCARBON.

pahoehoe Volcanic *lava that solidifies into
ropy or corded shapes with a smooth surface.
The name is a Hawaiian word meaning satin-
like.

palaearctic A *biogeographical region that
covers Europe, Asia, and North Africa.

Palaearctic faunal region The region that
includes Europe, Asia north of the Himalayan–
Tibetan physical barrier, North Africa, and
much of Arabia. Despite its size and great
range of habitats, the faunal variety in it is far
less than that of the *Ethiopian and *Oriental
faunal regions to the south of it (e.g. monkeys
are nearly absent and reptiles few in number).
The region is similar at the family level, and
rather less so at the generic level, to the *Nearctic region; the Bering *land bridge connected
the two for much of the *Cenozoic era.

Palaearctic realm A *biogeographical realm
that covers much of Europe and Asia, and contains a variety of *biomes including *tundra,
*grassland, *deciduous forest, *coniferous forest,
*chaparral, and *desert.

palaeo- A prefix meaning old or ancient, particularly *prehistoric. Spelled paleo in North America.

Palaeoarchaean The second of the four eras of the *Archaean eon, which lasted from 3600 to 3200 million years ago. The two *domains *Eubacteria and *Archaea evolved during the Palaeoarchaean.

palaeobiology The study of the origin, growth, and structure of *fossil animals and plants as living *organisms.

palaeobotany The study of *fossil plants.

Palaeocene The first epoch of geological time within the *Palaeogene, between 65.5 and 55.8 million years ago. With the disappearance of the *dinosaurs many new species of *mammals appeared.

(((🌐))) SEE WEB LINKS

• Palaeocene.

Palaeocene–Eocene thermal maximum A *climatic optimum that occurred about 55 million years ago, at the boundary of the *Palaeocene and *Eocene epochs, and that lasted for less than 100 000 years. At the onset of the optimum the global mean temperature increased by 5–8°C and the oceans warmed throughout their depths. A second temperature rise occurred briefly about 2 million years later.

palaeoclimate The *climate of a particular period in the geological past, before historical records or instrumental observations.

palaeoclimatology The study and reconstruction of past *climates and of *climate change.

palaeoecology The study of ancient *ecosystems.

palaeoenvironment A previous or ancient *environment.

palaeoenvironmental proxy Any of a number of remnants of past *environments (including *pollen grains, *tree rings, lake sediments, *ice cores, and *coral skeletons) that can be used to estimate how *climate and environment have changed through time.

palaeoenvironmental reconstruction The study of ancient *environments and of *environmental change.

Palaeogene A period of *geological time within the *Cenozoic era, dating from 65.5 to 23 million years ago; the early age of *mammals and a period of major *extinctions of species.

palaeogeographical map A map that shows the surface *landforms and *coastline of an area at some time in the geological past.

palaeogeography The study of the geography (particularly the *environment and distribution of physical features) of particular periods in the geological past.

palaeohydrology The study of the structure and dynamics of the *water cycle at particular periods in the geological past.

Palaeo-Indian The earliest, well-documented *archaeological cultures in North America, dating back some 6000 to 12 000 years before the present.

palaeolimnology The study of past *freshwater, *saline, and *brackish environments, based on analysis of sediment cores which preserve evidence of water chemistry and biology in the past.

Palaeolithic The second part of the *Stone Age, following the *eolithic, which began in Europe between about 750 000 and 500 000 BC and lasted until the end of the last *ice age about 8500 BC.

palaeomagnetism (magnetostratigraphy) The study of variations in the intensity and direction of the Earth's *magnetic field in the geological past, as recorded in *rocks. *See also* MAGNETIC REVERSAL.

palaeontological area An area in the USA which has been designated as containing significant (usually *fossil) remains of flora and (non-human) fauna dating from *prehistoric times.

palaeontology The study of ancient *fossil remains of plants and animals that are found in *sedimentary rocks, and of their geological contexts.

Palaeoproterozoic The first era of the *Proterozoic eon, which lasted from 2500 to 1600 million years ago. Several *glaciations occurred during this time. *Bacteria were probably the only forms of life until very late in the era, when *eukaryotes first appeared.

(((🌐))) SEE WEB LINKS

• The Palaeoproterozoic era.

palaeosol An ancient buried *soil that preserves evidence of past *environmental conditions and processes.

Palaeotropical floral kingdom A region whose geographical extent varies with the authority consulted. R. Good's definition (*The Geography of the Flowering Plants*, 1974) embraces the African (excluding the Cape), Indo-Malaysian, and *Polynesian floral subkingdoms. Other authorities adopt a more restricted definition, embracing most of Africa, Arabia, and the north-west part of the Indian subcontinent.

palaeotropics The tropical parts of the Old World (Africa and South East Asia). *See also* NEOTROPICS.

palaeowind The prevailing *wind direction in a particular area at some time in the geological past, inferred from the structure of ancient *sand dunes or the distribution of *volcanic ash.

Palaeozoic The first era of the *Phanerozoic eon of geological time that lasted from 542 to 251 million years ago, during which atmospheric *oxygen reached its present level and the *ozone layer formed, allowing life to flourish on land. All classes of *invertebrates except insects emerged, and seed-bearing plants, *amphibians, and *reptiles appeared.

(((●))) SEE WEB LINKS

• The Paleozoic era of the Phanerozoic eon.

palatable Pleasing to the taste.

palatable species Plants that are preferred by *grazing and *browsing animals, usually because they are sweeter or softer than other plants.

palatable water Water that is free from most colour, cloudiness, unpleasant tastes, and odour.

paleo- 1. North American spelling of *palaeo-. **2.** In North American *archaeology, a cultural period between 40 000 and 12 000 years ago.

palm A member of the Arecaceae (previously Palmae) family. This contains about 190 genera and about 2000 species, most tropical, solitary or clumped unbranched trees, many of which are economically important for food, fibre, canes, waxes, wood, thatch, and other uses. A common tree in *agroforestry.

Palmer drought severity index (PDSI) An index for classifying *droughts that measures the extent to which water supply deviates from what is normal in a particular area. It is widely used in the USA.

Palouse prairie A North American *prairie *grassland and meadow-*steppe vegetation dominated by bunch grasses, first identified in the Palouse region of south-eastern Washington state, but which also covers a large area of north-western Idaho, eastern Oregon, and northern Utah.

palsa A mound or ridge, largely made from *peat, which contains a perennial ice lens and is found in the damper sites of *mires in *periglacial areas. Widths are in the range 10–30 m, lengths 15–150 m, and heights 1–7 m. Probably palsas are a result of heaving associated with the growth of segregated ice. *See also* PINGO.

paludal Applied to organisms, soils, etc. that are of or associated with a *marsh.

paludification The spread of boggy conditions across an area as a result of the gradual rising of the *water table, as the accumulation of *peat impedes the drainage of water.

palustrine Relating to *wetland or *marsh *habitats.

palustrine wetland Any non-tidal *wetland that is dominated by trees, shrubs, persistent emergent plants, emergent *mosses or *lichens, and small, shallow open water ponds. Examples include *swamps, *marshes, *bogs, and *fens.

palynology *See* POLLEN ANALYSIS.

pampas The extensive grassy *prairie plains of *temperate South America.

pampas floral region Part of R. Good's *Neotropical floral kingdom (*The Geography of the Flowering Plants*, 1974); it lies east of the Andes, and between the tropical flora of Brazil and the temperate flora of Patagonia. The flora is relatively poor, with only about 50 *endemic genera, all of them small. In terms of vegetation the region is dominated by the pampa grasses. Few garden plants or important economic plants come from this region, although the pineapple (*Ananas comosus*) comes from Paraguay.

PAN *See* PEROXYACETYL NITRATE.

pan A compact soil horizon that has a high *clay content.

pandemic A *epidemic that occurs over a very wide area, and affects a large proportion of the population.

Pangaea The supercontinent that existed probably between 200 and 250 million years ago, and was surrounded by the *Panthalassa Sea. It broke apart by *continental drift into two portions, *Laurasia and *Gondwanaland, with the *Tethys Sea between them.

panorama A broad view, usually of an attractive natural *landscape or *scenery.

panplain (panplane, planplain) An area of very subdued relief that consists of coalesced *floodplains. It is produced by lateral stream migration and is a component of a *peneplain. Good examples are found in the Carpentaria region of Australia.

panplane See PANPLAIN.

Panthalassa The ancient *sea that covered most of the Earth's surface when all of the land that existed was in one large landmass (*Pangaea), probably between 200 and 250 million years ago.

pantropical Throughout the *tropics as a whole, between 23°30′S and 23°30′N latitude. *Contrast* NEOTROPICS; PALAEOTROPICS.

paper A thin sheet of material made of *cellulose pulp which is derived mainly from *wood, but also from rags and certain grasses. The pulp is processed into flexible leaves or rolls, which have many uses including for writing, printing, drawing, wrapping, and covering walls.

paper mill Mills (factories) that produce *paper from wood pulp.

parabiosis 1. The joining of two organisms that share one blood circulation. **2.** The condition of living together.

paradigm A worldview, shared set of assumptions, or widely accepted idea of how the world works, which forms the basis for *hypotheses and explanations.

paraffin 1. A *liquid fuel refined from *petroleum or shale. **2.** A flammable waxy solid that is made in the same way as the liquid fuel, and is used for sealing and waterproofing and in candles.

parallel drainage pattern A *drainage pattern in which small rivers flow generally parallel to one another over a sloping surface of uniform rock resistance.

parapatric speciation A form of *speciation in which the new *species evolves from *contiguous *populations.

paraquat A *defoliant *herbicide that is commonly used to kill particular types of crops (such as marijuana) and is *toxic to humans.

parasite A plant or animal that lives in or on a *host (an animal or plant of a different species) for at least part of its life, from which it obtains *nutrients. The relationship does not usually kill or benefit the host organism. *See also* ENDOPARASITE; ECTOPARASITE.

parasitism A win-lose form of *symbiosis between two different species in which one (the *parasite) benefits and the other (the *host) is harmed. *See also* BROOD PARASITISM.

parasitoid A *parasite that eventually kills its host.

parataxonomist A specialist in the monitoring of local *biodiversity, who is recruited locally and trained in the field.

Paratethys (Central European Sea) A large, arcuate seaway that, at its maximum development, extended a distance of 4500 km from just north of the Alps to just east of the Aral Sea. By the end of the *Oligocene it had been separated from the Boreal Sea by closure of the Ural, Polish, and Alsace straits. Towards the end of the *Miocene it became more lagoonal in character and by the *Pliocene was represented only by a series of land-locked lakes: Lake Balaton in Hungary, the Black Sea (rejoined to the Mediterranean Sea by *Quaternary faulting), the Caspian Sea, and the Aral Sea.

parathion The first *organophosphate insecticide, developed by the German company Bayer in the 1940s. It inhibits cholinesterase and is used to control aphids and other insects, mites, *nematodes, and woodlice on a wide range of crops. It is highly toxic by inhalation and ingestion, and moderately toxic by adsorption through the skin. It is toxic to aquatic invertebrates, fish, birds, and mammals, and its use is banned in many countries.

parc naturel et régional See NATIONAL PARK.

parent element An *isotope (parent) that is transformed into a different (*daughter product) isotope by *radioactive decay.

parent material The *mineral material from which a *soil develops, which is usually unconsolidated *weathered *bedrock or *sediment (*alluvium, *colluvium, or wind-blown deposits).

Pareto optimum In welfare economics, the optimum allocation of products and services to people in a particular setting (such as a country) that produces maximum benefit to the *population as a whole, and when it is impossible to make one or more individuals better off without making one or more other people worse off.

Parícutin An explosive *volcano that grew suddenly and rapidly in central Mexico in 1943. Over a 2-week period early that year, the area around Parícutin had been shaken by *earthquakes. On 20 February the ground cracked and a *vent opened up in a cornfield. First steam, then *volcanic dust, and then hot fragments started to pour out. Soon molten rock was pouring out, and it started to build up a cone around the central vent. The eruption continued for eight months, and the cone grew to a height of about 450 m. The accompanying *lava flows buried the village of Parícutin and nearby settlements. By 1952 the volcano had become *dormant.

Paris green See COPPER ACETOARSENITE.

park 1. In ancient farming systems, the enclosed fields lying between the inner fields next to the farm buildings and the larger, outer fields that were used only seasonally for pasture. **2.** Enclosed land on which deer are or were kept. **3.** In modern use: (a) an area of land set aside for public enjoyment and designed to resemble semi-natural land; (b) an enclosure for semi wild animals. **4.** See NATIONAL PARK.

park-like structure A stand of *vegetation that is dominated by large, scattered *trees with open spaces between them, and is usually maintained by natural ground *fires.

parthenogenesis Development of an egg without fertilization.

partial duration series Flow records that are used in *flood frequency analysis, which include all peak flows with a discharge greater than a chosen threshold (such as *bankfull discharge). Contrast ANNUAL MAXIMUM SERIES.

partial pressure The *pressure that is exerted by one *gas in a mixture of gases.

partial retention In *forest management, a method of tree harvesting in which only part of the *stand is removed, and the rest is left standing.

participation Engagement with and taking part in an activity. The process through which *stakeholders influence and share control over priority setting, policy-making, resource allocations, and access to public goods and services.

participation rate The portion of a *population that participates in a particular activity, such as a *recycling programme.

participatory action research (PRA) A type of *action research in which active collaboration between *stakeholders, practitioners, and researchers defines the content, process, and results of the research, and in which the activities are often designed to identify or monitor solutions to particular problems.

participatory monitoring and evaluation (PME) A process through which key *stakeholders actively engage in monitoring or evaluating a particular project, programme, or policy.

participatory rural appraisal (PRA, rapid rural appraisal) A group of participatory approaches and methods that emphasize local knowledge and enable local people to make their own appraisal, analysis, and plans, which helps development practitioners, government officials, and local people to work together to plan appropriate programmes.

participatory technology development (PTD) An approach to *rural development that is based on involving farmers in developing agricultural technologies that are appropriate to their particular situation, based on their own practical experience.

particle A tiny mass of solid or liquid material.

particle size The size of individual particles or grains of material, such as *soil or *sediment, expressed either in millimetres diameter or using the *phi (ϕ) scale. Size classes for sediments range from very fine *clays (less than 0.002 mm in diameter) and *silts (between 0.002 and 0.05 mm), to coarse *sands (range from 0.05 to 2.0 mm), and *gravels (larger than 2 mm).

particle-size analysis Determination of the size distribution of particles in a sample of *soil or *sediment, which is usually determined by sieving or *sedimentation (settling in liquid).

particulate Composed of *particles of solid or liquid matter, such as *soot, *dust, *aerosols, fumes, and *mists.

particulate filtration A procedure used in *air cleaning, in which *particles are removed by passing the air through fine filters.

particulate loading The concentration of particles in a sample of air or water, usually expressed as mass per unit volume (such as milligrams per litre, mg l^{-1}).

particulate pollution *Pollution in the form of small liquid or solid *particles suspended in the atmosphere or in water.

particulates Fine solid or liquid *particles in the air or in an emission. A *conventional or *criteria pollutant.

parts per billion (ppb) The number of parts of one substance that is present in a total sample of one billion (10^9) similar parts of another substance.

parts per million (ppm) The number of parts of one substance that is present in a total sample of one million (10^6) similar parts of another substance.

party A group of people who are engaged in a particular activity, such as a state (or regional economic organization such as the *EU) that agrees to be bound by a particular *treaty.

pascal (Pa) The SI unit of *pressure, which is equal to one hundredth of a *millibar, or one newton per square metre.

passenger pigeon A migratory pigeon (*Ectopistes migratorius*) that as late as the mid-19th century was one of the most abundant birds in North America. By 1900 it had become *extinct in the wild as a result of wholesale hunting for restaurants and other markets. The last known specimen died in captivity in 1914.

passive detector A measuring device that functions on its own, without any energy input or ongoing attention from the user.

passive heat absorption Using natural materials and structures without any moving parts to collect and store heat.

passive solar design Designing buildings in order to maximize the use of *solar radiation to warm and light the interior of a building, through such measures as careful siting and orientation, use of energy efficient windows, and provision of appropriate levels of insulation and heat storage.

passive solar heating A form of *solar heating that uses *solar radiation to heat build-ings directly, by trapping it within the structure of the building and then releasing it slowly. It relies on natural air flow rather than pumps to distribute the heat within the building. Glass greenhouses and conservatories are good examples. *Contrast* ACTIVE SOLAR HEATING.

passive solar power Using or capturing *solar energy (usually to heat water) without any external power.

passive use value *See* NON-CONSUMPTIVE VALUE.

pastoral Relating to shepherds or herdsmen, devoted to raising sheep or cattle, or more generally a romantic or idealized image of *rural life. *See also* BUCOLIC.

pastoral agriculture Farming based on rearing *livestock, such as beef cattle, dairying, and sheep. *Contrast* ARABLE.

pastoral nomad A *nomad who herds animals, and has no permanent place of residence.

pastoralism A form of *nomadism in which people move animals from place to place with no permanent human settlement. *See also* TRANSHUMANCE.

pasture A field covered with grass or herbs and suitable for grazing by livestock. *See also* ANNUAL PASTURE; NATIVE PASTURE; PERMANENT PASTURE; ROTATION PASTURE.

pasture management *Land management that is designed to ensure the sustainable growth of *pasture plants, in order to provide high quality feed and encourage the growth of desirable *grasses and *legumes while crowding out weeds, *brush, and inferior grasses.

pastureland Land that is used primarily for *pasture.

Patagonian floral region Part of R. Good's Antarctic floral kingdom (*The Geography of the Flowering Plants*, 1974); it has a small flora with a modest number of *endemic genera. It comprises the lowland regions of the southern extremities of South America. The Falkland Islands (Malvinas) are also included, but despite their isolation they have no well-known endemic genera. There are clear relationships with the flora of New Zealand.

patch An area of *vegetation that has a uniform structure and composition, and differs from the surrounding vegetation.

patch cut A *clearcut *logging operation that creates small openings in a *forest in patches of between about 10 to 100 acres, which are separated by living forest.

patch dynamics 1. Changes in the distribution of *patches of *habitat within a landscape that are caused by *disturbance and regrowth. **2.** The study and mathematical modelling of the proportion of feeding areas (patches) in a habitat that are occupied at a particular time by the species being studied.

patch residence time The length of time an animal spends foraging in a particular area (i.e. a patch) of its *habitat before diminishing returns compel it to move elsewhere.

patch size The size of a *patch of *vegetation or *habitat.

patent An *intellectual property right relating to inventions (innovative processes or products).

paternoster lake A lake that is formed on a *pro-glacial *floodplain after the glacier ice has melted. Such lakes are often found as a series, or chain resembling a paternoster in a rosary.

pathogen An *organism (such as a *bacterium, *fungus, or *virus) that can cause *disease in another organism.

pathogenic Capable of causing *disease.

pathological Related to or caused by *disease.

pathological waste Waste material that might contain *pathogens, making its disposal a possible hazard to public health, e.g. hospital wastes, some laboratory wastes, possibly infected materials.

pathway The physical route that a *chemical or *pollutant takes from its source to the exposed organism.

patterned ground A range of ground surface features that are found in *periglacial environments, and are the result of *freeze–thaw action (*physical weathering) at the top of the *permafrost. These may be sorted or unsorted, sorted varieties usually being outlined by coarse, stony material. The most common features of sorted ground are stone circles, *stone polygons, stone nets (on low-sloping ground), and *stone stripes (on higher slopes).

pavement Any rock that is exposed at the Earth's surface in the form of a more or less horizontal surface.

PCA *See* POLYCYCLIC AROMATIC.

PCB *See* POLYCHLORINATED BIPHENYL.

PCR *See* POLYMERASE CHAIN REACTION.

PDSI *See* PALMER DROUGHT SEVERITY INDEX.

PE *See* POTENTIAL EVAPOTRANSPIRATION.

peak The highest point (summit) of a *mountain.

peak discharge The maximum volume of flow at a particular point in a stream during a *runoff event.

peat 1. Partially decomposed vegetable matter that forms in boggy ground and can be cut and dried for use as a fuel. It forms in the initial stages of the *coal series. **2.** A *histosol in which the *O-horizon is at least 40 cm thick (it is often thicker) and the dry weight contains at least 65% organic matter.

peat bog *See* BOG.

peatland Any *wetland ecosystem that accumulates partially decayed plant matter. *Bogs and *fens are types of peatland.

pebble bed reactor An advanced design of *nuclear reactor which uses an inert or semi-inert gas (such as *helium, *nitrogen, or *carbon dioxide) as a coolant, at very high temperature, to drive a *turbine directly.

pecking order The name given to the hierarchical social organization found in some insect species (e.g. ants and bees) and in many vertebrate species. It is so called because the phenomenon was first described for chickens. Based on *dominance, it allows each member of the group to threaten (or actually peck) the individual immediately subordinate to it and so gain prior access to food or other resources.

ped A small unit (*aggregate) of *soil that is composed of individual particles of sand, silt, clay, and other soil material that stick together into a specific structure (such as a crumb or granule), and is formed by natural processes. *See also* SOIL STRUCTURE.

pedalfer An acid *soil in which *aluminium and *iron accumulate. It is produced by *laterization and *podsolization, and occurs mainly in humid climates.

pedigree The line of descent (list of ancestors) of an individual or a *purebred animal or plant.

pedigree breeding A system of *breeding plants or animals in which individuals are selected from a *cross on the basis of their desirability, judged individually and from their *pedigree record.

pediment A gently sloping surface, usually covered with *gravel, that has been created by *erosion in front of a mountain range in an *arid region.

pedocal An alkaline *soil in which *calcium accumulates. It is produced by *calcification and occurs mainly in subhumid, semi-arid, and arid climates.

pedogenesis The process of *soil formation.

pedology The study of the formation, characteristics, and distribution of *soils.

pedon The smallest three-dimensional unit of *soil, which defines a block (usually between 1 and 10 m^2 in area) with relatively uniform properties.

pedosphere The thin outer layer of the Earth's surface, which is made up of *soil.

PEL *See* PERMISSIBLE EXPOSURE LIMIT.

pelagic Of or relating to the *open sea or *ocean, free from any direct influence of the *shore or *sea-bed.

pelagic organism 1. A marine organism that inhabits open water where it moves freely upwards and downwards. Pelagic organisms are generally free-swimming (*nekton) or floating (*plankton), but *neuston are also included. **2.** A sea bird that spends most of its time out at sea and comes to land only to breed.

pelagic sediment Deep-sea sediments that are made up of fine-grained material (such as *clay, *radiolarian ooze, and *foraminiferal ooze) that slowly settles from surface waters.

pelt The fur coat of a *mammal.

peneplain A large flat or gently undulating area close to *sea level, formed by a long period of *erosion, which represents the end product of the ideal *cycle of erosion.

penesaline A level of *salinity intermediate between normal marine and hypersaline, ranging from 72‰ to 352‰. These salinity levels are high enough to be toxic to most marine organisms and can be tolerated only by a restricted range of fauna and flora.

penetrometer An instrument that is used to determine the resistance to penetration of a *soil, which reflects soil strength.

peptide A substance formed by two or more *amino acids; *proteins are made of multiple peptides.

peptide bond A chemical bond (–CO.NH–) by which one *amino acid molecule may be linked to the next in a chain.

per capita Literally 'each head', meaning each individual.

per capita consumption The amount of a particular commodity that is used by each individual, on average.

perceived risk The subjective appreciation of a danger by individuals, which may bear little relation to the statistical probability of harm. Risks that appear to be under voluntary control are perceived as smaller than those over which the individual has no control. Thus the risk of being injured in a road accident seems less than the risk of injury resulting from an accident at a nuclear plant, although the former is many thousands of times greater than the latter. *See* RISK ASSESSMENT.

perched aquifer (perched groundwater, perched water table) *Groundwater that is separated from the underlying main body of groundwater (*aquifer) by a layer of impermeable rock (*aquiclude).

perched groundwater *See* PERCHED AQUIFER.

perched water table *See* PERCHED AQUIFER.

percolate To drain or seep slowly through a *porous substance.

percolation The downward movement of water (*soil moisture) within a soil, through the *soil horizons, under the force of *gravity. This water may eventually pass into the underlying bedrock and become part of the *aquifer. *Contrast* INFILTRATION.

percoline (seepage line) A hollow at the base of a *hillslope where water (*soil moisture) seeps out onto the ground surface and becomes *overland flow.

perennation The survival of a plant from one growing season to the next, usually by entering a period of dormancy.

perennial Persisting from year to year.

perennial flow River flow that continues through the year, and dries up only during prolonged *drought. *Contrast* EPHEMERAL FLOW; INTERMITTENT FLOW.

perennial plant A plant that lives for more than two *growing seasons. Also known simply as a perennial. *Contrast* ANNUAL.

perennial stream A *stream or river that flows throughout the year, from source to mouth, and that dries up only during prolonged *drought and starts to flow again when regular *precipitation is restored.

perfluorocarbon (PFC) One of a group of human-made chemicals that are composed of *carbon and *fluorine only (CF_4 and C_2F_6). They were introduced as alternatives to *ozone-depleting substances, are emitted as *byproducts of industrial processes, and are used in manufacturing. They do not harm the *ozone layer in the stratosphere, but are powerful *greenhouse gases.

performance standard zoning Land use *zoning regulations that define broad criteria for determining the acceptability of certain industries, land uses, and buildings, rather than specification standards or detailed requirements.

performance-based resource estimate An estimate of the amount of a particular *mineral deposit that is available underground, based mainly on the ability of existing technology to extract the mineral under existing and probable future economic conditions.

periglacial Applied to the cold climate region adjacent to a *glacier or *ice sheet, in which the ground is largely permanently frozen (*permafrost) but may thaw during the summer.

perihelion The point in the orbit of any planet when it is closest to the Sun. For the Earth this occurs on 3 or 4 January each year. The opposite is *aphelion.

period A unit of time; in geological terms a unit that is shorter than an *era but longer than an *epoch.

periodic table A chart listing all of the known *elements of the universe, arranged in columns with similar chemical properties, in order of increasing *atomic number.

periphery The edge or outer part of an object, away from the centre.

periphyton Organisms, commonly *algae, that grow attached to rocks, stems, twigs, leaves, and bottom sediments in a freshwater lake or river.

permaculture Permanent *agriculture: a *sustainable form of *agriculture that is designed to enhance local *ecosystems and increase local *biodiversity, for example by providing *fuel, materials for shelter and home, and *habitat for livestock, as well as food.

permafrost Permanently frozen soil or ground, where the temperature has remained below freezing for at least two consecutive winters and the intervening summer. Permafrost covers approximately 26% of the Earth's land surface and is common in *periglacial environments such as the arctic *tundra. In some places it is very thick (up to 600 m on the North Slope of Alaska and 1400 m in Siberia). *See also* PATTERNED GROUND.

permafrost table *See* TJAELE.

permanent pasture A *pasture, usually created rather than natural, which consists mainly of *introduced *perennial plants that are permitted to remain for a number of years. *Contrast* ANNUAL PASTURE.

permanent retrievable storage Placing waste storage containers in a secure place (such as a special building, salt mine, or cavern in bedrock), where they can be inspected periodically and retrieved if necessary.

permanent water A watering place that supplies water to *wildlife and people at all times during the year or during a *grazing season.

permanent wildlife opening An area of land that is managed in order to create and maintain a *wildlife *habitat of grass, low shrub, and/or herbaceous ground cover.

permanent wilting percentage *See* PERMANENT WILTING POINT.

permanent wilting point (PWP, permanent wilting percentage, wilting coefficient, wilting point) As moisture is lost from the soil, the point reached at which the force with which the remaining moisture adheres to soil particles exceeds that exerted by plant roots. Plants are therefore unable to absorb moisture and wilting results. Since this condition arises from the amount of water present in the soil, plants will not recover unless water is added to the soil, i.e. the wilting is permanent. The permanent wilting point usually occurs when soil moisture is held with a force of about 15 MPa (150 bar). It is also measured as the percentage of moisture remaining in the soil after a specified test plant has wilted under defined conditions and will not recover unless water is added to the soil. *Compare* TEMPORARY WILTING.

permeability 1. (hydraulic conductivity) A measure of the rate at which water can *percolate through a soil or rock, usually expressed in cubic metres per second ($m^3 s^{-1}$). **2.** The ease with which a substance can pass through a membrane or other barrer.

permeable Applied to a material (e.g. a *soil or *rock) that permits fluids (e.g. *water) to pass through it in both directions. *Contrast* IMPERMEABLE. *See also* PERVIOUS; POROUS.

Permian The final *geological period in the *Palaeozoic era, between 299 and 251 million years ago, at the end of which an estimated 90% of all species died out in a *mass extinction (including many *corals, *brachiopods, and *trilobites), and *reptiles diversified and grew in dominance. All the continents merged to form the supercontinent of *Pangaea.

⊕ **SEE WEB LINKS**

• The Permian period of the Palaeozoic era.

permissible dose The maximum *dose of a *chemical that an individual may receive in a given period of time, without it causing significant harm.

permissible exposure limit (PEL) The permissible concentration of a harmful physical *agent (such as an air *contaminant) to which most workers can be safely exposed for 8 hours a day, 40 hours a week, over a working lifetime (40 years), without adverse effects.

permit A licence or legal document that gives the holder official permission to do something.

peroxyacetyl nitrate (PAN) An *air pollutant that is created by the action of sunlight on *hydrocarbons and *nitrogen oxides in the air, and is an ingredient of *photochemical smog.

perpetual resource Any *resource that is inexhaustible on a human time-scale.

persistence Continuity, such as the continued presence of a species at a particular location or of a *non-degradable chemical (such as a *pesticide) in the environment.

persistence time The time it takes for a *pesticide to become *inert.

persistent Long lasting or never ceasing.

persistent organic pollutant (POP) A chemical substance that is *persistent in the environment, *bioaccumulates through the *food web, and can damage human health and the environment.

persistent pesticide Any *pesticide (such as *DDT) that does not break down chemically or only breaks down very slowly, so it remains in the *environment after *a growing season. *Contrast* NON-PERSISTENT PESTICIDE.

person-rem A measure of the exposure of a *population to *radiation, calculated as the average dose per individual (in *rem) multiplied by the number of people exposed.

PERT *See* PROGRAMME EVALUATION AND REVIEW TECHNIQUE.

perturbation *See* RADIATIVE FORCING.

pervious Applied to a material (e.g. a *soil or *rock) that is able to let a liquid (e.g. water) penetrate or infiltrate it. *Contrast* IMPERVIOUS. *See also* PERMEABLE.

pessimist, environmental (ecodoom pessimist, miserabilist) A person who is inclined to take an unfavourable view of the *environmental crisis and what can be done about it. For example, such a person may believe that the human *population already exceeds the Earth's *carrying capacity, and this is reflected in global environmental problems such as the growing rate of *extinction of species, *global warming, and increased *poverty. *Contrast* OPTIMIST, ENVIRONMENTAL.

pest Any *animal that directly or indirectly damages or consumes food, fibre, or other material intended for human use or consumption. Like *weeds, many pests are harmless or even beneficial until their numbers increase in response to an abundant food supply.

pest control Any activities that are undertaken in order to restrict, reduce, or eliminate particular *pests in a given area.

pesticide A chemical (e.g. *insecticide, *fungicide, *nematicide, *rodenticide, *herbicide, or *germicide) that is used to kill or control *insect pests, *weeds, *fungi, *nematodes, *rodents, or *micro-organisms.

pesticide persistence The *persistence of a *pesticide, that is usually expressed in terms of *half-life (the length of time required for one-half of the original quantity to break down) and often divided into three categories: non-persistent (with a typical soil half-life of less than 30 days), moderately persistent (30 to 100 days), or persistent (half-life of more than 100 days).

pesticide resistance A situation in which a *population of *pests becomes *resistant to particular *pesticides so they are no longer affected by them. This can happen through behavioural change (which helps them to avoid the pesticide), biochemical change (which allows them to *detoxify the pesticide), or some other genetic characteristic that reduces their *susceptibility to the pesticide.

pesticide tolerance The amount of *pesticide residue that is permitted by law to remain in or on a *crop that has been harvested; this is set well below the point where the chemicals might be harmful to consumers.

pesticide treadmill The tendency of *pests to become resistant to the effects of particular *pesticides, as a natural part of the evolutionary process. New and more *toxic pesticides then have to be used, to which pests may eventually become resistant, and the spiral continues. *See also* PESTICIDE RESISTANCE.

pet A *domesticated *animal or *bird that is kept for companionship or amusement.

petiole *See* LEAF.

petrified forest The *fossilized remains of a former *forest, in the form of large logs and stumps, usually *in situ. See also* SILICIFICATION.

petrochemicals Chemicals that are derived from *crude oil or *natural gas and are used in the manufacture of many industrial chemicals, *fertilizers, *pesticides, plastics, synthetic fibres, paints, and medicines.

petroglyph A *prehistoric carving or drawing on a natural rock surface.

petrol *See* GASOLINE.

petroleum (crude oil) A naturally occurring liquid that is found in certain *sedimentary rocks and is composed of *hydrocarbons formed by the *anaerobic decay of organic matter. Petroleum can be *refined to produce *gasoline, *paraffin, and *diesel oil. *See also* MINERAL OIL; NATURAL GAS; OIL SHALE.

petroleum derivative A chemical that is formed when *petroleum breaks down in contact with *groundwater.

petroleum geology The study of the occurrence and exploitation of *oil and *gas fields.

petroleum product Any product that is derived from *petroleum or *natural gas.

petroleum refinery An installation (*refinery) that makes *petroleum products from *crude oil, unfinished oils, natural gas liquids, other *hydrocarbons, and alcohol.

PFA *See* PULVERIZED FLY ASH.

PFC *See* PERFLUOROCARBON.

pH A measure (short for potential hydrogen) of the concentration of hydrogen ions and thus the level of *acidity or *alkalinity of a solution. It is based on a (logarithmic) scale from 1.0 to 14.0, in which 7.0 represents a neutral state (such as distilled water), 1.0 is the most *acidic, and 14.0 is the most *alkaline or *basic.

phaeozems Any soil, apart from *chernozems and *kastanozems, with a surface *soil horizon that is dark in colour and contains (by weight) at least 1% organic matter or 0.6% organic carbon. Phaeozems are a reference soil group in the *World Soil Classification.

phalaenophily *Pollination by moths.

Phanerozoic The most recent eon of geological time, since the end of the *Proterozoic, which covers the last 542 million years, during which multicelled organisms appeared and left *fossil traces in rocks, and life on Earth has become more varied, complex, and abundant.

(((⊕))) SEE WEB LINKS

• The Phanerozoic eon.

pharmaceuticals Medicinal drugs which are prescribed by a doctor in order to cure, prevent, or treat diseases and relieve pains.

phase One of the four forms in which any matter can exist, as a solid (for water, in the form of ice), as a liquid, as a gas (*water vapour), or as a *plasma.

phase change A change from one *phase of matter to another. For water, the six phase changes are *melting, *freezing, *evaporation (vaporization), *condensation, *deposition, and *sublimation.

phenetic classification (phenetics) An approach to the classification of *organisms that is based on observable similarities and differences between taxa, with no assumptions about evolution. Largely replaced in recent years by *cladistics.

phenetic species concept The definition of *species as groups of individuals that look similar to each other and distinct from other groups. *See* BIOLOGICAL SPECIES CONCEPT; CLADISTIC SPECIES CONCEPT; ECOLOGICAL SPECIES CONCEPT; RECOGNITION SPECIES CONCEPT.

phenetics *See* PHENETIC CLASSIFICATION.

phenocryst A large *crystal in an *igneous rock, that is surrounded by a finer-grained *matrix.

phenol A white, crystalline compound (C_6H_5OH) that is derived from *benzene and used in the manufacture of some resins, weed killers, plastics, and disinfectants, and in the *petroleum refining process. It is *toxic to humans, and may be *carcinogenic.

phenology The study of periodic biological phenomena, such as flowering, breeding, and migration, especially in relation to climate.

phenotype The outward appearance, physical attributes, or behaviour of an *organism that develop through the interaction of the *environment and *genotype during growth and development. Individuals with the same genotype can have different phenotypes in different environments. *See also* ACQUIRED TRAIT; PHENOTYPIC ADAPTATION; TRAIT.

phenotypic adaptation A non-genetic form of biological *adaptation in *organisms, which occurs through behavioural changes in individuals.

pheromone A chemical substance that an animal releases into the environment and that elicits a response in another animal of the same species. For example, pheromones are used to attract mates, promote social cohesion, mark trails and territory, and as warnings.

pheromone trap A trap which uses either a natural or synthetic insect sex attractant *pheromone.

phi (ϕ) scale A scale that geologists use to measure the *particle size of *sediments, based on the logarithm of size rather than size in millimetres. The scale has zero in the fine sand range, with positive values for finer material (down to *clay) and negative values for coarser material (up to large *boulders).

philopatry Literally, love of one's native *habitat. It is the tendency of an individual not to disperse from its natal location, its home area. Most animal species show some degree of philopatry. One sex may be more philopatric than the other. For example, male birds tend to be more philopatric than females, and female mammals than males. *Compare* DISPERSAL.

philosophy 1. The love of and search for wisdom or knowledge, embracing logic, epistemology (the examination of the basis of knowledge), moral philosophy, ethics, etc. **2.** A statement or system of beliefs, which influence thought, action, and knowledge.

phloem The tissue in a *vascular plant that transports dissolved *nutrients from the leaves to the other parts of the plant.

phosphate A *non-metallic salt of *phosphorus and *oxygen which occurs naturally. Phosphates are a constituent of *nucleic acids and are essential for life. Plants use phosphates during *photosynthesis, and they are generally a *limiting factor. Phosphates are also released into the environment by *fertilizers and *detergents, act as a *nutrient pollutant in water, and contribute to *eutrophication.

phosphorescence A type of luminescence in which a substance absorbs energy and releases it slowly in the form of light. It should not be confused with *bioluminescence.

phosphorus (P) A *non-metallic element and one of the elements (*macronutrient) essential for the growth of *organisms. Phosphorus compounds are major constituents in the tissues of both plants and animals. Increased phosphorus levels result from the discharge of phosphorus-containing materials (such as *fertilizers) into surface waters, and this can contribute to *eutrophication.

phosphorus cycle The natural *biogeochemical cycle through which *phosphorus is moved through *environmental systems, from rocks through the *biosphere and *hydrosphere and back to rocks.

phosphorus plant Any *facility that uses electric furnaces to produce *phosphorus for commercial use, such as high grade phosphoric acid, *phosphate-based detergent, and organic chemicals.

photic Of, relating to, or caused by light. *Contrast* APHOTIC.

photic zone (epipelagic zone) The zone of a waterbody through which light penetrates, in which *photosynthetic organisms live. *Contrast* BATHYPELAGIC ZONE.

photoautotroph An *autotroph that uses light energy from the Sun to manufacture food, via *photosynthesis. *Compare* CHEMOAUTOTROPH.

photoblastic Applied to *seeds that use light to sense when conditions are right for germination.

photochemical oxidant A *conventional or *criteria pollutant that is created by the action of *sunlight on *nitrogen oxides and *hydrocarbons. *See also* PHOTOCHEMICAL SMOG.

photochemical pollutant Any chemical that reacts photochemically (in the presence of *sunlight) to destroy *ozone in the *stratosphere.

photochemical reaction A chemical reaction that is triggered by *sunlight.

photochemical smog A brownish atmospheric *haze that is often found above large urban or industrial centres during hot dry weather, and is caused by reactions between *air pollutants (particularly *ozone, *nitrogen oxides, and unburned *fuel from vehicle exhausts) in the presence of *sunlight. Such smogs were first observed in California in the 1940s, but they are becoming increasingly common in many heavily built-up areas. Many plants wilt and sometimes die when exposed to photochemical smogs, and people and animals suffer from irritation of the eyes and lungs. One way of controlling photochemical smogs is to cut down on the emissions of pollutant gases (particularly nitrogen oxides) from vehicle exhausts. Vehicle exhaust emission controls have been introduced in North America, the EU, and in many other countries to address this problem. *Catalytic converters on vehicle exhausts are designed to reduce exhaust gas emissions. *See* PHOTOLYTIC CYCLE.

photochemistry The branch of *chemistry that deals with the chemical action of light.

photodegradable Capable of being broken down by *ultraviolet light, for example in *sunlight.

photodissociation (photolysis) Chemical decomposition involving *sunlight, in which molecules are split into their constituent atoms.

photoelectric Relating to the conversion of light (*radiant energy) to electricity.

photolysis *See* PHOTODISSOCIATION.

photolytic cycle A naturally occurring sequence of chemical reactions that take place in the lower atmosphere in which *ultraviolet radiation supplies the energy for the *photodissociation of nitrogen dioxide (NO_2), which then reforms. Ozone that forms in the second reaction may leave the cycle to react with *hydrocarbons to produce *photochemical smog. The reactions are: $NO_2 + UV \rightarrow NO + O$ (1); $O + O_2 \rightarrow O_3$ (2); $O_3 + NO \rightarrow NO_2 + O_2$ (3).

photon A unit of *electromagnetic energy which has no electric charge and is generally regarded as a particle with zero mass.

photo-oxidant An oxidizing air pollutant (e.g. *ozone, *nitrogen dioxide, or *PAN) that is created by *photochemical reaction.

photoperiod The duration of the *daylight period.

photoperiodism The response of *organisms to changes in *day length, for example through changes in growth rate, feeding pattern, migration, and reproduction.

photophilous Tolerant of strong light. *Contrast* PHOTOPHOBIC, SCIOPHILOUS.

photophobic Very sensitive to light. *Contrast* PHOTOPHILOUS.

photorespiration A process in *C3 plants that occurs when CO_2 levels are low and that reduces the efficiency of *photosynthesis. The *enzyme (rubisco) that catalyses the fixation of CO_2 accepts either O_2 or CO_2, so the gases compete. While CO_2 is being consumed during photosynthesis its level falls and rubisco adds O_2 rather than CO_2 to the next stage of the cycle. This alters the sequence of reactions with the release of some of the CO_2 absorbed earlier. The process is called *respiration because it absorbs O_2 and releases CO_2, but it does so without yielding any energy.

photosphere The bright visible surface of the Sun.

photosynthate The *carbohydrate (including starch and sugar) that is synthesized during the process of *photosynthesis.

p

photosynthesis A complex process occurring within the cells of green plants and *cyanobacteria where the energy of sunlight, captured by *chlorophyll, powers the *reduction of *carbon dioxide and the synthesis of simple sugars, with the release of oxygen as a waste product (see Fig. 16). The sugars are used in the synthesis of proteins and other compounds, and provide a source of energy released through *respiration. *Contrast* CHEMOSYNTHESIS.

photosynthesizer A plant that carries out *photosynthesis.

photosynthetic efficiency The percentage of available light that is captured by *plants and used in *photosynthesis to make useful products.

photosynthetic rate The rate at which the reactions of *photosynthesis proceed, measured as either the rate at which a plant releases oxygen or the weight of *chlorophyll, per unit area or mass of green tissue.

phototaxis A change in the direction of movement of an organism in response to a change in light intensity.

phototroph An *autotroph that obtains energy from light, mainly by *photosynthesis.

phototropism The growth of plants towards *sunlight or other light source.

photovoltaic Technology for converting *sunlight directly into *electricity, usually with *photovoltaic cells.

photovoltaic cell (solar cell) An electronic device, consisting of layers of semiconductor materials, that is capable of converting incident light directly into an electric current.

photovoltaic energy The electrical energy produced when sunlight incident on a *photovoltaic cell is converted into electrical current.

Phragmites A genus of reed-grasses (family Poaceae) that grow in *wetland habitats such as *marshes, lake margins, or river banks.

phreatic Of or relating to *groundwater.

phreatic eruption A *volcanic eruption caused by the interaction of *magma with *groundwater, lake water, or seawater. The water adjacent to the magma is vaporized and expands, increasing the pressure on the surrounding water. When the pressure exceeds the confining pressure of the overlying water column the water vapour expands explosively, producing a steam-dominated eruption.

phreatic surface The upper surface of *groundwater within an *aquifer.

Fig. 16 Photosynthesis

phreatic zone *See* SATURATED ZONE.

phreatophyte *See* HYDROPHYTE.

phycobiont The principal algal or cyanobacterial *symbiont in a *lichen.

phycology (algology) The study of *algae.

phyletic evolution *Genetic changes that occur within the line of descent of a *species.

phyletic gradualism The belief that *evolution and *speciation occur over a long period of time through slow, progressive change. *Contrast* PUNCTUATED EQUILIBRIUM.

phylogenetic Relating to evolutionary development. *Contrast* ONTOGENETIC.

phylogenetic species concept *See* CLADISTIC SPECIES CONCEPT.

phylogenetic systematics *See* CLADISTICS.

phylogenetics The study of the relationships between *organisms; a branch of *systematics.

phylogeny The evolutionary history and line of descent of a *species.

phylum (*pl.* phyla) The third highest category in the scientific system of classification for animals and *fungi (*taxonomy), below *domain and *kingdom and above *class. Each kingdom comprises more than one phylum, and each phylum comprises more than one class. For example, the phylum Mollusca includes slugs, snails, clams, squid. The phylum Chordata includes all of the 'higher' animals (including fish, *amphibians, *reptiles, *birds, and *mammals), and the phylum Arthropoda (*arthropods) covers *insects, spiders, and *crustaceans. In older plant classifications phyla were sometimes called divisions; modern plant classification (*see* ANGIOSPERM PHYLOGENY GROUP) does not recognize phyla.

physical and chemical treatment Processes that are used to clean up pollution (including toxic materials in surface and *groundwater, *oil spills, and hazardous materials on or in the ground) and in large-scale *wastewater treatment facilities. Physical processes may include *air stripping or *filtration. Chemical treatment includes *coagulation, *chlorination, or *ozonation.

physical environment The *inorganic surroundings that are necessary for life, such as air, water, soil, rock, and sunlight.

physical factor Any non-living (*abiotic) factor, such as temperature, light, water, minerals, and climate, that influence an *organism.

physical oceanography The study of the world's *oceans, particularly in terms of water masses and their motions.

physical planning A form of *land use planning, particularly in *urban areas, which seeks to achieve a physically attractive environment by regulating the relationships between structures and their sites and surroundings.

physical quality of life A measure of economic welfare that is more sophisticated than *gross national product, and is based on three variables: percentage of the population which is literate, infant *mortality rate, and average *life expectancy after the age of one.

physical weathering *See* MECHANICAL WEATHERING.

physics The study of matter and energy, and their interactions.

physiognomic Based on physical features.

physiognomy 1. External appearance: an old-fashioned term to describe the *topography and other physical characteristics of a *landform and its *vegetation. **2.** The form and structure of natural communities.

physiographic climax *See* CLIMAX COMMUNITY.

physiographic province An area or region across which *elevation, *relief, *lithology, geological structure and geological history are similar, and different from those in surrounding regions.

physiographic region An area with similar *landforms.

physiography The natural physical features of the land surface.

physiological drought A condition caused by high salt levels in the *root zone of a soil, in which water in the soil is attracted to the salt, leaving less available for uptake from the soil by plants. This causes similar symptoms of stress in plants to those caused by normal *drought.

physiological race A geographically defined population of a *species that is physiologically distinct from other populations.

physiology The study of functions and processes in living things.

phyto- As a prefix (such as *phytoplankton), relating to plants.

phytochemical Relating to the *chemistry of plants, plant products, and plant processes.

phytohormone See PLANT GROWTH REGULATOR.

phytology See BOTANY.

phytomedicine The use of medicinal products that are based on plants.

phytonutrient Any *nutrient that is derived from plants.

phytophagous Plant-eating.

phytoplankton Microscopic floating aquatic plants, such as *algae and *diatoms.

phytoremediation *Remediation that uses plants to remove *contaminants from *soils, *sediments, and *groundwater. See PHYTOTREATMENT.

phytotoxic Harmful or poisonous to plants.

phytotoxin A substance that causes reduced growth in or kills plants.

phytotreatment The cultivation of specialized plants that absorb particular *contaminants from the soil through their roots or foliage. A form of *phytoremediation.

picocurie (pCi) A unit for measuring radioactivity, often expressed as picocuries per litre of air. One picocurie = one million millionth of a *curie = 0.037 *becquerel.

picoplankton *Planktonic organisms that range in size from 0.2 to 2.0 *micrometres.

piedmont An area of gently rolling hills at the base of a *mountain or mountain range.

piedmont glacier A lobe of ice that forms when a valley glacier extends beyond the walls of its valley and on to the adjacent lowland (piedmont).

piezometer An instrument that is used to measure *hydraulic pressure.

piezometric surface The surface of the static water level in a *confined aquifer.

pile 1. The *fuel element in a *nuclear reactor. **2.** A heap of material. **3.** A column of wood, steel, or concrete that is driven into the ground to support a structure.

pillow lava Volcanic *lava that has solidified under water and resembles heaps of pillows.

pilot balloon A small *meteorological balloon that is filled with helium and tracked as it rises through the *atmosphere at a predetermined rate, in order to determine how wind speed and direction change with altitude.

pilot test A small study that is carried out prior to a large-scale study, in order to test the suitability of a technique or procedure.

Pinchot, Gifford A US politician and conservationist (1865–1946) who served as the first Chief of the *US Forest Service (1905–10), was Republican Governor of Pennsylvania (1923–27 and 1931–35), and is remembered for advocating the conservation of resources, especially US forest reserves, through scientific approaches to their planned use and renewal.

pine barren An area of pine forest in which the various species of pine usually develop as small or medium-sized trees. The barrens coincide with poor, sandy, and to a lesser extent marshy soil, and owe their ecological character in part to centuries of burning. They occur in the south-eastern USA and on the coastal plain of the Atlantic and Gulf of Mexico from New Jersey to Florida (excluding its southern tip) and into Texas.

pingo An ice-cored, dome-shaped hill, oval in plan, 2–50 m high and 30–600 m in diameter, developed in an area of *permafrost. The larger examples have breached crests in which ice may be exposed. Fossil pingos take the form of circular or arced raised ramparts with depressions in their centres which usually contain water bodies, and often occur in groups. Such fossil geomorphological features provide evidence of past *periglacial conditions. See also PALSA.

pinnacle A tall peak on a mountain, or an isolated column of rock.

pinyon–juniper woodland A distinctive North American woodland vegetation with scattered trees of medium height, often mixed with sagebrush and other scrub, which is common in the dry arid mountain regions in the west.

pioneer species Species of plants, *lichens, and *micro-organisms that dominate the vegetation community in the early stages of *succession, because they can colonize bare sites.

pipe *See* SOIL PIPE.

piridaben A type of *insecticide that is used primarily in controlling *mites in tree fruit crops.

pisciculture *See* AQUACULTURE.

pit mining The extraction of material of value from below the surrounding land surface, by excavation of an *open cast mine or a *quarry.

pitchblende *See* URANINITE.

placer A deposit of a valuable *ore (such as mineral-bearing *gravel or *sand) that has formed by a concentration of heavy minerals in flowing water, for example by a stream or waves.

placer deposit A mass of *sand, *gravel, or similar *alluvial material, that can be extracted through *placer mining.

placer mining (hydraulic mining) The extraction of valuable heavy *minerals from a *placer deposit by washing sand and dirt away with a powerful jet of water, leaving behind the desired *mineral (e.g. *gold).

plaggen A *soil horizon, produced by human activity, which is more than 500 mm deep and results from long-continued manuring, often with materials enriched by *phosphate. The name is from the German *Plagge*, meaning sod.

plagioclimax A stable *climax community that arises from a *succession that has been arrested or deflected directly or indirectly as a result of human activities.

plain A large area of level, open land.

planation surface *See* EROSION SURFACE.

planet A body orbiting a *star that is sufficiently massive for its own gravity to make it spherical in shape, but insufficient to cause thermonuclear fusion within it, and that has cleared the region of space around it of *planetismals. *See also* MOON.

planetary albedo The fraction (approximately 30%) of incident *solar radiation that is reflected by the Earth–atmosphere system and returned to space, mostly by backscatter from *clouds in the atmosphere. *See also* ALBEDO.

planetary boundary layer The lowest level of the *atmosphere, where *friction is an important force and vertical mixing is common. Its depth varies but is usually less than about 500 m. *See* BOUNDARY LAYER.

planetary scale *See* GLOBAL SCALE.

planetismal A solid object that occurs during the formation of *planets. Gravity dominates its internal strength and its orbit is not significantly affected by drag from the surrounding gas. In the *solar system a planetismal is more than approximately 1 km in diameter.

planktivore An animal that eats *plankton, usually a fish that feeds on *zooplankton.

plankton *Aquatic organisms that are unable to swim because they have no motor power of their own, so they drift around with the *tide and ocean currents. *Phytoplankton comprise mainly *diatoms; these form the base of aquatic *food chains. *Zooplankton feed on phytoplankton and some have weak powers of locomotion. *Contrast* NEKTON.

planktonic Of or relating to the *plankton.

planktonic foraminifera Single-celled *protozoan *micro-organisms that live near the surface of the ocean and have skeletons made of *calcium carbonate. *See also* FORAMINIFERA.

planned grazing system A system of *grazing in which two or more grazing units are alternately rested from grazing, in a planned sequence, over a period of years.

planned ignition A fire that is started by a deliberate management action.

planned unit development (PUD) zoning *See* CLUSTER ZONING.

planning The act of drawing up plans and establishing a broad outline for goals, policies, and procedures that will accomplish agreed objectives. *See also* MANAGEMENT.

planning horizon The period of time which will be considered in the planning process to which a particular plan relates.

planosols Soils that have within 100 cm of the surface a *soil horizon that has been exposed to stagnant water for a prolonged period. Planosols are a reference soil group in the *World Soil Classification.

planplain *See* PANPLAIN.

plant A member of the *kingdom Plantae, which comprises *eukaryotes that possess *cellulose *cell walls, contain *chlorophyll *a* and *b* within *chloroplasts surrounded by two membranes, store *carbohydrate in the form of *starch, and have cells with two whiplash flagella (*see* FLAGELLUM) at some stage in the life cycle (these are often modified or have been lost in the course of evolution). The kingdom includes all land plants and green *algae.

plant breeding The deliberate improvement of *crops that are grown for food and fibre, based on selecting *genes that produce beneficial traits (such as increased production or decreased costs) and transferring them from one plant to another.

plant community A group of plants (e.g. *broadleaved *woodland) that grow together in a particular area, under given environmental conditions (soil, climate, etc.).

plant formation *See* FORMATION.

plant growth regulator (plant hormone, phytohormone) A substance or mixture of substances, other than a plant nutrient, trace element, or fertilizer, that will accelerate or retard the rate of growth or differentiation of a plant, affecting its maturation or produce. *Auxins, cytokinins, ethylene, and *gibberellins are the most important plant growth regulators. Hormones are classically described as being made at one site and functioning at another, but plant growth regulators are made in various tissues, transported actively or passively, and affect most tissues within the plant, so the term 'hormone' is misleading.

plant hormone *See* PLANT GROWTH REGULATOR.

plant kingdom The taxonomic *kingdom (*Plantae) that comprises all living or extinct *plants.

plant retrogression The reverse of *succession, in which a particular area is successively occupied by less-developed vegetation. In grassland management, for example, continuous *overgrazing of *pasture can cause the plant community to change from desirable, highly productive grasses to low quality, unproductive grasses.

Plantae (plant kingdom) In *taxonomy, the *kingdom of plants.

plantation An area of *forest that has been deliberately sown or planted to produce a cash crop of trees.

plantation agriculture A commercial *agricultural system found in tropical countries, in which specialized crops such as bananas, coffee, flowers, and cacao are grown primarily for export to *developed countries.

Plantlife A British nonprofit organization, founded in 1989 by the *Conservation Foundation, that works to protect wild plants and fungi.

(((🌐))) **SEE WEB LINKS**
• Home page of Plantlife.

planula The free-swimming *larval stage of coelenterates (animals with a fluid-filled body cavity, e.g. *corals).

plasma 1. A hot, electrically neutral gas of ions and free electrons. **2.** The liquid portion of blood, in which cells are suspended.

plasma membrane The outer membrane of a living cell.

plasma-arc reactor An *incinerator that operates at extremely high temperatures and destroys highly *toxic wastes that do not readily burn.

Plasmodium A *parasitic *protozoan that causes malaria in humans.

plastic limit The moisture content at which a *soil changes from solid to *plastic. *See* ATTERBERG LIMITS.

plasticity A property of any material that can flow.

plastics Durable, flexible, synthetic-based products that can be shaped by the application of heat or pressure, some of which (such as *PVC) are difficult to *recycle and pose problems because of their *toxic properties.

plastron 1. In turtles and tortoises (reptiles of the order Chelonia), the bottom part of the shell. *Contrast* CARAPACE. **2.** In some aquatic *insects, a gill consisting of water-repellant hairs that trap a bubble of air when the insect dives below the water surface.

plate *See* CRUSTAL PLATE.

plate boundary The margin between adjacent *crustal plates.

plate tectonics The theory that the Earth's surface is divided into rigid *crustal plates, which can move relative to each other (at an average speed of about 70 km per million years; 7 cm a year) because of the *plastic nature of the underlying *asthenosphere. It is believed that huge, slow-moving *convection currents within the upper *mantle move the crustal plates with them. Seven major plates (Eurasian, North American, South American, African, Pacific, Indian, and Antarctic) are recognized, together with a number of minor ones (e.g. Juan de Fuca, Philippine, Australian, Cocos, Caribbean, Nazca, Scotia, and Arabian). Active plate boundaries coincide with zones of *seismic and *volcanic activity, and plate movements are accompanied by the formation of new oceanic crust at *mid-oceanic ridges and the *subduction of plates at destructive margins. These large-scale crustal movements shape the Earth's surface and create all of its major natural features including *mountains, ocean basins, deep *ocean trenches, *volcanoes, and *earthquakes. The concept of plate tectonics draws together *continental drift, *sea-floor spreading, crustal structures, and volcanism into a coherent model of the way the outer layer of the Earth changes over time.

platy 1. Applied to soil *aggregates that are long and flat, rather than round or spherical. **2.** Applied to *minerals with a thin, flat, crystal structure (e.g. mica).

play 1. An underground source of *shale gas; the equivalent of a conventional gas field. **2.** The combination of factors that allow oil and gas to accumulate in a particular place.

playa A dry, flat-floored lake bed in a *desert, which may *flood from time to time, during *ephemeral flows after *storms. Many playas have a white, crusty layer of salts, formed by *salinization.

Pleistocene The first *epoch within the *Quaternary period, which began 2.588 million years ago and lasted until 11 800 years ago. During the Pleistocene climate switched between *glacial and *interglacial conditions through a number of cycles. Geological evidence from many locations throughout North America supports a four-phase model of glacial advances (called the *Kansan, *Nebraskan, *Illinoian, and *Wisconsinan), although there is evidence that many parts of Europe experienced five glacial periods. Ice covered much of the *northern hemisphere, largely removing all traces of earlier landscapes across much of Eur-

ope and North America and replacing them with distinctive glacial landforms, including the *Great Lakes. *Moraines indicate the outer limits of ice advance, which correlate closely with the distribution of glacial deposits and landforms. Most of the Pleistocene ice had melted by the start of the *Holocene, about 10 000 years ago, but valley glaciers remain in some high altitude mountain areas in both hemispheres and ice caps survive in Greenland and other parts of the *Arctic, and in *Antarctica.

(((@))) SEE WEB LINKS
• Pleistocene: The Ice Age.

Pleistogene *See* QUATERNARY.

plesiobiosis A rudimentary form of social *symbiosis, which involves the close proximity of nests of different species of social insects (such as ants).

pleuston *Organisms that float on the sea surface.

plinthite A constituent of a *mineral soil, comprising a large proportion of iron and aluminium oxides, *clay, and *quartz, which has developed through a combination of *leaching and *gleying in well-weathered tropical soils. On drying, plinthite changes irreversibly to an ironstone *hardpan.

plinthosols Soils that have an iron-rich *soil horizon containing more than 25% *plinthite within 50 cm of the surface. The plinthic material hardens when exposed to the air. Plinthosols are a reference soil group in the *World Soil Classification.

Pliocene The final *epoch of the *Neogene period, between 5.332 and 2.588 million years ago, when climate was relatively warm but cooling, with little *glaciation, and more and larger species of *mammal evolved. The appearance of new *land bridges led to extensive animal migration; three-toed horses crossed from North America into Eurasia and many mammals crossed from North America into South America.

(((@))) SEE WEB LINKS
• The Pliocene epoch of the Neogene period.

plot A small piece of land.

plough A farm tool with one or more heavy blades that break the soil surface, cut a furrow, and turn the soil over in preparation for sowing and growing crops. Spelled plow in North America.

plow See PLOUGH.

plucking See QUARRYING.

plug A comparatively small, steep sided body of *igneous rock which is approximately circular in plan. Some plugs are in-filled and solidified feeder channels for *volcanoes.

plugging 1. The process of stopping the flow of water, oil, or gas into or out of a rock formation through a *borehole or *well. **2.** The process of filling and abandoning a well.

plume A visible or measurable discharge of a *contaminant that is released from a particular source into the air, *groundwater, or surface water.

pluton See INTRUSION.

plutonic See INTRUSIVE.

plutonium (Pu) A heavy, *radioactive, metallic element (atomic number 94) that is similar to *uranium. It undergoes *fission when bombarded with *neutrons and is used in the production of *nuclear energy and the explosion of nuclear weapons. It occurs in nature in trace amounts, but is also produced as a *byproduct of the fission reaction in a uranium-fuelled nuclear reactor, and can be recovered for future use. See also BREEDER REACTOR.

pluvial A period during which the *climate is relatively wet. A pluvial period lasts for decades or longer, between *interpluvials.

pluvial lake A *lake that is formed during a *pluvial period.

pluvial period See PLUVIAL.

PM Particulate material.

PM₂.₅ Fine particulate material in the air which is less than 2.5 *micrometres in diameter. It is released by combustion, and their small size (about 1/30th the width of a human hair) allows these particles to penetrate deeply into the lungs when inhaled, so they are considered more harmful than PM_{10} particles.

PM₁₀ Particulate material in the air which is less than 10 *micrometres in diameter and includes soot, dust, smoke, fumes, and *aerosols. The particles are small enough to be inhaled by humans and can damage health. PM_{10} is a *criteria air pollutant that can cause reduced visibility.

PME See PARTICIPATORY MONITORING AND EVALUATION.

PNA See POLYNUCLEAR AROMATIC HYDROCARBON.

PNC See POTENTIAL NATURAL COMMUNITY.

pneumoconiosis A lung disease that is caused by the long-term inhalation of fine particulates.

PNV See PRESENT NET VALUE; POTENTIAL NATURAL VEGETATION.

Poaceae (Gramineae) The grasses, which comprise a large family of plants, most of which are *annual or *perennial herbs, but a few of which (e.g. bamboos) are woody. Ecologically, grasses are the most successful of all flowering plants; where forests have been cleared grasses have tended to replace trees as the dominant vegetation. Economically, the family includes the cereal crops: barley, maize, millet, oats, rice, rye, and wheat. Many species are important sources of fibre. There are 737 genera with about 7950 species distributed throughout the world.

poach To hunt, trap, or fish illegally.

poaching Hunting, trapping, or fishing illegally.

pocosin A swamp or marsh vegetation underlain by poorly drained, mostly organic soil, which is found on the southeastern coastal plain of the USA, particularly North Carolina.

podsol See PODZOLS.

podsolization See PODZOLIZATION.

podzolization (podsolization) A *soil-forming process by which the upper *horizon of a *soil becomes *acidic through the *leaching of bases which are deposited in the lower horizons (e.g. in a *pedalfer). It usually occurs under forests in areas with cool, moist climates and quite severe winters, where *decomposition of *organic matter is inhibited and a peaty mat of acidic organic material builds up on the soil surface. Mixing of organic matter and mineral matter within the soil is very limited because there are relatively few organisms.

podzols (podsol) Shallow, greyish-white *acidic soils with relatively little organic content and few soil organisms, which develop under *coniferous or heath vegetation in *temperate to cold moist climates. Podzols are usually infertile and unsuitable for agriculture. Podzols are a reference soil group in the *World Soil Classification.

p

poikilotherm An animal whose body temperature varies with the temperature of its surrounding environment. Fish and amphibians are poikilotherms. *Contrast* HOMEOTHERM.

point bar A low ridge of *sand and *gravel that is deposited along the inner bank of a *meandering *alluvial stream, where flow velocity is relatively low.

point of exposure The point at which an individual or *population may come into contact with a chemical of concern that originates from a particular site.

point source *Pollution that originates from a stationary source or a fixed facility, such as a pipeline or a factory. *Contrast* NON-POINT SOURCE.

poison A chemical that adversely affects health by causing injury, illness, or death.

polar At, near, or relating to the North or South Pole, or to the ends (poles) of a magnet.

polar air mass A cold *air mass that forms in a *high-latitude source region.

polar cell That part of the atmospheric circulation in which air subsides over one of the polar regions, flows away from the pole at low level, rises at the *polar front where it meets the *Ferrel cell, and flows towards the pole at high level.

polar climate A *climate zone that has no warm season, receives limited precipitation, and experiences penetrating cold with temperatures below 10°C throughout the year.

polar continental air mass An *air mass that develops over large land masses at high latitude, contains cold, dry, and stable air, and brings cool conditions in summer and cold conditions in winter.

polar easterlies Easterly winds that develop at high latitudes *poleward of the *subpolar low.

polar front The boundary in middle latitudes between polar and tropical air, where the *Ferrel cells and *polar cells meet.

polar front jet stream The *jet stream wind that is associated with the *polar front.

polar high One of two regions of persistent high surface atmospheric pressure that cover the Arctic Basin and Antarctica.

polar ice cap An *ice cap that forms close to the North or South Pole over land or sea. The interior of Greenland, West Antarctica, and East Antarctica are covered with what are more correctly termed *ice sheets.

polar maritime air mass An *air mass that develops over the oceans in higher latitudes, contains cool, moist air, and brings heavy cloud cover and dull conditions in winter and mild fair weather in summer.

polar molecule A molecule that does not carry a net electric charge, but in which the electrons are unequally shared between the atomic nuclei. In the water molecule, for example, the pull of the oxygen nucleus on the shared electrons is greater than the pull of the hydrogen nuclei. As a result, the oxygen end of the molecule carries a small negative charge and each of the hydrogen ends of the molecule carries a small positive charge. The molecule is said to have a dipole moment and can attract other molecules with a dipole moment.

polar region The area around the *poles, in which the climate is permanently cold and inhospitable.

polar stratospheric cloud (PSC) A type of cloud that forms in winter in the *stratosphere over Antarctica and less commonly over the Arctic at altitudes of 15–25 km. The clouds form in the very still air in the polar night vortex produced by the strong *geostrophic wind that circulates in winter. There are two principal types of PSCs. Type 1 consist of liquid droplets, about 0.001–0.1 mm in diameter, composed of a mixture of sulphuric (H_2SO_4) and nitric (HNO_3) acids dissolved in water. These clouds form at about 15 km where the temperature of approximately 195 kelvin (-78°C) is above the frost point. Type 2 PSCs are made from ice crystals and form at about 25 km where the temperature is approximately 188 kelvin (−85°C). Type 2 PSCs are seldom seen over the Arctic, where air temperatures are usually too high for them to form. The reactions that deplete stratospheric ozone (*see* OZONE HOLE) take place on the surface of PSC ice crystals.

polar wander The natural long-term cycle of movement of the Earth's *magnetic field. Evidence of polar wander is preserved in the pattern of changes in magnetic alignment (*palaeomagnetism) in rocks. As molten rock solidifies its particles align with the prevailing magnetic field, then retain that alignment. Rocks from different regions are aligned differently, showing that the rocks have moved since their formation.

This provides strong evidence for *continental drift. *See also* POLARITY REVERSAL.

polar-desert soil A *mineral soil that lacks identifiable *soil horizons, and has almost no surface *humus. It is associated with arid, polar-desert environments where precipitation is less than 130 mm annually, plant cover less than 25%, and thawed, active soil is 20–70 mm deep.

polarity Having a positive or negative charge.

polarity reversal A 180° change in the alignment of the Earth's magnetic field, so that the North and South magnetic poles exchange positions. Three such reversals have occurred every million years during the last 60 million years, but there have also been periods of up to 50 million years with no reversal.

polder A low-lying area of land that has been reclaimed from the sea by being artificially drained and protected from flooding by building *dykes, and is kept dry by continuous pumping.

pole 1. A point on the Earth where the axis of rotation intersects the surface. 2. One end of a magnetic dipole, e.g. one of the Earth's magnetic poles. *See also* NORTH POLE; SOUTH POLE. 3. A young tree. *See also* SAPLING.

poleward Towards one of the *poles.

policy A written plan of action that is adopted by an individual or group in order to accomplish some particular social or economic goal.

policy cycle The process by which problems are identified and acted upon in the public arena, for example by local and national government.

political ecology An umbrella term for a variety of projects that involve politics and the environment, including attempts to study politics using the language and methods of *ecology, the study of political struggles for control over *natural resources, and research on *biodiversity and *natural resource exploitation that is intended to inform public policy.

politics Social relations that involve authority or power; the science and methods of government.

pollard A traditional form of *woodland management in which mature trees are felled at about two metres above ground level in order to promote the regrowth of a crown of poles

above the reach of *grazing animals. *See also* COPPICE.

pollen Tiny, powdery grains derived from seed plants that contain the male reproductive cells. The pollen of each plant has a distinctive size and shape, which helps in *pollen analysis.

pollen analysis A technique that is used to reconstruct past *climate. Variations in the frequency of *pollen grains at different layers within a soil, sediment, or deposit can be analysed and the results plotted on a *pollen diagram. When *spores and micro-organisms are included in the study it is known as palynology.

pollen basket Part of the back (posterior) legs of the honeybee, in which it stores *pollen.

pollen diagram A graph of the results of a *pollen analysis for a particular site, which shows changes in the relative proportions of the *pollen of different plants over a period of time, and indicates changes in vegetation and, by inference, climate.

pollen rain The *pollen grains and *spores that fall on a particular site.

pollination The transfer of *pollen from the male part of a flower (stamen) to the female part of a flower (the style and stigma), by a *pollinator. *See also* MONOLECTIC; OLIGOLECTIC; POLYLECTIC.

pollinator An agent that carries *pollen to the female part of a flower, including beetles (*cantharophily), flies (*myophily), wasps (*specophily), ants (*myrmecophily), bees (*melittophily), butterflies (*psychophily), and moths (*phalaenophily).

pollutant A substance that *pollutes or causes *pollution. *See also* AIR POLLUTANT; WATER POLLUTANT.

pollutant pathway The route along which a particular *pollutant is distributed, for example within a building or through an *environmental system.

pollute To make impure or dirty with harmful or poisonous substances.

polluted Contaminated by *pollution.

polluter A person or organization that causes pollution of the environment.

polluter pays principle (PPP) The principle that the *polluter should pay the costs of controlling the *pollution they generate, and of cleaning up any environmental damage that is caused by that pollution.

pollution The process of contaminating or polluting. *See also* AIR POLLUTION; NOISE POLLUTION; WATER POLLUTION.

pollution charge The fee or charge that is levied per unit of pollution, based on the *polluter pays principle.

pollution control Any activities that are carried out in order to reduce or eliminate *pollution.

pollution episode (episode) A serious air pollution or water pollution incident in a particular area at a point in time.

pollution indicator Any *indicator that is used to show the presence of specific environmental conditions or *pollutants.

pollution permit An approach to the control of pollution emissions in which *polluters can bid for a *permit that allows them to create a given amount of *pollution. Permits can be resold, and the government can gradually reduce the number of permits that are available so that total pollution emissions can be controlled.

Pollution Prevention and Control (PPC) An approach to the control of *pollution in the UK, introduced under the EU *Integrated Pollution Prevention and Control Directive (IPPC Directive), that requires any operator of a factory or plant to obtain a *permit from the *environmental regulator and comply with the conditions in that permit. This replaced *integrated pollution control in 2000.

pollution prevention pays programme An approach to *environmental management that is based on preventing pollution (by elimination, reduction, or substitution) rather than dealing with it once it has occurred.

Pollution Standards Index (PSI) A system developed by the US *Environmental Protection Agency for measuring pollution levels for the major *air pollutants that are regulated under the *Clean Air Act, based on the health effects of several pollutants. It ranges from 0 (healthy) to 500 (extremely unhealthy). In 1999 the PSI was replaced by the *Air Quality Index (AQI).

polonium (Po) A *radioactive element that occurs in *pitchblende and other ores that contain *uranium.

polybrominated biphenyls (PBBs) Manufactured chemicals that were added as flame retardants to plastics used to make such goods as television sets, computer monitors, plastic foams, and textiles. PBBs were found to cause a variety of complaints when ingested. They are chemically stable and accumulate along food chains. Their manufacture and use is now banned in most countries.

polychlorinated biphenyl (PCB) A synthetic, *organic chemical that was once widely used in electrical equipment, specialized hydraulic systems, heat transfer systems, and other industrial products. It is highly *toxic and a potent *carcinogen, and the management of PCB wastes is tightly regulated.

polyculture *Crop cultivation in which a variety of different plants are grown together in the same *field. *Contrast* MONOCULTURE.

polycyclic aromatic (PCA) *See* POLYCYCLIC AROMATIC HYDROCARBON.

polycyclic aromatic hydrocarbon (PAH, polynuclear aromatics, PNAs, polycyclic aromatics, PCAs) A class of *organic compounds that contain hydrogen and carbon, found in products such as *petroleum and creosote. Some are *carcinogens.

polycyclic organic matter (POM) A broad class of compounds that are formed primarily from *combustion. POM is present in the air in *particulate form, and comes from diverse sources including vehicle exhaust, fires, and hazardous waste sites.

polyembryony Producing two or more young from the same egg.

polygamous Having more than one mate at a time.

polygenetic Caused by multiple processes, or created in a number of phases during which different processes were dominant.

polyhaline 1. Relating to *brackish water which has a *salinity between 18‰ and 30‰. *See* VENICE SYSTEM. **2.** Applied to a salt-tolerant species found in saline environments.

polylectic Applied to a *pollinator which collects *pollen from many species of plant. *Contrast* MONOLECTIC; OLIGOLECTIC.

polymer A substance that is made of many repeating chemical units or *molecules. Natural polymers include *proteins (polymers of amino acids) and synthetic polymers include *PVC (a polymer of vinyl chloride).

polymerase chain reaction (PCR) An enzymatic technique for producing a large number of copies of a specified type of *DNA segment. PCR may be specific to one particular DNA sequence within the *genome, or more general.

polymictic Applied to a *freshwater lake in which the water is circulating almost continuously.

polymorphic Occurring in two or more distinct forms.

polymorphism The occurrence of more than one distinct form of individual in a *population.

Polynesian floral region R. Good's Polynesian subkingdom within his *Palaeotropical floral kingdom (*The Geography of the Flowering Plants*, 1974), which contains a small, derived flora with only nine or ten *endemic genera, scattered through the various islands. The affinities are with Malesia and Australia, and there is no distinct 'Polynesian' flora as such. The great majority of the floral elements have been derived from adjacent floras. *See also* MELANESIA AND MICRONESIA FLORAL REGION.

polynuclear aromatic (PNA) *See* POLYCYCLIC AROMATIC HYDROCARBON.

polyp A small tube-like *marine animal which lives in warm, clear seas and grows with one end attached to the sea-bed, to rocks, or to other polyps. On the other end is a mouth surrounded by finger-like, stirging tentacles. Live *coral is made of polyps.

polyp bailout The process by which some stony *corals release themselves from their skeleton and drift to a new location, usually induced by stress.

polypeptide A linear *polymer composed of ten or more *amino acids linked by *peptide bonds.

polyphagous Feeding on or using many kinds of plant or animal, usually plant species from several families. *Contrast* MONOPHAGOUS.

polyphenism The occurrence of several *phenotypes in a *population that may be caused by environmental influences but is not due to different *genetic types.

polyphyletic A group of *species that do not have one common *ancestor species.

polyploid An organism that contains two or more sets of *genes or *chromosomes.

polytypic Applied to a *species that is divided taxonomically into *subspecies, or that varies geographically.

polyvinyl chloride (PVC) A tough *polymer plastic that has many everyday uses (including footwear, electrical cable, packaging, and toys), is not *biodegradable, and releases *hydrochloric acid when burned.

polyxenous In *symbiosis, having two or more *host families.

POM *See* POLYCYCLIC ORGANIC MATTER.

pond A pool of still water, often artificially created. A type of freshwater *wetland.

pool A shallow body of freshwater.

pool and riffle A common sequence of *bedforms in *alluvial channels, which tend to have narrow, deep sections (the pools) with fine *sediment on the bed, alternating with wider, shallower sections with *gravel beds (the riffles). This pool and riffle sequence appears to play an important role in the development of *meandering.

POP *See* PERSISTENT ORGANIC POLLUTANT.

population 1. A group of individuals of the same *species who are living in the same area at the same time and share a common *gene pool, which makes it possible for them to interbreed. **2.** In statistics, the complete set of individuals, alive or not. *Contrast* SAMPLE.

population at risk A subgroup of a *population, which is more likely to be exposed to a particular agent, or is more sensitive to that agent, than is the general population.

Population Bomb An influential book by Paul and *Anne Ehrlich (1968), in which they predicted imminent famine and disaster on a scale unprecedented in world history.

Population Connection A campaigning organization in the USA, originally called *Zero Population Growth, which was founded by *Paul Ehrlich in 1968 and adopted its new name in 2002. Its main focus is on the relationships between population, environment, and society.

population crash (dieback) A sudden sharp reduction in the size of a *population that can be caused by *disease, environmental stress (such as *pollution), or when its numbers exceed the *carrying capacity of its *habitat. *Contrast* POPULATION EXPLOSION. *See also* MAL-THUSIAN GROWTH.

population density The number of individuals of a *species occupying a particular area or volume (of water) at a specified time.

population dose The total *dose of *radiation that is received by individuals in a population that is exposed to a particular source or event.

population dynamics The study of the factors that affect the growth, stability, and decline of *populations, and of the interactions between those factors.

population explosion A sudden rapid rise in the number of individuals in a population in which the *birth rate exceeds *mortality rate. It generally brings increased environmental damage, through increased *resource use, *waste production, *pollution, and *land use change. A population explosion is also widely associated with social impacts such as low living standards, low education standards, unemployment and *poverty, *malnutrition and *starvation, civil unrest, large-scale *migration (both internal and international), the growth of huge *megacities and associated *shanty towns, and unsustainable pressures on government institutions and national economies. *Contrast* POPULATION CRASH. *See also* MALTHUSIAN GROWTH; OVERPOPULATION.

population genetics The study of the patterns and causes of variation in *genes among a group of individuals within a *population.

population momentum The tendency for *population growth to continue beyond *replacement level, because of a relatively large number of individuals of child-bearing age.

population policy A *policy or set of policies, usually agreed at national level, designed to manage population growth and improve the quality of life of individuals. *See also* INTERNATIONAL CONFERENCE ON POPULATION AND DEVELOPMENT.

population projection A *projection of the likely rate and pattern of growth of a population under particular conditions, particularly assumptions about future levels of *fertility, *mortality, and *migration. Every two years the *United Nations Population Division produces a set of population projections for every country, based on updated population data and revisions

in projection methodology. By 2050 the UN expects total world population to grow to between 7.3 billion and 10.7 billion. Under the high growth scenario world population will continue to increase after 2050; under the low growth scenario it will have slowly begun to decline. The medium growth projection of 8.9 billion people by 2050 is considered the most likely. Even under the low growth forecast, the world will have to meet the needs of an extra 1.3 billion people because *fertility in *developing countries is twice as high as that in *developed countries; developing countries have a younger age structure, which creates a momentum for continued *population growth for several decades ahead; and continued reductions in *mortality will add extra growth, particularly in countries with a relatively low *life expectancy.

population pyramid A bar chart that shows the distribution of the *population (within a country, region, or the world) by gender and age, usually with the younger ages at the bottom and with males on the left and females on the right. Slowly growing populations (such as the USA) typically have a relatively large elderly population, so they have a population pyramid of reasonably uniform width from bottom (young) to top (old). Rapidly growing populations (such as Kenya) have a disproportionately large number of young people and thus more of a true pyramid shape, becoming narrower towards the top. The pyramid for a population that is not growing, or is decreasing, often has a bulge in the middle-age range, with relatively few young and old people.

(((●))) SEE WEB LINKS

• Population pyramids, 1950–2050.

population viability analysis An analysis that estimates the minimum numbers that are required for a *population to be viable or self-sustaining.

pore space Spaces within a body of soil, *sediment, or rock.

Porifera The *phylum that comprises sponges.

porosity A measure of the amount of *pore space within a soil, sediment, or rock, which determines its capacity for holding water, and is expressed as the amount of pore space compared to the total volume of soil or rock, as a percentage.

porous Able to absorb fluids.

porphyritic Applied to an *igneous rock that contains relatively large crystals set within a finer grained *matrix.

positive charge An electrical charge that is created by having fewer *electrons than *protons.

positive feedback *Feedback that amplifies the response of the system. *Contrast* NEGATIVE FEEDBACK.

possibly extinct A *species which is known only from historical evidence, but for which there are hopes that it may be rediscovered.

post A pole or timber stake that is set up to mark something, or to support other structures for fencing.

post-closure The period of time after a waste management or manufacturing facility has been closed, which for monitoring purposes is often taken to be 30 years.

post-consumer material *See* SECONDARY MATERIAL.

post-consumer recycling The reuse of waste materials that have been generated from residential and consumer waste, such as converting wastepaper from offices into corrugated boxes or newsprint.

post-consumer waste Waste materials (such as office paper and *aluminium cans) that have been used by consumers and recovered from the *waste stream, which are then used as raw materials to make new products.

post-glacial After the *ice age, or after a *glacier has melted from a particular area.

post-industrial society A modern economy that is dominated by services and information, rather than by industry.

post-materialism A philosophy or worldview that emphasizes quality of life over the acquisition of material goods.

post-modern A late 20th-century view (in art, thought, and society) that what we take to be reality is in effect a human (social) construction rather than a physical entity, which promotes a distrust of objectivity, authority, universality, and moral and ideological absolutes.

post-modernism A belief that individuals are constructs of social forces, and that there is

no absolute transcendent truth that can be known.

postulate 1. A basic principle. 2. To make an assumption that is used as the basis for reasoning or hypothesizing.

potable water (drinking water) Water that safe to drink.

potamodromous Applied to the behaviour of fish that undertake regular migrations in large freshwater systems. *Compare* AMPHIDROMOUS; ANADROMOUS; CATADROMOUS.

potamon That part of a river in which the water is typically slow-moving, still-surfaced, deep, and relatively warm, favouring organisms that are thrifty in their use of dissolved oxygen. *Compare* RITHRON.

potash alum *See* ALUM.

potassium (K) A silver-white, soft, light, low-melting metallic element of the alkali metal group that occurs abundantly in nature and accounts for 2.59% of the Earth's *crust. It is a *macronutrient, one of three main *fertilizers (with *nitrogen and *phosphorus) that are essential for plant growth, and is generally not considered toxic.

potential dose *See* ADMINISTERED DOSE.

potential energy *Energy which is possessed by a body because of its position or state, such as water stored behind a *dam which can be used to produce *hydroelectricity.

potential evaporation The amount of water that could be evaporated if it was available, which depends on air temperature, *insolation, and wind speed. *Contrast* ACTUAL EVAPORATION.

potential evapotranspiration (PE) The amount of water that could be evaporated or transpired if it was available. *Contrast* ACTUAL EVAPOTRANSPIRATION.

potential instability *See* CONVECTIVE INSTABILITY.

potential natural community (PNC) The *biotic community that would become established on a site if all stages in the *succession were completed without interference from humans, under the present environmental conditions.

potential natural vegetation (PNV) The plant community that would develop on a site if all stages in the *succession were completed without interference from humans, under the present environmental conditions.

potential niche The maximum possible distribution of a species in the environment. *Contrast* REALIZED NICHE.

potential receptor Any organism or environmental medium that is in the pathway of a particular *contamination from a discharge.

potential resource Any part of the natural or human environment that is currently not thought to have *value, but which one day may become valuable as a result of developments in technology and know-how, and/or changes in market conditions.

potential temperature The temperature that a volume of fluid (most commonly air) would have if the pressure under which it was held were adjusted to average sea-level atmospheric pressure and its temperature were allowed to change adiabatically (*see* ADIABATIC).

potential yield The maximum annual *yield of a *renewable resource (such as timber from a forest or fish from the sea) that can be obtained on a *sustainable basis by using intensive management practices.

potentially responsible party (PRP) An individual or company that is potentially responsible for, or contributing to, contamination at a *Superfund site, and therefore potentially liable for *cleanup costs.

potentiation The ability of one chemical to increase the effect of another chemical.

potentiometric surface An imaginary surface that represents the level to which water rises in wells in a *confined aquifer: similar to the *water table of an *unconfined aquifer.

pothole 1. A small, rounded depression in the *bedrock of a stream bed, formed by *abrasion of small pebbles and cobbles in a strong current. **2.** A system of caves and underground rivers formed by water over a prolonged period of time.

POTW *See* PUBLICALLY OWNED TREATMENT WORKS.

powder snow Dry, loose, unconsolidated *snow.

power The rate at which *energy is supplied, usually measured in *watts.

power plant (power station) A place where *electricity is generated, either by burning *fossil fuels, controlling *nuclear reactions, tapping hot subsurface rocks (*geothermal), or diverting water to turn turbines (*hydroelectric).

power station *See* POWER PLANT.

Poza Rica incident An air pollution incident that occurred in 1950 at Poza Rica, Mexico, when equipment at the sulphur-recovery unit at an oil refinery failed, releasing a large quantity of *hydrogen sulphide which became trapped beneath an *inversion, killing 22 people and making approximately 320 ill.

p

POVERTY

The state of having little or no money and few or no material possessions. More than a fifth of the global population today live in poverty, subsisting on less than US $1 a day. There are clear links between poverty, population growth, and environmental problems. These are most evident at the level of individual households or communities, but they can also be detected at the national scale. Poverty is often accompanied by illiteracy, *malnutrition and poor *health, low status of women, and exposure to *environmental hazards. Poverty and lack of economic opportunities can force people to exploit marginal resources (e.g. by *overgrazing land or *overharvesting forests); this sets in motion a repeating cycle of *environmental deterioration, *marginalization, hardship, and poverty. Poverty is associated with a wide variety of health risks and problems, including inadequate *sanitation, unsafe *drinking water, *air pollution, and crowding. Poverty is linked to *fertility, and in many places women from low-income families have more children than women from richer families in the same society. Problems of rapid population growth are compounded by poverty and *inequality, and efforts are being made in many countries to reduce poverty as a means of improving the health of children and mothers, reducing the problems of rapid *urban development, and ensuring adequate nutrition for everyone. *See also* ABSOLUTE POVERTY; RELATIVE POVERTY.

ppb Parts per billion.

PPC *See* POLLUTION PREVENTION AND CONTROL.

ppm Parts per million.

ppmv Parts per million by volume.

PPP *See* POLLUTER PAYS PRINCIPLE.

PRA *See* PARTICIPATORY ACTION RESEARCH.

prairie A large area of flat or rolling *grassland, dominated by grasses and wildflowers, with no or few trees, that often grows on fertile soil. *See also* DRY PRAIRIE; HILL PRAIRIE; MESIC PRAIRIE; MIXED GRASS PRAIRIE; SAND PRAIRIE; SHORTGRASS PRAIRIE; TALLGRASS PRAIRIE; WET PRAIRIE.

prairie pothole A marsh type of vegetation dominated by small seasonally or permanently flooded depressions and emergent *hydrophyte vegetation, that is found in North America on the prairies of the upper Midwest and the Canadian plains, and provides a habitat for the majority of North American ducks during migratory nesting and the breeding season.

Precambrian The earliest unit of geological time, which ended with the beginning of the *Phanerozoic 542 million years ago, and accounts for about 90% of geological time. The first living *organisms appeared during the Precambrian. The term is now used only informally and has been replaced by the *Hadean, *Archaean, and *Proterozoic eons.

precautionary principle (do-no-harm principle) A proactive method of dealing with the environment based on the idea that if the costs of current activities are uncertain but are potentially both high and irreversible then society should take action before the uncertainty is resolved. The *Convention for the Prevention of Marine Pollution by Dumping from Ships and Aircraft (Oslo Convention) (1972) is an early example of the use of the precautionary principle since this convention, and subsequent ones, used a system of 'black' and 'grey' lists covering substances that could not be disposed of at sea and those for which a licence was required. Substances could be placed on the black list even if scientific evidence of harm was not fully available, so that discharges did not continue just because there was no proof of environmental damage. The *Vienna Convention for the Protection of the Ozone Layer (1985) and *Montreal Protocol (1987) were at the time quite unique amongst international environmental initiatives, because it was probably the first

time that serious attempts were made to avert a major environmental problem *before* the more serious consequences and side-effects were obvious. Previously governments would have insisted on waiting for conclusive scientific proof of cause–effect links before introducing appropriate preventive legislation and embarking on costly behaviour-changing strategies. Critics point out that the principle places the onus on those who propose an innovation to prove it harmless, which is inherently impossible because it is impossible to prove a negative, and that the principle can be used to prevent innovation of any kind. *Contrast* WAIT-AND-SEE PRINCIPLE. *See also* NO REGRETS POLICY.

precedent An act or decision that can be used as an example in dealing with subsequent similar situations.

precedent law *See* COMMON LAW.

precession A change in the orientation of the axis of a rotating body. The precession of the Earth's axis of rotation traces out the path of a cone over a period of about 23 000 years.

precious metal *See* NOBLE METAL.

precipitate A *solid that separates from a *solution.

precipitation 1. The process by which moisture (*water vapour) in the *atmosphere condenses and falls as *rain, *snow, *sleet, *hail, *dew, *frost, or *fog. 2. In chemistry, the action of causing a substance to be deposited in solid form from a solution.

precipitation fog *See* EVAPORATION FOG.

precipitation scavenging The process by which rain or snow removes *particulates from the *atmosphere and deposits them on the ground surface. *See also* RAINOUT.

precipitator An *air pollution control device that collects particles from an *emission by mechanical or electrical means.

precocial Applied to young mammals which are born with their eyes and ears open and are able to stand and walk, regulate their body temperature, and excrete without assistance. The young of grazing animals (e.g. cattle, sheep, and horses) are precocial. *Compare* ALTRICIAL.

pre-commercial thinning In commercial *forestry, removing some of the trees from a stand that are too small to be sold (for lumber or house logs), so that the remaining trees will grow faster.

pre-commitment period In *air pollution *emissions reduction, the period of time before the first *Commitment Period under the *Kyoto Protocol, when the operational framework is established and the involvement of signatories to the protocol is determined.

precursor A substance from which another substance is formed.

pre-cycling Making purchasing decisions that will reduce waste. This includes buying goods with less packaging, choosing products that will last longer, and avoiding single-use or disposable products, the most commonly cited example of disposable products being nappies.

predation An interaction between organisms in which one (the *predator) eats the other (the *prey). *See also* PARASITISM.

predator A *carnivore; an animal (such as a shark) that hunts and kills other animals (the *prey) for food.

predator control An interaction between *predator and *prey in which the predator controls the size of the prey population.

prediction An indication in advance based on observation, experience, or scientific reason. *Contrast* PROJECTION.

pre-existing use *Land use that existed before particular planning constraints were introduced.

preferable species *Plant species which are preferred by animals and are grazed out of choice.

pre-glacial Before *glaciation or before an *ice age.

prehistoric Dating back to before written historical records begin. In Europe this includes the *Stone Age, the *Bronze Age, and the *Iron Age. In North America prehistory is usually taken to refer any time before AD 1540.

Preliminary Assessment (PA) The initial step of a *site assessment of *Superfund sites, based on collecting and reviewing available records and information. *See also* SITE INSPECTION.

premature death A death that occurs before the average age within that population and which is usually attributable to a specific cause (such as an accident or *disease).

preparation The treatment of *waste materials prior to composting, which includes grinding, shredding, sorting, and adding sewage sludge.

preparatory cut In *forest management, the removal of trees towards the end of a *rotation in order to open the *canopy so the crowns of seed-bearing trees can enlarge, which improves seed production and encourages natural regeneration.

preparedness All measures that are taken before an event occurs, that allow for prevention, mitigation, and readiness. *See also* CONTINGENCY PLAN; DISASTER MANAGEMENT.

prescribed burn (controlled burn, prescribed fire) A planned fire in a predetermined area, in order to meet particular *resource management objectives such as to improve *silviculture, *wildlife management, *grazing, or reduction of fire hazard.

prescribed fire *See* PRESCRIBED BURN.

prescription Written instructions or a written statement that defines management objectives.

present net value (PNV, present net worth) A way of comparing the value of something now with the value of it in the future, which is used to compare alternative projects that have different cost and revenue flows. *See also* COST–BENEFIT ANALYSIS; DISCOUNT RATE.

present net worth *See* PRESENT NET VALUE.

preservation The activity of protecting something (such as old and historic buildings, sites, structures, and objects) from loss or danger. *Contrast* CONSERVATION.

preservative A chemical substance used to protect organic material (such as food or wood) from *decomposition or *fermentation.

preserve 1. To keep or maintain in an unaltered condition. 2. (reserve, nature reserve) A reservation in which plants, animals, and geological features are protected.

pressed wood product Material that is made from wood veneers, particles, or fibres that are bonded together with an adhesive under heat and pressure, and is used in making buildings and furniture.

pressure The force that is applied per unit area. *See also* ATMOSPHERIC PRESSURE.

pressure gradient (barometric gradient) The rate of change in *atmospheric pressure over a horizontal distance, indicated by the spacing of *isobars on a *weather map, that affects wind speed (a steep pressure gradient produces strong winds).

pressure group (interest group, special interest group) Any group of people who share special interests, are politically active, and advocate particular policies or approaches. Examples include *Friends of the Earth (FOE) and *Greenpeace. See also ENVIRONMENTALISM.

pressure-tube anemometer An instrument that measures *wind speed from the pressure exerted through a tube aligned to point into the wind.

pressurized water reactor (PWR) A type of *light-water *nuclear reactor in which water is used as a coolant, but it is kept under enough pressure so that it does not boil. Electricity is generated by turbines which are turned by steam that is formed in a secondary cooling system. Contrast BOILING WATER REACTOR.

pre-treatment A range of processes that are used to reduce, eliminate, or alter the nature of *wastewater pollutants from non-domestic sources before they are discharged into *publicly-owned treatment works.

prevailing westerlies (westerlies) The dominant *westerly winds that blow in middle latitudes on the *poleward side of the *subtropical high-pressure areas.

prevailing wind The direction from which the wind blows most often.

prevalence The number of individuals in a *population who have a particular *disease or condition at a given time. Contrast INCIDENCE. See also OCCURRENCE.

Prevention of Significant Deterioration (PSD) A programme, specified in the US *Clean Air Act, whose goal is to prevent *air quality from deteriorating significantly in areas of the country that currently comply with *ambient air quality standards.

prey An animal that is killed and eaten by other animals (the *predators).

price elasticity A measure of the sensitivity of *supply and *demand to changes in price.

Price-Anderson Act (1957) US legislation that established an insurance scheme for *nuclear power that is backed by taxpayers. It limits the amount of insurance that *nuclear power plant owners must carry, and shields nuclear power from free market forces by capping the liability of nuclear power plant owners in the event of a catastrophic accident or attack at levels which are significantly lower than likely costs.

primary ambient air quality standards *Air quality standards that are designed to protect human health. Contrast SECONDARY AMBIENT AIR QUALITY STANDARDS.

primary consumer A *herbivore, which eats *primary producers and so sits above them in a *food chain. Contrast SECONDARY CONSUMER. See also HETEROTROPH.

Primary Drinking Water Regulation A regulation that applies in the US to public water systems and specifies a contaminant level which it is judged will not adversely affect human health.

primary economic activities Agriculture, forestry, fishing, and mining. Contrast SECONDARY ECONOMIC ACTIVITIES; TERTIARY ECONOMIC ACTIVITIES.

primary effect See DIRECT EFFECT.

primary energy Energy that exists in natural resources (such as *coal, *crude oil, *sunlight, *uranium) that has not been converted or transformed by humans.

primary forest A *forest that is largely undisturbed by human activities. Contrast SECONDARY FOREST.

primary market The *marketplace into which shares are sold when they are first issued. Under the *Kyoto Protocol, the exchange of *emission reductions, *offsets, or *allowances between buyer and seller where the seller is the originator of the supply. Contrast SECONDARY MARKET

primary metabolite A product of *metabolism that is involved in the growth of the organism.

primary mineral 1. A *mineral such as *feldspar or *mica that has crystallized from a *magma and occurs or occurred originally in an *igneous rock. **2.** Any *mineral which occurs in the *parent material of the *soil. Contrast SECONDARY MINERAL.

primary nutrient The elements *nitrogen, *phosphorus, and *potassium, which must be taken up and used by plants in sufficient quantities for them to complete their *life cycles. *Contrast* SECONDARY NUTRIENT.

primary pollutant Chemicals (such as *carbon monoxide, *hydrocarbons, *nitrogen compounds, *particulate matter, and *sulphur dioxide) that are released directly into the air in a harmful form. *Contrast* SECONDARY POLLUTANT.

primary producer An *autotroph that captures energy from the environment and turns it into *biomass through *photosynthesis or *chemosynthesis, and forms the base (lowest *trophic level) of a *food chain. Examples include green plants on land and *phytoplankton in oceans. *See also* CHEMOTROPH.

primary production *See* PRIMARY PRODUCTIVITY.

primary productivity (primary production) The rate at which *autotrophs (principally green plants) produce *biomass by *photosynthesis and *chemosynthesis in the form of organic substances, some of which are used as food by the autotrophs themselves. Gross primary productivity (GPP) is the total rate of photosynthesis and chemosynthesis per unit ground area, including that portion of the organic material used in *respiration during the measurement period. Net primary productivity (NPP) is the rate of production minus the amount used in respiration. Net ecosystem production (NEP) is the rate of accumulation of organic material allowing for both autotroph respiration and consumption by *heterotrophs; i.e. NEP = GPP − (respiration by autotrophs + respiration by heterotrophs). Rates of storage at higher trophic levels are known as secondary productivities. Strictly, the primary production of an *ecosystem is the amount of organic material accumulated per unit ground area, but the concept is of little value unless a time period is specified. In practice, the terms productivity and production are often used interchangeably. The most productive ecosystems are *reefs and *estuaries, with natural *forests and freshwater a close second. The lowest productivities are found in the open *oceans and in *desert environments. Whilst mean NPP levels on land are more than four times as high as those in the oceans, when these productivities are weighed according to the total area involved the oceans far exceed land in area and so total net primary productivity on land is only twice that in the oceans. It is estimated that over 70% of terrestrial net production is concentrated between latitudes $30°N$ and $30°S$, which illustrates the ecological importance of the *tropical environment.

primary range A *grazing area (*range) which livestock prefers to use because it contains vegetation they like. When there is limited or no *range management animals are likely to over-graze these areas.

primary rock *See* IGNEOUS ROCK.

primary standard The pollution limit for *criteria air pollutants that is based on health effects. *Contrast* SECONDARY STANDARD. *See also* NATIONAL AMBIENT AIR QUALITY STANDARDS.

primary succession (prisere) An ecological *succession that begins on a newly formed soil or on a new surface that has been exposed for the first time (e.g. as the result of a landslide or volcanic eruption). *Contrast* SECONDARY SUCCESSION.

primary treatment (primary waste treatment) The initial treatment that is provided at a *wastewater treatment plant, in which solids and liquids are separated from *domestic sewage by screening and sedimentation. *See also* ADVANCED WASTEWATER TREATMENT; SECONDARY TREATMENT.

primary waste treatment *See* PRIMARY TREATMENT.

primary wave *See* P-WAVE.

primate Any of the 195 species of *mammal that belongs to the order Primates, which includes monkeys, apes, and humans.

prime agricultural land (prime farmland) The best available land which is capable of producing acceptable yields of *crops with acceptable inputs and minimal *environmental damage.

prime farmland *See* PRIME AGRICULTURAL LAND.

primeval Having existed from the earliest times. *See also* PRIMORDIAL.

Primitive Area A large tract of land within a US *National Forest, that has been set aside for *preservation in its natural condition with no alteration or development permitted except for measures to protect the spread of fire. Such areas were reclassified as *Wilderness Areas under the 1964 *Wilderness Act.

primitive area A category of land defined within the *recreation opportunity spectrum as an 'essentially unmodified natural environment of fairly large size', with few interactions between users. Motor vehicles are not permitted, and the area is managed to be largely free from evidence of human control.

primitive character In *cladistics, a character that is preserved from an ancestral stage in the evolution of the organism.

primitive cultivar A crop that has been developed from a *landrace.

primitive recreation Those types of *recreation activities that are associated with land having no roads, which includes hiking, backpacking, and cross-country travel.

primitive ROS A classification of *wilderness and *recreation opportunity on the ROS (*recreation opportunity spectrum) scale, based on an unmodified environment, where trails may be present but structures are rare, and where contact with other people is unlikely.

primordial First created or developed. *See also* PRIMEVAL.

principle of competitive exclusion *See* COMPETITIVE EXCLUSION PRINCIPLE.

principle of limiting factors The principle that the factor (such as a particular *nutrient, *water, or *sunlight) that is in shortest supply (the *limiting factor) will limit the growth and development of an *organism or a *community.

prion A small abnormal *protein that is found in brain cell membranes, which is responsible for *bovine spongiform encephalopathy ('mad cow disease') in cattle, scrapie in sheep, and new variant *Creutzfeld–Jakob disease in humans.

prior appropriation A doctrine of water law that allocates the rights to use a particular body of water on a first-come first-served basis.

prior informed consent In the context of the international trade in *hazardous chemicals, a procedure that seeks to share responsibility between exporting and importing countries in protecting *human health and the environment by sharing information about the hazards associated with those chemicals, and encouraging importing countries not to proceed without agreement.

priority habitat A category in the *EU Habitats Directive that is applied to *habitats that

are deemed to be of conservation importance within the *European Union.

priority pollutant A group of around 130 chemicals (of which about 110 are *organics) that appear on a US *Environmental Protection Agency list because they are toxic and relatively common in industrial discharges.

priority species Any species that is targeted in the *UK *Biodiversity Action Plan (BAP) for national conservation effort, and is the subject of a *Species Action Plan or *Species Statement in the UK BAP.

prisere *See* PRIMARY SUCCESSION.

pristine Natural, unspoiled, or undeveloped.

private forest *Forest land that belongs to individuals or corporations.

private good Any good or service whose consumption by one person excludes consumption by others. *Contrast* PUBLIC GOOD.

private land Land that belongs to individuals or corporations.

private opportunity cost The *opportunity cost of using a resource that is experienced by an individual, excluding any *externalities.

private property Things (*property or goods) that belong to individuals as opposed to public ownership, which gives those individuals the exclusive right to possess, use, or dispose of those things.

private value The value to an individual of using or not using a particular resource.

privatization The process of changing a government-owned resource (such as a *National Forest) to private control and ownership.

process waste Any *toxic pollutant or combination of pollutants that is an unavoidable product from any manufacturing process.

producer An *organism that synthesizes food molecules from inorganic compounds using an external energy source, usually by *photosynthesis. *Contrast* CONSUMER. *See also* PRIMARY PRODUCER.

product stewardship A product-centred approach to *environmental protection, which expects those in the product *life cycle (manufacturers, retailers, users, and disposers) to share responsibility for reducing the *environmental impacts of products.

product water *See* FINISHED WATER.

production 1. In *ecology, the total mass of organic matter that is manufactured in an *ecosystem during a certain period of time. Net production is the yield of the producers and consumers and is the amount of living matter in the ecosystem. **2.** In energy-flow studies, that part of the assimilated food or energy which is retained and incorporated in the *biomass of the organism, but excluding the reproductive bodies released by the organism. This may be regarded as growth. In energy-flow measurements, production is expressed as energy per unit time, per unit area. **3.** *See* PRIMARY PRODUCTIVITY.

production residues *See* CONSUMPTION RESIDUES.

production well A *well that has a high enough *yield that it can be used for public use, either for water supply or for industrial purposes.

productive Describing an area that is to provide goods and services and to sustain *ecological values.

productivity In general, the rate of output per unit of input, a measure of efficiency. In ecology, the rate of production of *biomass. *See also* GROSS PRIMARY PRODUCTIVITY; NET PRIMARY PRODUCTIVITY; PRIMARY PRODUCTIVITY; SECONDARY PRODUCTIVITY; TERTIARY PRODUCTIVITY.

profile 1. A cross-section through *topography or a *landscape. **2.** *See* SOIL PROFILE. **3.** Variations in the physical and chemical properties of water at different depths within a *waterbody.

profundal zone The bed of a body of deep freshwater, where insufficient light penetrates for rooted plants to become established.

progeny Children or offspring, the immediate *descendants of a plant or animal (including humans).

pro-glacial The area adjacent to (usually in front of) a *glacier.

pro-glacial lake A lake in front of a retreating *glacier or *ice sheet, which is usually fed by *meltwater. *See also* GLACIAL LAKE.

programme evaluation and review technique (PERT) *See* CRITICAL PATH METHOD.

programmed harvest The part of the *potential yield of a *crop that is planned for *harvest in any particular year.

prohibition zoning Any land use *zoning regulations which only allow particular types of use in certain kinds of areas, such as *floodplain zoning that only allows uses which do not reduce the flood water storage capacity.

project management The deliberate planning, control, and coordination of all aspects of a project (initiating, planning, executing, controlling, and closing), in order to achieve the agreed objectives.

project scenario The emission forecast made in an *emission reduction project, which is compared with the *business-as-usual (*baseline) scenario in order to determine the emission reductions that have been achieved.

projection A *forecast that is based on historic and current information. *Contrast* PREDICTION.

prokaryote A single-celled *organism that does not have a true nucleus containing genetic information, the *DNA being present as a loop in the *cytoplasm. *See also* EUKARYOTE.

proleg The fleshy, unsegmented false leg of a caterpillar.

promontory (headland) A narrow strip of land that extends out into the sea.

propagate 1. To increase the number of plants of a particular population by means of cuttings. **2.** To breed new lifestock through natural methods.

propagation Increasing or spreading of a plant or plants by natural reproduction.

propagule Any part of a plant that functions in *propagation or dispersal, e.g. *seeds or *spores.

propane (C_3H_8) A colourless, heavy gaseous *hydrocarbon that is found in *crude oil and *natural gas, and is used as *fuel and in *petrochemicals.

propanone *See* ACETONE.

propellant A substance, usually a gas (e.g. *butane, *propane, and *nitrogen oxides), that has a high *vapour pressure and is used to force material out of *aerosol spray cans.

proper resource pricing The pricing of *natural resources at levels which reflect their combined *economic values and *environmental values.

property A place or an object that is owned.

property rights The rights of an owner of *private property, which usually include the right to use the property as they see fit (within limits, such as *zoning) and the right to sell it when and to whom they decide.

proportionality principle The concept that control measures or a response should generally be proportional to the risk.

proposed species In the USA, any species of fish, wildlife, or plant that is proposed to be listed under the *Endangered Species Act.

prospect 1. To search for something useful or valuable. 2. The possibility of future success.

prospecting The search for *mineral deposits, for example by removing *overburden, or by drilling cores to obtain subsurface samples.

prospective study (cohort study) A study that follows a group (*cohort) of individuals over time, in order to determine whether exposure to particular factors produces adverse effects on the group or on different subgroups.

prospector A person who explores an area for useful or valuable *resources, such as *mineral deposits.

protandry 1. The maturing of male plant organs (anthers) before female organs (carpels). 2. In some animals (e.g. *nematodes), the production of sperm before the females produce eggs. 3. In some birds, the arrival of males at the breeding ground before females. *Contrast* PROTOGYNY.

protected area Land that is set aside, usually for *conservation purposes, where development is banned or seriously restricted. There are many different types of protected areas, ranging from *national parks (where conservation is one of a number of priorities) to *nature reserves and *biosphere reserves (where it is the main objective).

Protected Area Category Ia An *IUCN category of *protected area, a strict *Nature Reserve, which is a protected area managed mainly for scientific research or monitoring.

Protected Area Category Ib An *IUCN category of *protected area, a *Wilderness Area, which is a large area in an unmodified or slightly modified state which is protected and managed so as to preserve its natural condition.

Protected Area Category II An *IUCN category of *protected area, a *National Park, which is a protected area managed mainly for *ecosystem conservation and *recreation, which provides a foundation for scientific, educational, spiritual, recreational, and visitor opportunities, all of which must be environmentally and culturally compatible.

protected area system A system that legally establishes *protected areas and sites which are managed for *conservation objectives.

Protected Landscape or Seascape An *IUCN Management Category (V) for protected areas, which is designed 'to maintain nationally significant natural landscapes that are characteristic of the harmonious interaction of man and land while providing opportunities for public enjoyment through recreation and tourism within normal life style and economic activity of these areas'.

protection Defence against harm or danger: any activity (including insect and disease control, fire protection, and law enforcement) that reduces losses or risks, tends to maintain basic conditions and values, and reduces damage or injury to people and property.

protective plant Plants that are grown to protect crops, soils, or land from environmental damage.

protein A large organic molecule composed of one or more chains of *amino acids in a specific order, which is required for the structure, function, and regulation of cells, tissues, and organs. Each protein has unique functions. Examples include *hormones, *enzymes, and *antibodies.

Proterozoic An eon of geological time that followed the *Archaean, extending from 2.5 billion years ago to 542 million years ago (the start of the *Phanerozoic). During this time period the first bacteria and fungi and primitive multicelled organisms appeared and developed. Proterozoic means 'early life'.

( ) SEE WEB LINKS
• The Proterozoic eon of Precambrian time.

protese inhibitor A drug that inhibits the ability of a *virus to make copies of itself.

pruning

protist Any single-celled organism that belongs to the kingdom *Protoctista.

Protista *See* PROTOCTISTA.

protocol A code of correct conduct, or series of formal steps for conducting a test. *See also* MONTREAL PROTOCOL.

Protocol on Preparedness, Response and Co-operation to Pollution Incidents by Hazardous and Noxious Substances (2000) (HNS Protocol) An international *protocol that follows the principles of the *International Convention on Oil Pollution Preparedness, Response and Co-operation (1990), and seeks to ensure that ships carrying *hazardous and noxious liquid substances are covered, or will be covered, by regimes similar to those already in existence for oil incidents.

Protoctista In the five-kingdom and three-domain taxonomic systems, a *kingdom within the superkingdom or domain *Eukarya. The kingdom includes all of the aquatic, single-celled *eukaryotes (the *protozoa, *slime moulds, and *eukaryotic algae), as distinct from the multicelled *Plantae, *Fungi, and *Animalia. Previously known as Protista.

protogyny 1. The development of female reproductive organs before the appearance of the corresponding male feature. **2.** In some birds, the arrival of females at breeding grounds before males. *Contrast* PROTANDRY.

proton A subatomic particle that is found in all *atoms and has a positive electric charge. *See also* ELECTRON; NEUTRON.

protoplasm A term previously used to describe the components of living tissues. *See also* CYTOPLASM.

protoplast A plant, bacterial, or fungal cell that has had its cell wall removed.

prototroph A strain of *bacteria that has the nutritional requirements of the wild type or non-mutant species. *Compare* AUXOTROPH.

protozoa Single-celled *eukaryotes that feed as *heterotrophs, principally on *bacteria, although some are *symbionts of mammals, or *parasites causing human disease, including *malaria and *sleeping sickness. They live in the soil or freshwater. The groups of organisms described as protozoa are not closely related.

proven reserve Deposits of a mineral resource (such as a *fossil fuel) whose location and extent are known, as opposed to potential but unproved (discovered) deposits, and which can be extracted economically.

provenance Source area.

province A political or administrative region within a country.

provincial rank (S-rank) The conservation status rank of a species, subspecies, or variety of plant or animal within a country, based largely on the total number of known sites within that country and the degree to which they are potentially or actively threatened with destruction. *See also* GLOBAL RANK.

provinciality effect Increased *diversity of species caused by geographical isolation.

proximate cause The special or effective cause of a particular change, such as the combustion of *fossil fuel, which causes increased levels of *carbon dioxide in the atmosphere, which in turn causes *global warming.

proximate factor The general cause of a particular change, such as variations in day length, which affects the behaviour or organisms in various ways. *Contrast* ULTIMATE FACTOR.

proximity principle The principle that *wastes should be treated close to where they arise (ideally within the boundary of the plant or community in which they are generated), in order to avoid exporting them to other places.

proxy Substitute or surrogate.

proxy data Data that are used to represent a situation, phenomenon, or condition for which no direct information (such as instrumental records) is available.

proxy indicator An *indicator that is used to provide *proxy data. There are four main types of proxy climate indicator, for example, which are historical (oral or written records), biological (records of faunal and floral growth and distribution), geological (terrestrial deposits and features, and marine ocean sediment cores), and glaciological (*ice cores).

PRP *See* POTENTIALLY RESPONSIBLE PARTY.

pruning Cutting live or dead branches from plants (particularly the branches of trees, or the sides and tops of *hedges), in order to improve the quality of the growth. *See also* THINNING OUT.

psammon The microscopic flora and fauna of the interstitial spaces between sand grains of seashore and lake-shore areas.

psammosere The vegetation *succession that develops on *sand dunes.

PSC *See* POLAR STRATOSPHERIC CLOUD.

PSD *See* PREVENTION OF SIGNIFICANT DETERIORATION.

PSI *See* POLLUTION STANDARDS INDEX.

psychophily *Pollination by butterflies.

psychrometer An instrument consisting of a wet-bulb and a dry-bulb thermometer that is used to measure *humidity.

PTD *See* PARTICIPATORY TECHNOLOGY DEVELOPMENT.

pterygote An insect with wings or a wingless insect that evolved from winged ancestors. *Contrast* APTERYGOTE.

public estate *See* PUBLIC LAND.

public forest *Forest land in the USA that belongs to municipal, state, and federal governments.

public good Any good or commodity whose benefits are available to everyone, from which no one can be excluded, and from which no single individual can enjoy all of the benefits.

public health The health or physical well-being of a whole community.

public land (public estate) Land that is owned in common by all and is managed by the government (town, county, state, or federal).

Public Rangelands Improvement Act (1978) US legislation that amended the *Federal Land Policy Management Act (1976) to provide the *US Bureau of Land Management and the *US Forest Service with additional direction and authorities in managing public rangelands.

Public Utilities Regulatory Policy Act (PURPA) (1978) US legislation that requires utilities to buy power from eligible *cogeneration sources, small hydro, or waste-fuelled facilities, under contracts, at an agreed cost. It also requires utilities to provide a backup supply of *electricity to customers who choose self-generation.

publicly owned treatment works (POTW) A *municipal *wastewater treatment facility.

puddle 1. A small shallow area of water on the ground surface. **2.** To destroy the structure of the surface soil by physical methods such as the impact of raindrops, poor cultivation with implements, and trampling by animals.

puddled soil A dense *soil that is almost *impervious to air and water, having been *puddled when wet.

pulp Raw material (*cellulose fibres) that is made from *trees and used in producing paper products.

pulpwood Low quality *softwood that is harvested for use as a source of fibre in the manufacture of *pulp, for making products such as paper and textiles.

pulse *See* LEGUME.

pulverized fly ash (PFA) A by-product of coal-fired power stations that comprises the matter remaining after the carbon in the fuel (finely powdered coal) has been oxidized. The residual ash melts, then solidifies to form glassy, colourless, spherical particles most of which are the size of *sand and *silt particles. When wetted, PFA tends to set hard. It is used to make building blocks and, if organic matter and fertilizer are added to it, it will sustain plant growth.

pumice A light-coloured *volcanic rock that contains many trapped gas bubbles formed by the explosive eruption of *magma, is light enough to float on water, and can develop as layers to form *tuff when hardened.

pump and treat technology A treatment method in which *contaminated water is pumped out of the ground and then treated before being discharged back into the environment.

pumped storage scheme A *hydroelectric scheme in which the water that flows though the *turbines is recycled by pumping it back to the upper storage reservoir during off-peak periods, where it can be used again to produce *electricity during peak periods.

pumping level The level of the water surface in a *well when pumping is in progress.

pumping test A test that is conducted in a *well in order to determine the characteristics of the *aquifer or well.

punctuated equilibrium A model of *evolution in which change occurs in short, relatively rapid phases, followed by longer periods of stability (*stasis). This model helps to explain some important discontinuities in the *fossil record, including *mass extinctions (in which many different species appear to have died out at roughly the same time), and the lack of intermediate forms (fossil evidence of the existence of transitional forms between species, which would indicate stages in the long-term evolution of new species). *Contrast* PHYLETIC GRADUALISM.

pupa In an *insect, the stage of metamorphosis between being a larva and an adult, during which the body is transformed.

pupal paedogenesis The production of young by *pupae.

purebred An *animal (usually a horse) that has been bred for many generations from members of the same *breed or strain.

purification The process of making something pure; free from anything that debases, pollutes, or contaminates.

purine A nitrogen base (see BASE PAIR) composed of two adjoining ring structures, one of which has five members and the other six. The purine bases in the *nucleotides of *nucleic acids are adenine and guanine.

PURPA *See* PUBLIC UTILITIES REGULATORY POLICY ACT.

purse-seining A marine fishing technique in which a large fishing net is used to encircle and trap fish, then closed at the bottom to form a bag or purse that is hauled aboard the fishing vessel. Purse-seining often catches dolphins and other marine animals.

putrefaction The biological *decomposition of organic matter under *anaerobic conditions, which produces offensive smells. *See also* BUTYRIC FERMENTATION.

putrescible Material (usually *waste) that is able to rot quickly enough to cause offensive smells and attract flies.

puy 1. A volcanic hill in the Auvergne region of France. 2. Any steep-sided tower of volcanic rock (e.g. the Devil's Tower, Wyoming, USA, and Shiprock, New Mexico, USA). It consists of the resistant central plug or neck of a former volcano.

PVC *See* POLYVINYL CHLORIDE.

P-wave (primary wave) A type of *seismic wave, caused by an *earthquake, which is refracted (bent) as it passes through the liquid outer *core of the Earth and can be detected and measured at *seismograph stations. *Contrast* S-WAVE.

PWP *See* PERMANENT WILTING POINT.

PWR *See* PRESSURIZED WATER REACTOR.

pycnocline A layer in the *ocean where the water density increases rapidly with depth, which acts as a strong barrier to vertical mixing of seawater.

pyramid of biomass An *ecological pyramid that shows the relationship between total *biomass (weight of organic matter) and *trophic level within a *food web: biomass usually decreases at higher levels, because whilst the individual organisms are larger, there are fewer of them.

pyramid of energy An *ecological pyramid that shows the relationship between *energy (in calories per unit of area (square metres) over a given period of time, usually a year) and *trophic level within a *food web, as energy is lost through respiration so that relatively little of the original energy is ultimately available to the top *carnivores.

pyramid of numbers An *ecological pyramid which shows the relationship between the number of individuals and their *trophic level within a *food web. The number of individuals usually decreases at each level; a large number of *primary producers supports a small number of larger *consumers.

pyranometer An instrument which is used to measure *diffuse and direct *solar radiation.

pyrethrin A form of *organic *insecticide which is derived from certain species of chrysanthemums and breaks down in sunlight in a few days. In high *doses it kills many garden insect pests, but many insects can recover from exposure to low doses.

pyrethroid insecticides A group of synthesized compounds that resemble naturally occurring *pyrethrins. Insect *exoskeletons are porous to pyrethroids, which cause paralysis and death. They are used to control a wide range of insects including mosquitoes. Inhalation and skin exposure can cause irritation, but their toxicity is low. They are harmful to fish and aquatic organisms and to non-target insects.

pyrimidine A nitrogen base (*see* BASE PAIR) composed of a single, six-membered ring structure. The pyrimidine bases in the *nucleotides of *nucleic acids are cytosine and thymine in DNA and cytosine and uracil in RNA.

pyroclast Broken fragments of rock that are thrown out during a *volcanic eruption, including *lapilli, *pumice, *volcanic ash, and *volcanic bombs.

pyroclastic flow A hot, dense mixture of *ash, *pumice, *rock fragments, and *gas that is formed during an explosive *volcanic eruption and flows downhill at great speed.

pyroclastic rock A rock that is formed by the accumulation of fragments of volcanic rock scattered by a *volcanic explosion.

pyrolysis The chemical *decomposition of a substance by heat in the absence of oxygen, which produces various *hydrocarbon gases and a carbon-like residue.

p

QELRC *See* QUANTIFIED EMISSIONS LIMITATION AND REDUCTION COMMITMENT.

quadrat A sampling frame or square that is marked out for quantifying the number or percentage cover of a particular species within a given area. *See also* TRANSECT.

quadruped An animal that walks on four legs.

qualitative Relating to or expressed in terms of quality, rather than quantity. *Contrast* QUANTITATIVE.

quality assurance A programme or set of procedures and activities that are designed to ensure an acceptable level of quality.

quality of life The level of well-being of life style, and the physical conditions in which people live. *Contrast* STANDARD OF LIVING.

Quantified Emissions Limitation and Reduction Commitment (QELRC, Quantified Emissions Limitation and Reduction Objectives, QELROS). Legally binding targets and timetables defined under the *Kyoto Protocol for the limitation or reduction of *greenhouse gas emissions for *developed countries.

Quantified Emissions Limitation and Reduction Objectives (QELROS) *See* QUANTIFIED EMISSIONS LIMITATION AND REDUCTION COMMITMENT.

quantitative Relating to or expressed in terms of quantity (numbers), rather than quality. *Contrast* QUALITATIVE.

quarantine Enforced isolation or restriction of free movement of individuals, usually imposed to prevent the spread of a *contagious disease.

quarry 1. A surface excavation from which clay, stone, or minerals are extracted. *See also* MINE. **2.** An animal that is hunted or caught for food.

quarrying 1. (plucking) A process of *physical/mechanical weathering that involves repeated freeze–thaw cycles at the base of a *glacier or *ice cap, weakening the underlying rock, fragments of which are plucked out by the ice as it flows over it. **2.** Industrial scale surface extraction, using machinery, of minerals such as limestone for aggregates in road building or china clay for the pottery industry.

quartz The most common rock-forming *mineral, composed of crystals of silicon dioxide (SiO_2), which may be glassy or opaque.

quartzite A resistant *metamorphic rock in which individual sand grains are cemented together by *quartz, formed by applying great heat and pressure to *sandstone.

quassia An insecticide extracted from the roots and bark of *Picrasma excelsa* and *P. quassioides*, trees of the family Simaroubaceae, native to the Caribbean (where it is threatened by habitat loss) and temperate southern Asia, respectively. It has been used since 1825 to kill houseflies and later to control aphids. It is still used against aphids and caterpillars.

Quaternary (Pleistogene) The most recent period of *geological time, covering the last 2.588 million years, which includes the *Pleistocene and the *Holocene.

quickflow The portion of rainfall from a storm that moves rapidly to a stream channel where it produces a flood wave.

quicklime *See* LIME.

quiescence Dormancy, being at rest.

race *See* SUBSPECIES.

RACM *See* REASONABLY AVAILABLE CONTROL MEASURES.

RACT *See* REASONABLY AVAILABLE CONTROL TECHNOLOGY.

rad Short for 'radiation absorbed dose'. A unit of measurement that was used for the *absorbed dose of *radiation. It has been replaced by the *gray (1 rad = 0.01 *joules per kilogram = 0.01 gray).

radar Short for radio detection and ranging, an instrument that is used to detect and determine the range to distant objects (including rainstorms) by measuring the strength of the *electromagnetic signal reflected back from it.

radial drainage A *drainage pattern in which the rivers radiate outwards from a central high point, such as the dome of a uniform rock outcrop or the centre of a *volcano.

radiant energy *See* RADIATION.

radiant heat transfer The movement of heat between two surfaces that are exposed to each other but are not touching, and that have very different temperatures.

radiation (radiant energy) The transfer of heat, light, and other energy by means of *electromagnetic waves. The Earth's surface is warmed by shortwave radiant energy from the Sun, and contact with the warm surface warms the atmosphere by *convection. This heating process operates in much the same way as a domestic central heating radiator heats a room.

radiation balance (radiative balance) The balance on Earth between incoming short-wave solar *radiation and outgoing longwave radiation.

radiation budget A measure of all the inputs and outputs of *radiation relative to a particular system, such as the *Earth.

radiation dose The amount of *radiation that is absorbed by a material, system, or tissue in a given amount of time, expressed in *roentgens. *See also* ABSORBED DOSE.

radiation ecology The branch of *ecology concerned with the effects of radioactive materials on living systems and on the pathways by which they are dispersed through *ecosystems, including their dispersal through the *abiotic environment.

radiation exposure Most (82%) of the *radiation to which people are exposed comes from natural sources, including radioactive elements in the Earth and in our bodies, cosmic radiation from space, and radon gas. Of the 18% that comes from human activities, most is from medical *X-rays and *nuclear medicine.

radiation fog *See* GROUND FOG.

radiation inversion (nocturnal inversion) An increase in temperature with height in the atmosphere that is caused by radiational cooling of the ground surface.

radiation sickness The syndrome associated with intense acute exposure to *ionizing radiation, symptoms of which include nausea, diarrhoea, headache, lethargy, and fever.

radiation standard Regulations that define maximum exposure limits for protection of the public from *radioactive materials.

radiative balance *See* RADIATION BALANCE.

radiative cooling The process by which the surface of the Earth, and the air in contact with it, cools by the emission of longwave *radiation. This is continuous, but by day the absorption of solar radiation exceeds terrestrial radiation. Later in the day solar radiation diminishes and it ceases at night, and the continuing loss of warmth by terrestrial radiation makes nighttime temperatures lower than daytime temperatures. In summer days are longer than nights, so not all the warmth absorbed by day is lost at night, but in winter the night-time loss exceeds the daytime gain, which is why air temperatures are high in summer and low in winter.

radiative forcing (forcing, external forcing) The increase or decrease in the *radiation balance of the Earth, which is caused by the presence of a particular atmospheric constituent, such as *carbon dioxide or *aerosol. An increase leads to heating of the Earth's surface, while a decrease leads to cooling.

radiative transfer The movement of heat in the form of long-wavelength *infrared *radiation.

radiatively active gas Any gas (such as *water vapour, *carbon dioxide, *methane, *nitrous oxide, *chlorofluorocarbons, and *ozone) that absorbs incoming *solar radiation or outgoing *infrared radiation.

radical ecology The view that environmental problems can only be solved by a radical revision of attitudes and values, rather than through economic and political reform. *See also* DEEP ECOLOGY; ECOFEMINISM; SOCIAL ECOLOGY.

radio telemetry The science and technology of gathering and transmitting data automatically over great distances, for example from an artificial *satellite to a monitoring station on Earth.

radio tracking An observational technique used in field studies of animal behaviour, in which the animal is fitted with a battery-powered, fixed-frequency radio transmitter, usually attached to a collar, and the observer is equipped with a receiver and directional antenna.

radio wave A type of *radiant energy, with a wavelength of 3 to 30 gigahertz within the *electromagnetic spectrum, that is used to transmit radio and television signals.

radioactive Giving off or capable of giving off radiant energy (*radiation) in the form of particles or rays, as in *alpha particles, *beta particles, and *gamma rays.

radioactive decay The natural, spontaneous decay of the *nucleus of an atom to form another nucleus, which releases *alpha or *beta particles and/or *gamma rays at a fixed rate.

radioactive isotope *See* RADIOISOTOPE.

radioactive pollution *Contamination by a *radioactive material.

radioactive substance A substance that emits *ionizing radiation, and is thus *radioactive.

radioactive tracer A radioactive *isotope whose movement can be monitored and which is used to trace the pathways by which individual substances move through an organism, a living system, the *abiotic environment, etc. Non-radioactive chemical analogues of certain substances may be used for the same purpose if their movement can be monitored (e.g. caesium, which can be substituted for potassium).

radioactive waste (nuclear waste) Waste material that is *radioactive, is produced as a *byproduct of *nuclear reactions through power generation and nuclear research, and is classified into *low-level waste, *intermediate-level waste, and *high-level waste.

radioactivity The spontaneous decay or disintegration of an unstable atomic nucleus, which is accompanied by the emission of *radiation.

radiobiology The study of the principles, mechanisms, and effects of *radiation on living things. *See also* RADIOECOLOGY.

radiocarbon (^{14}C) A *radioactive *isotope of *carbon that is generated naturally in the atmosphere, has a *half-life of 5730 ± 30 years, and is used in *carbon dating.

radiocarbon dating *See* CARBON DATING.

radiochemical species Individual *radioactive elements that produce *radioactivity, such as radium-226, cobalt-60, strontium-90, and tritium.

radioecology The study of the effects of *radiation on plants and animals in natural communities. *See also* RADIOBIOLOGY.

radioisotope (radionuclide) A *radioactive *isotope.

radioisotope dating *See* RADIOMETRIC DATING.

Radiolaria A subclass of marine *protozoa that have skeletons made of *silica.

radiolarian ooze A silica-rich deep-sea sediment that is composed largely of the skeletons of *Radiolaria. *See also* PELAGIC SEDIMENT.

radiolarite A *lithified sedimentary rock formed from *radiolarian ooze.

radiological Relating to *radiology.

radiological monitoring Locating and measuring *radiation using instruments that can detect and measure ionizing radiation.

radiological weapon *See* NUCLEAR WEAPON.

radiology The diagnostic and therapeutic use of *radiation.

radiometric dating (radioisotope dating) A precise method of determining the *absolute age of rocks by measuring the different isotopes of elements within the rocks, e.g. *carbon-14 (half-life 5730 ± 30 years), uranium-238 (decays to lead-206, half-life 4.5 billion years), rubidium-87 (decays to strontium-87, half-life 50.0 billion years), and potassium-40 (decays to argon-40, half-life 1.5 billion years), and comparing them with known rates of decay of *radioisotopes.

radionuclide *See* RADIOISOTOPE.

radiosonde A package of instruments that is attached to a *weather balloon and transmits measurements of pressure, humidity, temperature, and winds as it ascends up to about 30 000 m. *See also* RAWINSONDE.

radium (Ra) A rare radioactive *isotope (radium-266) which occurs in *uranium ores, such as *pitchblende, and has a *half-life of 1622 years.

radius of influence **1.** The maximum distance from a *well over which vacuum or pressure occurs, which influences the movement of soil gas or *groundwater. **2.** The distance between a water well and the limit of the *cone of depression.

radius of vulnerability zone The maximum distance from the point of release of a *hazardous substance, over which the concentration in the air could reach the *level of concern under specified weather conditions.

radon (Rn) A naturally occurring, colourless, odourless *radioactive gas (radon-222) which is about eight times denser than air, is formed by the *radioactive decay of *radium, and has a *half-life of 3.82 days. It is one of the more important natural sources of *radioactivity in the environment, and causes health problems (including *cancer) in humans. Radon is released naturally from rocks, soils, and minerals that contain radium, and the gas is normally trapped in underground rocks, but when the rocks are weathered or crack the gas escapes. Some of it is dissolved in *groundwater, and can cause a health risk by contamination of water supplies. Most of the radon escapes directly into

the lower atmosphere, where it is mixed, dispersed, and diluted. It normally disappears quickly, because of its short half-life and rapid dispersion by winds, preventing the build up of dangerously high concentrations. The gas and its *radon daughter products emit *alpha particles, and may cause lung cancer.

radon daughter (radon decay product, radon progeny) A short-lived radioactive decay product of *radon that decays into lead *isotopes, and that can be spread through the air and cause health problems (particularly lung damage if inhaled) in humans.

radon decay product *See* RADON DAUGHTER.

radon progeny *See* RADON DAUGHTER.

RAFU *See* REASONABLY ANTICIPATED FUTURE USE.

rain Liquid *precipitation that falls as droplets of water. *See also* CONVECTION RAIN; FRONTAL RAIN; OROGRAPHIC PRECIPITATION; RAINFALL.

rain gauge An instrument that is used to measure the amount of *rainfall over a given period of time. A standard rain gauge consists of a cylinder 20 cm in diameter and closed at one end which is set on open ground with its rim 1 m above ground level. Rain falling into the gauge enters a collecting funnel which directs it into a calibrated measuring tube, 6.32 cm in diameter, inside the cylinder. The cross-sectional area of the measuring tube is 0.1 times the area of the mouth of the collecting funnel, so the amount of rainfall is calculated by dividing the depth of water in the tube by 10. Alternative designs include the tipping-buckets gauge in which rainwater falls into a bucket holding 0.25 mm of water; when full the bucket tips, making an electrical contact, and empties its water, while the second bucket is positioned to continue collecting.

rain making An attempt to induce *rainfall from a cloud that might not have released it.

rain shadow The reduction of rainfall to the lee side of a mountain barrier, which results in relatively dry surface conditions (e.g. in the mountains of the south-western USA, where the wetter western slopes of the Coast Range and the Sierra Nevada contrast with the desert areas of Nevada and eastern California on the lee side of the mountains).

rainbow An arc of coloured light that is formed in the sky when the Sun's rays are reflected and refracted (bent) by drops of water in rain or mist, and display the colours of the *visible light part of the *electromagnetic spectrum in sequence: violet (0.390–0.455 micrometres), blue (0.455–0.492 micrometres), green (0.492–0.577 micrometres), yellow (0.577–0.597 micrometres), orange (0.597–0.622 micrometres), red (0.622–0.770 micrometres), with violet on the inside of the arc and red on the outside. Sometimes a secondary bow is visible about 8° above the primary bow.

Rainbow Warrior A ship that is operated as a campaigning and research vessel by *Greenpeace; the first *Rainbow Warrior* was sunk by the French secret service in Auckland harbour, New Zealand, on 10 July 1985.

raindrop A drop of water that falls from a cloud. Raindrops are at least 1 mm across and typically 2–5 mm in size and they fall at 23–33 $km\ h^{-1}$.

raindrop erosion (rainsplash, splash erosion) *Erosion of exposed *soil on a bare, sloping surface that is caused by the impact of *raindrops, which loosens and splashes particles and moves them downslope.

rainfall 1. *Precipitation in the form of *rain. 2. The quantity of *precipitation that falls as *rain in a given period of time, usually expressed as depth of water (millimetres).

rainfall frequency A measure of how often *rainfall occurs in a particular place.

rainfall intensity The rate at which rain is falling at any given point in time, usually expressed in millimetres per hour (mm h^{-1}).

rainfall interception *See* INTERCEPTION.

rainfed farming Growing crops or animals under conditions of natural *rainfall, without the use of *irrigation.

rainforest A large, dense, evergreen forest that grows in a climate which has high humidity, constant temperature, and abundant rainfall (generally over 380 cm per year). There are both *tropical rainforests (such as the Amazon) and *temperate rainforests (such as in the Pacific Northwest of North America).

Rainforest Action Network (RAN) An international *environmental group that works to protect the Earth's *rainforests and support the rights of their inhabitants.

Rainforest Alliance An international *environmental group whose objective is to protect *rainforest *ecosystems and the people and wildlife that depend on them by transforming land use practices, business practices, and consumer behaviour.

rainout The removal from the air of particles that are small enough to act as *cloud condensation nuclei and fall inside *raindrops.

rainsplash *See* RAINDROP EROSION.

rainstorm A *storm with *rain.

rainwash *See* WASH.

raised beach A former *beach that is now situated above the present *sealevel as a result of earth movement or changes in global sea level.

raised bog A type of *bog that has a shallow dome-shaped cross-section, so that the bog surface (at least in the centre) is raised above the normal level of the *groundwater.

RAM *See* RELATIVE ATOMIC MASS.

Ramsar Convention An international convention on wetlands of international importance (1971), which was designed to promote the *conservation of internationally important *wetland *habitats, particularly in order to protect *waterfowl and other migratory water birds.

(⊕) **SEE WEB LINKS**

• The Ramsar Convention on Wetlands home page.

Ramsar site A *wetland that is of international importance and has been designated under the *Ramsar Convention.

RAN *See* RAINFOREST ACTION NETWORK.

random Lacking any predictable order or plan.

range 1. *See* RANGELAND. 2. *See* NATURAL RANGE. 3. *See* STATISTICAL RANGE.

range allotment *See* ALLOTMENT.

range condition The status of the vegetation and soil of a particular area of *rangeland, compared with the natural potential (*climax) for that site.

range management The management of *rangeland in order to sustain maximum livestock production and *conserve the *natural resources.

range of variability The observed limits of change in the composition, structure, and function of an *ecosystem over a given period of time, which results from both natural and human factors.

rangeland A large area of *grassland or open *woodland on which livestock can *graze and *browse. *See also* OPEN RANGE; PRIMARY RANGE; SECONDARY RANGE.

ranger A person who is responsible for managing and protecting a forest or park (such as a *national park), enforcing the laws that apply there, and offering information to visitors.

rank vegetation *Grassland or *marsh vegetation that has grown abundantly without being cut or grazed for some time, and as a result has become tall, tussocky, and dominated by coarse species of grass.

rapid needs assessment A group of techniques that are designed to document community needs (such as for food, shelter, healthcare, electricity, radio, and telephones) following a natural *disaster, usually within 48 hours.

rapid rural appraisal *See* PARTICIPATORY RURAL APPRAISAL.

rapids A section of a *river where *slope and flow *velocity both increase, so there is much *white water and many exposed rocks.

raptor A bird of prey (such as a falcon, hawk, eagle, or owl) that hunts and eats meat.

raptorial Adapted for catching and holding prey, often by having sharp claws and spines or bristles.

RARE *See* ROADLESS AREA REVIEW AND EVALUATION.

rare A *threatened category of species defined by the *IUCN (*Red Data Book) as 'taxa with small world populations that are not at present *endangered or *vulnerable, but are at risk. These taxa are usually localized within restricted geographical areas or habitats or are thinly scattered over a more extensive range'.

RARE II *See* ROADLESS AREA REVIEW AND EVALUATION II.

rare and endangered species *Species that have small *populations, either naturally or as a result of human impacts.

rare gas A name formerly given to a gas (e.g. helium or neon) that is *inert or unreactive and is thus very stable. The term is inaccurate because *argon, one of these gases, is not rare,

being present as a constant 0.93% of the atmosphere by volume. *See also* INERT GAS; NOBLE GAS.

rarity In *conservation assessment, seldom found or occurring.

rarity rank A rank (*G-rank, *N-rank, or *S-rank) that is assigned to a *species or ecological *community to indicate its degree of *rarity at the global, national, or subnational level, respectively.

ratification Making something valid by formally confirming it, e.g. by gaining parliamentary approval for a *convention, *protocol, or *treaty that the government of that country has signed.

ratite A flightless, running bird that has no keel on its sternum.

rattan A climbing *palm that has very long tough stems and is used for making baskets and furniture.

ravine A deep, narrow, steep-sided valley that has been eroded by running water.

raw humus *Humus that consists mainly of well preserved but fragmented plant remains.

raw land (undeveloped land) A North American term for land that has not been developed or subdivided in preparation for development.

raw material Natural, unprocessed material or resources that are converted by a manufacturer into a final product.

raw sewage Untreated domestic or commercial *wastewater.

raw water Untreated surface water or *groundwater.

rawinsonde A *radiosonde that carries a radar reflector so it can be tracked to monitor wind direction and strength.

RAWS *See* REMOTE AUTOMATIC WEATHER STATION.

Rayleigh scattering Scattering of light within the *atmosphere that is caused by gas molecules and fine particles of *dust, which reflects *radiation in all directions and makes the sky appear blue.

RCRA *See* RESOURCE CONSERVATION AND RECOVERY ACT.

REACH *See* REGISTRATION, EVALUATION, AUTHORISATION AND RESTRICTION OF CHEMICAL SUBSTANCES.

reach A stretch of stream or river that lies between inflowing *tributaries.

reaction 1. A chemical change: the interaction of two or more substances to form new substances. **2.** The acidity or alkalinity of a soil expressed as a value on the *pH scale. **3.** The fourth stage in plant *succession.

reactive waste *Hazardous waste which is normally unstable, reacts violently with water, can give off toxic fumes, and can explode if heated under pressure.

reactivity The ability of a material to undergo a chemical *reaction with the release of *energy, for example as a result of mixing or reacting with other materials, application of heat, or physical shock. One of the four *characteristics that is used to define *hazardous waste in North America.

reactor core (core) The innermost part of a *nuclear reactor that consists of the fuel, the *moderator (in a thermal reactor), and a coolant; it is where the *fission reaction takes place and the level of radiation is highest.

readiness In *disaster management, the phase of preparations that is designed to deal with an accident or incident.

reaeration The absorption of *oxygen into water from the *atmosphere.

reafforestation *See* REFORESTATION.

reagent A substance that is used to cause a *reaction, especially to detect another substance.

realized niche The actual distribution of an *organism in the environment. *Contrast* POTENTIAL NICHE.

real-time monitoring Monitoring and measuring events, processes, or changes as they are happening.

reasonable maximum exposure (RME) The maximum exposure to a particular *pollutant that is reasonably expected to occur at a particular site, such as a *Superfund site, combining all relevant pathways.

reasonably anticipated future use (RAFU) The likely future use of a site or facility given current use, local government planning, and *zoning.

reasonably available control measures (RACM) A broad term that is used in the USA to refer to technological and other measures for *pollution control that are reasonably available for use, technologically feasible, and economically viable.

reasonably available control technology (RACT) Pollution control technology that is reasonably available for use, technologically feasible, and economically viable.

rebound A recoil or movement back from an impact, particularly the *upwarping of the Earth's crust after additional weight (for example during *glaciation) is removed from it. *Contrast* SUBSIDENCE.

REC *See* RENEWABLE ENERGY CERTIFICATE.

recalcitrant Applied to a pollutant or substance that is not *biodegradable or is only biodegradable with difficulty, and that therefore accumulates in water, soil, and vegetation.

recalcitrant seed Seed that does not survive drying for long-term storage. Most tropical *rainforest trees produce seeds that can be stored for only a few days, rarely weeks, and must be preserved as growing plants.

recarbonization A process in which *carbon dioxide is added to water that is being treated to lower the *pH.

receiving water Any body of water into which *wastewater or treated *effluent are discharged.

receptor A species, population, community, habitat, or ecosystem that may be exposed to one or more particular *contaminants or *agents.

receptor site The site to which individuals of an *introduced species are taken in order to be introduced from another place (the *donor site).

recessional moraine *See* END MORAINE.

recharge To refill a *waterbody or an *aquifer with water by natural or artificial processes. *See also* GROUNDWATER RECHARGE.

recharge area (recharge zone) An area across which water enters (*recharges) an *aquifer via *infiltration.

recharge rate The quantity of water per unit of time that refills an *aquifer.

recharge zone *See* RECHARGE AREA.

reclaim To return something (such as land) to its original condition.

reclaimed land Land that has been brought into new productive use through *reclamation.

reclamation 1. *See* LAND RECLAMATION. **2.** *See* WASTE RECLAMATION.

recognition species concept The definition of *species as a set of organisms that recognize one another as potential mates, through a shared mate recognition system (such as a particular bird song). *See also* BIOLOGICAL SPECIES CONCEPT; CLADISTIC SPECIES CONCEPT; ECOLOGICAL SPECIES CONCEPT; PHENETIC SPECIES CONCEPT.

recombinant bacteria *Micro-organisms whose genetic makeup has been altered by the deliberate introduction of new *genetic elements, so that their offspring also contain these new genetic elements.

recombinant DNA *DNA that has been genetically engineered, such as new DNA produced by joining together pieces of DNA from different sources.

recombinant DNA technology *See* GENETIC ENGINEERING.

recombination The formation of new combinations of *genes, which occurs naturally in plants and animals during the production of sex cells (sperm, eggs, *pollen) and their subsequent joining in fertilization. It also occurs artificially, through *genetic engineering.

recommended maximum contaminant level (RMCL) The maximum level of a *contaminant in drinking water at which no known or anticipated damage to human health would occur.

reconnaissance survey A preliminary inspection or survey of an area (such as a *forest, *range, *watershed, or wildlife area), usually executed rapidly and at a relatively low cost, in order to gain general information that will be useful for future management.

reconstruction Rebuilding structures that have been damaged or destroyed, for example by a *natural hazard or *disaster.

record of decision (ROD) A document, associated with an *environmental impact statement (EIS), that publicly and officially discloses the decision of the responsible official concerning which alternative assessed in the EIS is to be implemented.

recoverability The ability of a *habitat, *community, or individual to recover from damage that is caused by an external factor.

recoverable Capable of being recovered, regained, or restored.

recoverable resource A *resource that can be recovered with current *technology, but whose recovery is not economical under current conditions.

recovered material Waste materials and *byproducts which have been recovered or diverted from *solid waste.

recovery 1. Return to an original state, such as the natural capacity of an open system for self-repair. **2.** In *conservation, the process by which the decline of an *endangered or *threatened species is arrested or reversed, and threats neutralized, so that its survival in the wild can be ensured. **3.** In *mineral processing, the amount of mineral that is separated and recovered in a mill, as a percentage of that calculated to be the original ore. **4.** In *waste management, the process of obtaining materials or energy resources from solid or liquid waste. **5.** In *disaster management, the coordinated process of supporting communities that have been affected by disaster in *reconstruction of the physical infrastructure and restoration of emotional, social, economic, and physical well-being.

recovery plan 1. A *plan to restore areas that have been affected by a particular *disaster. **2.** A plan for the conservation of an *endangered or *threatened species.

recovery rate The percentage of usable materials in a *solid waste stream that is recovered and *recycled, as a percentage of the total waste.

recreation Any activity that refreshes, satisfies, and brings enjoyment to people, in which they engage on a voluntary basis during *leisure time. *See also* CONCENTRATED RECREATION; DISPERSED RECREATION; INTENSIVE RECREATION; PRIMITIVE RECREATION.

recreation ecology The study of the effects of recreation on *ecosystems. Understanding the consequences of recreation upon ecosystems is becoming increasingly urgent with the rise in *ecotourism.

recreation land An area of land and water that is used primarily for *recreation.

recreation opportunity spectrum (ROS) A continuum of land types that is used in the USA to characterize *recreation opportunities in terms of setting, activity, and experience opportunities. The spectrum contains six classes: *primitive area, *semi-primitive non-motorized area, *semi-primitive motorized area, *roaded natural area, *rural area, and *urban area.

recreation resource A scenic or *wilderness feature or setting that has significance or value for *recreation, or a recreation facility.

recreation visitor day *See* VISITOR DAY.

recreational area An area of land or water that has been set aside for use by the public for *recreation activities and enjoyment.

recruitment The addition of new individuals to a *population by reproduction, which is commonly measured as the proportion of young in the population just before the *breeding season.

rectangular drainage pattern A *drainage pattern that is similar to the *trellis pattern, but with the pattern largely controlled by *faults or *joints that intersect at high angles.

recurrence interval (RI, return period) The average period, usually measured in years, between two successive *floods of a given size (*discharge) at a particular location within a river system, as calculated by *flood frequency analysis.

recurrent selection A *breeding method that is designed to increase the frequency of favourable *genes within a species, via repeated cycles of *selection and selected crossing of individuals.

recyclable Any material (such as glass, paper, *aluminium, and some plastics) that can be collected and sold for *recycling at a net cost no greater than the cost of collection and disposal.

recycle To reclaim or reuse old materials in order to make new products.

recycling The reprocessing of discarded *waste materials for reuse, which involves collection, sorting, processing, and conversion into raw materials which can be used in the production of new products.

recycling mill A facility where recovered (*recycled) materials are reprocessed into new products.

recycling scheme An organized scheme for *recycling solid waste materials. *See also* KERB-SIDE RECYCLING SCHEME.

red bag waste *See* INFECTIOUS WASTE.

Red Data Book A global list (*Red List) of *endangered and *threatened species, which is produced and regularly updated by the *World Conservation Union (IUCN). It contains colour-coded information sheets arranged by species: red for species that are *endangered, amber for *vulnerable, white for *rare, green for out of danger, and grey for species that are indicated to be endangered, vulnerable, or rare but with insufficient information to be properly classified. The three main groups of categories are *threatened, *unknown, and *not threatened.

Red Flag warning A term used by *weather forecasters to alert land managers to weather conditions that could lead to extensive *wildland *fires.

Red List The list of *endangered species that are included within a *Red Data Book.

red tide A reddish-brown discoloration of surface sea waters, usually along the *coast, caused by *nutrient pollution that encourages abnormally rapid growth and thus high concentrations of certain *dinoflagellates that produce *toxins which can be fatal to fish and other organisms. Such a tide can be red, green, or brown, depending on the coloration of the plankton; it is often transported by real *tides.

redox potential A scale that indicates the *reduction and *oxidation for a given material. The position on the scale is expressed as an electric potential in millivolts, normally in the range 0–1300 or 0–1400 millivolts. The *pH of the sample must be known since this can alter the reading.

redox reaction A reaction that involves simultaneous *reduction and *oxidation.

reduced tillage system A *tillage system (e.g. *minimum tillage) that preserves soil, saves energy and water, and increases crop yield by reducing the amount of cultivation.

reducer organism *See* DECOMPOSER.

reduction A chemical process that involves the addition of *hydrogen, removal of *oxygen, or the addition of *electrons to an element or compound. *Contrast* OXIDATION.

reduction potential (electrode potential) A quantitative measure of the ease with which a substance is oxidized or reduced. It represents the voltage necessary to prevent the flow of electrons to or from a half-cell containing aqueous solutions of the oxidized and reduced forms of the test substance when it is connected to a hydrogen half-cell.

reductionism The idea, which underpins modern science, that it is possible to explain phenomena in terms of their component parts, so that complex systems can be understood in terms of their constituents. *Contrast* HOLISM.

redwood Three species of coniferous trees that have red wood: *Metasequoia glyptostroboides* (dawn redwood); *Sequoiadendron giganteum* (Sierra redwood, big tree, giant sequoia, Wellingtonia); and *Sequoia sempervirens* (coast redwood).

reed A tall, woody, *perennial *grass (*Phragmites australis*) that has a thin hollow stem.

reedbed *Wetland dominated by stands of common reed (*Phragmites australis*).

reef A ridge of rocks, often made of *coral, that lies submerged near the surface of the sea and can pose a hazard to passing ships.

reef ball An artificial *reef that is built to restore damaged *coral reefs, and to create new fishing and scuba diving sites.

reef flat A pavement of naturally cemented, large skeletal debris and *reef debris which forms to the protected rear (leeward) of the crest of a reef. Water depth in this zone is shallow, only a few metres at most. Sand shoals and small islands or *cays may be present on the reef flat.

reef front An irregularly sloping ramp that extends from the *surf zone to a depth of approximately 100 m on the windward, open-sea side of a *reef.

reef knoll A dome-like mass of *limestone that has grown upwards from an active *coral reef.

reef trap A stratigraphic oil or gas trap produced by porous *reef limestones (the *reservoir rock) covered by impermeable strata.

reference site A sampling site that is selected for its relatively undisturbed conditions, which provides a *benchmark in comparative studies.

reference year The *benchmark year on which *environmental quality targets are established. For example, the *Kyoto Protocol uses 1990 as the reference year against which *Annex I nations are required to control their emissions of *greenhouse gases.

refine To remove unwanted substances from something such as *petroleum, which is refined to produce *petrol, *paraffin, and *diesel oil.

refinery A factory where a substance such as *petroleum is refined. *See also* PETROLEUM REFINERY.

reflection The return of light or sound waves from a surface.

reflectivity *See* ALBEDO.

reforestation (reafforestation) Replacing forest. *See also* AFFORESTATION.

reformer A device that extracts pure *hydrogen from *hydrocarbon fuels (such as *natural gas, *methanol, *ammonia, *gasoline, or vegetable oil) so it can be used in a *fuel cell.

reformulated gasoline A specially refined cleaner-burning blend of *gasoline that reduces emissions from vehicle exhausts, particularly *volatile organic compounds (VOCs) and *hazardous air pollutants.

refraction The deflection or bending of the path of a wave. 1. The bending of light as it passes obliquely from one transparent medium to another with a consequent change in its speed. The extent of the refraction is proportional to the difference in the speed of light in the two media and the angle at which the light enters. 2. The deflection of a sea *wave as it approaches the *shore.

refrigerant A chemical that cools air as it evaporates. Many refrigerants contain *CFCs and are harmful to the *ozone layer in the Earth's atmosphere.

refuge A safe place that offers protection or shelter, such as an area (for example a *nature reserve) that has been set aside for the purpose of conserving *species and their *habitats.

refugee A person who is forced to leave his/her home and seek safety in another region or

country as an exile, usually as a result of persecution.

refugium An area that remains unchanged
while the areas that surround it change a great
deal, and which therefore provides a *refuge for
*relict species or populations that require spe-
cific habitats.

refuse (trash, garbage) All forms of *solid
waste or *rubbish.

refuse-derived fuel Fuel that is made from
the *organic residue of *municipal solid waste,
which is shredded, formed into pellets or small
briquettes, then dried to make fuel for *power
plants.

reg A *desert surface that is covered by loose
stones and gravel, but with no *sand.

regelation The process by which a substance (for example the ice in a *glacier) melts
under pressure and then refreezes after the
pressure is released.

regeneration The regrowth, by either natural or artificial means, of vegetation and *ecological communities that have been damaged or
destroyed.

regeneration cut In *forest management, a
cutting strategy in which old trees are removed
while favourable environmental conditions are
maintained in order to promote and enhance
the natural establishment of new trees.

regeneration harvest In *forest management, a *clearcut that removes an existing
stand of trees in order to prepare the site for
*regeneration.

regenerative farming Farming techniques and methods of *land management that
are designed to restore soil productivity by measures such as *crop rotation, planting *ground
cover, protecting the surface with *mulch, and
reducing the input of synthetic chemicals and
mechanical compaction.

regime Any system of control, or more specifically a system of government. *See also* ENVI-
RONMENTAL REGIME.

regimen A treatment plan, formalized schedule, or strict, regulated plan that is designed to
reach particular goals.

region A geographical area of land and/or
water that is distinguished by certain natural

features, climatic conditions, or fauna or flora.
See also MORPHOGENETIC REGION; NATURAL RE-
GION; PHYSIOGRAPHIC REGION.

regional climate The climate of a moderately large area, such as north-western Europe
or the US Great Plains. *See* MACROCLIMATE.

regional diversity *See* GAMMA DIVERSITY.

regional haze Atmospheric *haze that extends over a large area and is produced by
many different sources.

regional metamorphism *Metamorphism of large areas of the Earth's *crust,
usually during mountain building at *convergent plate margins. *Contrast* CONTACT META-
MORPHISM.

regional plan The plan for a region, for
example to assist regional government or
authority to manage *natural resources on a
*sustainable basis or meet particular social or
economic goals.

regional planning The process of developing regional plans.

Regional Seas Programme A programme
launched in 1974 by the *United Nations Environment Programme to improve the management and exploitation of the marine and
coastal environment. More than 143 countries
participate in 13 regional seas programmes, and
there are associated programmes for the Antarctic, Arctic, Baltic Sea, Caspian Sea, and
North-East Atlantic.

• Regional Seas Programme.

**Regionally Important Geological/Geo-
morphological Site (RIGS)** In the UK, sites
(other than *SSSIs) that are considered worth
protecting for their educational, research, historical, or aesthetic importance, because of their
geology.

**Registration, Evaluation, Authorisa-
tion and Restriction of Chemical Substances (REACH)** An EU regulation on
chemicals and their safe use that came into
force on 1 June 2007. It requires manufacturers
to gather information on the properties of the
chemicals they produce and to register that
information on a central database run by the
*European Chemicals Agency. REACH calls for

the progressive substitution of alternatives to the most dangerous substances.

• REACH explained.

regolith The layer of *unconsolidated material (*soil and mineral *subsoil) that lies between the soil surface and the solid *bedrock below, composed mainly of weathered bedrock or *sediment.

regosolic soils An order in the Canadian system of *soil classification, comprising soils that are too weakly developed to be included in any other order. They lack *soil horizons and their properties are essentially those of the *parent material.

regosols A reference soil group in the *World Soil Classification that comprises all soils that do not belong to one of the other reference soil groups.

regression 1. A statistical method for studying and expressing the nature of relationships between two or more variables. 2. A slow lowering of *sea level that exposes land along the *shoreline.

regulated forest Forest land that is managed to produce a *sustained yield of timber.

regulated river A river in which the natural processes and/or the *river channel itself have been deliberately altered for management purposes, such as the construction of a large *dam for *water supply, to generate *hydroelectric power, or to reduce downstream *flooding.

regulation An authoritative rule; a principle or condition that normally governs behaviour. *See also* DIRECTIVE.

regulator An official or agency responsible for the control and supervision of a particular activity or area of public interest, or which oversees and applies legislation.

rehabilitate To restore to a good condition or bring back to an original condition.

rehabilitation The process of returning a disturbed site, *habitat, or *ecosystem to its original condition.

Reid Vapour Pressure (RVP) A measure of the volatility of petroleum products other than liquefied petroleum gases, but especially of gasoline, measured at 100°F (37.8°C). Refineries adjust the RVP seasonally because a high vaporization rate aids engine starting in cold

weather and a low RVP prevents fuel from vaporizing in the fuel lines.

reintroduction The renewed introduction of a species to an area from which it has almost or completely disappeared within historical times.

rejuvenation The process of restoring an *environmental system to a more youthful condition, such as the renewed downcutting of a river system as a result of *tectonic *uplift. *See also* LONG PROFILE.

relative abundance The number (*abundance) of *organisms of a particular kind which is present in a *sample or *community, relative to the total number of organisms in that sample or community.

relative age Age that is expressed relative to other ages ('younger than' or 'older than'), rather than in number of years. *Contrast* ABSOLUTE AGE.

relative atomic mass (RAM) The mass of an *atom of a particular chemical *element, relative to one atom of carbon (which has a RAM of 12). Formerly known as atomic weight.

relative chronology A *chronology that determines the age of a feature or event relative to the age of other features or events (for example, younger than or older than). *Contrast* ABSOLUTE CHRONOLOGY.

relative dating A range of methods for establishing the *relative age of an object or material, for example based on the relative position of individual *strata within *sedimentary rocks.

relative frequency *See* FREQUENCY.

relative humidity The amount of *water vapour that is present in the air, expressed as a percentage of the amount that the air could hold if it was saturated. *Contrast* ABSOLUTE HUMIDITY. *See also* HUMIDITY.

relative poverty A state of *poverty that is characterized by scarcity rather than lack of economic necessities, which does not immediately threaten life or health. *Contrast* ABSOLUTE POVERTY.

relative relief The difference between the highest and lowest points in a particular area. *Contrast* ABSOLUTE RELIEF.

relative risk A measure of comparative *risk of developing a particular *disease or condition, within a defined period of time.

relative scarcity A condition that exists when a particular *resource is in short supply in one or more areas, because of inadequate or disrupted distribution. *Contrast* ABSOLUTE SCARCITY. *See also* SCARCITY.

relay cropping A *cropping system in which two or more *crops are grown one after the other in the same field in the same year.

release 1. In general, to discharge or liberate something. **2.** In *pollution control, any process (including spilling, leaking, pumping, pouring, emitting, emptying, discharging, injecting, escaping, *leaching, dumping, or disposing) by which a *hazardous or *toxic chemical, or extremely hazardous substance, is discharged into the *environment.

release cutting The removal of competing vegetation in order to allow desired tree species to grow.

release rate The quantity of a *pollutant that is released from a *source into the *environment, over a given period of time.

relict An *organism or *species that survives as a remnant of an otherwise *extinct flora or fauna, in an *environment that has changed much from the one in which it originated.

relict distribution The distribution area of a *relict species, which is a remnant of a previously wider *range.

relief 1. The difference in *elevation between the high and low points of a land surface. **2.** Assistance in time of difficulty, such as the provision of immediate shelter, life support, and human needs to people who are affected by a *disaster.

rem The abbreviation for roentgen equivalent man, a former measurement of *radiation in terms of biological effect on human tissue. The rem has been replaced by the *sievert (1 sievert = 100 rem). *See also* DOSE EQUIVALENT.

remedial action Long-term *cleanup activities, including the cleanup, removal, containment, isolation, treatment, or monitoring of *hazardous substances that have been released into the *environment, in order to reduce or eliminate the long-term risks to *human health or the environment from exposure to *contaminants.

remediation (amelioration) Action that is taken to correct or treat a *pollution problem, which usually involves the *cleanup or other methods that are used to remove or contain a *toxic spill or hazardous materials from a

*hazardous waste site (such as a *Superfund site).

remedy A method, technique, or process that is designed to treat or clean up contaminated air, soil, sediments, or water. *See also* REMEDIATION.

remote automatic weather station (RAWS) A self-contained weather station that automatically acquires, processes, and stores local weather data which are then transmitted via radio, a landline, or through a *satellite (*GOES) to a receiving station elsewhere.

remote sensing Collecting information about an object or event from a distance, without being in physical contact with it, such as through *air photography or *satellite imaging. For example, satellite monitoring of the Earth's *radiation balance, atmospheric dynamics, the *oceans and ocean/atmosphere interactions, land resources, *glaciers, and *ice caps is proving to be particularly useful in building up a detailed picture of how the environment works and how it is being affected by human activities. Satellites are also being increasingly used in monitoring *natural hazards and *natural disasters. One promising development is the *World Environment and Disaster Observation System (WEDOS).

remotely operated vehicle (ROV) An unmanned submersible vehicle that is controlled from the sea surface, the uses of which include photographing and repairing underwater structures and collecting samples of sediment from the deep ocean floor.

removal action *See* SHORT-TERM CLEANUP.

removal cut In *forest management, the removal of the last seed-bearing trees or shelter trees after *regeneration is established. *See also* SHELTERWOOD CUT.

renewable Something that can be used again because it can be replaced or replenished: a *natural resource that is capable of being replaced by natural *ecological cycles or sound management practices.

renewable energy (renewables) *Energy that is obtained from sources that are for all practical purposes *inexhaustible, which includes moving water (*hydroelectric power, *tidal power, and *wave power), *thermal gradients in ocean water, *biomass, *geothermal energy, *solar energy, and *wind energy. Contrast this with energy from sources such as *fossil fuels, of which there is a finite supply which is exhaustible.

Renewable Energy Certificate (REC, Renewable Energy Credit) Under the *Kyoto Protocol, a tradable certificate of proof of the amount of *renewable energy that is used in the manufacture of a particular good or commodity. In many countries 1 REC = the equivalent of one megawatt hour (Mwh) of electricity from a renewable generation source. Known in the UK as Renewable Obligations Certificate. *See* RENEWABLE PORTFOLIO STANDARD.

Renewable Energy Credit *See* RENEWABLE ENERGY CERTIFICATE.

Renewable Obligations Certificate (ROC) *See* RENEWABLE ENERGY CERTIFICATE.

Renewable Portfolio Standard (RPS) A benchmark that defines the proportion of total annual energy sales that individual energy retail suppliers must obtain from *renewable energy sources, under the *Renewable Energy Certificate scheme.

renewable resource (flow resource, replenishable resource) A *natural resource (such as fresh water, a forest, or *renewable energy) that is replaced at a rate which is at least as fast as it is used, which has the ability to renew itself and be harvested indefinitely under the right conditions, but which can be converted into a *non-renewable resource if subject to *overexploitation. *See also* SUSTAINABLE YIELD.

renewables *See* RENEWABLE ENERGY.

replacement level A *population growth rate of zero, when the number of births equal the number of deaths in a population over a year. *See also* ZERO POPULATION GROWTH.

replacement-level fertility *See* ZERO POPULATION GROWTH.

replenishable resource *See* RENEWABLE RESOURCE. *Contrast* DEPLETABLE RESOURCE.

reportable quantity (RQ) The minimum amount of a *hazardous substance that, when spilled, must be reported to the proper authorities in the USA under *CERCLA.

repository A long-term storage *facility or archive. One preferred approach to the safe and sustainable management of *nuclear waste is long-term underground storage of the waste in specially developed and managed sites, but efforts to set up such repositories have been hampered by public opposition. Key site requirements for nuclear waste repositories include the following: the site must be away from major centres of population, the site must be accessible by road and rail, geological conditions must be suitable (it must be possible to tunnel, for example), prospects of minimizing *groundwater contamination must be good, it must be possible to store radioactive waste safely there for at least 10 000 years, and the site must be geologically stable (away from *fault lines and *earthquake zones). The controversy surrounding the proposed repository at *Yucca Mountain in Nevada illustrates some of the complexity of the issues involved.

representative area An area that is typical of its surroundings in terms of physical features and ecological patterns.

representative sample A *sample whose characteristics are the same as those of the original *population or reference population.

representativeness (typicalness) In *conservation assessment, the degree to which a sample is typical of a feature, habitat, or group of species.

reprocessing The chemical treatment of spent *nuclear fuel in order to separate potentially reusable constituents (such as *uranium and *plutonium) from unwanted *nuclear waste products.

reproduction The act of making copies; in biology, the process of generating offspring.

reproductive health hazard Any *agent that damages the reproductive system of an adult male or female, or the developing foetus or child.

reproductive isolation The isolation from each other of two *populations of a species, the individuals of which would otherwise be capable of interbreeding. Isolating mechanisms may be chromosomal (any *hybrid would either die or be infertile), mechanical (the species are different sizes or have genitalia of different shapes), behavioural (one species does not recognize the courting behaviour of the other), or ecological (the two species occupy different *microhabitats and seldom meet).

reproductive potential *See* BIOTIC POTENTIAL.

reptile Any *poikilothermic, air-breathing *vertebrate of the class Reptilia, which includes tortoises, turtles, snakes, lizards, alligators, and crocodiles. There are about 6000 species, found on all continents except Antarctica. *See also* HERPETOFAUNA.

rescue effect The reduction in the chance of extinction of a *species on an island that occurs when another member of that species arrives on the island; i.e. the incomer 'rescues' the resident. The rescue effect will be greater on islands that are closer to the mainland source of species than on more remote islands because the immigration rate will be higher.

research Systematic investigation that is designed to establish facts.

Research Natural Area An area that contains *natural resource values of scientific interest, which is managed primarily for research and educational purposes. *See also* NATURAL AREA PRESERVE.

reservation *See* RESERVE.

Reservation and Other Tribal Lands A North American term for all lands that lie within the boundaries of any Indian reservation, including rights of way and all lands that are held in trust for or supervised by any Indian tribe.

reserve (reservation) An area of land that is set aside and managed for a particular purpose, such as *nature conservation. *See also* BIOSPHERE RESERVE; GAME RESERVE; NATURE RESERVE.

reserves That part of an identifiable supply of *resources (such as a *mineral deposit) that can be extracted profitably, at present prices, with current technology.

reservoir A natural or artificial pond, lake, or basin that is used for the storage, regulation, and control of water. *See also* IMPOUNDMENT.

reservoir rock Any porous rock in which oil, gas, or water may accumulate; it is usually *sandstone, *limestone, or *dolomite, but sometimes fractured *igneous or *metamorphic rock.

residence time The period of time during which a substance remains in a particular area or in a particular part of an *environmental system, such as water retained in a *reservoir, or a *greenhouse gas retained in the *atmosphere. Typical residence time are: water vapour in the lower atmosphere, 10 days; carbon dioxide in the atmosphere, 5–10 days; aerosol particles in the lower atmosphere, one week to several weeks; aerosol particles in the upper atmosphere, several months to several years; water in the biosphere, two million years; oxygen in the biosphere, 2000 years; carbon dioxide in the biosphere, 300 years; surface water in the Atlantic Ocean, 10 years; deep water in the Atlantic Ocean, 600 years.

resident A permanent inhabitant or non-migratory animal.

residential land Land which is primarily used for permanent dwellings, such as houses and flats, including the associated infrastructure (such as roads, drains, and sewers).

residential sector A North American term for all private residences (occupied or vacant, owned or rented), including mobile homes as well as secondary homes such as summer homes. *See also* COMMERCIAL SECTOR; INDUSTRIAL SECTOR; TRANSPORTATION SECTOR.

residential waste *See* HOUSEHOLD WASTE.

residual 1. The difference between an observed and an expected or predicted value. **2.** The amount of a *pollutant that remains in the *environment after a natural or technological process has taken place, such as the *sludge that remains after initial *wastewater treatment, or the *particulates that remain in air after it has passed through *scrubbing or other processes.

residual herbicide A *herbicide that persists in the soil after it has been applied, and injures or kills germinating weed seedlings over a short period of time. *Contrast* CONTACT HERBICIDE.

residual risk The risk that remains after the application of selected safeguards, particularly the health risk from air pollutants that remains after the application of the *maximum achievable control technology.

residual stand In *forest management, the trees that are left standing after any cutting operation.

residuals *See* SLUDGE.

residue Matter that remains after other materials have been removed, such as the *fly ash that is left after *incineration, or the dry solids that remain after a sample of water or *sludge has been evaporated.

resilience The rate at which a system regains structure and function following a stress or perturbation. *Contrast* RESISTANCE. *See also* SENSITIVITY.

resin A thick, sticky liquid that is exuded by certain plants and becomes hard when exposed to the air. Fossilized resin is known as *amber.

resistance 1. Any mechanical force that slows or opposes motion. **2.** A measure of the degree to which a body opposes the passage of an electric current. **3.** The ability of a system to withstand being disturbed by an external factor. *Contrast* RESILIENCE. *See also* INERTIA; STABILITY.

resistor A device that is used to control the flow of electric current by providing *resistance.

resolution 1. The accuracy with which something can be measured, or the scale at which it is measured. **2.** Finding a solution to a problem. **3.** A decision to do something or to behave in a certain manner.

resource An available supply of something that is valued because it can be used for a particular purpose, usually to satisfy particular human wants or desires. *See also* AESTHETIC RESOURCE; CULTURAL RESOURCE; NATURAL RESOURCE.

resource allocation The deliberate distribution and use of *resources in an organized and efficient way, in order to meet defined goals or objectives, or to complete particular tasks in a timely and efficient manner.

resource conservation An approach to the *conservation and *sustainable use of *natural resources that is based on reducing the amount of *solid waste that is generated, reducing overall resource consumption, and using recovered resources.

Resource Conservation and Recovery Act (RCRA) (1976) US legislation that amended the *Solid Waste Disposal Act (1965) by establishing a regulatory system for the *Environmental Protection Agency to regulate and manage *solid waste, including *hazardous waste, requiring safe and secure procedures to be used in treating, transporting, storing, and disposing of hazardous wastes, and preventing new *Superfund sites from arising.

resource depletion Using a *non-renewable resource and/or using a *renewable resource faster than it can naturally be replaced.

resource management 1. The deliberate *management of *natural resources. **2.** A task within *project management that ensures that adequate resources are allocated to a particular activity (for example after a *disaster).

resource management system (RMS) A system that integrates *conservation practices and *resource management techniques in order to maintain or improve soil, water, plant, and related resources.

resource partitioning The sharing of resources by different *species within a biological community, through the development of specialized *niches, thus reducing direct competition.

resource plan A *plan that is prepared by government and used to guide public policy and action on the use, treatment, and management of soil and water resources.

resource recovery The recovery of materials, fuel, or energy, particularly from *solid waste.

resource recovery facility Any *facility at which *solid waste is processed in order to extract, convert to energy, or otherwise separate and prepare solid waste for *reuse.

resource recovery system A solid *waste management system that is designed for the collection, separation, recycling, and recovery of solid wastes, including the disposal of non-recoverable waste residues.

Resource Reserve An *IUCN Management Category (VI) for *protected areas, which is designed 'to protect resources of the area for future use and prevent or contain development activities that could affect the resource pending the establishment of objectives that are based upon appropriate knowledge and planning'.

resource scarcity A shortage or deficit of a particular *resource. *See also* ECONOMIC SCARCITY.

resource values A broad term used in North America to describe products or services that depend upon *ecological processes, including *water quality and quantity, *forage, *fish, *wildlife, *timber, *recreation, *energy, *minerals, and cultural and heritage resources.

resource war A military conflict that is driven by the attempt by one country to dominate and appropriate the *natural resources (such as the oil reserves) of another country.

Resources for the Future An independent environmental organization that is based in the USA, and whose mission is 'to improve environmental and natural resource policymaking worldwide through objective social science research of the highest caliber'.

SEE WEB LINKS

• Resources for the Future home page.

respiration 1. A cellular metabolic process in which food substances are sequentially oxidized with the release of the high-energy compound ATP (adenosine triphosphate), with carbon dioxide and water as byproducts. It is the precise opposite of *photosynthesis. **2.** The transport of oxygen to and carbon dioxide from tissues. **3.** The action of breathing.

respiration rate The rate at which the concentration of *oxygen is reduced by *respiration.

response action Action that is taken by an agency in order to address the risks posed by the release or threatened release into the environment of *hazardous substances.

rest To remain inactive. In land management, to leave an area of *grazing land ungrazed or unharvested for a particular period of time such as a year or a *growing season.

restitution The act of making good, or of giving the equivalent, for any loss, damage, or injury. *See also* RESTORATION.

restoration The act of restoring, renovating, or re-establishing something to close to its original condition, such as the structure and function of a *damaged habitat or *ecosystem.

restoration cost The estimated likely total cost of cleaning up a site and restoring it to a natural condition after resource-using activities (such as *mining) have ceased there.

restoration ecology The study of the structure and *regeneration of plant and animal *communities, particularly the deliberate *colonization and revegetation of *derelict land, for example after activities such as *mining and *waste disposal and after land has been released from *agricultural use.

restricted use area (RUA) In North America, an area of land that is closed to particular activities in order to protect damaged or fragile *habitats and *ecosystems, and allow them to recover naturally.

retardation The extent to which something is delayed or held back, such as the retention of *contaminants in soils and deposits by one or more physical, chemical, or biological factors.

retention The process of holding back or retaining, such as the portion of an original stand of trees that is retained after felling, or the amount of *precipitation on a drainage area that does not escape as *runoff.

retention time (flushing rate, turnover rate) The average period of time for which *water resides in a *lake or *reservoir.

retrofit (backfit) To add machinery or equipment to an existing piece of equipment or system in order to correct a defect or add capability, such as the addition of a *pollution control device on an existing facility without making major changes to the generating plant.

return period *See* RECURRENCE INTERVAL.

return stroke An electrical discharge that carries positive charge upward along a *lightning channel from the ground to the cloud.

reuse The repeated use of a product or material in its same form, for either the same or a different purpose. *Contrast* RECYCLING.

revegetation Re-establishing and developing plant cover, by either natural or artificial means, such as reseeding. *See also* REFORESTATION.

revenue–cost analysis A method of comparing alternatives which is based on analysing the monetary income that each alternative would generate in relation to its cost. *See also* COST–BENEFIT ANALYSIS.

reverse fault An overhanging type of vertical displacement *fault, in which one side is pushed upwards over the other at an angle (the *dip of the *fault line), as a result of strong *compression pressure.

reverse osmosis A method for the *desalination of water, which involves passing the *saline water through a *permeable membrane (film) under pressure. Relatively pure water passes through the membrane, leaving much of the dissolved salt behind.

reversible change A change that can be reversed to give a return to the original state without a major alteration in the surroundings.

reversible effect An effect that is not permanent, such as an adverse effect that decreases when exposure to a *toxic chemical stops.

reversible reaction A *chemical reaction that can proceed in either direction, depending on the concentration of reacting materials.

review To reappraise or evaluate, particularly to reconsider objectives and policies, or to evaluate progress against objectives and policies.

revolving door 1. In general, an organization or institution that has a high rate of turnover of personnel or membership. **2.** A US term for the movement of people in and out of government in a manner that implies that, while the individual is not working for the government, he or she is working for an interest group that benefited from the policies that the individual pursued while working for the government.

Reynolds number (Re) A dimensionless number associated with fluid flow, which represents the relative importance of *viscous forces and *inertial forces in a fluid, i.e. the extent to which the fluid flows smoothly or turbulently. As *Re* increases, inertial forces become more important. If *Re* <500, flow is laminar (*see* LAMINAR FLOW); if *Re* >1000, flow is turbulent (*see* TURBULENT FLOW).

rhizome A horizontal, underground plant stem that bears *roots and leaves. *Compare* STOLON.

rhizosphere The soil zone that immediately surrounds plant roots, which is modified by the increased number of *micro-organisms that live there in association with plant roots.

R-horizon *See* D-HORIZON.

rhourd *See* DRAA.

rhyolite A fine-grained *extrusive *volcanic rock, similar in composition to *granite.

RI *See* RECURRENCE INTERVAL.

ria A drowned river valley.

ribbon development A narrow strip of continuous building development, for example along a road or along the *coast.

ribonucleic acid (RNA) A molecule with a similar structure to *DNA that is involved in a number of cell activities, especially *protein synthesis (because it decodes the instructions that *genes carry for protein synthesis).

richness, species The number of species in a community, habitat, or sample. *See also* DIVERSITY.

Richter scale A scale for describing the magnitude of an *earthquake, devised by Charles Richter (1900–85) in 1935 and based on the amount of energy generated. It is a logarithmic scale that ranges along a progression from zero (minor event) to nine (major event): severe earthquakes have magnitudes greater than seven. It was replaced in the 1970s by the *moment magnitude scale, which gives similar values to earthquakes but is calculated differently. The scale is given in Appendix 7. *Compare* MERCALLI SCALE.

ride An area (often a strip) of *woodland that has been cleared, in order to provide access, fire breaks, and open areas for game and wildlife.

ridge 1. A tongue-like protrusion of relatively high pressure in the atmosphere into a region of lower pressure. **2.** A poleward deviation in the *polar front jet stream. **3.** A long section of high ground between adjacent *valleys.

ridge planting A *conservation farming method in which seeds are planted in ridges, which creates warmer soil temperatures and traps rainwater in the furrows between the ridges.

ridging The formation or intensification of a *ridge of *high pressure in the atmosphere.

riffle A rocky shoal or *sandbar that lies just below the surface of a *stream. *See also* POOL AND RIFFLE.

rift valley A *valley that has formed along a *rift zone where tensional forces have pulled the Earth's *crust apart.

rift zone A system of crustal fractures arising from tensional forces, similar to that which occurs at *mid-oceanic ridges.

rifting The geological process by which a long trough bounded by normal faults is formed by fractures of the Earth's *crust where adjacent *crustal plates have been pushed apart, similar to that which occurs at *mid-oceanic ridges.

right of way The legal right for members of the public to cross land or *property that is owned by someone else, including the strip of land that is used for a road, railroad, or power line, to which the operating company has special right of access.

right to roam A UK campaign by the Ramblers Association and others to be allowed to walk across private land and land owned by the Ministry of Defence. In 2000 the UK government enacted legislation granting a limited right to roam in England and Wales. In Scotland, as well as the Scandinavian countries, the public has access to all land, provided that right is exercised responsibly.

rights Entitlements that are assured by custom, law, or property.

RIGS *See* REGIONALLY IMPORTANT GEOLOGICAL/GEOMORPHOLOGICAL SITE.

rill A small *gully or channel that is formed by *soil erosion on a hillslope or a gently sloping surface, such as a bare *spoil heap or recently ploughed field.

rill erosion The *erosion of exposed *soil on a sloping surface that is caused by the cutting of small water channels by concentrated *surface runoff. It is intermediate between *sheet erosion and *gully erosion.

rime A form of *frost that is created by the freezing onto solid objects of supercooled water droplets in *fog, and appears as a mass of ice crystals on surfaces such as grass.

ring net *See* SEINE NET.

Ringelmann chart A series of shaded illustrations that are used to measure the *opacity of *air pollution emissions, ranging from light grey (number one) to black (number five). The chart is used to set and enforce *emission standards.

Rio Declaration on Environment and Development A general statement of intent which was agreed in 1992 at the *United Nations Conference on Environment and Development and centres on the well-being of people, on the right of states to control their own natural resources, and on their obligation not to damage the environment of other countries. Amongst other things it recommends the *precautionary principle, internalization of *environmental costs, use of *environmental impact statements, and the *polluter pays principle. *See also* SUSTAINABLE DEVELOPMENT.

Rio Earth Summit *See* UNITED NATIONS CONFERENCE ON ENVIRONMENT AND DEVELOPMENT.

rip current A current that flows strongly away from the *shore through gaps in the *surf zone at intervals along the *shoreline.

riparian Relating to the banks of a *stream, *lake, or *waterbody.

riparian forest (gallery forest) Trees and shrubs that grow alongside a river or lake.

riparian rights The *rights of an owner of land which borders a *waterbody to use or control all or part of that waterbody, including the right to prevent diversion or misuse of upstream waters.

riparian vegetation Plants that are adapted to grow in the moist conditions found along the banks of streams, lakes, and other waterbodies.

riparian zone A stream and all of the vegetation on its banks.

ripple A very small-scale *bedform, like a miniature sand dune, which is created at low *flow velocity in the fine sediment of an *alluvial channel. Ripples are always found in a group.

rip-rap A layer of medium to large rocks or logs that is used to stabilize banks along shorelines, ponds, lakes, rivers, and reservoirs.

rising tide *See* FLOOD TIDE.

risk A measure of the likelihood or probability that damage to life, health, property, and/or the environment will occur as a result of a particular *hazard. *See also* ACCEPTABLE RISK; AVOIDABLE RISK; UNACCEPTABLE RISK.

risk analysis The process of identifying where *risks might arise, estimating the likelihood of them happening, and analysing the trade-off of risk against costs and benefits.

risk assessment Methods that are used to estimate short- and long-term harmful impacts on human health or the environment which arise from exposure to *hazards associated with a particular product or activity.

risk avoidance Management that is designed to help ensure that risks will not occur. *Contrast* RISK MITIGATION.

risk–benefit analysis A comparison of the relative *risks and benefits associated with a particular *hazard, in order to determine its acceptability.

risk characterization A summary of what is known about the adverse health, safety, and environmental impacts that are likely to arise from exposure to a particular *hazard.

risk communication A process of providing the public with information about the *risks associated with particular products, substances, activities, and technologies.

risk estimate An assessment of the likelihood that *organisms that are exposed to a particular *pollutant will develop an adverse response (such as *cancer).

risk evaluation The process of determining the acceptability of a particular *risk, based on perceived costs and benefits.

risk factor Any factor that increases the chance of an individual developing or aggravating a particular medical condition, such as heart disease or *cancer.

risk management The systematic application of *management policies, procedures, and practices to the tasks of identifying, analysing, evaluating, treating, and monitoring *risk.

risk mitigation The management of undesirable events as they occur, when the associated *risk could not be avoided. Contrast RISK AVOIDANCE.

risk perception The perception by people of the health, safety, or environmental *risks that are or may be associated with particular activities or in particular settings.

risk reduction Any action that is taken to reduce the likelihood and impact of a particular *risk, which includes education, *regulation, and *remediation.

risk-based targeting The direction of *resources (for example in *disaster management) to those areas that have been identified as having the highest potential or actual adverse impact on *human health and/or the *environment.

risk-specific dose The *dose that is associated with a specified level of *risk.

Riss The third phase of *glaciation in Europe during the *Pleistocene; equivalent to the *Illinoian in North America.

rithron That part of a river in which the water is typically fast-moving, broken-surfaced, shallow, and relatively cold, favouring cold-water organisms with a high demand for dissolved oxygen. Compare POTAMON.

river A large natural *stream of water that flows along a *channel.

river bank See RIPARIAN; STREAM BANK.

river basin See DRAINAGE BASIN.

river bed See STREAM BED.

river blindness (onchocerciasis) A disease in humans caused by an *infestation with slender threadlike *nematodes (Onchocerca volvulus) which are deposited under the skin by the bite of blackflies (Simulium species). The disease can cause blindness and is common in Africa and tropical America.

river capture See RIVER PIRACY.

river channel See STREAM CHANNEL.

river diversion scheme An engineering scheme that is designed to redirect *flood water on a *floodplain and make it flow away from built-up areas, normally by constructing artificial channels.

river equilibrium An *equilibrium channel form that is maintained by adjustments of *hydraulic geometry, *channel pattern, and *slope, in order to preserve a balance of energy moving through the system. Equilibrium exists when the energy provided to do work (transport the sediment and shape the river landscape) is just enough to perform the work that has to be done. See also DYNAMIC EQUILIBRIUM.

river flow The water that flows along a river, ultimately to the sea, as part of the *water cycle. It includes water from *overland flow, *throughflow, *interflow, *soil pipes, *percolation, and *groundwater, as well as *precipitation that falls directly into rivers and lakes. See also EPHEMERAL FLOW; INTERMITTENT FLOW; PERENNIAL FLOW.

river form The *morphology of a river channel, which differs between *alluvial channels and *bedrock channels, which display different forms of *river equilibrium.

river network See DRAINAGE NETWORK.

river piracy The *erosion of large rivers in which one actively eroding river captures the *headwater of an adjacent river, altering the pattern of its *drainage network.

river regulation See REGULATED RIVER.

river terrace A flat platform of land that lies above the level of the valley floor, which may be a surviving remnant of an abandoned *floodplain (see Fig. 17). Contrast TERRACE.

river valley A *valley that has been eroded by a *river.

riverine Of or related to a *river. See also ALLUVIAL; FLUVIAL; RIPARIAN.

Fig. 17 River terrace development

riverscape The *landscape of or surrounding a *river.

RMBK reactor A Soviet *nuclear reactor that was developed by scaling up a reactor originally designed to produce weapons-grade fissile material. The RMBK used unenriched uranium oxide fuel, a graphite *moderator, and water for cooling, carried in pipes through the core. To reduce the risk of water reacting explosively with graphite the core was bathed in nitrogen, but the close proximity of graphite and water led to the rejection of the design in all countries other than the USSR. It was an RMBK reactor that failed at *Chernobyl, after which the RMBK programme was halted and no more were built.

RMCL *See* RECOMMENDED MAXIMUM CONTAMINANT LEVEL.

RME *See* REASONABLE MAXIMUM EXPOSURE.

RMS *See* RESOURCE MANAGEMENT SYSTEM.

RNA *See* RIBONUCLEIC ACID.

road An open way, generally public rather than private, which is used for travel or transportation.

roaded natural area A category of land defined within the *recreation opportunity spectrum as 'predominantly natural appearing environments with moderate evidence of the sights and sounds of man', with moderate to high interaction between users, conventional motorized use allowed and catered for in the design of the facilities, and resource use practices that are evident but harmonized with the natural environment.

Roadless and Undeveloped Area A large area of a *National Forest in the USA which contains no roads and is suitable for designation as a *wilderness area.

Roadless Area Review and Evaluation (RARE) The US national inventory of roadless and undeveloped areas that lie within the *National Forests and *National Grasslands, which was carried out during the 1960s.

Roadless Area Review and Evaluation II (RARE II) An updated version of the *Roadless Area Review and Evaluation that was conducted by the *US Forest Service in 1979, which included consideration of potential *wilderness designations for these areas.

roadway Any surface that is designed, improved, or normally used for vehicle travel.

ROC *See* RENEWABLE OBLIGATIONS CERTIFICATE.

rôche moutonnée (rock knob) An outcrop of bare, resistant rock which has been carved by *glacier ice moving over it. The upstream (*stoss) side is shaped by *abrasion, and is usually smoothed, rounded, and streamlined and often has *striations. The downstream (*lee) side is usually steep and angular because it is eroded by *quarrying processes.

rock A solid, cohesive, aggregate of one or more crystalline minerals. *Oxygen makes up about 47% of exposed rocks, *silicon makes up about 28%, and a further 24% is made of *aluminium, *iron, *potassium, *calcium, *sodium, and *magnesium. *Contrast* IGNEOUS ROCK; METAMORPHIC ROCK; SEDIMENTARY ROCK. *See also* ROCK CYCLE.

rock cycle (geological cycle) The never-ending series of natural geological processes that continuously refashions, redistributes, and recycles material from and on the Earth's *crust, including *weathering, *erosion, *sediment transport, *deposition, and *lithification of *sedimentary rocks, *metamorphism, and all the processes that create *igneous rocks. The rock cycle operates in much the same way as the major *biogeochemical cycles and the global *water cycle, but much more slowly over the full span of *geological time (see Fig. 18).

rock flour A *glacial sediment composed of finely ground rock particles, which is formed by *abrasion of rocks underneath a moving *glacier.

rock glacier A mass of rock (*talus) that is held together by *ice that moves downslope, like a *glacier.

rock knob *See* RÔCHE MOUTONNÉE.

rock salt (halite) Common salt, or *sodium chloride, a white, crystalline, evaporate mineral.

rock type A division of *rocks into three major groups (*igneous rocks, *sedimentary rocks, and *metamorphic rocks), depending on how they were formed.

rock varnish A thin, dark coating of manganese that forms on the surface of *rocks in *arid climates.

rockfall A very sudden, rapid *mass movement *erosion process, involving the fall of weathered rocks down very steep slopes or cliffs. These rocks are often deposited as a *scree slope.

rockslide A *landslide of rocks.

Rocky Flats The site near Denver, Colorado, USA of a weapons production facility run by the US Atomic Energy Commission, which operated from 1952 to 1989. Cleanup of the site began in 1992 in preparation for turning the site into a *national wildlife refuge.

ROD *See* RECORD OF DECISION.

rodent Any member of an order (Rodentia) of relatively small gnawing mammals (such as a mouse, a squirrel, or a beaver) that have in each jaw a single pair of teeth with a chisel-shaped edge. Rodents are *herbivores or *scavengers. There are 1500–2000 species.

rodenticide A chemical *pesticide that is used to control or kill *rodent pests (such as rats and mice) and prevent them from damaging food and crops.

roentgen (R) A unit of exposure to ionizing *radiation from *gamma rays or *X-rays. The roentgen has been replaced by the *SI unit of coulombs per kilogram of pure, dry air; $1 R = 2.58 \times 10^{-4}$ C kg^1. *See also* REM.

roguing The removal of undesirable plants from *hybrid seed production plots, in order to produce a better quality of seed.

Roman Warm Period The period from 200 BCE to 400 CE during which global average temperatures were at least equal to those of the early 21st century and in some parts of Europe were 2–2.5°C higher.

Romanticism An early 19th century movement which emphasized the personal, emotional, and dramatic through the use of exotic, literary, or historical subject matter. The movement affected political, philosophical, and artistic thought throughout Western Europe. *See also* TRANSCENDENTALISM.

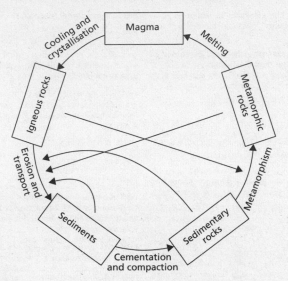

Fig. 18 Rock cycle

rookery A colony of breeding animals, usually birds or seals.

roost A perch or place where birds or bats rest or sleep, often in groups.

root The lower (usually underground) part of a *plant, which anchors it in the soil and absorbs *water and mineral *nutrients from the soil by means of the *root hairs.

root climber A plant (such as ivy) that raises itself up by means of *adventitious roots, which adhere to the plants that support it. *See also* SCRAMBLER; TWINER.

root hair The thin hair-like growth from the *root, through which a plant absorbs *nutrients from the *soil.

root nodule A small, gall-like growth on the roots of certain plants, especially *legumes but also others including alder (*Alnus* species), bog myrtle (*Myrica gale*), sea buckthorn (*Hippophaë* species), sumach (*Coriaria* species), California lilac (*Ceanothus* species), and cycads. The nodules develop as a consequence of infection of the roots by *bacteria. Bacterial colonies then inhabit the root nodules and benefit the plant by fixing atmospheric nitrogen, much of which becomes available to the plant.

root zone The upper part of a *soil that is penetrated by *plant roots.

ROS *See* RECREATION OPPORTUNITY SPECTRUM.

rosette A short, circular cluster of leaves on a plant, close to the ground. Rosette plants (e.g. daisy, *Bellis perennis*) are less likely to be grazed (or mown) than taller plants.

Rossby wave A horizontal wave-like motion, with a wavelength of 4000–6000 km, that is found in the *mid-latitude westerly circumpolar air stream. It occurs in the middle and upper *troposphere, forms and decays over a period of one or two months, and is followed by *geostrophic winds as they flow around the world.

rotary kiln incinerator An *incinerator that has a rotating combustion chamber that is designed to keep waste moving, thus allowing it to vaporize and burn more easily.

rotating-cup anemometer An instrument that measures *wind speed from the speed of rotation of small cups on its top.

rotation 1. The spinning of a body (such as the Earth) about its axis. **2.** A planned recurrent sequence, for example of *crops. *See also* CROP ROTATION.

rotation cycle The planned number of years between successive planting of crops within a *rotation.

rotation pasture A *pasture composed of *introduced *perennial plants and/or self-seeding *annual species, which is one unit in a *crop rotation of five years' duration or less.

rotational cropping *See* CROP ROTATION.

rotational set-aside A form of *crop rotation in which the location of *set-aside land is periodically switched from place to place within a farm holding.

rotenone An organic *insecticide that is derived from the roots of some *legumes and is used to control beetles and similar insects.

rotifers A phylum (Rotifera) of unsegmented animals lacking a fluid-filled body cavity (coelom), in which normally a complete alimentary canal is present, as is a muscular pharynx possessing well-developed jaws. Their name is derived from the ciliated crown, which in many species gives the appearance of a rotating wheel when it beats. The largest individuals reach 3 mm in length, but most are much smaller. There are about 1800 species.

rotor cloud A turbulent *altocumulus or *cumulus cloud formation that is found in the *lee of some *mountain barriers when winds cross the barrier at high speed.

rough fish Any species of *fish that is considered to be useless for food or sport, or even as bait. *Contrast* GAME FISH.

roughage Indigestible parts of food, that are high in fibre but low in *nutrients.

roundwood The trunk or large branch of a tree that has been felled, with or without its bark but before it is squared or cut into planks. *See* INDUSTRIAL TIMBER.

route of exposure The way in which an organism might come into contact with a chemical substance, such as by drinking (*ingestion), breathing (*inhalation), or bathing (skin contact).

ROV *See* REMOTELY OPERATED VEHICLE.

row crop A *crop that is grown agriculturally in rows (e.g. beans, brassicas).

row intercropping Growing two or more *crops simultaneously, in rows.

RPS *See* RENEWABLE PORTFOLIO STANDARD.

RQ *See* REPORTABLE QUANTITY.

r-selection *Natural selection for species with high reproductive rates, which can quickly colonize an area when favourable conditions occur. Such species flourish in rapidly changing environments. *Contrast* K-SELECTION.

r-strategy A life strategy in which *species are best adapted to live in a variable *habitat by having a high rate of reproduction. *Contrast* K-STRATEGY.

RUA *See* RESTRICTED USE AREA.

rubber *See* LATEX.

rubbish *See* SOLID WASTE.

rudaceous rocks Coarse-grained *clastic *sedimentary rocks (such as *conglomerates) which have *particles larger than two millimetres across.

ruderal A plant, or applied to a plant, that is associated with human dwellings or agriculture, or that colonizes waste ground. Ruderals are often weeds that have high demands for nutrients and/or are intolerant of competition.

ruminant An animal (such as a cow or goat) that chews the cud, having a multichambered stomach that allows it to digest *cellulose.

runoff That part of *precipitation, *snow or ice melt, or *irrigation water which flows across the land to *streams or other *waterbodies.

rural Living in or characteristic of farming or country life; beyond the limits of a *city, *town, *village, *hamlet, or any other designated residential or commercial area.

rural area A category of land defined within the *recreation opportunity spectrum as 'a natural environment that has been substantially modified by development of structures, vegetative manipulation, or pastoral agricultural development'. In a rural area resource use practices may be used to enhance specific recreation activities and to maintain vegetative cover and soil, sights and sounds of humans are readily evident, and interaction between users is often moderate to high. Many facilities are designed for use by a large number of people and facilities are often provided for special activities; facilities for intensive motorized use and parking are available.

rural development The development of the *countryside, in order to improve living conditions, increase employment, and enrich cultural life.

rural diversification Increasing the number and variety of ways of making a living in the countryside, beyond traditional activities such as *farming, and including new activities such as *recreation and tourism, and craft industries.

rural settlement A group of houses in the *countryside, which can take the form of a *dispersed settlement, a *hamlet, or a *village. *See also* URBAN SETTLEMENT.

rural–urban fringe Where a *town or *city meets the *countryside.

rural–wildland interface A North American term for where *rural development and *wildland meet and intermix, with no clearly defined zone of separation.

rustic Simple, characteristic of *rural life.

rusting The *corrosion of *iron.

RVP *See* REID VAPOUR PRESSURE.

ryolite A relatively viscous, *extrusive type of *granite; a typical *felsic rock.

sabkha A wide area of coastal flats bordering a *lagoon, where evaporites, dominated by carbonate–sulphate deposits, are formed. It is named after such an area on the south-eastern coast of the Arabian Peninsula.

SAC *See* SPECIAL AREA OF CONSERVATION.

sac Any membranous bag or cavity.

sacred grove A stand (*grove) of trees that is regarded as having spiritual value or meaning.

sacrifice area/site A patch of land in which overuse is allowed or even encouraged, in order to protect other more fragile areas or to optimize the overall benefits of *natural resource use across an area.

sacrificial seed crop *Seed that would normally be sown for a commercial harvest (such as *cereal) but which is sown instead to be consumed by seed-eating animals and birds.

safe 1. Free from danger or *risk. **2.** A *not threatened category of species defined by the *IUCN (*Red Data Book) as 'neither rare nor threatened'.

Safe Drinking Water Act (SDWA) (1974) US legislation that sets standards for drinking water quality and oversees the states, localities, and water suppliers who implement those standards. It is used with the *Resource Conservation and Recovery Act and the *Comprehensive Environmental Response, Compensation, and Liability Act to protect and clean up *groundwater by setting *water quality standards.

safe water *Water that is considered safe for drinking because it does not contain harmful *bacteria or *toxic materials, although it may have taste, odour, colour, and certain mineral problems.

safe yield The amount (*yield) of water that can be taken from a source of supply each year, over a period of years, without depleting the source beyond its ability for natural replenishment.

safety Freedom from danger or *risk.

Saffir–Simpson scale A scale for measuring the strength of *hurricanes, which runs from one (minimal damage likely) to five (catastrophic damage potential), based on the maximum sustained wind speed generated by the hurricane. The scale is given in Appendix 4.

Sagebrush Rebellion (Wilderness Lands Sagebrush Rebellion) An organized resistance movement which gathered momentum in the 1960s in the western USA, and especially in the state of Nevada, calling for a return of the control of federal lands to individual states.

Sahara A *sand desert which stretches across much of northern Africa, and is the world's largest *desert (nine million km^2). As recently as 6000 years ago the Sahara was covered with grasses and shrubs, and climate modelling of why it suddenly turned into the driest region on Earth shows that the transition from grass to sand could have occurred in just 300 years. The model starts with a slow reduction in solar heating of the atmosphere (to simulate the effect of changes in the Earth's tilt and orbit), which gradually weakened the monsoons over India and North Africa, thinning the vegetation cover. After a few thousand years of gradual change, the impoverished vegetation could no longer preserve soil moisture and maintain the cycle of evaporation, atmospheric circulation, and precipitation that drove the African monsoon. It is suggested that this triggered an abrupt switch to a desert climate about 5400 year ago, producing the initial Sahara Desert that has since changed in response to climate change and human disturbance.

salination *See* SALINIZATION.

saline Salty, a solution of salts (*sulphates and *chlorides of *sodium and *calcium).

saline deposit A deposit of salt (*sulphates and *chlorides of *sodium and *calcium) in or on a soil, which reduces soil *fertility and inhibits the growth of *vegetation or *crops.

SAHEL

A narrow zone of land about 500 km wide that runs across much of northern Africa, south of the *Sahara and north of the *equatorial zone. Annual rainfall is normally between 100 mm and 200 mm, and most of the rain falls between June and September. The natural vegetation is mainly sparse savanna grassland and shrubland, and traditional forms of agriculture include nomadic herding and (in some places) the cultivation of peanuts and millet. The area has always been marginal because of the limited rainfall and naturally arid conditions. Water is always in short supply in the Sahel region because of the low total rainfall, the concentration of rain into the wet season, and the persistently high temperatures (and thus rapid rates of evaporation). But water shortage became particularly serious between 1968 and 1974, when rainfall in the Sahel was significantly below the long-term average. This triggered the worst drought in North Africa in about 150 years and was probably associated with an increasingly arid regional climate. Between 1969 and 1990 rainfall in the Sahel was below the long-term average in every year. During the drought of 1973–4, for example, an estimated 100000 people died, mostly through starvation. Millions of cattle died too. The situation grew worse in the 1980s as the continued lack of rainfall caused widespread famine. Initially many people died through lack of drinking water. But as the drought continued, lack of water caused crop failures and livestock had nothing to graze. The land became completely barren and the soil was baked by the sun to form a hard surface which is impossible to plough.

saline giant A thick and extensive salt deposit, produced by the evaporation of a large hypersaline sea. In north-western Europe, for example, the Zechstein salts, which are mined in northern Germany for rock salt and potash, were formed during the *Permian by the evaporation of water from a partially barred marine basin covering more than 250 000 km^2. Similar extensive *evaporate deposits were also formed during the *Miocene by the evaporation of part of the Mediterranean.

saline intrusion *See* SALTWATER INTRUSION.

saline soil A soil that contains enough soluble salts (*sulphates and *chlorides of *sodium and *calcium) to reduce its fertility. Saline soils are common in hot climates, and usually have fairly uniform *profile and contain little *humus.

salinity A measure of the concentration of dissolved salts (*sulphates and *chlorides of *sodium and *calcium) in water, normally expressed as parts per thousand (‰). *Freshwater has a salinity of less than 0.5‰ (it is described as *limnetic), *seawater has a salinity greater than 30‰ (it is *euhaline), and *brackish water an intermediate salinity. Salinity is not a fixed property of water, because it can be increased (usually inadvertently, through *salinization) or decreased (on purpose, by *desalination). Seawater is saline, because it contains dissolved salts, the most important of which are sodium chloride (77.8‰), magnesium chloride (9.7‰), magnesium sulphate (5.7‰), and calcium sulphate (3.7‰). These are derived from weathering and erosion of rocks on the conti-

nents, as well as material derived from natural forest fires, volcanic eruptions, and air pollution. Seawater in the open ocean away from obvious sources of pollution has an average salinity of about 35‰, varying between about 34‰ and 36‰. Runoff in rivers normally has a salinity of more or less zero, whereas salinity in the Great Salt Lake in the USA is more than 150‰ because of the high evaporation loss in the hot, dry climate.

salinity gradient The change in *salinity with depth in a *waterbody, such as the *ocean.

salinization (salination) A process in which high concentrations of dissolved salts (*sulphates and *chlorides of *sodium and *calcium) accumulate near the surface of a soil, usually by *capillary action from *saline *groundwater. Salinization may result from large-scale *irrigation schemes in *semi-arid areas that lack adequate drainage to remove surplus water, so that much of the soil water *evaporates, drawing groundwater to the surface and leaving behind a salt residue. Salts can accumulate over time to threshold concentrations at which they become toxic and inhibit commercial agriculture. Salt damages the root hairs on plants (through which they take in water and nutrients from soil moisture) and reduces yields. Through time *salinity in the upper soil increases and plants start to show symptoms of stress.

salmonid A member of the *fish family Salmonidae, which includes salmon, trout, and char. There are about 70 species.

SALR *See* SATURATED ADIABATIC LAPSE RATE.

salt 1. The product of the reaction between an *acid and a *base, dissolved in water. **2.** The common name for the salt *sodium chloride (NaCl).

salt dome A structure formed by the upward movement of *evaporates, accompanied by the downward movement of denser material overlying them. Most salt domes are circular to lozenge-shaped in plan and extend vertically for many kilometres.

salt field An area underlain by recoverable deposits of salt.

salt flat A site with poor drainage in an *arid climate, where the water evaporates, leaving behind salts (*sulphates and *chlorides of *sodium and *calcium) in and on the soil.

salt lake A lake in which the concentration of mineral salts is typically about 100‰ or greater, and dominated by dissolved chlorides (e.g. the Dead Sea, which contains 64‰ NaCl and 164‰ $MgCl_2$).

salt pan A basin in a semi-arid region where *evaporates are deposited. The least soluble salts (calcium and magnesium carbonates) are precipitated first, on the outside of the pan, followed by sodium and potassium sulphates. Finally, sodium and potassium chlorides and magnesium sulphate are deposited in the centre.

salt spray *See* SEA SPRAY.

salt weathering A type of *physical weathering of rocks that is most common in *arid climates, where occasional rain dissolves salts from the rocks, the water evaporates leaving salt crystals, and subsequent hydration or heating causes the crystals to expand, widening cracks in rocks and detaching rock flakes.

salt wedge An intrusion of seawater into an *estuary in the form of a wedge that advances beneath the less dense freshwater.

saltation A process of *bedload movement in a river, which involves the hopping or bouncing of small *sand-sized particles along the river bed in the *turbulent water flow. Small particles move in the same way on land, in arid environments such as sandy deserts.

saltatorial Adapted for hopping or moving by leaping.

saltmarsh An area of low-lying ground along a *coast (usually within a sheltered *bay), which is regularly flooded by *seawater at average *high tide during the *growing season, and where salt-tolerant plants grow.

saltwater The water of the *sea and *ocean, which has a much higher *salinity than *freshwater.

saltwater intrusion (saline intrusion) The *contamination of *groundwater by seawater in coastal areas, which occurs mainly where large quantities of fresh groundwater are abstracted for supply purposes (usually by pumping it out) and more is taken out than naturally flows in to replenish it. It is a principal cause of *salinization in many coastal areas because saltwater, which is permanently stored in *sediments beneath the *sea-bed, can percolate inland beneath the freshwater *aquifer. Saltwater intrusion has affected coastal aquifers in many areas, particularly in arid climates. The United Nations Environment Programme estimates that by the early 1990s it had already affected 70 000 km^2 in China, 200 000 km^2 in India, 32 000 km^2 in Pakistan and the Near East, and 52 000 km^2 in the USA. It also affects parts of southern Europe.

salvage To save from ruin, harm, or destruction, including by the *reuse of waste materials.

salvage logging In *forest management, the logging of dead, damaged, or diseased trees in order to improve the overall health of a forest.

sample In statistics, the particular set of individuals, alive or not, about which measurements are taken. *See also* REPRESENTATIVE SAMPLE. *Contrast* POPULATION.

sampling The process of selecting a representative set of specimens from the full *population, so that the subset can be used to make inferences about the population as a whole.

San Andreas fault A major *fault line system that runs for 1040 km up the west coast of California, defined by the boundary between the Pacific *crustal plate and the North American plate. The Pacific plate is sliding northwest at a speed of a few centimetres a year. Recent *global positioning system measurements put the rate of movement along the San Andreas fault between 1990 and 1993 at about 46 mm a year. The San Andreas fault is the source of a number of major destructive *earthquakes along western California, including the 1906 San Francisco earthquake, a similarly large earthquake at Fort Tejon in 1857, and the smaller Loma Prieta earthquake of 1989.

sanction The granting of formal and explicit approval or authorization, or a penalty that is imposed for failure to observe a command or agreed policy.

sand Mineral rock fragments (*sediment) which have a *particle size between 0.06 mm and 2.0 mm, which is between −1.0 and 4.0 on the *phi (ϕ) scale.

Sand County Almanac A book by Aldo *Leopold (1948), which describes the changing nature, seasons, and his reflections through the year, during which he lived with his family on a run-down farm in rural Wisconsin.

sand desert A type of hot *desert (such as the *Sahara), which is often covered by *sand dunes and dominated by wind action.

sand dune A ridge (*dune) of *sand that is formed when sand grains are blown by the wind, and which migrates forward as the individual sand grains are pushed downwind.

sand mining The deliberate extraction of *sand from beaches and other deposits for use elsewhere (for example by the construction industry). *Contrast* BEACH REPLENISHMENT.

sand prairie A type of *prairie that grows on extensive *sand deposits, which are usually well-drained and leached, and have nutrient-poor soils.

sand storm The lifting of sand and dust particles, often to great altitude, by turbulent winds. Visibility is greatly reduced.

sandbar A ridge (*bar) of *sand that has been built up by water *currents, especially in a *river or in *coastal waters.

sandblasting 1. A *physical weathering process in which rock is eroded by the impact of sand grains carried by the wind. *See also* VENTIFACT. **2.** A mechanical process that uses sand at high pressure to remove surface material from an object, for example to remove rust from metal objects, or to clean buildings from discoloration.

sandflat A flat area of *sand on a *coast or in an *estuary.

sandstone A *clastic *sedimentary rock composed of compacted and cemented grains of sand (mostly *quartz); it varies in colour, depending on what *mineral it contains and what material cements it together.

sanitary Clean and virtually free from germs (*micro-organisms), thus posing little if any danger of infecting something that comes into contact with it.

sanitary landfill A traditional approach to *solid waste management, in which material is simply dumped in holes in the ground (*landfill) and then covered with soil

sanitary sewer An underground pipe (*sewer) that carries off domestic or industrial *wastewater but not storm water.

sanitary waste Waste material (such as *refuse) that is generated by normal housekeeping activities and is not hazardous or *radioactive.

sanitary water Domestic wastewater that comes from kitchen, bathroom, and laundry sinks, baths, and washing machines. Also known in the United States as gray water.

sanitation The control of physical factors in the environment that could harm human health.

sanitation salvage In *forest management, the removal of dead, damaged, or susceptible trees, mainly in order to prevent the spread of *pests or *disease and thus to promote forest health.

sanitization The process of cleaning to levels judged safe by public health standards.

Santa Ana The name given to a warm, dry *foehn wind which blows downslope on the *lee side of the mountains in the Los Angeles basin (USA), most commonly in autumn and winter. *See also* CHINOOK; FOEHN.

sap A watery solution of sugars, salts, and minerals that exudes from plant vascular tissues that are damaged.

saprophyte A type of *heterotrophic *organism that feeds on soluble organic compounds from dead plants and animals. Some absorb compounds that are already dissolved, others (including some *fungi and many *bacteria) break down undissolved foods by secreting digestive *enzymes onto them.

sapling (pole) A young tree, usually less than 10 cm in diameter.

saponin Any member of a class of glycosides that form colloidal solutions in water and foam when shaken. Saponins have a bitter taste, hydrolyse red blood cells, and are very toxic to fish. They occur in a wide variety of plants, including *Saponaria officinalis* (soapwort), which produces a lathery liquid, once widely used for washing wool and still used for cleaning delicate textiles, including antique ones.

saprobe *See* SAPROTROPH.

saprolite A soft, fully decomposed *rock that is formed *in situ* in tropical areas by the *chemical weathering of *igneous or *metamorphic rocks.

sapropel Organic ooze or sludge accumulated in anaerobic conditions in shallow lakes, swamps, or on the seabed. It contains more hydrocarbons than *peat. When dry it is dull, dark, and tough and it may be a source of oil and gas.

saprophagous Feeding on dead or decaying organic matter.

saprophyte *See* SAPROTROPH.

saprotroph (saprobe, saprovore) An organism that absorbs soluble organic nutrients obtained from inanimate sources (e.g. dead plant or animal matter). If the organism is plant-like it is called a saprophyte, if it is animal-like it is called a saprozoite.

saprovore *See* SAPROTROPH.

saprozoite *See* SAPROTROPH.

sapwood The outer zone of wood in a *tree, that lies between the *bark and the *heartwood and contains active *xylem cells.

SAR *See* SODIUM ADSORPTION RATIO.

SARA *See* SUPERFUND AMENDMENTS AND RE-AUTHORIZATION ACT.

satellite 1. A natural object that orbits a *planet. **2.** An artificial object that is placed in orbit around the Earth or another planet in order to collect information or for communication. *See also* REMOTE SENSING.

saturated Filled to capacity (for example, with water).

saturated adiabatic lapse rate (SALR) The rate at which the *temperature of a parcel of *saturated air decreases as it rises through the *atmosphere. The rate depends on temperature; typical SALR rates are between about 5°C and 9°C per kilometre (the higher the moisture content, the lower the lapse rate) and the average SALR is 6°C km^{-1}. *Contrast* DRY ADIABATIC LAPSE RATE. *See also* LAPSE RATE.

saturated air Air that contains as much *water vapour as it can possibly hold under existing conditions (of temperature and pressure), so that *condensation will occur if any more water vapour is added.

saturated flow The movement of water in a soil that is completely filled with water. *Contrast* UNSATURATED FLOW.

saturated zone (phreatic zone, zone of saturation) That portion of a soil or an *aquifer in which all of the pore space is filled with water. *Contrast* UNSATURATED ZONE.

saturation The act of making something totally *saturated.

saturation point The maximum concentration of water vapour that a parcel of air can hold at a given temperature and pressure.

saturation vapour pressure The *vapour pressure at which the layer of air immediately above the surface of water is saturated with *water vapour at a given temperature.

savanna Extensive open tropical *grassland, with scattered *trees and *shrubs, which covers large areas of Africa, North and South America, and northern Australia.

savanna woodland A type of savanna in which trees and shrubs form a generally light canopy. Most trees and bushes are *deciduous but usually *evergreens are also well represented. Some tall trees occur, but most are stunted and gnarled. They frequently have thick, corky, fire-resistant bark.

sawlog A log that is large enough to be cut into sawn *timber.

sawtimber Trees that are large enough to be cut into *timber.

saxicolous Growing on stones, rocks, walls, etc.

SBS *See* SICK BUILDING SYNDROME.

scarcity A shortage or lack of something (such as a particular *natural resource), so that *supply is insufficient to meet *demand. *See also* ABSOLUTE SCARCITY; RELATIVE SCARCITY.

scarification Loosening *topsoil by mechanical action (for example by scratching the surface of it) in order to prepare the ground for regrowth by direct seeding or natural seed fall.

scarp *See* ESCARPMENT.

scattered clouds The sky condition when between one-tenth and five-tenths is covered by *clouds.

scattered showers *Showers that cover between a quarter and a half of an area.

scattering Dispersing or spreading wide, such as the process in which a beam of light is diffused by collisions with *particles that are suspended in the *atmosphere.

scavenge 1. In ecology, to feed on *carrion or refuse. **2.** In meteorology, to remove particles from the air by *precipitation.

scavenger A *detritivore.

scavenger fish *See* ROUGH FISH.

scavenging *See* PRECIPITATION SCAVENGING.

scenario A description of how a situation might develop, based on a particular set of assumptions and factors, which is used to evaluate available options and select ways of dealing with uncertainty. *See also* WORST CASE SCENARIO.

scenery The appearance of the natural and human-made features of a *landscape.

scenic Having attractive (usually natural) *scenery.

Scenic and Recreational River Part of the *National Wild and Scenic Rivers System in the USA, which includes rivers or sections of rivers that are readily accessible by road or railway, may have some development along their shorelines, and may have undergone some impoundment or diversion in the past.

scenic area Any place that is designated as containing particularly attractive *scenery, and which is specially managed in order to preserve these qualities.

scenic corridor A North American term for the view seen from a road. *See also* VISTA.

schist A medium-grained *metamorphic rock in which the *minerals are compressed into a plate-like arrangement, formed by the applying of great heat and pressure to banded *gneiss.

Schistosoma Blood fluke; a genus of *parasitic flatworms (class Trematoda) that causes *schistosomiasis in humans.

schistosomiasis (bilharzia) A disease in humans caused by an infestation of, or an infection caused by, a *parasite of the genus *Schistosoma*, that is common in the tropics and South East Asia. The symptoms depend on the part of the body infected.

school Loosely, an aggregation of fish or marine mammals that are observed swimming together, possibly in response to a threat from a predator. More strictly, a grouping of fish, drawn together by social attraction, whose members are usually of the same species, size, and age, the members of the school moving in unison along parallel paths in the same direction.

science The systematic study of the natural world and its physical and biological processes, through observation, identification, description, experimental investigation, and theoretical explanations.

Science and Survival A book by Barry *Commoner (1963), in which he writes that 'the separation of the laws of nature among the different sciences is a human conceit; nature itself is an integrated whole', and 'technology has not only built the magnificent material base of modern society, but also confronts us with threats to survival which cannot be corrected unless we solve very grave economic, social, and political problems'.

Scientific Committee on Problems of the Environment (SCOPE) A nongovernmental organization, founded in 1969, comprising a global, interdisciplinary group of scientists and scientific institutions that assembles, reviews, and assesses the information available on induced environmental changes and the effects of these changes on people. It works closely with *UNEP and *UNESCO.

(((●))) **SEE WEB LINKS**
• SCOPE home page.

scientific method The approach that *science uses to gain knowledge, based on making observations, formulating laws and theories, and testing theories or hypotheses by experimentation.

scientific name *See* LATIN NAME.

scientific notation A method of writing numbers in terms of powers of ten. For example the number 0.000118 would be represented as 1.18×10^{-4} or 1.18E−04 where E stands for exponent, as in the exponent that ten is raised by.

Scientific Reserve/Strict Nature Reserve An *IUCN Management Category (I) for protected areas that are designed 'to protect nature and maintain natural processes in an undisturbed state in order to have ecologically representative examples of the natural environment available for scientific study, environmental monitoring, education, and for the maintenance of genetic resources in a dynamic and evolutionary state'.

sciophilous See SKIOPHILOUS.

sclerite A general term for any single plate of the *exoskeleton of an *organism.

schlerophyll forest A type of forest found in *Mediterranean climates that is dominated by scattered woody *scrub and widely spaced trees, most of which are less than six metres high.

sclerophyllous Applied to plants with hard, woody, small, and often spiky *evergreen leaves.

SCOPE See SCIENTIFIC COMMITTEE ON PROBLEMS OF THE ENVIRONMENT.

scoping A process for identifying which potential environmental impacts, alternatives, and other issues will be addressed in an *environmental impact statement.

scoria Loose, rubbly, *basalt rocks ejected by a volcano that accumulate around vents, eventually building up as a scoria cone, the height of which may range from a few tens of metres to up to 300 m, with a slope determined by the angle of repose of the loose material.

scour The effect of *abrasion, usually by sand or gravel, on the bed of a *river or the *sea.

scrambler A *root climber plant that raises itself above other vegetation with the aid of thorns or hooks. Contrast TWINER.

scrap 1. A small fragment of something. **2.** Waste material that is discarded from manufacturing operations but may be suitable for *reprocessing.

scrap metal Discarded metal that is suitable for *reprocessing.

scree (talus, talus cone) A slope that is covered with loose rock fragments that have broken off a cliff or steep slope above as a result of *frost action and *rockfall.

screening 1. The sifting of *sewage through a screen in order to remove coarse *solids that are floating and suspended in it. **2.** Testing a large

number of individuals from a population in order to identify which ones have a particular genetic trait, characteristic, or biological condition.

scrub Dense vegetation consisting of stunted *trees or bushes which colonize open ground, particularly *grassland. See also MAQUIS.

scrub oak–mountain mahogany shrubland A North American *shrubland vegetation dominated by mountain mahogany, serviceberry, and/or Gambel oak, accompanied by numerous *grass and *forb species, which is found in temperate areas such as the Central Rockies.

scrubber An *air pollution control device that uses a spray of water to trap *pollutants and cool *emissions.

scrubbing The process of purifying a gas by washing it with a liquid in a tower. See FLUE GAS SCRUBBING; LIMESTONE SCRUBBING.

S-curve A curve that describes *logistic growth in a *population, so-called because of its shape. Contrast J-CURVE.

Scyphozoa The class comprising true jellyfish (phylum Cnidaria), which are marine, mainly *pelagic animals.

SDWA See SAFE DRINKING WATER ACT.

SEA See STRATEGIC ENVIRONMENTAL ASSESSMENT.

sea Part of an *ocean or a large body of *saltwater that is at least partially enclosed by *land.

sea breeze (onshore breeze) A coastal *breeze that blows from sea to land during the day, when the land surface is warmer than the water surface, triggering *convection over the land and drawing air in from over the sea. Contrast LAND BREEZE.

sea defence wall An artificial structure that is built along a *coastline in order to protect cliffs or property from *erosion by *waves and *tides.

sea ice *Ice that is formed by the freezing of seawater and can extend out from the land as *pack ice, for example around *Antarctica.

sea level The level of the surface of the *ocean, based on the average level between high and low *tides, which is used as a *datum when calculating the height of features on land or depth in the ocean. It is used as a standard base for measuring heights and depths on the Earth, and it is the baseline for plotting the global *hypsometric curve, and for calculating the heights of *mountains and the depth of *ocean trenches. *Atmospheric pressure readings are usually expressed as sea level equivalents in order to eliminate the effects of *altitude.

sea level change A long-term change in the relative level of land and sea, which can be caused by *isostatic adjustment of the land (as a result of *tectonic forces), and/or by *eustatic change (change in the volume of water that is stored in the *oceans). Geological evidence suggests that during the height of the last *glaciation (about 18000 years ago) sea level was between 110 m and 140 m lower than it is today, and large areas of the *continental shelves were dry land. Sea level has risen through the post-glacial period (the so-called *Flandrian *transgression), rapidly at first, but levelling off about 5000 to 6000 years ago. It has remained relatively close to its present position over the last 5000 to 6000 years. Global warming has caused a global rise in sea level of between 15 and 20 cm over the last century; roughly 2–5 cm of the rise has been caused by melting of *glaciers and *ice caps, and another 2–7 cm has resulted from the expansion of ocean waters as they warm.

sea spray (salt spray) The spray that blows from the tops of *ocean waves.

sea-bed The bottom of a *sea or *ocean.

sea-bed mining Extracting *natural resources (such as nodules of *manganese) from the *sea-bed.

sea-floor spreading The process by which *crustal plates beneath the *oceans are pushed apart as new *magma is pushed upwards from within the Earth's crust to the surface of the ocean floor, in the central trough of the *mid-ocean ridge, where it cools. The new rock mirrors and preserves the *magnetic polarity of the Earth at the time of formation. *See also* CONSTRUCTIVE PLATE BOUNDARY; PLATE TECTONICS.

seamount (guyot) An isolated, flat-topped, submarine *mountain, rising more than 1000 m from the ocean floor.

search and rescue In *disaster management, the process of locating and recovering victims and applying first aid and basic medical assistance.

seascape A coastal or maritime *landscape. *See also* PROTECTED LANDSCAPE OR SEASCAPE.

season A natural division of the year, defined by the *equinoxes and *solstices (the four seasons: *winter, *spring, *summer, and *autumn/fall) or by atmospheric conditions (e.g. the *monsoon season).

seasonal Occurring, during, or dependent upon a particular *season.

seasonal plant A plant that flowers and completes its life cycle within a single wet–dry season in equatorial regions.

seasonal polyphenism A type of *polyphenism in which different forms of a species are produced at different times of the year. It is a common form of *phenotypic plasticity among insects.

seaward In the direction of the *sea. *Contrast* LANDWARD.

seaweed Any of the large marine *algae. They comprise three groups: green seaweeds (Chlorophyta); brown seaweeds (Rhaeophyta); and red seaweeds (Rhodophyta). Kelp is a brown seaweed, genus *Laminaria*.

Secchi disc A disc that is lowered into a waterbody in order to determine the clarity or transparency (*opacity) of the water, based on the depth at which its black and white markings can no longer be seen from the surface.

second growth *See* SECONDARY FOREST.

Second World Centrally planned economies, such as those of Eastern Europe between 1948 and 1990. *Contrast* FIRST WORLD; THIRD WORLD.

secondary ambient air quality standards *Air quality standards that are designed to protect human welfare, including the effects on vegetation and fauna, visibility, and structures. *Contrast* PRIMARY AMBIENT AIR QUALITY STANDARDS.

secondary consumer A *carnivore that occupies a higher *trophic level than the *primary consumers in a *food chain because it eats them. Examples include: on land, lions that eat wildebeest, hawks that eat field mice; in the oceans, herring that eat copepods.

secondary economic activities Manufacturing activities. *Contrast* PRIMARY ECONOMIC ACTIVITIES; TERTIARY ECONOMIC ACTIVITIES.

secondary effect *See* INDIRECT EFFECT.

secondary enrichment (supergene enrichment) The re-precipitation of sulphides and oxides from descending acidic *groundwater that has *leached the surface zone of an *ore deposit, thereby enriching the ore at lower levels.

secondary forest (second growth) A *forest that grows on land after the original mature *old growth forest has been *harvested, or died because of *fire or insect attack. *Contrast* PRIMARY FOREST.

secondary growth *See* SECONDARY THICKENING.

secondary market The exchange (under the *Kyoto Protocol) of *greenhouse gas *emission reductions, *offsets, or *allowances between buyer and seller where the seller is not the originator of the supply. *Contrast* PRIMARY MARKET.

secondary material (post-consumer material) A material that is recovered from *post-consumer wastes and is reused in the manufacture of a product.

secondary mineral *Minerals (such as *clays and *oxides) that are formed from the material released by *weathering. *Contrast* PRIMARY MINERAL.

secondary nutrient The elements *sodium, *calcium, and *magnesium that must be taken up and used in sufficient quantities for plants to complete their life cycles. *Contrast* PRIMARY NUTRIENT. *See also* ESSENTIAL ELEMENT.

secondary pollutant A *pollutant that is created when *primary pollutants combine with each other and with other substances, as happens for example when *sulphur dioxide reacts with *oxygen and moisture to form *sulphuric acid that falls as *acid rain. *Contrast* PRIMARY POLLUTANT.

secondary production *See* SECONDARY PRODUCTIVITY.

secondary productivity (secondary production) The amount of new biomass (weight) that is produced by plant-eating animals (*herbivores) in a given period of time. *Contrast* PRIMARY PRODUCTIVITY; TERTIARY PRODUCTIVITY.

secondary range A *grazing area (*range) that is lightly used or unused by livestock when there is limited or no *range management. It will not normally be fully used until the *primary range has been overused.

secondary recovery The extraction of more *oil or *gas from a reservoir than can be recovered by normal flowing and pumping operations, for example by pumping pressurized gas, steam, or water containing chemicals into a *well.

secondary rock *See* SEDIMENTARY ROCK.

secondary standard The pollution limit for *criteria air pollutants that is based on environmental effects (such as damage to property, plants, or visibility). *Contrast* PRIMARY STANDARD.

secondary succession The re-establishment of *vegetation on land that has had a vegetation cover at some time in the past but which might have been destroyed by natural processes (including *lightning fires, severe *storms, and *volcanic eruptions) or by human interference (including *forest clearance, building construction, and fires). *Contrast* PRIMARY SUCCESSION. *See also* SUCCESSION.

secondary thickening (secondary growth) The formation of new tissue by the repeated lateral division of cells in the *cambium of a woody plant, adding successive layers of new growth that increase the girth of the stem or root and that can be seen as *growth rings.

secondary treatment (secondary wastewater treatment) The second treatment that is provided at a *wastewater treatment plant, in which *bacteria consume suspended organic matter in the waste that remains from the *primary treatment of sewage. This process removes only limited amounts of *nitrogen and *phosphorus, which must be removed by *advanced wastewater treatment. *See also* PRIMARY WASTE TREATMENT.

secondary use Use that is incidental to the main purpose of an area or building.

secondary wastewater treatment *See* SECONDARY TREATMENT.

secondary wave *See* S-WAVE.

secondary woodland *Woodland on a site that has not been continuously wooded since 1600 AD. *Contrast* ANCIENT WOODLAND.

second-growth forest A *forest that has grown back after being logged, as a result of *secondary succession.

sector A segment or part of the *economy of a country in which particular activities take place. *See also* COMMERCIAL SECTOR; INDUSTRIAL SECTOR; RESIDENTIAL SECTOR; TRANSPORTATION SECTOR.

secular 1. Long term change that takes place slowly, as opposed to *seasonal or *cyclical changes. 2. Not sacred or religious, relating to the worldly.

secure landfill A solid waste disposal site (*landfill) that is lined and capped with an *impermeable barrier in order to prevent leakage or *leaching.

sedentary Not moving, staying in one place. *See* SESSILE.

sedentism Living in one main place all year round; having a *sedentary lifestyle. *Contrast* NOMADISM.

sedge A plant of the family Cyperaceae, which resemble *grasses but have solid stems, and often grow in *wetlands. There are about 4500 species.

sediment Grains of solid (usually *mineral) material that have been deposited by some natural process.

sediment delivery ratio The proportion of the *soil that is eroded from upland sources that actually reaches a *stream channel or storage *reservoir.

sediment discharge *See* SEDIMENT LOAD.

sediment load (sediment discharge, sediment yield) The amount of *sediment that is transported through a *stream cross section over one year, which includes chemicals carried in solution (the *dissolved or *solution load), small particles carried in suspension (the *suspended load), and larger particles that are rolled along the river bed (the *bedload).

sediment pond A natural or artificial *pond that is used for the recovery (by settling) of solids from *effluent or *runoff.

sediment yield *See* SEDIMENT LOAD.

sedimentary rock (secondary rock) A type of *rock that is formed by deposition, either of cemented fragments of rocks that have been eroded from the land (*clastic sedimentary rocks), organic materials (*organic sedimentary rocks), or chemicals that are deposited from water (*chemical precipitates). *See also* ROCK CYCLE; DIAGENESIS.

sedimentation (siltation) The deposition of *sediment from a state of *suspension in water or air.

sedimentation basin *See* CLARIFIER.

sedimentation tank A *wastewater tank in which floating wastes are skimmed off and settled *solids are removed for disposal elsewhere.

sedimentology The study of the nature and character of *sediments, and of how they form.

seed The body from which a new plant develops, comprising an outer seed coat containing a store of food and an *embryo plant.

seed bank A special type of *gene bank that is designed for the *ex situ conservation of individual plant varieties through the preservation and storage of *seeds.

seed productivity The amount of *viable *seed that is produced by an individual plant.

seed shrimp *See* OSTRACOD.

seed tree In *forest management, a tree that is left standing in order to provide *seed for the natural *regeneration of the area that has been harvested.

seedbed The *soil in which seeds are deposited and *germinate.

seeding Putting seeds in or on soil where they will *germinate and grow. *See also* BROADCAST SEEDING; DRILL SEEDING.

seedling The young plant that grows from a seed that has *germinated.

seep A small *spring, *pool, or other place where water trickles naturally from the ground.

seepage The slow movement or *percolation of water through *soil or *rock.

seepage lake A *lake that has either an inlet or an outlet but not both and which receives water mainly from *precipitation and *groundwater rather than from inflow along *tributary streams.

seepage line *See* PERCOLINE.

seiche A *wave on the surface of a *lake or landlocked *bay that is caused by local atmospheric changes, tidal currents, or *earthquakes.

seif dune A type of *sand dune that is common in hot *deserts, in which long ridges of wind-blown sand are aligned parallel to the dominant wind direction.

seine net (ring net) A traditional form of *ocean fishing involving the use of curtain nets that are drawn out and pulled along, in order to enclose a shoal of fish.

seismic Relating to *earthquakes, particularly the energy waves that are generated by *earthquake activity.

seismic activity *Earthquake activity.

seismic seawave See TSUNAMI.

seismic survey A technique for determining the detailed structure of the *rocks beneath a particular area, which is based on sending acoustic *shock waves into the rocks and measuring the signals that are reflected back.

seismic wave A *shock wave that is generated by an *earthquake and measured using a *seismograph. The waves travel at different speeds, depending on the density of the material they pass through. There are two main types of seismic wave, the *S-wave (secondary wave) and the *P-wave (primary wave).

seismicity The geographical and historical distribution of *earthquakes, or the number of earthquakes in a particular period of time.

seismograph An instrument for measuring and recording Earth tremors and *earthquakes, based on recording the passage of *seismic waves through the ground.

seismology The study of *earthquakes and *seismic activity.

selection Choice between available options. See also ARTIFICIAL SELECTION; NATURAL SELECTION.

selection pressure A measure of the effectiveness of *natural selection in altering the *genetic composition of a *population.

selective breeding See ARTIFICIAL SELECTION; CAPTIVE BREEDING.

selective cutting See SELECTIVE THINNING.

selective pesticide A chemical *pesticide that is designed to affect only particular types of *pests, leaving other plants and animals unharmed.

selective thinning (selective cutting) In *forest management, the periodic removal (*thinning) of individual trees or groups of trees in order to improve or regenerate a *stand. See also LINE THINNING; MECHANICAL THINNING.

selenium (Se) A relatively rare *non-metallic element that occurs naturally in rock and soils in certain regions. It is released from *copper and *lead refineries and municipal wastewater. It is essential to humans and animals in low concentrations and is toxic at very high concentrations. See also ACID MINE DRAINAGE.

self-pollinated See INBRED.

self-sufficient Able to look after yourself, and provide for all of your needs yourself without help from others.

seller In *greenhouse gas *emissions trading, under the *Kyoto Protocol, a legally recognized entity (such as an individual, corporation, not-for-profit organization, or government) that sells reductions, *credits, or *allowances to another legally recognized entity through a sale, lease, trade, or other means of transfer.

selva See TROPICAL RAINFOREST.

semelparity The condition of an organism that has only one reproductive cycle during its lifetime.

semi-arid climate A moderately dry climate, with amounts of rainfall between 250 and 500 mm a year, which is usually enough to support the growth of short, sparse *grass. See also STEPPE.

semi-confined aquifer An *aquifer that is partially overlain by a rock formation which has low *permeability, through which water can pass only slowly to *recharge the aquifer. Contrast CONFINED AQUIFER.

semi-desert scrub A transitional formation type situated between true *desert and more thickly vegetated areas (e.g. between *thorn forest and desert or between *savanna and desert). The vegetation is sparser than that of the thorn forest and succulents are more common, as a consequence of the drier climate. Most of the plants are shallow-rooted, and so able to exploit any precipitation that percolates into the surface layer of the soil before it evaporates.

semi-improved   grassland *Grassland that has been modified by the application of *fertilizers and/or *herbicides, and by intensive *grazing or *drainage. Contrast IMPROVED GRASSLAND.

semi-natural habitat A habitat which has been affected directly or indirectly by human activity. Contrast NATURAL HABITAT.

semi-natural woodland An *ancient woodland site that has been managed over a period, resulting in some change in structure and species composition, and which consists of stands of mainly *native trees that have not been obviously planted. On a recent woodland site, the term includes all stands that have originated mainly by natural regeneration.

semiochemical A naturally occurring message-bearing *biochemical that organisms use to communicate with each other, and to interrogate their environment. *See also* ALLOMONE; KAIROMONE; PHEROMONE.

semi-permeable A material that will allow some but not all substances to pass through it. *Contrast* IMPERMEABLE; NON-PERMEABLE; PERMEABLE.

semi-primitive motorized area A category of land defined within the *recreation opportunity spectrum as 'a predominantly natural or natural appearing environment of moderate to large size', with a low concentration of users, motorized recreation use permitted only on unmade local primitive roads, and the area managed to have subtle minimum on-site controls and restrictions.

semi-primitive non-motorized area A category of land defined within the *recreation opportunity spectrum as 'a predominantly natural or natural-appearing environment of moderate to large size', with low interaction between users, motorized recreation use not permitted, local roads possibly used on a limited basis for other resource management activities, and the area managed to have minimal but subtle on-site controls and restrictions.

semi-volatile organic compound (SVOC) A group of *organic compounds that are composed primarily of *carbon and *hydrogen, and have a tendency to *evaporate (volatilize) into the air from water or soil.

senescence The loss of function that accompanies aging, for example in a plant or animal or in a *waterbody that is subject to *eutrophication.

sensible heat Heat that causes a change in temperature (for example of air in the atmosphere) by changing the speed at which the *molecules move.

sensible heat flux The transfer of heat that is associated with thermal heating of parcels of air.

sensible temperature The sensation of temperature that a human body feels, rather than the actual temperature of the *environment as measured with a *thermometer.

sensitive species Plant or animal *species which are susceptible to changes in *habitat or to impacts from human activities.

sensitivity The degree of change in a system that is associated with a given degree of stress or perturbation. *See also* CLIMATE SENSITIVITY; SUSCEPTIBILITY.

septic system A domestic *wastewater treatment system (consisting of a *septic tank and a soil absorption system) into which wastes are piped directly from the home. *Bacteria *decompose the waste, *sludge settles to the bottom of the tank, and the treated *effluent flows out into the ground through drainage pipes.

septic tank An underground tank for storing *wastewater from a home. *See also* SEPTIC SYSTEM.

sequential cropping A pattern of *multiple cropping in which one *crop follows another on the same land, either with or without a break, in successive seasons.

sequester To separate or lock up. *See also* SEQUESTRATION.

sequestration The removal (*sequestering) of *greenhouse gases (particularly *carbon dioxide) from the *atmosphere by *biomass (such as trees, soils, and plants), via *photosynthesis, in order to help reduce the *greenhouse effect and control *global warming. *See also* CARBON SEQUESTRATION; FOREST SEQUESTRATION.

sequoia 1. (coast redwood) The *coniferous tree *Sequoia sempervirens*, native to Southern California, that grows up to 120 m tall. **2. (Sierra redwood, giant sequoia, Wellingtonia)** The tree *Sequoiadendron giganteum*, native to California, which grows up to 100 m tall. *See also* REDWOOD.

serac Jagged pinnacles of ice on the surface of a *glacier or *ice sheet.

seral Of or relating to the series of stages (*seres) in ecological or plant *succession.

seral stage A recognizable step or stage in the development of an ecological *community through *succession.

sere A transitional stage in the development of a plant community as it changes, through *succession, from bare ground to *climax. The full sequence of seral communities is a *prisere.

sericulture The culture of silkworms (*Bombyx mori*) for the production of silk.

serir A veneer of mixed sand and gravel mantling a Saharan plain and transported originally by *sheet-wash and *braided-river activity. Subsequently it was weathered and modified under more arid conditions.

serotiny In certain plants, especially trees (e.g. jack pine (*Pinus banksiana*), lodgepole pine (*P. contorta*), and many species of *Eucalyptus*), the retention of seeds in pods or cones on the tree, often for many years, until a disaster, most commonly the heat of a fire, causes their release. After fire, the seeds fall on ground fertilized by ash in a site cleared of competitors.

serpentine barrens Impoverished, often scrubby or *heathland vegetation associated with serpentine rocks. On weathering these rocks release an excess of *magnesium into the soil, and this often inhibits the development of the natural *climax in the areas concerned.

sesquioxide A general term for the hydrated oxides and hydroxides of iron and aluminium.

sessile 1. Applied to an organism that is *sedentary, fixed, or attached to a substrate and unable to move at will. *Contrast* MOTILE. **2.** Applied to a leaf that has no stalk, and is attached to the plant directly at the stem.

seston *Particulate matter that is suspended in *seawater.

set-aside Agricultural land that is removed from food production as part of the *Common Agricultural Policy, which allows farmers to claim special payments and creates an opportunity to adopt land management practices that benefit *wildlife.

settleable solids Suspended material that is heavy enough to sink to the bottom of a *wastewater treatment tank.

settlement 1. An area where one or more groups of families live together, either in the *countryside (*see also* RURAL SETTLEMENT) or in towns and cities (*see also* URBAN SETTLEMENT). **2.** The act of establishing a *colony. **3.** A legal agreement that is reached between two or more individuals or parties.

settling A gradual sinking to a lower level by *gravity, such as the deposition of suspended solids on the bed of a *waterbody.

settling basin *See* CLARIFIER.

settling tank A storage tank for the treatment of drinking water and *wastewater, in which heavy particles sink by *gravity to the bottom from where they can be removed and disposed of. *See also* SEPTIC TANK.

severe storm A major *storm that damages property or endangers life. In the USA, the National Weather Service defines a severe storm as one producing hailstones at least 19 mm across, wind gusts of at least 93 km h^{-1}, a *tornado, or more than one of these.

severe thunderstorm A *thunderstorm that produces heavy *precipitation, frequent *lightning, strong, gusty surface winds, or *hail, and can cause *flash floods and damage structures.

Seveso A village near Milan, Italy, that was the site of a major *air pollution incident on 10 July 1976, when a cloud of chemicals containing *dioxin was released from the Icmesa factory, manufacturing the *herbicide 2,4,5-T, to which an estimated 37 000 people were exposed between Milan and Lake Como. Seveso (pop. 700) was evacuated and more than 600 domestic animals had to be destroyed. There were no fatalities, but those most heavily exposed suffered from chloracne, a skin complaint, and later evidence suggested a link with certain cancers and injury to the immune and reproductive systems.

Seveso II Directive A directive of the *European Union on the control of major accident hazards involving dangerous substances, that is designed to help prevent such hazards in the wake of the *Seveso accident by making information more widely available about the distribution of hazardous substances, and by the adoption of major accident prevention policies and strategies.

Seveso site A site where hazardous substances are located, as defined under the *Seveso II Directive. Such sites are referred to as either upper tier or lower tier, depending on the level of *risk.

sewage The *organic waste and *wastewater that is produced by residential and commercial establishments, and is discharged into *sewers.

sewage contamination The introduction of untreated *sewage into a *waterbody.

sewage lagoon *See* OXIDATION POND.

sewage outfall The point at which *sewage is discharged, often from a pipe, into a *waterbody.

sewage sludge (biosolids, sludge) The solid portion of *sewage that contains *organic matter along with the *algae, *fungi, *bacteria, and *protozoans that consume it.

sewage system (sewerage) The system of pipes (*sewers) that carries *sewage.

sewage treatment *See* WATER TREATMENT.

sewage treatment plant A facility that is designed to receive the *wastewater from domestic sources, and to remove from it any materials that reduce *water quality and threaten public health and safety when they are discharged into receiving streams or *waterbodies.

sewer A channel or network of pipes that carries *wastewater and *stormwater runoff from the source to a treatment plant or receiving stream. *See also* SANITARY SEWER; STORM SEWER.

sewerage *See* SEWAGE SYSTEM.

sex ratio The number of females per thousand males within a *population.

sexual dimorphism The occurrence of morphological differences (other than primary sexual characters) that distinguish males from females of a species of organism (e.g. male deer often have larger antlers than females, and the males of many birds have differing (often more brightly coloured) plumage). These are secondary sexual characters, but not all sexual dimorphism is directly sex-related. For example, female sparrowhawks (*Accipiter nisus*) are bigger than males, possibly due to resource partitioning of prey, females taking larger birds, or to the needs of incubation.

sexual reproduction The production of new individuals through the fusion of *haploid nuclei, usually male and female *gametes.

sexual selection *Natural selection favouring characteristics that increase the likelihood of attracting a mate. Such characteristics might be used in male displays, e.g. a peacock's tail (intersexual selection) or in threats or combat between rival males, e.g. deer antlers (intrasexual selection).

shade intolerant Plants (particularly trees) that need a lot of *sunlight to regenerate and grow.

shade temperature The temperature of the air, conventionally measured in a standard shelter or screen that protects the thermometer from rain and from direct sunshine, but allows the free passage of air.

shade tolerant Plants (particularly trees) that can regenerate and grow in the shade of surrounding vegetation.

shadow price The *social value of a resource (such as habitat or wilderness), for which a meaningful economic price is difficult to calculate.

shale A fine-grained, grey or black *clastic *sedimentary rock that is composed of compacted and hardened *silt and *clay, with clear *laminations.

shale gas *Natural gas that is held within *shale rocks several kilometres below ground. Recoverable deposits of shale gas are believed to be extremely large. Britain may have 150 billion m^3, the United States 24 trillion m^3, Mexico 19 trillion m^3, South Africa 13.7 trillion m^3, Argentina 22 trillion m^3, Australia 11 trillion m^3, and China 36 trillion m^3. There are also large deposits in France, Poland, Canada, Libya, Algeria, Brazil, and other countries. Access to the gas is gained by *hydraulic fracturing.

(((•))) SEE WEB LINKS

• 'Shale Gas: Applying Technology to Solve America's Energy Challenges'.

shale oil A *petroleum-like substance that is found in high concentrations in some *shale rocks. *See also* KEROGEN.

shallow ecology A *worldview or set of beliefs which reflects a utilitarian and *anthropocentric attitude to nature, based on materialism and *consumerism. It seeks technological solutions to major environmental problems, rather than a change in human behaviour and values. For example, shallow ecology promotes the recycling of waste rather than preventing waste in the first place. *Contrast* DEEP ECOLOGY.

Shannon–Wiener index A measure of *biodiversity, based on the number of *species (species richness) and the way in which the individuals are apportioned into those species (evenness) within a given area. The index number is large when the species diversity is large and/or apportioned evenly amongst the species, and it is small when the species diversity is small and/or apportioned unevenly amongst the species. This method is based on information theory, and it is used when there are too many individuals within the sample area for each one to be identified and counted. The index (H) is calculated using the formula $H = -\sum_{i=1}^{N_0} [p_i \times log\ p_i]$, where i is the total number of individuals in one species, p_i is the number of individuals of one species in relation to the number of individuals in the population, and N_O is the total number of species in the sample. *See also* SPECIES DIVERSITY INDEX.

shanty town A peripheral area of a town or city that is inhabited by the very poor. It usually consists of simple houses with little or no infrastructure or services and is located in marginal environments with low *environmental quality and high environmental *risk. *See also* SQUATTER SETTLEMENT.

shear *See* WIND SHEAR.

shear strength The resistance of a material to *shear stress. This varies with temperature, the confining pressure, and the shape, size, and loading factor of the surface particles, and the amount of pore liquid present.

shear stress The *stress on a *particle acting parallel to a plane to which a force has been applied. It occurs because gravity pulls objects downhill so it promotes downslope movement.

shear wave *See* S-WAVE.

shearing 1. To cut the fleece off an animal using electric or hand-held shears. 2. To trim back and shape tree branches. 3. To deform a body by moving one part of it relative to another.

sheep dip A liquid *disinfectant and *insecticide in which sheep are immersed to protect them from pests and diseases.

sheet erosion The *erosion of a layer of exposed *soil from a sloping surface by *runoff water or wind.

sheet flow *See* OVERLAND FLOW.

sheet lightning *Lightning seen as a general flash rather than a bright fork. It is forked lightning flashing either between two clouds and seen through an intervening cloud, or between two regions inside a single cloud.

sheet-wash A geomorphological process in which a thin, mobile sheet of water flows over the surface of a hill-slope and may transport the surface *regolith. It is important in semi-arid regions, and may also be significant in temperate zones if the vegetation cover has been removed.

shelf break The sharp change in slope on the ocean floor between the *continental shelf and the *continental slope.

shelter *See* COVER.

shelterbelt (windbreak, windstrip) A barrier composed of rows of *trees and *shrubs that are planted to block wind flow and drifting snow, reduce *soil erosion, and protect buildings, gardens, orchards, or sensitive crops from high winds.

sheltered In terms of *wave exposure, applied to coasts that are protected from danger or bad weather.

shelterwood cut In *forest management, the gradual removal of the entire *stand of trees over a period of partial cuttings, which allows an *even-aged stand to regenerate in the partial shade. *See also* REMOVAL CUT.

shepherd A person who herds sheep on an open *range.

shield In a nuclear power plant, a wall to protect people from exposure to harmful *radiation.

shield area *See* CRATON.

shield volcano A *volcano that is built from repeated non-explosive flows of *lava, covers a large area, and has relatively shallow slopes, like many of the volcanoes in Hawaii.

shifting cultivation *See* SLASH AND BURN.

shingle 1. A general term for coarse *beach material, which is often well-rounded and composed of hard resistant rock, and a mixture of *gravel, pebbles, and larger material. 2. Wood or slate building material that is used as roofing or siding on a building.

shoal 1. A *sandbank in a river or stream, that is visible under low flow. 2. A large group of *fish.

shock disease In animals, a response to overcrowding in which physiological changes to the *endocrine system lead to physical deterioration, reduced reproductive success, and fighting, which may be followed by a catastrophic decline in numbers.

shock load The arrival at a *water treatment plant of water that contains high amounts of *algae, *suspended solids, or other *pollutants.

shock wave A large *compression wave (such as a *seismic wave or *sonic boom) that is caused by a shock to the medium through which the wave travels.

shoot The above-ground portion of a *plant, on which the leaves grow. *Contrast* ROOT.

shooting Killing wildlife, often *game as a *field sport, by gunfire.

shopping arcade *See* SHOPPING MALL.

shopping centre *See* SHOPPING MALL.

shopping mall A North American term for a building or set of buildings that contain stores and have interconnecting walkways that may or may not be enclosed, and which make it easy for people to walk from store to store. In the United Kingdom and Australia these are called shopping centres or shopping arcades. *Contrast* STRIP MALL.

shore The strip of land that borders a relatively large *waterbody (such as a *lake or *ocean) and is above the *high water mark. *See also* LITTORAL.

shore zonation The division of the seashore into zones, each with its own characteristic fauna and flora.

shoreline *See* COASTLINE.

short term A brief period of time, in environmental terms often defined as less than about three to five years. *Contrast* LONG TERM; MEDIUM TERM.

short-day plant A plant in which flowering is favoured by short days and correspondingly long nights. There are two groups of such plants: some species in which there is an absolute requirement for these conditions and others in which flowering is merely hastened by them. The term is somewhat misleading, in that the critical factor is the period of darkness and short-day plants require a night of more than a minimum duration.

short-distance migration A pattern of *migration in which species move within, rather than between, *temperate or *tropical zones.

shortgrass A North American *prairie *grassland vegetation dominated by grasses that are short and can tolerate drought conditions, which is common on the dry upland plains east of the Rocky Mountains.

shortgrass prairie A type of *prairie that grows in areas that receive between 30 and 40 centimetres of precipitation per year and have high *evaporation rates.

short-range planning Planning ahead up to five years. *Contrast* LONG-RANGE PLANNING. *See also* SHORT TERM.

short-term cleanup (removal action) Cleanup of a *contaminated site that seeks to minimize immediate threats to public health and the environment, for example after an emergency fire, spill, or release.

shortwave radiation *Radiant energy in the visible and near-ultraviolet *wavelengths (between about 0.1 and 2.0 micrometres), such as that emitted by the Sun. *Contrast* LONGWAVE RADIATION.

shower A short period of *precipitation from a convective cloud that begins and ends abruptly and is often followed by sunshine and a blue sky.

shredding **1.** Reducing the size of a particular material (such as waste paper for *recycling) by tearing or chopping it. **2.** Mixing and grinding *soil in order to make it more homogeneous and increase *permeability.

shrink–swell clay *Clay that expands (swells) when wet and shrinks when dry. Most such clays contain the *mineral montmorillonite, which can hold a large amount of water in its structure.

shrub A low, woody, *perennial *plant that has no trunk but several major branches at or near the base giving a bushy appearance, usually less than six metres tall.

shrub layer In the stratified structure of a forest, the layer of woody plants shorter than the *brush, comprising *shrubs and *saplings of those tree species that form the *canopy.

shrubbery A collection of *shrubs that are growing together, which may have been planted.

shrubland An open or closed *stand of *shrubs up to about two metres tall.

SI *See* SYSTÈME INTERNATIONALE.

sial Part of the Earth's *crust, which is named after its two main chemical constituents, silica (Si) and alumina (Al). It has a lower density than *sima, and forms the *continental crust.

Siberian high The region of high average pressure in the colder seasons of the year over Siberia, produced by the density of the very cold air at the surface over the Siberian plains.

sibling species Species that look so alike that human observers find it hard to distinguish between them.

sick building syndrome (SBS) A set of symptoms that affect some people while they are inside a particular building but which disappear when they leave the building, and which cannot be traced to specific *pollutants or sources within the building.

side effect An effect (often undesired or negative) other than the one intended.

Sierra Club A US environmental organization founded by John *Muir in 1892 that promotes public education, litigation, and outings and conferences.

(SEE WEB LINKS)

• Sierra Club home page.

sievert (Sv) The *SI unit of *radiation dose equivalent equal to 1 joule of energy per kilogram of absorbing tissue. The sievert replaced the rem (1 Sv = 100 rem).

significant effect A serious adverse impact in terms of such things as size, geographical extent, duration, frequency, or degree of reversibility.

silage *Fodder that is made by storing and fermenting green *forage plants in a *silo.

Silent Spring A book written by Rachel *Carson, published in 1962, which described the loss of birds killed by *pesticide poisoning from agricultural *insecticides, and which had a significant impact on attitudes towards the *environment, and on the development of modern *environmentalism.

silica *Silicon dioxide, a compound that occurs in many *minerals, which is found in all *volcanic rocks, and is an important ingredient in the Earth's *crust.

silicate A compound of *silicon and *oxygen (SiO$_4$). Silicates are the most abundant of rock-forming *minerals.

siliceous Mainly or entirely composed of *silicon.

silicification The process in which *silica replaces the original material of a substance, such as wood or a non-*siliceous rock. See also PETRIFIED FOREST.

silicon (Si) A naturally occurring, *non-metallic *element, which is a major component of many types of rocks and minerals and accounts for 27.2% of the Earth's *crust.

silicon dioxide (SiO$_2$) A white or colourless solid that becomes soluble at high temperatures. See also SILICA.

silicosis A type of *pneumoconiosis that is caused by the inhalation of *silica dust.

sill A sheet-like horizontal intrusion of *magma between existing rock strata.

silo A tall, cylindrical structure (or pit) in which *fodder is stored to make *silage.

silt Fine *sediment with a *particle size between 0.002 and 0.06 mm, which is between 4.0 and 9.0 on the *phi (ϕ) scale; coarser than *clay but finer than *sand.

siltation See SEDIMENTATION.

siltstone A fine-grained *clastic *sedimentary rock composed of compacted and hardened *silt-size particles.

Silurian The third period of the *Palaeozoic era, covering the period from 443.7 to 418 million years ago, during which marine life flourished, the first species of plants and *arthropods appeared, and the first terrestrial *ecosystem became established.

(SEE WEB LINKS)

• The Silurian period of the Palaeozoic era.

silver (Ag) A naturally occurring, soft, white, *precious metallic element that is used in coins and jewellery, and has many other uses.

silviculture The care and cultivation of *forest trees. See also FORESTRY.

silvopastoral system An *agroforestry land use system in which *trees or *shrubs are grown and animals graze or browse. See also FOREST GRAZING

silvopisciculture Growing trees as part of a fish-farming enterprise.

sima The *oceanic crust of the Earth, which is named after its two main chemical constituents (*silica (Si) and *magnesium (Ma)), is denser than *sial that covers it in places, and where it is not covered by sial it comprises the ocean bed.

simazine A selective *herbicide that is used to control broadleaved weeds and annual grasses in a variety of crops and, at higher applications, for total weed control on waste ground, paths, etc. It is moderately persistent, but almost completely non-toxic to humans and wildlife.

Simon, Julian US academic and environmental *optimist (1932-98) who is best known for his work on population and natural resources, including the controversial book *The *Ultimate Resource.*

simulation An experiment run as a model of reality, often using a computer, to predict the behaviour of a *system under certain conditions.

single To reduce the regrowth from a *coppice stool to allow a single pole to grow on to form a standard tree.

single occupancy vehicle (SOV) A privately operated vehicle whose only occupant is the driver, who uses it mainly for personal travel and daily commuting to work. *Contrast* HIGH OCCUPANCY VEHICLE.

sink 1. A place where a substance can be stored naturally, such as plants which are a sink for *carbon dioxide (because they transform it by *photosynthesis into *organic matter, which either stays in the plant or is stored in the soil). *Contrast* SOURCE. *See also* CARBON SINK. **2.** *See* SINKHOLE.

sink habitat A *habitat that is a net importer of individuals, because local reproduction is not sufficient to balance local *mortality. *Contrast* SOURCE HABITAT.

sink population A population that occupies a *sink habitat. *Contrast* SOURCE POPULATION.

sinkhole (doline, sink) A steep-sided depression that is found in some *limestone (*karst) areas and is caused by the collapse of an underground channel or cavern as a result of *solution weathering.

sinking A method of controlling an *oil spill, using a *sinking agent to trap the oil and sink it to the bottom of the *waterbody where the mixture of oil and agent eventually undergoes natural *biodegradation.

sinking agent A chemical additive that is added to a floating *oil spill in order to sink it below the water surface.

Sino-Japanese floral region Part of R. Good's *Boreal Realm (*The Geography of the Flowering Plants*, 1974), which corresponds geographically with the Sino-Himalayan-Tibetan mountains, northern and central China, and Japan. The region is differentiated by more than 300 *endemic genera and contains the richest flora in the northern temperate zone.

sinter A chemical *precipitate that is formed from the minerals (mainly *silica) in *geothermal water, especially from *geysers.

sinuosity A measure of the degree of *meandering within a river, defined as the ratio of stream length to valley length. Tightly meandering rivers travel much further over a given length of valley and so they have high sinuosity.

sinuous Winding, with many curves or turns.

SIP *See* STATE IMPLEMENTATION PLAN.

sirocco A dry *desert wind that blows, most commonly in spring, from the Sahara in north Africa across the Mediterranean Sea (where it picks up moisture) towards Sicily and southern Italy, where it is experienced as a hot, humid wind.

SITE *See* SUPERFUND INNOVATIVE TECHNOLOGY EVALUATION.

site A piece of land on which something is located.

site assessment The formal process by which the US *Environmental Protection Agency determines whether a potential site should be placed on the *National Priorities List (NPL). It can consist of a *Preliminary Assessment (PA) or a combination of a PA and a *Site Inspection (SI).

site capacity The *carrying capacity of a particular *site for a particular use.

site class A form of *land classification based on ecological factors and the potential production capacity (such as *crop or *forest yield) of a particular site.

Site Inspection (SI) A stage in *site assessment in the USA, following the *Preliminary Assessment, during which the *Environmental Protection Agency gathers information from a *Superfund site in order to use the *Hazard Ranking System to determine whether the site should be placed on the *National Priorities List.

Site of Special Scientific Interest (SSSI) A *conservation site of national importance in

S

the UK that has been designated for special protection under the Wildlife and Countryside Act 1981 because of its plants, animals, or geological or physiographical features.

site preparation The treatment of a site (for example with mechanical clearing, burning, or *herbicides) to prepare it for planting, such as *reforestation.

site remediation The process of cleaning up a *hazardous waste disposal site. *See also* REMEDIATION.

siting The process of choosing a location for a *facility.

size class In *forest management, one of three categories of tree stem diameters that is used to classify timber, which are seedling/sapling (less than five inches (12.7 cm) in diameter), pole timber (five to seven inches (12.7 to 17.8 cm), and sawtimber (greater than seven inches (17.8 cm)).

Skeptical Environmentalist, The A book by Bjorn Lomborg, published in 2001, which challenges the belief that the global environment is progressively getting worse, using statistical information from reputable international research institutes. It is one of the most controversial books on the environment in recent years. *See also* OPTIMIST, ENVIRONMENTAL.

skidding Hauling logs by sliding them from where they are cut to a collection point.

skimming Using a machine to remove a physical *pollutant (such as *oil) from the surface of a *waterbody.

skin absorption The ability of some *hazardous chemicals to enter the human body by passing directly through the skin and entering the bloodstream.

skiophilous (sciophilous) Applied to the response to light of an organism adapted to living in shade. *Contrast* PHOTOPHILOUS; PHOTOPHOBIA.

sky The *atmosphere and outer space beyond it, viewed from the ground.

skyline logging (skyline yarding) A method of *logging in which timber is transported from where it is cut to a collecting point by means of an overhead trolley that runs along a cable system.

skyline yarding *See* SKYLINE LOGGING.

slack A low-lying area of ground in an area of coastal *sand dunes, which is often damper than the surrounding sand and may even contain temporary *pools.

slack water The minimum velocity of a *tidal stream, at the point of cross-over between successive *flood currents and *ebb currents, when water is relatively calm.

slag The non-metallic residue from the *smelting of metallic *ores. It generally forms as a molten mass floating on top of the molten metal.

slaked lime *See* LIME.

SLAPP *See* STRATEGIC LAWSUIT AGAINST PUBLIC PARTICIPATION.

slash *See* LOGGING RESIDUE.

slash and burn (milpa, swidden agriculture, shifting cultivation) A traditional agricultural system practised by semi-nomadic people in which a patch of *forest land is cleared for *cultivation by felling and then burning the trees (which adds *nutrients to the soil). Crops are grown for 1–5 years before the soil becomes depleted, weeds invade, and yields fall. The site is then abandoned and work commences on another site. Sites are cleared and cultivated in rotation, ideally allowing each one a *fallow period long enough for its fertility to recover.

slash disposal The removal of *logging residue, often in order to reduce the risk of *fire spreading.

slashing In *forest management, cutting back the less tough, competing vegetation (such as *ground cover like bracken) to improve tree growth.

slate A black or grey, fine-grained *metamorphic rock that is formed by applying great heat and pressure to *shale and *mudstone. It is useful as a building and roofing material.

sleeping sickness (sleepy sickness) *Encephalitis lethargica, a form of encephalitis that is caused by a *virus, which was *epidemic between 1915 and 1926, and whose symptoms include paralysis of the eye muscles associated with abnormal eye movements, tremors, catatonia, extreme muscular weakness, and Parkinsonism.

sleepy sickness *See* SLEEPING SICKNESS.

sleet **1.** In the UK, a mixture of rain and snow falling together. **2.** In North America, small *raindrops that freeze into ice pellets while they are falling.

slickenside A polished rock surface that is created when one mass of rock slides over another in a *fault plane.

slide *See* LANDSLIDE.

slime mould A *eukaryotic organism that is single-celled while food is plentiful, but in times of scarcity forms a feeding structure consisting of either a mass of acellular *protoplasm (plasmodium) with a single nucleus or a mass of amoeboid cells (pseudoplasmodium) with many nuclei, which is able to move in search of food. They feed on *bacteria, *algae, and *fungi, and reproduce by producing many brightly coloured fruiting bodies that release *spores. Slime moulds were formerly classed as fungi, which they resemble, but are now known to be unrelated to the fungi, comprising three main groups that are not closely related to each other.

(SEE WEB LINKS)

• Introduction to slime moulds.

sling psychrometer An instrument that is used to measure the amount of *water vapour in the air, using wet and dry bulb *thermometers mounted on a frame.

slip *See* LANDSLIP.

slop Poles produced by *coppicing.

slop tank *See* LOAD ON TOP.

slope (gradient) The angle at which something is inclined, which is normally expressed as fall (drop in height) per unit horizontal distance, sometimes converted to a percentage.

slope stability The resistance of an inclined surface to failure by sliding or collapsing.

SLOSS principle An acronym for Single Large Over Several Small, the proposal that a single large *nature reserve will contain more *species than several small reserves with the same total area. Whether this is so depends on the extent to which the species in the small reserves overlap. If there is little overlap between reserves (i.e. each small reserve contains many species that are not found in any of the other reserves), several small reserves may be preferable to a single large one. Small areas of *habitat may also afford more protection against disease or the accidental introduction of predators.

slough A *stagnant *swamp type of vegetation that is dominated by grasses, sedges, and rushes and is commonly found on the muddy backwater of a river, marsh, or tidal flat.

slow sand filtration A *water treatment process in which water is drained slowly through a bed of *sand in order to remove particles from it.

sludge (residuals) Solid matter that is removed during the treatment of *water or *wastewater. *See also* SEWAGE SLUDGE.

sludge digester A tank in which organic *sewage sludge is decomposed by *micro-organisms, which releases energy and converts much of the sewage to *methane, *carbon dioxide, and *water.

sludge processing *See* AEROBIC DIGESTION.

slum An area in a *city that has poor-quality living conditions and marked poverty.

slump A *landslide in which the rock mass tilts back as it slides down from a *cliff or *escarpment.

slurry A *suspension of fine solid *particles in a liquid, such as liquified animal *manure.

small game *Birds and small *animals (*game) that are hunted or trapped.

smallholding A small plot of land on which fruit and vegetables are cultivated, usually for sale. *See also* HORTICULTURE; MARKET GARDEN.

smart growth Comprehensive planning and environmentally sensitive development of land that is designed to restore sense of community, enhance natural and cultural resources, expand choice in transportation, employment, and housing, reduce air pollution, promote public health and healthy communities, and increase the efficiency of investments in infrastructure.

Smart Growth Network A US non-profit group which is a partnership of government, business, civic, and conservation organizations. It promotes the principles and practice of *smart growth as a way of reconciling the tensions between *conservation and *development. *Compare* WISE USE MOVEMENT.

(SEE WEB LINKS)

• Smart Growth website.

smelter An industrial plant for *smelting.

smelting The process of extracting *metal from *ore by heating and melting, which separates out the impurities.

Smith-Lever Act (1914) US legislation that established a federal–state cooperative extension programme to provide education for the public about agricultural and *natural resources.

smog 1. A mixture of *smoke and *fog that was once common in industrial cities (*see* GREAT LONDON SMOG). **2.** *See* PHOTOCHEMICAL SMOG.

smoke A type of *air pollution in the form of a visible cloud of solid and liquid particles, most less than 1 micrometre across, which is produced by the burning of *fossil fuels, particularly *coal.

smokeless fuel Fuel that emits no visible *smoke when it burns and that is permitted for use in designated smokeless zones.

smokestack *See* STACK.

Smokey the Bear A mascot of the *US Forest Service, which was adopted in 1944 to educate the public on the dangers of forest fires. Royalties from licensed use of the mascot are used to fund education programmes on prevention of forest fire.

SMR *See* STANDARDIZED MORTALITY RATIO.

SMSA *See* STANDARD METROPOLITAN STATISTICAL AREA.

smudge pot *See* ORCHARD HEATER.

smudging The burning of materials (e.g. oil) to produce a smoke layer that reduces the effect of radiation cooling in the air above the ground surface. It is used as a protective measure against *frost damage (e.g. in fruit-growing areas, especially in frost hollows).

SMZ *See* STREAMSIDE MANAGEMENT ZONE.

snag A standing dead or decaying *tree, which provides nesting sites, feeding sites, and *habitats for *wildlife.

snout The steep, terminal zone of a *glacier; it is usually heavily loaded with debris.

snow Frozen *water vapour in the atmosphere that falls in light white flakes (*snowflakes) and settles on the ground as a white layer. A form of *precipitation.

snow advisory A statement (*advisory) that is issued in the USA when *snow is expected to create hazardous travel conditions.

snow avalanche The rapid downslope movement of large quantities of *snow.

snow cornice A mass of *snow or *ice that projects over a mountain ridge.

snow density The mass of *snow per unit volume, which is equal to the water content of the snow divided by its depth.

snow flurry An intermittent light shower of *snow.

snow gauge A modified *rain gauge used to measure the amount of snowfall. Snowfall is always reported as its rainfall equivalent if the information is needed for meteorological purposes, most simply by melting the snow, because snowflakes vary greatly in size, depending on temperature, and the smaller they are the more air they trap between them, increasing the bulk of the snow.

snow line 1. The lower limit of permanent *snow cover on a mountainside. This decreases with latitude, from the *equator (around 5000 m) towards the *poles (close to *sea level). **2.** The boundary between an area covered by snow and the adjacent area that is not.

snow melt The conversion of *snow into *runoff and *groundwater, as *temperature rises.

snow pellet (graupel) A form of *precipitation that consists of a *snow crystal and a *raindrop frozen together.

snow shower *See* SNOW SQUALL.

snow squall (snow shower) An intermittent heavy shower of snow, accompanied by strong wind, that greatly reduces visibility.

snowbank A mound or heap of *snow.

snowdrift A mass of *snow that has been heaped up by the wind, often in the *lee of an obstruction.

snowfall The rate at which *snow falls or accumulates on the ground, which is usually expressed in depth of snow (in centimetres) over a six-hour period.

snowfield A permanent large area of *snow on the ground, most commonly found at high *altitude or *latitude.

snowflake A six-pointed cluster of ice crystals which falls from a *cloud.

snowpack The total amount of *snow and *ice on the ground, including fresh new snow and older snow and ice which has not melted.

snowstorm A *storm accompanied by heavy *snowfall.

soakaway A place where water soaks into the ground.

soap A natural cleaning agent that is made by the reaction of a fat or oil and an *alkali. *See also* INSECTICIDAL SOAP.

soapwort *See* SAPONIN.

social capital The degree of social cohesion which exists in a community, which is reflected in social networks, norms, and trust.

social class A collection of people with similar position or social rank.

social construction of reality A process in which people's experience of reality is determined by the meaning they attach to that reality. *See* POST-MODERNISM.

social cost (non-market cost, opportunity cost) The value of the best alternative use of a particular scarce *resource, or the potential benefit that is foregone from not following the best alternative course of action.

social Darwinism The 19th-century belief that the strongest in society should flourish and the weak should be allowed to perish, i.e. 'might is right'. *See also* NATURAL SELECTION.

social ecology The view that environmental problems arise from fundamental social problems, and that they cannot be understood or solved without dealing with problems within society, including economic, ethnic, cultural, and gender conflicts. *See also* RADICAL ECOLOGY.

social forestry Planting and looking after trees or shrubs in order to maintain or improve the quality of life of local communities. *See also* COMMUNITY FORESTRY.

social impact The changes in social and cultural conditions, which can be positive or negative, which directly or indirectly result from an activity, project, or programme. *Contrast* ENVIRONMENTAL IMPACT.

social inequality A condition in which different members of a society have unequal amounts of income, prestige, and social power.

social justice The objective of creating a fair and equal society in which each individual matters, their rights are recognized and protected, and decisions are made in ways that are fair and honest.

social movement A large number of people who act together in order to pursue some shared objective, such as *environmentalism.

social sciences Those disciplines that are concerned with the study of human behaviour, which include anthropology, economics, psychology, geography, political science, and sociology.

social value The non-economic value that society puts on a resource and that is recognized by most, if not all, people, such as the benefits to human health of clean air and water. *See also* SHADOW PRICE.

socialism (socialist economy) An *economic and political system in which the means of production, distribution, and exchange are owned by society as a whole and controlled by co-operatives or the central government. The system may operate within a market economy. *Contrast* CAPITALISM. *See also* MARXISM.

socialist economy *See* SOCIALISM. *Contrast* CAPITALIST ECONOMY; MARKET ECONOMY.

society A broad grouping of people (including a community or nation) that shares common traditions, institutions, collective activities, and interests.

sociobiology The study of behaviour in social animals (including humans), based on the assumption that such behaviour is biologically based, genetically encoded, and evolves through the process of *natural selection.

socioeconomics The social and economic conditions of a particular area or population.

sociology The study and classification of social groups and human societies.

SOCs *See* SYNTHETIC ORGANIC CHEMICALS.

sod 1. Established grass, *turf, or *sward. **2.** A strip of turf that is cut and transplanted to establish grass cover in another place.

sodar A device that is used to detect and determine the range to distant objects or changes in temperature or humidity in the atmosphere, based on the scatter and reflection of sound energy. Short for 'sound detection and ranging'. *See also* SONAR.

sodgrass A North American *grassland vegetation dominated by grasses (such as big bluestem, *Andropogon gerardii*) that spread horizontally, like the grass in a lawn, and are characteristic of *tallgrass prairies.

sodicity The accumulation of *sodium in *soil, which adversely affects soil structure and increases *toxicity to plants.

sodium (Na) A naturally occurring, silver-white, soft, waxy, ductile element of the *alkali metal group, that can form various salts with *halogens and *metals, is abundant in nature, and is not generally considered to be *toxic. When dissolved in water it can be used to indicate *salinity.

sodium adsorption ratio (SAR) The tendency for sodium *cations to be adsorbed at *cation-exchange sites in soil at the expense of other cations, calculated as the ratio of sodium to calcium and magnesium in the soil (as the amount of sodium divided by the square root of half the sum of the amounts of calcium and magnesium, where *ion concentrations are given in moles per gram). A low sodium content gives a low SAR value. In practice, allowance must be made for other reactions within the soil that do not involve sodium but affect concentrations of calcium and magnesium. The SAR value is most likely to be changed by irrigation water.

sodium chlorate A *systemic and *soil-acting herbicide used for total weed control on land that is not intended for cropping. It persists in the soil after application and makes dry plant residues highly flammable. It is an eye, skin, and respiratory irritant and toxic if ingested. Its use is banned under the *Montreal Protocol on Substances That Deplete the Ozone Layer.

sodium chloride (NaCl) Common salt.

SOFAR channel (sound channel) An acronym for the *SO*und *Fi*xing *A*nd *R*anging channel, a zone in the oceanic water column at a depth of about 1500 m, where the velocity of sound is at a minimum value. Sound passing through the zone is refracted upwards or downwards back into the zone, with little loss of energy, causing sound energy to be trapped in a zone of well-defined depth. The SOFAR channel may be used for the transmission of sound over long distances, exceeding 28 000 km, and can be used to track free-drifting, subsurface, neutrally buoyant floats.

SEE WEB LINKS
• Discovery of sound in the sea.

soft detergent A cleaning agent (*detergent) that breaks down naturally in the environment.

soft energy path An approach to *economic development that relies on renewable sources of *energy, including *solar power, *wind power, and *water power. *Contrast* HARD ENERGY PATH.

soft mast Soft, fleshy fruits potentially eaten by wildlife (examples include persimmon, wild grapes, blackberries, blueberries, huckleberries, mulberries, plums, autumn olive, and crab apples).

soft water Water that does not contain a significant amount of dissolved minerals such as salts of *calcium or *magnesium. *Contrast* HARD WATER.

softened water Water that is treated in order to reduce its hardness (due to *calcium and *magnesium).

softwood A general term for a *coniferous tree and for the wood from such trees. *Contrast* HARDWOOD.

soil The layer of disintegrated rock particles, organic matter, water, and air that covers most of the land surface. Soil is a typical *open system with inputs, throughputs, and outputs of matter and energy, and it is intimately linked with other *environmental systems, particularly climate and vegetation. Through *weathering and *erosion, soils are linked to the lithosphere system and have a place (albeit a short-term one) within the *rock cycle. *See also* PEDOGENESIS.

soil acidification Soil that becomes *acid, due to the production of nitric acid and sulphuric acid by *bacteria followed by *leaching. *See also* ACIDIFICATION.

soil aeration The process by which air in the soil is replenished by air from the atmosphere. The degree of *aeration depends mainly on the *porosity of the soil, and poorly aerated soils contain more *carbon dioxide and less *oxygen.

soil aggregate Individual *soil particles stuck together, forming the smallest unit of *soil texture. Thus, for example, a soil with a granular structure is composed of relatively small, rounded aggregates, and a soil with a blocky structure is made up of aggregates with sharp corners and irregular shapes.

s

soil amendment *See* SOIL ENHANCEMENT.

soil and water conservation practices Control measures that are adopted in order to reduce the loss of soil and water from a particular area.

Soil and Water Resource Conservation Act (1977) US legislation that provides for a continuing appraisal of soil, water, and related resources, including fish and wildlife habitats, and a soil and water conservation programme to assist landowners and land users in furthering soil and water conservation.

Soil Association A UK environmental campaigning and certification organization, whose mission is to promote *sustainable *organic food and farming.

(⊕) SEE WEB LINKS
• Soil Association home page.

soil association A group of named *soil taxonomic units that occur together in a characteristic pattern over a geographical region.

soil bulk density The mass of *soil per unit of volume, which is a measure of *compaction.

soil class A group of soils that have a definite range in a particular property such as *acidity, *slope, *texture, or *structure.

soil classification (soil taxonomy) The systematic arrangement of *soils into groups or categories on the basis of their characteristics. *See also* COMPREHENSIVE SOIL CLASSIFICATION SYSTEM; WORLD SOIL CLASSIFICATION.

soil climate The moisture and temperature conditions that exist within a particular soil.

soil compaction The reduction of soil volume as a result of applied load, vibration, or pressure, which leads to a decrease in *soil bulk density and *soil porosity.

soil complex A mapping unit (smaller than a *soil association) that is used in detailed *soil surveys where two or more defined *taxonomic units are so completely intermixed geographically that separating them is impossible.

soil concretion *See* CONCRETION.

soil conditioner Any substance (such as *compost) that enriches the physical condition of *soil and increases its *organic content as part of *soil enhancement.

soil conservation Methods that are used to reduce *soil erosion, prevent depletion of soil nutrients and soil moisture, and enrich the *nutrient status of a soil.

Soil Conservation Act (1935) US legislation that provided for control and prevention of *soil erosion, delegated all activities relating to soil erosion to the Secretary of Agriculture, and established the Soil Conservation Service.

Soil Conservation and Domestic Allotment Act (1936) US legislation that established the Agricultural Conservation Program, which provides cost-sharing funds to landowners for the protection of soil and water resources, including practices to improve tree planting and timber stands.

soil creep *See* CREEP.

soil drainage *See* DRAINAGE.

soil enhancement (soil amendment, soil improvement) Adding material (including *fertilizers, *organic materials, *sand, or *lime) to a *soil in order to improve its fertility, long-term chemical or physical status, or stability. *See also* SOIL CONDITIONER.

soil erodibility A measure of the inherent susceptibility of a *soil to *erosion, regardless of *topography, *vegetation cover, *management, or *weather conditions.

soil erosion The removal of *topsoil by *raindrop erosion and *sheet erosion, as a result of human activities, particularly if the protective vegetation has been removed. A number of factors promote soil erosion, including *deforestation, *overgrazing, *compaction (which destroys soil structure), farming on steep slopes without *terraces, and the practice of leaving ground barren for long periods in winter. The erosion of soil by running water can be tackled in a number of ways, including: maintaining a protective plant cover on vulnerable soils, perhaps by planting crops in alternate strips (grass and grains); reducing the amount of time for which bare soil is exposed, by using *mulch or reintroducing *crop rotations; *contour ploughing; building terraces that intercept and stop the downslope movement of soil; and netting, a temporary form of erosion control in which netting is placed over bare soil surfaces after they have been seeded. The erosion of soil by wind can be reduced by maintaining a plant cover to reduce wind speed (thus energy), contour ploughing, planting strips of row crops in intervals across a field of cereals, and using

S

trees and shrubs as shelter belts or windbreaks. *See also* ACCELERATED EROSION.

soil fabric The arrangement, size, shape, and frequency of the particles in a *soil.

soil factor *See* EDAPHIC FACTOR.

soil fertility The ability of a *soil to support plant growth by providing water, *nutrients, and a medium in which growth can occur.

soil formation (pedogenesis) The process by which *soil is formed as a result of interactions over time between parent material (*rock), *climate, *topography, and *organisms.

soil gas Gas (such as *radon) that is contained in the pore spaces between *soil particles.

soil horizon A relatively uniform layer within a *soil profile that has distinct characteristics (see Fig. 19). *See also* A-HORIZON; B-HORIZON; C-HORIZON; D-HORIZON.

soil improvement *See* SOIL ENHANCEMENT.

soil loss equation *See* UNIVERSAL SOIL LOSS EQUATION.

soil map A map that shows the location and extent of the different *soil associations and *soil complexes in a particular area.

soil moisture *See* SOIL WATER.

soil moisture deficit The difference between the current amount of *soil moisture and the moisture which would be in that soil at *field capacity.

soil monolith A vertical section through a *soil, which is often preserved with resin and mounted for display.

soil order The highest level within the *Comprehensive Soil Classification System. There are eleven soil orders: *alfisols, *andosols, *aridisols, *entisols, *histosols, *inceptisols, *mollisols, *oxisols, *spodsols, *ultisols, and *vertisols.

soil organic matter *See* HUMUS.

soil phase A subdivision of a *soil series, based on characteristics (such as slope) that affect the use and management of the soil but not enough to create a separate soil series.

soil pipe 1. A drain that conveys liquid waste from toilets. 2. (pipe) A natural small-scale tunnel within a *soil, usually part of a network, that plays a part in *soil erosion and *gully development.

soil productivity The capacity of a *soil to produce a particular *yield of crops or other plants, under a given specified system of *management.

soil profile A vertical cross-section through all the horizons in a *soil, from the surface to the unaltered *parent material. *See also* SOIL HORIZON.

soil reaction A measure of the degree of *acidity or *alkalinity of a *soil. *See also* PH.

soil region An area across which *soils are relatively uniform. There are 50 soil regions in the USA, which vary with climate and vegetation.

soil resource inventory *See* SOIL SURVEY.

soil salinization The accumulation of salts near the soil surface, usually resulting from *irrigation under conditions of poor or impaired drainage. *See also* SALINIZATION.

soil seed bank The ungerminated but viable *seeds that lie in the soil.

soil series A group of *soils that have similar *soil profile characteristics and are derived from similar *parent materials.

soil solution The water and *solutes that are dissolved within it present in the soil.

soil structure The arrangement of *soil particles into larger particles or clumps.

soil survey (soil resource inventory) The systematic examination, description, classification, and mapping of *soils within an area.

soil taxon A named group of *soils within a *soil classification system (soil taxonomy).

soil taxonomic unit *See* SOIL TAXON.

soil taxonomy *See* SOIL CLASSIFICATION.

soil texture The relative proportion of the various size groups of individual particles (*sand, *silt, and *clay) in a *soil.

soil type A subdivision of a *soil series defined in terms of surface *soil texture.

soil water (soil moisture) *Water that is contained in the *pore spaces of a *soil, as *gravitational water, *capillary water, and *hygroscopic water.

soil-acting herbicide A *herbicide that is applied to the soil prior to the emergence of aerial parts of weeds.

O-horizon
Surface litter

A-horizon
Topsoil

E-horizon
Zone of
leaching

B-horizon
Subsoil

C-horizon
Weathered
parent material

D-horizon
Bedrock

Fig. 19 **Soil horizon**

soil-forming factor Any natural factor that influences *soil formation, the most important of which are *parent material, climate, natural vegetation, living organisms, slope, and time.

soil-forming process The processes by which *soil formation occurs, which include *leaching, *eluviation, *illuviation, *laterization, *podsolization, *calcification, *acidification, and *salinization.

soiling index A measure of the darkening potential of smoke and soot suspended in one cubic metre of air.

solar activity Activity of the *Sun.

solar architecture The design and building of structures that are energy efficient in terms of *solar energy, involving a combination of technologies including *solar panels and *photovoltaic systems.

solar cell (photovoltaic cell) A means of indirectly harnessing *solar energy, using panels made from a semiconductor material (usually *silicon) that generate electricity when illuminated by *sunlight. Solar cells can be used at any *latitude, and large installations are required because of the low efficiency of the technology (currently about 15%). The energy they produce is relatively expensive.

solar collector A device that collects *solar energy, concentrates it, and converts it to useful forms of energy. Typical systems are based on heat-absorbing (usually black) panels containing pipes through which air or water is circulated, either by thermal convection or by a pump. The air or water is heated as it passes through the panel, and the heat is usually circulated around a building through pipes. Such collectors require a lot of sunshine to work efficiently, and are not really suited to high latitudes. The energy produced is relatively expensive because of the high capital cost of installing the heater systems. A form of *active solar heating.

solar constant The rate at which *solar energy is received just outside the Earth's atmosphere, which is about 1360 *watts per square metre (W m^{-2}). The exact rate varies a little through time, depending on variations in the total amount of energy released by the Sun, variations in the Earth's *rotation around its axis, and variations in the Earth's orbit around the Sun.

solar cycle (sunspot cycle) The natural regular cycle of variation in the frequency or number of *sunspots, which has a length of roughly 11 years. *See also* DALTON MINIMUM; MAUNDER MINIMUM; SPÖRER MINIMUM.

solar energy (solar power) Energy that is derived from the *radiation of the *Sun, which is a *sustainable, *renewable, non-polluting, and relatively reliable energy source. Nearly all the energy we use is ultimately solar, except for *tidal energy (which is generated mainly by the gravitational pull of the Moon) and *nuclear energy. *Fossil fuels and *biomass fuels are ultimately derived from solar energy. *Hydropower and *wind power are generated from air and water circulations, which are ultimately driven by solar heating. Solar radiation (*insolation) arrives at the Earth's surface at a fairly low temperature, so sunshine is often thought of as low-grade energy that is not suitable for most uses. It can be made much more useful by concentrating the energy, using *solar collectors, or by *using solar cells.

solar flare A bright eruption of hot gas in the Sun's outer atmosphere, usually associated with active groups of *sunspots.

solar furnace A device that uses a curved mirror or array of mirrors to focus *solar radiation on to a target, thereby concentrating the solar energy. Such furnaces can attain temperatures high enough to melt steel.

solar heating The use of solar *energy or *sunlight to heat buildings. Traditional approaches to heating buildings have relied heavily on *passive solar heating, particularly in sunny places. More recently, technologies have been developed to pump heat around buildings, using *active solar heating or passive solar heating. There is great scope for expanding the use of solar heating systems because the energy supply is inexhaustible and the technology is already fairly well developed and is likely to become cheaper and more efficient in the future. This type of energy use produces less *pollution than burning *fossil fuels or running *nuclear reactors and most places receive enough *sunlight to make this approach possible, even if it supplements other types of heating systems that can be switched on when there is insufficient sunlight.

solar luminosity A measure of the brightness of the *Sun, which is determined by the amount of *solar radiation it is emitting.

solar power *See* SOLAR ENERGY.

solar radiation Energy that comes from the *Sun in the form of *electromagnetic radiation, mostly at *wavelengths of between 1.0 and 0.1 micrometres (μ). Very shortwave (high-energy) *gamma and *X-rays are absorbed in the upper *atmosphere and none reaches the surface. Much of the radiation within the *ultraviolet (UV) range (0.2–0.4 μ) is filtered by atmospheric gases, particularly at wavelengths below 0.29 μ where most of the UV (which causes sunburn) is absorbed by stratospheric *oxygen and *ozone. The atmosphere is transparent to wavelengths longer than 0.29 μ, but *water vapour absorbs energy in a series of narrow bands between 0.9 and 2.1 μ. As well as its composition, the amount of solar radiation also changes as it passes through the Earth's atmosphere. Less than half of the radiation that arrives at the edge of the atmosphere (the *solar constant) eventually reaches the Earth's surface. Most of what is lost is reflected back into space, and has no further impact on the Earth or its atmosphere. About 10% of what is lost is absorbed or scattered by ozone, water vapour, and particles of dust in the atmosphere. *See also* INSOLATION; RAYLEIGH SCATTERING.

solar system The collection of *celestial bodies that orbit the *Sun.

solar thermal electric technology A range of technologies that are similar in concept to *solar heating technologies in using *sunlight to generate heat, but they create enough heat to power a *generator, which is then used to produce *electricity.

solar wind The steady stream of charged particles (mostly *hydrogen and *helium) that flows away from the *Sun out into the *solar system at all times. The solar wind creates *auroras and *geomagnetic storms when it interacts with the Earth's upper atmosphere. It also deflects some of the *cosmic radiation bathing the Earth, thereby influencing the formation of clouds and, from that, surface temperatures. *See* CLOUD.

solar year The time it takes the Earth to make one orbit around the *Sun, which is roughly 365.24 days.

solarization (heliosis) The inhibition of *photosynthesis at very high light intensities, due mainly to the photo-oxidation of certain of the compounds involved.

solder A *metallic compound of tin and *lead that is used to seal joints between pipes.

solfatara A *fumarole that releases sulfurous gases. When cooled in the atmosphere the gases deposit a variety of *minerals. The name is from the Solfatara crater, near Naples, Italy.

solid waste (garbage, refuse, rubbish) Solid materials which are discarded from industrial, commercial, mining, or agricultural operations, and from community activities.

solid waste disposal The placement of *solid waste that is not *salvaged or *recycled into its permanent, final location, such as a *landfill.

Solid Waste Disposal Act (1965) US legislation on *waste disposal that provided states with money for research on the disposal of solid wastes. It was replaced by the *Resource Conservation and Recovery Act (RCRA) (1976).

solid waste management The systematic collection, source separation, storage, transportation, transfer, processing, treatment, and disposal of *solid waste.

solidification (chemical fixation) The conversion of a liquid into a solid, either naturally (such as the freezing of water into ice) or by adding material (like cement) to a liquid *waste stream to make it more solid and less soluble.

solifluction A type of *soil creep that occurs in areas underlain by *permafrost, under *periglacial conditions.

soligenous mire A *mire that receives water from rain and slope run-off.

solitary Living alone, not in *colonies. *Contrast* GREGARIOUS.

solonchaks Soils with a layer enriched in soluble salts that is more than 15 cm thick and lies at the surface or only a little way below it. Solonchaks are a reference soil group in the *World Soil Classification.

solonetz A type of *grassland *soil that is found in a *subhumid or *semi-arid climate, under grass and shrub vegetation. It falls within the *soil order *aridisols.

solstice One of the two days each year when the Sun at mid-day is either highest or lowest in the sky, which determines the *seasons. In the *northern hemisphere the Sun is highest in the sky when it is directly above the *Tropic of Cancer on 21–22 June, and this defines the summer solstice; the Sun is lowest in the sky when it is over the *Tropic of Capricorn on

22–23 December, which defines the winter solstice. The solstices, and thus the seasons, are reversed in the *southern hemisphere.

solubility The ability of a substance to dissolve into another. *See also* GAS SOLUBILITY.

soluble Capable of being dissolved. *Contrast* INSOLUBLE.

solum That part of the *soil that is capable of supporting life, which is mainly the *A-horizon and *B-horizon within a *soil profile.

solute A substance that can be dissolved into another substance (a *solvent).

solute load *See* SOLUTION LOAD.

solution A mixture of one or more *solutes dissolved in a *solvent.

solution load (dissolved load, dissolved solids, solute load) The *sediment that is carried in *solution by a *river.

solvent A substance that has the ability to dissolve another (a *solute). *See also* UNIVERSAL SOLVENT.

soma The entire body of an *organism, excluding the *germ cells.

somatic Relating to or characteristic of the *body (*soma).

somatic cell Any cell other than a *germ cell.

somatic damage Damage that is caused to the *chromosomes in individual body tissue cells (such as skin cells or lung cells) by environmental factors (for example, *UV light in the case of skin cells and tobacco smoke/air pollution or radiation from *radon decay products in lung cells), which can accumulate over successive cell divisions and lead to *cancer. *Contrast* GENETIC DAMAGE.

sonar A device for detecting and locating objects by means of sound waves which are sent out and reflected back by the objects. Short for 'sound navigation and ranging'. *See also* SODAR.

sonde *See* RADIOSONDE; RAWINSONDE.

sonic boom A loud explosion-like sound in the air that is caused by a shock wave from an aircraft (or any object) travelling at or above the speed of sound.

Sonoran Desert One of the largest and hottest *deserts in North America, which straddles part of the border between the USA and Mexico and covers large parts of the states of Arizona,

California, and Sonora. It has a dry, clear climate and contains some unique plants and animals, such as the saguaro cactus.

soot Fine *carbon dust that is formed by the incomplete *combustion of *fossil fuels, and gives *smoke its colour.

sorption The action of soaking up (*absorption) or attracting (*adsorption) substances, which is used in many *pollution control systems.

sorted ground *See* PATTERNED GROUND.

sorting An expression of the range of grain sizes present in a *sediment. A well-sorted sediment is characterized by a narrow range of grain sizes; a poorly sorted sediment contains a wide range of grain sizes.

sound wood *Timber that is in a good condition, free from damage, decay, or defects.

sounding 1. A measure of the depth of water. **2.** A plot of variation in height of one or more atmospheric parameters (such as temperature, humidity, pressure, or wind speed) at a particular point in time, usually based on data from a *radiosonde.

soundscape The full range of noises that are heard in a particular place or area.

sour gas *Natural gas that contains high levels of *hydrogen sulphide; natural gas containing little or no hydrogen sulphide is known as sweet gas.

sour water *Wastewater that contains foul-smelling material, usually *sulphur compounds.

source Any area (such as a *city), place (such as a *power plant), or object (such as a *chimney stack) from which particular *pollutants are released, or at which *waste materials are produced. *Contrast* SINK.

source habitat A *habitat that is a net exporter of individuals. *Contrast* SINK HABITAT.

source population A population that occupies a *source habitat. *Contrast* SINK POPULATION.

source reduction The elimination or reduction of *waste material at the *source, by modifying the process which produces the waste. *See also* BACKYARD COMPOSTING; INTEGRATED WASTE MANAGEMENT.

source region A region where *air masses originate and acquire their properties (particularly temperature and moisture).

source separation Segregating *waste materials where they are generated, such as separating paper, metal, and glass from other wastes in order to make *recycling simpler, more efficient, and more cost-effective.

south 1. The compass point that is at 180° from *north. **2.** A general term ('the South') for the less developed countries that are located in the *southern hemisphere and are often referred to as the *Third World.

south Brazilian floral region Part of R. Good's *Neotropical floral kingdom (*The Geography of the Flowering Plants*, 1974), which contains a large flora with about 400 *endemic genera; a high proportion of its several thousand *species is also endemic. Many important economic and ornamental plants derive from this region (e.g. cassava).

South Pole The most southerly point on Earth, at 90°S latitude in the *southern hemisphere; the southern end of the Earth's rotational axis. *Contrast* NORTH POLE. *See also* ANTARCTICA.

south temperate oceanic-island floral region Part of R. Good's Antarctic floral kingdom (*The Geography of the Flowering Plants*, 1974), which contains a very small flora scattered among the islands of the oceans surrounding Antarctica. There are only two *endemic genera, one of which is *disjunct between several islands. Despite the great distance separating the islands, and their varying latitudes, there is a notable floristic constancy. A characteristic vegetation is tussocky grassland, dominated by vicarious species of *Poa* (*see* VICARIANCE).

southern hemisphere The half of the Earth that lies *south of the *equator. *Contrast* NORTHERN HEMISPHERE.

southern lights *See* AURORA.

Southern Ocean The area of *ocean that lies within the *Antarctic Convergence.

Southern Oscillation A periodic reversal of the distribution of surface *atmospheric pressure across the tropical parts of the Pacific Ocean, measured at Tahiti and Darwin, Australia, which occurs on average every 1–5 years, and is associated with *El Niño events, accompanied by variations in wind speed, ocean currents, sea-surface temperatures, and variations in precipitation in the surrounding areas. *See also* ENSO.

southern pine forest A *coniferous forest *biome in the USA that is characterized by a warm, moist climate.

south-west Australian floral region Part of R. Good's Australian floral kingdom (*The Geography of the Flowering Plants*, 1974), which is a very rich floral region with a high degree of *endemism, in many respects rivalling that of the Cape region of South Africa. The same families are prominent in both floras and they have many growth forms in common.

SOV *See* SINGLE OCCUPANCY VEHICLE.

sovereignty The exercise by a state of absolute power over its territory, system of government, and population.

SPA *See* SPECIAL PROTECTION AREA.

space 1. An empty area or the distance between two or more objects. **2.** The area in which the solar system, stars, and galaxies exist.

Spaceship Earth The metaphor of the *Earth as a spaceship, travelling through *space as a self-contained system, dependent on its own vulnerable supplies of natural resources (including air, water, and soil). There are some interesting implications of the Spaceship Earth metaphor. For example: spaceships are self-contained, and as such must carry all the resources they require; spaceships are small relative to the vastness of space through which they travel; spaceships are complex systems (involving many computer control systems, air conditioning, wiring, and so on) with many components fitted together into a stable, working whole; no spaceship would be able to operate for long without a constant supply of energy to power all of its systems; in many spaceships some of the energy comes from within (from batteries and other non-renewable fuel sources) and some from outside (they use solar energy by means of solar panels, for example); conditions in spaceships are carefully controlled to suit human life; if conditions in a spaceship change too much or too fast they can become unsuitable for human survival; spaceships don't last for ever!

spatial distribution The arrangement of individuals in a particular area or *space.

spawn The eggs of certain *aquatic *organisms (particularly fish and *amphibians), or the act of producing such eggs or egg masses.

SPCC *See* SPILL PREVENTION, CONTROL AND COUNTERMEASURE.

Special Area of Conservation (SAC) An area within the *European Union that is designated for protection under the *Habitats Directive, because of its *natural habitats and/or populations of *species. *See also* NATURA 2000.

special interest group A large group of people who share a common cause, interest, or issue, which uses its organizational power to promote change which is beneficial to its members. *See also* PRESSURE GROUP.

Special Protection Area (SPA) An area within the *European Union that has been designated for protection because it contains important populations of *birds and habitats for birds. *See also* NATURA 2000.

special risk group A group of people (such as children or the elderly) which is at high risk because of its *sensitivity or *exposure to one or more particular *hazards.

special waste Items of *solid waste, such as household hazardous waste, bulky wastes (including refrigerators and furniture), tyres, and used oil.

specialist In ecology, a species that has a very narrow *range in terms of *habitat or food requirements. *Contrast* GENERALIST.

speciation The process by which new species evolve through *mutation and *natural selection, dividing one species into two populations which at least in theory are unable to interbreed. Rapid speciation is known as *adaptive radiation. *Contrast* EXTINCTION.

species A population of organisms that resemble one another closely and that reproduce with one another but not with other populations. Their reproductive isolation means they cannot exchange genes outside their own group. Species are defined in various ways, including the *biological species concept, *cladistic species concept, *ecological species concept, *phenetic species concept, and *recognition species concept. *See also* BIODIVERSITY; BIOLOGICAL CLASSIFICATION; LATIN NAME.

Species 2000 An international project that was set up to index all of the known *species of organisms (*animals, *plants, *fungi, and *micro-organisms) on Earth, in order to provide a baseline dataset for comparative studies of global *biodiversity.

⊕ SEE WEB LINKS

• Species 2000 home page.

species abundance A measure of the total number of individuals of a particular *species in a defined area, population, or community. *Contrast* SPECIES RICHNESS.

Species Action Plan A special part of a *biodiversity action plan, which sets objectives and targets for the maintenance or enhancement of the population and range of particular species, and the actions necessary to achieve them, over a period of 10–15 years. *See also* LOCAL BIODIVERSITY ACTION PLAN.

species–area relationship In *island biogeography, the relationship between the area of the island and the number of species that occur within it; as area increases, the number of species present (*diversity) usually also increases.

species at risk *Species whose future is at risk, either globally or within a particular region. The *IUCN classification defines species in terms of the degree of threat they face, as *extinct, *possibly extinct, *endangered, *vulnerable, *rare, *no longer threatened, and *status unknown.

species composition The types and number of *species that occupy a particular area.

species concept The basis on which a *species is defined. *See also* BIOLOGICAL SPECIES CONCEPT; CLADISTIC SPECIES CONCEPT; ECOLOGICAL SPECIES CONCEPT; PHENETIC SPECIES CONCEPT; RECOGNITION SPECIES CONCEPT.

species diversity The number and relative abundance of *species that are present in a particular community. *See also* BIODIVERSITY.

species diversity index The ratio between the total number of *species in a particular *community, and some measure of the relative importance of individual species (for example, in terms of number, *biomass, or *productivity). *See also* SHANNON–WIENER INDEX.

species extinction *See* EXTINCTION.

species name *See* LATIN NAME.

species of concern A North American term for a *native species that is not listed as *endangered or *threatened but whose population is declining fast enough to cause concern among biologists.

species recovery plan A plan that is designed to halt the decline of an *endangered species, and increase its population, through protection, *habitat management, *captive breeding, disease control, or other techniques.

species richness (alpha diversity) The number of *species that are present in a *habitat or *ecosystem.

Species Statement Within the UK *Biodiversity Action Plan, an overview of the status of *species and broad policies developed to conserve them.

species survival plan A *captive breeding programme, usually within a *zoo or *aquarium, that is designed to aid the recovery of a particular species by breeding a healthy, genetically diverse, and self-sustaining captive population.

species turnover *See* BETA DIVERSITY.

specific conductance A measure of the *conductivity of a sample of water (its ability to conduct an electrical current), which reflects its content of *dissolved solids.

specific gravity The relative weight of a *mineral compared with the weight of an equal volume of pure water, which has a specific gravity of one.

specific heat The amount of heat that is required to raise the temperature of one gram of a substance by 1°C. *See also* HEAT CAPACITY.

specific heat capacity *See* HEAT CAPACITY.

specific humidity The ratio of the mass of *water vapour in a unit volume of air to the mass of a unit volume of that air including the water vapour, usually expressed as grams per kilogram (g kg^{-1}): a measure of *humidity.

specific name *See* LATIN NAME.

specific retention The ratio of the undrained water to the total water in a rock, the undrained water being water contained in rock voids or *pore spaces, from which it cannot be recovered by drainage or pumping. It is retained against the action of gravity by molecular attraction and *capillary action.

specific yield The amount of water that a unit volume of *saturated *permeable rock will yield when drained by *gravity.

specimen An individual, item, or part that is considered typical of a group, class, or whole.

specophily *Pollination by wasps.

spectrum The distribution of *electromagnetic radiation in order of *wavelength. *See also* ELECTROMAGNETIC SPECTRUM.

spent fuel *Nuclear fuel from a *commercial reactor that is no longer capable of sustaining the fission process. *See also* NUCLEAR FUEL CYCLE; REPROCESSING.

spill The deliberate release of water from a *dam, through the *spillway. *See also* OIL SPILL.

Spill Prevention, Control and Countermeasure (SPCC) A North American plan that outlines how a facility will prevent *oil spills, and how it plans to control and contain an oil spill to keep it from reaching surface water.

spillway The overflow structure of a *dam, through which excess or flood flows are released.

spire A young timber tree, the lowest branch of which is at a considerable height.

spit A low ridge or *bar of sand and gravel that projects from the shore into the sea, and is formed by the *deposition of *sediment moved along the *coast by *longshore drift.

splash erosion *See* RAINDROP EROSION.

splitting the atom *See* NUCLEAR FISSION.

spodic horizon The B-horizon in a *spodosol, in which *aluminium and *organic matter accumulate.

spodosol A soil *order in the *Comprehensive Soil Classification System, comprising sandy soils that develop under forests (particularly *coniferous forest), are *acidic, and have accumulations of *organic matter and *iron oxides and *aluminium oxides in the *B-horizon.

spoil The *overburden of rock and soil that is removed to gain access to the coal or mineral material in *surface mining.

spoil bank (spoil heap) A mound of mine refuse that is created by the deposit of *overburden or waste rock.

spoil heap *See* SPOIL BANK.

spore 1. The microscopic seed-like, *haploid cells of *fungi, *algae, *bryophytes, and ferns that grow directly into a new organism. **2.** A bacterial cell that functions as a *propagule, allowing the bacterium to survive a period of adverse environmental conditions.

Spörer minimum A period of low *sunspot activity from about 1460 to 1550 that coincided with low global average temperatures. The minimum was recorded by the German astronomer Gustav Spörer (1822–95) and named after him by the American astronomer John A. Eddy (1931–2009).

sport fish See GAME FISH.

sports utility vehicle (SUV) A vehicle that has the load-hauling and passenger-carrying capacity of a large station wagon or minivan, which may or may not be suitable for off-road driving.

SPOT Système Probatoire d'Observation de la Terre, a *satellite *remote sensing system which was launched in 1986 and provides information on a commercial basis for environmental research and monitoring, ecology management, and for use by the media, environmentalists, and legislators.

spot forward See FORWARD CONTRACT.

spot zoning A special type of land use *zoning that allows particular activities in an isolated plot of land which would not be allowed in the surrounding area.

sprawl Low density development on the edge of cities and towns, which is usually poorly planned, occupies much land, and depends heavily on vehicles. See also SUBURBAN SPRAWL.

spray A jet of *vapour or small droplets.

spraying The application of a liquid (such as a *fertilizer, *herbicide, or *insecticide) in the form of small particles which are ejected from a sprayer.

spread To extend, scatter, or disperse, for example to expand the geographical distribution of an *organism within a particular area.

spreading zone The area around a *mid-ocean ridge, under the sea, where newly formed *crust is moving away from the central axis of the ridge, at rates of 1–10 cm per year.

spring 1. A place where *groundwater flows naturally from the *water table in rock onto the land surface. 2. The *season of growth, between *winter and *summer, when temperatures at mid-latitudes increase as the Sun approaches the summer *solstice. Astronomically this is the period between the *vernal equinox and the summer *solstice, which covers the months of March, April, and May in the northern hemisphere, and September, October, and November in the southern hemisphere.

spring line A line of *springs, usually defined by changes in rock type.

spring tide A *tide which occurs about every two weeks and coincides with the new and full moon, which has a large tidal range because the gravitational forces of the Moon and Sun complement each other. Contrast NEAP TIDE.

springwood 1. High forest that has developed from shoots growing from tree stumps. 2. The ground growth or shoots of new *coppice that emerge from the *stools of a felled coppice. 3. See EARLYWOOD.

sprinkler irrigation A method of *irrigation that uses mechanical devices that sprinkle water over crops to simulate rain.

squall A sudden, brief storm, often accompanied by rain, in which the wind speed increases by up to 50% to at least 30 km h^{-1} for at least two minutes, then dies away slowly.

squall line A series of vigorous *cumulonimbus clouds that merge to form a continuous line up to 1000 km long that advances at right angles to the line itself, generating *squalls as it passes.

squatter Someone who settles upon land without permission or authority.

squatter settlement A *shanty town that occupies land without the owner's permission.

S-rank See PROVINCIAL RANK.

SSSI See SITE OF SPECIAL SCIENTIFIC INTEREST.

St Elmo's fire A bright electric discharge that is projected from objects when they are in a strong electric field, such as during a *thunderstorm.

stability 1. A condition of the *atmosphere that exists when the *dry adiabatic lapse rate is greater than the *environmental lapse rate, so that a parcel of air that is caused to rise will tend to sink back to its original height without cooling to the *dew point, so no *condensation occurs. 2. The propensity of a system to attain a steady state or stable oscillation. See also PERSISTENCE; RESILIENCE; SENSITIVITY.

stabilization The process that is used to convert harmful bacteria and odours in sludge into inert, harmless material, which usually involves *aerobic or *anaerobic *digestion.

stabilization pond See LAGOON.

stable air Air that has little or no tendency to rise, which is usually accompanied by clear dry *weather. See also STABILITY.

stable equilibrium A *system that tends to return to the same *equilibrium after disturbance.

stable isotope An *atom whose *nucleus is not *radioactive and therefore does not alter (*decay) through time.

stack 1. (smokestack) A large, tall *chimney through which combustion gases and smoke are released into the air. **2.** An isolated pillar of rock in the sea, the remnant of a former *cliff that has been eroded by *wave attack.

stack effect An upward flow of air in a building that is caused by warm air rising, which creates positive pressure at the top of a building and negative pressure at the bottom. It can disrupt *ventilation and air circulation within the building.

stack gas See FLUE GAS.

stade (stadial) A brief cold period within a generally warmer climate, which is too short-lived for an *ice sheet or *glacier to form. Contrast INTERSTADE.

stadial See STADE.

stage The level of the water surface relative to a given *datum, at a given location, such as in a *stream channel.

stage hydrograph See HYDROGRAPH.

stagnant Not in a current or stream, and thus still rather than moving or flowing.

stagnation A state of inactivity.

stakeholder A person or group with a vested interest in a particular project, activity, or issue because they are involved in it or affected by it.

stakeholder analysis An analysis of the interests of different *stakeholders in a project, activity, or issue, such as a conservation project.

stalk The main *stem of a *herbaceous plant.

stand A group of similar plants in a particular area. See also TIMBER STAND.

stand density The degree of crowding of trees in a *stand or a *forest, often expressed as the number of trees per unit area.

standard 1. A basis for comparison, such as the maximum concentration of a particular *air pollutant or *effluent that is adopted by a regulatory authority as enforceable. **2.** A tree that grows to its full height. **3.** A tree with a single trunk that is suitable for making sawn timber. **4.** A cultivated plant that has been grafted on to a robust, upright stem and therefore stands without support.

standard atmosphere 1. A hypothetical vertical distribution of temperature, pressure, and density of air in the *atmosphere which, by international consent, is regarded as representative of the overall atmosphere, for example for use in designing missiles and aircraft. **2.** In meteorology, the average atmospheric pressure at sea level, assuming the atmosphere to be a perfect gas at a temperature of $15°C$ (188.16 kelvin) and the acceleration due to gravity to be 9.80655 m s^{-1}. The standard atmosphere is then $0.101\,325$ megapascals 1013.25 millibars).

standardized mortality ratio (SMR) The ratio of the number of deaths in a population to the expected number of deaths in a standard population adjusted for age and possibly other factors such as gender or race.

Standard Metropolitan Statistical Area (SMSA) An *urban region in the USA that has at least $100\,000$ inhabitants, and has strong economic and social ties to a central *city of at least $50\,000$ people.

standard of living The level of material well-being of an individual or group, in terms of goods and services available to them. A measure of *quality of life.

standing crop The total amount of *biomass in an *ecosystem at a particular point in time, usually expressed as the weight (in grams) of living material per unit area or volume.

standing wave 1. A wave in which the water surface oscillates vertically between fixed points (nodes), without any forward progression, the crest at one moment becoming the trough at the next. The points of maximum vertical rise and fall are called antinodes. At the nodes the water particles show no vertical motion but exhibit the maximum horizontal motion. Standing waves may be caused by the meeting of two similar wave groups travelling in

S

opposite directions. *See also* HYDRAULIC JUMP. **2.** A *lee wave.

starch A complex *carbohydrate that is found mainly in the seeds, fruits, roots, and other parts of plants, particularly in corn, potatoes, wheat, and rice.

star dune A complex sand dune in which a series of slip faces radiate about a central point, producing a rough star shape. Such dunes are the product of highly variable wind directions.

starter castle *See* MCMANSION.

starting delivery date The first specified future date when the *forward contract *emissions reductions will be delivered under the *Kyoto Protocol.

starting price The price of the *emissions reductions at the *starting delivery date in the bid or offer for a *forward contract, under the *Kyoto Protocol.

startling coloration The presence of very strong colours in a species. *Contrast* CAMOU-FLAGE; DISRUPTIVE COLORATION.

starvation A state of extreme hunger that results from lack of *essential nutrients over a prolonged period of time.

stasis A period of little or no detectable change, for example in the *evolution of a *species.

State Implementation Plan (SIP) A detailed description of the programmes a state in the USA will use to carry out its responsibilities under the *Clean Air Act, which must be approved by the *Environmental Protection Agency.

state land Land that is owned and administered by the state in which it is located.

state of matter One of the four normal states of matter, which are *solid, *liquid, *gas, and *plasma.

state of the environment report A report that provides up-to-date information relating to *environmental quality and *natural resources, which usually includes an inventory of what is there, an assessment of their state and quality, a baseline against which to compare changes, and the prospect of monitoring of changes through time.

state park A park or recreation area in the USA that is owned and administered by the state in which it is located.

Statement of Forest Principles The informal name of a non-legally binding framework for international action in dealing with the causes and impacts of *deforestation, particularly within the tropics, that was agreed at the *United Nations Conference on Environment and Development in 1992. Its formal title is Non-Legally Binding Authoritative Statement of Principles for a Global Consensus on the Management, Conservation and Sustainable Development of all Types of Forests.

static electricity Electricity that is at rest, rather than flowing. A static charge develops when the surfaces of certain materials come into contact and electrons move from one to the other, leaving one with a positive charge and the other with a negative charge, and the materials then move apart and are separated by an insulating material (e.g. dry air).

static equilibrium A type of *equilibrium that occurs where force and reaction are balanced, and the properties of the system remain unchanged over time. *Contrast* STEADY-STATE EQUILIBRIUM.

static instability *See* CONVECTIVE INSTABIL-ITY.

stationary front A *front between warm and cold air masses, which is moving very slowly or not at all. Air on either side is moving approximately parallel to the front.

stationary source A source of *pollution (such as a *smokestack) that does not move. *Contrast* MOBILE SOURCE.

statistic A measure that is calculated from a *sample of data.

statistical range The difference between the upper and lower values in a set of data.

statistical significance The condition in which the difference between two means is equal to or greater than 1.96 times the standard error of the mean. Since there is an approximately 20 : 1 likelihood that such a difference occurs by chance, 95% of the means will be enclosed, assuming a normal distribution of the data. The result is thus significant at the 95% level or, to express it more precisely, it is significant at level $p = 0.05$. Higher levels of significance are possible and yet more convincing, e.g. $p = 0.01$ is equivalent to 1 chance in 100

(99% probability) that the original (null) hypothesis of the means being acceptably the same is correct.

statistics A branch of mathematics that deals with the collection, analysis, interpretation, and presentation of large amounts of numerical data.

status unknown An *unknown category of species that is defined by the *IUCN Red Data Book as 'no information is available with which to assign a conservation category'.

statute An *act that is passed by a legislative branch of government, which declares, commands, or prohibits something, and which describes *law and defines the time within which parties must take action to comply.

statutory Applied to a legal requirement, authorized by *statute.

statutory agency A government body which has powers defined in law, such as the *Environment Agency in the UK and the *Environmental Protection Agency in the USA.

statutory law Law which is enacted by the legislative branch of government, in contrast to case law or common law.

steady state (equilibrium state) A state in which the properties of a *system remain constant and there are no net exchanges of mass or energy with the surrounding *environment over time. *See also* HOMEOSTASIS.

steady-state economy An *economy in which birth and death rates are relatively low, and the use of renewable energy sources and recycling of materials is relatively constant over time.

steady-state equilibrium A type of *equilibrium in which the average condition of the system remains unchanged over time. *Contrast* STATIC EQUILIBRIUM.

steam fog *See* EVAPORATION FOG.

Stefan–Boltzmann equation An equation that can be used to calculate the *black body temperature of a body (including a *planet, such as the *Earth).

Stefan–Boltzmann law The physical law that relates the amount of radiation a body emits to its temperature. The law is expressed as: $E = \sigma T^4$, where E is the amount of radiation emitted in watts per square metre T is the tem-

perature in kelvins, and σ is the Stefan–Boltzmann constant (= 5.67×10^{-8} $Wm^{-2}K^{-4}$).

stem The upright structure (*stalk) that supports a *plant or *fungus, usually above the ground and in a direction opposite to the *roots.

stemflow The water (*precipitation after *interception) that trickles down the *stems of plants and eventually reaches the ground below the vegetation as part of the *throughfall.

steno- A prefix denoting the ability of an *organism to tolerate only a narrow range of environmental conditions. *Contrast* EURY-.

stenoecious Applied to an organism that can live in only a restricted range of *habitats.

stenohaline Tolerant of a narrow range of *salinity.

stenophagic Applied to organisms that have a highly specialized diet.

stenothermal Tolerant of a narrow range of *temperature.

stenotopic Appled to an organism that tolerates only a narrow range of environmental conditions.

steppe An extensive, mid-latitude, *temperate, grassland *biome that covers much of Eurasia, particularly Russia.

sterile Incapable of reproducing.

sterile male release An approach to fly pest control, which is based on releasing sterile males with which females mate only once, producing eggs that do not hatch.

sterilization (disinfection) The removal or destruction of all *micro-organisms, using heat, irradiation, gas, or chemicals.

stewardship Responsibility for the sustainable management and use of a particular *resource or place. *See also* LAND ETHIC.

stewardship management *See* TOTAL RESOURCE MANAGEMENT.

stochastic A process or event that involves a *random variable or behaviour, or a pattern that results from random effects, but with some direction. *Contrast* DETERMINISTIC.

stock **1.** Farm animals that are bred and kept for meat or milk. *See also* LIVESTOCK. **2.** A plant or stem onto which a *graft is made. **3. (boss)** A *discordant *intrusive igneous feature that is smaller than a *batholith, with no distinct shape.

stock resource See NON-RENEWABLE RESOURCE.

Stockholm Conference See UNITED NATIONS CONFERENCE ON THE HUMAN ENVIRONMENT.

Stockholm Declaration A statement of 'common principles to inspire and guide the peoples of the world in the preservation and enhancement of the human environment' which was agreed at the 1972 *United Nations Conference on the Human Environment.

(())) SEE WEB LINKS

• Text of the Stockholm Declaration.

stocking density The number of *livestock per unit area of land.

stockpile A reserve, held in store for future use or a special purpose.

stoichiometric Pure. A chemical compound is stoichiometric when its component elements are present in the precise proportions represented in its formula. A stoichiometric mixture is one consisting of elements in exactly the proportions required to yield a stoichiometric compound on reaction, utilizing all the components of the mixture.

stolon A plant stem that runs horizontally along the ground surface (e.g. of a strawberry). *Compare* RHIZOME.

stoma See STOMATA.

stomata (*sing.* **stoma**) The small openings in the leaves and herbaceous stems of plants through which carbon dioxide, oxygen, and *water vapour are exchanged with the surrounding air.

Stone Age The *prehistoric period of human culture in Europe that lasted up to about 2000 BCE (up to the dawn of the Bronze Age), during which stone was the main material used for making tools and weapons. Archaeologists usually divide the Stone Age into four periods: the *eolithic, the *Palaeolithic, the *Mesolithic, and the *Neolithic.

stone polygon A type of *patterned ground on low slopes, in which stones are moved across the ground surface by *freeze-thaw action and are aligned in the shape of polygons. *Contrast* STONE STRIPE.

stone stripe A type of *patterned ground on steep slopes, in which stones are moved across the ground surface by *freeze-thaw action and are aligned in stripes oriented downhill. *Contrast* STONE POLYGON.

stool 1. A tree stump that is capable of producing new shoots. **2.** The permanent base of a *coppiced tree.

storage General term for the temporary holding (for example in containers, tanks, waste piles, and surface impoundments) of *waste material while it awaits treatment or disposal.

storm A violent weather episode that often includes extreme conditions, such as strong *winds (force 11 on the *Beaufort scale), heavy rain, hail, or snow, often accompanied by *thunder and *lightning.

storm flow The rapid runoff on a river *hydrograph that is created directly by the input of *precipitation from a *storm.

storm hydrograph See HYDROGRAPH.

storm sewer A *sewer system that collects and carries rain and snow runoff to a point where it can soak back into *groundwater or flow into surface waters.

storm surge An abnormally high wall of seawater that is pushed ashore by high winds, and is normally associated with the approach of a *hurricane.

storm warning A *warning that is issued about an impending *storm, which involves sustained surface winds of greater than about 90 km h^{-1}.

stormwater The portion of *precipitation which flows over land into storm sewers or surface waters.

stormwater collection system The equipment (which includes pipes, pumps, and conduits) that is used to collect and transport surface water from *precipitation, and/or *wastewater, to and from storage or treatment areas.

stoss The side of a slope that faces the direction of flow of ice, wind, or water. *Contrast* LEE.

strain 1. A genetic variant, or group of organisms within a *species that differ very little from similar groups. *See also* CULTIVAR. **2.** Deformation of a material as a result of applied force. *See also* ISOSTATIC ADJUSTMENT.

strangler A plant that uses another plant for physical support, ultimately suppressing and strangling that plant by enclosing it in its own. Most stranglers occur in *tropical rainforests (e.g. the strangling fig, several *Ficus* species).

strata *See* STRATUM.

strategic environmental assessment (SEA) The systematic process of evaluating the *environmental impacts of a policy, plan, or programme and its alternatives, including the preparation of a report on the evaluation and the use of the findings in publicly accountable decision-making. *See also* ENVIRONMENTAL IMPACT ASSESSMENT.

strategic lawsuit against public participation (SLAPP) A lawsuit that has no merit in itself but is brought against private citizens who act in the public interest, usually by a large corporation or a wealthy individual, in order to intimidate them and silence them by burdening them with huge costs of legal defence.

strategic mineral Any *mineral that a country uses (for example for defence purposes) but which it cannot produce itself.

strategic plan A plan that an organization develops in order to help align its structure and resources with defined priorities, missions, and objectives.

strategy A statement or framework that describes how a particular programme will achieve its desired goals and objectives.

stratification To separate into layers (*strata), such as the layers (*lamination) within a *sedimentary rock, or the layers of vegetation within a *tropical rainforest. *See also* THERMAL STRATIFICATION.

stratified Layered. *See also* STRATIFICATION.

stratified drift Well-sorted layers of sand and gravel that have been deposited by glacial *meltwater.

stratified estuary An *estuary in which *freshwater from the land lies on top of denser *saltwater from the sea.

stratified seed *Seed that has been stored in a cool, moist environment in order to develop to the point where it can *germinate.

stratified vegetation The layers (*strata) of vegetation within a forest, which are defined by species, age, or size of plant into the tree layer, shrub layer, and herb layer. *See also* CANOPY; OVERSTOREY; UNDERSTOREY.

stratiform A *cloud that develops horizontally rather than vertically.

stratigraphic Relating to or determined by the layers (*strata) within a sediment or *sedimentary rock.

stratigraphic sequence The series of layers (*strata) within a sediment or *sedimentary rock, which can be interpreted by *stratigraphy.

stratigraphic trap (lithologic trap) An oil or gas trap formed as a result of lithologic (*see* LITHOLOGY) variations (e.g. interbedded lenses of sands and silts in a deltaic environment).

stratigraphic unit A group of closely related layers (*strata) within a *sedimentary rock.

stratigraphy The study of the origin, composition, distribution, and succession of *strata in sedimentary rocks, on the basis of fossil content (*biostratigraphy) and lithology (*lithostratigraphy).

stratocumulus (Sc) A genus of soft, grey, rolling low *cloud with a base below 2000 m. It has a flat base and rounded top, is thicker than *stratus, and is often accompanied by weather changes and *precipitation.

stratopause The boundary in the *atmosphere between the *stratosphere and the *mesosphere, at a height of about 50 km, where the air temperature is about 0°C.

stratosphere The layer of the *atmosphere between the *troposphere (below) and the *mesosphere (above), the lower level of which varies with latitude from about nine km at the poles to 16 km near the equator, and which extends to an altitude of around 50 km. In this layer there is little *water vapour but much *ozone, and temperature remains stable or rises slightly with altitude. The stratosphere is not uniform, and conditions change between the lower and upper parts of it. The lower part of the stratosphere, up to an altitude of about 35 km is a transitional zone above the *tropopause in which air temperature is fairly constant in the region of $-55°C$. Temperature rises with height in the upper stratosphere, between about 35 and 60 km, reaching about 0°C at the stratopause. *See also* OZONE DEPLETION; OZONE LAYER.

s

stratospheric ozone *Ozone that is found in the *stratosphere. It blocks out harmful *ultraviolet rays from the Sun, including those that may cause damage to human health and the environment. *Contrast* TROPOSPHERIC OZONE. *See also* OZONE LAYER.

stratotype A sequence of sediment or rock at a particular place, in which a *stratigraphic unit or boundary is defined, which is used as a global standard for comparing all other stratigraphic units of its kind (defined by age and *lithology).

stratovolcano A *volcanic cone that consists of both *lava and *pyroclastic rocks.

stratum (*pl.* strata) A horizontal or originally horizontal layer of *sedimentary rock, or a horizontal layer of vegetation. *See also* STRATIFICATION.

stratus (St) A genus of grey, featureless, low *cloud, with a base below 2000 m. It can produce *drizzle or *snow but rarely produces heavy *precipitation, and is *fog when its base is at ground level. Stratus clouds are commonly found during the winter in humid climates in middle and high latitudes, and can persist for days or weeks.

straw The plant residue that remains after *seeds are removed in threshing.

streak The colour of a *mineral when it is in powdered form.

stream A natural body of running water that flows along a *channel. *See also* CREEK; RIVER.

stream bank (river bank) The sides of a *stream channel.

stream based standard *See* RECEIVING WATER QUALITY STANDARDS.

stream bed (river bed) The bottom of a *stream channel.

stream channel (river channel) A *watercourse, or natural *channel along which water flows.

stream discharge The rate of flow of water along a stream over a given period of time, which depends on volume and velocity of flow, and is usually expressed in cubic metres per second ($m^3 s^{-1}$).

stream frequency The number of *stream segments per unit drainage area (usually per square kilometre). Dense networks have high stream frequencies. *Contrast* DRAINAGE DENSITY.

stream order The relative position or rank of a *stream segment in a drainage network, with the smallest permanent streams defined as first order, second order defined as where two first-order streams join, third order as where two second-order streams join, and so on.

stream power The rate at which a stream can do work, especially the transport of its load, and measured over a specific length. It is largely a function of channel slope and discharge and is expressed by $\Omega = \gamma Qs$, where Ω is the power, γ is the specific weight of water, Q is the discharge, and s is the slope. Streams tend to adjust their flow and channel geometry in order to minimize their power.

stream segment A reach of a *stream channel, usually defined as between two successive tributaries.

stream use classification A system for classifying *streams according to the intended use of the water, such as for *recreation or *irrigation.

streamflow Discharge that occurs in a natural *stream channel, which includes *runoff and water that is added or removed through *diversion or flow in a *regulated river.

streamline The curved path of any medium (such as a parcel of air or a flow of water or ice) that flows steadily over or around an obstacle.

streamside buffer A *buffer zone or strip of permanent undisturbed vegetation (usually forest or grass) that is left between a *stream and an adjacent area of more intensive land use (such as agriculture or urban development). It is designed to reduce *soil erosion and protect water quality by filtering out pollution before it reaches the water. *See also* RIPARIAN.

streamside management zone (SMZ) An area adjacent to a *stream in which vegetation is maintained or managed in order to protect water quality, provide diversity of habitat, and create wildlife *travel corridors.

street Any public thoroughfare or residential road that leads off a main road.

stress 1. The force per unit area that is applied to a body, and produces *strain on that material. **2.** A physical or chemical process that causes a response within an *organism, *population, or *ecosystem.

stressor *See* AGENT.

stria *See* STRIATION.

striae Plural of stria. *See* STRIATION.

striation (stria) A scratch mark that is caused by *abrasion of the surface of a rock by a *glacier, is aligned in the direction of ice movement, and is very useful in reconstructing directions of ice movement in the past.

Strict Nature Reserve *See* SCIENTIFIC RESERVE/STRICT NATURE RESERVE.

strike 1. (*noun*) The compass direction of a horizontal line on an inclined plane (i.e. it is at right angles to the angle of inclination, known as the dip). The direction or trend of a *bedding plane or *fault, relative to the horizontal. (*verb*) To lie in the direction of such a line. **2.** (*noun*) The discovery of an economically valuable source of a mineral. (*verb*) To make such a discovery.

strike-slip fault (transcurrent fault) A horizontal displacement *fault (such as the *San Andreas fault in California), in which movement occurs along the fault line as a result of *shearing.

strip cropping *See* STRIP FARMING.

strip cutting In *forest management, a system of *clearcutting in narrow strips in order to minimize edge effects and allow natural *regeneration of the forest.

strip development A sprawling form of commercial land use in which each establishment is given direct access to a major thoroughfare, which usually has many large signs designed to attract passers-by. Visitors drive to and from the strip, which therefore requires extensive parking areas.

strip farming (strip cropping) Planting different *crops in alternating strips along land contours, so that when one is harvested the other remains to protect the soil and prevent erosion.

strip mall North American term for a shopping centre (*shopping mall) that consists of a continuous line of single-storey shops, stores, businesses, and restaurants along a road or busy street, usually opening onto a car park. *Contrast* SHOPPING MALL.

strip mining The mining of *ore or *coal from an *open mine, which usually involves the use of large machines (bulldozers, power shovels, or stripping wheels) that scoop out the material in long, narrow strips. The two main types are *area mining and *contour mining.

Strong, Maurice A Canadian industrialist and public servant (born 1929) who was the first Executive Director of the *United Nations Environment Programme. He served as Secretary-General of the 1992 *United Nations Conference on Environment and Development and as a senior advisor to UN Secretary-General Kofi Annan.

strontium (Sr) A reactive, metallic element that resembles *calcium and can replace it in biological processes. The *radioisotope ^{90}Sr is a health hazard because it can lodge in bone.

strophic balance The state of balance that is reached when the *pressure gradient (which forces air to move from high to low pressure) and the *Coriolis effect act in the opposite directions, causing air to flow at right angles to the *pressure gradient (deflected to the right in the *northern hemisphere and to the left in the *southern hemisphere); i.e. anticlockwise around centres of low pressure in the northern hemisphere.

structural trap A trap formed by the deformation of porous and non-porous rock strata as a result of folding, faulting, etc., in which oil, gas, or water may accumulate.

structure 1. The way in which something is organized, such as the pattern of plant species within an *ecosystem. **2.** Anything that is built for the support, shelter, or enclosure of people, animals, goods, or property.

Structure Plan A statutory *land use plan agreed by a county planning authority in the UK, which sets out strategic policies for town and country planning within that county. *Contrast* LOCAL PLAN.

stubble The short stalks that are left behind in a *field after a cereal *crop has been harvested.

stubble mulch A soil covering that is composed of the unused stalks of crop plants (*stubble).

stump The lower part of a tree that remains standing after the tree has been felled or *coppiced.

stumpage The commercial value of standing trees.

stylet 1. A barb found in the proboscis of certain worms in the pharynx of *tardigrades (water bears). **2.** A long mouth part of certain *insects, mainly bugs (Hemiptera), used to extract fluids.

Stylops A genus of minute (males are 1–1.75 mm long) insects (order Strepsiptera), which in their larval state are *parasitic on other insects.

subaerial Located on or near the ground surface.

subarctic The high latitude area in the northern hemisphere, generally between 50°N and 70°N, which has a *subarctic climate.

subarctic climate A *climate zone that is found across much of North America and most of northern Eurasia, north of the *humid continental climate and south of the *polar climate in the *northern hemisphere, and is characterized by bitterly cold winters and short cool summers.

subatomic Smaller than an *atom, or relating to the constituents of an atom or the forces within an atom.

sub-bituminous coal (black lignite) A rank of *coal that is intermediate between *lignite and *bituminous coal.

subclimax A late stage in a *succession to a climatically controlled *climax, especially one that persists for a long time because the succession has been arrested or deflected by factors such as natural fires, storms, lack of long-term environmental stability, or management (e.g. a succession to forest that is converted to pasture at the grassland stage, and held there because grazing herbivores destroy tree and shrub seedlings).

subcommunity A subdivision of a *community.

subdivision The act of subdividing land (for example into sites, blocks, or lots with streets or roads and open spaces), or the area of land that has been divided up.

subduction The process at a *convergent plate boundary, where the denser plate is drawn downwards into the *mantle beneath the less dense plate.

subduction zone A zone in the Earth's crust where one *crustal plate is drawn downwards into the *mantle beneath an adjacent, less dense one.

subgenus One of two or more groups of closely related *species that constitute a *genus.

subglacial Beneath a *glacier or *ice cap. *Contrast* ENGLACIAL; SUPRAGLACIAL.

subglacial stream A *meltwater *stream that flows underneath a *glacier or *ice cap.

subhumid climate A warm, moist *climate which supports *grassland or *prairie vegetation.

sublimation The direct alteration (*phase change) of *ice (solid) to *water vapour (gas).

sublittoral Of or relating to the region of the *continental shelf, lying between the sea *shore and the edge of the continental shelf.

sublittoral fringe The upper part of the *sublittoral zone, which is uncovered at *low tide.

sublittoral zone 1. A zone within the *ocean that extends from the *low tide mark to the edge of the *continental shelf, with depths of up to about 200 m. **2.** *See* LIMNETIC ZONE.

submarine Beneath the surface of the *sea.

submarine canyon An underwater *canyon in the *continental shelf.

submerged aquatic vegetation *Vegetation that lives at or below the surface of a *waterbody.

submergence marsh The lower zone of a *saltmarsh, from the mean high-water level of *neap tides to the general level of mean high water. Typically, this zone experiences more than 360 submergences per annum, usually with more than one hour of submergence during daylight each day. Continuous exposure never exceeds nine days. *Compare* EMERGENCE MARSH.

subpolar and arctic climate zone The coldest of the world's *climate zones that is found at high *latitudes, and contains *continental subarctic, *marine subarctic, and *arctic and *ice cap climates.

subpolar climate (boreal climate, taiga climate) A *climate zone that is found in the *northern hemisphere, south of the *polar climate, and is characterized by severely cold winters and short, cool summers.

subpolar low A belt of low atmospheric pressure between 60° and 70° latitude in both hemispheres where easterly winds generated by the *polar high converge with westerly winds from the *subtropical high. Weather here is often very unsettled, with extensive cloud cover.

subpopulation A subset of a natural or artificial breeding *population. *See also* VARIETY.

subshrub A plant that is smaller than a *shrub and produces wood only at its base, and has abundant growth branching upwards from the base, the upper stems dying back at the end of each growing season.

subsidence **1.** In meteorology, the slow sinking of air that is usually associated with *high pressure areas. **2.** In geology, a settling of the ground surface as a result of the collapse of *porous formations from which large amounts of *groundwater, *oil, or other underground materials have been withdrawn.

subsidence inversion A temperature *inversion that develops in the atmosphere as a result of air gradually sinking over a wide area and being warmed by *adiabatic compression, often associated with *subtropical high pressure areas.

subsidy A grant that is paid by government to the supplier of a good or service that benefits the public.

subsist To support oneself.

subsistence The means of obtaining food and other items that are essential for basic survival.

subsistence economy An *economy in which production meets the minimum needs of the population, but produces no surplus.

subsistence farming Cultivation of *crops and *livestock in order to provide for the basic needs of the farmer and his/her family, without producing surpluses that can be sold at market. *Contrast* CASH CROP.

subsoil The lower part of a *soil profile, beneath the *topsoil, which generally contains little *organic matter.

subsoiling The breaking up of subsoils, usually because they are compacted, without inverting them. Subsoiling is usually performed with a chisel-like device which is pulled through the soil.

subspecies (race) A geographically isolated or physiologically distinct group within a *species, which is capable of interbreeding with other members of the subspecies but rarely does so. *See also* CULTIVAR; VARIETY.

substance A material of a particular kind or composition.

substance of very high concern (SVHC) Under the *Registration, Evaluation, Authorisation and Restriction of Chemical substances (REACH) regulations, a chemical substance that has been identified in the first step towards requiring authorisation for its use, usually leading to restrictions on use, because the substance is harmful to human health or the environment.

substitutability The degree to which one material can be replaced or exchanged for another.

substrate (substratum) The surface on which a plant or animal lives and grows; for example a rocky or sandy substrate.

substratum *See* SUBSTRATE.

subsurface drainage The removal of excess water from within a soil or deposit, often by means of *tile drains.

subsurface mining The extraction of *metal ore or *fossil fuel resources from beneath the surface of the ground.

subtropical The region between the *tropical and *temperate regions, which extends between about latitudes 35° and 40° North and South.

subtropical front A boundary in *subtropical latitudes, where warm air that is carried towards the poles by the *Hadley cells meets the cooler air of the middle latitude *Ferrel cells.

subtropical high One of several semipermanent zones of *high pressure that are found in *subtropical latitudes. They are most strongly developed in summer and influence weather to the east of them by blocking the eastward movement of midlatitude *depressions.

subtropical jet A strong, generally westerly wind in the upper *troposphere that blows over *subtropical latitudes. *See also* JET STREAM.

suburb (suburbia) The outer part of a *city or *urban area, close to the urban-*rural boundary, with limited commercial land use and low-density residential development. *See also* EXURBIA.

suburban Relating to, characteristic of, or situated in *suburbs. *See also* URBAN.

suburban sprawl (sprawl, urban sprawl, Los Angelization) The growth of a metropolitan area, particularly the *suburbs, over a large area.

suburbia *See* SUBURB.

succession 1. In general, a sequence or the action of following in order. 2. In ecology, the gradual and orderly sequence of different plant *communities that develop over time in the same area, as one community replaces another through a predictable series of stages (*seres), until a stable climax is established. The sequence normally involves five stages, beginning with creation of an area of bare land (*nudation), followed by the arrival of the first plant seeds (*migration), establishment of the seeds and growth of the plants (*ecesis), competition between the established plants, and their effects on the local environment (*reaction), until the populations of species eventually reach an equilibrium condition, in balance with the surrounding environment, which is sustainable (*stabilization). A typical succession in a temperate area might take up to 150 years from open ground to mature woodland, and each sere would have its characteristic plants and animals. *See also* PRIMARY SUCCESSION; SECONDARY SUCCESSION.

successional stage *See* SERE.

succulent A plant (such as a desert cactus) that is adapted to life in very dry conditions, often by having a soft fleshy body which can store water for use during times of drought.

sucker A *shoot that grows from the *stem of the plant below ground level.

Sudanese park-steppe floral region Part of R. Good's African floral subkingdom within his *Palaeotropical floral kingdom (*The Geography of the Flowering Plants*, 1974), which has a not very rich flora. Species of *Acacia*, grasses, and palms tend to dominate the vegetation.

sudden oak death A disease caused by the *oomycete *Phytophthora ramorum* that has resulted in extensive tree death in the United States and has been reported in many parts of Great Britain. *P. ramorum* infects a wide range of trees, including oaks, but is also found in some shrubs, such as *Rhododendron* and *Viburnum*.

suffocate To die due to a lack of *oxygen.

suitable forest land (suitable timber land) A North American term for land that is managed for timber production.

suitable range A North American term for land that produces or is capable of producing enough *forage for *grazing by *livestock on a *sustainable basis, under intensive management, without causing environmental damage.

suitable timber land *See* SUITABLE FOREST LAND.

sulphate (SO₄) An *ion that contains *sulphur and *oxygen (SO_4), which react easily with *hydrogen to become *sulphuric acid (H_2SO_4). It is one of seven major ions that are found naturally in most *waterbodies, and is a good *indicator of *water pollution.

sulphate aerosol An *aerosol that consists of compounds of *sulphur formed by the interaction of *sulphur dioxide and sulphur trioxide with other compounds in the *atmosphere. These come from natural sources (particularly *volcanic eruptions) and from the combustion of *fossil fuels and the eruption of volcanoes like Mount Pinatubo.

sulphate reducer A *micro-organism that exists in an *anaerobic environment and reduces *sulphate to *hydrogen sulphide.

sulphur (S) An abundant, tasteless, odourless, yellowish, non-metallic solid element that is found in *hydrocarbons, which release *sulphur dioxide when burned. It is one of nine *macronutrients which plants require for healthy growth, and is an important but small constituent of some *proteins.

sulphur content The amount of *sulphur that is found in a particular coal, which strongly influences the amount of *sulphur dioxide that is released on combustion and thus affects *acid rain.

sulphur cycle The *biogeochemical cycle by which *sulphur circulates within the *biosphere. The sedimentary and atmospheric phases are both important in the sulphur cycle (unlike the *nitrogen and *carbon cycles), and they are of comparable size. One source of sulphur is volcanoes. Although major volcanic eruptions are relatively infrequent, and so release relatively small amounts of sulphur overall, when they do occur they produce sudden increases in atmospheric sulphur. Sulphur compounds are also released by *weathering of rocks. Roughly

S

similar amounts of sulphur reach lakes and rivers from the atmosphere and from rock weathering. The oceans also play an important role in the sulphur cycle. Several species of marine phytoplankton produce *dimethyl sulphide (DMS), much of which breaks down in water. But some of the DMS enters the air where it is oxidized to *sulphur dioxide and *sulphate aerosol, which fall to the surface in rain. This is the principal route by which sulphur moves from the oceans to the land. The oxidization of DMS sulphate has implications for the control of *acid rain in many coastal areas, because it can be as important a source of sulphur as air pollution. Sulphate aerosols can act as *cloud condensation nuclei, further complicating the situation. In terrestrial ecosystems *bacteria break down sulphate and release gases, mainly *hydrogen sulphide. Human activities have doubled the amount of sulphur in the atmosphere since the Industrial Revolution in the 18th and 19th centuries. By far the most significant human impact is the burning of fossil fuels, particularly *coal (which contains on average 1–5% sulphur) and *oil (containing 2–3% on average).

sulphur dioxide (SO₂) A colourless, poisonous gas that is formed by burning *sulphur to create an *oxide, most commonly by the burning of *fossil fuels that contain sulphur in order to generate electricity in power stations. The sulphur dioxide is released into the atmosphere as an *air pollutant, and can cause *acid rain. It is a conventional or *criteria pollutant, and can give rise to *trans-frontier pollution. The amount of sulphur that enters the atmosphere from the burning of fossil fuel is similar to that produced by natural processes, but is not so widely distributed. Combustion emissions are spatially concentrated in major industrial regions and so they often overload regional *biogeochemical cycles. Much effort has been invested in devising ways of reducing sulphur dioxide emissions at source, particularly from the burning of fossil fuels in power stations. Strategies include burning less fuel, switching to fuel with a lower sulphur content, reducing the *sulphur content of the fuel before burning it, and reducing the sulphur content of the fuel at combustion (by *fluidized bed technology) or the sulphur content of the waste gases (by *flue gas desulphurization).

sulphur hexafluoride (SF₆) A colourless gas that is soluble in alcohol and ether. It is a powerful *greenhouse gas that is widely used in the electrical utility industry to insulate high-voltage equipment. It has a global warming potential of 24900 and persists in the atmosphere for up to 3200 years. It is one of the six greenhouse gases to be limited under the *Kyoto Protocol.

sulphur trioxide A compound (SO_3) that forms in the atmosphere by the *oxidation of *sulphur dioxide (SO_2): $2SO_2 + O_2 \rightarrow 2SO_3$. This reaction occurs most readily on the surface of water droplets, leading to the immediate formation of *sulphuric acid (H_2SO_4).

sulphuric acid (H_2SO_4) A *toxic, *corrosive, strongly acid, colourless compound that is formed when *sulphur oxides combine with atmospheric *moisture, and is a major ingredient of *acid rain.

summer The warmest *season of the year, between *spring *and autumn/fall, when the Sun is highest in the sky. Astronomically this is the period between the *summer solstice and the *autumnal equinox, which covers the months of June, July, and August in the northern hemisphere, and December, January, and February in the southern hemisphere.

summer solstice *See* SOLSTICE.

sump A pit or tank that is used to catch liquid *runoff for drainage or disposal.

Sun The star at the centre of our *solar system, around which the planets (including the Earth) orbit. The Earth is on average about 150 million km away from the Sun, but this varies between 147 million and 152 million during the elliptical orbit. With a diameter of nearly 1.4 million km, the Sun is 109 times bigger than the Earth and has a volume equivalent to that of 1.3 million Earths. The Sun accounts for almost 99% of the mass of the solar system. The Sun is composed mostly of *hydrogen (about 70%) and *helium (30%); other elements make up less than 1%. It generates energy by nuclear fusion reactions that burn hydrogen into helium in its interior. These reactions produce temperatures of about 5530°C at the surface and about 15 000 000°C at the centre, as a result of which the Sun radiates energy (particularly heat and light).

suncup A small, bowl-shaped depression in ice that is melted by *insolation.

sundown *See* SUNSET.

sunlight The light or rays from the *Sun. *See also* SOLAR HEATING.

sunlight zone *See* PHOTIC ZONE.

sunrise The first light of day, as the *Sun rises above the horizon in the morning.

sunset (sundown) The time in the evening at which the *Sun begins to fall below the horizon.

sunspot A dark-coloured region on the surface of the *Sun that represents an area of cooler temperatures and intense magnetic fields. The number of sunspots is greater when the Sun is more active. Sunspots vary in size from about 1500 km to groups up to 200000 km in diameter. They constantly change size and appearance. Most spots appear and disappear within a day or so, but some last longer than a month. Quite why sunspots vary so much is not known, but they might be caused by strong magnetic fields that block the outward flow of heat to the Sun's surface.

sunspot cycle *See* SOLAR CYCLE.

super-adiabatic lapse rate A fall of temperature with increasing altitude that is greater than the usual *dry adiabatic lapse rate; it occurs in conditions of intense heating over land or sea.

supercell A type of *convection cell that may develop inside a very vigorous *cumulonimbus cloud. Upcurrents rise at an angle to the vertical, so precipitation falling vertically through the cloud travels to the side of the upcurrents rather than directly into them, thus cooling and eventually suppressing the upcurrents and causing the cloud to dissipate. Consequently, the supercell continues to grow. Supercell storms are capable of generating *tornadoes.

supercity *See* MEGALOPOLIS.

supercooled Cooled below *freezing point.

supercooled water Liquid water droplets at temperatures well below 0°C that would freeze immediately if particles were present to start the freezing process.

supercritical water Water which has undergone a thermal treatment in which moderate temperatures and high pressures are used to increase its ability to break down large organic molecules into smaller, less toxic ones by combining *oxygen with simple organic compounds to form *carbon dioxide and water.

Superfund (Superfund Trust Fund) A fund established by Congress in the USA under the 1980 *Comprehensive Environmental Response, Compensation, and Liability Act, financed by fees paid by toxic waste generators and by cost recovery from cleanup projects, in order to pay for the cleanup of inactive and abandoned *hazardous waste sites or *hazardous materials that have been accidentally spilled or illegally dumped.

Superfund Amendments and Reauthorization Act (SARA) (1986) US legislation that amended the 1986 *Comprehensive Environmental Response, Compensation, and Liability Act to provide additional funding for environmental cleanup of hazardous waste sites.

Superfund Innovative Technology Evaluation (SITE) In the USA, a programme of the *Environmental Protection Agency designed to promote the development and use of innovative treatment technologies in the cleanup of *Superfund sites.

Superfund Program *See* COMPREHENSIVE ENVIRONMENTAL RESPONSE, COMPENSATION, AND LIABILITY ACT.

Superfund Trust Fund *See* SUPERFUND.

supergene enrichment *See* SECONDARY ENRICHMENT.

superimposed river A *river network in which an initial pattern, determined by original rock structures and types, has been preserved as the river has cut down through underlying rocks, superimposing the original pattern on underlying structures and rock types to which it bears no relation.

superparasitism The infestation of *parasites by other parasites.

superposition, principle of The basis for interpreting the *stratigraphic sequences within *sedimentary rocks, based on the assumption that older rocks are overlain by younger rocks so long as the rocks have not been disturbed by *folding, *faulting, or other geological processes. This helps geologists to establish a *relative chronology of deposition, and to make geological associations from place to place.

supersaturated air Air in which the *relative humidity is greater than 100%.

supersaturation A *relative humidity of more than 100% in the *atmosphere.

supersonic Faster than the speed of sound in the surrounding air. *See also* MACH.

supersonic transport A jet aeroplane that flies faster than the speed of sound (*Mach > 1).

supertramp A *species that disperses efficiently, colonizes readily, and has a wide *range, but is excluded by *competition from *habitats supporting a rich variety of species.

supplementarity A requirement within the *Kyoto Protocol that adequate domestic energy and other policies exist to ensure the achievement of long-term *emissions reduction goals. *See also* FLEXIBILITY MECHANISM.

supplementary feed Feed (such as hay or *silage, feed blocks or concentrates) that is used to supplement the dietary requirements of *livestock, usually during the winter.

supply The quantity of a good or service that producers are willing to provide at the specified price, time period, and condition of sale. *Contrast* DEMAND. *See also* MARKET EQUILIBRIUM; SUPPLY SCHEDULE.

supply chain A series of business transactions that starts with raw material and ends with the sale of the finished product or service.

supply schedule The relationship between price and the quantity of a good or service that producers are willing to provide.

suppressed (overtopped) One of the four major *crown classes in trees, in which trees which have crowns below the general level of the crown cover receive no direct light either from above or from the sides.

suppression In *fire management, all of the activities involved in extinguishing or containing a fire, starting with its discovery.

supraglacial On top of a *glacier or *ice cap. *Contrast* ENGLACIAL; SUBGLACIAL.

supraglacial stream A *meltwater *river that flows over the surface of the ice in a *glacier or *ice cap.

supralittoral zone The seashore zone immediately above the uppermost edge of the *littoral zone and beyond the reach of tidal submergence, though it is affected by sea spray.

surf *Waves breaking on the *shore.

surf zone The zone of *wave action that extends from the *shore out to the most seaward point of the zone (the *breaker zone) at which waves approaching the coastline start to break.

surface air temperature The *temperature of the air near the surface of the Earth, the global average of which is 15°C.

surface boundary layer *See* BOUNDARY LAYER.

surface current The horizontal movement of seawater at the surface of a *sea or *ocean.

surface drainage The removal of excess water from the surface of the ground, either naturally by a *stream, or artificially by means of a *drainage ditch.

surface fire A *forest fire of moderate intensity in which low vegetation (such as *shrubs) and some of the surface (*bark) of trees are burned, but not the *crowns of trees, so the trees survive.

surface hoar A deposit of *ice crystals that builds up on a surface when the temperature of the surface is colder than the air above and colder than the frost point of that air. *See also* HOAR.

surface impoundment Any natural or constructed facility that is used to store liquids on the ground surface, including *water storage ponds and *lagoons.

surface inversion *See* RADIATION INVERSION.

surface layer The lowest few metres of the *atmosphere, or the upper few metres of the *ocean, within which the air or water is mixed by the *wind.

surface mining *See* OPEN CAST MINING.

Surface Mining Control and Reclamation Act (1977) US legislation that established a programme for the regulation of surface mining activities and the reclamation of coal-mined lands, under the administration of the Office of Surface Mining, Reclamation and Enforcement, in the Department of the Interior.

surface resource Any *renewable resource (such as *timber) that is found on the surface of the Earth, in contrast to resources such as *groundwater and *minerals which are found beneath the surface.

surface rights Ownership of or rights to use the surface of the land. Subsurface rights (including *mineral rights) are often treated separately.

surface runoff *Runoff that flows overland to a *stream channel.

surface storage All forms of natural storage of water (Including *ponds and depressions) on the ground surface.

surface tension The tension of the surface film of a liquid, caused by mutual attraction of molecules in the liquid, which controls the shape of the liquid surface and makes it seem as though a thin, flexible skin covers the surface.

surface water All water that is naturally open to the atmosphere, including *rivers, *lakes, *reservoirs, *ponds, *streams, *impoundments, *seas, *estuaries, and *wetlands.

surface wind The wind blowing close to the Earth's surface, the velocity of which is usually measured at a standard height of 10 m. Surface-wind velocity is reduced by the frictional effect of the underlying surface. The actual wind is a balance of *pressure-gradient force, *Coriolis effect, and frictional effects.

surfactant A *soluble chemical compound that reduces the surface tension between two liquids, as used in many *detergents.

surge 1. A sudden forceful flow, for example in the flow of a *glacier. **2.** A large, destructive *ocean wave that is created by very low *atmospheric pressure and *strong winds, for example associated with a *hurricane.

surplus Excess; a quantity that exceeds what is needed.

surrogate A substitute. *See also* PROXY.

surveillance The ongoing systematic collection, collation, and analysis of data and the timely distribution of information to those who need to know so that action can be taken.

survey 1. A drawing showing the legal boundaries of a property. **2.** A count or *census of the number of individuals in an area, from which inferences about the *population can be made.

survival The act of living or continuing to exist.

survival of the fittest *See* NATURAL SELECTION.

survivorship The condition of outliving others; the likelihood of a representative newly born individual surviving to various ages. *Contrast* LONGEVITY.

survivorship curve The curve that describes changes in *mortality rate as a function of age.

susceptibility The degree to which an organism is sensitive to a particular factor, such as *infection by a *pathogen. *See also* SENSITIVITY.

suspended load *See* SUSPENDED SEDIMENT.

suspended sediment (suspended load) The fine particles of *sediment that are carried in *suspension by a *river, when turbulent mixing exceeds gravitational sinking.

suspended solids Solids (*colloidal and particulate matter such as *clay, *sand, and finely divided *organic material) that either float on the surface of water or are suspended in it. Suspended solids can usually be removed by filtering.

suspension A mixture in which fine particles are suspended in a fluid, supported by buoyancy.

suspension feeder (filter feeder, suspensivore) Any *organism (such as sponges and corals) that feeds on particulate *organic matter (including *plankton) that is suspended in a water column.

suspensivore *See* SUSPENSION FEEDER.

sustainability A concept that is used to describe community and *economic development in terms of meeting the needs of the present without compromising the ability of future generations to meet their needs. *See also* ECOLOGICAL SUSTAINABILITY; SUSTAINABLE DEVELOPMENT.

sustainability indicator A measure (*indicator) of *sustainable development.

sustainable Capable of being sustained or continued over the long term, without adverse effects.

sustainable agriculture An *agricultural system that is ecologically sound, economically viable, and socially just. Sustainable agriculture uses techniques to grow crops and raise livestock that conserve soil and water, use organic *fertilizers, practice biological control of *pests, and minimize the use of non-renewable *fossil fuel energy.

sustainable community A *community of people that is capable of maintaining its present level of growth without damaging effects.

SUSTAINABLE DEVELOPMENT

According to the *World Commission on Environment and Development (WCED), sustainable development is 'development that meets the needs of the present without compromising the ability of future generations to meet their own needs', which includes *economic growth together with protection of the quality of the environment, each reinforcing the other. Many of the symptoms of the *environmental crisis illustrate what can go wrong if environmental resources are over-used or used in ways that create environmental damage or instability. This is particularly true in *developing countries, where developed-world notions of development have often been transplanted with dire consequences. A central objective of the 1992 *United Nations Conference on Environment and Development was to establish the need to replace existing exploitative and environmentally damaging forms of *economic development with more sustainable and environmentally friendly forms of development. *Sustainability is an in-built feature of all natural environmental systems provided that human interference is absent or minimized. It relates to the capacity of a system to maintain a continuous flow of whatever each part of that system needs for a healthy existence. Human use of environmental resources and interference with environmental systems disturbs this in-built capacity, which can make a system unsustainable. Economists argue that resource use and depletion can stimulate research and development, substitution of new materials, and the effective creation of new resources, but there are limits to what is possible. Conservationists and ecologists have long been aware of the significance of sustainability within natural environmental systems. However, it was not until the late 1980s that the broader concept of sustainable development was first introduced by the WCED. The search for a single definition of 'sustainability' seems elusive, partly because it embodies a number of ideas imported from different disciplines—including *economics (no growth or slow growth), *ecology (integrity of the *biosphere, *carrying capacity), *sociology (critique of *technology), and *environmental studies (*ecodevelopment, resource–environment links). Whilst the WCED definition has been widely accepted, there has none the less been widespread debate about what sustainability might actually mean in practice, and about how it might best be applied to different cultures and economies. It is generally accepted that development can be sustainable only if it is based on sound *ecological principles and practices, but beyond that there is little real consensus. Some *environmentalists argue that too much attention has been focused on defining the meaning of sustainability, and not enough on exploring the implications of sustainability as it is likely to affect the status quo within and between countries. One significant effect of the sustainable development debate has been to raise awareness of the need to adopt wider perspectives when making decisions that affect the environment. Moving towards a more sustainable way of living will inevitably require some radical changes in attitudes, *values, and behaviour. There is no clear answer to the question of how we can create a vibrant global economy that does not destroy the *ecosystems on which it is based. The environmentally sustainable 'brave new world' will have to be less polluting, probably heavily reliant on solar energy, make extensive use of new ways of using and reusing materials, adopt less resource-intensive means of growing food, and develop effective strategies for preserving forests. There would also need to be radical changes in energy systems, tax systems, international economic structures, and provision of international aid. A strategy for building a sustainable society was proposed in *Caring for the Earth, which suggested a set of principles for sustainable development which include respect and care for the community of life, improving the quality of human life, conserving the Earth's vitality and *diversity, minimizing the depletion of *non-renewable resources, keeping within the Earth's *carrying capacity, changing personal attitudes and practices, enabling communities to care for their own environments, providing a national framework for integrating development and conservation, and creating a global alliance.

S

Sustainable Development Commission See UNITED NATIONS COMMISSION ON SUSTAINABLE DEVELOPMENT.

sustainable livelihood approach An approach to *sustainable development which involves public participation and integrates environmental, social, and economic issues into a holistic framework for analysis and management.

sustainable management Managing the use, development, and protection of *natural resources in a way or at a rate which enables people and communities to provide for their social, economic, and cultural well-being and for their health and safety. See also SUSTAINABLE DEVELOPMENT.

sustainable use The use of an *organism, *ecosystem, or other *renewable resource at a rate that is within its capacity for renewal.

sustainable yield (sustained production, sustained yield) The rate at which a *renewable resource may be used in a *sustainable way. Traditional ways of harvesting natural renewable resources, such as fish from the *oceans, wood from the *forests, and plants and products from natural *ecosystems, have usually been sustainable so long as the quantities extracted were not greater than natural processes were able to replace. Many ways in which *natural resources are used are now intensive and unsustainable, without deliberate management intervention to limit the quantities removed to below *threshold sustainable yields.

sustained production See SUSTAINABLE YIELD.

sustained yield See SUSTAINABLE YIELD.

SUV See SPORTS UTILITY VEHICLE.

Sv See SIEVERT.

SVHC See SUBSTANCE OF VERY HIGH CONCERN.

SVOC See SEMI-VOLATILE ORGANIC COMPOUND.

swale A low-lying depression on the ground surface, which is often marshy or swampy, or may contain small lakes.

swamp A low-lying area of *wetland that is usually flooded throughout the year. In European usage, a swamp is covered with grasses and trees, has better drainage than a *bog, has more woody plants than a *marsh, and does not accumulate deposits of *peat. Swamps may be *freshwater or *saltwater, and *tidal or non-tidal. In North America, a swamp is equivalent to a European marsh.

swamp gas See METHANE.

sward The above-ground component of *grassland vegetation, which comprises *grasses and *herbs.

swash A thin sheet of water that moves up a beach after a wave breaks on the *shore. See also SURF.

S-wave (secondary wave, shear wave) A type of seismic wave, created by an *earthquake, that causes *shear stress in the material it moves through. Contrast P-WAVE.

sweet gas See SOUR GAS.

swell A relatively smooth ocean *wave (up to two metres high and 30 m long) that may travel great distances from its source.

swidden agriculture See SLASH AND BURN.

swinging-plate anemometer See ANEMOMETER.

symbiont One of two or more *organisms that are engaged in *symbiosis. See also FACULTATIVE MUTUALIST.

symbiosis A situation in which two different species live together and interact, with one benefiting and the other either benefiting (*mutualism), not being significantly affected (*commensalism), or being harmed (*parasitism).

symbiotic Applied to a relationship between members of two different *species which results in a mutual benefit (*symbiosis).

sympatric Describing closely related species that have naturally overlapping *ranges but do not interbreed. Contrast ALLOPATRIC.

synanthrope An animal that benefits from environmental modifications made by humans to such an extent that it becomes closely associated with humans. Examples include the feral pigeon, house sparrow, and house mouse.

synchronous Coinciding in time. Contrast ASYNCHRONOUS.

syncline A concave *fold of rock *strata, with the youngest rocks at the centre of the downfold. Contrast ANTICLINE.

synclinorium A complex type of *fold in rock, in which there are many small folds superimposed on the major *syncline.

syndrome A collection of characteristics that occur together, such as the symptoms that are characteristic of a particular *disease.

synecology The branch of *ecology that deals with whole *communities of plants and animals, and the interactions of the *organisms within them. *Contrast* AUTECOLOGY.

synergetic Working together in *synergy.

synergism The combined effect of cooperative interaction between two or more changes that is greater than the sum of their separate effects. *Contrast* ADDITIVE EFFECT.

synergy The combination of two or more influences that are mutually reinforcing, making an overall impact greater than the sum of their separate effects.

synfuel *See* SYNTHETIC FUEL.

synoptic Overall, or relating to a large-scale or broad view.

synoptic chart *See* WEATHER MAP.

synoptic meteorology The branch of *meteorology that deals with weather phenomena occurring simultaneously over a large area. *Contrast* MESOSCALE METEOROLOGY.

synroc A synthetic rock-like material into which *intermediate-level waste may be incorporated for final disposal.

synthesis The combination of discrete items to form a new whole, such as the development of new ideas from existing ones, or the combination of separate elements to form a new complex product, synthetic chemical compound, or material.

synthetic Produced artificially. *Contrast* NATURAL.

synthetic fuel (synfuel) A liquid or gaseous *fossil fuel produced from *coal, *lignite, or other solid *carbon sources.

synthetic organic chemicals (SOCs) Artificial (*anthropogenic) *organic chemicals, some of which are *volatile and others of which tend to stay dissolved in water without undergoing *evaporation.

system Any collection of components that work together to perform a function, such as the hardware and software that comprise a computer system, or the *biotic and *abiotic elements that make up an *ecosystem. *See also* CLOSED SYSTEM; OPEN SYSTEM.

systematics The study of *species, which includes their description (identification) and naming (*taxonomy), and the study of relationships among and between *taxa (*phylogenetics).

Système Internationale (SI) The international system of units; the metric system of measurements used in science. Some SI units and conversions are given in Appendix 10.

Système Probatoire d'Observation de la Terre *See* SPOT.

systemic Affecting or spread through the whole body (for example of a plant or animal), not localized.

systemic herbicide A *herbicide that kills the whole of a plant, not just the part it is sprayed on. *Contrast* CONTACT HERBICIDE.

systemic insecticide An *insecticide that is absorbed by a plant, then distributed throughout the plant, rendering all parts of the plant toxic to insect pests. It is effective even if only a small part of the plant is treated. The insecticide does not harm insects that do not feed on the treated plant.

systems analysis The study of how the component parts of a *system interact and contribute to the functioning of the system.

systems ecology A branch of *ecology that analyses mathematically, usually with the help of computer models, the way components of *ecosystems retain, exchange, or cycle energy and materials.

tableland A large, relatively flat area of high ground.

tagma *See* TAGMATA.

tagmata (*sing.* **tagma**) A specialized group of segments in the body of an *arthropod.

tagmosis The fusion of individual segments to form a body wall, which occurs in some *insects.

taiga *See* CONIFEROUS FOREST.

taiga climate *See* SUBPOLAR CLIMATE.

tail water The *surface water that drains from the lower end of an irrigated field.

tailings 1. Rock and other waste materials that are separated from crushed *ore in the *mining process. **2.** *See* TAILINGS DAM.

tailings dam A dam made from material that is sufficiently permeable for moisture to drain through it over a regulated period. The dam is constructed to retain the water-sodden, fine-grained materials (tailings).

tailpipe The exhaust pipe through which gases from an engine (for example in a motor vehicle) are released into the air.

tailpipe standard *Emission gas limitations that are applicable to the exhausts of mobile source engines.

take 1. The *abstraction of water from surface water or groundwater. **2.** A North American verb meaning to harass, harm, pursue, hunt, shoot, wound, kill, trap, capture, or collect any wild species.

taking A North American term for government appropriation of private property or property rights, without compensation.

taku The name of a strong *katabatic wind in southeastern Alaska, in the region of the Taku River, which occurs on average four times a year between October and April.

tall stacks policy A North American approach to the reduction of *air pollution, by using tall *stacks (chimneys) which release gas emissions high into the *atmosphere, from which they are dispersed by wind.

tallgrass A North American *prairie *grassland vegetation dominated by grasses (such as big bluestem, *Andropogon gerardii*) that are tall and that flourish with abundant moisture. This type of grassland originally covered portions of 14 states from Texas to Minnesota, but more than 90% of it has been lost to urban sprawl and converted to cropland.

tallgrass prairie A type of *prairie that grows in areas that receive more than 50 cm of precipitation per year and have *loamy or *clay-based soils.

talus Angular rock debris (*scree) at the base of a *cliff.

talus cone *See* SCREE.

taluvium A hill-slope deposit that consists of a mixture of coarse, rocky rubble and finer particles. The term is a hybrid, derived from *talus and *colluvium.

tannin A naturally occurring substance occurring in many plants, including the skins, seeds, and stems of grapes, or sometimes in oak barrels, that gives red wine its dry, slightly bitter taste. Tannins are astringent and toxic, serving the plant by deterring *herbivores.

Tansley, Arthur George (1871–1955) A British ecologist and conservationist who emphasized *ecology as an 'approach to botany through the direct study of plants in their natural conditions' (*Practical Plant Ecology*, 1923). He also pointed out that since plants exist in communities the ecologist should be concerned with the structure of communities, or 'plant sociology'. This view became central to most British and American ecological theory. Tansley coined the term *ecosystem in 1935 (in 'The use and abuse of vegetational terms and concepts',

Ecology 16: 284–307), although it may have been used earlier by his colleague Roy Clapham. Tansley's book *Types of British Vegetation* (1911) paved the way for vegetation description in Britain. Tansley was a lecturer at the University of Cambridge (1907–23), where much of his ecological work was done, and professor of botany at the University of Oxford (1927–37). He was instrumental in founding the British Ecological Society (1913) and was its first president. His many books include *The British Islands and their Vegetation* (1939) and *Britain's Green Mantle* (1949).

tap root A large plant *root that grows vertically downwards into the *soil until it reaches either an impenetrable layer or a layer that lacks oxygen or moisture.

tap water Drinking water that comes directly from a tap, usually in a home. *See also* POTABLE WATER.

tar sand A *sedimentary deposit that consists of a mixture of *clay, *sand, *water, and a tar-like heavy oil (*bitumen), which can be extracted by heating, and can then be refined to produce synthetic *crude oil.

tardigrades (water bears) A phylum (Tardigrada) of very small (most less than 0.5 mm long), specialized animals, most of which live in the films of water that surround the leaves of terrestrial mosses and lichens; some are found between sand grains in marine and freshwater deposits. The body is short, plump, and cylindrical, with four pairs of *ventral legs that end in claws or toes. There are 400 species.

target area The area at which an application of *agrochemicals (such as an *insecticide or *pesticide) is targeted.

target level The desired or threshold value of an *environmental indicator, defined in terms of human health, safety, and environmental quality.

target species The intended catch of a *fishery. *Contrast* BYCATCH.

tarn A *freshwater *lake in a *cirque.

taungya A Burmese word that is now widely used to describe the practice, in many tropical countries, of establishing tree plantations by planting and tending tree seedlings together with food crops. Food cropping ends after 1–2 years as the trees grow up.

taxon (*pl.* **taxa)** A group of *organisms that are regarded as distinct enough to be treated as a separate unit.

taxonomic Of or relating to *taxonomy.

taxonomy The science of naming and classifying organisms into systematic hierarchies comprising groups (*taxa) based on shared characteristics and natural relationships. A branch of *systematics. There are eight levels of classification in modern taxonomy, with *domain at the top, followed by *kingdom, *phylum, *class, *order, *family, *genus, and *species, although plant taxonomy has only clade between family and kingdom (Plantae). *See also* LINNAEAN CLASSIFICATION.

Taylor Grazing Act (1934) US legislation that authorized the Secretary of the Interior to establish grazing districts from unreserved public domain lands, and to make rules and regulations for their occupancy and use.

TBT *See* TRIBUTYLTIN.

TDS *See* TOTAL DISSOLVED SOLIDS.

TEA-21 *See* TRANSPORTATION EQUITY ACT FOR THE 21ST CENTURY.

tebufenozide A type of *insecticide that works by accelerating the *moulting process, and is used to control larval insects (butterflies and moths) in apple orchards.

technocentric Based on *technology and science, or reflecting trust in science. *Contrast* ANTHROPOCENTRIC; ECOCENTRIC.

technocracy The control or strong influence of society and government by people with well-developed technical skills, particularly scientists and engineers.

techno-fix Reliance on engineering and *technology to find solutions to major human problems, including environmental problems.

technological disaster (man-made disaster) A disaster that is caused by non-natural causes, including biological, chemical, *nuclear and transport disasters, and terrorism. *Contrast* NATURAL DISASTER.

technological hazard A hazard created by people, as opposed to a *natural hazard. Examples include the release of *air pollutants such as *CFCs, serious *industrial accidents such as *oil spills at sea and explosions at nuclear power stations and toxic chemical plants, and the creation of waste materials (such as *nuclear

technological imperative

wastes) that are *toxic and *persistent and which natural *environmental systems are incapable of breaking down.

technological imperative The view that if we *can* do something, we *should* do it, such as generating energy from *nuclear power, even if it has many risks and unknowns associated with it. *Contrast* PRECAUTIONARY PRINCIPLE.

technological optimist *See* OPTIMIST, ENVIRONMENTAL.

technology The application of scientific processes, methods, or knowledge to produce goods and services that people consider useful.

technology transfer The process of transferring scientific findings from research laboratories into useful products by the commercial sector.

tectonic Relating to the deformation of rocks in the Earth's *crust.

tectonic forces Geological forces that buckle, distort, and fracture the Earth's *crust, including *warping, *folding, *faulting, and *volcanic activity.

tectonic plate *See* CRUSTAL PLATE.

tectonics The study of the large-scale movements of rocks in the Earth's *crust, including *diastrophism, *orogenesis, and *plate tectonics.

teleconnection A linkage between changes in ocean and atmosphere circulations in widely separated parts of the globe, through which weather patterns in one region influence the weather patterns in a distant place. The best known example is the *El Niño/Southern Oscillation. *See also* BUTTERFLY EFFECT.

telemetry Sending and receiving data over long distance communication links, such as *satellite or telephone.

temperate Relating to the *mid-latitude area of the Earth's surface, between the *tropics (23.5°) and the *polar circles (66.5°) in both *hemispheres.

temperate climate A *mid-latitude *climate with mild temperatures and moderate levels of rainfall, both of which vary from *season to season.

temperate desert A *mid-latitude *desert *biome that is hot in the summer and cool in the winter, such as the Mojave Desert in the USA.

temperate forest A *biome that is characterized by *deciduous *broadleaved trees, which includes *humid continental mixed forest and *marine west coast forest.

temperate grassland A *grassland *biome that is found in the warm climates of the continental interiors, such as the *prairie of North America, *pampas of South America, *veld of South Africa, and *steppe of Eurasia.

temperate rainforest A type of *rainforest *biome that is found in the mid-latitude zone, such as the cool, dense, rainy forest of the northern Pacific coast of North America, which is dominated by large *coniferous trees.

temperature A measure of the heat content of an object or substance, described using a number of different scales, particularly the commonly used *Fahrenheit and *Celsius scales, and the *Kelvin scale (which is used by scientists).

temperature inversion *See* INVERSION.

tempered air *See* CONDITIONED AIR.

temporary wilting Wilting that occurs in hot weather when the rate of *transpiration exceeds the rate at which a plant can absorb moisture from the soil. The plant recovers when the temperature falls. *Compare* PERMANENT WILTING POINT.

Tennessee Valley Authority (TVA) An agency established by the US Congress in 1933 to assist in the development of the Tennessee River and adjacent areas.

tension A force or stress that causes stretching, for example of *glacier ice as it passes over a rock step, or of crustal rocks stretched by *tectonic activity. *Contrast* COMPRESSION; SHEAR.

tephra Volcanic ash and dust that is thrown out into the air during an explosive *volcanic eruption.

tephrochronology The study of layers of *volcanic ash (*tephra) to determine their *relative ages or *absolute ages.

teratogen A chemical substance or other factor (such as *radiation) that alters the formation of cells, tissues, and organs, thereby causing abnormal development of an embryo and thus birth defects. *See also* CARCINOGEN; MUTAGEN.

terbutryne A selective, *soil-acting herbicide that inhibits *photosynthesis. It is used to control most grasses and many broadleaved weeds in a range of crops and to control floating and submerged weeds in reservoirs, fishponds, and slow-moving water. Its toxicity is low.

term 1. The period of time in which a *mammal completes gestation; from conception to birth. **2.** The period of time during which a contract (such as the *Kyoto Protocol) is in force.

terminal moraine *See* END MORAINE.

terminator technology The *genetic engineering of plants to produce *sterile seeds, which makes it impossible for farmers to save and replant seeds from their harvest and makes them reliant on the commercial seed market. The technology has not been incorporated in seeds sold commercially anywhere in the world. *See also* TRAITOR TECHNOLOGY.

terminus The end or snout of a *glacier.

termitophile Applied to a species that must spend part of its life closely associated with termites. It may scavenge or steal food, or may prey on the termites.

terpenes *See* ISOPRENE.

Terra A *satellite *remote sensing system that was launched by *NASA in 1999 and began returning data in 2000. It is the flagship of the *Earth Observing System and transmits information on how the oceans, continents, and atmosphere interact. Its sensors could scan the entire planet every one to two days.

(**⊕**) SEE WEB LINKS
• Latest Terra news.

terra firme *See* AMAZON FLORAL REGION.

terrace 1. A relatively flat, natural surface along a *river valley, above the level of the *floodplain. **2.** An artificial flat surface constructed on sloping ground in order to produce land for growing *crops and to reduce *soil erosion.

terracing Construction of a series of horizontal levels built on a hillside, in order to retain water and reduce soil *erosion.

terrain The natural surface features of an area of land, particularly the *landforms.

terrain analysis The collection, analysis, evaluation, and interpretation of information on the features of the terrain in a particular place, such as *slope, *aspect, and *relief.

terrain evaluation *See* LAND EVALUATION.

terrane A region of the Earth's *crust, usually defined by major *fault systems, in which the *geology differs significantly from that of surrounding regions.

terrarium A box, usually made of glass, which is used for the keeping and observation of small animals or plants.

terrestrial Related to, or living or growing in or on, land.

terrestrial ecosystem Any land-based *ecosystem, such as a *forest, *desert, *grassland, or *cropland.

terrestrial radiation Longwave *electromagnetic *radiation that is emitted by the Earth at a wavelength inversely proportional to the absolute temperature of the surface.

territorial Applied to the behaviour of an animal establishing and defending an area against others of its own kind.

territorial sea A zone of the *high seas adjacent to each coastal state, that is generally either 5.6 or 22 km wide, was established by the *Convention on the Territorial Sea and Contiguous Zone, and within which the state has sovereignty over air space, water, and the *sea-bed.

territoriality The defence of a given area (*territory), in order to partially or totally exclude others from it.

territory 1. A specific area of the Earth's surface over which a state exercises sovereignty. **2.** The area in which an animal or group of animals *lives and defends against intruders. This is usually smaller than its *home range.

terrorism Using acts or threats of violence to civilians, for example as a political weapon to draw attention to a group's goals or to gain those goals through fear and intimidation.

tertiary consumer The top *carnivore, which occupies the top of a *food chain because it eats *herbivores and *carnivores.

tertiary economic activities Service activities, such as trade and transport. *Contrast*

PRIMARY ECONOMIC ACTIVITIES; SECONDARY ECONOMIC ACTIVITIES.

Tertiary period In *geological history, the name formerly given to the first period of the *Cenozoic era, which began 65.5 million years ago and ended 2.588 million years ago. The term is no longer used, and what used to be the Tertiary is now divided into the *Palaeogene and *Neogene periods.

tertiary productivity The amount of new biomass (weight) that is produced by meat-eating animals (*carnivores) in a given period of time. *Contrast* PRIMARY PRODUCTIVITY; SECONDARY PRODUCTIVITY.

tertiary rock *See* METAMORPHIC ROCK.

tertiary sector That part of the *economy that produces services and information.

tertiary treatment *See* ADVANCED WASTE-WATER TREATMENT.

Tethys Sea The sea that geologists believe lay between *Laurasia and *Gondwanaland in the original landmass *Pangaea, probably between 200 and 250 million years ago. *See also* CONTINENTAL DRIFT.

tetrachloromethane *See* CARBON TETRACHLORIDE.

tetra-odotoxin *See* TETRODOTOXIN.

tetrodotoxin (tetra-odotoxin) A powerful poison that can cause general paralysis in humans after ingestion. It is found in the body, particularly the intestines, liver, and gonads, of pufferfish (Tetraodontidae) and their relatives. These fish can be eaten safely only after careful filleting.

texture, rock The characteristics of the particles of an individual *rock, including grain size, size variability, degree of rounding or angularity, and preferred *orientation.

thalweg The line of deepest water in a *stream channel as seen from above, where the water usually flows fastest.

thatch Plant stalks (straw, reeds, or even living grass) that are used as roofing material.

thematic mapper (TM) A *remote sensing device that is found on *Landsat *satellites, which scans images of the Earth's surface in seven spectral bands from visible to thermal infrared, with a spatial resolution of about 30 m.

theoretical Based on theory or speculation, rather than on observation, experiment, or *empirical testing.

theory A coherent explanation or description, reasoned from known facts. *See also* HYPOTHESIS.

thermal 1. Relating to or caused by heat. 2. A small rising column of air occurring as a result of surface heating, which allows birds and gliders to soar.

thermal capacity *See* HEAT CAPACITY.

thermal conductivity A measure of the capacity of a material (such as a rock) to transfer heat by direct contact.

thermal cover *Cover (such as shade beneath trees) that is used by animals to lessen the adverse effects of *weather.

thermal delay In climate change, the potentially long *time lag before ocean warming affects *global warming.

thermal enrichment *See* THERMAL POLLUTION.

thermal equator The zone of highest mean temperature over the Earth, either in the annual or long-term average or at a given moment. On the long-term average, it is located around 5°N latitude. This position north of the geographical equator results from the generally rather higher temperature of the northern hemisphere as compared with the southern hemisphere; this is because the glaciated Antarctic continent maintains colder summers in the southern hemisphere than does the Arctic, with a much smaller land area, in the northern hemisphere. *See also* COLD POLE.

thermal equilibrium A condition that exists between two objects when they have reached the same *temperature, so that heat energy ceases to flow between them.

thermal expansion Expansion (for example of the volume of air) caused by an increase in temperature.

thermal flux *See* HEAT FLUX.

thermal low A non-frontal *depression associated with strong daytime heating of land surfaces, mainly in summer, which occurs, for example, in Arizona, Spain, and in northern Indian low-pressure cells. The occurrence of thermal lows is also influenced by imbalances in the main wind-streams in the upper *tropo-sphere.

thermal plume A *plume of hot water that is discharged into a *stream or *lake by a source of heat, such as a power plant.

thermal pollution (thermal enrichment) Artificially raising or lowering the temperature of a *waterbody in a way that damages *aquatic organisms or *water quality.

thermal radiation See INFRARED.

thermal reactor A *nuclear reactor in which the *fission *chain reaction is sustained mainly by slow (thermal) *neutrons.

thermal stratification The *stratification of layers of water of different temperature and density within a deep *waterbody.

thermal treatment The use of heat to treat *hazardous waste by changing its chemical, physical, or biological character or composition, for example by *incineration.

thermistor A *resistor with a *resistance that changes with temperature, and which can be used as a temperature sensor.

thermoclastis See INSOLATION WEATHERING.

thermocline A horizontal layer in which the temperature of a body of water changes more rapidly than in the layers above or below. In a thermally *stratified *lake or *reservoir in summer, the thermocline lies between the *epilim-nion above and the *hypolimnion below. In the oceans the thermocline begins 10–50 m below the surface and continues to a depth of more than 1500 m. See also METALIMNION.

thermodynamics The study of heat and energy flow in chemical reactions.

thermodynamics, first law of (law of conservation of energy) A physical law that states that energy is conserved; it is neither created nor destroyed under normal conditions. See also THERMODYNAMICS, SECOND LAW OF; THERMODYNAMICS, THIRD LAW OF; THERMODYNAMICS, ZEROTH LAW OF.

thermodynamics, second law of A physical law that states that less *energy is available to do work with each successive energy transfer or transformation in a system. See also THERMODYNAMICS, FIRST LAW OF; THERMODYNAMICS, THIRD LAW OF; THERMODYNAMICS, ZEROTH LAW OF.

thermodynamics, third law of In a perfectly crystalline solid there is no further increase in *entropy when the temperature falls to *absolute zero. See also THERMODYNAMICS, FIRST LAW OF; THERMODYNAMICS, SECOND LAW OF; THERMODYNAMICS, ZEROTH LAW OF.

thermodynamics, zeroth law of If two isolated systems are each in *thermal equilibrium with a third, then they are in thermal equilibrium with each other. See also THERMODYNAMICS, FIRST LAW OF; THERMODYNAMICS, SECOND LAW OF; THERMODYNAMICS, THIRD LAW OF.

thermograph An instrument that measures and records variations in air *temperature through time. See also THERMOMETER.

thermohaline Relating to density currents in the *ocean, associated with the combined effects of *temperature and *salinity.

thermohaline circulation Large-scale vertical motions of water in the *ocean which are driven by density differences caused by variations in *temperature and *salinity.

thermokarst A low-relief landscape dominated by irregular shallow depressions caused by selective thawing of ground ice (*permafrost).

thermometer An instrument that is used to measure *temperature, using either the *Fahrenheit or *Celsius scale. See also THERMOGRAPH.

thermonuclear reaction A *nuclear reaction that is self-sustaining and is triggered by the *fusion of light nuclei under very high temperatures, which releases a large amount of heat. The basis of a nuclear bomb and the subject of intensive research to build a fusion reactor.

thermopause The top of the *atmosphere; a transitional layer between the *thermosphere (where temperature increases with height) and the *exosphere. Its height above the ground varies between about 200 and 500 km depending on *solar activity.

thermophile An *extremophile (domain *Archaea) that thrives in environments where the temperature is high, typically up to 60°C.

thermophilous Warmth-loving.

thermosphere The top layer within the upper *atmosphere that lies above the *meso-sphere. Its base is about 90 km above sea level and it has no precise upper boundary. The air in the thermosphere is very thin and temperature increases with altitude, sometimes up to 1100°C.

thicket A dense growth of *bushes or *trees. *See also* BRUSH.

think-tank A group of individuals who seek collectively to generate new ideas or approaches to solving particular problems. Examples of US environmental think-tanks include the *Cato Institute, the *Heartland Institute, and the *Heritage Foundation.

thinning (thinning out) The act of removing some of the plants from a *crop, or immature trees from a *forest, in order to improve the growth of the remainder. *See also* LINE THINNING; MECHANICAL THINNING; SELECTIVE THINNING.

thinning out *See* THINNING.

thiocarbamate pesticides A group of compounds used as *fungicides to control several fungal diseases including early and late blight of potatoes and tomatoes, and to protect seeds and seedlings, and used as *herbicides on a wide range of crops. Some are skin, eye, and respiratory irritants. They are of low to moderate mammalian toxicity.

Third World *See* DEVELOPING COUNTRY.

Thirty Percent Club A group of countries that committed themselves to reduce their emissions of *sulphur dioxide by 30% between 1980 and 1993 in order to reduce the problem of *acid deposition.

Thomson, Sir Charles Wyville (1830–82) An Irish biologist and oceanographer, who was appointed professor of natural history at Edinburgh University in 1870. He was especially interested in life in the deep oceans and proposed and then led the five-year *Challenger* expedition (1827–6), in the course of which 4717 new marine species were discovered. Following the expedition, Thomson began the arrangement of the collections and publication of the results. His studies of temperature differences led him to postulate the circulation of ocean waters.

Thoreau, Henry David US writer and social critic (1817–62) who is best known for the book *Walden* (1854), an account of his experiment in simple living, and for the essay *Civil Disobedience* (1849), which outlined a doctrine of passive resistance that was subsequently to influence the views of Mahatma Gandhi and Martin Luther King Jr.

thorium (Th) A naturally occurring *radioactive metal that is found at very low levels in soil, rocks, and water. It is a soft, *ductile, silver-grey, heavy metallic element which has a *radioactive *isotope, thorium-232, with a *half-life of 14 million years.

thorn forest A *deciduous forest of small thorny trees which grows in a *tropical *semi-arid climate.

thorn shrub A dry, open *woodland or *shrubland that is dominated by sparse, spiny shrubs.

Thornthwaite climate classification A system for describing climates devised in 1931 and revised in 1948 by the American climatologist Charles Warren Thornthwaite (1889–1963), which divides climates into groups according to the vegetation characteristic of them, the vegetation being determined by precipitation effectiveness (P/E). The sum of the monthly P/E values gives the P/E index, which is used to define five humidity provinces, with associated vegetation. In 1948 the system was modified to incorporate a moisture index, which relates the water demand by plants to the available precipitation by means of an index of *potential evapotranspiration (PET) calculated from measurements of air temperature and day length. The system also uses an index of thermal efficiency, with accumulated monthly temperatures ranging from 0, giving a frost climate, to more than 127 for a tropical climate. *Compare* KÖPPEN CLIMATE CLASSIFICATION.

threatened Applied to a *species or *community that is likely to become *endangered if limiting factors are not reversed. *Contrast* ENDANGERED; EXTINCT; EXTIRPATION; VULNERABLE SPECIES.

threatened species A category of species under threat, developed as *IUCN (*Red Data Book) Conservation Categories, and widely used around the world. The categories within this group are *extinct, *endangered, *vulnerable, *rare, and *indeterminate.

Three Gorges project A major engineering project along the Yangtze River in China to build the world's largest *hydroelectric *dam. The dam was designed as part of a large multipurpose water resource project, designed to achieve four main goals, namely flood control (to prevent flooding along the densely populated middle and lower reaches of the Yangtze), energy generation (to generate 80 terawatt hours of electricity needed for industrial expansion in central-south and east China), water supply (to significantly increase the availability of water for agriculture, industry, and domestic users in the region), and navigation improvement (to improve the navigation of modern boats between Chongqing and Yichang, which in the past had been severely restricted by a series of rapids, shoals, and shifting shallows). The scheme displaced up to 1.2 million people from that portion of the Yangtze valley, from more than 320 villages and 140 towns. Construction began in December 1994 and was completed in October 2008. Its generating turbines became fully operational in May 2012.

Three Mile Island A narrow island in the middle of the Susquehanna River near Harrisburg, Pennsylvania, USA, which is also the site of a *nuclear accident at the Three Mile Island Nuclear Generating Station on 28 March 1979, when one of the *nuclear reactors suffered a partial core *meltdown.

three Rs Common term for three methods of *waste management, which are *reduce, *reuse, and *recycle.

three-cell model An approximate representation of the general circulation of the atmosphere. Air rises over the equator and subsides over the sub-tropics; these are *Hadley cells. Air subsides over polar regions and spreads into lower latitudes; these are *polar cells. The Hadley and polar cells drive a third set of *Ferrel cells in middle latitudes.

threshold A fixed value (such as the concentration of a particular *pollutant) at which an abrupt change in the behaviour of a *system is observed.

threshold dose The minimum *dose of a substance that will produce a measurable effect.

threshold level The concentration or amount of a particular substance or condition below which it cannot be detected, or below which a significant *adverse effect is not expected.

threshold limit value (TLV) The *concentration of a particular substance (such as an air *pollutant) to which most workers can be exposed without *adverse health effects.

threshold velocity The *flow velocity (of wind or water) that is needed to cause sediment to start to move.

throughfall The *precipitation that falls directly through vegetation to the ground surface

below, and that which falls off leaves after *interception.

throughflow Water (*soil moisture) that moves downslope within a soil, along *impermeable *soil horizons. *Contrast* INTERFLOW.

throughput Output relative to input; the amount that passes through a *system from input to output.

throughput tax *See* DISPOSAL CHARGE.

thrust fault A vertical displacement *fault associated with low-angle *fault planes.

thunder The loud cracking or deep rumbling noise that is usually heard a short time after a *lightning strike within a *thunderstorm, and is generated by a shock wave caused by the rapid and violent expansion of atmospheric gases when they are suddenly heated (to perhaps 15000°C) by *lightning. The delay between seeing the lightning and hearing the thunder increases with distance, generally by about one second per 350 metres.

thundercloud The dark, towering, thick, flat-topped *cumulonimbus clouds associated with *thunderstorms, caused by strong updraft.

thundershower A brief *rainstorm with *thunder and *lightning.

thunderstorm A *storm that results from strong rising air currents, which brings heavy *rain or *hail, and *thunder and *lightning. *See also* AIR MASS THUNDERSTORM; FRONTAL THUNDERSTORM.

tidal bore *See* BORE.

tidal current (tidal stream) The cyclical rise and fall of the water level in confined coastal areas (such as *estuaries and inlets) that is caused by the *tide. Each tidal current lasts for about six hours 12 minutes, which corresponds to the two phases of high water and low water each *lunar day. *See also* FLOOD CURRENT; EBB CURRENT; SLACK WATER.

tidal cycle (tidal period) The 14 day period from one *spring tide to the next spring tide, or from one *neap tide to the next neap tide.

tidal flat (tidal marsh) A broad, flat *coastal wetland of muddy, marshy, or sandy sediment, which is covered and uncovered in each *tidal cycle.

tidal marsh *See* TIDAL FLAT.

tidal period *See* TIDAL CYCLE.

tidal power Energy that is generated by using the motion of the *tides to drive water turbines that run electricity generators. Most tidal power schemes are based on barrages (dams), usually across natural inlets. The reservoir is filled with water as the tide rises and the sluice gates are shut at high tide. As the tide falls water drains out from the reservoir. In traditional systems as the water rushed out it turned a water wheel to provide direct mechanical energy for grindstones and pulleys. In modern systems the water turns turbines to generate electricity. Some tidal energy schemes use only the out-flowing tide to produce energy and they operate for about 30% of the time. Others use both in-flowing and out-flowing tides, to generate energy for about 60% of the time. This is a traditional form of power generation, used in ancient Egypt and throughout Europe until the middle of the 20th century. It is sustainable and non-polluting, and in theory it could provide around 20% of present global energy production. Large tidal range schemes have been operating in France, China, and the former Soviet Union for some years, and they have proved that this approach is both sustainable and cost-effective. Ecologists warn, however, that barrages built in *estuaries alter the flow of water downstream, and therefore also alter sedimentation, with possible effects on wildlife.

tidal power station (tidal station) A *hydroelectric plant that exploits the rise and fall of *tides to drive *turbines to generate *electricity using *tidal power.

tidal range The difference in height between successive high and low *tides at a particular place, which varies through time because of the *solar tides.

tidal station See TIDAL POWER STATION.

tidal stream See TIDAL CURRENT.

tidal wave An unusually high destructive water level along the shore, usually caused by a *storm surge. The term is often, but incorrectly, applied to a *tsunami.

tidal wetland Any *saltwater or *freshwater *wetland that is influenced by the cyclical movements of tidal waters.

tide The cyclical rising and falling of the water of the *oceans that occurs twice each day and results from the gravitational attraction of the Moon and Sun acting on the rotating Earth. See also TIDAL CURRENT; TIDAL CYCLE; TIDAL RANGE.

tile drain A perforated pipe (often made of plastic, concrete, or pottery) that is buried in *soil in order to drain off excess water.

till A collective term for the group of *sediments laid down by the direct action of glacial ice without the intervention of water. The sediments may be classified in terms of particle size or grouped according to the basic process of debris release. Subglacial melt gives rise to lodgement till; surface *ablation gives ablation till, followed by flow till after further movement; and the general thaw of static ice produces melt-out till. Although the material is unsorted by water action, the alignment of stones within till can indicate the direction of ice movement. See also BOULDER CLAY.

till fabric The alignment of elongated pebbles within *boulder clay, which gives an indication of the direction in which the *ice was moving when the sediment was deposited.

till plain An extensive, relatively flat or gently undulating land surface covered by *boulder clay, which was deposited by a retreating *glacier.

tillage The cultivation of land, particularly through ploughing, preparing the soil for sowing and raising crops, and weeding. See also CONSERVATION TILLAGE.

tillite A lithified deposit of *boulder clay or *till.

tilth The physical condition of a soil that determines its suitability for plant growth, and depends upon texture, structure, consistency, and the amount of *pore space.

timber 1. A general term for forests or other clusters of trees. 2. (lumber) Wood or wood products that are used for construction.

timber belt See WINDBREAK.

timber line A line that marks the altitudinal limit of trees that are in a *closed canopy and grow erect and tall. It occurs below the *tree line proper, and is commonly depressed to below its natural level by fires caused by human activities.

timber stand A community (*stand) of trees of similar species, size, and age.

timberland *Forestland that produces or is capable of producing crops of industrial wood. Previously known as commercial forestland.

time lag See LAG.

time of travel The time it takes for *ground-water to move a given horizontal distance.

time scale The division of geological history into eras, periods, and epochs, usually on the basis of *stratigraphy and *palaeontology.

time zone A region across which clocks are set to the same time. The 360° circumference of the Earth is divided into 24 time zones on the basis of *longitude, each one roughly 15° wide and defined as one hour different from the adjacent time zone. The *International Date Line marks the cross-over from one day to the next.

time zoning A particular form of land use *zoning that allows a particular activity in a particular place only for a defined period of time, after which it becomes illegal.

timeline The sequence of events over time.

Times Beach A town near St Louis, Missouri, that was bought in its entirety in February 1983 by the federal government and declared unfit for human habitation. In the 1970s chemical wastes mixed with used oil had been spread to control dust on dirt and gravel roads. Severe flooding in December 1982 exposed inhabitants to high levels of *dioxin, revealing extensive contamination of the *groundwater.

tissue culture A technique that is used to grow body tissue of a plant or animal outside the body (*in vitro*) in a culture medium, for example in test tubes.

titanium (Ti) A lightweight non-ferrous metal element that is very strong, non-reactive and does not cause allergic reactions in humans.

tjaele (frost table) A frozen surface at the base of the *active layer, which moves downwards as thaw occurs. The tjaele should not be confused with the upper limit of *permafrost, the permafrost table.

TLV *See* THRESHOLD LIMIT VALUE.

TM *See* THEMATIC MAPPER.

TMDL *See* TOTAL MAXIMUM DAILY LOAD.

TNC *See* NATURE CONSERVANCY, THE.

TNT *See* TRINITROTOLUENE.

toad Any of various semiaquatic and terrestrial *amphibians that have stout bodies, dry skin, no tail, and long back limbs for leaping. *Contrast* FROG.

tolerable soil loss The amount of *soil that can be lost by *accelerated erosion over 100 years without significant or permanent reduction of soil productivity.

tolerance The ability of an *organism to survive exposure to potentially harmful amounts of a substance without showing an adverse effect.

tolerance limit The limit to which an *organism can withstand changes in the environment (such as exposure to a potentially harmful *pollutant). *See also* LIMITING FACTOR.

tolerant Not sensitive to adverse environmental conditions (such as shade or drought) and thus able to withstand them. *Contrast* INTOLERANT.

toluene A colourless, flammable liquid that is derived from *petroleum or *coal tar, and is used as a solvent for gums and lacquers and in high-octane fuels. *See also* TRINITROTOLUENE.

tombolo A coastal depositional landform (*bar) that grows by *longshore drift to join a small island with another island, or with the mainland.

TOMS *See* TOTAL OZONE MAPPING SPECTROMETER.

tonne *See* METRIC TON.

top carnivore The creature occupying the highest *trophic level in a *food web (such as a lion). It is generally not consumed by other organisms whilst it is alive.

topogenous mire A type of *bog that forms under climatic conditions of reduced rainfall, with consequent lower humidity and summer drought, which restrict the growth of wetland vegetation to areas where precipitation is concentrated (e.g. valley bottoms).

topographic map A map that shows the *topography of an area, usually by means of *contour lines.

topography The character of the surface of an area, particularly its *relief and the position of its features.

toposequence *See* CATENA.

topsoil The upper layer within a *soil profile (comprising the *A-horizon and *B-horizon), which normally contains *organic matter, in which plants grow.

tor A rocky outcrop or hill. The distinctive granite tors on Dartmoor in Devon, England, are believed to have been formed by the *chemical decomposition of *granite under *tropical climates during the *Palaeogene period and subsequent erosion of the debris.

Torino scale A ten-point scale for assessing the risk of an *asteroid or *comet hitting the Earth; the higher the Torino value the greater the risk. The scale is given in Appendix 6.

tornado (twister) A violent storm with extremely high wind speeds in the form of a rapidly rotating column of air. Tornadoes can form when a *supercell develops in a massive *cumulonimbus cloud and begins to rotate, forming a *mesocyclone. The rotation then extends downwards, becoming narrower and intensifying through the conservation of angular momentum as it emerges below the cloud base. The funnel is visible because the low pressure causes moisture to condense around the core. The funnel becomes a tornado when it touches the ground (and a waterspout if it touches a lake or the sea).

tornado advisory A notification issued to the public and emergency and other agencies within a designated area when atmospheric conditions are such that tornadoes could occur.

tornado scale See FUJITA SCALE.

tornado warning A *warning that is issued to warn the public and emergency and other agencies when a *tornado is imminent or is occurring.

tornado watch A *watch that is issued to the public and emergency and other agencies when atmospheric conditions are favourable for producing *tornadoes. *Contrast* TORNADO WARNING.

torpor A dormant state.

torrent 1. A very fast-moving stream of water. 2. A heavy downpour of rain that may cause flooding.

Torrey Canyon A large *oil tanker that sank and broke apart off southwest England in 1967 and caused a large *oil spill that polluted the *sea, *coastline, and marine *food chain.

total dissolved solids (TDS, dissolved solids) The amount of dissolved substances (such as *salts or *minerals) in a sample of water, which reflects *salinity and is measured by *electrical conductivity.

total economic value The overall economic *value of a particular *natural resource,

taking into account both use and non-use values.

total exchange capacity See CATION EXCHANGE CAPACITY.

total fertility rate A measure of *fertility, based on the average number of children in a family. See also REPLACEMENT-LEVEL FERTILITY.

total growth rate The net rate of growth of a particular population, which results from births, deaths, *immigration, and *emigration.

total maximum daily load (TMDL) A North American term for the amount of a particular *pollutant that a *waterbody can receive and still meet *water quality standards.

Total Ozone Mapping Spectrometer (TOMS) An instrument carried on a *NASA satellite that makes global measurements of atmospheric *ozone on a daily basis. Three TOMS are operational.

total quality management (TQM) An approach to *management that focuses on achieving a high quality product and customer satisfaction.

total resource management (stewardship management) An approach to *natural resource management in which all resources are managed as a whole, responsibly, and on a *sustainable basis.

total solids All of the *organic and *inorganic matter that is suspended or dissolved in water.

total suspended particles The particulate matter that is present in the air at a given place and time.

total suspended solids (TSS) A measure of the amount of *suspended solids that is present in *wastewater, *effluent, or a *waterbody, which can usually be removed by *filtration.

totally effluent free See ZERO DISCHARGE.

towering cumulus A tall *cumulus cloud (cumulus congestus, Cu_{con}) that extends through low and middle cloud levels, and that is likely to grow into *cumulonimbus.

town An *urban settlement with a fixed boundary that is smaller than a *city. The threshold size for distinguishing between a town and a city varies from country to country.

townscape The *landscape of a *town or built-up area.

toxaphene An *insecticide that was developed as a substitute for *DDT. It causes adverse health effects if it contaminates in domestic water supplies, and is *toxic to freshwater and marine aquatic life. It is a *critical pollutant whose use is now restricted in North America.

toxic Poisonous; harmful to living organisms.

toxic chemical A chemical that can cause severe illness, poisoning, birth defects, disease, or death when ingested, inhaled, or absorbed by living organisms, even at low doses.

toxic cloud A *plume of gases, *vapours, *fumes, or *aerosols in the air, which contains *toxic materials.

toxic colonialism General name for the export, usually by shipping, of *toxic wastes to a weaker or poorer nation.

toxic concentration The *concentration at which a particular substance produces a *toxic effect.

toxic dose The *dose level at which a particular substance produces a *toxic effect.

toxic emission The release of *toxic materials into the air or water or onto the land.

toxic pollutant Any *pollutant that is listed as *toxic by a national agency, usually because it can cause death, disease, or birth defects in organisms that ingest or absorb it.

Toxic Release Inventory (TRI) A database of *toxic releases in the USA which is compiled from *SARA reports.

toxic site A site where *toxic wastes have been dumped or released, which has been designated for cleanup.

toxic substance Any material that can cause illness, death, disease, or birth defects when organisms are exposed to it, even in very low quantities.

Toxic Substance Control Act (TSCA) (1976) US legislation that seeks to ensure that the impacts of chemical substances on human health and the *environment are identified (by the *Environmental Protection Agency) and properly controlled before those materials are made available in the market, in order to protect people and the environment.

toxic waste Any waste that is poisonous to humans, animals, or plants. *Contrast* HAZARDOUS WASTE.

toxicant Any *poison or *toxic substance that may injure an *organism exposed to it. *See also* TOXIN.

toxicity The degree to which a particular substance is harmful or poisonous. *See also* ACUTE TOXICITY; CHRONIC TOXICITY.

toxicity assessment The process of defining the nature of injuries that may be caused to an *organism by *exposure to a given *toxic substance, and how these are affected by the time and *concentration of exposure.

toxicity test A controlled laboratory test to determine the *toxicity of a substance, using living organisms.

toxicological disaster An environmental *disaster caused by the large-scale, accidental release of a *toxic substance into the air, soil, or water, which damages organisms and *environmental systems.

toxicological profile The detailed analysis and description of a *toxic substance in order to determine safe levels of *exposure.

toxicology The study of the effects of poisons or *toxic substances on living organisms.

toxification Poisoning.

toxin 1. A poisonous substance produced by an animal or plant. **2.** A substance produced by a micro-organism that is poisonous to plants or animals. *See also* TOXICANT.

TQM *See* TOTAL QUALITY MANAGEMENT.

trace A very small amount of a material, such as a concentration of less than one to ten parts per million.

trace element *See* MICRONUTRIENT.

trace gas A *gas (e.g. *ammonia, *nitrogen dioxide, *sulphur dioxide, and *hydrogen sulphide) that is present in the *atmosphere in only small amounts, either because of its very *reactive nature or because it is produced or emitted at a very low rate. Many are *greenhouse gases.

trace metal A *metal (such as *cadmium, *copper, *chromium, *mercury, *nickel, *lead, and *zinc) that is naturally found in extremely small quantities in animal and plant cells and tissue but is necessary for growth.

tracer Any substance (such as *radioactive isotopes and certain dyes) that is used to find out how something else moves through an *organism or an *environmental system.

traction A process of river *bedload movement that involves the rolling or sliding of particles (coarse *sand and *gravel) along the bed of the river.

tractor logging A method of *logging in which *timber is dragged or carried by tractor from where it is cut to a collecting point.

tradable emission permit (tradable permit) In *greenhouse gas *emissions trading, an authorization that allows an emitter to emit a specified number of tonnes of emission within a given period of time. This allow emitters to determine the most economic way of covering their emissions, including buying additional permits, selling excess permits, and/or taking actions to reduce emissions.

tradable permit *See* TRADABLE EMISSION PERMIT.

trade The commercial exchange (buying and selling) of goods and services.

trade wind A major *wind belt that circles the Earth, beyond the *equatorial low pressure zone up to about 30° latitude in each *hemisphere, in which the prevailing winds blow towards the equator, from the northeast in the northern hemisphere and from the southeast in the southern hemisphere. *See also* INTER-TROPICAL CONVERGENCE ZONE.

trade-off An exchange that occurs as a compromise.

traditional agriculture *Agriculture that is based on traditional farming practices such as *crop rotation, use of animal *manures instead of chemical *fertilizers, and use of animal power rather than machines.

traditional knowledge (indigenous knowledge) The body of knowledge and beliefs that is handed down from generation to generation, within communities.

traditional resource rights The bundle of rights associated with long-term *natural resource use within traditional communities, which includes *intellectual property rights, human rights, land rights, and religious rights.

Tragedy of the Commons The title of a parable told in *Two Lectures on the Checks to Population* published in 1833 by the English economist William Forster Lloyd (1795-1852) and revived in a paper published in 1968 in *Science* magazine (13 December, Vol. 162, pp. 1243-8) by American biologist Garrett Hardin (1915-2003), in which Hardin discusses present-day attitudes towards the environment as being similar to how medieval villagers viewed common grazing land: all of the herdsmen had a right of access to the common pasture that (in those pre-enclosure times) had no field boundaries and was open to all. Each herdsman would be inclined to graze as many cows as possible on the common land, because that way he would get the maximum return. Such an arrangement, of use without restriction, would work well so long as the number of people and cattle remained below the *carrying capacity of the common land (perhaps because of disease and poaching). Once the carrying capacity is exceeded, each cow gets relatively less grass to eat so its yield declines, and *overgrazing decreases *environmental quality and leads to *soil erosion. Because each person is trying to maximize their income, they are all trapped in a system that can tolerate only certain levels of use, competing against each other for a larger share of the available resources (space and grass in this case). As Hardin concludes, 'each man is locked into a system that compels him to increase his herd without limit — in a world that is limited. Ruin is the destination toward which all men rush, each pursuing his own best interest in a society that believes in the freedom of the commons. Freedom in a commons brings ruin to all.' The 'Tragedy of the Commons' analogy applies just as well to common property resources, including the *atmosphere, the *oceans, and *wilderness. *See also* SUSTAINABLE DEVELOPMENT.

(((()))) SEE WEB LINKS

• Full text of 'The Tragedy of the Commons'.

trail A North American term for a relatively narrow path that is designed for use by pedestrians, horse riders, and/or off-road vehicles; a designated corridor that is not classified as a highway, road, or street.

trait A genetically inherited feature of an organism. *See also* GENETIC ANALYSIS; PHENOTYPE.

traitor technology (genetic use restriction technology) In *genetic engineering, the use of an external chemical to switch a plant's genetic traits on or off. *See also* TERMINATOR TECHNOLOGY.

tramp species *Species that have been spread around the world inadvertently by human commerce. For example, *Sargassum* *muticum* (japweed or strangleweed) was inadvertently introduced into British coastal waters, probably with the importation of the Japanese oyster (*Crassostrea gigas*); it clogs pipes and fouls outboard engines. *Eichhornia crassipes* (water hyacinth), taken to the USA from Venezuela by Japanese exhibitors at the 1884 Cotton Exposition in New Orleans, escaped and is now a serious weed of many rivers in low latitudes throughout the world. The brown rat (*Rattus norvegicus*), originally from south-east Asia, and the house mouse (*Mus musculus*), originally from the Russian–Turkish border region, are well-known animal examples.

trample To walk on and flatten.

trampling Physical damage to plants and/or soil that is caused by many people or animals walking over it.

Trans-Alaska Pipeline An *oil pipeline that runs 1200 km from *oil wells at Prudhoe Bay in the north to the port of Valdez in the south, crossing large areas of *permafrost by being raised above the ground.

trans-basin diversion *See* INTERBASIN TRANSFER.

trans-boundary pollution *See* TRANS-FRONTIER POLLUTION.

Transcendentalism A literary and philosophical movement that was begun during the early 19th century in New England by Ralph Waldo *Emerson and others. It was a reaction against the rationality of the Enlightenment movement, was strongly influenced by the Romantic movement, emphasized the essential unity of all creation and the inherent goodness of humans. Transcendentalists believed that insight would reveal more about fundamental truths than would logic and experience, and emphasized nature as a source of human inspiration. Transcendentalism played an important part in the emergence of the *environmental movement in the USA during the early 20th century, through such writers as Emerson and *Thoreau. *See also* ROMANTICISM.

transcurrent fault *See* STRIKE-SLIP FAULT.

transect A (usually straight) line on the ground along which observations are made at some (usually regular) interval.

transform fault A special type of *strike-slip fault which forms the boundary between two moving *crustal plates, usually along an offset segment of a *mid-oceanic ridge.

transform plate boundary A junction between adjacent *crustal plates which are moving alongside and parallel to one another.

transformation Progressive change that removes evidence of an earlier state, such as the conversion of land from one use to another (such as *deforestation).

transformer A device that is used to raise or lower the voltage of an electric current in distribution or transmission lines.

trans-frontier pollution (international pollution, trans-boundary pollution) The transport of a pollutant pollutant (such as *acid rain) across national or state borders by natural processes (the movement of air or water). *Contrast* INTERSTATE POLLUTION.

transgenic Containing *genes from another *species, which have probably been introduced using *recombinant DNA technology. *See also* GENE SPLICING.

transgression A rise in *sea level relative to the land. *See also* SEA LEVEL CHANGE.

transhumance A type of *pastoralism in which people and animals move seasonally in search of *pasture, with winters usually spent in snow-free lowlands and summers spent in the cooler uplands. *See also* NOMADISM.

transient Lasting only for a short period of time.

transition The change from one state to another.

transition zone The outer area of a *biosphere reserve where reserve management is broadened to make it compatible with local socio-economic development.

transitional nation A country whose *economy is changing to advanced industrial and agricultural practices. *Contrast* DEVELOPED COUNTRY; DEVELOPING COUNTRY.

transitional zone A zone in which populations from two or more adjacent *plant communities meet and overlap.

translocated herbicide *See* SYSTEMIC HERBICIDE.

translocated species A *native species that has been introduced into suitable habitats within its own country, having previously been excluded by natural barriers. *See also* INTRODUCED SPECIES.

translocation 1. In *genetics, the switching of a segment of a *chromosome to another chromosome. 2. In biology, the movement of water, nutrients, or chemicals within a plant. 3. In ecology, the deliberate movement of whole habitats or populations of species, by people, from one place to another.

transmissible disease A *disease that is transmitted from one individual to another by *infection, through physical contact.

transmission line A pipeline that moves a liquid or gas, or wires or cables that move electric power from place to place.

transmissivity The rate at which *groundwater can flow through an *aquifer.

transmutation The conversion of one *element into another by a process that takes place in the *nucleus, such as the change from one *isotope of an element into another one by irradiating or bombarding it with *radioactive particles.

transnational corporation A company that is controlled from its home country but has large operations in many different countries. *Contrast* MULTINATIONAL CORPORATION.

transpiration The *evaporation of water from plants through tiny holes (*stomata) in their leaves and stems (lenticels).

transplant To transfer a plant from one location to another, or transfer an organ from one individual to another.

transport To move or carry.

transportation The activity of moving things from one location to another, for example using vehicle to *transport people or goods.

Transportation Equity Act for the 21st Century (TEA-21) (1998) US legislation that replaced the *Intermodal Surface Transportation Efficiency Act, and authorized and funded highway, highway safety, transit, and other surface transportation programmes from 1998 to 2003.

transportation sector A North American term for all of the private and public vehicles that move people and commodities, including cars, trucks, buses, motorcycles, railways (including trains), aircraft, ships, barges, and natural gas pipelines. *Contrast* COMMERCIAL SECTOR; INDUSTRIAL SECTOR; RESIDENTIAL SECTOR.

transuranic elements Elements beyond *uranium in the periodic table, i.e. elements with an atomic number higher than 92. All are radioactive and all were first discovered in the laboratory, although neptunium (93) and *plutonium (94) were later found to occur naturally.

transuranic waste (TRU) *Waste that arises mainly from weapons production, and consists of clothing, tools, rags, and similar items that are contaminated with small amounts of *radioactive elements (mostly *plutonium) with *half-lives greater than 20 years.

transverse dune A relatively straight, long *dune that is oriented at right angles to the prevailing wind or current.

trash Common term for *refuse.

trash-to-energy plan Burning *solid waste in order to produce *energy.

travel corridor The strip of land beside a *road or *trail that is normally visible from it.

travel cost method In *economic evaluation, a method for determining the value of things (such as recreational resources) that are generally not bought and sold, based on the assumption that the costs met by individuals who travel to a particular site can be used as surrogate prices.

travertine *See* TUFA.

trawl A type of *fishing net that is towed in the water or on the sea-bed behind a vessel. It has a wide mouth and tapers to a small, pointed end.

treated wastewater *Wastewater that has been processed (physically, chemically, or biologically) in order to reduce its potential to cause health problems.

treatment Any physical, chemical, or biological process that makes a hazardous substance less hazardous.

Treatment, Storage, and Disposal Facility (TSDF) A site in the USA that is regulated by the *Environmental Protection Agency, where a *hazardous substance is treated, stored, or disposed.

treaty A formal, binding, written agreement between two or more countries, arrived at by negotiation.

tree A large, *perennial, woody plant that usually has one main trunk, a number of branches, and a *crown of foliage.

tree cavity A hollow in a tree that provides a resting or nesting place for *wildlife.

tree dieback (forest death) The large-scale death of trees that is caused by, or associated with, *air pollution.

tree farm A *stand of planted trees that are of the same age and species. When mature they will usually be harvested by *clearcutting, followed by replanting.

tree farming (farm forestry) Any *agroforestry practice that includes management of *trees within the *farmland.

tree line The upper limit of normal tree growth in mountains or high *latitudes, above which the climate is too cold or windy for trees to grow.

tree ring A *growth ring in the cross section of a tree trunk, which indicates growth during one year. The number of rings corresponds to the age of the tree, and variations in ring width reflect the pattern of weather during the life of the tree. *See also* DENDROCHRONOLOGY; DENDROCLIMATOLOGY.

trellis drainage pattern A *drainage pattern in which tributaries join at high angles, often approaching right angles, which is common in areas with rocks of different strengths (thus resistance to erosion) and in areas with regular series of folds (*anticlines and *synclines).

trench 1. A long, narrow ditch, often dug either to improve drainage or to install a pipe. **2.** *See* OCEAN TRENCH.

TRI *See* TOXIC RELEASE INVENTORY.

triallate A selective *thiocarbamate herbicide used to control grasses in a variety of crops. Depending on the crop, it is applied before or after planting. It is very slightly toxic to humans if ingested, but non-toxic by inhalation or skin exposure. It is highly toxic to fish and other aquatic animals.

Triassic The first period of *geological time in the *Mesozoic era, between 251 and 200 million years ago, when the supercontinent Pangaea straddled the equator and large predatory *reptiles (*dinosaurs) evolved.

 SEE WEB LINKS
• The Triassic.

tribal peoples *See* INDIGENOUS PEOPLES.

tributary A *stream or *river that flows into another river or a *lake.

tributyltin (TBT, organotin) A *synthetic *organic compound based on tin, which is sprayed on the hulls of ships to control the growth of barnacles and other organisms and is extremely *toxic to *marine life. Its use has been banned by the *International Maritime Organisation.

trichloromethane *See* CHLOROFORM.

2,4,5-trichlorophenoxyacetic acid (2,4, 5-T) A synthetic *auxin used as a *herbicide to defoliate broadleaved weeds. It is moderately toxic to humans, but the manufacturing process left it with traces of 2,3,7,8-tetrachlorodibenzo-*p*-dioxin (TCDD), a highly toxic *dioxin. 2,4,5-T was widely used until 1985, when it was banned in the United States, followed by its phasing-out in other countries.

trickle irrigation *See* DRIP IRRIGATION.

trickling filter A *wastewater treatment system in which the water is trickled over a bed of stones that are covered with *bacteria. The bacteria break down the *organic waste and produce clean water.

trilobite A class of marine *arthropod with three segments to its body. Trilobites were abundant in the *Palaeozoic era but became extinct during the *Permian.

trinitrotoluene (TNT) An explosive consisting of a pale yellow crystalline compound ($C_7H_5N_3O_6$) that is a *flammable and *toxic derivative of *toluene.

triphenyltin *See* TRIBUTYLTIN.

trivial name *See* LATIN NAME.

troglobion *See* TROGLOBITE.

troglobite (troglobion) An animal that lives its entire life within a cave and is specifically adapted to life in total darkness.

troglodyte A cave-dweller.

trophic Relating to food or nutrition, or to levels in a *food chain.

trophic level A level in a *food chain that is defined by the method of obtaining food and defines the number of steps (energy transfers) up from the original source of energy, from *primary producer, to *primary consumer, *secondary consumer, and *tertiary consumer (see Fig. 20).

Trophic levels and energy flow

Fig. 20 Trophic level

trophic state/status The degree of biological *productivity of a *waterbody, which largely reflects the availability of *nutrients within it. It may be *oligotrophic (nutrient poor), *mesotrophic (moderately productive), or *eutrophic (very productive and fertile).

trophic structure The organization of feeding relationships in an *ecosystem into the different levels in a *food chain, such as *producers (plants), *primary consumers (herbivores), and *secondary consumers (carnivores).

Tropic of Cancer The line of *latitude that runs 23°27' north of the *equator, which is the farthest north that the *Sun can appear directly overhead, and marks the northern limit of the *tropics.

Tropic of Capricorn The line of *latitude that runs 23°27' south of the *equator, which is the farthest south that the *Sun can appear directly overhead, and marks the southern limit of the *tropics.

tropical Relating to, situated in, or characteristic of the *tropics, the region on either side of the *equator, between the *Tropic of Cancer and

the *Tropic of Capricorn, in which climate varies relatively little from season to season.

tropical air mass A warm/hot *air mass that forms in the *tropics.

tropical climate A *climate zone which covers much of the *equatorial and *tropical regions, in which temperatures remain high throughout the year and precipitation can be very high at least during part of the year. There are five different climate zones within the tropics: *equatorial wet, *tropical wet-and-dry, *monsoon, *tropical steppe and desert, and *west coast desert.

tropical continental air mass An *air mass that develops over large land masses in *subtropical latitudes, contains hot dry air, and brings clear skies and low *relative humidity.

tropical cyclone An extensive area of low surface pressure that develops in the *tropics and matures to become the biggest and most violent type of atmospheric disturbance on Earth. It develops only if the sea-surface temperature is at least 27°C over a large area, if there is an area of low pressure within 5°

latitude of the equator, and if there is no *wind shear at higher levels to disorganize the structure of the storm. A typical tropical cyclone has a diameter of 150–1500 km, is circular in shape, and has a calm area (the *eye) of warm, subsiding air at the centre which is surrounded by a band of powerful up-draught (the *eye wall), having great turbulence, thick cloud cover, and torrential rainfall. Further concentric bands of cloud surround the eye wall, weakening with distance from the core and separated by bands of relatively clear skies. Strong winds spiral inwards towards the centre of the storm (down the pressure gradient); this wind blows anticlockwise in the northern hemisphere and clockwise in the southern hemisphere. The strong winds cause extensive damage. The word hurricane is used in the North Atlantic Ocean, Caribbean Sea, Gulf of Mexico, and eastern North Pacific Ocean; a tropical cyclone is known as a typhoon in the western Pacific and a cyclone in the Indian Ocean. The storm becomes a tropical cyclone when its sustained wind speeds exceed 120 km h^{-1}.

tropical depression An area of low pressure that develops in the *tropics through the convergence of air at low level.

tropical desert A *desert *biome that is hot throughout the year, such as the Sahara.

tropical disturbance A vigorous low-pressure system that develops in the *tropics, is not linked to a weather *front, and is likely to grow into a *tropical storm.

tropical forest Forest that grows in *tropical climates with high temperatures and generally high annual rainfall. The two main types are *tropical rainforest and *monsoon forest.

tropical maritime air mass An *air mass that develops over *tropical or *subtropical oceans, contains hot moist air, and often brings convectional rain in summer and *drizzle in winter.

tropical montane forest Two distinct formations, lower and upper montane forest, each of which has a characteristic structure, *physiognomy, and flora; the two are usually sharply bounded. Lower tropical montane forest is tall. Upper tropical montane forest usually comprises trees 10–12 m high in a single stratum. When their trunks and boughs are misshapen and covered in mosses, *lichens, and liverworts this is *mossy forest, which coincides with belts of mist and cloud at heights of 2000–3000 m. Above the cloud zone (e.g. in New Guinea), the trees are taller and the 'mosses' less in evidence. On the highest mountains, *tropical subalpine forest occurs as a further zone.

tropical rainforest clearance *Deforestation of *tropical rainforests that is caused by many things, including over-intensive *shifting cultivation, the collection of *fuelwood for cooking and heating and for making charcoal, encroachment and clearance by landless peasant farmers, clearance for *pasture or *crops, commercial *logging, *grazing, road construction, ranching, mining, and fire. Ecologists are concerned at the pace and pattern of the clearance of tropical rainforest, which once covered about a tenth of the Earth's surface. More than 40% of the rainforest has been cleared since the 1940s. Overall, about a quarter of the loss is due to forestry, but the balance of factors varies from place to place. Much of the wood felled from rainforests is destined for the international timber market, where tropical hardwood commands a high price. Environmentalists argue that if clearance continues at recent rates all of the world's primary (undisturbed) rainforest is likely to disappear or be damaged by 2020. This would mean the loss of an irreplaceable biological asset, because rainforests contain about half of all the wood growing on the Earth and at least 40% of all known species of plants and animals. They are amongst the most diverse and complex *ecosystems on the planet. As well as a significant loss of *biodiversity, clearance of rainforests causes the loss of valuable natural resources including hardwoods (such as mahogany, rosewood, and teak) and tree products (such as quinine, vegetable gums, and rubber). Tropical rainforest clearance may also contribute to the *greenhouse effect and *global warming, by removing an important *carbon sink. Various attempts have been made to conserve the remaining rainforests. For example, some governments (including those of Costa Rica, Panama, Brazil, and the Democratic Republic of the Congo) have designated forest reserves to conserve representative tracts of this important biome, and some endangered tropical hardwood species have been listed in the *Convention on International Trade in Endangered Species (CITES). In recent years the rate of clearance has slowed. At present it amounts to about 54 000 km^2 a year. In the period 2000–2005 the annual loss was: Africa 2200 km^2 (1.0% of the total area); Asia 18 700 km^2 (2.0%); America 31 000 km^2 (0.6%); Madagascar (400 km^2 (0.3%); and Papua New Guinea 1400 km^2 (0.5%).

t

tropical seasonal forest A *tropical forest *biome comprising a mixture of forest, open woodland, and grassy *savanna that grows in a hot climate that has distinct wet and dry seasons.

tropical steppe and desert climate zone A very hot, dry *tropical climate zone beyond the *tropical wet-and-dry climate zone, at higher *latitudes, dominated by relatively stable subtropical high pressure cells throughout the year. Many of the world's great deserts (including the Sahara, the Sonoran, and the Great Australian) are found in this climate zone.

tropical storm A *tropical depression that has deepened and that produces winds of 61-120 km h^{-1}. Tropical storms are given names that they retain if they grow into *tropical cyclones.

tropical subalpine rainforest A formation of low, stunted trees with tiny leaves which is found just below the *tree line on the very tallest mountains in the humid tropics.

tropical wave *See* EASTERLY WAVE.

tropical wet climate A *tropical climate with enough rainfall to allow a dense *tropical rainforest to grow.

tropical wet-and-dry climate A *tropical climate zone that lies outside the *tropical wet climate and has a summer wet season and a winter dry season. This promotes the growth of *savanna landscapes, dominated by scattered trees within extensive *grassland.

tropics The part of the Earth's surface that lies between the *Tropic of Cancer and the *Tropic of Capricorn, which has a hot climate and no cold season. In America this zone is known as the *neotropics and in Africa and South East Asia as the *palaeotropics.

tropopause The boundary in the *atmosphere between the *troposphere and the *stratosphere, which is located at an altitude of about 16 km in the *tropics, 11 km in middle latitudes, and 8 km at the poles.

troposphere The portion of the *atmosphere closest to the Earth's surface, which extends to the *tropopause, and throughout which temperature decreases with increasing height (*see* LAPSE RATE), except locally in *temperature inversions. The average temperature at the tropopause is -65°C over the equator (where the tropopause is highest), -55°C in middle latitudes, and -30°C over the poles. Vertical *convection currents cause the air to be turbulent and well mixed. The turbulent transport of heat combined with the vertical transport of heat by convection and the transport of *water through *evaporation and *condensation mean the troposphere contains almost all of the atmosphere's moisture and ensures it is the region in which all weather phenomena occur. Because air is compressible, the troposphere holds about 90% of the mass of the atmosphere, and about 50% of the atmospheric mass is in the lowest 6 km.

tropospheric ozone *Ozone that is located in the *troposphere. It is created by air pollution through the interaction of *nitrogen oxides, *volatile organic compounds, and sunlight, is a significant *greenhouse gas, and causes widespread human health problems via *photochemical smog. *Contrast* STRATOSPHERIC OZONE.

trough 1. The lowest point in a wave of air or water; the opposite of *ridge. **2.** A tongue-like protrusion of low atmospheric pressure into a region of higher pressure. **3.** A meander towards the equator in the *polar front jet stream. **4. (equatorial trough)** A synonym for the *Intertropical Convergence Zone.

troughing The deepening of a centre of low pressure in the atmosphere.

Trout Unlimited A US-based non-profit conservation organization that is committed to conserving, restoring, and managing the country's trout and salmon fisheries and their *watersheds.

TRU *See* TRANSURANIC WASTE.

true cost The sum of the *market and non-market (*social) costs associated with the production and use of goods and services.

true north The direction of the Earth's actual *North Pole, as opposed to *magnetic north.

true south The direction of the Earth's actual *South Pole, as opposed to *magnetic south.

truncated spur A former headland in a *river valley which has been sliced off by an advancing valley *glacier.

trunk The main stem of a tree.

TSCA *See* TOXIC SUBSTANCE CONTROL ACT.

TSS *See* TOTAL SUSPENDED SOLIDS.

TROPICAL RAINFOREST (EQUATORIAL FOREST, SELVA)

A *rainforest *biome which is found in the hot, wet *tropical climate zone, mostly between latitudes 5° and 10°. In this humid zone temperatures remain uniformly high throughout the year. There are high *diurnal variations in temperature, each month receives at least 60 mm of rainfall (so there is no dry season), annual rainfall usually exceeds 1500 mm, and there are periodic torrential downpours accompanied by thunder and lightning. The rainforest environment is hot, wet, and humid. Ecologists also believe that it has been remarkably stable over exceedingly long periods of time. This has encouraged plants and animals to adapt to their environment, which in turn has promoted *speciation and the evolution of unparalleled *biodiversity. More than half of the remaining rainforests are in Central and South America (particularly in Amazonia), and the rest are in South East Asia (particularly Sumatra, Borneo, and Papua New Guinea) and in Africa (particularly the Congo Basin). The forest is dominated by tall *evergreen trees and dense *undergrowth and it usually has very distinct *stratification. The vegetation is dominated by tall broadleaved *evergreen trees, *epiphytes (plants such as mosses which grow on other plants but are not parasitic on them), and lianas (climbing vines) and giant ferns. Rainforest trees are closely spaced, and they are often tied together by lianas and epiphytes. Most are tall and straight, have very shallow root systems, and are anchored to the ground by a series of buttresses. Many different tree species are present in even quite small areas of rainforest. Animal life within the rainforest is rich and varied. It includes forest elephants (whose ivory tusks are highly prized by poachers), many different reptiles (including snakes, alligators and crocodiles, turtles, and lizards), a range of primates (including monkeys and apes), some predatory big cats, and a huge variety of birds and insects. Contrary to popular belief (because they look so abundant and productive) rainforests grow on very poor soils. Most of the *nutrients within the rainforest ecosystem are stored within the *biomass rather than in the soils, and the decomposer part of the *food web (which includes fungi, bacteria, and insects) rapidly breaks down organic material including dead trees, broken limbs and branches, leaf litter, and dead animals. The nutrients are quickly recycled through the forest soil into tree roots, so that forest soils have little organic matter and only a very thin cover of leaf litter. Because the forest soils contain so few nutrients, they are not suitable for continuous cultivation after the forest has been cleared. Rapid *leaching caused by heavy tropical rainfall makes the problem even worse. Soil productivity quickly declines (after between three and six years) and cultivated areas are then abandoned. *Secondary succession leads to the growth of scrubby vegetation, and then to *savanna (if the cleared area is large) or secondary rainforest (if it is a relatively small patch which can revegetate and self-repair). *See also* TROPICAL RAINFOREST CLEARANCE; TROPICAL FOREST.

tsunami A giant *wave (a seismic wave not a tidal wave) that is triggered by a submarine *earthquake or *volcanic eruption and moves across the ocean at a speed of more than 700 km h^{-1}. The word tsunami is Japanese for 'harbour wave', and tsunamis cause widespread damage when they reach the coast. In the open ocean these giant waves have long wavelengths (up to several hundred kilometres) and small heights (less than a metre). When they reach shallow water at the *coast they slow down and build up, which creates large, powerful waves that can sweep inland and cause widespread damage and destruction, with great loss of life.

tufa (travertine) A light-coloured *limestone that is formed in caves and around hot springs where *groundwater saturated in *carbonate is exposed to the air.

tuff A general term for an *extrusive *volcanic rock formed of compacted *volcanic ash and dust. *See also* PUMICE.

tumour Any abnormal mass of cells that results from uncontrolled cell division and multiplication, and can be *benign (not cancerous) or *malignant (cancerous).

tundra A treeless *biome found at high latitudes in *arctic and *subarctic regions that have long freezing winters and brief summers and where grasses, mosses, lichen, low shrubs, and a few flowering plants survive. The land is usually a flat or gently rolling plain, with black soil and permanently frozen subsoil (*permafrost), and is usually very wet.

tunnel In *mining, a lateral or horizontal underground passage that is dug to reach a *vein or mineral deposit.

turbidimeter A device that measures the density of *suspended solids in a liquid, based on the cloudiness of the mixture.

turbidite A deposit of sediment from a *turbidity current.

turbidity The degree of cloudiness in water (or air) that is caused by the presence of *suspended solids.

turbidity current A dense, flowing mass of water and *suspended sediment, that is heavier than clear water and thus flows downhill along the bottom of the sea or a lake, often at high speed. *See also* DENSITY CURRENT.

turbine A device in which blades on a wheel are turned by the force of moving water or steam. The blades are connected by a shaft to a generator in order to produce electricity.

turbulence Unstable flow of a gas or liquid, or instability in the *atmosphere that produces *gusts and eddies.

turbulent flow A *flow type that involves mixing within moving air or water, caused by irregular *eddies. *Contrast* LAMINAR FLOW.

turbulent mixing The physical mixing of air or water by *turbulent flow.

turf The surface layer of *soil that includes a matted layer of *grass and grass roots. *See also* SWARD.

turgor The rigidity of a plant and its cells and organs, resulting from hydrostatic pressure exerted on the cell walls.

turnover (overturn) The process by which the water in a large body of *freshwater is completely mixed by circulation during *spring and *autumn. *See also* MIXING CYCLE.

turnover rate *See* RETENTION TIME.

tussock A clump of *grasses or *sedges that are bound together by their roots.

TVOC Total volatile organic compound. *See also* VOLATILE ORGANIC COMPOUND.

twilight *See* DUSK.

twilight zone *See* MESOPELAGIC.

twiner A *root climber plant that raises itself up by twisting itself around another upright plant. *Contrast* SCRAMBLER.

twister The popular name in the USA for a *tornado.

type locality The location of the first described specimen of a *species or *subspecies, or where a particular rock type, *stratigraphic unit, *fossil, or *mineral, was first identified.

typhoid fever An acute, highly infectious and often fatal disease caused by the typhoid bacillus (*Salmonella enteric*) which is transmitted by food or water contaminated by faeces from an infected person.

typhoon The name for a *severe storm or *hurricane in the western Pacific.

typicalness *See* REPRESENTATIVENESS.

t

ubiquitous Widely present, being or seeming to be everywhere.

Udall Scholarship The most prestigious scholarship awarded to undergraduate students in the USA, given to those 'who have demonstrated outstanding potential and a commitment to pursuing careers related to the environment'.

UK *See* UNITED KINGDOM.

UK Biodiversity Action Plan *See* BIODIVERSITY ACTION PLAN.

UKMET The medium-range numerical *weather prediction model that is used in the United Kingdom.

ultimate disposal The process of returning *waste materials to the environment in a form which will have the minimal *environmental impacts.

ultimate factor Aspects of the environment (such as food) that are directly important to the well-being and fitness of an *organism. *Contrast* PROXIMATE FACTOR.

Ultimate Resource A controversial book by Julian *Simon (1996) that attacks *neo-Malthusian thinking and supports continued population and economic growth, arguing that there are few physical limits to the availability of *natural resources or the ability of environmental systems to assimilate wastes.

ultisol A type (*order) of soil that develops in the *tropics and *subtropics. It is created largely by *chemical weathering, has more *clay in the *B-horizon than the *A-horizon, and has an *acid subsoil.

ultrabasic (ultramafic) Applied to an *igneous rock that has a relatively high content of *magnesium and *iron, but very little *silica.

ultraclean coal Coal that has been washed, ground into fine particles, then chemically treated to remove *sulphur, ash, and other substances.

ultramafic *See* ULTRABASIC.

ultraplankton Any *plankton organism that is less than two micrometres in size.

ultrasheltered In terms of *wave exposure, a fully enclosed *coast with a *fetch of up to a few hundred metres.

ultraviolet (UV) *Radiation from the Sun that is within the non-visible portion of the *electromagnetic spectrum, beyond violet light, with a *wavelength between 10 and 400 nanometres. It can be useful or potentially harmful, depending on its wavelength. Type A (UV-A) (315–400 nm) is generally beneficial to plants. UV-B (280–315 nm) induces the production of vitamin D in human skin and lack of exposure can lead to deficiency of this vitamin, but excessive exposure can cause a variety of skin problems (including sunburn, skin cancer, and premature aging) and cataracts in humans, and is directly affected by levels of *ozone in the atmosphere; a decrease in ozone levels leads to increased UV-B radiation on the ground.

umbrella species A species of plant or animal that has a large home *range and broad *habitat requirements, both of which overlap with other species, so that if it is given a large enough area for its own protection the other species will also benefit.

umbrisols Soils with a dark-coloured subsurface *soil horizon containing at least 1% organic matter or 0.6% organic carbon and with a base saturation of less than 50%. Umbrisols are a reference soil group in the *World Soil Classification.

UN *See* UNITED NATIONS.

unacceptable risk The level of *risk above which specific action by a manager or government is regarded as necessary in order to protect life and property, and to achieve stated

objectives. *Contrast* ACCEPTABLE RISK; AVOID-
ABLE RISK.

unavailable water Water that is held so
tightly in the *pores of the soil that it cannot
be taken up by plant roots. *Contrast* AVAILABLE
WATER.

unbuffered Lacking a resistance to change
in *pH, having a low *buffering capacity.

UNCBD *See* UNITED NATIONS FRAMEWORK
CONVENTION ON BIOLOGICAL DIVERSITY.

UNCCC *See* UNITED NATIONS FRAMEWORK
CONVENTION ON CLIMATE CHANGE.

UNCCD *See* UNITED NATIONS CONVENTION
TO COMBAT DESERTIFICATION.

UNCED *See* UNITED NATIONS CONFERENCE ON
ENVIRONMENT AND DEVELOPMENT.

UNCHE *See* UNITED NATIONS CONFERENCE
ON THE HUMAN ENVIRONMENT.

UNCLOS *See* UNITED NATIONS CONVENTION
ON THE LAW OF THE SEA.

UNCOD *See* UNITED NATIONS CONFERENCE
ON DESERTIFICATION.

unconfined aquifer An *aquifer that contains water which is not under pressure, so the
water level in a *well is the same as in the water
table outside the well.

unconformity A gap in the rock record (particularly within a *stratigraphic sequence) at
a particular place, caused by the *erosion of
existing rocks before younger rocks are subsequently deposited on top.

unconformity trap A *stratigraphic trap
formed by the folding, uplift, and *erosion of
porous *strata, followed by the deposition of
later beds that seal oil, gas, or water. Although
common structures, these traps contain only 4%
of the world's oil, perhaps because of losses that
occur during uplift and erosion.

unconsolidated Loose, separate, or unat-
tached, for example the individual particles in
a sediment such as *alluvium.

uncontrolled fire Any fire that threatens to
destroy life, property, or *natural resources.

unconventional oil *Natural resources
such as *shale oil and *tar sands that can be
liquefied and used like *oil.

unconventional pollutant *See* NON-
CRITERIA POLLUTANT.

UNCSD *See* UNITED NATIONS COMMISSION ON
SUSTAINABLE DEVELOPMENT.

UNCTAD *See* UNITED NATIONS CONFERENCE
ON TRADE AND DEVELOPMENT.

underburn A fire that can consume ground
vegetation but not *trees or *shrubs.

underfit stream *See also* MISFIT STREAM.

underground mining A technique for extracting *minerals that consists of subsurface
excavation with minimal disturbance of the
ground surface.

underground storage tank A large tank
buried underground, used for storing hazardous substances or petroleum products such
as *gasoline or heating oil. *See also* LEAKING
UNDERGROUND STORAGE TANK.

undergrowth *See* BRUSH.

undergrowth layer *See* UNDERSTOREY.

underplant To plant young trees or sow seed
under an existing *stand of vegetation.

understorey (undergrowth layer) The
plants beneath the *canopy in a stand of *stratified vegetation. *Contrast* OVERSTOREY.

underwood *See* BRUSH.

undesirable species Any species of plant
that is not desirable for a particular reason, for
example because it is unpalatable, poisonous,
or can injure animals.

undeveloped land *See* RAW LAND.

undiscovered resource A *natural resource that is assumed to exist, or has yet
to be thought about. *Contrast* UNIDENTIFIED
RESOURCE.

UNDP *See* UNITED NATIONS DEVELOPMENT
PROGRAMME.

unenclosed land Land that has not been
enclosed with a fence or wall.

UNEP *See* UNITED NATIONS ENVIRONMENT
PROGRAMME.

UNESCO *See* UNITED NATIONS EDUCATIONAL,
SCIENTIFIC AND CULTURAL ORGANIZATION.

uneven-aged stand A forest stand composed of trees of different ages and sizes, all

growing together. *Contrast* ALL-AGED STAND; EVEN-AGED STAND.

ungrazed Land or plants that have not been grazed by animals.

ungulate **1.** A *grazing animal (e.g. a cow, deer, bison, or sheep) that has hooves and in most cases is adapted for running. **2.** Hoof-like.

unidentified resource A *mineral resource that is assumed to be present within known geological areas, but has not yet been specifically located or described in detail. *Contrast* UNDISCOVERED RESOURCE.

UNIDO *See* UNITED NATIONS INDUSTRIAL DEVELOPMENT ORGANIZATION.

uniform effluent standard A pollution control *standard that is designed to regulate the discharge of *point sources of pollution by enforcing compliance with *effluent quality standards.

uniformitarianism The belief that the geological processes that have shaped the Earth through geological time are the same as those operating and observable today, that is they are uniform through time. *Contrast* CATASTROPHISM.

unimproved grassland *Grassland that has not been agriculturally improved by being treated with chemical *fertilizers or *herbicides, so it is usually rich in *wildlife.

unintended release Any non-deliberate release into the environment of *genetically modified organisms.

unique species A *native species that is found in only one place.

unit **1.** A single undivided whole (thing or person). **2.** A fixed quantity (for example of length, time, or value) that is used as a standard of measurement.

unit hydrograph *See* HYDROGRAPH.

United Kingdom (UK) The nation state that consists of England, Scotland, Wales and Northern Ireland.

United Nations (UN) An international organization of countries that was established in 1945 with 51 members, which by 2012 had expanded to 193 members. Its purpose is 'to preserve peace through international cooperation and collective security'.

(⊕) SEE WEB LINKS

• UN home page.

United Nations Commission on Sustainable Development (UNCSD) A commission of the *United Nations that was created in December 1992, as a result of the *United Nations Conference on Environment and Development, in order to monitor and report on implementation of the UNCED agreements at the local, national, regional, and international levels.

United Nations Conference on Desertification (UNCOD) A major international conference which met in Nairobi in August 1977, and agreed a Plan of Action to Combat Desertification which was designed to prevent and stop the advance of *desertification and, where possible, to reclaim desertified land for productive use.

United Nations Conference on the Human Environment (UNCHE) The first major international conference to address the relationships between human activities and the *environment, held in Stockholm, Sweden, in June 1972. It produced a set of principles in the Stockholm Declaration, led to the founding of the *United Nations Environment Programme, and was a catalyst for development of the modern *environmental movement. It was followed up in 1992 by the *United Nations Conference on Environment and Development.

United Nations Conference on Trade and Development (UNCTAD) An organization set up by the United Nations in 1964, which 'promotes the development-friendly integration of developing countries into the world economy . . . with a particular focus on ensuring that domestic policies and international action are mutually supportive in bringing about sustainable development'.

United Nations Convention Concerning the Protection of the World Cultural and Natural Heritage An international convention that was adopted in November 1972 and came into force in 1975, under which each state that signed it 'recognizes [its] duty of ensuring the identification, protection, conservation, presentation and transmission to future generations of the cultural and natural heritage'.

United Nations Convention on the Law of the Sea (UNCLOS) (1982) An international convention that came into force

u

UNITED NATIONS CONFERENCE ON ENVIRONMENT AND DEVELOPMENT (UNCED)

A major international conference that was held in Rio de Janeiro, Brazil, in June 1992 and is popularly known as the Earth Summit. The conference was the culmination of more than a decade of preparatory work, and it established the tone, pace, and direction of the international environmental agenda for the foreseeable future. The seeds for the Earth Summit were sown in Stockholm in 1972, where the first international *United Nations Conference on the Human Environment was held. A series of preparatory meetings were held between 1990 and 1992 in various countries, at which governments, *non-governmental organizations (NGOs), and expert scientists discussed and largely reached agreement on a series of basic documents which would be formally debated at Rio. Most (178) countries were represented and more than 100 heads of state attended the Rio summit. Five important agreements were reached: the *Rio Declaration on Environment and Development; *Agenda 21; a *United Nations Framework Convention on Biological Diversity; a *United Nations Framework Convention on Climate Change; and a *Statement of Forest Principles. Despite the huge amount of media coverage it attracted, and the promising tone of the conventions and other items which were agreed, the Rio Earth Summit has had a mixed reaction. *Environmentalists from *developed countries hailed the conference as the 'last chance to save the planet', whilst delegates from *developing countries saw it as an opportunity to redress long-standing economic grievances. Supporters argue that although the conference attracted a great deal of bad press coverage, and was widely criticized by environmental *pressure groups, it did mark a welcome and substantial change in international political attitudes towards the environment. They also applaud the recognition formally given at Rio of the need to tackle over-consumption in industrialized states, and *poverty and *resource scarcity in the developing world. Agenda 21 recognized that growth, the alleviation of poverty, *population policy, and *environmental protection were mutually reinforcing and supporting. Critics argue that whilst UNCED delivered an impressive number of international agreements on a variety of topics, it hardly began to address the fundamental driving forces of global environmental change—such as trade, population growth, and institutional change. They also point out that the legal agreements signed at Rio are relatively weak and lack binding commitments and timetables. On balance, even though some aims were not achieved at Rio, it was nonetheless an important step on the long-term path towards environmentally *sustainable development.

in 1994 and was designed 'to regulate all aspects of the resources of the sea and uses of the ocean'. Amongst other things, it introduced the concept of the 200-mile (322-km) *Exclusive Economic Zones.

United Nations Convention to Combat Desertification (UNCCD) (1992) An international convention that is designed to promote a new, integrated approach to the problem of land degradation in arid, semi-arid, and dry sub-humid areas, emphasizing action to promote *sustainable development at the community level.

United Nations Development Program (UNDP) The global development network set up by the United Nations in 1965, which operates by 'advocating for change and connecting countries to knowledge, experience and resources to help people build a better life', and provides technical support for *development.

United Nations Educational, Scientific and Cultural Organization (UNESCO) An agency of the United Nations that was created in 1946 to promote collaboration between countries through education, science, and culture. It has headquarters in Paris, France, and national commissions in many countries.

United Nations Environment Programme (UNEP) A major programme that was established in 1972 at the *United Nations Conference on the Human Environment, to stimulate and coordinate *sustainable environmental practices worldwide. *See also* EARTHWATCH.

United Nations Food and Agriculture Organization (FAO) The first specialized United Nations agency that was created in 1945 to combat hunger and poverty, with a mission to raise living standards, agricultural productivity, nutrition levels, and rural living conditions.

United Nations Framework Convention on Biological Diversity (UNCBD) A framework for international action in protecting *biodiversity that was agreed at the *United Nations Conference on Environment and Development in 1992. It calls on countries to identify *endangered species and conserve the places where they live, and under it each nation agreed to prepare a National Action Plan or Biodiversity Strategy.

United Nations Framework Convention on Climate Change (UNCCC) A framework for international action in tackling the prospect of *global warming associated with emission of *greenhouse gases which was agreed at the *United Nations Conference on Environment and Development in 1992. It called for the stabilization of greenhouse gas emissions by the year 2000 to prevent serious induced global warming, and led to the *Kyoto Protocol. Oil-producing countries (particularly the USA) were concerned that limitations on the burning of *fossil fuels would be a direct threat to their economies, so there was heated debate and a great deal of behind-the-scenes negotiation was required to get the convention accepted.

United Nations Industrial Development Organization (UNIDO) A part of the *United Nations whose mission is to improve people's living conditions and promote global prosperity through offering tailor-made solutions for the sustainable industrial development of developing countries and countries with economies in transition.

United Nations System-wide Earthwatch See EARTHWATCH.

universal soil loss equation (soil loss equation) A formula that is used to estimate rates of *soil erosion by considering climate, soils, and topographic conditions at a site, as well as the extent to which the use and management of the soil reduce erosion. It has the general form $A = R \times K \times L \times S \times C \times P$ in which A is the amount of soil lost from that field each year, R is the *erosivity of the rainfall (based on amount and type of rainfall), K is erosivity of the soil (liability of the particular soil to erosion), L is the length factor of the field (ratio of the length of the field to a standard field of 22.6 m), S is the slope factor (ratio of the soil lost to the amount lost from a field with a 9% gradient), C is the crop management factor (ratio of soil loss to that from a field under cultivated bare fallow), and P is the soil conservation practice factor (ratio of soil loss to that from a field where no care is taken to prevent erosion). See also WIND EROSION EQUATION.

universal solvent A *solvent that can dissolve anything, including both *bases and *acids, as well as gold, that was sought by the alchemists. No such solvent exists, but a wide range of substances are soluble in water, which is sometimes called the universal solvent.

Universal Time See GREENWICH MEAN TIME.

univoltine Having one brood and generation in a year or season. See also VOLTINISM. Contrast BIVOLTINE; MULTIVOLTINE.

unknown (threat) category of species A category for species under threat that is defined by the *IUCN *Red Data Book as including *status unknown and *insufficiently known.

unleaded fuel *Petrol that has not been treated with *lead. Contrast LEADED FUEL.

unpalatable species Species that are not readily eaten by animals because they taste unpleasant.

unplanned ignition A *fire that has started at random by either natural or human causes, or on purpose by an arsonist.

unregulated harvest Tree *harvest that is not part of the *allowable annual harvest, which can include the removal of dead material or non-commercial species.

unsaturated flow The movement of water in a *soil that is not completely filled with water. Contrast SATURATED FLOW.

unsaturated zone (vadose zone) That portion of a soil or an *aquifer in which not all of the pore space is filled with water, although some water may be present. Contrast SATURATED. See also AERATION ZONE.

unstable air Air that continues to rise once it has begun to do so, because the *environmental lapse rate is greater than the *dry adiabatic lapse rate, so that rising air cools more slowly than the surrounding air and remains warmer than the surrounding air at every height. See also INSTABILITY.

unsuitable forestland *Forestland that is not managed primarily for *timber production.

updraught A local current of rising air, often within a *cloud.

u

upland (highland) High, hilly, or mountainous country. *Contrast* LOWLAND.

uplift The lifting up of a region of the Earth's *crust, for example during *mountain building.

upslope fog A *fog that forms when moist, stable air is cooled when it is lifted up a mountain slope.

upslope precipitation *Precipitation that forms when moist, stable air is forced to rise along an elevated plain. *See also* RAIN SHADOW.

upslope wind *See* ANABATIC WIND.

upstream In the direction from which the flow is coming; against the current. *Contrast* DOWNSTREAM.

upwarping The *warping or bending upwards of the Earth's *crust.

upwelling The rising to the surface of a large lake or ocean of cold water from a lower depth. In the open ocean it is caused by the divergence of two surface currents, the upwelling water replacing the diverging waters. Near coasts it is caused by the *Ekman effect induced by winds blowing away from the coast. The cold upwelling water is often rich in nutrients.

upwelling current A type of *ocean current that lifts cold, nutrient-rich water from the ocean floor.

upwind In the direction from which the wind is blowing; against the wind. *Contrast* DOWNWIND.

uracil herbicides Compounds derived from uracil, a pyrimidine base that occurs in *ribonucleic acid (RNA), that are used to inhibit photosynthesis in weeds in orchards, vineyards, soft fruits, and a range of other crops. They are of low toxicity.

uraninite (pitchblende) Uranium dioxide (UO_2), a strongly *radioactive mineral that is the main *ore of *uranium. It is found in *veins with the minerals of *lead, tin, and *copper, and in *sandstone deposits.

uranium (U) A silver-coloured, heavy, *radioactive metal that is found especially in *uraninite, exists naturally as a mixture of three *isotopes (U-234, U-235, and U-238), and is used in *nuclear reactors and the production of *nuclear weapons.

urban Relating to, characteristic of, or situated in a *city. *See also* SUBURBAN.

urban and built-up area/land A land use category in the USA that consists of residential, industrial, commercial, and institutional land. This includes construction sites, railway yards, cemeteries, airports, golf courses, *sanitary landfills, *sewage treatment plants, water control structures and spillways, small parks, and highways.

urban area A geographical area that constitutes a *town or *city.

urban canyon The deep, narrow passage formed by a city street lined by tall buildings on both sides. Wind tends to be funnelled along the street, especially if the street is aligned with the wind direction, and the airflow may become helical, moving up the faces of the buildings on the windward side and down those on the lee side.

urban climate A local climate that is affected by the presence of a *town or *city, which can include lower *relative humidity, lower *wind speeds, and higher *rainfall. *See also* URBAN HEAT ISLAND.

urban development The development of fabric and infrastructure in an *urban area.

urban district A subdivision of a county that covers an *urban area in the United Kingdom.

urban forestry The management of naturally occurring and planted trees in *urban areas.

urban heat island (heat island) A dome of raised air temperatures that lies over an *urban area and is caused by the heat emitted from buildings and structures into air trapped beneath a *temperature inversion.

urban planning (city planning) The design and organization of *urban areas and activities.

urban renewal The redevelopment or rehabilitation of property in an *urban area.

urban runoff *Runoff that is generated from *urban areas.

urban settlement A densely populated settlement, which can take the form of a *town, *city, *metropolis, *conurbation, *megalopolis, or *world city. *See also* RURAL SETTLEMENT.

urban sprawl *See* SUBURBAN SPRAWL.

urbanization The social, *demographic, and economic processes involved in the growth of *towns and *cities.

urea A compound $(CO(NH_2)_2)$ formed from carbon dioxide and ammonia by the breakdown of *amino acids in animals and some plants.

urea herbicide A group of three compounds (diuron, siduron, and tebuthiuron) that inhibit *photosynthesis and are used to control weeds in a range of crops and on non-agricultural land. They are of low toxicity.

urtication A burning or itching sensation which is usually caused by an *allergic response to insect bites or food or drugs.

US United States.

US Army Corps of Engineers (ACE) A US federal agency whose mission is to provide engineering services, including planning, designing, building, and operating dams and other civil engineering projects, designing and managing the construction of military facilities for the Army and Air Force, and providing design and construction management support for other defence and federal agencies. The Corps has played a major role in altering the US landscape.

US Bureau of Land Management (BLM) A federal agency of the *US Department of the Interior that administers large areas of public land which is located mostly in 12 western states. Its mission is to sustain the health, diversity, and productivity of the public lands for the use and enjoyment of present and future generations.

US Bureau of Reclamation (BR) A federal agency of the *US Department of the Interior that was established in 1902 to provide public funds for irrigation projects in arid regions. The BR played a major role in the construction of *dams, *reservoirs, and *irrigation systems designed to reclaim arid and semi-arid lands in western states, especially since in the 1930s.

US Department of Agriculture (USDA, Agriculture Department) The federal department of the US government that develops and executes policy on agriculture, food, forestry, and soil conservation.

US Department of the Interior (DOI, Interior Department) A Cabinet department of the US Government that manages and con-serves most federally owned land. It is not responsible for local government or for civil administration, except in the cases of Indian reservations.

US Fish and Wildlife Service (FWS, Fish and Wildlife Service) The federal agency of the *US Department of the Interior that is responsible for managing and preserving the country's *wildlife.

US Forest Service (Forest Service) The federal agency of the *US Department of Agriculture that is responsible for, among other things, managing the country's *National Forests.

USA United States of America.

USDA See US DEPARTMENT OF AGRICULTURE.

use district An area within a city that is covered by a *zoning ordinance that prescribes what land use is permitted, and what type of structures may be placed on it.

use value The economic value of a particular *resource for a specific use. *Contrast* NON-CONSUMPTIVE VALUE.

U-shaped valley (glacial trough) A deep *valley with steep sides and a flat floor, usually eroded by a *glacier. *Contrast* V-SHAPED VALLEY.

UT See GREENWICH MEAN TIME.

utilitarian Having a useful function.

utilitarianism A philosophy that judges everything in terms of its utility or usefulness, and which argues that all action should be directed towards achieving the greatest happiness for the greatest number of people.

utility 1. The quality of being of practical use. *See also* UTILITARIAN. **2.** A company that performs a public service (such as delivering water or energy to a region), subject to government regulation.

utility corridor A North American term for a strip of land that forms a passageway through which commodities such as oil, gas, and electricity are transported.

UV See ULTRAVIOLET.

u

vaccination (inoculation) Taking a *vaccine as a precaution against contracting an *infectious disease, through a needle injection, by mouth, or by aerosol.

vaccine A product that produces immunity from an *infectious organism and therefore protects the body from the *disease.

vadose zone *See* AERATION ZONE; UNSATURATED ZONE.

vagile Wandering; freely motile, mobile. *Contrast* SESSILE.

vagrant An individual of a *species that naturally wanders, moving from place to place outside its usual range or away from the usual migratory routes, without being part of a self-regenerating population.

valence The number of hydrogen atoms that typically bond to an atom of an *element, which indicates the charge of the atom. For example, oxygen has a valence of two in water (H_2O).

valence electrons The outermost electrons in an atom, which are particularly active in bonding.

validation The process of establishing the integrity and correctness of data. *See also* GROUND TRUTH.

valley Any long area of low-lying land that has higher ground on either side, and usually contains a *river.

valley bog A *mire community that develops in wet valley bottoms, in valleys with some downstream impedance, or in badly drained hollows. This type of mire is flow-fed (rheotrophic), so technically it is a poor *fen type of community rather than a true *bog. The supply of nutrients is determined by the concentration of elements in the drainage water (which is usually low) and the rate of water flow through the system. In extensive valley mires the acidic, lateral mire expanses may become elevated and *ombrotrophic if rainfall is adequate. *Compare* BLANKET BOG; OMBROGENOUS BOG; RAISED BOG.

valley breeze A daytime local *anabatic wind in a *mountain environment that occurs when the air warms in the valley bottom, becoming less dense, and cooler air subsides over the centre of the valley, displacing the warmer air and lifting it up the valley sides.

valley fog *See* RADIATION FOG.

valley glacier *See* GLACIER.

valley train A glacial *outwash plain that is confined within a narrow valley.

valuation The act of determining or estimating the *value or worth of an object.

value An expression of monetary worth of a particular object, or its power to command other things in exchange.

value judgement A judgement of the rightness or wrongness of something, based on a particular set of *values.

value system *See* VALUES.

values (value system) A set of ethical beliefs and preferences that determine our sense of right and wrong. *See* VALUE JUDGEMENT.

vanadium (V) A naturally occurring, white, soft, ductile, toxic *heavy metal that is *carcinogenic and is used to make *alloys in iron and steel making.

vantage point *See* VIEWPOINT.

vaporization The conversion of a *liquid or *solid to a *vapour.

vapour The gaseous form of a substance that is normally in the solid or liquid state at room temperature and pressure, such as *water vapour.

vapour density The density of a *gas relative to the density of *hydrogen at the same temperature and pressure.

vapour pressure The *partial pressure exerted on a surface by atmospheric *water vapour. This is determined by the *humidity and is a measure of the tendency of a material to *evaporate. See also SATURATION VAPOUR PRESSURE.

variability Absence of uniformity.

variable Liable to, or capable of, change.

variety In *botany, a genetically distinct division of a *species, next below the rank of *subspecies. See also CULTIVAR.

varve A thin layer of *sediment that is deposited in a lake within one year by *glacial outwash.

varzea See AMAZON FLORAL REGION.

vascular plant Any plant (including ferns, *conifers, and *flowering plants) that contains a system of vessels (*phloem and *xylem) which transport water and nutrients between different parts of the plant, for example from the roots to the leaves. Contrast NON-VASCULAR PLANT.

VC See VINYL CHLORIDE.

vector A carrier. **1.** Any organism that is capable of transmitting *disease. Examples include flies, mites, ticks, rats, and dogs. **2.** In *genetic manipulation, the agent by which *DNA is transferred from one cell to another.

vector quantity A physical quantity that acts in a direction, so its description must include both its magnitude and its direction (e.g. wind, given as speed and direction).

veering winds Wind that changes direction in a clockwise manner.

vegan A *vegetarian who also excludes from their diet all other animal products, such as milk and eggs.

vegetarian A person who only eats plants, not meat. A *herbivore.

vegetation All of the plants and trees that grow in a particular region or area.

vegetation cover type See COVER TYPE.

vegetation succession See SUCCESSION.

vegetative Applied to plant parts or structures that are concerned with feeding and growth, and are not involved in the production of seed, such as the roots, stems, and leaves.

vehicle Any non-living means of transport (usually made by humans), including cars, motorcycles, trains, ships, and aircraft.

vehicle emission The emission of *pollution (including *carbon monoxide, *hydrocarbons, and *nitrogen oxides) by a motor vehicle.

vein **1.** A layer of *ore between layers of rock. **2.** A structural part of a *leaf. **3.** In the human body, a blood vessel that carries blood from the capillaries towards the heart.

veld *Temperate grassland in South Africa.

velocity (flow rate, flow velocity) Speed, or distance travelled per unit time.

Venezuela and Guiana floral region Part of R. Good's *Neotropical floral kingdom (The Geography of the Flowering Plants, 1974), a region that has affinities with the adjacent Andean and Amazon floral region, but nevertheless constitutes an independent unit with about 100 *endemic genera. The flora is poorly known and has yielded no plants of any great value.

Venice system A system for the classification of *brackish water based on the percentage of chloride contained in the water. The system was adopted at a symposium held in April 1958 in Venice, sponsored by the International Association of Limnology and the International Union of Biological Sciences. The system classifies waters by percentage salinity as: hyperhaline ($>\pm 40$); euhaline (± 40–± 30); mixohaline ((± 40) ± 30–± 0.5); mixoeuhaline ($>\pm 30$ but less saline than the adjacent sea); mixopolyhaline (± 30–± 18); mixomesohaline (± 18–± 5); mixo-oligohaline (± 5–± 0.5); limnetic ($<\pm 0.5$). The $\pm$ symbol indicates that the values are approximate.

(((●))) SEE WEB LINKS

• The Venice System for the Classification of Marine Waters According to Salinity.

vent A vertical pipe in a *volcano, up which the molten *magma moves to the surface. See also HYDROTHERMAL VENT; VOLCANIC PLUG.

ventifact A stone that has flat surfaces that are often highly polished and have been formed by *sandblasting in strong winds; often found across a *desert floor.

ventilation The movement of air, particularly the process of supplying fresh air to, or removing contaminated air from, a building or structure. See also AIR CONDITIONING.

V

ventilation index (clearing index) A measure of the potential of the atmosphere to disperse *airborne pollutants from a stationary source, based on the product of the *mixing depth and transport wind speed.

venturi effect The speeding up of the flow of air or water as it passes through a constriction (such as a pipe or narrow channel), caused by the pressure rise on the upflow side of the constriction and the pressure drop on the downflow side as it diverges.

venturi scrubber An *air pollution control device exploiting the *venturi effect that uses water to remove fine particles from volatile, hazardous, or corrosive gas streams, or from gas streams containing solid materials that are difficult to handle.

vermiculite The mineral *mica that has been processed and expanded by heat. It is used as a medium for starting seedlings and root cuttings.

vermiculture A *composting process that uses worms and *micro-organisms to convert *organic wastes into nutrient-rich *humus.

vermin The collective name for various small animals (including mice, rats, and birds) and insects (including cockroaches and flies) that are regarded as *pests.

vernal Of or relating to *spring.

vernal equinox The *equinox at which the sun crosses the equator, entering the hemisphere where it will then be spring. This occurs on 20–21 March in the *northern hemisphere and on 22–23 September in the *southern hemisphere. *Contrast* AUTUMNAL EQUINOX.

vertebrate An animal (such as an *amphibian, *bird, fish, *mammal, or *reptile) that has a backbone and a spinal column. *Contrast* INVERTEBRATE.

vertical Up and down, as opposed to *lateral or sideways.

vertical stratification The vertical distribution of *subcommunities within a *community of plants and animals. *See also* STRATIFICATION.

vertisol A type (*order) of clay soil in the *Comprehensive Soil Classification System that develops in climates with clear wet and dry seasons. Vertisols expand when wet and crack when dry.

very exposed In terms of *wave exposure, an open *coast that faces into prevailing winds and receives wind-driven waves and *swell with a *fetch of at least several hundred kilometres, but where deep water (50 m) is no closer to the shore than about 300 m.

very sheltered In terms of *wave exposure, a coast with a *fetch of less than about three kilometres where it faces prevailing winds, or about 20 km where it faces away from prevailing winds, or which has offshore obstructions (such as *reefs).

vesicle A small air pocket that forms in *volcanic rock as it solidifies.

vessel 1. General name for a boat or ship. **2.** Any tube that carries fluids within a body, such as *veins in humans or the *xylem tissue in plants.

vestigial A structure that no longer serves a useful purpose, such as an organ whose original function has been lost during *evolution of the organism (e.g. the appendix in humans, hind limbs in whales).

viability The ability to survive, or to live and develop normally.

viable Capable of living, developing, or germinating normally.

viable population A self-sustaining *population with a high probability of survival because it has sufficient numbers and *reproductive potential.

vicariance *Speciation that occurs as a result of the separation and subsequent isolation of portions of an original population by a geographical barrier, such as a mountain or a *waterbody.

vicariant Species that occupy similar *niches but in geographical isolation from each other, as a result of *vicariance.

Vienna Convention for the Protection of the Ozone Layer (1985) An international agreement designed to minimize human destruction of the *ozone layer, mainly by reducing the production and emission of *CFCs into the atmosphere. The *Montreal Protocol fits within the framework of this convention.

viewpoint (vantage point) A place from which the surrounding *landscape or *scenery can be viewed or observed.

viewscape The visible *landscape.

V

viewshed Those parts of a *landscape that can be seen from a particular point. *Contrast* AIRSHED; WATERSHED.

village A *rural settlement that is much smaller than a *town. Sometimes used to refer to local centres within a *city, that were previously separate villages.

vinclozalin A *fungicide used to control diseases in vines, other fruits, vegetables, and ornamental crops, and on turf. It is moderately persistent in soil. It causes slight nose and throat irritation but is otherwise of low toxicity. It is moderately toxic to fish, but does not harm insects or earthworms.

vineyard A place where grapes are grown for making wine.

vinyl chloride (VC) A *halogenated, *hydrocarbon compound that is used in producing some plastics (including *PVC), and is believed to be *carcinogenic.

viral agent An *agent that is known to cause particular diseases, which may be used for example as a *biological warfare agent. *See also* DISEASE AGENT.

virga (fallstreak) Precipitation that falls from a cloud but evaporates before reaching the ground. It appears as a veil beneath the cloud.

virgin forest An area of *old growth forest in its natural state, untouched by humans.

virgin material 1. Any undeveloped *resource that is or could become a source of raw materials. **2.** Previously unused raw material, such as *copper, *aluminium, *lead, *zinc, *iron, or other *metal or metal ore.

virucide A chemical substance that destroys *viruses.

virulence The ability of an organism to cause *disease.

virus An ultra-microscopic non-cellular infectious agent (the smallest known type of *organism) that contains genetic information but replicates itself only within the cells of living *hosts. Many are *pathogens and can cause disease (such as *AIDS) in humans.

viscosity A measure of the resistance of a liquid to flow.

viscous Possessing a high *viscosity.

visibility Ability to be seen or the distance a person can see with normal vision.

Visibility Protection Program The programme specified by the Clean Air Act in the USA, which is designed to restore visibility caused by air pollution and prevent future reduction of visibility.

visible light The portion of the *electromagnetic spectrum that includes light that can be seen by humans, which we see as colours ranging from red (longer *wavelengths, around 0.77 micrometres) to violet (shorter wavelengths, around 0.4 micrometres), as in a *rainbow.

visitor day (recreation visitor day) A way of measuring the use of a particular site or facility by visitors, defined as the use of an area for a total of 12 person-hours by one or more people, either continuously or spread over several visits.

vista A point or area along a route which offers a panoramic, unusual, or very attractive view of a *landscape or *scenery.

visual blight Any change to a *landscape that adversely affects *visual quality.

visual impact Any positive or negative change in the appearance of the *landscape as a result of development.

visual quality The nature and quality of a *visual resource, and how it is perceived and valued by the general public.

visual resource The visible physical features of a *landscape.

vitamins Organic *micronutrients that are present in minute quantities in natural foodstuffs, that the body needs in small amounts to grow and stay strong but is unable to produce in sufficient quantities for itself.

vitrification A process for treating *radioactive waste that immobilizes it by mixing it with glass-forming chemicals, so that as it cools it solidifies into a type of glass.

viviparous Applied to animals (including most *mammals, some *reptiles, and some *fish) that are born live and do not hatch from eggs, to plants (e.g. mangroves) that produce seeds that germinate inside the fruit and obtain nourishment from it, and to plants (e.g. some grasses) that reproduce vegetatively from a shoot rather than from a flower.

VOC *See* VOLATILE ORGANIC COMPOUND.

void A space within something solid, for example within a *soil or a *sedimentary rock.

volatile A substance that evaporates readily at normal temperatures and pressures.

volatile organic compound (VOC) Compounds (such as *gasoline, *alcohol, and the solvents used in paints) that contain carbon and evaporate readily into the air. They contribute to the formation of smog and may be toxic.

volcanic Relating to, produced by, or consisting of *volcanoes.

volcanic activity (vulcanism) Any activity of a *volcano, which includes both underground activity (*intrusive volcanic activity) and activity on the Earth's surface (*extrusive volcanic activity).

volcanic aerosol The cloud of particles which is thrown into the *stratosphere by explosive *volcanic eruptions. *See also* VOLCANIC RADIATIVE FORCING.

volcanic ash *See* TEPHRA.

volcanic bomb A small lump of *magma that is thrown up into the air during an explosive *volcanic eruption as molten rock and then cools into a solid fragment before it reaches the ground.

volcanic breccia A *pyroclastic rock formed from large pieces of *volcanic rock, including *volcanic bombs. *Contrast* BRECCIA.

volcanic cone (volcanic dome) A conical mountain that is built up around a central *vent by *lava and *pyroclastic materials released when a volcano erupts.

volcanic dome *See* VOLCANIC CONE.

volcanic dust *See* TEPHRA.

volcanic eruption The eruption of a *volcano as a result of *extrusive volcanic activity, which causes molten *magma to reach and spill out over the Earth's surface, and large amounts of *volcanic gas and steam to be released. Products include *volcanic bombs, *tephra, *lava flows, and the build-up of *volcanic cones.

volcanic gas Dissolved *gases contained in *magma that are released into the atmosphere during *volcanic eruptions.

volcanic glass *See* OBSIDIAN.

volcanic plug A volcanic landform that is formed when *lava hardens within a *vent in an active *volcano. A volcanic plug can cause a buildup of pressure in the magma trapped

behind it which may be followed by a violent explosive eruption.

volcanic radiative forcing The effect of *volcanic aerosols on radiation transfers within the atmosphere. Regional air temperature is directly affected via changes in *albedo.

volcanic rock *See* IGNEOUS ROCK.

volcanic steam Hot steam that is released into the air in *volcanic eruptions, and from *fumaroles and *solfataras.

volcanic zone An area in which there are active or dormant *volcanoes.

volcano A mountain formed by *volcanic activity and material.

voltinism The number of generations or broods that an individual has each year. *See also* BIVOLTINE; MULTIVOLTINE; UNIVOLTINE.

volume A measure of how much space an object occupies, expressed in *SI units as cubic metres (m^3).

volume reduction An approach to *waste management that involves reducing the volume of *waste, usually by compacting, shredding, *incineration, or *composting.

voluntary Without being required to; by free will.

voluntary commitment The formal name, under the *Kyoto Protocol, for any actions that a government or organization takes to reduce *pollution emissions on a voluntary basis, outside what is required by regulations.

voluntary simplicity Deliberately choosing a *lifestyle that is based on a lower level of *consumption, for environmental or ethical reasons.

volunteer plant A crop plant that has grown as a result of natural propagation, as opposed to having been deliberately planted by humans. Most volunteer plants grow from seed left in the soil from a previous crop.

vortex A whirling mass of air or water in the form of a vertical column or spiral.

vorticity A measure of the amount of local rotation in an airflow.

voucher specimen A preserved and archived specimen of a plant or animal that documents the use of a particular name, or its presence in a particular place.

V

V-shaped valley A river *valley that has relatively uniform gently sloping walls and has been eroded by *fluvial processes. *Contrast* U-SHAPED VALLEY.

vulcanism *See* VOLCANIC ACTIVITY.

vulnerability (fragility) The *sensitivity, *resilience, and capacity of a system to adapt to stress or perturbation.

vulnerability analysis The process of estimating the *vulnerability to potential *natural hazards or *environmental change (such as the release of a particular pollutant) of specified elements at risk (such as elderly people or rare species).

vulnerable species A category of species defined by the *IUCN *Red Data Book as 'taxa believed likely to move into the *endangered category in the near future if the causal factors continue operating'. *Contrast* ENDANGERED; EXTINCT; EXTIRPATED; THREATENED.

vulnerable zone An area over which the concentration of a chemical that has been accidentally released into the air could reach the *level of concern.

wader (wading bird) A general term for long-legged birds that wade in water in search of food and *overwinter in the *intertidal zone in *estuaries.

wadi An *ephemeral river channel in a *desert area, that contains water only immediately after a storm.

wading bird *See* WADER.

wait-and-see principle A conservative approach to *environmental management, in which action is postponed until complete, correct, and detailed predictions of the likely impacts of different courses of action are available. *Contrast* PRECAUTIONARY PRINCIPLE.

wake The region of turbulence immediately behind a solid body caused by the flow of air over or around the body.

Walden A book by Henry David *Thoreau (1854), in which he describes his retreat from civilization between 1845 and 1847 to live in a small wooden cabin by Walden Pond in Massachusetts. The book also outlines Thoreau's philosophy of self-reliance and his *transcendentalist beliefs, both of which were heavily influenced by the writings of Ralph Waldo *Emerson.

Wallace, Alfred Russel (1823–1913) An English naturalist who was a contemporary of Charles *Darwin. While collecting biological specimens in the East Indies (now Indonesia), Wallace came independently to the theory of *evolution by *natural selection. His ideas were presented together with those of Darwin at a meeting of the Linnean Society of London on 1 July 1858.

Walter climate diagram A graphic representation of climatic conditions at a particular place, showing seasonal variations and extremes as well as mean values and therefore providing a succinct and easily accessible summary of a local climate. The diagram shows the height above sea level, the number of years during which temperature and precipitation observations continued, mean annual temperature and precipitation, mean daily minimum temperature in the coldest month and maximum in the warmest month, the lowest and highest temperatures recorded, mean daily variation in temperature, mean monthly temperature and precipitation, relative period of drought and relative humid season, mean monthly rainfall in excess of and below a given value, reduced supplementary precipitation curve, months in which the mean daily minimum temperature was below freezing, months with frosts, and the mean duration of frost-free days. The diagram was devised in 1979 by the German-Russian biogeographer Heinrich Walter (1898–1989).

warm cloud A cloud that contains only liquid droplets. *Compare* COLD CLOUD; MIXED CLOUD.

warm front An advancing *front with warmer air behind it. *Contrast* COLD FRONT. *See also* FRONT; FRONTAL LIFTING.

warm occlusion A *frontal zone formed when the warm air has been lifted from the surface and the *warm front extends to the surface, so that the air behind the front and beneath the warm air is not so cold as the air ahead of the front. *Contrast* COLD OCCLUSION.

warm sector The region of warm air between a *warm front and the following *cold front. *Contrast* COLD SECTOR.

warm-blooded (endothermic) Applied to an animal whose body temperature is internally regulated. The term is misleading and no longer used, because while they are active *ectotherms (e.g. reptiles) also maintain constant body temperatures. *Contrast* COLD-BLOODED.

warning A message to alert emergency services and the general public about impending danger from extreme conditions (e.g. a *tornado) that are already occurring or that have been detected, and to inform them of appropriate action that should be taken immediately. *Contrast* ADVISORY; WATCH.

warp soil Soil consisting mainly of *silt deposited by floodwater. *See* WARPING.

warping 1. The gentle deformation of the Earth's crust over a large area, without *folding or *faulting, which can be upwards (*upwarping) or downwards (*downwarping), as a response to great pressure. **2.** A traditional farming practice in which a river is allowed to flood low-lying ground in order to deliver a load of nutrient-rich *silt.

wash 1. A common form of *slope erosion process, involving *overland flow across a sloping surface. **2.** The usually dry channel of an *intermittent or *ephemeral stream in a *semi-arid area.

wash zone The depth zone in which sediments are disturbed by *wave action near the *shoreline.

washout The removal of solid particles from the air by collision with *raindrops.

wastage zone (zone of wastage) The area on a *glacier where there is a net loss of snow and ice. *Contrast* ACCUMULATION ZONE.

waste 1. (garbage, refuse, trash) Any material that is unused and rejected as worthless or unwanted. **2.** An area of unenclosed land used for common pasture.

waste characterization The process of identifying the chemical and microbiological constituents of a particular *waste material.

waste disposal Getting rid of (*disposal) of *toxic, *radioactive, or other *waste materials, most commonly by *landfill or *incineration, rather than by *reuse, *recovery, or *recycling.

waste disposal system A system for the *disposal of *wastes, including *sewer systems, *treatment works, and *disposal wells.

waste exchange An arrangement in which companies exchange their *waste materials, for the benefit of both parties.

waste feed The flow of *waste materials into an *incinerator, which can be either continuous or intermittent.

waste generation The amount of *waste material generated by a particular source, or that enters the *waste stream before *recycling,

*composting, *landfilling, or *incineration takes place.

waste heat Heat that is left after useful energy generation, such as in the warm water discharged into a storage pond after cooling a commercial *nuclear reactor.

waste heat recovery Using *waste heat that would otherwise be released into the environment to provide space heating or water heating in buildings.

waste load allocation The maximum amount (relative or absolute) of *pollutants that an individual discharger of wastes is allowed to release into a particular waterway.

waste management The management of *waste materials, usually based on the management of wastes at all stages (production, handling, storage, transport, processing, and ultimate disposal) in such a way as to minimize the risks to human health, wildlife, and environmental systems. Traditional approaches to the management of non-toxic solid waste rely heavily on *sanitary landfill. Disposing of *toxic wastes in this manner is unsuitable, largely because of the risk of contaminating *groundwater. The nuclear industry produces sizeable amounts of waste, much of which is safe and can be disposed of in traditional ways. But some *nuclear waste is highly radioactive, poses serious health risks to people and wildlife, and remains dangerously radioactive for long periods of time (hundreds of thousands of years or longer for many isotopes).

waste minimization *See* WASTE REDUCTION.

waste reclamation The reclamation of solid wastes by converting them into useful products. Examples include composting *organic waste into soil and separating *aluminium and other metals for *recycling.

waste reduction (waste minimization) The process of reducing the amount of *waste that is disposed of, for example by avoiding and/or reducing the generation of waste in the first place, or by reusing, recycling, and recovering waste through *resource recovery.

waste site A dumping ground.

waste stream The output of wastes from a particular area, which includes *domestic waste, *yard wastes, and industrial, commercial, and construction *refuse.

w

waste treatment The process by which *hazardous waste materials are stored or treated in order to minimize their impacts on the environment.

waste treatment lagoon A storage pond in which *wastewater is stored for biological treatment.

waste-to-energy facility *See* MUNICIPAL WASTE COMBUSTOR.

wastewater Water that carries *wastes from homes, businesses, and industries and usually contains *dissolved solids and/or *suspended solids.

wastewater reclamation Any process which involves the reuse of *wastewater (for example for cooling or *irrigation), with or without treatment.

wastewater treatment Chemical, biological, and mechanical procedures that are applied to *wastewater in order to remove, reduce, or neutralize *contaminants before the water is discharged into a *waterbody. *See also* ADVANCED WASTEWATER TREATMENT; PRIMARY TREATMENT; SECONDARY TREATMENT.

wastewater treatment plant A *facility that contains a series of tanks, screens, filters, and other means by which *pollutants are removed from *wastewater.

watch An announcement to alert emergency and other services and the public to the possibility of a specified hazard (e.g. a *tornado watch) in a defined area. A watch is issued as far in advance of the event as possible and on receiving one people should take steps to protect their lives and property. *Contrast* ADVISORY; WARNING.

water (H_2O) An odourless, tasteless, colourless liquid formed by a combination of hydrogen and oxygen which, at sea-level pressure, freezes at $0°C$ ($32°F$) and boils at $100°C$ ($212°F$) and is a major constituent of all living matter.

water balance *See* WATER BUDGET.

water bears *See* TARDIGRADES.

water budget (water balance) An assessment of all of the inputs, outputs, and net changes to a particular *water resource system (such as a *drainage basin) over a given period of time, usually a year.

water catchment *See* DRAINAGE BASIN.

water chemistry The chemical composition and characteristics of *water. *See also* WATER QUALITY.

water column The area between the surface and the bottom of a *waterbody.

water conservation Any practice that promotes the efficient use of *water, such as minimizing losses, reducing wasteful use, and protecting availability for future use.

water consumption The use of water.

water cycle (hydrological cycle, hydrogeological cycle) The continuous natural cycling of water from the *atmosphere to the land and oceans and back (see Fig. 21). The basic structure of the global water cycle is quite simple. Water is evaporated from the oceans, seas, lakes, rivers, and vegetated land areas, and it becomes part of the atmospheric store of water vapour. Global and regional wind systems redistribute the water vapour across the Earth's surface. Condensation creates *clouds and *precipitation, and the latter brings water back to the surface where it enters the soil or *groundwater, or flows directly into rivers or lakes. Rivers transport water (as *runoff) from land surfaces into the oceans. Naturally, much of the precipitation falls directly over seas and oceans, effectively short-circuiting the land phase of the water cycle. The total volume of water in the global cycle is estimated at about 1384 million km^3. Just over 2% of the total water in the global cycle is freshwater, and most of that is locked up as polar ice caps and in glaciers. If all of the ice were to melt it would release enough water to keep the world's rivers flowing at their normal rates for up to 1000 years. The major stores are the *oceans (97.41%), *ice caps and *glaciers (1.9%), *groundwater (0.5%), *soil moisture (0.01), *lakes and *rivers (0.009%), and the *atmosphere (0.0001%).

water equivalent The depth of *water that would result from the melting of a sample of *snow or *ice.

water filter A filter (such as charcoal or a fine *membrane) that is used to remove impurities from water.

Water Framework Directive A directive of the *European Union that was introduced in October 2000 and is designed to promote a *sustainable water policy within the European Union.

Fig. 21 Water cycle

water harvesting The process of capturing and saving rainwater for later use (for example storing water in barrels for use in watering a garden).

water inventory 1. An inventory to show how water is consumed, used, or otherwise involved in a particular process or place (e.g. within a factory or private house). **2.** Globally, 97.41% of the Earth's water occurs in the oceans. Of the fresh water, 75% is locked up in *ice sheets and *glaciers and almost 25% is *groundwater. Lakes, reservoirs, swamps, river channels, biospheric water, atmospheric water, and soil moisture together account for the remainder. The amount of water at each stage of the *water cycle is called the water storage.

water management The planned development, distribution, and use of *water resources.

water mass A discrete body of *seawater in which physical properties (such as *temperature and *salinity) are uniform, but different from surrounding water masses with which it will mix only very slowly. *Contrast* AIR MASS.

water mill A mill that is powered by a water wheel, a traditional form of *hydropower. *Contrast* WINDMILL.

water moulds *See* OOMYCETES.

water pollutant Any material (usually a chemical) that *pollutes freshwater.

water pollution The *pollution of fresh water (for example through *eutrophication,

*acidification, and *groundwater pollution), which decreases its purity and often makes it unsuitable for use as a *water resource if not dangerous to human health.

water power *See* HYDROPOWER.

water purification The process of removing *contaminants from a water supply in order to make it safe and *palatable for human use.

water quality The chemical, physical, and biological characteristics of a particular *waterbody, usually in relation to its suitability for a particular use. *See also* WATER CHEMISTRY.

water quality criteria Standards that are used to protect *water quality for designated uses such as drinking, swimming, raising fish, farming, or industrial use.

water quality objective A statutory target for *water quality that is used to provide a common framework for dischargers and regulators.

water quality standard A *standard that defines the management goals for a particular *waterbody, by designating the beneficial uses to be made of the water and by setting *water quality criteria appropriate for protecting those uses.

water quality testing Monitoring *water quality to ensure that it is safe for particular uses (such as protection of fish, drinking, and swimming).

water resource Any source of water that is useful to people (for example, for drinking, recreation, irrigation, livestock production,

W

industry). Less than 3% of the water within the *water cycle is *freshwater, and 99% of that is frozen in *ice caps and *glaciers, or is stored as *groundwater. As a result, only 1% is readily available for use. Water shortage is a major and recurrent problem in many regions, including most of Africa, the Middle East, much of South Asia, a large proportion of the western USA and northwest Mexico, parts of South America, and nearly all of Australia. Less than 20% of the population in many developing countries has access to clean drinking water. Water supplies to an area can be increased in various ways (including building *dams, *canals and pipelines, and building *desalination plants), but these engineering solutions are expensive. Access to and shared use of water are major issues for many neighbouring countries, and *hydropolitics can led to major confrontation between countries. World-wide, irrigation agriculture consumes over 70% of all the water used by people, industry accounts for a further 20%, and domestic and municipal uses account for most of the remaining 8%.

water resource management The deliberate *management (protection, allocation, and development) of *water resources in order to benefit people and/or the environment.

water softening The reduction or removal of *calcium and *magnesium ions from water in order to reduce its *hardness.

water storage pond (water treatment lagoon) An artificial pond or holding tank in which liquid *wastes are stored before treatment.

water supply The total amount of *water that is available within a particular area for human and other uses.

water supply system The collection, treatment, storage, and distribution of *potable water from source to use.

water table The level beneath the ground below which *permeable *rock is saturated with *groundwater. *See also* AQUIFER; PERCHED AQUIFER.

water treatment (sewage treatment) Any method of cleaning water for a specific purpose (such as drinking water, irrigation water, or discharge to a stream).

water treatment lagoon *See* WATER STORAGE POND.

water vapour *Water that has evaporated into the air as an invisible gas (it accounts for up to 5% of air by volume), which is an important part of the *water cycle and also the most important *greenhouse gas. When it condenses it turns into a *liquid state to form *mist, *fog, *rain, *sleet, *hail, or *snow.

water well A vertical shaft that is sunk into the ground, usually to a depth of less than 100 m, in order to access an underground *water supply (*aquifer).

water year A 12-month period, usually selected to begin and end during a relatively dry season, which is used a basis for consistent processing and reporting of hydrological data.

water yield The total amount of water (*streamflow and *groundwater) that drains from a *drainage basin over a given period of time (usually a year), usually expressed as equivalent depth of water spread evenly across the basin area.

waterbar A diversion ditch or hump that is used on a road or trail in order to remove water and prevent *erosion.

waterbody Any body of surface water, such as a *lake, *river, or *pond.

waterborne Floating on, supported by, or transmitted in *water.

waterborne disease A *disease that is spread by *contaminated water.

watercourse *See* CHANNEL.

waterfall A cascade of water over resistant rocks or a cliff. *See also* LONG PROFILE.

waterfowl Any bird that spends much of its life in *wetland, particularly lakes, rivers, or streams

water-holding capacity The amount of water that a particular soil can hold.

waterhole A natural depression in the ground, in which *rainwater collects.

waterlogged Saturated with *water.

waterlogging The *saturation of soil with water, often because of *impeded drainage.

watershed *See* DRAINAGE BASIN; DRAINAGE DIVIDE.

watershed approach *See* WATERSHED MANAGEMENT.

watershed area All of the land and water within a *drainage divide.

watershed management (watershed approach) The planned use of all of the *natural resources of *drainage basins in order to meet agreed objectives.

waterspout A column of rotating air over a body of water; in effect a *tornado over the water. *Contrast* LANDSPOUT.

waterway A navigable *watercourse, such as a *river or *canal.

watt (W) The *SI unit of power that is equal to one *joule per second (J s^{-1}).

wave A movement up and down or back and forth, such as a rhythmic movement on the surface of the *ocean, produced by wind as it blows over the water, or the intersection of a *warm front and a *cold front.

wave amplitude The distance between the mean level and the top of the *wave crest or bottom of the *wave trough; it is equal to half the *wave height.

wave base The depth beneath a water mass below which wave action ceases to disturb the sediments. Wave-base depth is approximately equal to half the wavelength of the surface waves.

wave crest The highest part of a *wave. *Contrast* WAVE TROUGH.

wave cyclone (wave depression) A low-pressure centre (*cyclone) that forms and moves along a *front.

wave depression *See* WAVE CYCLONE.

wave diffraction An effect seen as waves pass through an opening in a breakwater into protected waters. The waves fan out from the opening into the region beyond, but as they do so their height is diminished.

wave energy *See* WAVE POWER.

wave frequency The number of *waves per second to pass a given point (f), which is the speed of the wave (c) divided by the *wavelength (λ): $f = c/\lambda$.

wave height The vertical distance between the *wave trough and *wave crest.

wave ogive *See* OGIVE.

wave period The time that elapses between the passage of two successive *wave crests or *wave troughs past a fixed point.

wave power (wave energy) The energy in the motion of ocean *waves, some of which can be captured and converted into usable *energy (*electricity). Records of wave size and frequency, collected using a wave recorder, can be used to compute the potential for wave power in a given area. Various approaches have been tested since the early 1970s, including transforming the motion of the water surface into a flow of air, which can then drive a turbine, or transforming the motion of the water surface using floating devices which rise and fall at different rates. Wave power currently contributes very little to the global energy supply, but it has great potential, up to 1 terawatt according to some estimates. It also has minimal *environmental impacts.

wave refraction The bending of *wave crests to parallel the topography of the sea floor as they arrive *onshore. *See also* LONGSHORE DRIFT.

wave steepness The ratio of *wave height to *wavelength, which affects the stability of ships and marine structures. It is represented by the angle between the base and hypotenuse of a right-angled triangle the other sides of which are the wavelength and wave height.

wave train A series of *waves from the same direction.

wave trough The lowest part of a wave, between two *wave crests.

wavelength 1. The horizontal distance between two successive *wave crests or *wave troughs. *Contrast* WAVE HEIGHT. **2.** The wavelength of *electromagnetic radiation was formerly measured in *angstroms (Å), although scientists now prefer to express wavelengths in micrometres (μm) or nanometers (nm). 10 000 Å = 1 μm; 1000 μm = 1 nm. Very long wavelengths are usually expressed in terms of frequency, as *hertz (Hz).

WBCSD *See* WORLD BUSINESS COUNCIL FOR SUSTAINABLE DEVELOPMENT.

WCED *See* WORLD COMMISSION ON ENVIRONMENT AND DEVELOPMENT.

WCMC *See* WORLD CONSERVATION MONITORING CENTRE.

WCS *See* WILDLIFE CONSERVATION SOCIETY; WORLD CONSERVATION STRATEGY.

weak acid An *acid that does not ionize completely in water. *Contrast* STRONG ACID.

weakening In *synoptic meteorology, a decrease in pressure gradient around a pressure system over time. Changes of this kind bring about a weakening of the winds. *See also* INTENSIFICATION.

wealth The state of being rich and affluent, or having an abundance of material possessions and resources.

weapons of mass destruction (WMD) Weapons that kill or injure large numbers of civilians as well as military personnel. These include *biological weapons, *chemical weapons, and *nuclear weapons.

weather The physical condition of the *atmosphere at a particular place and time, particularly in terms of moisture, temperature, pressure, and wind.

weather balloon A balloon, about 1.5 m in diameter and filled with helium, which lifts a *radiosonde aloft to measure temperature, pressure, and humidity, or lifts a *rawinsonde also to track winds, as it rises through the air. *See also* WIND SONDE.

weather forecast The *prediction of future *weather for a place and over a specified time period, based on knowledge of meteorological principles and processes, and information about current and recent weather conditions.

weather front *See* FRONT.

weather map (synoptic chart) A map that shows the *meteorological conditions over a particular geographical area at a given time.

weather modification The deliberate management of weather systems to benefit humans, for example through *cloud seeding to encourage rainfall over dry places.

weather side *See* WINDWARD SIDE.

weathering The chemical *decomposition and physical disintegration of rocks *in situ* by the action of external natural factors. Not all of these are associated with the weather. *See also* CHEMICAL WEATHERING; MECHANICAL WEATHERING.

WEDOS *See* WORLD ENVIRONMENT AND DISASTER OBSERVATION SYSTEM.

weed A plant that is growing where it is not wanted, or where is does not normally grow,

and which is considered undesirable or unattractive. *Compare* PEST.

weed control The process of reducing the growth of *weeds to an acceptable level, for aesthetic, economic, public health, or other benefits.

weeding Removing unwanted plants (*weeds), particularly at the *seedling stage.

weedkiller *See* HERBICIDE.

Weeks Law (1911) US legislation that authorized purchase and addition to *National Forest System lands within the *watersheds of navigable streams, in order to regulate the flow of navigable streams or to produce timber.

weir A low *dam that is built across a *stream in order to raise the water level or divert the flow.

welfare An index of well-being.

well A deep hole or shaft that has been dug or drilled in order to access underground resources (particularly water, *oil, *gas, or *brine).

well field An area that contains one or more productive *wells.

well injection Putting fluids underground by means of a *well.

well monitoring Measurement of *water quality in a *well, using on-site instruments or laboratory methods.

well plug A watertight and gastight seal that is installed in a *well in order to prevent the movement of fluids.

wellhead The top of a *well, at ground level.

wellhead protection area A designated area around a public water supply *well that is protected from *contaminants that may damage human health.

west The compass point that is at 270° from north.

West African rainforest floral region Part of R. Good's African floral subkingdom (*The Geography of the Flowering Plants*, 1974), which contains a rich flora that has provided some valuable economic plants (e.g. *Coffea liberica*) and others of more local importance, including timber trees.

West and Central Asiatic floral region Part of R. Good's *Boreal Realm (*The Geography of the Flowering Plants*, 1974), which contains a limited, specialized flora, because much of the region comprises dry mountains and deserts. There are about 150 *endemic genera, virtually all small. Barley and some types of wheat probably originated in this region.

West Wind Drift *See* ANTARCTIC CIRCUMPOLAR CURRENT.

west-coast desert climate zone A *tropical climate zone of dry *desert climates that is confined to narrow bands along the west coasts of all continents except Eurasia and Antarctica.

westerlies (prevailing westerlies) The predominant winds that blow from the west in middle latitudes on the *poleward side of the *subtropical high-pressure areas.

western intensification The tendency of ocean currents flowing along the western margins of all oceans to be stronger, swifter, and narrower than currents flowing along the eastern margins. The currents flow northwards in the northern hemisphere and southwards in the southern hemisphere.

wet deposition The deposition of *pollutants from the atmosphere by rain or snow. *Contrast* DRY DEPOSITION. *See also* ACID RAIN.

wet meadow A *grassland with *waterlogged soil.

wet prairie A type of *prairie that grows in sites that have *waterlogged soils throughout much of the *growing season.

wetfall The delivery to surface communities of nutrients carried in precipitation, in solution (e.g. sulphur and nitrogen oxides) or as insoluble particles (e.g. dust and ash particles). *Compare* DRYFALL.

wetland Land that is covered with water for at least part of each year, and is thus transitional between *terrestrial and *aquatic ecosystems. It supports aquatic vegetation that is specifically adapted for *waterlogged soil conditions, as found for example in *swamps, *bogs, *fens, *marshes, and *estuaries.

wetland soil *See* HYDRIC SOIL.

whale Any of the larger *cetacean mammals that have a streamlined body and breathe through a blowhole on the head.

whaling The intentional hunting and killing of *whales for their meat, blubber, and other products.

whirlwind *See* DUST DEVIL.

white frost *See* HOAR.

white water Water that moves across *rapids or a *waterfall, and has white foam on the surface. It is created by breaking waves.

white-out Reduced daylight *visibility caused by heavy *fog, *snow, or *rain.

WHO *See* WORLD HEALTH ORGANIZATION.

whole-tree removal In *forest management, felling and transporting the whole tree with its crown and sometimes even its roots, for chipping or trimming and cutting at a mill.

wild 1. In a natural state, not tamed, *domesticated, or *cultivated. **2.** The wild; an uninhabited area in a primitive state.

Wild and Scenic River Corridor The area on both sides of a *wild or scenic river.

Wild and Scenic Rivers Act (1968) US legislation that provided for designation of *wild and scenic rivers and for comprehensive studies of other rivers designated as potential additions to the *National Wild and Scenic Rivers System.

wild animal *See* WILDLIFE.

wild river A river or section of a river designated under the *Wild and Scenic Rivers Act, which is unpolluted, free of impoundments, generally inaccessible except by trail, and flows through primitive countryside.

wild species An organism that naturally lives in the *wild and has not been subject to breeding to alter it from its *native state.

wild type The normal form of an *organism, which occurs most frequently in nature.

wilderness Defined by the US *Wilderness Act (1964) as 'an area where the earth and its community of life are untrammelled by man, where man himself is a visitor who does not remain'. In this formal sense, wilderness is a place where vehicles are not allowed, where no permanent camps or structures can be made, and where *wildlife and its *habitat would be kept in as primitive a condition as possible.

Wilderness Act (1964) US legislation that defined *wilderness, established the *National Wilderness Preservation System, and created a process by which Congress could in future add areas to the national system of national forests, parks, and wildlife refuges.

w

Wilderness Area A large area of *wilderness in the USA that has been set aside for preservation by the US Congress by including it in the *National Wilderness Preservation System. Previously known as Primitive Area.

Wilderness Lands Sagebrush Rebellion *See* SAGEBUSH REBELLION.

wildfire An unplanned *fire, often in *wildland, that is burning out of control. *See also* PRESCRIBED FIRE.

wildflower A wild or uncultivated flowering plant.

wildfowl Any *game bird, such as ducks, swans, and geese.

wildland Land that is covered mainly by natural vegetation.

wildland fire Any fire that occurs on undeveloped land.

wildlife (wild animal) Any *animal which is now or historically has been found in the *wild, or in the wild state, within a particular area (such as a country). This includes *mammals, *birds, *reptiles and *amphibians, and including both *game species and non-game species and *vermin. *See also* CONSUMPTIVE WILDLIFE; NON-CONSUMPTIVE WILDLIFE.

Wildlife Conservation Society (WCS) One of the first *conservation organizations in the USA, established in 1895, whose mission is to advance wildlife conservation, promote the study of zoology, and create and manage urban wildlife parks.

(🌐) SEE WEB LINKS
• Wildlife Conservation Society home page.

wildlife corridor (wildlife travel corridor) A linear *habitat or feature (such as a *canal or *hedgerow) that allows animals and plants to move between isolated sites.

wildlife habitat An area of land and water that supports particular *wildlife or groups of wildlife, such as *woodland, *cropland, *rangeland, and *wetland.

wildlife refuge *See* WILDLIFE SANCTUARY.

wildlife sanctuary (wildlife refuge) An area that is designated for the protection of wild animals (*refuge), where animals can breed without interference or danger and *hunting and *fishing are either prohibited or

strictly controlled. *See also* MANAGED NATURE RESERVE/WILDLIFE SANCTUARY.

wildlife travel corridor *See* WILDLIFE CORRIDOR.

wildlife tree A standing live or dead tree that provides a *habitat for the *conservation or enhancement of *wildlife.

wildscape A rugged or *wilderness *landscape.

wildwood Original *woodland cover, unaffected by human activity.

willingness to accept The amount of compensation that an individual is willing to accept in exchange for giving up a particular good or service.

willingness to pay The amount that an individual is willing to pay to acquire a particular good or service.

willow Any of the large number of *deciduous trees and shrubs of the *genus *Salix*.

willy-willy The name given to *severe storms in some South Pacific islands.

wilt To lose strength; a plant wilts if it has insufficient water.

wilting coefficient *See* PERMANENT WILTING POINT.

wilting point The water content of a soil below which plants are no longer able to draw water from it, so they *wilt. *See* PERMANENT WILTING POINT.

wind The horizontal movement of air, that is caused by variations in *atmospheric pressure.

wind belt A zone of the Earth's surface over which particular *wind systems flow.

wind direction The direction from which the wind is blowing, reported with reference to *true north.

wind energy (wind power) Energy from moving air, usually in the form of *electrical energy that is produced by wind-driven *turbines. Wind energy has been traditionally exploited to drive *windmills, and more recently by *wind turbines and *wind farms. The use of wind power around the world has risen rapidly since the early 1980s. Electricity generation from wind power looks likely to increase further in the future, because it is environmentally clean, and eases distribution problems in remote areas beyond the reach of the grid.

wind erosion (aeolian erosion) The process by which soil is detached, transported, and deposited by *wind.

wind erosion equation A formula that is used to estimate rates of *soil erosion from a field that has particular characteristics, by considering *erodibility, roughness, climate, shelter, and vegetation.

wind farm A group of *wind turbines that generate electricity, usually owned and operated by one company.

wind field The three-dimensional spatial pattern of *winds at a particular place and time.

wind power *See* WIND ENERGY.

wind power plant *See* WIND FARM.

wind rose A circular diagram that shows, for a given place or area, the frequency and strength of the *wind that blows from various directions.

wind shear A change in *wind speed or direction with vertical or horizontal distance.

wind sock/cone An open-ended fabric cone that is used to indicate the direction and relative speed of the *wind, often at airfields. *Compare* WIND VANE.

wind sonde A *weather balloon that carries only a radar reflector and is tracked to determine wind speed and direction. There are about 500 upper air weather stations in the world as a whole. Each station releases two wind sondes each day, at 0600 and 1800 UTC (coordinated Universal Time), midway between the launches of *radiosondes. *See also* RAWINSONDE.

wind speed The average speed at which *wind blows in a particular place, which is usually measured in kilometres per hour (km h^{-1}) or as a force on the *Beaufort scale.

wind turbine A mechanical device that converts the energy of *wind into *electricity; a modern form of *windmill.

wind vane An instrument that is attached to a high structure, and rotates freely to show *wind direction. *Compare* WIND SOCK.

wind wave A wave in a large *waterbody (such as an ocean) that is generated by the flow of air over the water surface.

windbreak *See* SHELTERBELT.

windchill The cooling effect of strong wind and low temperature, due to the removal of the layer of warm air next to the skin. The effect can be measured and is usually reported in degrees Celsius (or Fahrenheit). Wind chill can cause *hypothermia in people.

windfall **1.** Fruit that has fallen from a tree. **2.** A tree that is blown down by the wind. **3.** An unexpected financial gain.

windmill A mill that is powered by the wind, traditionally used to grind grain for flour. *Contrast* WATER MILL.

windrow A streak of foam or row of floating debris, aligned in the prevailing wind direction, that forms on the surface of a lake or ocean. Where winds blow across a water surface, vertical circulation cells are set up in near-surface waters. These circulation cells are alternately right- and left-handed vortices, and windrows form at the water surface along the lines of convergence between adjacent cells.

windstrip *See* SHELTERBELT.

windthrow Trees that have been uprooted by strong *wind.

windward The side towards the *wind. *Contrast* LEEWARD.

winter The coldest *season of the year between *autumn/fall and *spring, when the Sun is mainly in the opposite hemisphere. Astronomically this is the period between the *winter solstice and the *vernal equinox, which covers the months of December, January, and February in the northern hemisphere, and June, July, and August in the southern hemisphere.

winter cover *Cover that is required for *overwintering, such as *den trees for squirrels or dense evergreen *thickets for deer.

winter range *Rangeland at low altitude that is used by *migratory animals (such as deer, elk, caribou, and moose) during the winter months.

winter solstice The shortest day of the year, when the Sun is lowest in the sky (because of the Earth's tilt), which marks the start of the *winter season. This occurs in the northern hemisphere on 22–23 December, and in the southern hemisphere on 21–22 June. *See also* SOLSTICE; SUMMER SOLSTICE.

w

winterkill The death of *aquatic organisms during the winter that is caused by a lack of *dissolved oxygen in the frozen water.

Wisconsinan The North American name for the fourth and most recent period of ice advance (*glaciation) of the *Pleistocene *ice age, starting about 75000 years ago and ending with the start of the Holocene around 10000 years ago. It is approximately equivalent to the *Devensian in Britain and the Würm in Central Europe.

Wise Use Movement A US non-profit *anti-environmental *front group comprising a loosely affiliated network of people and organizations (including ranchers, loggers, miners, industrialists, hunters, off-road vehicle users, and land developers) who favour widespread privatization and oppose environmental regulation, particularly any which restricts access to *natural resources and public lands. *Compare* SMART GROWTH NETWORK.

withdrawal The removal of water from *surface water or *groundwater.

WMD *See* WEAPONS OF MASS DESTRUCTION.

WMO *See* WORLD METEOROLOGICAL ORGANIZATION.

Wolf minimum A period of low solar activity that lasted from 1280 until 1340. It was accompanied by a fall in global temperatures that marked the start of the transition from the *Medieval Warm Period to the *Little Ice Age.

wolf tree A large older tree (such as an oak or beech) that has a broad *crown and little or no *timber value, but is valuable for *wildlife. Often a remnant from a previous *stand.

wood 1. The structural parts of woody *perennial plants, especially *trees. *See also* TIMBER. **2.** A small *grove of trees of mixed species, including *undergrowth.

wood energy Wood products that are used as fuel, which include *industrial timber, wood chips, *bark, sawdust, forest residues, *charcoal, and pulp waste.

wood pasture Land on which trees grow and where farm livestock or deer are grazed systematically. *See also* POLLARD.

woodland (open canopy forest, open forest) A landscape with widely spaced, mature trees. The crowns spread more widely than those in a *closed canopy, and do not touch.

woodlot A small plot of land on which trees are grown and managed for *timber.

woodscape A wooded or *woodland *landscape.

woody perennial A plant with thick, tough, *lignified stems which usually lives longer than three years and increases in size each year.

work The energy that is transferred by a force to an object as the object moves.

World Bank The popular name for the International Bank for Reconstruction and Development, an international financial institution that provides funds for development, which was established in 1947.

World Business Council for Sustainable Development (WBCSD) A coalition of 175 international companies drawn from more than 30 countries and 20 major industrial sectors, who share a commitment to *sustainable development through *economic growth, ecological balance, and social progress.

world city A *city which is important nationally and globally as a centre of trade, banking, finance, industry, and markets.

World Commission on Environment and Development (WCED) An international committee that was set up by the United Nations General Assembly in 1983 to examine international and global environmental problems and to propose strategies for *sustainable development. It was chaired by the then Norwegian Prime Minister Gro Harlem Brundtland, and is also known as the Brundtland Commission. Its report, *Our Common Future* (1987), defined and popularized the notion of sustainable development through global cooperation, and was a major catalyst for the 1992 *United Nations Conference on Environment and Development.

World Conservation Monitoring Centre (WCMC) A research centre for monitoring *endangered species that was set up in 1979 by the *World Conservation Union, and established in 2000 as the world *biodiversity information and assessment centre of the United Nations Environment Programme, which seeks 'to promote wiser decision-making and a sustainable future by providing information on the conservation and sustainable management of the living world'.

World Conservation Strategy (WCS) A major international *nature conservation initiative that was launched in 1980 and presented a single integrated approach to global problems based on the concepts of helping species and populations, conserving planetary life support systems, and maintaining genetic diversity.

World Conservation Union (IUCN) A *non-governmental organization that was founded in 1948. It promotes scientifically based action for the conservation of wild living resources and publishes the *Red List and the *Red Data Book. Previously called the International Union for Conservation of Nature and Natural Resources.

World Environment and Disaster Observation System (WEDOS) A proposed environmental *remote sensing system based on launching 26 Earth observation *satellites at low altitude, which would allow any area of the world to be observed at least once a day with a 20 m resolution.

World Environment Day Occurring on 5 June each year, World Environment Day was designated in 1972 by the *United Nations Conference on the Human Environment as a day to focus on environmental problems.

World Health Organization (WHO) An agency of the *United Nations that was founded in 1948, is based in Geneva, and serves to promote cooperation among nations in controlling *disease.

(⊕) SEE WEB LINKS
• WHO home page.

world heritage Natural and cultural *heritage sites that belong to all the peoples of the world, irrespective of the territory in which they are located.

World Heritage Convention See CONVENTION CONCERNING THE PROTECTION OF THE WORLD CULTURAL AND NATURAL HERITAGE.

World Heritage Fund A trust fund that was established by *UNESCO, under the 1972 *Convention Concerning the Protection of the World Cultural and Natural Heritage, for 'the protection of the world cultural and natural heritage of outstanding universal value'. It funds the protection of *World Heritage Sites. *Contrast* GLOBAL HERITAGE FUND.

World Heritage List The formal list of *World Heritage Sites administered by *UNESCO.

(⊕) SEE WEB LINKS
• Full list of World Heritage Sites.

World Heritage Site An *IUCN Management Category (X) for protected areas, a specific site (such as a forest, mountain range, lake, desert, building, complex, or city) that has been nominated for the international World Heritage programme administered by UNESCO, under the *United Nations Convention Concerning the Protection of the World Cultural and Natural Heritage.

World Meteorological Organization (WMO) An intergovernmental organization that was established by the *United Nations in 1947 to monitor and standardize collection of global weather data. It is based in Geneva, Switzerland.

(⊕) SEE WEB LINKS
• WMO home page.

world park An international version of a *national park, which belongs to no single nation but is the responsibility of all nations. None have yet been declared, although the *Antarctic Treaty envisaged it as a means of protecting the unique landscape of Antarctica.

World Population Conference, Bucharest (1974) An international conference organized by the *United Nations which brought together representatives from more developed and less developed countries for the first time. The conference agreed that 'development is the best contraceptive', and proposed the *World Population Plan of Action. It was followed up by the *International Conference on Population which was held in Mexico City in 1984.

World Population Plan of Action A plan of action that was developed at the 1974 *World Population Conference, which recognized that population growth and economic development are mutually related. Amongst other things, the plan was designed to encourage countries to develop their own population policies, reduce mortality and infant mortality, make family planning education and services available for all individuals, promote regional and rural development policies in order to reduce urban pressure, improve national population and development planning, and promote legal, educational, and employment equality for women.

world problematique A concept created by the *Club of Rome to describe the complex

w

set of the crucial problems (political, social, economic, technological, environmental, psychological, and cultural) that humanity faces, and that need solving.

World Resources Institute (WRI) An environmental *think-tank and independent research organization based in Washington, DC, that was set up in 1982 to address global environmental issues.

(⊕) SEE WEB LINKS
• WRI home page.

World Soil Classification (FAO–UNESCO Classification) An international system of soil classification devised by the *United Nations Food and Agriculture Organization (FAO), the *United Nations Educational, Scientific and Cultural Organization (UNESCO), and the International Society of Soil Science (ISS). Work on the project began in 1961 and was completed in 1974. It is based on diagnostic *soil horizons and in its original form it divided soils into 26 major groups, subdivided into 106 soil units. The classification was updated in 1988 and has been amended several times since. In its present form it comprises 30 reference soil groups and 170 possible subunits.

World Summit on Sustainable Development (WSSD) An international gathering of governments, *UN agencies, and *nongovernmental organizations that met in Johannesburg, South Africa, in August to September 2002, in order to assess progress in dealing with *sustainable development since the 1992 *United Nations Conference on Environment and Development.

World Trade Organization (WTO) An international organization with 136 member countries that was set up in 1994 to replace the *General Agreement on Tariffs and Trade, in order to regulate international trade.

World Wide Fund for Nature (WWF) The world's largest and most experienced independent *conservation organization, founded in 1961 as the World Wildlife Fund, whose mission is to protect nature and biological diversity around the world. It has 4.7 million supporters

and a global network active in around 100 countries.

World Wildlife Fund (WWF) *See* WORLD-WIDE FUND FOR NATURE.

worldview A largely unconscious but generally coherent set of presuppositions and beliefs that every person has that shape how we make sense of the world and everything in it. This in turn influences such things as how we see ourselves as individuals, how we interpret our role in society, how we deal with social issues, and what we regard as truth. *See also* ANTHROPOCENTRISM; ECOCENTRISM.

Worldwatch Institute An independent research organization that was founded in 1974. It is based in the USA and 'works for an environmentally sustainable and socially-just society, in which the needs of all people are met without threatening the health of the natural environment or the well-being of future generations'.

(⊕) SEE WEB LINKS
• Worldwatch Institute home page.

worst case scenario The *scenario that produces the worst outcome imaginable for a given set of assumptions and conditions.

wrack 1. A brown seaweed of the family Fucaceae **2.** Seaweed, other organic matter, and drift material (including solid wastes and other pollutants) that accumulates on a *beach, usually at the *high tide mark.

wrack zone The collection of material (*wrack) at the *high tide mark on a beach.

WRI *See* WORLD RESOURCES INSTITUTE.

WSSD *See* WORLD SUMMIT ON SUSTAINABLE DEVELOPMENT.

WTO *See* WORLD TRADE ORGANIZATION.

Würm The Central European equivalent of the *Wisconsinan *glaciation, the fourth and final phase of glaciation during the *Pleistocene.

WWF *See* WORLD WIDE FUND FOR NATURE.

w

xenobiosis A form of *symbiosis among ants in which two colonies of different species live together on friendly terms without rearing their broods in common.

xenobiota A plant that is displaced from its normal *habitat, or a chemical that is not normally found in a particular biological system.

xenobiotic A chemical substance that enters the environment, where no organism has previously encountered it. Many *pesticides, preservatives, and cleaning chemicals fall into this category.

xenolith (inclusion) A fragment of pre-existing rock that is embedded inside an *igneous rock.

xenon (Xe) A heavy, colourless, relatively inert *gas that is a trace element in the Earth's *atmosphere, present at 0.08 parts per million by volume.

xeric Having very little moisture, tolerant of or adapted to dry conditions. *Contrast* MESIC; HYDRIC.

xerophilous Able to withstand dry ground and *drought.

xerophyte A plant that is adapted to grow in very dry conditions. *Contrast* HYDROPHYTE; MESOPHYTE.

xerosere The vegetation *succession that begins in a dry *habitat where little moisture is freely available, such as solid bedrock, broken rocks, or fine rock and sand particles.

X-ray diffraction In *mineralogy, a method for studying microscopic crystal form and structure, using *X-rays.

X-rays *Electromagnetic radiation of very short *wavelength and very high energy, which can penetrate many substances (including skin tissue), hence X-rays are used for photographing internal tissues, bones, and organs in humans, and for detecting flaws in metal objects.

xylem The layer of cells in the trunk of a *tree that carries water and nutrients, which are absorbed from the soil by the roots, to the leaves. *See also* GRAIN.

xylophagous Feeding on wood, which certain insects or insect larvae do.

yard A North American term for the enclosed land around a house or building.

yard waste A North American term for *solid waste in the form of grass clippings, leaves, twigs, branches, and other garden refuse.

yarding In forest management, moving logs from where the tree fell to a central place (*landing) for hauling away from the *stand.

year The period of time that it takes for a *planet (such as the *Earth or Mars) to make a complete revolution around the *Sun, measured from one *vernal equinox to the next. An Earth calendar year is 365.129 days, but a Pluto year is almost 250 Earth years. A sidereal year is measured against the fixed stars; it averages 365.256 days.

yellowcake An impure mixture of *uranium oxides (U_3O_8) that is extracted from crushed uranium *ore during processing.

yellow-fever mosquito The mosquito (*Aedes aegypti*) that transmits yellow fever and dengue.

Yellowstone National Park The world's first national park, established in 1872, located in the US states of Idaho, Montana, and Wyoming. It is famous for its *geysers, *hot springs, and other *geothermal features, and is home to grizzly bears and wolves and free-ranging herds of bison and elk.

yield The amount of a *natural resource (such as freshwater, fish, or crop growth) that is harvested over a given period of time, usually a year.

yield-depression curve A graph on which the *draw down is plotted against the yield of a pumped well or borehole. The resulting plot is invariably curved, and is used to determine the optimum pumping rate for a water supply.

Younger Dryas A *stade or relatively cold period from about 12 900 to 11 600 years ago, which interrupted the warming of the Earth after the last *ice age.

youth **1.** The first part of the *life cycle of an organism, before it reaches *maturity. **2.** An early stage in the *cycle of erosion in which a landscape has been uplifted and is beginning to be dissected by canyons cut by young streams. *Contrast* MATURITY; OLD AGE.

Yucca Mountain The site in southern Nevada, USA, of a controversial development of an underground *repository for long-term storage of *high-level radioactive waste. The plan for the repository was scrapped in 2010.

yushō An illness caused by mass poisoning, which occurred in Kyūshū, Japan, in 1968. Rice bran oil contaminated with *polychlorinated biphenyls and polychlorinated dibenzofurans was sold as a feed supplement for poultry and as cooking oil. Poultry began dying and about 2000 people who had consumed the oil fell sick; there were no deaths. The name means 'oil symptoms'.

Z *See* GREENWICH MEAN TIME.

zephyr A prevailing light and warming breeze from the west at the time of the summer solstice (in the northern hemisphere).

zero discharge (totally effluent free) A condition in which no *pollutants are released into the environment.

zero population growth (ZPG, replacement-level fertility) 1. A stable *population, with a *growth rate of zero, which is achieved when births plus *immigration equal deaths plus *emigration. **2.** The name of an environmental *pressure group that was founded by Paul *Ehrlich in 1968 and which in 2002 changed its name to *Population Connection.

zero till *See* NO TILL.

zero-emission vehicle A vehicle (usually powered by *electricity, *fuel cells or *hydrogen) that theoretically produces no *pollution when stationary or operating.

zero-grazing Animal husbandry that is based on bringing *fodder to the animals rather than letting them *graze freely.

zinc (Zn) A blue-white, lustrous, *metallic element, one of the eight *micronutrients that are essential for plant health. It is soluble and found naturally in air, soil, water, and foods. It is an essential nutrient for humans but is harmful in large amounts. It is brittle at ordinary temperatures but *malleable when heated, and is used in a wide variety of *alloys and in galvanizing *iron.

zineb A dithiocarbamate *fungicide used to control a range of diseases in fruit and vegetable crops, including potato blight and downy mildews. It is a skin, eye, and respiratory irritant and slightly to moderately toxic if ingested.

zircon A hard *mineral that is common in all types of *igneous rock and many *metamorphic rocks, that yields clear gemstones called cubic zircons which are a cheap alternative to diamond.

zonal Along a line of *latitude. *Contrast* MERIDIONAL.

zonal soil A mature soil that has well-developed characteristics typical of the *climatic zone in which it occurs. *Contrast* AZONAL SOIL; INTRAZONAL SOIL. *See* GREAT SOIL GROUP.

zonal wind The large-scale movement of air in a dominantly west-east or east-west direction, with little movement north-south or south-north.

zonation The distribution of plants and animals into different geographical zones, such as the variations in water depth in the *intertidal zone.

zone fossil *See* INDEX FOSSIL.

zone of ablation *See* ABLATION ZONE.

zone of accumulation *See* ACCUMULATION ZONE.

zone of aeration *See* AERATION ZONE.

zone of leaching The layer of soil, just beneath the *topsoil, from which soluble *nutrients are removed (leached) by water.

zone of saturation *See* SATURATED ZONE.

zone of wastage *See* WASTAGE ZONE.

zoning In North America, the rules and regulations that are established by local government to govern the use of land, particularly the size, type, structure, nature, and use of buildings. *See also* AESTHETIC ZONING; AGRICULTURAL ZONING; CLUSTER ZONING; CONSERVATION ZONING; EXCLUSIVE USE ZONING; FLOODPLAIN ZONING; FOREST USE ZONING; LARGE-LOT ZONING; NATURAL RESOURCE ZONING; OPEN SPACE ZONING; PERFORMANCE STANDARD ZONING; PROHIBITION ZONING; SPOT ZONING; TIME ZONING; ZONING ORDINANCE; ZONING PERMIT.

zoning ordinance In North America, a local law or regulation that is established by a city council or similar body to govern land use within a particular designated area (zone) and the nature of the buildings within each zone. *See also* ZONING; ZONING PERMIT.

zoning permit In North America, an official finding that a planned use or structure complies with existing *zoning ordinances, or is allowed by the granting of a special exception.

zoning variance In land use *zoning, a licence to act contrary to the usual rule.

zoo Short for zoological garden. A place (usually a garden or park) where live animals are kept for exhibition or for *captive breeding programmes for *endangered species. *See also* BOTANICAL GARDEN.

zooecology The study of the relationship between animals and their environment. *Contrast* ZOOLOGY.

zoological area An area in the USA that has been designated by the US Forest Service or others as containing *animals, animal groups, or animal communities that are natural and important in some particular way.

zoological garden *See* ZOO.

zoological kingdom *See* ANIMAL KINGDOM.

zoology The study of animals (including *mammals, *birds, *reptiles, *amphibians, *fish, *insects, spiders, and *molluscs) and their structures and functions. *Contrast* ZOOECOLOGY. *See also* BOTANY.

zooneuston Those animals associated with the surface of water, mainly in freshwater *habitats, and influenced by surface tension. The group is divided into those associated with the upper surface of the film, to which the term 'epineustic' is applied, and those associated with the lower surface, described as 'hyponeustic'. Many organisms show adaptation to this environment (e.g. some bugs of the order Hemiptera have pads at the ends of their legs that enable them to walk across the water surface). *See also* NEUSTON.

zoonosis An *infection or infectious *disease that occurs mainly in wild and domestic animals but can be transmitted to humans.

zooplankton The animal component of the *plankton community, which feed on *phytoplankton and other zooplankton, and are eaten by tiny fish.

zooxanthellae Brownish *algae that live in a *symbiotic relationship with certain *corals, clams, and some sponges and are responsible for the brilliant green, yellow, and blue colours in corals and clams.

ZPG *See* ZERO POPULATION GROWTH.

zygote A fertilized egg. *See also* FERTILIZATION; GAMETE.

Appendix 1. Sources of online data on the environment

The most useful and accessible general source of up-to-date information are the *GEO: Global Environment Outlook* reports, published by the United Nations Environment Programme, both in print and online (the reports can be downloaded in full as PDF files from http://www.unep.org/geo). The GEO Indicators section contains data on atmosphere, disasters caused by natural hazards, biodiversity, coastal and marine areas, freshwater, urban areas, and global environmental issues.

Useful online sources of information and data on particular environmental issues include:

Biodiversity   Global Biodiversity Information Facility (GBIF); http://www.gbif.org/

Biodiversity   Species 2000; http://www.sp2000.org/

Carbon dioxide   Carbon Dioxide Information Analysis Center (CDIAC); http://cdiac.ornl.gov/

Chemicals   European Chemicals Agency; http://echa.europa.eu/

Climate change   Intergovernmental Panel on Climate Change (IPCC); http://www.ipcc.ch/

CLOUD   http://cloud.web.cern.ch/cloud/

Conservation   World Conservation Monitoring Center (WCMC); http://www.unep-wcmc.org/

Conservation   World Conservation Union (International Union for the Conservation of Nature – IUCN); http://www.iucn.org/

Conservation   World Wildlife Fund (WWF); http://www.wwf.org/

Development   Organization for Economic Co-operation and Development (OECD); http://www.oecd.org

Development   United Nations Development Programme (UNDP); http://www.undp.org/

Development   United Nations Educational, Scientific and Cultural Organization (UNESCO); http://www.unesco.org

Development   World Bank; http://data.worldbank.org/indicator

Energy   International Energy Agency (IEA); http://www.iea.org/

Energy   World Energy Council (WEC); http://www.worldenergy.org/

Environment   Environmental Protection Agency Envirofacts Data Warehouse; http://www.epa.gov/enviro/

Environment   United Nations Environment Programme GEO Data Portal; http://geodata.grid.unep.ch/

Environment   World Resources Institute (WRI); http://earthtrends.wri.org/

Environment   Worldwatch Institute; http://www.worldwatch.org/

Fauna and Flora   Fauna and Flora International; http://www.fauna-flora.org/

Food and agriculture   United Nations Food and Agriculture Organization (FAO); http://faostat.fao.org/

Food safety   European Food Safety Authority; http://www.efsa.europa.eu/en/pesticides/mrls.htm

Forests   Forest Stewardship Council (FSC); http://www.fsc.org/

Global warming   Global Warming Policy Foundation; http://www.thegwpf.org/

Greenhouse gases   United Nations Framework Convention on Climate Change (UNFCCC); http://ghg.unfccc.int/index.html

Green Revolution   International Food Policy Research Institute; http://www.ifpri.org/sites/default/files/pubs/pubs/ib/ib11.pdf

Health   United Nations World Health Organization (WHO); http://www.who.int/en/

Heritage   UNESCO World Heritage Centre; http://whc.unesco.org/

Human settlements United Nations Human Settlements Programme (UN-HABITAT); http://www.unbrussels.org/agencies/habitat.html

National and global statistics United Nations Statistics Division (UN-STAT); http://unstats.un.org/unsd/default.htm

Natural disasters International Disasters Database; http://www.emdat.be/

Nuclear energy International Atomic Energy Agency (IAEA); http://www.iaea.org/

Ozone United Nations Environment Programme Ozone Secretariat; http://www.unep.ch/ozone/DataReport99.shtml

Population United Nations Population Division; http://www.un.org/esa/population/unpop.htm

Regional seas Regional Seas Programme; http://www.unep.org/regionalseas/

Resources Global Resource Information Database; http://www.grid.unep.ch/

Soils International Soil Reference and Information Centre (ISRIC); http://www.isric.org/

Sustainable development International Institute for Sustainable Development (IISD); http://www.iisd.org/

Weather World Meteorological Organization; http://www.wmo.int/pages/index_en.html

Wetlands Ramsar Convention on Wetlands; http://www.ramsar.org/

Appendix 2. International environmental treaties

Up-to-date information on international environmental treaties, and on which countries have signed up to which treaties, can be found online at the FBI *World Factbook* web site (http://www.cia.gov/cia/publications/factbook/appendix/appendix-c.html), on which this appendix is based.

a. Subjects

Air Pollution   *See* CONVENTION ON LONG-RANGE TRANSBOUNDARY AIR POLLUTION

Air Pollution-Nitrogen Oxides   *See* PROTOCOL TO THE 1979 CONVENTION ON LONG-RANGE TRANSBOUNDARY AIR POLLUTION CONCERNING THE CONTROL OF EMISSIONS OF NITROGEN OXIDES OR THEIR TRANSBOUNDARY FLUXES

Air Pollution-Persistent Organic Pollutants   *See* PROTOCOL TO THE 1979 CONVENTION ON LONG-RANGE TRANSBOUNDARY AIR POLLUTION ON PERSISTENT ORGANIC POLLUTANTS

Air Pollution-Sulphur 85   *See* PROTOCOL TO THE 1979 CONVENTION ON LONG-RANGE TRANSBOUNDARY AIR POLLUTION ON THE REDUCTION OF SULPHUR EMISSIONS OR THEIR TRANSBOUNDARY FLUXES BY AT LEAST 30%

Air Pollution-Sulphur 94   *See* PROTOCOL TO THE 1979 CONVENTION ON LONG-RANGE TRANSBOUNDARY AIR POLLUTION ON FURTHER REDUCTION OF SULPHUR EMISSIONS

Air Pollution-Volatile Organic Compounds   *See* PROTOCOL TO THE 1979 CONVENTION ON LONG-RANGE TRANSBOUNDARY AIR POLLUTION CONCERNING THE CONTROL OF EMISSIONS OF VOLATILE ORGANIC COMPOUNDS OR THEIR TRANSBOUNDARY FLUXES

Antarctic - Environmental Protocol   *See* PROTOCOL ON ENVIRONMENTAL PROTECTION TO THE ANTARCTIC TREATY

Biodiversity   *See* CONVENTION ON BIOLOGICAL DIVERSITY

Chemicals   *See* REGISTRATION, EVALUATION, AUTHORISATION and RESTRICTION OF CHEMICAL SUBSTANCES.

Climate Change   *See* UNITED NATIONS FRAMEWORK CONVENTION ON CLIMATE CHANGE

Climate Change-Kyoto Protocol   *See* KYOTO PROTOCOL TO THE UNITED NATIONS FRAMEWORK CONVENTION ON CLIMATE CHANGE

Desertification   *See* UNITED NATIONS CONVENTION TO COMBAT DESERTIFICATION IN THOSE COUNTRIES EXPERIENCING SERIOUS DROUGHT AND/OR DESERTIFICATION, PARTICULARLY IN AFRICA

Endangered Species   *See* CONVENTION ON THE INTERNATIONAL TRADE IN ENDANGERED SPECIES OF WILD FLORA AND FAUNA (CITES)

Environmental Modification   *See* CONVENTION ON THE PROHIBITION OF MILITARY OR ANY OTHER HOSTILE USE OF ENVIRONMENTAL MODIFICATION TECHNIQUES

Hazardous Wastes   *See* BASEL CONVENTION ON THE CONTROL OF TRANSBOUNDARY MOVEMENTS OF HAZARDOUS WASTES AND THEIR DISPOSAL

Law of the Sea   *See* UNITED NATIONS CONVENTION ON THE LAW OF THE SEA (LOS)

Marine Dumping   *See* CONVENTION ON THE PREVENTION OF MARINE POLLUTION BY DUMPING WASTES AND OTHER MATTER (LONDON CONVENTION)

Marine Life Conservation   *See* CONVENTION ON FISHING AND CONSERVATION OF LIVING RESOURCES OF THE HIGH SEAS

Nuclear Test Ban   *See* TREATY BANNING NUCLEAR WEAPONS TESTS IN THE ATMOSPHERE, IN OUTER SPACE, AND UNDER WATER

Ozone Layer Protection   *See* MONTREAL PROTOCOL ON SUBSTANCES THAT DEPLETE THE OZONE LAYER

Polar Bears   *See* AGREEMENT ON THE CONSERVATION OF POLAR BEARS

Ship Pollution   *See* Protocol of 1978 Relating to the International Convention for the Prevention of Pollution from Ships, 1973 (MARPOL)

Tropical Timber 83   *See* International Tropical Timber Agreement, 1983

Tropical Timber 94   *See* International Tropical Timber Agreement, 1994

Wetlands   *See* Convention on Wetlands of International Importance Especially As Waterfowl Habitat (Ramsar)

Whaling   *See* International Convention for the Regulation of Whaling

b. Treaties

Antarctic Treaty
opened for signature 1 December 1959
entered into force 23 June 1961
objective to ensure that Antarctica is used for peaceful purposes only (such as international cooperation in scientific research); to defer the question of territorial claims asserted by some nations and not recognized by others; to provide an international forum for management of the region; applies to land and ice shelves south of 60°S latitude
parties 48
further details http://www.scar.org/treaty/at_text.html

Basel Convention on the Control of Transboundary Movements of Hazardous Wastes and Their Disposal
shown in the table below as Hazardous Wastes
opened for signature 22 March 1989
entered into force 5 May 1992
objective to reduce transboundary movements of wastes subject to the Convention to a minimum consistent with the environmentally sound and efficient management of such wastes; to minimize the amount and toxicity of wastes generated and ensure their environmentally sound management as close as possible to the source of generation; and to assist less developed countries in environmentally sound management of the hazardous and other wastes they generate
parties 179
further details http://www.basel.int/

Convention for the Conservation of Antarctic Seals
shown in the table below as Antarctic Seals
opened for signature 1 June 1972
entered into force 11 March 1978
objective to promote and achieve the protection, scientific study, and rational use of Antarctic seals, and to maintain a satisfactory balance within the ecological system of Antarctica
parties 16
further details http://www.antarctica.ac.uk/about_antarctica/geopolitical/treaty/update_1972.php

Convention on Biological Diversity
shown in the table below as Biodiversity
opened for signature 5 June 1992
entered into force 29 December 1993
objective to develop national strategies for the conservation and sustainable use of biological diversity
parties 193
further details http://www.biodiv.org/convention/articles.asp

Convention on Fishing and Conservation of Living Resources of the High Seas
shown in the table below as Marine Life Conservation
opened for signature 29 April 1958
entered into force 20 March 1966

objective to solve through international cooperation the problems involved in the conservation of living resources of the high seas, considering that because of the development of modern technology some of these resources are in danger of being overexploited

parties 38

further details http://untreaty.un.org/ilc/texts/instruments/english/conventions/8_1_1958_fishing.pdf

Convention on Long-Range Transboundary Air Pollution

shown in the table below as Air Pollution
opened for signature 13 November 1979
entered into force 16 March 1983
objective to protect the human environment against air pollution and to gradually reduce and prevent air pollution, including long-range transboundary air pollution
parties 51
further details http://www.unece.org/env/lrtap/lrtap_h1.htm

Convention on Wetlands of International Importance Especially as Waterfowl Habitat (Ramsar)

shown in the table below as Wetlands
opened for signature 2 February 1971
entered into force 21 December 1975
objective to stem the progressive encroachment on and loss of wetlands now and in the future, recognizing the fundamental ecological functions of wetlands and their economic, cultural, scientific, and recreational value
parties 160
further details http://www.ramsar.org/cda/en/ramsar-home/main/ramsar/1_4000_0__

Convention on the Conservation of Antarctic Marine Living Resources

shown in the table below as Antarctic-Marine Living Resources
opened for signature 5 May 1980
entered into force 7 April 1982
objective to safeguard the environment and protect the integrity of the ecosystem of the seas surrounding Antarctica, and to conserve Antarctic marine living resources
parties 38
further details http://www.ccamlr.org/pu/e/e_pubs/bd/pt1.pdf

Convention on the International Trade in Endangered Species of Wild Flora and Fauna (CITES)

shown in the table below as Endangered Species
opened for signature 3 March 1973
entered into force 1 July 1975
objective to protect certain endangered species from overexploitation by means of a system of import/export permits
parties 175
further details http://www.cites.org/

Convention on the Prevention of Marine Pollution by Dumping Wastes and Other Matter (London Convention)

shown in the table below as Marine Dumping
opened for signature 29 December 1972
entered into force 30 August 1975
objective to control pollution of the sea by dumping and to encourage regional agreements supplementary to the Convention
parties 87
further details http://www.imo.org/OurWork/Environment/SpecialProgrammesAndInitiatives/Pages/London-Convention-and-Protocol.aspx

Convention on the Prohibition of Military or Any Other Hostile Use of Environmental Modification Techniques

shown in the table below as Environmental Modification
opened for signature 10 December 1976

entered into force 5 October 1978
objective to prohibit the military or other hostile use of environmental modification techniques in
   order to further world peace and trust among nations
parties 60
further details http://www.opcw.org/html/db/cwc/more/enmod.html

International Convention for the Regulation of Whaling
shown in the table below as Whaling
opened for signature 2 December 1946
entered into force 10 November 1948
objective to protect all species of whales from overhunting; to establish a system of international
   regulation for the whale fisheries to ensure proper conservation and development of whale stocks;
   and to safeguard for future generations the great natural resources represented by whale stocks
parties 89
further details http://iwcoffice.org/

International Tropical Timber Agreement, 1983, 1994, 2006
shown in the table below as Tropical Timber 83
opened for signature 18 November 1983
entered into force 1 April 1985; this agreement expired when the International Tropical Timber
   Agreement, 1994, went into force with the aim of ensuring that by the year 2000 exports of
   tropical timber originate from sustainably managed sources; to establish a fund to assist tropical
   timber producers in obtaining the resources necessary to reach this objective; it was updated in
   2006
objective to provide an effective framework for cooperation between tropical timber producers
   and consumers and to encourage the development of national policies aimed at sustainable
   utilization and conservation of tropical forests and their genetic resources
parties 36 (EU counted as one party)
further details http://treaties.un.org/doc/source/RecentTexts/XIX_46_english.pdf

Kyoto Protocol to the United Nations Framework Convention on Climate Change
shown in the table below as Climate Change-Kyoto Protocol
opened for signature 16 March 1998
entered into force 23 February 2005
objective to further reduce greenhouse gas emissions by enhancing the national programmes of
   developed countries aimed at this goal and by establishing percentage reduction targets for the
   developed countries
parties 192
further details http://unfccc.int/resource/docs/convkp/kpeng.html

Montreal Protocol on Substances That Deplete the Ozone Layer
shown in the table below as Ozone Layer Protection
opened for signature 16 September 1987
entered into force 1 January 1989
objective to protect the ozone layer by controlling emissions of substances that deplete it
parties 197
further details http://ozone.unep.org/pdfs/Montreal-Protocol2000.pdf

Protocol of 1978 Relating to the International Convention for the Prevention of Pollution From Ships, 1973 (MARPOL)
shown in the table below as Ship Pollution
opened for signature 17 February 1978
entered into force 2 October 1983
objective to preserve the marine environment through the complete elimination of pollution by oil
   and other harmful substances and the minimization of accidental discharge of such substances
parties 150
further details http://www.imo.org/about/conventions/listofconventions/pages/international-con-
   vention-for-the-prevention-of-pollution-from-ships-(marpol).aspx

Protocol on Environmental Protection to the Antarctic Treaty
shown in the table below as Antarctic-Environmental Protocol
opened for signature 4 October 1991
entered into force 14 January 1998
objective to provide for comprehensive protection of the Antarctic environment and dependent and associated ecosystems; applies to the area covered by the Antarctic Treaty
consultative parties 48
further details http://www.antarctica.ac.uk/About_Antarctica/Treaty/protocol.html

Protocol to the 1979 Convention on Long-Range Transboundary Air Pollution Concerning the Control of Emissions of Nitrogen Oxides or Their Transboundary Fluxes
shown in the table below as Air Pollution-Nitrogen Oxides
opened for signature 31 October 1988
entered into force 14 February 1991
objective to provide for the control or reduction of nitrogen oxides and their transboundary fluxes
parties 34
further details http://www.unece.org/env/lrtap/nitr_h1.html

Protocol to the 1979 Convention on Long-Range Transboundary Air Pollution Concerning the Control of Emissions of Volatile Organic Compounds or Their Transboundary Fluxes
shown in the table below as Air Pollution-Volatile Organic Compounds
opened for signature 18 November 1991
entered into force 29 September 1997
objective to provide for the control and reduction of emissions of volatile organic compounds in order to reduce their transboundary fluxes so as to protect human health and the environment from adverse effects
parties 24
further details http://www.unece.org/env/lrtap/vola_h1.html

Protocol to the 1979 Convention on Long-Range Transboundary Air Pollution on Further Reduction of Sulphur Emissions
shown in the table below as Air Pollution-Sulphur 94
opened for signature 14 June 1994
entered into force 5 August 1998
objective to provide for a further reduction in sulphur emissions or transboundary fluxes
parties 29
further details http://www.unece.org/env/lrtap/fsulf_h1.html

Protocol to the 1979 Convention on Long-Range Transboundary Air Pollution on Persistent Organic Pollutants
shown in the table below as Air Pollution-Persistent Organic Pollutants
opened for signature 24 June 1998
entered into force 23 October 2003
objective to provide for the control and reduction of emissions of persistent organic pollutants in order to reduce their transboundary fluxes so as to protect human health and the environment from adverse effects
parties 31
further details http://www.unece.org/env/lrtap/pops_h1.html

Protocol to the 1979 Convention on Long-Range Transboundary Air Pollution on the Reduction of Sulphur Emissions or Their Transboundary Fluxes by at Least 30%
shown in the table below as Air Pollution-Sulphur 85
opened for signature 8 July 1985
entered into force 2 September 1987
objective to provide for a 30% reduction in sulphur emissions or transboundary fluxes by 1993
parties 25
further details http://www.unece.org/env/lrtap/sulf_h1.html

Treaty Banning Nuclear Weapon Tests in the Atmosphere, in Outer Space, and Under Water
shown in the table below as Nuclear Test Ban
opened for signature 5 August 1963
entered into force 10 October 1963
objective to obtain an agreement on general and complete disarmament under strict international control in accordance with the objectives of the United Nations; to put an end to the armaments race and eliminate incentives for the production and testing of all kinds of weapons, including nuclear weapons
parties 123
further details http://www.un.org/disarmament/WMD/Nuclear/pdf/Partial_Ban_Treaty.pdf

United Nations Convention on the Law of the Sea (LOS)
shown in the table below as Law of the Sea
opened for signature 10 December 1982
entered into force 16 November 1994
objective to set up a comprehensive new legal regime for the sea and oceans; to include rules concerning environmental standards as well as enforcement provisions dealing with pollution of the marine environment
parties 162
further details http://www.un.org/Depts/los/convention_agreements/texts/unclos/unclos_e.pdf

United Nations Convention to Combat Desertification in Those Countries Experiencing Serious Drought and/or Desertification, Particularly in Africa
shown in the table below as Desertification
opened for signature 14 October 1994
entered into force 26 December 1996
objective to combat desertification and mitigate the effects of drought through national action programmes that incorporate long-term strategies supported by international cooperation and partnership arrangements
parties 194
further details http://www.unccd.int/

United Nations Framework Convention on Climate Change
shown in the table below as Climate Change
opened for signature 9 May 1992
entered into force 21 March 1994
objective to achieve stabilization of greenhouse gas concentrations in the atmosphere at a low enough level to prevent dangerous anthropogenic interference with the climate system
parties 194
further details http://unfccc.int/resource/docs/convkp/conveng.pdf

C. Countries that had ratified by June 2005

Country	Air Pollution	Air Pollution-Nitrogen Oxides	Air Pollution-Persistent Organic Pollutants	Air Pollution-Sulphur 85	Air Pollution-Sulphur 94	Air Pollution-Volatile Organic Compounds	Antarctic-Environmental Protocol	Antarctic-Marine Living Resources	Antarctic Seals	Antarctic Treaty	Biodiversity	Climate Change	Climate Change-Kyoto Protocol	Desertification	Endangered Species	Environmental Modification	Hazardous Wastes	Law of the Sea	Marine Dumping	Marine Life Conservation	Nuclear Test Ban	Ozone Layer Protection	Ship Pollution	Tropical Timber 83	Tropical Timber 94	Wetlands	Whaling
Afghanistan														X	X	X			X		X						
Albania											X	X		X			X					X				X	
Algeria											X	X		X	X	X	X	X				X	X			X	
Andorra																	X										
Angola											X	X		X			X	X				X	X				
Antigua & Barbuda											X	X	X	X	X	X	X	X	X		X	X	X			X	X
Argentina	X						X	X	X	X	X	X	X	X	X	X	X	X	X		X	X	X			X	X
Armenia	X										X	X		X			X	X			X	X				X	
Australia	X	X		X	X		X	X	X	X	X	X	X	X	X	X	X	X	X	X	X	X	X	X	X	X	X
Austria	X	X		X	X	X				X	X	X	X	X	X	X	X	X	X		X	X	X	X	X	X	X
Azerbaijan		X		X	X	X					X	X	X	X	X		X	X	X			X				X	
Bahamas											X	X	X	X			X	X				X	X			X	
Bahrain											X	X		X			X	X				X				X	
Bangladesh											X	X	X	X	X	X	X	X			X	X				X	

(continued)

C. Countries that had ratified by June 2005 (contd)

Country	Air Pollution	Air Pollution-Nitrogen Oxides	Air Pollution-Persistent Organic Pollutants	Air Pollution-Sulphur 85	Air Pollution-Sulphur 94	Air Pollution-Volatile Organic Compounds	Antarctic-Environmental Protocol	Antarctic-Marine Living Resources	Antarctic Seals	Antarctic Treaty	Biodiversity	Climate Change	Climate Change-Kyoto Protocol	Desertification	Endangered Species	Environmental Modification	Hazardous Wastes	Law of the Sea	Marine Dumping	Marine Life Conservation	Nuclear Test Ban	Ozone Layer Protection	Ship Pollution	Tropical Timber 83	Tropical Timber 94	Wetlands	Whaling
Barbados	X	X									X	X	X	X	X		X	X	X			X	X			X	
Belarus	X	X		X							X	X		X	X		X		X			X	X			X	
Belgium		X			X	X	X	X	X	X	X	X	X	X	X	X	X	X	X	X	X	X	X	X	X	X	
Belize											X	X		X	X	X	X	X				X	X			X	
Benin												X		X	X	X	X	X				X	X				
Bhutan												X															
Bolivia											X	X	X	X	X		X	X	X	X	X	X		X	X	X	
Bosnia & Herzegovina	X										X	X					X	X			X		X	X	X	X	
Botswana								X			X	X		X	X	X	X	X		X	X	X	X	X	X	X	
Brazil							X	X	X	X	X	X	X	X	X	X	X	X			X	X	X	X	X	X	X
Brunei								X										X				X	X				X
Bulgaria	X	X				X	X			X	X	X		X	X		X				X	X	X			X	
Burkino Faso		X				X					X	X		X	X		X					X	X			X	
Burma		X									X	X	X	X	X						X	X			X		
Burundi											X	X	X	X	X		X	X				X	X	X			

Country																						
Cambodia	X						X	X	X		X	X	X	X		X	X				X	
Cameroon	X						X	X	X		X	X	X	X		X	X		X		X	
Canada	X	X	X	X			X	X	X		X	X	X	X		X	X	X	X		X	
Cape Verde	X						X	X	X		X	X	X	X		X		X			X	
Central African Republic							X	X	X		X	X	X	X					X			
Chad			X	X	X		X	X	X	X	X	X	X	X		X	X				X	X
Chile	X	X	X				X	X	X	X	X	X	X	X	X	X	X		X		X	X
China	X						X	X	X	X	X	X	X	X		X	X		X		X	X
Colombia	X						X	X	X	X	X	X	X	X		X	X	X			X	X
Comoros						X	X	X	X		X	X	X	X		X		X			X	X
Congo, Democratic Republic							X	X	X		X	X	X	X	X							
Congo, Republic							X	X	X		X	X	X	X	X			X	X			X
Cook Islands						X	X	X	X	X	X	X	X	X	X			X			X	X
Costa Rica							X	X	X	X	X	X	X	X	X		X	X	X		X	
Cote D'Ivoire	X						X	X	X		X	X	X	X	X		X	X	X		X	
Croatia	X						X	X	X	X	X	X	X	X	X			X	X		X	
Cuba	X					X	X	X	X	X	X	X	X	X	X		X	X			X	
Cyprus	X	X	X				X	X	X	X	X	X	X	X			X	X	X		X	
Czech Republic	X	X	X				X	X	X	X	X	X	X	X		X	X	X	X		X	X
Denmark	X	X	X				X	X	X	X	X	X	X	X		X	X	X			X	
Djibouti							X	X	X	X	X	X	X	X	X		X		X			
Dominica							X	X	X		X	X	X	X		X	X					X
Dominican Republic							X	X	X		X	X	X	X	X		X	X				
Ecuador	X					X	X	X	X	X	X	X	X	X	X		X	X	X		X	X
Egypt	X						X	X	X	X	X	X	X	X		X	X	X			X	X
El Salvador	X						X	X	X	X	X	X	X	X		X	X	X			X	X
Equatorial Guinea							X	X	X		X	X	X	X	X				X			

(continued)

C. Countries that had ratified by June 2005 (contd)

Country	Air Pollution	Air Pollution-Nitrogen Oxides	Air Pollution-Persistent Organic Pollutants	Air Pollution-Sulphur 85	Air Pollution-Sulphur 94	Air Pollution-Volatile Organic Compounds	Antarctic-Environmental Protocol	Antarctic-Marine Living Resources	Antarctic Seals	Antarctic Treaty	Biodiversity	Climate Change	Climate Change-Kyoto Protocol	Desertification	Endangered Species	Environmental Modification	Hazardous Wastes	Law of the Sea	Marine Dumping	Marine Life Conservation	Nuclear Test Ban	Ozone Layer Protection	Ship Pollution	Tropical Timber 83	Tropical Timber 94	Wetlands	Whaling
Eritrea	X									X	X	X		X	X		X	X				X	X			X	
Estonia	X	X		X		X					X	X		X	X		X	X				X	X			X	
Ethiopia											X	X		X	X			X				X					
Fiji	X	X		X	X	X	X	X		X	X	X	X	X	X	X	X	X	X	X	X	X	X	X	X	X	X
Finland	X	X		X	X	X	X	X	X	X	X	X	X	X	X	X	X	X	X	X	X	X	X	X	X	X	X
France	X						X	X	X		X	X		X	X	X	X	X	X	X		X	X	X	X	X	
Cameroon											X	X		X	X			X				X	X	X	X		
Gabon											X	X		X	X			X			X	X	X	X	X	X	
Gambia											X	X		X	X		X	X			X	X	X	X	X	X	
Georgia	X	X		X							X	X	X	X	X	X		X				X	X			X	X
Germany	X	X		X	X	X	X	X	X		X	X	X	X	X	X	X	X	X		X	X	X	X	X	X	X
Ghana					X		X	X			X	X	X	X	X	X	X	X			X	X	X	X	X	X	
Greece	X	X					X			X	X	X		X	X	X	X	X	X		X	X	X	X	X	X	
Grenada											X	X		X	X			X				X	X				X
Guatemala										X	X	X	X	X	X			X			X	X	X			X	
Guinea											X	X	X	X	X	X	X	X	X			X				X	X

Guinea-Bissau									X	X	X	X		X	
Guyana						X	X	X	X	X	X	X	X		X
Haiti						X	X	X	X	X	X	X	X		X
Holy See (Vatican City)									X	X					
Honduras						X	X	X	X	X	X	X	X		X
Hong Kong															
Hungary	X		X	X	X	X	X	X	X	X	X	X	X	X	X
Iceland	X		X		X	X	X	X	X	X	X	X	X	X	X
India		X	X	X		X	X	X	X	X	X	X	X	X	X
Indonesia			X		X	X	X	X	X	X	X	X	X	X	X
Iran			X			X	X	X	X	X	X	X		X	
Iraq															
Ireland	X		X	X	X	X	X	X	X	X	X	X	X	X	X
Israel		X	X	X	X	X	X	X	X	X	X	X	X	X	X
Italy	X		X	X	X	X	X	X	X	X	X	X	X	X	X
Jamaica	X		X	X	X	X	X	X	X	X	X	X	X	X	X
Japan	X		X	X	X	X	X	X	X	X	X	X	X	X	X
Jordan			X	X	X							X		X	
Kazakhstan	X		X		X					X		X			
Kenya			X		X	X	X	X	X	X	X	X	X	X	X
Kiribati										X					
Korea, North			X	X			X		X	X	X	X			
Korea, South			X	X	X	X	X	X	X	X	X	X		X	X
Kuwait	X		X			X			X	X	X	X			
Kyrgystan			X		X	X	X	X	X	X	X	X			
Laos			X			X		X	X	X	X	X			
Latvia	X		X		X	X	X	X	X	X	X	X		X	X
Lebanon			X		X	X	X	X	X	X	X	X		X	X
Lesotho			X	X	X	X	X	X	X	X	X	X	X		
Liberia			X	X	X	X	X	X	X	X	X	X	X	X	X

(continued)

C. Countries that had ratified by June 2005 (contd)

Country	Air Pollution	Air Pollution-Nitrogen Oxides	Air Pollution-Persistent Organic Pollutants	Air Pollution-Sulphur 85	Air Pollution-Sulphur 94	Air Pollution-Volatile Organic Compounds	Antarctic-Environmental Protocol	Antarctic-Marine Living Resources	Antarctic Seals	Antarctic Treaty	Biodiversity	Climate Change	Climate Change-Kyoto Protocol	Desertification	Endangered Species	Environmental Modification	Hazardous Wastes	Law of the Sea	Marine Dumping	Marine Life Conservation	Nuclear Test Ban	Ozone Layer Protection	Ship Pollution	Tropical Timber 83	Tropical Timber 94	Wetlands	Whaling
Libya	X										X	X		X			X		X			X				X	
Liechtenstein	X	X		X	X	X					X	X		X	X		X					X				X	
Lithuania				X	X						X	X			X		X					X				X	
Luxembourg	X	X	X	X	X	X					X	X		X	X	X	X					X				X	
Macedonia	X										X	X		X	X		X	X				X				X	
Madagascar											X	X	X	X	X	X	X	X	X	X	X	X	X	X	X	X	
Malawi											X	X		X	X	X	X	X		X	X	X	X			X	
Malaysia											X	X		X	X		X	X		X	X	X	X				
Maldives											X	X	X	X	X		X	X		X	X	X	X	X	X	X	
Mali											X	X		X	X		X	X	X		X	X				X	
Malta	X										X	X	X	X	X		X	X	X		X	X	X			X	
Marshall Islands											X	X					X	X				X	X			X	
Mauritania											X	X	X	X	X	X	X	X		X	X	X	X			X	
Mauritius											X	X	X	X	X		X	X		X	X	X	X			X	
Mexico											X	X	X	X	X		X	X	X		X	X	X			X	X

Country
Micronesia, Federated States
Moldova
Monaco
Mongolia
Morocco
Mozambique
Namibia
Nauru
Nepal
Netherlands
New Zealand
Nicaragua
Niger
Nigeria
Niue
Norway
Oman
Pakistan
Palau
Panama
Papua New Guinea
Paraguay
Peru
Philippines
Poland
Portugal
Qatar
Romania
Russia

(continued)

C. Countries that had ratified by June 2005 (contd)

Country	Air Pollution	Air Pollution-Nitrogen Oxides	Air Pollution-Persistent Organic Pollutants	Air Pollution-Sulphur 85	Air Pollution-Sulphur 94	Air Pollution-Volatile Organic Compounds	Antarctic-Environmental Protocol	Antarctic-Marine Living Resources	Antarctic Seals	Antarctic Treaty	Biodiversity	Climate Change	Climate Change-Kyoto Protocol	Desertification	Endangered Species	Environmental Modification	Hazardous Wastes	Law of the Sea	Marine Dumping	Marine Life Conservation	Nuclear Test Ban	Ozone Layer Protection	Ship Pollution	Tropical Timber 83	Tropical Timber 94	Wetlands	Whaling
Rwanda											X	X		X	X			X			X	X	X				
Saint Kitts & Nevis											X	X		X	X		X	X				X	X				X
Saint Lucia											X	X	X	X	X	X	X	X	X			X	X				X
Saint Vincent & the Grenadines											X	X		X	X	X	X	X					X	X			X
Samoa											X	X		X	X			X			X	X					
San Marino											X	X		X	X						X						
Sao Tome & Principe											X	X	X	X	X	X		X				X	X				
Saudi Arabia											X	X		X	X		X	X	X	X	X	X					
Senegal											X	X	X	X	X		X	X		X	X	X	X			X	X
Serbia & Montenegro	X										X	X		X			X	X			X	X	X			X	X
Seychelles											X	X		X	X		X	X	X		X	X	X				
Sierra Leone											X	X		X	X		X	X		X	X	X	X			X	

Singapore		X			X		X	X		X			X	X						
Slovakia		X		X	X	X	X		X	X			X	X					X	X
Slovenia			X	X	X	X		X	X				X	X					X	X
Solomon Islands						X		X					X							
Somalia																				
South Africa	X	X		X	X	X	X	X		X		X	X	X						
Spain	X		X	X	X	X	X	X	X	X	X	X	X	X	X		X	X		X
Sri Lanka			X	X	X	X	X	X	X		X	X	X	X		X				X
Sudan				X	X		X	X				X	X	X						
Suriname			X	X	X	X	X	X				X	X	X	X	X				
Swaziland				X	X	X	X	X				X	X	X						
Sweden	X	X	X	X	X	X	X	X	X	X	X	X	X	X	X	X	X	X	X	X
Switzerland	X	X	X	X	X	X	X	X	X	X	X	X	X	X	X	X	X	X	X	X
Syria				X	X	X	X	X		X		X	X	X						
Taiwan																				
Tajikistan				X	X	X	X	X	X			X	X	X					X	X
Tanzania				X	X	X	X	X		X		X	X	X		X			X	X
Thailand				X	X	X	X	X	X	X		X	X	X		X	X		X	X
Togo				X	X	X	X	X				X	X	X		X	X			
Tonga					X	X	X	X		X		X	X	X		X	X			
Trinidad & Tobago			X	X	X	X	X	X	X	X		X	X	X		X			X	X
Tunisia				X	X	X	X	X				X	X	X						
Turkey	X		X	X	X	X	X	X		X		X	X	X					X	X
Turkmenistan				X	X	X	X	X				X	X	X						
Tuvalu													X							
Uganda				X	X	X	X	X				X	X	X				X		
Ukraine	X	X		X	X	X	X	X	X	X		X	X	X					X	X
United Arab Emirates				X	X	X	X	X		X		X	X	X						

(continued)

C. Countries that had ratified by June 2005 (contd)

Country	Air Pollution	Air Pollution-Nitrogen Oxides	Air Pollution-Persistent Organic Pollutants	Air Pollution-Sulphur 85	Air Pollution-Sulphur 94	Air Pollution-Volatile Organic Compounds	Antarctic-Environmental Protocol	Antarctic-Marine Living Resources	Antarctic Seals	Antarctic Treaty	Biodiversity	Climate Change	Climate Change-Kyoto Protocol	Desertification	Endangered Species	Environmental Modification	Hazardous Wastes	Law of the Sea	Marine Dumping	Marine Life Conservation	Nuclear Test Ban	Ozone Layer Protection	Ship Pollution	Tropical Timber 83	Tropical Timber 94	Wetlands	Whaling
United Kingdom	X	X			X	X	X	X	X	X	X	X		X	X	X			X	X	X	X	X	X	X	X	X
United States	X	X					X	X	X	X				X	X	X			X	X	X	X	X	X	X	X	X
Uruguay							X	X		X	X	X	X	X	X	X	X	X				X	X		X	X	
Uzbekistan											X	X	X	X	X	X	X					X			X	X	
Vanuatu								X			X	X	X	X	X				X			X					
Venezuela										X	X	X		X	X		X	X		X	X	X	X	X	X	X	
Vietnam											X	X		X	X	X	X	X				X	X		X	X	
Western Sahara																											
Yemen											X	X		X	X	X	X	X				X					
Zambia											X	X		X	X		X	X			X	X				X	
Zimbabwe											X	X		X	X			X				X					

Appendix 3. The Beaufort scale of wind strength

Force	Wind speed (kilometres per hour)	Description	Evidence of impact on land
0	1.5 or less	Calm	The air is still, smoke rises vertically
1	1.6–5	Light air	Wind vanes and flags do not move, but rising smoke drifts
2	6–12	Light breeze	Wind is felt on the face, leaves rustle, wind vanes move
3	13–20	Gentle breeze	Leaves rustle, small twigs move, and the wind extends light flags
4	21–29	Moderate breeze	Dust, loose leaves, and pieces of paper blow about
5	30–39	Fresh breeze	Small trees that are in full leaf wave in the wind
6	40–50	Strong breeze	Large branches move, telephone wires whistle, it becomes difficult to use an open umbrella
7	51–61	Moderate gale	Trees start to sway, people walking into the wind start to have difficulties
8	62–74	Fresh Gale	Small twigs are torn from trees
9	75–87	Severe gale	Slight structural damage (chimneys are blown down, slates and tiles are torn from roofs)
10	88–101	Storm	Seldom experienced inland, but causes considerable structural damage; trees are broken or uprooted
11	102–120	Violent storm	Very rarely experienced, but causes widespread damage; trees are uprooted and blown some distance, cars are overturned
12	Greater than 120	Hurricane	Widespread devastation, with buildings destroyed and many trees uprooted

Appendix 4. The Saffir–Simpson hurricane scale

Hurricane category	Wind speed (kilometres per hour)	Evidence of impact on land
Category 1 hurricane	118–152	No real damage to buildings, but damage to mobile homes and poorly constructed signs. Some coastal flooding and minor damage to piers
Category 2 hurricane	153–176	Some damage to building roofs, doors, and windows, considerable damage to mobile homes, and some trees blown down. Piers damaged by flooding, and small boats in unprotected moorings may break loose
Category 3 hurricane	177–208	Some structural damage to small residences and utility buildings, large trees blown down, mobile homes and poorly built signs destroyed. Coastal flooding destroys smaller structures, with larger structures damaged by floating debris; flooding may extend well inland
Category 4 hurricane	209–248	More extensive structural damage, including collapse of roofs on small residences. Major erosion of beach areas, and flooding well inland
Category 5 hurricane	More than 248	Complete roof failure on many residences and industrial buildings, some complete building failures, small utility buildings blown over or away. Flooding causes major damage to lower floors of all structures near the shoreline. Large-scale evacuation of low-lying residential areas may be required

Appendix 5. The Fujita scale of tornado intensity

F-scale number	Description	Wind speed (kilometres per hour)	Type of damage
Weak			
F0	Gale tornado	64–115	Some damage to chimneys, branches broken off trees, shallow-rooted trees pushed over, sign boards damaged
F1	Moderate tornado	116–179	Surface peeled off roofs, mobile homes moved or overturned, moving vehicles pushed off road, attached garages may be destroyed
Strong			
F2	Significant tornado	180–251	Considerable damage; roofs torn off houses, mobile homes destroyed, train carriages blown over, large trees snapped or uprooted, light objects blown around
F3	Severe tornado	252–330	Roof and some walls blown off well-constructed buildings, trains overturned, most trees uprooted
Violent			
F4	Devastating tornado	331–416	Well-constructed buildings are flattened, structures with weak foundations are blown some distance, vehicles blown over, large objects blown around
F5	Incredible tornado	417–509	Strong buildings lifted off foundations, blown around and disintegrated, vehicles fly through the air, reinforced concrete structures badly damaged
F6	Inconceivable tornado	510–606	Very unlikely, and very localized (surrounded by F4 and F5 winds); serious damage caused by large objects, including vehicles, blowing around

Appendix 6. Torino asteroid and comet impact hazard scale

Torino level	Category	Description
0	No hazard (white zone)	Zero likelihood of a collision
1	Normal (green zone)	Routine discovery in which a pass near the Earth is predicted, but the chance of collision is extremely unlikely
2	Meriting attention by astronomers (yellow zone)	Discovery of an object making a close but not highly unusual pass near the Earth, with an actual collision very unlikely
3		Close encounter, with a 1% or greater chance of collision capable of localized destruction
4		Close encounter, with a 1% or greater chance of collision capable of regional devastation
5	Threatening (orange zone)	Close encounter that poses a serious but still uncertain threat of regional devastation
6		Close encounter by a large object which poses a serious but still uncertain threat of global catastrophe
7		Very close encounter by a large object, which (if occurring within 100 years) poses an unprecedented but still uncertain threat of global catastrophe
8	Certain collisions (red zone)	Collision is certain, capable of causing localized destruction
9		Collision is certain, capable of causing unprecedented regional devastation
10		Collision is certain, capable of causing global climatic catastrophe

Appendix 7. Richter earthquake magnitude and modified Mercalli earthquake intensity scales

Richter magnitude	Mercalli intensity (at epicentre)	Experience of observers
1–2	I	Felt by very few people, barely noticeable
2–3	II	Felt by a few people, especially on upper floors
3–4	III	Noticeable indoors, especially on upper floors, but may not be recognizable as an earthquake
4	IV	Felt by many indoors, few outdoors
4–5	V	Felt by almost everyone, some people awakened, small objects moved, trees and poles may shake
5–6	VI	Felt by everyone, difficult to stand, some heavy furniture is moved, some plaster falls, chimneys may be slightly damaged
6	VII	Well-built structures may have slight to moderate damage, poorly built structures may be badly damaged, some walls may collapse
6–7	VIII	Little damage in specially built structures, considerable damage to ordinary buildings, severe damage to poorly built structures, some walls collapse
7	IX	Considerable damage to specially built structures, buildings moved off foundations, large ground cracks, large-scale destruction, landslides
7–8	X	Destruction of most structures and foundations, severe ground cracking, landslides, large-scale destruction
8	XI	Total damage, few structures left standing, bridges destroyed, wide cracks in the ground, waves seen on the ground
8 or greater	XII	Total damage, waves seen on the ground, objects thrown up in the air.

Appendix 8. The geological time-scale

Eon	Era	Sub-era	Period	Epoch	Starting (millions of years ago)
Phanerozoic		Quaternary	Pleistogene	Holocene	0.012
				Pleistocene	2.588
	Cenozoic		Neogene	Pliocene	5.332
				Miocene	23.03
			Palaeogene	Oligocene	33.9
				Eocene	55.8
				Palaeocene	65.5
	Mesozoic		Cretaceous		146
			Jurassic		200
			Triassic		251
	Palaeozoic	Upper Palaeozoic	Permian		299
			Carboniferous		359
			Devonian		416
		Lower Palaeozoic	Silurian		444
			Ordovician		488
			Cambrian		542
Proterozoic					2500
Archaean					3800
Hadean					4567

Appendix 9. Chemical elements

Details of the properties of each element can be found online at http://www.lenntech.com/Periodic-chart-elements/alphabetic.htm

Chemical element	Symbol	Atomic number	Chemical element	Symbol	Atomic number
Actinium	Ac	89	Gold	Au	79
Aluminium	Al	13	Hafnium	Hf	72
Americium	Am	95	Hassium	Hs	108
Antimony	Sb	51	Helium	He	2
Argon	Ar	18	Holmium	Ho	67
Arsenic	As	33	Hydrogen	H	1
Astatine	At	85	Indium	In	49
Barium	Ba	56	Iodine	I	53
Berkelium	Bk	97	Iridium	Ir	77
Beryllium	Be	4	Iron	Fe	26
Bismuth	Bi	83	Krypton	Kr	36
Bohrium	Bh	107	Lanthanum	La	57
Boron	B	5	Lawrencium	Lr	103
Bromine	Br	35	Lead	Pb	82
Cadmium	Cd	48	Lithium	Li	3
Calcium	Ca	20	Lutetium	Lu	71
Californium	Cf	98	Magnesium	Mg	12
Carbon	C	6	Manganese	Mn	25
Cerium	Ce	58	Meitnerium	Mt	109
Caesium	Cs	55	Mendelevium	Md	101
Chlorine	Cl	17	Mercury	Hg	80
Chromium	Cr	24	Molybdenum	Mo	42
Cobalt	Co	27	Neodymium	Nd	60
Copernicium	Cn	112	Neon	Ne	10
Copper	Cu	29	Neptunium	Np	93
Curium	Cm	96	Nickel	Ni	28
Darmstadtium	Ds	110	Niobium	Nb	41
Dubnium	Db	105	Nitrogen	N	7
Dysprosium	Dy	66	Nobelium	No	102
Einsteinium	Es	99	Osmium	Os	76
Erbium	Er	68	Oxygen	O	8
Europium	Eu	63	Palladium	Pd	46
Fermium	Fm	100	Phosphorus	P	15
Fluorine	F	9	Platinum	Pt	78
Francium	Fr	87	Plutonium	Pu	94
Gadolinium	Gd	64	Polonium	Po	84
Gallium	Ga	31	Potassium	K	19
Germanium	Ge	32	Praseodymium	Pr	59

Promethium	Pm	61	Tellurium	Te	52
Protactinium	Pa	91	Terbium	Tb	65
Radium	Ra	88	Thallium	Tl	81
Radon	Rn	86	Thorium	Th	90
Rhenium	Re	75	Thulium	Tm	69
Rhodium	Rh	45	Tin	Sn	50
Roentgenium	Rg	111	Titanium	Ti	22
Rubidium	Rb	37	Tungsten	W	74
Ruthenium	Ru	44	Ununhexium	Uuh	116
Rutherfordium	Rf	104	Ununoctium	Uuo	118
Samarium	Sm	62	Ununpentium	Uup	115
Scandium	Sc	21	Ununquadium	Uuq	114
Seaborgium	Sg	106	Ununseptium	Uus	117
Selenium	Se	34	Ununtrium	Uut	113
Silicon	Si	14	Uranium	U	92
Silver	Ag	47	Vanadium	V	23
Sodium	Na	11	Xenon	Xe	54
Strontium	Sr	38	Ytterbium	Yb	70
Sulphur	S	16	Yttrium	Y	39
Tantalum	Ta	73	Zinc	Zn	30
Technetium	Tc	43	Zirconium	Zr	40

Appendix 10. SI units and conversions

SI Unit	Quantity	Symbol	Conversion
BASE UNITS			
metre	length	m	1 m = 3.2808 feet
kilogram	mass	kg	1 kg = 2.205 pounds
second	time	s	
ampere	electric current	A	
kelvin	thermodynamic temperature	K	1 K = 1°C = 1.8°F
candela	luminous intensity	cd	
mole	amount of substance	mol	
SUPPLEMENTARY UNITS			
radian	plane angle	rad	$\pi/2$ rad = 90°
steradian	solid angle	sr	
DERIVED UNITS			
coulomb	quantity of electricity	C	
cubic metre	volume	m^3	1 m^3 = 35.3213 feet^3
farad	capacitance	F	
henry	inductance	H	
hertz	frequency	Hz	
joule	energy	J	1 J = 0.2389 calories
kilogram per cubic metre	density	$kg\ m^{-3}$	1 $kg\ m^{-3}$ = 0.0624 lb ft^{-3}
lumen	luminous flux	lm	
lux	illuminance	lx	
metre per second	speed	m/s	1 $m\ s^{-1}$ = 3.281 ft s^{-1}
metre per second squared	acceleration	$m\ s^{-2}$	
mole per cubic metre	concentration	$mol\ m^{-3}$	
newton	force	N	1 N = 7.218 lb force
ohm	electric resistance	Ω	
pascal	pressure	Pa	1 Pa = 0.145 lb in^{-2}
radian per second	angular velocity	$rad\ s^{-1}$	
radian per second squared	angular acceleration	$rad\ s^{-2}$	
square metre	area	m^2	1 m^2 = 10.764 feet^2
tesla	magnetic flux density	T	
volt	electromotive force	V	
watt	power	W	1W = 3.412 Btu/h
weber	magnetic flux	Wb	

Prefixes used with SI units

PREFIX	SYMBOL	VALUE
atto	a	$\times 10^{-18}$
femto	f	$\times 10^{-15}$
pico	p	$\times 10^{-12}$
nano	n	$\times 10^{-9}$
micro	μ	$\times 10^{-6}$
milli	m	$\times 10^{-3}$
centi	c	$\times 10^{-2}$
deci	d	$\times 10^{-1}$
deca	da	$\times 10$
hecto	h	$\times 10^{2}$
kilo	k	$\times 10^{3}$
mega	M	$\times 10^{6}$
giga	G	$\times 10^{9}$
tera	T	$\times 10^{12}$

SI unit	Imperial unit
LENGTH	
centimetre	0.394 inch
2.54 cm	inch
kilometre	0.6214 statute miles
1.609 km	statute mile
1.852 km	nautical mile
AREA	
square centimetre	0.155 inch^2
6.452 cm^2	square inch
hectare	2.471 acres
0.4047 ha	acre
square kilometre	0.386 mile^2
2.59 km^2	square mile
VOLUME	
litre	1.76 pints
0.568 l	pint
4.546 l	UK gallon
3.785 l	US gallon
16.387 cm^3	cubic inch
0.028 m^3	cubic foot
MASS	
tonne	0.984 UK ton
tonne	1.102 US ton
UK ton	1.016 t
US ton	0.906 t